"Noam Zion has written another cl[_____]
and insights from the full spectrun[_____]
tion, uncensored, from the Bible an[_____] down to modern liberal
rabbis and feminists, might be called *The Art of Halachic Loving* because
it is not just a static anthology; it is shaped to guide and enhance the
pleasure of sex and the depth of development of intimacy, communication and relationship. This is a book to be read, savored, reflected
on, discussed, and applied to life."

—**BLU GREENBERG AND YITZ GREENBERG**, authors respectively of
   On Women and Judaism and *The Jewish Way*

"Combining exacting, serious textual analysis with entertaining, often
comical stories of rabbis and their sexual habits, Noam Zion takes us for
a ride through the highways and byways of the Jewish erotic imagination. He deserves high praise for his erudition, creativity, and courage."

—**SHAUL MAGID**, professor of Jewish Studies, Dartmouth College,
   and author of *American Post-Judaism: Identity and Renewal in a
   Postethnic Society*

"Noam Zion masterfully illuminates how two thousand years of commentary and debate have amplified the subject of sex in Jewish tradition
and enriched it with nuance. Engage your mind, open your heart, and
take this book to your bed!"

—**RACHEL BIALE**, author of *Women and Jewish Law* and *Growing Up
   Below Sea Level: A Kibbutz Childhood*

"Who knew that there was so much marital drama in rabbinic literature? Noam Zion has provided the definitive anthology and comparative commentary on this subject."

—**DAVID BIALE**, Emanuel Ringelblum Distinguished Professor of Jewish History, University of California, Davis, and author of *Eros and the Jews* and *Hasidism: A New History*

"Moving effortlessly between traditional Jewish sources produced throughout history, Noam Zion makes us reflect, as Jews and simply as humans, on what's actually at stake in conjugal relationships. I strongly recommend this erudite, accessible, sensitive, and witty guide to all."

—**MICHAEL SATLOW**, professor, religious and Judaic studies, Brown University, and author of *Tasting the Dish: Rabbinic Rhetorics of Sexuality*

"*Sanctified Sex* is a learned, insightful, and engaging treatment of Jewish teachings concerning love and sex. For the rabbi who thinks s/he already knows it all or the graduate student who wants to know it all, there is no better resource. Noam Zion is a scholar who writes with a clear, accessible voice, and readers who are willing to dive deep into this subject will find themselves immensely rewarded by his masterful treatment."

—**DAVID KRAEMER**, professor of Talmud and Rabbinics, Jewish Theological Seminary, and author of *A History of the Talmud*

"*Sanctified Sex* is both timeless and timely. For the mainstream Jewish community, which tends to default to saying that Judaism is sex-positive (in contrast with Christianity), this deeper examination is warranted. For the academic community, the different eras the book encompasses guarantee a broad range of applicability. For the general community, Noam Zion is asking a key human question: what tools can I find to strengthen a long-term marriage?"

—**RABBI LISA GRUSHCOW**, senior rabbi, Temple Emanu-El-Beth Sholom, Montreal, and editor of *The Sacred Encounter: Jewish Perspectives on Sexuality*

Sanctified Sex

University of Nebraska Press

Lincoln

Sanctified Sex

The Two-Thousand-Year Jewish Debate on Marital Intimacy

NOAM SACHS ZION

The Jewish Publication Society
Philadelphia

Acknowledgments for the use of copyrighted material appear on
pages xvii–xix, which constitute an extension of the copyright page.

All rights reserved. Published by the University of
Nebraska Press as a Jewish Publication Society book.
Manufactured in the United States of America.

Library of Congress Cataloging-in-Publication Data
Names: Zion, Noam Sachs, author.
Title: Sanctified sex: the two-thousand-year Jewish
debate on marital intimacy / Noam Sachs Zion, The
Jewish Publication Society, Philadelphia.
Description: Lincoln: University of Nebraska Press, [2021] |
Includes bibliographical references and index.
Identifiers: LCCN 2020041733
ISBN 9780827614666 (paperback)
ISBN 9780827618725 (epub)
ISBN 9780827618732 (mobi)
ISBN 9780827618749 (pdf)
Subjects: LCSH: Sex—Religious aspects—Judaism. |
Rabbinical literature—History and criticism.
Classification: LCC BM720.S4 Z57 2021 |
DDC 296.3/664—dc23
LC record available at https://lccn.loc.gov/2020041733

Designed and set in Garamond Premier Pro by L. Auten.

Dedicated to a Beloved Partner in Life, Marcelle Zion,

and a Lifelong Hevruta, David Dishon

"Either companionship or death!" (TB *Ta'anit* 23a)

Contents

Part Five. Modern North American Rabbis:
Confronting the Sexual Revolution

Acknowledgments

For this publication, my deep gratitude is extended to the steadfast Rabbi Barry Schwartz, director of The Jewish Publication Society (JPS), and to the dedicated and inventive Joy Weinberg, JPS managing editor, both of whom were unflagging in their support and constructive criticism; and to the University of Nebraska Press and its highly professional staff for their role as a publishing partner in this volume.

For emotional love and support, I owe so much to my wife, Marcelle, and our children and grandchildren.

For the academic content of this monograph, stretching from the giving of the Torah to today, I owe much to the breadth of David Biale's pioneering work *Eros and the Jews*, to Moshe Idel's and Yehuda Liebes's understandings of kabbalist lovemaking, and to Benjamin Brown's eye-opening investigation of the debate on marital intimacy among contemporary Haredim.

For intellectual excellence, for educational vision and financial support, I owe everything to the institution that has inspired, nurtured, and sponsored my lifelong research—the Shalom Hartman Institute in Jerusalem, my *beit midrash*. Its founder is my seminal teacher of Torah, Rabbi David Hartman; its current director and visionary institution builder is his son, Donniel Hartman; its North American director is Yehuda Kurtzer; and its talented scholars are my colleagues, my study partners, and my friends for forty years who have generously shared with me their curiosity, intellectual breadth, and wisdom in small and large ways.

My singular gratitude for this book project encompasses many. My beloved, enthusiastic, insightful *hevruta* partners are David Dishon, Peretz Rodman, and Randall Zachman. My generous scholarly consultants and critical readers included David Biale, David Golinkin, Elliot Dorff, Yoni (Jonathan) Garb, Rivka Neriya-Ben Shahar, Kimmy Caplan, Zvi Zohar, Eliezer Papo, Avner Holtzman, Marty Lockshin, Avishalom Westreich, Ronit Irshai, Mark Washofsky, Yitz Greenberg, Steven Greenberg, Ariel Picard, Leonard Gordon, Shraga Bar-On, Biti Roi, Melila Hellner-Eshed, Arthur Green, Rut Kagan, Dror Yehoshua, Dov Linzer, Shlomo Zacharow, Lisa Grushcow, Avi Ferzig, Ira Stone, Geoffrey Claussen, Naamah Kelman, Leon Morris, Alan Flashman, and Janet and Sheldon Marder. My resourceful, widely knowledgeable and ever-helpful research librarian is Daniel Price of the Hartman Institute, and my talented digital editor, himself a scholar of mysticism, Gene Matanky. My tireless copy editors and proofreaders were Virginia Perrin, Sam Mellins, Danny Weininger, Leah Linfield, David Estrin, Michael Milgrom, Shelly Horowitz, Marc Rosenstein, Sigalit Ur, Kathy Aron-Beller, Lynn Pollak Golumbic, Sherman Rosenfeld, Helen Senor, Renee Rothberg, Sophie Wolle, Eli Katz, Rachel Adelman, and Deborah Morse.

Note to the Reader

TB and TJ are abbreviations for the Babylonian and Jerusalem Talmuds. Italics in quotes are the author's emphasis (unless otherwise noted). All English translations from the Bible, the Talmud, and other rabbinic texts, except for kabbalist sources, are the author's (unless otherwise noted).

The author gratefully acknowledges permission to quote from the following copyrighted material.

Introduction: Reproduced from *Engendering Judaism: An Inclusive Theology and Ethics* by Rachel Adler by permission of the University of Nebraska Press. Copyright 1998 by Rachel Adler. Published by The Jewish Publication Society, Philadelphia. *Standing at Sinai* by Judith Plaskow. Copyright © 1990 by Judith Plaskow. Used by permission of HarperCollins Publishers.

Chapter 4: Debra Kamin, "In the Boudoir with Orthodox Jewish Women," *Guardian*, September 2, 2015.

Chapter 12: Irving Greenberg, "Dr. Greenberg Discusses Orthodoxy, YU, Viet Nam and Sex," *The Commentator*, April 28, 1966. Copyright 1966 by Irving Greenberg.

LaDaat LeEhov by Avraham Shmuel (pseudonym). Copyright 2017 by Raphael Ostroff.

Chapter 13: Reproduced from the *Second Jewish Catalog: Sources and Resources*, edited by Sharon Strassfeld and Michael Strassfeld, by permission of the University of Nebraska Press. Copyright 1976 by The Jewish Publication Society of America.

Chapter 14: "Sex, Relationship and Single Jews" by Jeremy Kalmanofsky, in *The Observant Life: The Wisdom of Conservative Judaism for Contemporary Jews*, edited by Martin S. Cohen. Copyright 2012 by Rabbinical Assembly. Used by permission.

Introduction

For one human being to love another: that is perhaps the most difficult of all our tasks, the ultimate, the last test and proof, the work
for which all other work is but preparation. . . . That is why young
people, who are beginners in everything, are not yet capable of love:
it is something they must learn. . . .

    Love is a high inducement to the individual to ripen, to become
something in himself, to become world for himself [and] for another's sake. It is a great exacting claim upon him, something that
chooses him and calls him to vast things.

—RAINER MARIA RILKE (1875–1926, Austrian poet),
   Letters to a Young Poet

On the day of my marriage in the Old City of Jerusalem in 1975, my
bride and I spent the morning studying Maimonides' laws of marriage with my Talmud teacher Rav Menahem Froman. Later in his
career, Froman attracted media attention as a religious peace activist
living on the West Bank and engaging in interreligious dialogue
with Muslim imams associated with the radical Islam of Hamas.

    One day, when asked by a journalist to be photographed, Fro-
man instructed the cameraman to include God in the picture. So
Froman invited his wife, Hadassah, to stand next to him and then
directed the photographer to focus on the space between himself
and his wife, because, he explained, the Shekhinah fills the space
between a loving husband and a wife, just as Rabbi Akiba teaches:
"Man (*ish*) and woman (*isha*)—if they merit it, Shekhinah (*ya*) is
between them. If they do not merit it, fire (*esh*) is between them"
(TB *Sotah* 17a).[1] For Froman, the pursuit of sanctity encompasses

an all-consuming devotion to Torah and, equally, to the sacred labor of perfecting his relationship with his wife.

At the core of this book about marital intimacy is the halakhic (i.e., legal) debate between two Jewish understandings of sanctity and their practical implications for sexuality: holiness via ascetic self-control of one's sexual desire or holiness via joyous emotional and erotic union with one's spouse. One approach to sanctity is chiefly defined negatively, by what one should not do—namely, by refraining from illicit intercourse and suppressing sexual impulses and thoughts in order to preserve the sanctity of a pious Jew (primarily, male) and of Israel, its land and people. The other involves positive actions that celebrate the expression of erotic intimacy in intimate bonds of fidelity, mutuality, and pleasure as the royal road to enhancing sanctity, peace, love, and unity in the world.

The contemporary feminist theologian Rabbi Rachel Adler connects these two types of the sacred with two ceremonies—*kiddushin* and *nisuin*, betrothal and commencement of married life—performed at every classic rabbinic wedding. In kiddushin the groom usually presents a ring to his bride and pronounces her sanctified to him in an exclusive sexual bond. (After kiddushin, unlike an engagement, a divorce is required to sever the marriage ties.) In the nisuin ceremony, while standing under the marital canopy (huppah), the couple is blessed with seven wishes for marital joy and togetherness. Adler summarizes the difference: "If *kiddushin* represents sanctification through separation [from sexual relations with any other man], the *Sheva Brakhot* [seven nuptial blessings] celebrate a sanctification through the holy coming together [of husband and wife] that is covenant."[2]

The ideal of sanctity through control of sexual urges (separation from impurity) is, Adler argues, at the heart of the betrothal symbolized by the Talmudic ritual of *kiddushin* (literally, the sanctification of the bride by and to the groom) recited over the first cup of wine. In offering the bride a ring, the husband designates her as his wife, as one dedicated to her husband alone; thereby her adulterous intercourse with any other man is prohibited because it violates her exclusive bond with her husband and it would constitute a scandalous desecration of the holiness of Israel.

The idea of holy matrimony as "sanctification through separation" originates in the Torah in the central mitzvah of the Holiness Code of Leviticus (Lev. 18–26), where God commands the people: *You shall be holy for I Adonai your God am holy* (Lev. 19:2). To be intimate with a sacred God means to make one's community sacred, so, as God says, *I can dwell among them* (Exod. 25:8). Operationally, to become a sacred people, Israel must obey some positive ethical directives (Lev. 19:10,18—*love your fellow as yourself; leave produce in your field for the poor and the resident alien*). Most of Leviticus, however, highlights negative commandments of sanctification through separation that are designed to restrain powerful natural urges from within and to rebuff insidious cultural influences from without— including illicit sexual unions with inappropriate partners (such as incest, adultery, intermarriage with idolaters, and intercourse with one's spouse at inappropriate times, such as *niddah*, menses) (Lev. 18–20). Therefore, the blessing over kiddushin at a wedding reaffirms a negative sanctity maintained by strictly monitored sexual behavior.

Positive sanctity is introduced in the traditional wedding's second ceremony: the recital of the seven nuptial blessings (*Sheva Brakhot*) over the second cup of wine, which initiates the *nisuin*, literally, "the marriage," as the couple begins to live together in the home, symbolized by the tent-like canopy (huppah). In nisuin, Adler identifies the second type of *kedushah*: sanctification through covenantal coming together. The marital contract (*ketubah*), usually read and delivered to the bride before the Seven Blessings, obligates the husband to support his wife financially and to provide regularly for her sexual needs. From that moment on, sexual union is permitted and mandated in what Adler calls the positive sanctity of loving intimacy.

For normative Jewish tradition, the ideal place for sexual relations is within the sanctified and committed relationship governed by mutual obligation under law—marriage—whose mutual duties are formalized in the ketubah designed (in principle) to protect the dignity of each spouse and deliver reciprocally the wife's and husband's physical, financial, and emotional needs. While procreative sex is highly valued, the chief obligation to one's spouse is the regularly scheduled satisfaction of erotic desire (especially the wife's). Almost every other item in bilateral relations between spouses may be renegotiated in the ketubah, such as who earns the money, where the couple resides, and whether the husband may take a second wife. But the *right* to sexual satisfaction cannot be forfeited, even if the husband and wife consent to temporarily forgo that right to let one's spouse devote full attention to study or business.[3]

Understanding historically and conceptually the halakhic debate about the centrality of sex and emotional intimacy within marriage is the theme of this book.

While the topic is ancient, contemporary trends have destabilized the institution of marriage, in general, and within the Jewish (and even the Orthodox) world, in particular. In the West, a series of ideological revolutions in the public square have transformed interpersonal relations in the private sphere. First, the democratic revolution has prioritized self-autonomy and self-concern, with individuals placing their own needs ahead of their families' needs. Second, the feminist, or gender, revolution has challenged patriarchal patterns, casting into confusion what spouses may appropriately expect from one another, so that everything is up for negotiation. Third, the sexual identity revolution destabilizes heterosexual identities by calling into question whether identity is biological or cultural, inborn or preferential, and whether gender is binary or fluid. Fourth, the revolution of sexual civil rights, reaching its apex in the

United States in the 2015 U.S. Supreme Court's marriage equality ruling, has liberated private life from the supervision of religion and law that enforced and often legislated private sexual morality. The increasingly acceptable options of living together and no-fault divorces (since 1970), combined with changing lifestyles and greater longevity, have resulted in marriage no longer being the societal norm in North America and Western Europe. Fifth, the romantic revolution has made a person's love life, at times volatile, more crucial to the sense of personal meaning than ever before.

Finally, sixth, the sexual revolution has opened up erotic options inside and outside matrimony without regard to procreation, and has elevated sexual satisfaction to a sine qua non of daily life. The contemporary couples therapist Esther Perel summarizes sociologist Anthony Giddens's insight in this regard:

> Sex . . . became . . . a marker of our identity . . . that we define and redefine throughout our lives. It is an expression of who we are, no longer merely something we do. . . . Sex is a human right linked to our individuality, our personal freedom, and our self-actualization. Sexual bliss, we believe, is our due—and it has become a pillar of our new conception of intimacy.[4]

In response, worried that marriage as an institution and its traditional values have been deeply undermined, rabbis affiliated with Judaism's diverse religious movements (from ultra-Orthodox to Jewish Renewal) have mobilized to creatively reformulate approaches to sexuality within marriage and to reeducate their followers to bolster or reshape spousal relations. They formulate their positions toward contemporary issues by revisiting authoritative sources and critically engaging in classic legal debates, as rabbis have always done.

Sanctified Sex draws on two thousand years of rabbinic thought and law to address questions about achieving loving intimacy, strong emotional bonds, frank spousal communication, and passionate sexual union in the context of sanctity in marriage. What can Judaism, in particular Jewish law with its penchant for detailed hands-on directives, contribute to the intersection between sanctity and intimacy in erotic relationships? What halakhic precedents are relevant, and how are rulings changing? What can we learn from the burgeoning literature of rabbinic guidebooks for newlyweds? While not providing any panaceas, the advice rabbis offer in response to the dilemmas they face can give us two thousand years of perspective and insight as we ourselves struggle to nurture our love relationships.

The Two-Thousand-Year Debate

Jews, of course, and especially rabbis, seldom agree. On marital sex there is no coherent, monolithic rabbinic position, but rather, over time, rabbis' clashing traditions have generated competing halakhic rulings and religious rationales. Halakhic Judaism, a legal civilization of contending ideals and practices, finds strength in internal diversity and vitality in robust disagreements. Hence this book's subtitle is *The Two-Thousand-Year Jewish Debate on Marital Intimacy*.

In light of contemporary value questions facing modern Jews, this book investigates and juxtaposes classical texts and competing schools of thought in a pluralist manner, without assuming "normative Judaism" has only one take on marital intimacy. As my teacher Rabbi David Hartman taught me: "Judaism is an invitation to participate in a multigenerational conversation, and that is the meaning of Oral Torah." Jews share in a lively discussion with their ancestors and contemporaries in which they hope to learn from those with whom they most disagree as well as from those who inspire them most. In this multigenerational conversation within the halakhic tradition, we find moments of great insight and sensitivity as well as hurtful practices I think ought to be shunned, but that judgment will be the reader's to make.

Within the entire halakhic tradition on marital law and lovemaking, there is an ongoing struggle between polar views of sexuality. While some rabbinic traditions promote sacred life over and at the expense of sexuality, others regard the two as complementary. Some rabbis wish to minimize spousal intimacy in order to suppress the anarchic evil inclination, especially in males, while others want to enhance sexual passion to bring harmony to interpersonal relationships (*shalom bayit*), to achieve mystical union (*yihud*), and to repair the cosmos (*tikkun olam*).

The contemporary Jewish feminist theologian Judith Plaskow succinctly describes Jewish law's unresolved "ambivalence toward sexuality":

> The sexual impulse is given by God and thus is a normal and healthy part of human life. Sexual relations are appropriate only within the framework of heterosexual marriage, but within marriage, they are good, indeed, are commanded (a *mitzvah*). Yet sexuality—even within marriage—also requires careful, sometimes rigorous control in order that it not transgress boundaries. . . .
>
> Although the lenient attitude [to marital duties] is enshrined in halakhah, many rabbis and commentators adjured Jews to follow a stricter standard than the law permitted [a restrictive or ascetic ethic].[5]

Plaskow correctly identifies the tension within the halakhah between what is *permitted* (thus enabling couples to shape their own love life with greater latitude for individual taste) and what is *commended*. After issuing a permissive ruling, the same rabbi may recommend that the pious elites refrain voluntarily from that same permitted behavior in order to achieve a higher spiritual ideal in accord with a more stringent ascetic code.

Furthermore, a deeper conflict within halakhic Judaism emerges between two evolving schools of thought on the compatibility of marital sexuality and kedushah, whether erotic desire may help fulfill the divine mitzvah *Be holy for I [God] am holy* (Lev. 19:2) or whether sexual drives detract from the image of God within humanity.

The dialectical evolution of halakhic attitudes toward marital intimacy extends from the opening chapters of Genesis to the latest developments among Haredim (the ultra-Orthodox) in Israel and Jewish feminists in America. At each stage, as we will see, participants in this universe of discourse express their values by reinterpreting inherited texts in new ways.

Functions of Halakhah in Guiding Marital Relationships

How, some readers may ask, can the deliberations on the halakhah of marital intimacy as surveyed in *Sanctified Sex* be helpful even for those who do not regard halakhah as legally binding in their daily lives, especially in their bedrooms? This question is relevant even to Orthodox Jews committed to the binding nature of Jewish law as God's commandments. After all, contemporary Jews, even the ultra-Orthodox, reside in democratic societies where halakhic laws are not enforced by the power of the state. Thus, practically speaking, it is each Jew's choice as an individual in accord with one's worldview, to adopt a certain halakhic practice, interpret it in a particular way, choose the community that mandates that practice, and determine which scholars or rabbis will be their authority or advisors in setting policies and settling disputes. Furthermore, the relevance of halakhah depends, importantly, on how its norms are categorized: as (1) coercive, (2) prescriptive, or (3) advisory.

HALAKHAH AS A COERCIVE SYSTEM

As a *coercive* system, halakhah provides a formal legal framework, an external scaffold of rights and duties for the institution of marriage, supported by societal sanctions. Precisely because the emotional foundations of relationships are subject to fickle feelings of passionate love that can turn into vicious hatred, various nations and communities have legislated binding norms to stabilize those relationships upon which families and societies are built. Chiefly, the coercive power of law provides a legal remedy for gross spousal abuse where essential boundaries and redlines have been violated, and then a process for negotiating separation and dividing up assets fairly (at least in principle). Thus in Judaism, the classic role of the ketubah (marriage contract) is to determine the financial settlement when a couple (or, formerly, the husband unilaterally) decides to divorce, and the ketubah's provisos define the grievances by which monetary compensation is allocated to the aggrieved party. For example, since the law of *onah* (marital duties) prohibits coerced sex between husband and wife, an act of marital rape is grounds for compelling a husband who sexually violates his wife to issue a divorce and pay her the amount specified in the ketubah. Historically the ketubah's monetary penalties served as a substantive deterrent to marital misconduct.

In a democratic country with separation of religion and state, legal coercion of halakhah is absent, yet one's chosen community has quasi-coercive social regulation. In Orthodox communities, with their close-knit social webs, members, though voluntary, can be pressured to avoid deviant behavior by penalizing them with gossip, critical comments, and refusal to countenance marriages between children of normative families and those seen as violators of community standards. In Conservative or Reform communities, social pressure on fellow congregants to observe halakhic codes are absent (except, perhaps with the ritual committee's rules for synagogue ceremony and decorum), but rabbis are often expected to conform to the policies on conducting marriages prescribed by their respective rabbinical associations.

As a *prescriptive* system, halakhah (literally, "walking the path") stipulates normative behaviors and values as a way of life to which Jews are expected to aspire. For example, according to halakhah, it is religiously wrong to have sex with a spouse when drunk because the ideal sexual union ought to express mutuality of heart, mind, and body. But no one is ever punished by the community or the courts for such less-than-ideal behavior. While Rabbis of all denominations teach the values of modesty, marital love, and sanctity, they interpret and apply them in radically different ways. Contemporary Haredim interpret modesty (*tzinus*) as a demand for gender segregation, for wearing clothing that covers up potentially sexually arousing parts of the body (including hair and ankles), and for condemning all public forms of sexual expression as pornographic. Yet various kinds of ultra-Orthodox Jews often disagree about how modesty should impact marital intimacy and whether passionate conjugal lovemaking is sinfully immodest or sacred. So too Conservative, Reform, Jewish Renewal, and Reconstructionist rabbis often disagree, not about the values of sanctity and love, but about how to apply them. Some, but not all, Liberal rabbis firmly disapprove of premarital sex, especially among teenagers, though they have no coercive authority to enforce their strictures as binding norms and would not want their views to be legislated by the state. But Jewish Renewal rabbis give their blessings to unmarried couples living together.

The Reconstructionist rabbi David Teutsch observes: "Contemporary [liberal] thinking about sexual ethics does not begin with norms . . . [but] with values and ideals."[6] For example, in their sexual ethics curricula Reform rabbis have formulated a tablet of ten *values*, rather than Ten *Commandments*, through which students and couples can discuss their aspirations and evaluate the moral and spiritual health of their relationships. Like the Orthodox, Liberal rabbis count modesty as one of the top ten values, but its embodiment in particular practices depends on each couple's choices after studying texts and engaging in reasoned deliberation. Principled halakhic debates, such as those about the permissibility of nonmarital sex (see Part Five), highlight the value conflicts for deliberation, though for most Liberal rabbis, rabbinic precedent has no coercive power over personal practice.

HALAKHAH AS AN ADVISORY SYSTEM

As an *advisory* system, halakhah seeks less to obligate, legally, morally, or spiritually, than to counsel wisely—and here, I believe, is where this book, *Sanctified Sex*, finds its greatest potential benefit. It focuses less on the regulatory legal *forms* of marriage and divorce—an arena determined by rabbis and institutions—and instead stresses halakhic advice about the dynamic psychological and erotic *content* of intimate interpersonal relationships, whose implementation depends on couples' choices and self-discipline. Since Christian and Western notions of law are understood more narrowly as coercive systems enforced by punishment, many contemporary readers may miss this vital educational role of halakhah as a source of wisdom and disciplined practices for self-improvement, self-care, and monitoring ethical conduct.

For Maimonides (12th century, Egypt), God's law is the *Torah*, literally, "a book of teachings," a useful guidebook filled with *wisdom and understanding acknowledged in the eyes of the nations* (Deut. 4:6):

> The sole object of the Law is to benefit us . . . *for our good always, that God might preserve us alive* (Deut. 4:24). . . . Every one of the six hundred and thirteen mitzvot serves to inculcate some truth, to remove some erroneous opinion, to establish proper relations in society, to diminish evil, to train in good manners or to warn against bad habits.[7]

The greater part of the rules in the Law are but *counsels from of old* (Isa. 25:1), from One who is *great in counsel* (Jer. 32:19), to correct our moral qualities and to keep straight all our doings.[8]

This Volume: Inclusions and Exclusions

In mapping approaches to marital intimacy and their historical development, *Sanctified Sex* follows a chronological timeline: seminal Biblical texts and their rabbinic interpretation (Part One), Talmudic literature coalescing around the tales of three famous rabbis (Part Two), debates among medieval codifiers and mystical commentators (Part Three), contemporary Israeli Haredi disagreements and their novel rulings and practices (Part Four), and the liberal North American rabbis facing the sexual revolution (Part Five).

Part One, "Marital Duties and Scheduled Sex: Torah and Mishnah" (chapter 1), elucidates how Torah and Talmud treat marital sex as a legal obligation, mainly a duty of husbands toward their wives. Romantic love may flow spontaneously, but for the Rabbis, long-term marital love must be cultivated under law, and sex must be scheduled in accord with the marital agreement. Therefore, they codify marital intimacy by setting standards for both its quality and quantity.

Part Two, "Talmudic Disputes: *Kama Sutra* versus Ascetic Modesty in Three Rabbis' Bedrooms" (chapters 2–4), delves into the Talmudic debate evolving from three idiosyncratic stories about the bedroom activities of famous rabbis: Rav with his jocular lovemaking (chapter 2), Rabbi Eliezer and Imma Shalom with their micro-managed, highly circumspect midnight intercourse (chapter 3), and Rav Hisda's provocative sex education for his adolescent daughters (chapter 4). The Talmud contrasts Rav's joyous sexual playfulness and erotic pillow talk, on the one hand, with Rabbi Eliezer's meticulous, silent, forced march to a hasty climax with

Imma Shalom as if he were "coerced by a demon," on the other hand. For Rav Hisda, the art of marital intercourse is orchestrated by the wife, who engages the husband in a wordless dialogue of desire, coy postponement, and finally orgasm. While each story originally appeared as a personal anecdote about a particular rabbi's bedroom modus vivendi, the Talmudic editor (sometimes hundreds of years later than the Rabbis cited) arranges these tales, rabbinic quotes, and arguments into literary units of two or three pages of Talmud each called a *sugya*. Afterward, the medieval codifiers of Jewish law transform the first two exceptional tales into exemplary halakhic practices—required or at least recommended for all couples. These biographical tales spawned two competing canons of arousal or suppression in performing one's marital duties.

Part Three, "Medieval Mysticism and Law: Sacred Love and Legal Limits" (chapters 5 and 6), examines how, beyond codifying Talmudic marital practices, the medieval era witnesses spectacular innovation in mystical thought and hence halakhic guidance about marital lovemaking. In the Kabbalah's literary apogee, the Zohar prescribes mutual joy in the sexual union of man and woman, which welcomes the divine spirit into the human experience of sanctified sex (chapter 5).

Kabbalah's mythic imagination about the divine life of eros spills over into halakhic discipline in shaping the quality of onah (marital sexual obligations). Ra'avad and Joseph Ibn Gikatelia (12th–13th century, Provence and Spain) are the first mystic rabbis to compose kabbalist halakhic manuals for onah (chapter 5). Later, however, the Lurianic interpreters of the Zohar (16th century, Safed, Ottoman Empire) generate a contradictory legal legacy that constrains joyful marital intercourse in the law code of the Shulhan Arukh composed by the mystic legalist Joseph Karo (chapter 6). If Ra'avad and Ibn Gikatelia (probably the author of *The Holy Letter*) are inspired by the model of Rav's playful marital sex, Karo, in the footsteps of

Rabbi Eliezer and Imma Shalom, legislates these idiosyncratic stringencies as mainstream practice.

Part Four, "Contemporary Haredim: Hasidim versus Litvaks on Marital Intimacy" (chapters 7–11), reveals how these internal halakhic battles about the quality and sanctity of ideal marital intercourse have played out innovatively and contentiously, initially in the nineteenth-century Hasidic (chapter 7) and Litvak Mussar movements (chapter 8), and later within the milieu of contemporary Haredim, especially in Israel since 1948. The protagonists of this later debate are Hasidic rebbes (originating in Eastern Europe) and Litvak Talmud scholars (stemming from Lithuanian-style yeshivot). Initially, in 1948, the (Hasidic) Gerer Rebbe issued a newly stringent ascetic ruling exhorting sacred sexual practices that minimize marital intimacy (chapter 7). Then, in the 1950s, in response, the Litvak scholar called the Hazon Ish proclaimed that sanctity in the halakhah of onah demands enhanced emotional and erotic intimacy, nuanced communication and listening, and heightened physical pleasure (chapter 9). Crusading Litvak Haredi halakhic educators are still in the midst of an educational campaign to rebuff the spiritual forces of sexual asceticism represented by Ger Hasidim and to inculcate the sanctity of eros and emotional intimacy for young Haredi couples (chapters 10–11).

Part Five, "Modern North American Rabbis: Confronting the Sexual Revolution" (chapters 12–16), investigates another period of innovative halakhic thinking about the sanctity of marital intimacy: North American Jewish denominations reacting to the sexual revolution of the late 1960s up through the present. Wrestling with transformations in lifestyles and values among their constituencies, the rabbis of the Modern Orthodox (chapter 12), Reform, Conservative, Reconstructionist, Havurah, and Jewish Renewal movements (chapters 13–15) revisit and redefine their halakhic policies and norms regarding nonmarital sexual relations. For many, their new understanding of the sanctity of lovemaking is inspired by Martin Buber's philosophical ethics of the I-Thou relationship and/or the neo-mystical sexuality nurtured by the revival of Kabbalah studies. Out of their allegiance to a sacred notion of marriage, these rabbis seek to combat promiscuity as a desecration of love. They debate whether to restrict, regulate, or, for some, elevate the phenomenon of "living together" without holy matrimony. The last chapter (chapter 16) examines the groundbreaking work of two feminist Jewish theologians, Judith Plaskow and Rachel Adler, whose trenchant critique of halakhic marriage as a patriarchal system necessitates calls not only for liberal reform but for radical revolution. For them, not the law of the Torah and Talmud, but the prophecy and poetry of the Bible, especially Hosea, Malachi, and the Song of Songs, offer solace and inspiration for envisioning an egalitarian marriage, a partnership in love.

The innovative worldviews shaking up the laws and rationales of bedroom practice have periodically buffeted and revitalized a two-thousand-year-old rabbinic ethos of love and marriage. Thus medieval Jewish neo-Aristotelian philosophers like Maimonides circumscribe sexual activity in terms of the ethics of the golden mean and the medical regimen of a healthy life, while suppressing physical desire and prioritizing philosophic contemplation. Simultaneously, some medieval kabbalists elevate marital lovemaking to a sacred mystical practice on which the fate of the Divinity and the cosmos depends. With the opposite valence, early modern Lurianic and Hasidic thinkers pursue sanctity by minimizing sexual desire and emotional intimacy between spouses. Modern Jewish existentialists shift the focus of marital eros from the body to interpersonal communication and thereby influence the halakhic rulings of modern rabbis on sexual ethics. Contemporary psychology suffuses halakhic rulings, sermons, and guidebooks about Jewish couple relations not only in liberal but also in ultra-Orthodox (non-Hasidic) settings.

All these schools of thought reflect on the role of sexuality in the striving for a holy and wholesome life.

Space limitations in this book preclude worthy discussion of many important and related matters. The focus, per the book's subtitle (. . . *on Marital Intimacy*), is interpersonal *marital* relations, and, in this volume, these are also chiefly heterosexual. The halakhic issues around LGBTQ lovemaking and marriage, which are beyond the competency of this author, have been treated by other scholars elsewhere.[9] Nonetheless, LGBTQ couples may find general halakhic principles about intimate interpersonal relationships originally developed for heterosexual couples applicable to their relationships.

A number of readers may be dismayed to find almost no women's voices (except for chapter 16, which is devoted to contemporary Jewish feminist theologians Plaskow and Adler). They may well be disturbed and, moreover, encounter presumptuous assumptions by men about women's sexual and emotional needs concomitant with male rabbis' legal prescriptions for "the good" of women. Classical halakhic traditions are androcentric, hierarchical, and paternalist. With the recent entrance of female rabbis into Liberal Judaism and female scholars filling the equivalent of rabbinic roles in Modern Orthodoxy, we may soon expect to find alternative norms and laws regarding marital relations. Unfortunately, only very few have so far written on the halakhic issues of heterosexual marital intimacy investigated in this book.

Traditional halakhic codes on marital relations may—and often should, to my mind—arouse irritation, resentment, and, when it affronts human dignity, righteous indignation. Yet it is not this author's purpose to defend or to condemn rabbinic culture's gendered treatment of marital relations, but to appreciate the debates and their rationales from these rabbis' historic perspectives and allow readers to evaluate their relevance on their own terms. Admittedly, however, I have my own egalitarian value commitments, and I would not have undertaken this book had I not found some ancient and contemporary Jewish insights about the practice of loving intimacy beneficial and valuable enough to share with my readers without claiming they represent the essence of Judaism or the majority rabbinic view. Given my emphasis on the halakhic treatment of psychological and erotic intimacy, I do not analyze the institution of marriage or the laws of niddah (menstrual impurity) and their implications for intimacy, researched already by other scholars.[10] Further, the book does not address the question, "Is Judaism pro-sex or anti-sex?," which has been exhaustively addressed in previous scholarship.[11]

Contemporary halakhic marital advice often overlaps with contemporary how-to books about happy marriages—passionate sex, consent, communication, problem solving, mutual respect, and navigating gender differences. This book interweaves these and other vital ideas by viewing them through Jewish legal, religious, and societal lenses. In particular, Judaism's legal culture legislates about interpersonal sexual relations through the prism of sanctity and intimacy.

While surveying halakhic texts selectively to emphasize *value* debates implicit in the legal tradition, the author attempts to avoid deciding *the* halakhah (*psak*) by evaluating the validity of legal arguments, or declaring whose voice is *most* authoritative. My aim is to ground readers in understanding the unfolding dynamics of halakhic traditions and their diverse worldviews, though inevitably my own biases will emerge.

Rabbinic tradition is clear on one point: studying Torah has never been about seeking emotional "safe spaces" where one never hears upsetting counternarratives. The opponent's principled opposition is the welcome stimulus for developing counterarguments. Hillel's school was chosen to anchor and preside over the transmission of rabbinic tradition because of its famous commitment to open debate and pluralism of interpretation: "The students of Hillel were kind and humble. They taught their own ideas as well as the ideas from the students of Shammai. Furthermore, they even taught Shammai's opinions first" (TB *Eruvin* 13b).

In the spirit of Hillel, I ask the reader to keep an open heart and mind to various views and try to learn without reticence about the Jewish ideas of marital intimacy. To that end, the book's motto is the witty retort of the Talmudic disciple Rav Kahana, who (as we see in chapter 2) audaciously hid under his master's bed to learn, by eavesdropping, about his master's art of lovemaking. When asked to justify his hutzpah, he replied: "It is Torah and I must learn it" (TB *Hagiga* 5b).

Personally, I hope and recommend, in accordance with the Mussar teacher Rav Isaac Sher (20th century), that readers, especially as couples, study the laws of onah reviewed in *Sanctified Sex* in order to enrich their relationships with kedushah (sanctity), *shalom bayit* (domestic peace), and passionate love.[12] As the Zohar (13th century) teaches:

> One must make one's wife joyful at that moment [of sexual union] in order to . . . share a common desire. Both of them as a unity . . . in soul and in body . . . are called "[the complete] human being" (Gen. 5:2). Then the Holy One may dwell in this unity, granting it a spirit of sanctity.[13]

Sanctified Sex

PART ONE

Marital Duties and Scheduled Sex

TORAH AND MISHNAH

Legislating Marital Sexuality I

BIBLICAL AND RABBINIC MANDATES

Solon was right to legislate that men should make love to their wives at least three times a month, not just for pleasure but to renew the marriage treaty and to wipe out grievances. It follows that husbands should be physically faithful, for in marriage it is better to love than to be loved.

—PLUTARCH (Greece, d. 120 CE), *Advice to Bride and Groom*

Introduction

For the peace and happiness of his city, Solon, the wise ruler of Athens (6th century BCE), legislated that married couples schedule sex at least three times a month "to renew the marriage treaty and to wipe out grievances."[1] Judaism, too, prescribes regular marital sex for a variety of purposes, but defining the parameters of mandatory sex is quite a complex matter. As we will see, Talmudic Rabbis view some sexual relations between husband and wife as permissible, others as prohibited; some as optional, and others as obligatory; some as commendable, and others as disgusting. Among themselves, the Rabbis often disagree, but they all legislate that wives have an irrevocable right to regularly scheduled intercourse in marriage.

From a twenty-first-century liberal democratic perspective, some of us may ask: What right do the Rabbis have to supervise and control the most intimate, personal, and hence private aspect of our lives? Rabbi Michael Gold put this question succinctly in the title of his book *Does God Belong in the Bedroom?* (1992). Still, even if we moderns believe that religion generally and halakhah specifically should not have a coercive role within the bedroom, we might nev-

3

ertheless ask what wisdom God or Judaism may have for our often complex love lives. Rather than looking for *the* Jewish answer, that is, the halakhic bottom line, we may benefit from examining more than two thousand years of debates concerning the whys and hows of sexuality in married life. What aspirational norms does Jewish law foster and what dilemmas does it expose in Rabbinic attempts to define good and bad marital sex?

That the Rabbis understood the multivalent qualities of sex can be seen in the varied Rabbinic euphemisms for intercourse. *Oseh tzrakhav* is "doing his biological needs," and *derekh eretz* is "the way of the world," a universal activity among humans and animals. "Eating fish" and "drinking from a cup" are culinary metaphors for sex (TB *Nedarim* 20a–b). "Taking" (*vayikah*) and "bringing" a woman into a man's house are biblical euphemisms for consummating a marriage with intercourse, as in the case of Isaac, *who brought her* [Rebecca] *into the tent of his mother Sarah and there she became his wife, he loved her and Isaac was comforted after his mother's* [death] (Gen. 24:67). Other graphic idioms refer to the man's physical act of penetration: for example, *bi'ah* is "entering/coming inside," and *b'ila* means "climbing on top" or "taking possession." Traditionally a husband is called *ba'al*, "proprietary master."

Other names for marital sex, however, emphasize mutuality in the act of sexual union, such as "becoming one flesh" (*vhayu l'basar ehad*), sexual "union" (*yihud, hibur*), and "coupling" (*zivug*, pairing). Some terms relate to spousal duties: *onah* refers to the husband's regular conjugal duties and the wife's contractual rights. *Devar mitzvah* (doing a mitzvah), a divine commandment, metaphorically alludes to God's mandate for husbands to make their wives happy sexually. My personal favorites are "a time for love" (*et dodim*); "private or intimate matters between him and her" (*devarim beino l'veina*); and "talk and play" (*sah v'sahak*)—erotic conversation, hugging, and kissing as foreplay that leads to intercourse (Gen. 26:8; TB *Hagiga* 5b).

As we will see, both the Torah and its subsequent Rabbinic interpreters create standards for marital sexuality by defining conjugal duties qualitatively and quantitatively. Fundamental to evaluating these *hows* of prescribed marital sex is understanding their *whys*. Two different explanations as to why appear in the two inconsistent Creation stories of Genesis that recount the mythic origins of man and woman.

Torah's Two Foundational Narratives of Human Sexuality

Human sexuality is so central to the Torah's worldview that it begins with two contradictory stories: God's creation of male and female (Gen. 1) and God's formation of the first woman in the Garden of Eden (Gen. 2). The two narratives offer opposing perspectives regarding divine intentions or purposes in creating men and women as sexual creatures.

GENESIS 1

Genesis 1 highlights male and female cooperation in both reproduction and mastery of God's Creation:

> *God created humanity* (ha-Adam) *in the divine image,*
> *in the image of God God created it,*
> *male and female God created them.*
> *Then God blessed them saying:*
> *"Be fruitful and multiply, and fill the earth and conquer it, rule over*
> *the fish of the sea, the birds of the sky, and the animals that crawl on*
> *the earth."* (Gen. 1:27–28)

The Hebrew verbs for the commands *be fruitful, multiply, fill, conquer,* and *rule* appear in plural form, thus making explicit that both male and female humans are assigned the role of stewards of God. Both are created in God's image. Both are created simultaneously and equally. Their labor is collaborative, not hierarchal, and so jointly they conquer and rule the animals of land, sea, and air. Together they are both necessary to reproduce in order to fill the earth, and thus expand civilization across the world under their shared dominion as divinely mandated. Genesis 1 uses the terminology of *zakhar* (male) and *nekeva* (female, lit., "hole," as in 1 Kings 12:10), perhaps referring to their interlocking reproductive anatomy.

In this version of the narrative, no mention is made of emotional intimacy, love, or pleasure. Male and female are not created for their own good but to fulfill their lofty purpose as procreators and co-masters of Creation.

GENESIS 2

Genesis 2, an independent account of Creation, tells a different story. Here, God forms the woman for Adam's own good, and human sexuality has nothing to do with reproduction. Rather, God's motivation for forming the woman (*isha*) out of the man (*ish*) is to assuage Adam's emotional, erotic, and existential loneliness. As God says: *It is not good for the human being* (ha-Adam) *to be alone; I will make a helpmate corresponding to him* (ezer kenegdo) (Gen. 2:18). In Biblical Hebrew *ezer* connotes someone who can save Adam, just as God is called *ezer* (Ps. 54:6), and *kenegdo* describes the mate God seeks for Adam as juxtaposed (not subordinate) to him.

Serving as creator, therapist, and matchmaker, God forms, from the same earth from which he made Adam, a menagerie of animals endowed with a life force (*nefesh haya*) like Adam's, and then submits them as candidates to be Adam's one and only partner in a monogamous relationship. None, however, meet Adam's standard. Rashi (Rabbi Shlomo ben Isaac, the classic Ashkenazi commentator on Bible and Talmud, 11th century, France and Germany) makes no bones about why Adam is dissatisfied with these proposed companions. Noting that it is only when God brings him the woman—not the animals—that Adam exclaims, *This time [she-is-it]!* (Gen. 2:23), Rashi comments: "*This time* teaches us that Adam had sex with every domesticated [literally, "herd animal"] and wild animal, but in them his ardor was not cooled."[2]

After his first frustrated efforts, God decides that what the human needs is another human who is more like him and yet complementary to him. God fills that lacuna with a physician's skill: anesthetizing Adam with a deep slumber, surgically dividing his body into two halves (*tzela*, often rendered as "rib," is better translated as "side"), closing up the flesh neatly, and constructing from that side the woman to fit with and complete the human being (*ha-Adam*).

Not sure she will match up to Adam's exacting expectations, God brings her to him for final approval. Overjoyed, Adam exclaims, in poetic verse, the first love song of the Bible:

> *This time [she-is-it]! Bone from my bones, flesh from my flesh!*
> *This one [she] shall be called Woman/Isha,*
> *for from Man/Ish this one was taken!* (Gen 2:23)[3]

Note the poem's poetic rhythm, its threefold refrain of "this" (*zot*), which concludes: *This one is it!* As if pointing at her, Adam recognizes "this" as his other half, the fitting complement for which he has longed.

The Israeli scholar of mysticism Moshe Idel explains the Biblical myth in terms of the quest for a lost unity:

> The erotic or sexual attraction is therefore envisioned in terms of an attempt to return to the initial state. . . . The sexual union [is] a reconstruction of the lost state of organic union between male and female.[4]

In the Torah itself existential loneliness, rather than raw sexual desire, appears to drive the prolonged search for a fitting partner.

At the completion of the matchmaking process, Adam's mellifluous poem of discovery expresses his longing and now his fulfillment.

After God's triumphant success with matchmaking, the Torah's narrator steps back from the play-by-play report of events in the Garden in order to reflect on the paradigmatic import of this mythic origin for marriage: *Therefore a man leaves his father and his mother and clings to his wife, and they become one flesh* (Gen. 2:24). Paradoxically, the man must cut himself off from his organic flesh and blood (his parents) before beginning a journey to find someone, a woman, outside his nuclear biological family whom he feels is his own—his flesh and bone, in a new and more powerful sense than he had with his mother and father.

The discovery of a suitable wife leads the man to "cling" to her, "attach" (*davak*) himself in a physical (most probably, sexual) bonding so as to become "one flesh." Attachment also connotes loyalty, just as the people of Israel hold on tight (*davak*) in their devotion to God (Deut. 4:4). Even though the woman comes from biologically distinct origins (except for the first woman), the man sees her as his original other half returned to him as a lost other half in accord with the myth of the formation of the first woman from the first man. The new kinship bond of marriage is stronger and, in some sense, more natural than the parent-child bond that must necessarily be broken to enable creating this new bond.

In sum, the implicit purpose of marriage according to Genesis 2 is the human search for existential unity. The text makes it clear that marriage is not created for momentary sexual release, as Rashi suggests above, but rather for a stable new kinship relationship. God facilitates the union of man and woman not for *reproduction*, but for *reunion* of the basic man-woman unit that God had earlier divided into two halves (Gen. 2:21, 24), neither of whom was self-sufficient without the other. Note that, in this narrative, reproduction is not yet on the divine or human agenda, because mortality is not yet part of their consciousness.

As we have seen, then, in both models of marriage (Genesis 1 and 2), sex plays a central role, but the quality of procreative sex is very different than unitive intercourse by which two become one flesh. With procreation, male and female look forward—beyond their coupling—to the next generation that transcends them, while with existential lovemaking man and woman are united in the now in fulfilling emotional and perhaps erotic longing.

Talmudic Interpretations of Adam and Eve's Relationship

In Rabbinic midrash (a genre of imaginative interpretation of Biblical verses composed chiefly in the Land of Israel, 1st to 7th centuries CE), the Biblical narratives reveal God's broad-ranging purpose in establishing marriage, and the primal couple itself represents a model for every human couple to follow:

And God said: *It is not good for the human (ha-Adam) to be alone* (Gen. 2:18).

The school of Yaakov taught: "One who has no wife remains without good, without help, without joy, without blessing, and without atonement." ...

Rabbi Shimon in the name of Rabbi Yehoshua the son of Levi said: "Also without peace, for it says, *And your dwelling is peace*" [1 Sam. 25:6].

Rabbi Yehoshua of Sikhnin said: "Also without life, for it is written, *Enjoy life with a woman whom you love*" [Eccl. 9:9].

Rabbi Hiyya the son of Gumadi said: "Also he is not a complete human, for it says, *Male and female God created them and blessed them and called their name: Adam*" (Gen. 5:2). (*Genesis Rabbah* 17:2; *Ecclesiastes Rabbah* 9:9)

In this discussion among Rabbinic interpreters, they are not really disagreeing but supplementing one another in elevating and ramifying the significance of the marital union. Like guests at a wedding asked to bless the new couple, they compete to pile on praise of this relationship. They do not interpret the benefits of the woman narrowly, as a servant for man or as a necessary partner in procreation. Rather, the union of man and woman facilitates the fulfillment of the greatest human blessings: goodness, joy, atonement, peace, and a life of love (even though love is not explicitly mentioned in Genesis 1 or 2). Finally, Rabbi Hiyya identifies marriage as the achievement of human completeness, for only when Adam the man is united with the woman does God truly apply to both together the honorific term *Adam/human in the likeness of God* (Gen. 5:1–2). Marital intimacy must serve all these ends.

Marital Duties in Torah, Mishnah, and Talmud

In the Garden of Eden there is no society and hence no institution of marriage, so the union into one flesh has no contractual implications. But once the covenant at Mount Sinai establishes Jewish society, law codes are needed to actualize the aspirational purposes of marriage implicit in the two Genesis narratives.

THE LAW OF WIVES

The first Biblical legal text about marriage is the "law of wives" (*mishpat ha-banot*), which appears in the Bible's first code of law (Exod. 21–23) imparted to Moses immediately after the Ten Commandments. This law stipulates standard obligations for every husband, so as to prevent a polygamous husband from neglecting his marital duties to his first wife, should he take a second wife:

He shall deal with her according to the law of [married] *women and if he marries another* [woman], *he must not deprive her of her* she'eir, *her* kesut, *and her* onah. . . . *If he does not provide these three, she shall go free.* (Exod. 21:9b–11)

Classic medieval Bible commentators understand the wife's three inviolable rights differently. Rashi summarizes the basic Talmudic exegesis that "her *she'eir,* her *kesut,* and her *onah*" are her allowances for food, clothing, and sexual intercourse.[5] By contrast, Nahmanides (13th century, Spanish kabbalist, Bible commentator, and Talmudist) argues that all three provisions refer specifically to the quality of physical contact, the nuanced language of expressing love through sexual union:

She'eir is a term for a "flesh" and blood relative. It recalls Adam and Eve who became in the garden *one flesh,* one family [a second meaning of *she'eir*]. But it may also mean, literally, that she may not be deprived of the touch of her husband's flesh. Hence he is not to follow the Persian custom of having intercourse in his clothes.

Kesut is her bed "clothes," her linens. She must be wooed in her bed, in an honorable fashion, and not [mounted] while lying on the floor, like a prostitute.

Onah is her "times" of lovemaking *(et dodim),* regularly scheduled, even if he takes a second wife.[6]

Explicating Nahmanides, Rabbi Isaac Sher (20th century, Israel) insists that "one who has sexual relations with his spouse without great desire has violated the Torah's prohibition on denying one's wife her *onah* (conjugal rights)."[7] A student of Nahmanides, Ritba (Rabbi Yom Tov Asevilli, 14th century, Barcelona), transforms this commentary into a binding and more egalitarian law. A husband's refusal to make love with his wife in the nude is grounds for [her to sue for] divorce from her husband, even if he claims his refusal is for the sake of modesty. The same ruling applies should she insist on [performing intercourse while clothed], for then she is rebelling against her sexual obligations. Sex [when clothed lacks closeness of flesh, and hence] does not qualify as an embodiment of *the way of affection (hibah).*[8]

Further, according to Nahmanides, marital intimacy embodies three dimensions of the conjugal bond—free choice, commitment, and love—all of which derive from the natural foundations of marriage within the Creation story.[9] Free choice plays a crucial role in Adam's selection of a mate. Therefore, "it is good that the mate stands opposite him (*ezer kenegdo*, "face-to-face"), so that he can see the other. Then he can either separate from or unite with the mate according to his will."[10] Already in the Garden, before eating from the Tree of Knowledge, says Nahmanides, both man and woman demonstrate the capacity for free choice, rational decision making, and sexual union.

Nahmanides elucidates the second dimension of the marital bond, commitment to companionship, by pointing out that, unlike most animals, human beings are meant to mate for life:

Domestic and wild animals have no commitment to their females, but rather the male copulates with any female he should chance upon and then goes on his way. But it is because of this [difference from animal mating] that the verse states that the female of the man is *bone of my bone and flesh of my flesh* (Gen. 2:23). She will be in his bosom as part of his own body; and he will desire her and want to be with her constantly.

And just as this was with Adam, so it was integrated into the nature of his progeny, that males would be committed to their wives, *abandoning their fathers and mothers*, and viewing their wives as if they were *one flesh* with them.[11]

For Nahmanides, the third dimension necessary to marriage is a shared life of eros. Human sexuality is not just a mechanism of Nature for promoting procreation and childrearing, but a means to express love, union, and affectionate companionship. As the contemporary Judaica scholar James Diamond explains: "By synchronizing sex with the emotional and psychological needs of the woman, Nahmanides has constructed an encounter that is mutual—*between* partners—rather than a one-sided fulfillment of duty performed *on* the other."[12]

Indeed, the duty to give one's newlywed wife happiness appears in the laws of Deuteronomy, with the onus of lovemaking on the husband:

> *When a man has taken a bride, he shall not go out with the army and not be assigned to it for any purpose. He shall be exempt one year for the sake of his household, to make happy the woman he has married.* (Deut. 24:5)

The Torah enables a new groom to make his new bride happy by granting him a yearlong exemption from army service. Thus, regardless of its procreative potential, it is a mitzvah for him to engage in marital intercourse, generating joy by devoting time and intensive attention to his wife. And beyond year one, the mitzvah of onah continues, as Rabbah (4th century, Babylonia) says: "A man is [always] obligated to make his wife happy with *devar mitzvah*" (a euphemism for onah) (TB *Moed Katan* 8b; TB *Pesahim* 72b; see TB *Baba Batra* 10b). Thus it is that the Torah's law of wives and its Rabbinic interpreters establish a mandatory societal system to define and enforce a wife's right to happiness, so defined as regular sexual intimacy.

TALMUDIC LAWS OF MARITAL SEXUALITY

Many centuries after the Torah's code of law is promulgated (dates of its composition have been estimated from the 12th century to the

5th century BCE), the Talmudic Rabbis (from the 1st century CE) begin to institutionalize sexual relations in marriage in accordance with the Biblical purposes in Genesis 1 and 2: procreation, on the one hand, and emotional solidarity and erotic pleasure, on the other.

Following Genesis 1, in which male and female are partners for procreation, the Rabbis ask themselves: What legal conditions should shape reproductive marital sex? First, we turn to the Mishnah (canonized ca. 200 CE by Rabbi Judah HaNasi in the Land of Israel), and then to the Talmud that comments on the Mishnah (completed in two versions in the Land of Israel and in Babylonia between the 5th and 7th centuries). The Mishnah establishes restrictive guidelines for choosing a fertile partner, by stipulating that she must be capable of reproduction and, if she proves to be infertile, she must be divorced and replaced:

> No man may abstain from keeping the law, *Be fruitful and multiply* (Gen. 1:28), unless he already has children: according to the School of Shammai, two sons; according to the School of Hillel, a son and a daughter, for it is written, *Male and female God created them* (Gen. 5:2). If he married a woman and lived with her ten years and she bore no child, it is not permitted for him to abstain [any longer from fulfilling this legal obligation]. (*Mishnah Yevamot* 6:6)

Given this procreative mandate, we might expect the Rabbis to stipulate a sexual position that maximizes the possibility of fertilization (such as the missionary position with the man on top), while prohibiting anal intercourse or other sexual practices that may waste procreative semen. Some halakhic authorities prefer that missionary position, but the dominant Talmudic tradition permits sex in any posture one likes (see chapters 3 and 6). We might also expect the Rabbis to prohibit scheduling intercourse that cannot lead to pregnancy (such as with a woman who is already pregnant or who is postmenopausal), or to make such nonprocreative marital sex optional. Yet the Rabbis, nevertheless, *obligate* husbands to make love regularly with their wives, regardless of whether the wives are fertile or not. After producing the requisite two children for the mitzvah of *be fruitful and multiply*, a man may marry a woman who is congenitally infertile, and then too he is obligated to engage in marital sex regularly.[13]

Furthermore, over time, Jewish tradition abandoned the enforcement of the mishnah restricting a man's choice of a wife to a fertile woman in order to maintain *shalom bayit* (harmonious emotional relationships in the home) in an infertile marriage. In the fourteenth century, Ribash (Rav Isaac bar Sheshet Perfet, 14th century, Barcelona) reports that the courts no longer compel divorce in such cases:

> [The obligation to compel divorce] is the letter of the law, but what can we do? For many generations we have not heard that a court forced a man to divorce a wife who had borne him no children in ten years of marriage. . . . If courts had to apply the letter of the law and force couples to divorce . . . then strife and argument would abound. Our Sages looked the other way and did not prevent [infertile] matches, let alone break up marriages.[14]

A charming Talmudic tale reveals the power of love in marriage to suspend the law that prioritizes having children:

> Rabbi Idi [3rd century, Land of Israel] said: Once there was a woman in Sidon [Lebanon] who remained for ten years with her husband and she did not give birth. They came before Rabbi Shimon ben Yohai, and they wanted to be divorced from each other [in accord with the Mishnah]. He said to them: "By your life, just as you became coupled to each other with feasting and drinking, so too you should not part without feasting and drinking." They went their way and made for themselves a feast, and made a great meal and he drank too much.

When he regained his senses, he said to her: "My daughter [i.e., his wife], see any good thing that I have in this house. Take it and go to your father's house." What did she do? After he went to sleep, she summoned her slaves and maidservants and she said to them: "Lift him up with the bed and take him and bring him to the house of [my] father." . . .

When the wine wore off, he said to her: "My daughter, where am I being taken?" She said: "To [my] father's house." He said to her: "Why am I going to your father's house?" She said to him: "Didn't you say to me last night: 'Take any good thing that is in my house with you and go to your father's house'? There is nothing as good for me as you!"

They went to Rabbi Shimon ben Yohai, he prayed for them, and they conceived. [This tale] teaches you that just as the Holy One visits (*pokeid*) sterile women [granting them fertility, as God did for Sarah—Gen. 21:1], so too, righteous men ought to visit sterile women [i.e., continue sexual relations even after years of sterility]. (*Song of Songs Rabbah* 4:5; *Pesikta de-Rav Kahana* 22:2)

In this fairytale ending all is well: the husband stays with his barren wife and she eventually gives birth. But the larger point is that a man may disregard the law of procreative marriage, staying as long as he wants with the infertile wife he loves. Clearly, then, procreation is not always a necessary component of marital sex, and not the exclusive reason for making regular intercourse mandatory. Biblical and Rabbinic conjugal duties derive from alternative purposes of marriage—marital intimacy, mutual pleasure, biological release, and channeling of desire.

The Revolutionary Rabbinic Marriage Contract

Recognizing that wives are largely disadvantaged in relation to their husbands (socially, economically, and legally, as explained below), the marital laws about sexual relations that the Rabbis enact are (generally, but not always) intended to protect wives from possible neglect, shame, and exploitation by their husbands. In contrast to the legal and social practices of the Torah, Talmudic marriage is nothing short of revolutionary within the Jewish legal tradition.

According to the Torah, a marriage begins when a man "takes" a woman and performs intercourse, and then he may divorce her whenever he finds in her something profoundly repulsive or, according to some interpreters, something mildly off-putting (Deut. 24:1) (TB *Gittin* 90a–b). The Torah never explicitly states that a woman must consent to the marriage, or that she has the right to divorce her husband if he fails to live up to his obligations to provide food, clothing, and sexual needs (Exod. 21:9–11). No marital contract is mentioned; rather, custom dictated that the bride's parents negotiate the financial arrangements. For example, Laban marries off his daughters Leah and Rachel to Jacob in exchange for fourteen years of shepherding (Gen. 29:18–27).

By contrast, the Rabbinic institution of marriage involves a more egalitarian process of negotiating a contract. Betrothal must be concluded solely by the legal authority of the couple, regardless of the parents' opinion, for their commitment must be the product of the exercise of their own joint legal autonomy. As Maimonides sums up the Talmudic law: "No woman can be betrothed except by her free will."[15] For this reason, child marriages (in which it is assumed a minor cannot yet formulate an independent judgment about the suitability of a prospective spouse) are condemned, and face-to-face encounters between bride and groom are strongly recommended so the two can evaluate their mutual attractiveness to one another.[16] Whereas in the Bible wives are bought with bride-prices paid generally to their parents, in the Talmud women usually consent to betrothal (*kiddushin*) simply by accepting a symbolic gift worth less than a *prutah* (the smallest coin).[17]

While the Torah never mentions a written contract concluded between the couple, the Rabbis insist on the negotiation of a written contract (*ketubah*) in which both spouses determine their reciprocal obligations. Grounded in mutual consent, the Rabbinic ketubah specifies frequency of sexual relations, constraints on unilateral changes of the couple's residence or the husband's profession, visits to and from in-laws, clothing and jewelry allowances, and much more. Its most important innovation stipulates the husband's hefty financial debt to his wife in case of his death or his unilateral decision to divorce her. Should he fail to fulfill the provisos of their contract, the courts can force him to either live up to his obligations or divorce his wife and pay her the ketubah settlement. For example, a man who fails to meet his wife's sexual needs has given her grounds for suing for divorce and receiving the ketubah settlement. Similarly, should she refuse to live up to her agreement, he may divorce her without paying her ketubah settlement (*Mishnah Ketubot* 5:6–7; 7:1–6). The ketubah's large payment provides the wife with some economic security in case she becomes a divorcée or a widow, but equally important is its deterrent or punitive dimension in case of malfeasance by husband or wife.[18]

The ketubah, read aloud at traditional weddings, employs global language stipulating that the husband owes "whatever Jewish men usually owe their wives." By default, most couples then and now simply accept those conditions, though if they wish they can modify or add their own provisos before the wedding. Even though the Torah commands that husbands support their wives financially (Exod. 21:11), and the standard ketubah requires the man to buy his wife clothing, jewelry, and bedding, in theory almost every financial duty between spouses may be altered by prior consent.[19] For example, Rabbi Akiba's son stipulated that his wealthy wife would support him for as long as they were married, so he could study rather than work (*Tosefta Ketubot* 4:7).

Exceptionally, the sexual duties and rights stipulated in the ketubah are not fully negotiable. While a wife may temporarily forgo her right to onah, a woman may *not* irreversibly renounce her right to sexual relations.[20]

Two rationales explain the unique status of the woman's irrevocable right to intercourse in marriage. First, the Rabbis consider sexual satisfaction a basic human need. If a wife loses her right to onah, how will she fulfill her needs? Won't her unrequited biological urges lead to extramarital affairs and social anarchy? Second, the Rabbis believe that intercourse is constitutive of emotional intimacy, and marriage without sexual intimacy is an empty formality that does not address human loneliness. Thus, for the Rabbis, permanent abstinence is not valid in a marriage contract.[21]

So it is that in a straightforward marital dispute, when a woman demands that her sexual rights be honored and a husband refuses, the Mishnaic law is clear: the man is to do his duty or pay the ketubah compensation and release his wife to seek another partner. Maimonides equates the denial of sexual duties to one's wife with the economic and moral crime of withholding wages due to a day laborer: "There is no difference between one who holds back payment of wages to a day laborer, and one who does this to one's wife."[22]

By this time, careful readers may have noticed that Rabbinic law speaks about men's sexual obligations but not their rights. As we saw, Ritba and many later halakhic authorities assume that a man's conjugal rights are self-evident, but the Talmudic texts do not detail those rights—only the wife's entitlement to sex. In the Rabbis' eyes, special legislation is needed to protect women because three other marital laws profoundly disadvantage them.

First, according to classical Jewish law, men, but not women, may have multiple marital partners (polygamy). Only in the Ashkenazi world of Catholic France and Germany did Rabbenu Gershom

(Germany, ca. 1000) proclaim that polygamy was prohibited for Jewish men as it was for Christians.[23] In fact, in Jewish law in most Muslim lands until the establishment of the State of Israel, polygamy was an option for Jewish men, as it was and still is according to the sharia law for Muslim men.[24] (Israeli Ashkenazi and Sephardi rabbis convened in 1950 to forbid polygamy, and the Israeli Knesset made bigamy a crime in 1959, though Jews from Muslim lands such as Yemen who made *aliyah* together with more than one wife continued to practice polygamy in Israel.[25])

Second, women are further disadvantaged compared to men in that husbands can unilaterally divorce their wives, but wives can at best sue the courts to compel their husbands to divorce them when the men are at fault for violating the ketubah.[26] Rabbenu Gershom would attempt to help equalize this situation in the eleventh century by establishing that Jewish men could not divorce their wives without their wives' consent.[27] From then on, for Ashkenazim (whose family origins were originally from France and Germany and later Eastern Europe) both to marry and to divorce required mutual consent.

In the subsequent century, Maimonides (12th century, Egypt) would codify in his great compendium of Jewish law, the *Mishneh Torah*, a revolutionary position even more supportive of women's sexual rights. Appealing to the human freedom to mastery over one's own body, Maimonides rules that a woman has a right to a *unilateral no-fault divorce* if she cannot stand to have sexual relations with her husband anymore:

> If she says: "I have come to loathe him and I cannot willingly submit to intercourse with him," then [the court must] force him to divorce her immediately [even by applying corporal punishment until he consents] since she [a wife] is *not like a captive who must accede to intercourse with one whom she hates* [such as a captor who has kid-

napped her]. Let her go out [i.e., be divorced] though without [the right to] any ketubah payment at all.[28]

This ruling, however, has not been accepted broadly by other rabbis, then or now. Therefore, in a contested divorce, Rabbinic courts can compel a husband to issue a divorce only for due cause, but not simply when she claims emotional incompatibility.

Third, a wife is disadvantaged because, if a husband engages in extramarital sex, the violation is regarded as at most a misdemeanor equivalent to prostitution, but a wife who partakes in an extramarital liaison is considered guilty of the capital crime of adultery. Thus a husband can find sexual satisfaction alongside his marriage, while a wife has no legal recourse to sexual intimacy outside of the husband-wife relationship. And so, within the provisos of the ketubah, the Rabbis created *affirmative action legislation* specifically for wives so as to obligate their husbands to provide them with sex in a timely fashion.

Rules for *Onah's* Frequency

For the Talmudic Rabbis, building trust and intimacy in marriage necessitates both a certain quantity as well as quality of conjugal intimacy. However, devoting countless hours to the family's livelihood and to raising children makes it difficult for couples to set aside time for interpersonal sexual affection. The mishnah we examine below (*Mishnah Ketubot* 5:6) tries to balance two competing marital duties—loving and financially supporting one's spouse—within the then standard setting of a family where the male is the breadwinner.

But just how frequently is a husband expected to renew sexually his union with his wife? Emerging in the ensuing discussions are three different rabbinic approaches toward the frequency of marital relations:

1. Daily, unless limited by the time, travel, and energy constraints of the husband's occupation. (*Mishnah Ketubot* 5:6)

2. Variable, determined by the wife's physiological and emotional desires (Rashi et al.).

3. Negotiable, decided by the husband and wife themselves (Ra'avad, 13th century, Provence), though the wife retains veto power over whatever consensual arrangement the couple reaches.

SCHEDULING SEX BY THE HUSBAND'S OCCUPATION

The mishnah legislates the wife's right to regular sexual intimacy, but regulates and restricts its frequency based on the husband's business schedule and his leftover energy for sex:

The [frequency of the] times (*onah*) for performing one's marital duty [to one's wife] is prescribed in the Torah (Exod. 21:10)....

For men who are *tayalin* [an unknown term, perhaps a day laborer or a student], every day.

For laborers, twice a week.

For mule-drivers, once a week.

For camel-drivers, once in thirty days.

For sailors, once in six months. (*Mishnah Ketubot* 5:6)

If the legislation of onah is intended to enforce a woman's rights, then, the question arises: Why give priority to the man's pursuit of his livelihood? It seems absurd to grant the wife of a sailor such a limited right to sex, especially since Maimonides calculates that the wife of a polygamous sailor with four wives (one in each port?) is entitled to intercourse only once every two years.[29]

Nevertheless, Rabbi Moshe Feinstein (20th century, New York City) justifies this law because one cannot obligate the husband to a scheduled onah beyond his ability: "The Torah does not subject a person to an obligation for intercourse that surpasses his capabilities, his health, and his available time."[30] In any case it is the wife who consented to this arrangement when she knowingly married a sailor.

SCHEDULING SEX BY THE WIFE'S SPONTANEOUS DESIRE

Several halakhic authorities find the strict scheduling of the husband's minimal marital duties in the mishnah an inadequate response to a woman's basic needs. Rather, they say, the husband is obligated to cause his wife joy in sexual intercourse whenever she so desires. Commenting on Rava's (4th century, Babylonia) Talmudic statement, "A man is obligated to make his wife happy by doing the mitzvah [of onah]," Rashi explains: "Even if it is beyond her scheduled onah, [he is obligated to make her happy] whenever the husband sees that his wife desires it" (TB *Pesahim* 72b). Therefore, whenever a husband sees his wife adorning herself to attract his attention, he is duty-bound to respond by making love to her.[31]

Even this approach has some shortcomings. Some wives may be too embarrassed to make their sexual needs known to their husbands, and/or some husbands might miss their wives' subtle signals about when they feel the need for intimacy. In such cases, the aforementioned mishnah offers a safety net: a set minimum number of marital encounters not triggered by a wife's explicit request.[32]

Rabbi Moses ben Joseph di Trani (Safed, 1500–80 CE) comments on the mishnah that onah belongs to the wife: "It is her right, not his right."[33] Therefore, husbands who feel a need for intercourse more often than the mishnah's schedule may suggest to their wives that they engage in sexual intimacy, but they have no such right to sex on demand and are dependent each time on their wives' consent.

The third option, articulated by Ra'avad, overrides the frequency requirements of the mishnah by asserting that the husband and wife are free to reach a mutual agreement about onah without regard to the husband's occupation. Ra'avad explains: "The Rabbis estimated that the woman will reconcile herself to what her husband can provide in accordance with his capability and his pleasure," but she is not obligated to consent, and he may agree to commit to more frequent onah.[34] The mishnah's schedule is not binding unless the couple agrees at the time of their marriage.

Based on the principle of mutual consent, Maimonides rules: "After marriage a wife may permit her husband to refrain from satisfying her *onah*" altogether.[35] Rav Solomon Luria, the Maharshal (16th century, Lithuania), however, rules that even if the wife states explicitly that she forfeits her right to intimate marital duties, her forfeiture (*mhila*) is invalid, for "one may say yes but really mean no."[36] Negotiations, then, are not always the result of freely given consent. The wife, warns the Maharshal, is probably deferring to her insistent husband even though she wants and needs more sexual intimacy. Contra Maimonides, he would not treat her verbal consent to abstinence as an expression of fully voluntary agreement, since the husband wields authority over her—legal, social, economic, and even physical. In a similar vein, the Israeli Prevention of Sexual Harassment Law (5758/1998) stipulates that a person having authority over another (army officer, boss, teacher, rabbi) who urges a subordinate to have intercourse is guilty of harassment, even if the subordinate ultimately consents, since his or her consent under duress is defective.

Further challenges arise in this model of onah set by mutual negotiation. For one, what if, after marrying, the husband wishes to make a fundamental change of career that is liable to affect the couple's pattern of intimacy and the wife does not agree to the change?

In this scenario, the Rabbis offer the following guidance:

> Rabbah, son of Rabbi Hanan, said to Abbaye: "What [is the frequency of onah when] a mule driver [a local teamster on short transport routes who is available to have intercourse with his wife once a week] becomes a camel driver [going on longer caravans and available only once a month]?"
>
> [Abbaye] replied [with a folk proverb]: "A woman prefers one *kab* [bushel-like measure of grain] with sexual satisfaction to ten *kab* with abstinence." (TB *Ketubot* 61b)

Abbaye (Babylonia, d. 339) explains that camel drivers make more money than mule drivers. Nevertheless, Abbaye assumes that most wives prefer a husband's greater proximity and more intimacy over his larger income and her improved lifestyle. In effect, according to Abbaye, the woman wields ultimate veto power regarding her husband's career changes.

Abbaye's view becomes the accepted rabbinic law. According to Rabbi Jacob ben Asher's halakhic code, the Tur (14th century, Spain):

> A husband is *not* permitted to change his profession from one [that enables and therefore requires] frequent fulfillment of marital obligations to one with less frequent onah, such as a mule driver who becomes a camel driver without permission [of the spouse] even if the new profession is more profitable. (Tur: Even HaEzer 76)

In essence, since the husband's occupation affects the most intimate aspect of the couple's life together, pursuing one's own professional growth after becoming married is no longer an individual decision. While spouses are expected to flexibly renegotiate the conditions of their shared life from a place of love and understanding, the woman still wields the halakhic upper hand to veto proposed changes that will inevitably affect her marital life.

What is more, according to the tradition, even a wife who *has* consented to her husband's job change (or to a long business trip) that deprives her of her onah may always revoke her permission unilaterally. The medieval commentator Abraham Hiyya de Boton (Salonica, d. 1605) explains:

> Even when she gives permission to stay away longer, this is not a formal forfeiture of her rights. As long as she does not demand sexual intimacy and she gives him permission to be away, the husband may abstain from intercourse with her. But the right to make a claim [for more frequent intimacy] is always hers, to be activated anytime she wishes.[37]

While in principle wives seem to have the legal upper hand in negotiations involving their husbands' absences, say for business trips, in reality this is not always the case. As the Maharshal argues above, "One may say yes but really mean no." In practice, husbands may often cajole their wives into assenting, and traditional women may often defer their needs in order to maintain domestic tranquility. The husband may (subtly, or not) pressure the wife to relinquish her best interests out of her love for him or a shared idealism for his higher spiritual calling to study Torah away from home. She may also decide pragmatically that compromise is the better part of valor.

Aware that the acquiescing wife's internal dialogue may well be, *I said yes, as you knew I would, but I really wanted to say no!*, the Talmud considers this issue in determining the length of a scholarly husband's study furlough. On one hand, the mishnah stipulates:

"Students may go away to study the Torah, *without* the permission [of their wives, for a period of at most] thirty days." (Presumably, prospective brides were to be made aware of this stipulation before they agreed to marry a student.) On the other hand, the Talmud queries: "For how long [may the students go away] *with* the permission [of their wives]?—For as long as they desire. [But] what should be the usual period [of such a trip]?" (TB *Ketubot* 61b).

In their interpretation of the Talmudic question about "the usual period" of such a permitted trip requested by the husband and granted at the discretion of the wife who has consented, two great medieval commentators capture the way in which formal consent may mask the husband's power to intimidate his wife, even if he is not fully aware of his hidden tyranny. According to Rashi:

> "The usual period" [of a professional furlough for which a husband may ask his wife's indulgence] is the standard acceptable length of absence [for a study trip, i.e., thirty days]. But the husband who has asked and even received permission [from his wife] to go away for longer will be held accountable for a sin, even if he succeeded in *seducing* his wife into granting a permit to stay abroad longer.

Rabbenu Asher (13th century, Spain) explains that "even if his wife grants him permission to be away longer, because he placated her or because she was embarrassed [to say "no"], in truth her heart is still distressed."[38] For both Rashi and Rabbenu Asher, the woman's vulnerability to her husband's pressure undermines the validity of her consent to his absence.

In sum, the chief marital duty is to maintain sexual intimacy in quality and quantity. Exemptions may be permitted only by truly free and mutual consent. Perhaps the best metaphor for rabbinic marriage is "a life of ongoing negotiations" to sort out conflicting interests and desires.

Romantic and Liberal Critiques of the Mishnah's Obligatory Sex

So far, by examining the details of the Mishnah's law of onah, this chapter has shown how the Rabbis sought to protect women's rights and needs within a patriarchal society in which men could and often did take advantage of their power differential over their wives. Stipulating the frequency and quality of sexual duties within a negotiated contract is the Rabbis' primary mechanism to defend wives and to upgrade love and emotional intimacy in marriage. Yet, it is precisely the notion of halakhically regimented marital relations imposed by rabbinic authority that is intolerable from the modern perspectives of a romantic ethos of spontaneous love and of political liberalism.

For believers in romance, obligatory scheduled sex is by definition insincere, perfunctory, and dehumanizing, and thus vitiates its meaning as an act of love. If onah is supposed to be about love, then spontaneity, individuality, and creativity are essential. As the philosopher Friedrich Nietzsche (19th century, Germany) wrote, "the free spirit hates all habituation and rules."[39] In this view, the mishnah's quantitative stipulation of acts of marital sex can at best address the wife's need to satisfy her biological urges, but marital duties so defined have nothing to do with romantic lovemaking as a qualitative experience.

The liberal objection to the mishnah's legislation highlights the injury to individual liberty and the law's invasion into matters of personal taste. Society should not violate one's privacy and autonomy, especially in one's most intimate personal space—the marital bed.

These weighty contemporary criticisms, which appeal intuitively to the author and to many readers, make it difficult to appreciate sympathetically the logic of the rabbinic approach to marital intimacy. Therefore, let us consider briefly how one might plausibly respond, first to the liberal critique of the law of onah, and afterward to the romantic objections.

The classic philosopher of liberalism, John Stuart Mill (19th century, England), proclaims the doctrine that every citizen has a right to liberty of action limited only by the constraint "to prevent harm to others."[40] By that definition, a liberal government ought to intervene in private familial affairs so as to defend women who are being abused by more powerful husbands. Here Mill's liberalism is proactive: The state has a responsibility to "beneficially employ its powers" and promote "the public welfare."[41] Therefore he supported the Bill for the Better Prevention and Punishment of Assaults on Women and Children (1853), and spoke out against "domestic tyranny."[42]

By the same liberal logic, the Torah and the Mishnah regard the denial of a woman's right to sexual intimacy as an abuse of the weaker member in the marital framework. Leaving the fulfillment of sexual needs to a couple's erotic spontaneity is not a reliable way to handle drives that if unsatisfied may endanger the health of either spouse, their relationship, and the larger society. Well-defined contractual rights that can be enforced by legal coercion can help remedy social and legal injustices against women in a patriarchal society that takes men's sexual hegemony for granted. Thus the Rabbis replaced a hierarchal, status-based marriage with a consensual, contractual one. In its ideal functioning, the law of onah should not enforce the ethos of marriage coercively (except in the most egregious situations) but educationally, by instructing members of a couple to make their expectations explicit so that each spouse will become more sensitive to the other's needs. Then the couple should negotiate a contract for their common good, and honor their commitments out of love and responsibility.

Furthermore, turning to the objections raised to the Mishnah's legislation by the romantic ethos, how might the Rabbis defend the scheduling of obligatory marital duties of intercourse? How might they interpret the law of onah in light of Romanticism's assumptions about the gender distinctions between the erotic mentalities of men and women?[43] Other chapters address the controversial issues surrounding assumed gender differences between male and female sexual desire (chapters 2 and 9–11). Here I examine two unusual responses from ultra-Orthodox halakhic authorities of the last 150 years who take seriously the importance of sexual passion in women in marriage.

Two Ultra-Orthodox Rejoinders to the Romantic Critique of *Onah*

Rabbis Chaim Sofer and Moshe Feinstein, ultra-Orthodox halakhic authorities who lived in societies that were subject to the modernizing ethos of love and marriage, responded to implicit romantic objections to the mishnah's schedule of obligatory marital sex by issuing innovative rulings. Both rabbis reject in principle the Western idea of romantic love, and yet in practice adjust their understanding of onah to suit romantic sensibilities that highlight sexual passion in lovemaking. They reinterpret the halakhah to give prevalence to spontaneous unscheduled sexual desires and to meet, what they presume, are divergent erotic and emotional needs of men and women.

SOFER'S RULING: MUTUAL PASSION

Rav Chaim Sofer (Hungary, d. 1886) bolsters the view that halakhic onah means a couple owes each other natural, hot-blooded, even irrational sexual passion:

> The husband is obligated to his wife and the wife is obligated to her husband in the mitzvah of *onah*. . . . For the Torah understood the heart of human beings that the madness of impulse (*shigyonot ha-yetzer*) is implanted by Nature so human beings might have pleasure.

The path to approach the affection of intercourse is to lie together with bodily contact with hugs and kisses and so on. . . .

Therefore the Talmud teaches that one who wishes to have intercourse while he is clothed and she is clothed must divorce her and pay her ketubah, for pleasures like this are also included in the mitzvah of *onah*.[44]

While the mishnah obligates only the husband to satisfy his wife, Sofer makes the obligation mutual and ascribes an equally passionate drive for sexual intimacy to both men and women.

FEINSTEIN HARMONIZES THE HALAKHAH OF *ONAH* WITH NATURAL SEXUALITY

By contrast, Rav Moshe Feinstein (Minsk, Russia; New York City, 1895–1986), the preeminent American Orthodox halakhic decisor of the twentieth century, asserts that a study of natural sexuality reveals that men and women possess wholly different needs for intimacy and sexual satisfaction: Men want sex all the time and women prefer emotional attention. Since the mishnah on scheduled marital intercourse specifies the frequency of a husband's conjugal obligations to his wife but fails to mention a wife's sexual duties to her husband, Feinstein must radically reinterpret this mishnah and the halakhah of onah so they correspond to what he believes to be true about natural, God-given gender differences in libidinal drives. Thus Feinstein rules:

The wife is obligated to serve *his* sexual needs *at any time* that he wishes, even if it is not the scheduled *onah*, as long as she is healthy [and pure of menstrual blood]; but the husband is not obligated to provide her with sexual intercourse, except in accordance with [1] the [mishnah's] prescribed the schedule of *onah*, [2] the night she is purified in the *mikveh* [the ritual bath after the termination of her period], [3] just before he goes on a trip, and [4] whenever he notices that she is making an effort to please him by adorning herself before him.[45]

The husband can demand sex any time, and the wife is legally bound to be cooperative (though elsewhere Feinstein clearly prohibits a husband from coercing his wife against her will). So, too, Feinstein rules that the wife has a right to intercourse whenever she hints to him that she is interested:

> Whenever he sees that the woman is filled with desire and longing, then his response fulfills the Torah's obligation, for that is the main requirement of the Torah regarding onah. . . . So, just as in eating and dressing, onah is not dependent on a particular time but only on one's desire.[46]

Husbands are instructed to be ready for intimacy, especially when wives are most likely to want that physical closeness—immediately *after* the two-week moratorium on touching during her menstrual period and its one-week aftermath, and immediately *before* he goes on a trip, when anticipated distance presumably makes her heart grow fonder. No schedule minimizes the mutual marital duty that allows either partner to initiate intimacy, whether its focus is more sexual (men) or more emotional (women).

Contra Feinstein's ruling, the Torah and the Talmud do not specify the frequency with which a woman has to provide sexual satisfaction to her husband. Some authorities, such as the Maharit (Rabbi Joseph di Trani, Greece, d. 1639), rule that a wife is obligated to satisfy his needs *only* when he is obligated to her in accordance with his professional capabilities; he has no right to demand sex at a higher frequency. In fact, the Maharit adds a proviso that limits the husband's right to insist even on that limited frequency of onah: "Of course she is not obligated to meet his needs at any *particular* time if she does not want it."[47] As a result, husbands must successfully woo their wives, arouse them, and thereby persuade them to make love each time they are aroused.

How does Feinstein justify his surprising reinterpretation of the mishnah? He assumes that the halakhah that God gave Israel must harmonize with (what he believes is) God's design for Creation as revealed in the differential physiology and psychology of men and women. Feinstein authoritatively states that "a man always desires sex,"[48] so the mishnah on the frequency of onah could not possibly set a limit on men's right to unscheduled sex or exempt women from fulfilling those needs, as the Maharit assumed. Further, Feinstein concludes from his study of female desire that the mishnah could *not* really demand that husbands provide their wives with frequent intercourse, as that would make no sense, since women by nature do not want sex at the high frequency men do. When women do want marital relations, and only when they do—and, then, as often as they wish—men must be available for onah.

To Feinstein, what women *do* want at a higher frequency than men is attention to their emotional needs for intimacy, especially their unverbalized desires. Since Feinstein assumes and even prescribes that women be reticent about verbalizing their unmet expectations, husbands need to become more attentive to their wives' unspoken needs. He instructs husbands to learn to do what does not come as second nature to them: to be solicitous, attend to their wives at all times (to hear what is unexpressed), and take the initiative to make themselves accessible.

In Feinstein's calibration, onah as a fixed schedule of sexual relations becomes a default position:

> Since most women, however, are modest, and their desire is not externalized, and there are many men who will not notice that she wants sex as indicated by her expression of affection to him.... Therefore,

the Rabbis established a schedule based on their estimation of the man's strength and the woman's desire.[49]

A husband must check in with his wife in case he has not noticed that she feels moved by sexual and more likely emotional needs. Since a woman's need for *onah* is often psychological more than physiological, Feinstein rules that a husband must demonstrate his interest in his wife, even if neither he nor she has a sexual urge at that moment:

> For she may think: if he really loved her, he would have intercourse with her. For she knows that a man always desires sex, even more than a woman does (TB *Ketubot* 64b). Then [if he does not initiate sexual intimacy] she will think that his refraining from intercourse with her is a sign that he does not love her. Then she will feel very hurt by his restraint, even more than from the actual denial of the satisfaction of intercourse. That is why the Rabbis stipulated [with the exception of her period of niddah, ritual impurity] that wives have a right to *onah* on a daily basis [at least for nonscholars], even if it is unusual for a woman to feel desire daily.[50]

While Feinstein regards the difference between males and females as natural, rooted in God's Creation, he acknowledges that changing social mores can modify a woman's felt needs. Because in the modern world in America, where Feinstein came to live from a rural village in Lithuania, social and cultural pressures on women stimulate their sexual desires to a higher pitch than in the past, and so he says the mandated frequency of onah must be adjusted upward. For example, scholars, who have been taught since the Talmudic era that they are obligated to have intercourse with their wives only once a week, must now initiate sexual relations with their wives twice a week. Feinstein cites a precedent and then applies it to the modern era:

[Rabbi Eliyahu HaCohen of Casablanca, d. 1729] says: "The sexual promiscuity of this generation and the envy women feel of one another [i.e., their competitive jealousy of what they presume is the greater sexual satisfaction of their female neighbors] have generated greater desire than can be provided [by intercourse only] once a week."[51]

Thus [explains Feinstein] the essence of the mitzvah of onah [is the husband's duty to provide his wife's sexual needs]. Even if the husband does not notice her added desire, [the scholar is obligated not once but] twice a week, because she may be too ashamed and modest to show him [what she needs].[52]

Feinstein's approach to halakhah is radical. Whatever the legal texts say about onah, he insists that they be reinterpreted in light of scientific and sociological truths about human sexuality. For him, the Torah and the Oral Law promulgated by the Creator cannot disregard actual human needs differentiated by gender and society. The Torah, understood broadly as the God-given Jewish way of life, does not require that Jews sacrifice their sexual or emotional needs in order to obey the letter of the law. Rather, in this case the halakhah must be interpreted to reflect what Feinstein thinks is the original purpose of the mitzvah adjusted to changing times.

Modern Applications: Perel's Scheduling of Intimacy and the Youngs' Sexperiment

While romantics insist on spontaneous, passion-driven sexual union and oppose prescribing sexual intercourse as a duty owed to one's partner, some contemporaries—in particular, a famous Jewish psychotherapist and a popular Evangelical preacher—have campaigned in favor of scheduling intimacy in advance. Thus, some of the lessons of the mishnah's timetable for scheduled, obligatory, and frequent onah with one's partner (whether both spouses feel like it or not) find renewed plausibility in the books of marital therapist Esther Perel and of the Reverend Ed Young and his wife, Lisa Young.

THE MARITAL THERAPIST ESTHER PEREL ON SCHEDULING INTIMATE TIME

Perel reports that in her private practice many long-term couples find it difficult to maintain erotic desire in sexual relations, since their familiarity with one another often breeds boredom. Therefore Perel encourages them to make advance appointments for sexual encounters, because "anticipation is part of building a plot; that is why romance novels and soap operas are filled with it."[53] Moreover, preplanning bestows a level of importance on the intentionality of one's sex life—which is typically more characteristic of a date, during which one woos a potential sexual partner.

Nonetheless, Perel often meets with resistance to her suggestion, for two reasons. First, her clients protest that, by this stage in their relationship, they should not have to court one another deliberately:

> Quite a few of my patients balk at the idea of deliberateness when it comes to sex . . . believing [these strategies] should no longer be necessary after the initial conquest. . . . This reluctance is often a covert expression of an infantile wish to be loved just as we are, without any effort whatsoever on our part, because we're so special. "You're supposed to love me no matter what!"[54]

The second objection to scheduling sex in advance is that passion should be spontaneous, not artificially programmed. But Perel criticizes that romantic cult of spontaneity:

Just because you live with someone doesn't necessarily mean he's readily available. If anything, he requires more attention, not less. If you want sex to remain humid, this is the kind of attention you have to bring to it.[55]

By eliminating the comfortable but lazy assumption that sexual arousal is automatic, the couple is compelled to work at cultivating desire and intensifying their emotional intimacy.

Perel's therapeutic advice resonates with the mishnah's duty to schedule onah regularly. Yet she also echoes the Talmudic advice to court one's wife each time, before onah, so one's wife will consent to sex willingly and passionately (see chapter 3). Perel, too, upends the assumption that conjugal intercourse should be a taken-for-granted right or a perfunctory duty.

THE PASTOR'S SEXPERIMENT:
A DISCIPLINED SCHEDULE OF LOVEMAKING

Another modern parallel of the mishnah's idea of predetermining the frequency of marital intimacy began in 2008, when the Reverend Ed Young and his wife, Lisa, challenged husbands and wives of his twenty-thousand-member Fellowship Church in Grapevine, Texas, to strengthen their marital unions through a "Sexperiment." Each married couple was asked to take a vow to perform the discipline of "intentional sex" for seven days in a row. Like it or not, whether moved by passion or not, congregants made a commitment and placed daily sexual intimacy on their calendar.

Young explained that the Sexperiment was "not a gimmick or a publicity stunt" but a spiritual discipline and a biblical commandment: "Christians tend to think that sensuality is carnality, but in actuality it's spirituality. We've kicked the bed out of church and

God out of the bed. We need to bring the bed back in the church and God back in the bed. . . . Sex is a beautiful thing, because it comes from God."[56] He cited Genesis 2:24, that a couple *shall become one flesh*, and 1 Corinthians 7:5, *Do not deprive each other of sexual relations.*

The Youngs' book about their approach, *Sexperiment: Seven Days to Lasting Intimacy with Your Spouse* (2012), explains that it is a "sin [to] depriv[e] your spouse of his or her sexual needs."[57] For the Youngs, however, the Sexperiment was not primarily about sex alone but about intimacy as a broad sharing of life:

> Regular sex will deepen your marriage, because it's an outward reflection of an inward connection. The more you have sex, the more you're saying emotionally, physically, and spiritually, "We are one. We're connected."[58]

Sure enough, as the pastor had anticipated, members of his community reported significant marital benefits in just seven days:

> [Dear] Ed, I thank God for you and your wife! Thank you for finally teaching us the truth! My husband and I are on day nine, so that should tell you something, LOL.
>
> Ed, This seven-day sex challenge . . . is golden! Showers of praise from my wife and I, whose sex life over the years has stagnated and become, I suppose, a little rusty.
>
> Ed, We have a ritual now, my wife and I: after dinner, sit by our fire and share a cup of tea, bagging our usual TV indulgences in favor of talking and sharing our days, which leads not only to emotional intimacy but, now with your challenge, a desire to turn that back into physical intimacy as well.[59]

For spouses "to retrieve and revive [their marital] vows,"[60] an ethic of continuous, hard, intentional, purposeful work is needed.

Lovemaking has to be given a higher priority among one's various obligations in life, and couples have to stop giving perennial excuses for evading it. Rather, they need to learn to communicate about and negotiate their needs, while also recognizing and accommodating their differences. Intentional, planned "whoopee" (as the Youngs call it) can save one's whole marriage from mediocrity and even divorce, because, as they observe, increased frequency of sex within marriage transforms the whole emotional relationship. In particular the Youngs highlight two interpersonal benefits, honesty and forgiveness, both of which contribute to deep intimacy:

> When sexual intimacy takes place, we're emotionally naked, we're spiritually naked, and we're physically naked. Nakedness assumes intimacy. . . . When you make love regularly, it forces you to come to terms with issues such as forgiveness, which has a huge effect on every other aspect of your relationship.[61]

Many of the guidelines and practical benefits for marriage that the Youngs have developed can be directly compared to Jewish practice. What the Rabbis can learn from the Sexperiment is the down-to-earth felicity of its persuasive rhetoric; and what the Rabbis can offer to Protestant Christianity, as it experiments with delineating the details of marital duties, is a longstanding, nuanced legal tradition that makes the practice of scheduled lovemaking mandatory.

Conclusion

To summarize Rabbinic Judaism teaches that "planned lovemaking" need not be an oxymoron. In contemporary society, when spouses face increasing demands on their time, scheduling may be the most effectual technique to realize nurturing, and authentic, lovemaking. Planning creates a space for intimacy in a crowded schedule, and the mitzvah of onah makes it an obligation to invest consistently in that relationship. Law and love are not opposites, just as scheduled sex is not necessarily less passionate.

By now it should also be clear that for this mishnah and its classic Rabbinic commentators, as well as its modern parallels in Perel and the Youngs, marital intercourse, onah, is not to be understood as orgasmic release per se. Rather, intercourse becomes the focal point within a full spectrum of interpersonal relations comprising emotional intimacy and trust, wooing and foreplay, pleasuring and passion. What is necessary and obligatory is not merely to express and satisfy one's own desire, but to take responsibility for the well-being of another—emotionally and sexually.

PART TWO

Talmudic Disputes
KAMA SUTRA VERSUS ASCETIC MODESTY IN THREE RABBIS' BEDROOMS

Talmudic Proprieties of Pillow Talk 2

INVADING THE PRIVACY OF RAV'S BEDROOM

Sometimes, treating one's spouse with respect and
with the awe of polite distance manifests a lack of intimacy (closeness).
One must behave with intimacy rather than with respectful distance.
Telling jokes and behaving lightheartedly is more loveable
than seriousness and awesome respect.
One must make every effort to behave in a more intimate way.
—HAZON ISH, Rav Avraham Isaiah Karelitz, *The Holy Letter* (1953)

Introduction

The Talmudic bedroom story of Rav (given name: Abba Arikha, 175–
247 CE), founder of the academy of Sura in Persian Babylonia, is fundamental to the traditional Rabbinic understanding of the relationship
between marital communication and sexuality. As the story goes, Rav's
student (and future rabbi) Kahana (d. 290 CE) has come to spy on his
master and his wife in their bedroom during intercourse. He sets out
on an audacious reconnaissance mission that will preserve for posterity
the pillow talk of his teacher. The novice disciple soon discovers, to
his apparent horror, his august master's secret life of sexual passion,
erotic foreplay and jesting banter. Out of Kahana's espionage grows a
multigenerational jurisprudential investigation of the implications of
Rav's bedroom etiquette, or lack thereof, for marital couples.

Kahana's Espionage in Rav's Bedroom

The Talmud is filled not only with reports of heated debates between
veteran scholars, but also painful Oedipal exchanges between up-

43

and-coming disciples and their rabbinic masters. In rabbinic education it is imperative for the student to absorb and memorize his teacher's Oral Torah and to observe and imitate his personal behavior, in public and in private, his lived and embodied Torah. Yet, as he matures, a successful student also challenges his master's intellectual authority and establishes his own sacred path. This brief Talmudic tale reveals the friction at the point where the student's urge to learn metamorphosizes into his ambition to establish his independence as a rabbi in his own right:

> Rav Kahana entered under Rav's bed. He heard him chatting, jesting [i.e., playing, laughing, or engaging in foreplay[1]] and gratifying his needs.
>
> Rav Kahana said to him: "It seems as if the mouth of Abba [i.e., Rav] had never before tasted that dish!"
>
> Rav replied: "Kahana, are you *there*? Get out, for this is not the way of the world" [i.e., it is not good manners (*derekh eretz*) to spy on us in our bedroom].
>
> Rav Kahana answered back: "This is Torah and I must learn it!" (T B *Brakhot* 62a; see also T B *Hagiga* 5b)

Just as Kahana is scandalized by Rav's behavior, so Rav is shocked by Kahana's hutzpah in invading his privacy and its unintended outcome of embarrassing Rav and presumably his wife. Beneath those spontaneous reactions, let us investigate the halakhic and ideological issues that underlie the mutual recriminations of master and disciple and their implications for determining the Talmudic ethos of marital intimacy.

Rabbinic Views on Privacy

We ought to view Kahana's behavior as particularly egregious, since he would have been familiar with his teacher Rav's two oft-quoted statements conveying the inappropriateness of violating a couple's privacy in the bedroom. The first reads:

> Regarding anyone who sleeps in a room where a husband and wife are [sleeping and thus interferes with their sexual privacy], we pronounce the [condemnatory] verse, *You expel the women of my people from the house of pleasures* (Mic. 2:9). (TB *Eruvin* 63b)

Here, Rav's prophetic curse can clearly be applied to Kahana's home invasion. The philosopher and halakhic scholar Moshe Halbertal explains that the invasion of privacy destroys the notion of home essential to human selfhood, dignity, and intimacy. Home is supposed to be a place where one does not have to be on guard or on alert, or maintain appearances before the gaze of another. It is meant to be a space where each of us can "be ourselves" without the burdens of social expectations.[2] For this reason, Maimonides teaches that a homeowner may insist on building a wall on his property, "so a neighbor cannot see his fellow when one is using one's own part of the courtyard, for there is a category of damage caused by gazing" into another's sphere of intimacy.[3]

The social philosopher Leon Kass speaks of the gift of trust that loving couples offer one another in private:

> When in the presence of love, clothing is eventually removed; the mutual and willing exposure of sexual nakedness will be understood by each partner as a gift to one's beloved and will be received gladly and without contempt. Thanks to modesty and shame, love of the beautiful elevates human longings and declares itself triumphantly indifferent to our frailty and our finitude.[4]

Taking sexual privacy further, Maimonides summarizes the Talmudic laws that require a couple to keep their pillow talk and sexual experiments secret, thereby protecting a spouse from exhibitionist abuse. His synopsis refers obliquely to the tale of Rav:

A husband who uses a vow to coerce his wife to tell others what he said to her, or what she said to him, regarding words of jesting (*s'hok*) and lightheadedness (*kalut rosh*) that a man and woman say to one another about matters of intercourse is required to grant a divorce and obligated to pay the full ketubah settlement. He may not be so brazen before her face and not coerce her to say to others such shameful things.[5]

In short, as an unwanted, outside observer, Kahana takes by force the knowledge of another's erotic play, which is supposed to be shared between lovers as a gift of trust in the privacy of the marital lair.

The second relevant adage often taught by Rav, that Kahana must have known, states that one ought to die rather than shame another person: "It is better to cast oneself into a fiery furnace than publicly to put to shame one's fellow creature" (TB *Baba Metzia* 59a). Not only has Kahana shamed a fellow creature, but his own honored teacher!

Angrily, yet also educationally, Rav tries to teach Kahana that his manner of learning Torah "is not the way of the world" (good manners), because both the secret intimacy of the marital bed and the honor of a teacher must be guarded zealously. In this case, he implies that the Torah of lovemaking is taught *not* by watching or eavesdropping on the master and *not* by entering surreptitiously and violating his personal space and the intimate sanctuary of his marriage. Rather, one must approach lovemaking by respecting the privacy of the bedroom, and therefore Rav expels Kahana forthwith.

Akiba: Torah over Privacy

Kahana is not the only Rabbinic disciple to aver that Torah learning must transcend the bounds of civil propriety and respectful deference for one's venerated teacher. Earlier, according to the Talmud, Akiba (2nd century CE) as a student already behaved with similar lack of proper distance toward the privacy of his master, Rabbi Joshua (ca. 100 CE). The story goes as follows:

> Rabbi Akiba said: "Once I entered after Rabbi Joshua into the out-house, and I learned three things: one defecates facing, not from east-to-west, but from north-to-south;[6] one defecates not standing up but sitting down; and one wipes not with the right but with the left hand."
> Ben Azzai [Akiba's fellow student] told him: "Even to that extent you were brazen before your rabbi's face?!"
> Rabbi Akiba answered: "This is Torah and I must learn it!" (TB *Brakhot* 62a)

Here, Akiba audaciously spies on his teacher tending to his own physical needs in the outhouse. Appropriately called a "privy" in England, the bathroom is another private space where undesired exposure of one's physicality may impugn one's dignity.

Akiba regards the disciple's quest for knowledge as essential to Torah—and, as such, believes it is to be prioritized over propriety and even over reverence for one's master. Paradoxically, to both Akiba and Kahana, impropriety is the sole way to discover what constitutes proper behavior in private. Others vehemently disagree: Ben Azzai rebukes Akiba for violating decorum ("the way of the world"), just as Rav later rebukes Kahana. Nonetheless, these two zealous disciples hold their ground: "This is Torah and I must learn it!"

The fact that the narrator gives both Akiba and Kahana the last word suggests that both are vindicated in the exchange. Even when a disciple is unbridled in pursuing knowledge, the end justifies the means, and both impudent students Akiba and Kahana become great scholars.

The Gaon of Vilna, Elijah Kremer the Hasid (18th century, Lithuania), for one, extols *shimush talmidei Torah*, learning by serving the physical needs and imitating the lived Torah of one's masters. He teaches that Torah embodied in daily routines is greater than theoretical Torah acquired from an oral teaching or a text.[7] Therefore, to learn the secret ways of his master, a student is called upon to perform for him the same menial tasks a slave would render his master, for the master lets down his guard when served by a personal valet, and then his true character is revealed.

Kahana's True Character?

In my view, however, Kahana's exchange with Rav deserves a different reading. While in Akiba's case, the disciple simply watches in silence, never interrupting his master on the toilet, Kahana speaks up in the bedroom at the most inopportune moment and accuses his master of acting like a ravenous glutton. By so doing, it can be argued, Kahana is not interrogating Rav in the interest of learning Torah; but rather he is *intentionally* trying to shame Rav into desisting from ravenous sex Kahana believes to be uncouth. In fact, Kahana's gutter language shows him to be as vulgar as the libel of which he accuses his own master. When in response to Rav's reproach Kahana cites his predecessor Rabbi Akiba's retort—"This is Torah and I must learn it!"—his rationale appears dissembling. Kahana does *not* regard his teacher's lovemaking as Torah to be learned. To him, Rav's pillow talk is not a normative model to be followed. Rather, Kahana seeks to discredit Rav's behavior so that it will *not* be accepted as a halakhic paradigm.

Ascribing impious and subversive motives to Kahana's foray into Rav's bedroom is in keeping with what we know of Kahana's behavior elsewhere, when he rashly causes someone's death. In that incident, Kahana confesses to the tragic effects of his own impetuosity: "I came to do good and I ended up sinning."[8]

Furthermore, it is possible to conjecture that Kahana acted not out of youthful indiscretion but out of a self-serving desire to catch

Rav in an embarrassing situation in order to expose his master's double standards and thereby challenge his authority. As Rav's student, Kahana would have known that Rav had cautioned husbands to be discrete in their pillow talk: "Rav says: 'Even a superfluous conversation between husband and wife is reported at the hour of death (Judgment Day)'" (TB *Hagiga* 5b). Spouses will be held culpable for their bedroom indiscretions—including personal dialogue—in the divine court where embarrassing exchanges will be quoted back to them verbatim in the world to come. Thus, by intentionally spying on Rav's pillow talk, Kahana could have intended to expose his master as a hypocrite who asserted one standard for others while flagrantly disobeying it himself.

Indeed, in yet another episode in the Talmud (TB *Baba Kamma* 117a), Kahana intentionally humiliates Rabbi Yohanan, publicly challenging this elder sage with questions Yohanan cannot answer in order to promote himself to the first row of scholarship. The Talmud's description of the seating arrangement in houses of study can be likened to the hierarchical ranking of seating arrangements of musicians in an orchestra, where the positioning of the chairs—for example, the first violinist nearest the conductor and ahead of the less esteemed violinists—reflects the relative professional status and knowledge of the performers. With each unanswered question, Kahana moves up in the seven rows of distinguished students arrayed before the master, while Rabbi Yohanan comes down a rung from his perch on seven pillows. A passion for power—rather than for knowledge—may be Kahana's true motive.

Alternatively, Kahana may simply rank the pursuit of wisdom, for which he came to study with his master, so far above the pursuit of physiological pleasure that he disdains his teacher's investment of excitement in such (seemingly) lower instincts. In this, Kahana might well concur with Rabbi Shimon bar Yohai's unfulfilled wish:

Had I been on Mount Sinai at the moment the Torah was given, I would have asked the Holy One to create for human beings two [separate] mouths: one to engage with Torah and one to handle all his [physiological] needs. (TJ *Brakhot* 8a; 1:2)

Apparently Bar Yohai wishes to model the purity of his intellectual study of Torah after the prophet Moses, who refrained from eating, drinking, and intercourse for forty days and nights while on Mount Sinai receiving the Torah (Exod. 38:28). So too Kahana may believe it is aesthetically disgusting for the same mouth to consume a woman's flesh as if it were a delicious dish and to speak Torah. He also insists on a strict separation between the mundane and the sacred, the physical and the spiritual. If so, then from Kahana's perspective, his teacher Rav ought to treat intercourse as a necessary evil to propagate children and as a legally requisite act of taking care of his wife's needs but no more. Kahana may even concede that Rav is so overwhelmed by his libidinal drives that he must find physiological release in intercourse. But that is no excuse to behave lightheadedly in sex as if Rav were a sex-starved adolescent reveling in his first sexual encounter.

A thousand years later, the Aristotelian philosopher Maimonides would assert that the Torah prohibits discussion of sexual matters. In the Maimonidean hierarchy, intellectual aspiration is above one's bodily needs, the man above the woman, the Torah scholar above the *am ha-aretz* (ignorant laborer), the Jew above the idolatrous Gentile, the spiritual above the political and economic, and the heavenly above the earthly. Men are thus to minimize discussions with women, lest these conversations whet men's appetites, corrupt their character, and damage their health.[9]

From that philosophical perspective, with roots that go back to Jewish Hellenism (beginning in the third century BCE, even before the Talmud), Kahana may view Rav as undermining the hierarchy of the mind over the passions by arousing unnecessary desire through salacious talk with a woman. True speech, from this perspective, is not to be shared with women unlearned in Torah, but solely with like-minded men of Torah in the palace of verbal creativity: the *beit midrash* (house of study). In this light, one might conclude that Kahana is understandably shocked by Rav's lack of scholarly restraint in initiating an irreverent erotic conversation with his wife.[10]

Halakhic Debate on Pillow Talk

Ironically, Rav, who sought to protect the secrecy of his bedroom, certainly never intended his practice of onah to set a legally binding paradigm for all couples. For his part, Kahana also would not have intended to disseminate knowledge of Rav's bedside manners as a model to emulate. Yet, in succeeding generations the Jewish legal tradition came to employ Rav's lived Torah to mandate that onah must be accompanied by joyous, playful, and erotic conversation with one's wife in preparation for sexual union.

This legal code, however, would come to stand alongside an opposing legal code on the same subject. Rav and Kahana would come to embody two strands of Rabbinic tradition at loggerheads about the proper halakhic approach to spousal communication before and during sexual activity. Let us analyze Rav's position first, and then Kahana's.

As we see, Rav invests great efforts in engaging his wife with his humorous conversation. He undertakes what is called *ritzui*: the wooing and courting ritual, in which a husband seeks his wife's willing consent and arouses her desire to have intercourse with him (since Jewish law stipulates that onah must be accompanied by a woman's consent). Surprisingly, the Rabbis idealize the courting behavior of roosters as a positive model to emulate. "A rooster woos/appeases/courts [the hen] before performing intercourse," as one sees when the rooster prances before the hen, stretches his wings, and scrapes his feet. Rav himself explains the rooster's courting gestures anthropomorphically, as if the rooster were promising to buy the hen a lovely coat (TB *Eruvin* 100b). (Interestingly, the French seventeenth-century term "to make love" originally meant "to court.")[11]

Later Jewish codes of law regard Rav's jovial foreplay and jesting as an example of such obligatory wooing or conciliation (*ritzui*).[12] The Shulhan Arukh (the authoritative code of medieval Jewish law) concludes: "A husband may not possess his wife sexually unless she consents freely. If she is not desirous of intercourse, then he must court her until she is willing."[13] Further, Rav Isaac Sher (d. 1952), the head of the ultra-Orthodox Slabodka Yeshiva in Jerusalem, celebrates the fact that Rav makes love with such lightheaded gusto as if "he had never before tasted that dish!"

> One should learn from the case of Rav that it is a mitzvah to act lightheadedly (*kalut rosh*) with one's wife exactly as she wishes as if he were a bridegroom just emerging from the wedding canopy who had never had intercourse in his life. She wants [him to behave] that way, so that she too will feel like a bride at the moment of her wedding. . . . And that is the way they should behave their whole lives . . . as it says, *I am to my beloved and my beloved is to me* (Song of Songs 6:3).[14]

By contrast, Rav Kahana takes an alternative halakhic stance: A husband does *not* need to woo and ingratiate himself with his wife each time he wishes to exercise his marital rights. To Kahana, his master should no longer find any fascination in the sexual chitchat that gratifies an unrefined, sensuous palate, and he should not be talking to his wife more than necessary. Torah is the only ever-new and exciting dish worthy of expansive discussion.

Similarly, the Mishnah relays that "Yossi ben Yohanan of Jerusalem said: 'Do not converse [*siha*] too much with the woman.

This refers to one's wife and even more so (*kal vahomer*) [does this warning apply to expanded conversation] with one's fellow's wife.'" From this, the Rabbis extrapolate: "Anytime a person converses too much with women—it causes him damage, nullifies words of Torah and eventually he inherits hell" (*Mishnah Avot* 1:5). Furthermore, to Kahana, talking with one's wife even for the express purpose of facilitating sexual relations is not necessary, as intercourse is the husband's unilateral prerogative, even without wooing his wife and even against her will (see TB *Nedarim* 15b).

Rav's Worldview: Love and Pleasure

Meanwhile, Rav himself is not as steadily focused on the needs of his wife as one might deduce from this story alone. The Talmud tells us that Rav avails himself of a characteristically Persian marital practice (*nikah mut'ah*) found among Zoroastrians from Babylonia and still practiced by some Shiite sects of Iranian origin.[15] Whenever Rav would journey far from his wife, upon arrival at his destination, he would announce his need for a sexual partner that night, and marry her for just one night, as it says: "When Rav happened to be in the city of Darshish, he would proclaim: 'Who wishes to be my wife for the night?'" (TB *Yoma* 18b).

For Rav, it seems, sexuality is not just a legitimate biological need and a permitted, morally neutral pleasure, but also a commendable religious value. Worldly pleasures are not just a necessity to assuage bodily urges, as Rabbi Shimon Bar Yohai believes, but rather a divine gift to be savored and an occasion for blessing God. Rav teaches: "In the world to come, one will be called to account for everything one's eye saw, but which one did not eat" (TJ *Kiddushin* 4:12, 48b; TJ *Brakhot* 4:12, 66d). God's bounty must not be treated with disdain, but enjoyed. In the spirit of the book of Ecclesiastes (1:2–3; 2:24; 3:12–13), with its heightened sense of the ephemeral nature of human life, both Rav and his Babylonian sparring partner Shmuel advise their students to enjoy this world while it lasts:

> Shmuel said [to his student Rav Judah, who was known for his big teeth]: "Big Teeth, snatch and eat, snatch and drink, for the world we are leaving is analogous to a wedding celebration."
>
> Rav said to Rav Hamnuna: "If you have [material resources,] use them well. For there is no pleasure in Sheol [the nether world of death]. Don't wait for death!" (TB *Eruvin* 54a)

Their message echoes the simple pleasures of the otherwise pessimistic book of Ecclesiastes:

> *Go, eat your food with happiness, and drink your wine with a joyful heart, for God has already approved what you do. . . . Enjoy life with your wife, whom you love, all the days of this transitory life that God has given you under the sun—all your ephemeral days. For this is your lot in life and in your toilsome labor under the sun.* (Eccles. 9:7, 9:9)

Apparently, Rav takes the Talmudic maxim about dining—"Any meal served without salt is no meal" (TB *Brakhot* 44a)—to mean: add spice to your life, and enjoy your wife and this world with gusto.

Rav asserts that it is natural for a husband's love for his wife to depend on the degree of her physical allure. To explain why King Ahashverosh *loved Esther above all the women and found favor and grace in his eyes beyond all the virgins* (Esther 2:17), Rav praises Esther for satisfying the king's taste for erotic variety: "When he wanted the taste of virginity, [she provided him] that taste, and when he wanted the taste of an experienced woman, [she provided him] that taste" (TB *Megillah* 13a). Maintaining as well that women must be given the beauty aids necessary to maintain their husbands' sexual interest, Rav says that even in the desert, along with manna, God rained down jewelry for the women to adorn themselves. With the jewels, spices also descended from Heaven to prepare perfumes to enhance their attractiveness (TB *Yoma* 75a).

Without these aids to reinforce sexual interest, and without erotic pleasure, which might be adversely impaired by bodily defects in female beauty, Rav fears that a husband may not be capable of observing the mitzvah to love his spouse as himself. Rather, if a man is yoked in marriage to a woman he does not desire, he will come to resent and hate her, and eventually he will divorce her. It is therefore better to avoid an ill-starred entanglement that would lead a husband to sin by hating and then perhaps hurting his wife.

Hence, in an era in which matchmaking at a distance, mediated through parental negotiations, was normative, Rav introduces the following novel—and undoubtedly revolutionary—legislation: You may not betroth a woman until you meet her face-to-face.

> Rav says: "One should never betroth himself to a woman without having seen her; for one might subsequently discover a blemish in her, and then he might come to loathe her and thus transgress the commandment: *You shall love your fellow as yourself*" (Lev. 19:18). (TB *Kiddushin* 41a)

While this directive is phrased in terms of the husband's erotic desire that underlies the persistence of his marital love, Rav simultaneously looks out for the wife's needs in the marital relationship. The dissatisfied husband can always divorce his wife unilaterally if he wishes, but by Talmudic law the wife cannot divorce him. Therefore, before she consents to the marriage, it is important that she be granted the opportunity to evaluate her husband's character and his sexual appeal to her in a face-to-face encounter—specifically, for her to be able to say "I want to marry this one."

Rav's concern to ensure a woman's informed consent to a prospective husband is explicit in another novel ruling. He insists that if a daughter is a minor, her father must postpone her betrothal: "One is prohibited from betrothing one's minor daughter until she grows up and she says, 'I want to marry this one'" (TB *Kiddushin* 41a). When she is no longer a minor, her thinking will hopefully be more independent of her parents' preferences and her judgment more rational as well.

Rav's concern for the wife is manifest in other rulings as well.[16] Asserting that *shalom bayit* (domestic tranquility) is incompatible with an authoritarian husband who speaks in anger and evokes fear, Rav says, "Anyone who casts excessive awe in his household will eventually cause three transgressions: adultery, bloodshed, and the desecration of Shabbat" (TB *Gittin* 6b). Rashi elucidates this psychological dynamic by explaining that, in order to escape the husband's awesome rage at the *slightest* error, his terrorized wife, who may have forgotten to immerse herself in the *mikveh*, will end up lying to him and then he will sleep with her when she is still impure. Or she will finish cooking his dinner even after sundown on Shabbat eve, lest her husband fly into a rage that the food is underdone. Or she will hastily flee her abusive husband and end up falling off a bridge or into a pit and dying. Thus, a stringent husband's wrath will backfire, bringing both his wife and himself to sin. Rav adds that such a marriage is unbearable because "no one can live with a snake in the same basket" (TB *Ketubot* 77a). Only trust creates a home environment for love.

Maimonides, Elazar Hasid, and Hirsch

Subsequent medieval codes attempted to extricate consistent halakhic norms from Rav's bedroom story by balancing between the contradictory approaches to marital intimacy of Rav and Kahana. The great rationalist Sephardi codifier Maimonides (12th century, Egypt), on the one hand, and the great Ashkenazi pietist Rabbi Elazar Hasid (13th century, Germany), on the other, both appreciate

Kahana's concern lest what he heard from under Rav's bed set a dangerous precedent for sexual revelry in word and deed that could deteriorate into a mandate for vulgarity. Yet, unlike Kahana, they value Rav's desire to woo his wife and make sure she consents to make love willingly and passionately, and so they affirm his joyful physical language of lovemaking even when it is expressed without words.

MAIMONIDES' RULINGS: RESPECT AND DIGNITY WITHOUT UNCOUTH BEHAVIOR

Attempting to bridge both the permissive and the dismissive strands in Rav and Kahana's Talmudic tale, Maimonides cites both the positive and the negative approaches to marital communication. On the one hand, he stipulates that sexual intimacy requires conversational intimacy in order to secure anew a wife's consent to each new act of intercourse: "One shall not coerce [his wife] and force her into intercourse against her will, but rather [perform intercourse only] with her consent and as an outcome of conversation (*siha*) and joy (*simha*)."[17]

In the legal traditions of the ancient Near East and thereafter, the phrase "with joy" means "with voluntary consent."[18] If a wife comes to detest her husband, then her intercourse would no longer be joyous but rather involuntary. This logic leads Maimonides, as we saw, to coin a new rationale: a woman has a right to control access to her own body, even in marital relations with her husband:

> If she says: "I have come to loathe him and I cannot willingly submit
> to intercourse with him," then [the court must] force him to divorce
> her immediately since she [a wife] is *not like a captive who must accede
> to intercourse with one whom she hates*.[19]

For Maimonides, disgust with one's husband is grounds for divorce, because forcing a wife to have intercourse with someone she hates violates her basic human freedom. Therefore, joyful conversation with one's spouse is not just an erotic technique, but an essential way to respect the wife's human dignity and her freedom of choice. Freedom as well as love characterizes marital duties that emerge "as the outcome of a conversation and joy."

On the other hand, Maimonides also expresses disgust at talking about sexual intimacy more than necessary. In this he sounds more like Kahana than Rav:

> Sexual intercourse need not be spoken of more than what our pure Torah has said about this disgusting topic; and one is forbidden to mention or converse about it at all. The sense of touch is a shameful aspect of human beings, as Aristotle said, so even more shameful is the dirtiness of intercourse. . . . The sense of touch belongs to us because we are animals, nothing more, and it shares nothing of our humanness.[20]

To Maimonides, avoiding sex talk is precisely what elevates human beings above animals in heat. Spouses—and especially scholars with their wives—are to avoid frivolous or uncouth talk:

> A scholar . . . should not be too lightheaded and should not be foul-mouthed . . . even in intimate relations between him and her.[21]

> A woman should be modest at home, minimize laughter and light-headedness in the presence of her husband, and she should not verbally demand sexual satisfaction of her needs.[22]

Maimonides' view is consistent with the Talmudic teaching: "Rabbi Akiba says: 'Laughter and lightheadedness (frivolity) lead to [illicit] sexual intercourse'" (*Mishnah Avot* 3:13).

Thus, Maimonides balances two opposed concerns and contradictory Talmudic sources. On the one hand, he wants to ensure that marital relations are founded on a wife's joyful consent, and, on the other, he wishes to minimize spousal conversations whose quality and quantity may lead to vulgar speech or to acts of uncontrolled sexuality. In his rulings, Maimonides manages to maintain support for both views without admitting they are contradictory.

ELAZAR HASID'S RULING:
ALL KINDS OF HUGS WITHOUT VULGAR TALK

Rabbi Elazar Hasid's German school of mystical piety famously extolled penitential practices such as rolling in the snow naked. Nevertheless, he did not disdain physical pleasure and emotional intimacy with one's wife as a path to greater sanctity, as long as one refrains from vulgar talk. The night after the wife has purified herself in the *mikveh*, he instructed each pious husband to initiate joyous erotic intercourse:

> After immersion he should make her joyful, hug her, and kiss her. One should sanctify oneself in the act of intercourse by refraining from vulgar talk and avoiding gazing at anything revolting in his wife. But he should delight (*sha'shua*) her with touching, with all forms of embraces, to gratify his own desire and her desire. He should not think about anyone but her, for she is his bosom wife, and he should show her affection and love.[23]

Here Elazar Hasid never mentions pillow talk as a positive expression of building a relationship or cultivating consent to intercourse, as Rav and Maimonides do. He worries about vulgar talk, which he proscribes, as do Kahana and Maimonides, and condemns gazing at one's wife's genitalia, which he finds pornographic. Perhaps Elazar Hasid is put off by animalistic fascination with dirty sex, so he instructs the pious to refrain from what he considers wanton behavior, just as Kahana abhors what he sees as Rav's lascivious talk and his open desire for sexual gratification.

And yet, Elazar Hasid does not demonize the woman and her body as a source of temptation for the pious husband and of contamination of his mystical mindset. Rather, one must think of one's beloved wife to the exclusion of other women and focus on one's emotional relationship to her as a bosom companion (see Mic. 7:5). Prohibiting vulgar talk and thoughts opens a sacred clearing for interpersonal love, by eliminating the man's tendency to dehumanize his wife by treating her as a sex object for his narcissistic gratification. Yet Elazar Hasid does not polarize dualistically between body and soul, between material and spiritual. He does not treat the body—his or hers—as shameful. Apparently he disagrees with Maimonides' philosophical view that the sense of touch is shameful in human beings. Rather, within boundaries, he wishes to "make her joyful, hug her, and kiss her" upon her return from the mikveh.

After maintaining a separation of some ten to fourteen days during and after her menstrual bleeding, in which they never touch one another at all, what was forbidden is now commanded, what was unsacred to touch is now mandatory to kiss and hug. Yet Elazar Hasid does not describe the husband's motivation in terms of marital obligations, scheduled sex, or procreation, but rather love, affection, and desire. He urges each pious husband to "delight her with touching, with all forms of embraces, to gratify *his* own desire and *her* desire." In place of verbal wooing, he elevates fervent, full-bodied embraces as a means to "show her affection and love." Emotional, physical, and intellectual are combined in their interpersonal union, and that is made possible because what can be dirty, vulgar, and revolting about sex has already been excluded.

Conclusion: Takeaways for a Modern Marriage

What we might learn from Rav and his school of wooing one's spouse depends on controversial assumptions about the divergent emotional natures of men and women. Rav seems to operate on conventional assumptions still maintained by many couples therapists in the modern era—whether true or stereotyped and prejudicial—about a wife's heightened emotional sensitivity. Rav warns husbands to uphold their responsibilities to preemptively avoid causing pain to their wives: "A man must always be wary of causing pain to his wife, for her tears are ever-present and her sensitivity to (emotional) pain is near" (TB *Baba Metziah* 59a). In contemporary language, we might say a woman's threshold of emotional pain—vulnerability to insult and feeling her dignity impugned—is low. Or, we might say, women tend to be more focused on relationships than men, so for them intercourse tends to be more about lovemaking than sexual climax, and therefore they might take offense more readily if not wooed properly before intercourse. Even for those who do not agree with these presumed gender differences, they may be able to derive advice about how to manage a spouse of whatever gender when emotionally raw and hypersensitive, because there is often an explosive potential for marital strife.

How can spouses approach marital tensions? Maimonides advises, as the Talmud does, that intercourse be avoided while a couple is quarreling, when husband and wife feel animosity, or when the wife is fearful of her husband.[24] Some contemporary marriage therapists observe that men often wish to cope with marital tensions by engaging in pleasurable intercourse without prior discussion of the emotional issues.

Many Talmudic Rabbis like Rav agree with those women who say that emotional equilibrium needs to be restored before engaging in sexual intimacy. Those women typically insist that intimate, honest conversation, which exposes the roots of the emotional pain separating husband and wife, ought to precede sexual intimacy.[25] In their eyes, intercourse without prior emotional resolution is more likely to exacerbate marital strains.

Rav, as we have seen, is careful to open lines of communication with his wife before making love, in part to speedily unearth emotional obstacles that might otherwise stay submerged and undermine their delicate relationship. In short, emotional sharing can help heal bruised relationships, and then marital harmony can facilitate optimal sexual union.

Similarly, the halakhic commentator Rabbi Joel Sirkis (Poland, 1561–1640) stresses the importance of the couple's pre-onah communication, especially on Shabbat, when one is obliged to engage in the mitzvah of lovemaking:

> Even before nightfall [on Friday night], a husband is obligated to demonstrate additional affection and love for his partner. It is not just that one must avoid arguments on Friday afternoon before Shabbat and make amends for past fights with one's wife. One must be careful to pursue love and fraternity every Friday afternoon so that nothing untoward will cause the cancellation of the mitzvah of onah on Shabbat.[26]

Sirkis expands the role of marital conversations from making amends for unresolved arguments to proactively expressing love in words and gestures as the recommended path to lovemaking.

Perhaps even more important in our age is the question of how husbands treat their wives not just on Shabbat but throughout the course of their lives together. Spousal conversations can focus not only on resolving acrimony, arousing desire, and expressing love, but also intellectual exchanges of ideas. For that reason, Rabbi Samson R. Hirsch (19th century, Germany), the founder of Modern Orthodoxy, rehabilitates the spiritual and intellectual standing of wives by envisioning them as full partners in serious intellectual and moral discussions. With that, he upgrades the quality of marital communication—and indeed the purpose of marriage itself—above mere arrangements for procreation and sexual release. Here he reinterprets the halakhic limitations on talking to one's wife so as to distinguish between worthwhile conversations that should be encouraged and *siha* (i.e., gossip) that should be minimized:

> *Siha* [which is prohibited in *Mishnah Avot* 1:5] does not refer to serious conversation, but to merely idle talk and gossip. A man who truly respects his wife will have more to offer than just trivial talk and idle chatter for her amusement. He will want to discuss with her serious concerns of life and will derive enjoyment from the resulting exchange of views and counsel.[27]

Hirsch's understanding of spousal communication is unprecedented in rabbinic tradition. Kahana, Maimonides, and Elazar were anxious lest marital intimacy generate vulgar talk, though Rav and Maimonides appreciated the art of verbal wooing in the art of lovemaking. Other rabbis, like Sirkis, believed conversation between spouses could settle quarrels and enhance affection. But only Hirsch imagines an intellectual and spiritual exchange with one's wife that can emerge once vulgar talk and gossip are suppressed. Thus, he finds a balance between Rav and Kahana's two poles, and yet transcends them both in the spirit of a more egalitarian and more robust communicative reciprocity between husband and wife.

How, then, might we understand Rav and Kahana's dispute today? In my judgment, while Kahana's actual rebuke of his teacher's sexual passion is misguided, his stated rationale for spying on his teacher is fully justified. Torah as a valuable way of life is not restricted to academic intellectual exchanges but encompasses intimate relations (sexual, emotional, and intellectual). Rav's passionate bedroom relationship with his wife and his many revolutionary rulings about marriage redeem the romantic dimension of Jewish marriage, and, centuries later, Maimonides codifies Rav's playful, joyful conversations as the definitive prescription for fulfilling the mitzvah of onah.

Modesty or License in the Marital Bed

3

Take an admonition concerning the modesty and continence of married people.

For some are such swine that they think that in marriage they are permitted to do anything they please with their wives. But they are decidedly in error.

And they should know that they may indulge in that wretched pleasure and embracing—but not as though it were clean....

—MARTIN LUTHER (Protestant Reformation, 1483–1546, Germany),
Lectures on Genesis

Introduction

Without ever intending to make his bedroom love nest a halakhic precedent for the whole world, Rav's exuberant and talkative behavior in bed (see chapter 2) sets an erotic norm for subsequent halakhah—"to chat and jest, to play and laugh, while gratifying his needs" (TB *Brakhot* 62a). By contrast, as we see in this chapter, the pious asceticism of speech, sight, and touch practiced by Rabbi Eliezer ben Hyrcanus (Yavneh, Land of Israel, ca. 100 CE) and his wife, Imma Shalom, models the path of sanctity for medieval ascetics and today's Hasidic sects (see chapter 7).

The tale of Imma Shalom's bedroom is recounted in the context of a Talmudic sugya (TB *Nedarim* 20a–b) that assesses these two divergent ideals of the marital bed—modesty and ascetic restraint versus freestyle eroticism—by artfully juxtaposing Rabbi Eliezer's extremely conservative views with Rabbi Judah HaNasi and Rav's scandalously libertarian views on couple sexuality. The Talmudic discussion opens by bolstering Rabbi Eliezer's ascetic reticence with a report on human sexual practices distasteful to angels. Then the sugya reverses course, by citing Judah HaNasi, Rav, and Rabbi Yohanan bar Nafha, who permit husbands to do whatever they like sexually with their wives. The roller-coaster dialectics of these Talmudic debates illuminate the spectrum of rabbinic opinion on fitting conjugal behavior.

Eliezer's Bedroom Etiquette

Before hearing an eyewitness report on the bedroom of Rabbi Eliezer and Imma Shalom, it is important to realize how important these protagonists are in the Mishnaic era after the destruction of the Second Temple by the Romans in 70 CE. Rabbi Eliezer is a follower of the more stringent and conservative rabbinic school of Shammai, though he was a prime disciple of Rabban Yohanan ben Zakkai, who was in turn a disciple of the more humanist and lenient school of Hillel (Jerusalem, 1st century BCE). With his auditory memory, which loses not a "drop" of the Oral Torah he learns (*Mishnah Avot* 2:8), Rabbi Eliezer was able to preserve all he heard from his teacher Rabban Yohanan ben Zakkai, a rabbinic refugee from the destruction of Jerusalem (70 CE). In the Mishnah and Talmud he is very often quoted, as we saw above (chapter 1). In his personal life Rabbi Eliezer ben Hyrcanus demonstrates single-minded devotion to sacred preoccupations, and he brags, "I never engaged in a conversation about secular matters in my life" (TB *Sukkah* 28a).

His wife, Imma Shalom, a famous Talmudic personage in her own right, is the sister of Rabban Gamliel II, head of the Sanhedrin, a descendant of Hillel. Her honorific title "Imma" (Mother) parallels the Roman term "matron," applied to aristocratic women. Parallel to the Aramaic term "Imma" is "Abba" (Father), which refers to several great Rabbis such as Rav, who is called Abba Arikha. (Similarly, Aramaic-speaking Christian heads of monasteries and convents are called "Abbots" and "Mothers Superior," respectively.)[1]

The Talmud reports on this legendary Rabbinic couple's practice of ascetic sexuality, but not in Rabbi Eliezer's name. We know about his sexual modesty from his loquacious wife, to whom people came seeking advice on how to produce good-looking male heirs, as Imma Shalom and Rabbi Eliezer had done. She responded that they engage in rushed sexual encounters that minimize direct physical contact and take place at the darkest, most silent time of night—midnight.

> They asked Imma Shalom: "How do you merit such particularly beautiful children (sons)?"
>
> She answered: "[My husband, Rabbi Eliezer] does not have intercourse [literally, "talk" (*m'sapeir*)] with me—neither at the beginning nor at the end of the night, but only around midnight. Then, when he is having intercourse, he uncovers only a handbreadth [of the garment covering the sexual organs] and then he [immediately] covers over a handbreadth [which is defined as sufficient erotic exposure of female flesh to distract a man in the midst of prayer. See TB *Brakhot* 24a]. He acts as if a demon were coercing him [to have intercourse].
>
> I once asked him: 'Why [do we always have intercourse at midnight]?'
>
> He answered me: 'So that I do not direct my eyes to another woman!'"—Lest [the Talmudic sugya explains] his children become *mamzerim* [i.e., the moral equivalent of children of adulterous relations]. (TB *Nedarim* 20a–b)

This anecdote about the private practice of an exceptionally pious husband, recounted by a woman in a casual conversation, has given birth to a long legal history.

Why is Imma Shalom so frank in publicizing unmentionable details from her and her husband's most intimate moments? In immodestly revealing her husband's clandestine bedroom habits (the likes of which Rav too would have been glad to hide from his students), her intention is not to "kiss and tell" or to teach the art of loving, but to impart her husband's scientific recipe for generating beautiful offspring.

An alternative version of our tale addresses how Imma Shalom overcomes her initial timidity and consents to publicize her husband's sexual secrets to others:

> At first when they said to her that her children were beautiful, she blushed and would not say anything in return. So they said to her: "There is a topic in Torah that we need to learn, but we are embarrassed to ask. . . . How does he [Rabbi Eliezer] behave with you during sex?" When she saw [that their question was motivated by a quest for purity], she told them the whole story.[2]

Essentially, Imma Shalom is asked to reveal a trade secret regarding eugenics. According to the Greek theory of regeneration, not only do the physical and moral traits of the parents determine the child's health and beauty, but so does the father's and mother's mental state at the moment of impregnation. The Rabbis adopt this theory of eugenics, as we see in the tale of Rabbi Yohanan bar Nafha, who is famed for being physically beautiful:

> One who wishes to see the beauty of Rabbi Yohanan should bring a brand-new silver cup and fill it with the red seeds of the pomegranate and place around its rim a garland of red roses, and let him place it at the point where the sun meets the shade, and that vision is the beauty of Rabbi Yohanan. (TB *Baba Metzia* 84b)

The Talmud relays that Rabbi Yohanan always stationed himself near the *mikveh*, so that after immersion women would see him and think of his beauty when they were having intercourse with their husbands that night. Thus these women were enabled to produce a beautiful generation of young Jews (TB *Baba Metzia* 84a). (Of course, Rabbi Eliezer is diametrically opposed to adulterous thoughts such as these, lest his illicit fantasies about another woman damage his offspring.[3])

From the perspective of eugenics, Rabbi Eliezer's timing and physical gestures during intercourse can be decoded as methods for shaping his mental intentions:

1. Scheduling onah at midnight concentrates his mind on his wife to the exclusion of other women.

2. Keeping the couple's genitalia covered as much as possible even during intercourse enhances their sense of shame, a Rabbinic virtue.

3. Very gingerly covering and uncovering his or her body and rushing to ejaculation, like one coerced by a demon, minimize tactile contact and hence arousal in order to preserve the purity of his mental state.

Thus the cultivation of a father's state of mind is Rabbi Eliezer's secret to producing beautiful (i.e., optimal traits) in his children (who apparently owe little to Imma Shalom herself, whose mindset is not mentioned).

Let us explore each of these bedroom behaviors.

SCHEDULING INTERCOURSE AT MIDNIGHT

Rabbi Eliezer sets his sexual clock to the middle of the night (TB *Brakhot* 3a), presumably because there will be no conversations in the street, the courtyard, or the next apartment that might trigger his thoughts of other women.[4] Overhearing other people's talk will not only disturb his concentration, but may trigger alien thoughts in his mind:

From the phrase, *Do not go astray after your hearts* [*and after your eyes after which you prostitute yourselves*] (Num. 15:39), Rabbi Judah HaNasi learns: "One should not drink from one cup [i.e., not have intercourse with one woman], while one's eyes are looking in another cup." (TB *Nedarim* 20b)

Rabbi Eliezer enlists his wife's ready consent to midnight intercourse by explaining his aims to his curious spouse. Adulterous fantasies, it is feared, will translate into children born with physical defects (see below Rabbi Levi's list of nine birth defects). Intercourse amid the quiet of midnight upholds the purity of Eliezer's mental state, which benefits his wife by helping her give birth to lovely children. Meanwhile, he is devoted solely to her and thinks of no one else.

His effort to explain his motives and thereby enlist his wife's voluntary cooperation with an extremely inconvenient time for onah suggests he cares about her emotional needs, even if his choreography of intercourse is unlikely to give her sexual satisfaction or physical intimacy.

Ruth Calderon, a scholar of Talmudic narratives, understands the conversation between Imma Shalom and Rabbi Eliezer as an instance of remarkable candor in their relationship.[5] The couple is able to converse forthrightly about intimate matters. Imma Shalom takes the initiative and demonstrates the courage to ask him about his sexual practices—and the husband answers honestly, without any qualms. He reveals to her his inner struggles with *yetzer ha-ra* (the evil impulse), and how easily he is distracted by other women passing by. Although she could have rebuked him for his wandering eye and sexual fantasies, she does nothing of the sort. In fact, she is not jealous or angry. She appears to esteem him for his frankness and for taking proper precautions that generate the beautiful children of whom she is so justly proud.

From the perspective of Talmudic ethics, bashfulness about one's body is a moral trait, and Rabbi Eliezer's modesty in bed contributes to refining his ethical character. Talmudic ethics speaks highly of sexual modesty as the source of a nuanced sense of shame that functions like a guilty conscience: "Shame leads to fear of sin. From this we learn: It is a good sign for a person to experience embarrassment (*baishan*)" (TB *Nedarim* 20b).

One who respects divine judgment is ashamed to be exposed in sin before God. As the contemporary neo-Hasidic theologian Abraham Joshua Heschel says: "I am afraid of people who are never embarrassed at their own pettiness, prejudices, envy, and conceit; never embarrassed at the profanation of life. . . . Religion depends upon what man does with his ultimate embarrassment."[6]

In Rabbi Eliezer's view, sexuality, even with one's spouse, and even as part and parcel of performing the mitzvah of onah, embodies the ugliness of the animality of human beings that ought to be hidden from one's eyes and barely touched by one's hands. This is consistent with his teaching, "One should always flee from ugliness and from whatever is similar to ugliness" (*Tosefta Hullin* 2:24). So he "makes love" as if fleeing from something contaminating, something arousing spiritual disgust.

Rabbenu Asher (13th century, Spain) defines the halakhic intent of Rabbi Eliezer's practices, which is "to minimize his pleasure."[7] But total sexual abstinence is not a halakhic option when the man has not fulfilled his reproductive duties and his wife has not given up her right to onah. Rabbi Eliezer must expose his phallus minimally to perform procreative intercourse, just as a woman must expose her breast to feed a nursing child. And so, this unavoidable physical maneuver must be kept to a functional minimum, to preclude arousal. Mutual pleasure and emotional and tactile intimacy, suppressed to protect Rabbi Eliezer's sanctity of mind, render his wife's only benefit—from this highly circumscribed sexual contact—the beauty of their offspring.

RUSHING LIKE ONE "COERCED BY A DEMON"

To purify his inner consciousness, Rabbi Eliezer wants to contain both the physiological and mental aspects of sexual arousal. While Imma Shalom sees her husband as someone practicing scientific eugenics to produce more beautiful children, Rabbi Eliezer treats his intercourse with his wife as a manifestation of involuntary coercion, as if he is "coerced by a demon" (TB *Nedarim* 20a–b).

How are we to understand this powerful and disturbing literary metaphor for a husband's mindset while performing onah? Three states of mind have been proposed:

1. **Perils of Sex.** Rabbi Eliezer may regard marital relations, which are hedged about by many restrictions, as a dangerous liminal state. The longer one dallies, the more sins one may commit. Therefore, he may say to himself, *I will hurry my marital duty, for so much might go wrong with this mitzvah. Let me speed through this sexual act as if I am escaping the clutches of a demon tempting me to sin.*

2. **Engulfment of Sex.** Rabbi Eliezer may be concerned lest libidinal forces engulf his core self. In the wish to distance himself—his mind—from whatever physiological arousal (*yetzer ha-ra*) accompanies intercourse, he may rally himself, saying: *I split myself into body (not me) and mind (me). My body is a captive usurped by an external force from which I am alien. Satan has possessed me in the form of a sexual drive that makes me do things I cannot control. I protest that whatever physiological reactions my body manifests, they are against my will.*

Just as a woman being raped may dissociate her mind from what is happening to her body, so Rabbi Eliezer dissociates himself from sex with his wife. While taking the sexual initiative, he acts as if he is the one being raped, coerced to have sex with her. He may think: *I refuse to cooperate in this travesty of my will and this insult to my dignity. By remaining passive and rushing through this act, I will experience no desire, no joy, and no identification.* Herein Rabbi Eliezer resembles the midrashic description of Queen Esther when King Ahashverosh takes her by force. She adamantly remains stone cold in her passivity as if she were "inanimate earth" (*karka olam*) (TB *Sanhedrin* 74b).

In the ancient Near East and later in Rabbinic literature, one who manifests joy (*simha*) in doing something is tantamount to one who acts voluntarily, willingly.[8] By refusing to enjoy sex and by simulating the behavior of someone acting under duress, Rabbi Eliezer demonstrates that his act is involuntary. He performs his marital duties "against his will," under compulsion, not to serve his own sexual desires, which invade him like a foreign god that has taken over his body (TJ *Nedarim* 9:1, 41a; TB *Shabbat* 105b; TB *Sanhedrin* 74b).

3. **Sex for the Sake of the Mitzvah.** Another understanding of being "compelled by a demon" interprets "compulsion" abstractly as a symbol for "commandedness" and "demon" as a reference to God. Rabbi Eliezer wants to perform the mitzvah of onah for its own sake, not egotistically for his own physical pleasure. He may think: *My motivation for doing this mitzvah is not animalistic or narcissistic. Rather, I want to fulfill a higher obligation to which I am bound.*

In part, Rabbi Eliezer's obedience to this mitzvah can be compared to Rabbi Elazar ben Azariah's concept of *hukkim*, laws that have no utilitarian or moral purpose beyond obedience to God:

> Rabbi Elazar ben Azariah says: . . . "Do not say: 'I am disgusted by the flesh of swine' such that it is my natural will and desire to refrain

from eating such meat, but rather say: 'I do want to eat it, but what can I do, my Father who is in heaven has decreed: *You shall be holy for Me, for I, Adonai, am holy and, therefore I have separated you from all the nations in order to be Mine* (Lev. 20:26).' (Sifra on Lev. 20:26; *Kedoshim* 9,12)

Thus, seemingly senseless commandments provide an opportunity to demonstrate selfless, uncritical capitulation to God's will, which paradoxically elevates the human being's dimension of sanctity. By seeing his act as an expression of submission to God's command, Rabbi Eliezer places God's will over and above desire in order to achieve sanctity (TJ *Yevamot* 13:2).

The Angelic Code of Modesty

After telling the tale of Imma Shalom's beautiful children, the Talmud introduces Rabbi Yohanan ben D'havai's angelic code of sexual modesty for bedroom decorum. Like Rabbi Eliezer, Rabbi Yohanan insists on maintaining ascetic propriety, especially when performing the mitzvah of onah. The angels caution married couples to hide their eyes, constrain their hands, and close their mouths during contact with their shameful private parts:

Rabbi Yohanan ben D'havai says: "Four things were communicated to me by the ministering angels:

Why are fetuses born with a limp? Because they [i.e., the parents] turned their tables upside down [i.e., their sexual position placed either the woman on top or the man entering her from behind].

Why are fetuses born dumb? Because they [i.e., the fathers] kissed that place [i.e., the woman's vagina].

Why deaf? Because they spoke during the time of intercourse.

Why blind? Because they [i.e., their fathers] gazed at that place." (TB *Nedarim* 20b)

The angels thus provide strict guidelines to limit the "excesses" in sensory experience during intercourse: seeing another's sexual organs, hearing an erotic voice, and perhaps tasting, by kissing, the genitalia.

Rabbi Yohanan ben D'havai's tradition is not reported as a normal part of oral law passed down from teacher to student; nor does it take the form of a midrash on an authoritative verse. Its validity derives from its status as a direct revelation by angels.

Why attribute these rules to angels? First, knowledge gleaned from the angels may reveal the hidden determinants associated with procreation, for they have access to the heavenly process of determining the nature of the fetus based on the moral purity of the parents. Second, only the angels can conduct espionage in the bedroom, seeing and recording the private sexual excesses of married couples. As God's spies, angels collect this incriminating evidence to facilitate divine judgment. Thus the Rabbis report: "Even [the content] of a superfluous conversation between husband and wife is [recorded and] reported back to the perpetrator at the hour of death (Judgment Day)" (TB *Hagiga* 5b). Rabbi Yohanan ben D'havai wants to warn couples that, thanks to angelic surveillance, they must avoid sexual indiscretions because their secret bedroom exploits are not beyond divine scrutiny and punishment.

Why would angels who have no sex life of their own be anxious to scrutinize human beings' erotic life? Perhaps they wish to instruct the pious about how to transcend their demeaning physicality. By distancing themselves from what Resh Lakish calls the place of *tinofet* (the vagina as a defiling, impure place, the origin of secretions that soil and disgust), men can raise themselves above animals, and thereby approach the supramaterial standing of angels.

The Rabbinics scholar David Brezis points out that noncanonical works found within the Qumran Library (100 BCE–68 CE) instruct humans to imitate the angels by denigrating their own physiological needs.[9] According to the book of Jubilees, a spiritual human being like Enoch (Hanokh) who *walked with God* (Gen. 5:22) can be redeemed from sin and mortality and become angelic. Taken heavenward directly, Enoch "stands with the army of holy ones and joins the assembly of the children of heaven."[10] But even angels in heaven are subject to sexual temptation, such as the rebellious angels who *descended* in order *to have sex with the daughters of Adam . . . whom, they saw, were good-looking* (Gen. 6:2, 6:4). Instead, Enoch calls upon humans to *ascend* to an angelic state (Enoch 15:3ff), and perhaps Rabbi Yohanan ben D'havai's endeavor to purify human sexuality with angelic guidance represents a similar trend. He preaches disdain of sexuality in order to elevate the sanctity of the spiritualized self so as to reap benefits in this world (children without birth defects) and the next.

Contesting Ascetic Traditions

At this point in the sugya, the Talmudic editor of this debate begins to contest the ascetic traditions of Rabbi Eliezer and Ben D'havai it has just reported by four means: (1) permitting intimate pillow talk, (2) repudiating the angelic code, (3) moralizing the causes of birth defects, and (4) praising sexual hutzpah in wives and assuring them outstanding offspring.

PERMITTING INTIMATE PILLOW TALK

The first refutation of the ascetic code is designed to permit and commend talking to one's wife about erotic matters during intercourse. To prove this point, the editor of the sugya interprets, against the grain, the story of Rabbi Eliezer so as to attribute *to him* erotic pillow talk!

The linguistic trigger for their discordant reinterpretation of Rabbi Eliezer's bedroom practices is his wife's report that "he is *m'saper* with me in the middle of the night." While *m'saper* in context is a euphemism for having intercourse, the Talmudic editor deliberately misunderstands it not metaphorically, but literally, as "talking," as it is used in Rabbi Yohanan ben D'havai's warning that those "talking" (*m'saprim*) during intercourse will be punished by giving birth to deaf children. Thus the editor generates an artificial contradiction between Rabbi Eliezer's purported pillow talk and Rabbi Yohanan ben D'havai's warning. Now the editor may query: How can the pious wife of Rabbi Eliezer ben Hyrcanus brag that she has given birth to exquisitely beautiful sons, presumably without birth defects, when she reports that her husband "talks with me" in the middle of the night? According to Ben D'havai, Imma Shalom's children should have been born deaf as a suitable punishment for verbal immodesty. The artificial halakhic contradiction between authoritative texts must now be resolved.

Characteristically, the editor's "solution" argues that Imma Shalom and Ben D'havai were referring to different situations. Some conversations during marital intercourse are commendable and produce beautiful offspring, while others are uncouth and generate birth defects:

> It is not a contradiction! Here [the source about Rabbi Eliezer] refers to talking [with one's spouse during sexual relations] about *topics related to intercourse* [and hence it is permitted]; and there [Rabbi Yohanan ben D'havai] refers to *talking about other matters* [not related to intercourse and those and only those are prohibited]. (TB *Nedarim* 20a–b)

Calderon, the Israeli Talmudist and humanist educator, observes that in Hebrew *m'saper* unites two meanings of the word "intercourse," just as they do in English—sexual union and social communication.[11] However forced it may seem to imagine Rabbi Eliezer engaging in a rousing erotic conversation with his wife like that of Rav with his wife (Tractate *Kallah* 1:21; but TB *Sukkah* 28a), the Talmudic dialectic generates a surprising halakhic consensus that mandates conversing about lovemaking with one's wife. And in so doing, it undermines the originally ascetic intent of Rabbi Eliezer's bedroom practices.

Medieval commentators explicate this Talmudic distinction in terms of the importance of nurturing emotional bonding between husband and wife:

> Rabbenu Nissim (14th century; Gerona, Spain): "Talking for the sake of intercourse is permitted in order to appease one's wife."

> Menahem HaMeiri (13th century, Provence): "A wife is permitted to talk to him to appease her husband with her words in order to make herself beloved (*l'hitaheiv*)."[12]

The practical halakhic result of this distinction between permitted and prohibited topics of bedroom marital communication can be quite comic. The sugya declares that one should not accustom oneself to talk with women too much: "Do not become accustomed to make conversation with women, for it leads to adultery" (TB *Nedarim* 20a–b). Yet, while a scholar ought never to discuss anything with his wife beyond a bare minimum of practical matters, he may be expansive in discussing erotic issues, at least when performing his marital duties.

REPUDIATING THE ASCETIC CODE

Our Talmudic sugya now makes a U-turn by citing "the Rabbis," an amorphous majority, who stand in judgment on all the halakhic prescriptions previously proposed. In an unusually authoritative statement they declare: "The Rabbis said: 'The law does *not* follow Rabbi Yohanan ben D'havai, rather a person does whatever he wants to do with his wife'" (TB *Nedarim* 20a–b). In short order, the rigorous bedroom decorum of the angels—whether a direct communication from supernatural beings or simply the opinions of other Rabbis—is dismissed as lacking in halakhic authority. And not only do these Rabbis reject the ascetic angelic code; they assert positively that "a person does whatever he wants to do"! Broadly, the sugya calls for an end to almost all invasive legislation about marital intercourse in order to enable couples to work out their own style of lovemaking without regard to judgmental codes of ascetic modesty.

Could this be construed as secularization of intercourse and liberation of sexual fantasy? Yes, but not necessarily for *both* spouses. Talmudic sexual license is asymmetrical, establishing a regime of arbitrary male control over one's wife's sexual practices. Utilizing an analogy to consuming meat or fish, her body is compared to dehumanized prey at the mercy of her rightful predator, her husband, or *ba'al* (owner). Incidentally, the Talmud often uses the words "meat" and "fish" to refer metaphorically to sex (see TB *Yoma* 75a):

> To what may she be compared? To a slab of meat coming from the slaughterhouse/butcher's shop which may be prepared for consumption [by the man, the customer] in any way he wishes—he may eat it with salt, or broil it and eat it, or cook it and eat it, or seethe it and eat it. So too she is comparable to a fish coming from the house of the fisherman [literally, the hunter]. (TB *Nedarim* 20a–b)

Brazenly, the Rabbis, who have just overruled the restrained asceticism of the angels, now hand the woman over to a ravenous husband who may treat her in bed however he wishes, as if she were just flesh to be consumed at his culinary pleasure. Given this U-turn, one might appreciate Rabbi Eliezer's self-restraining bedroom ethics in a newly positive light: as an antidote to men's sense of entitlement over their wives' bodies. Rabbi Eliezer and Ben D'havai sought to keep in check the crass tyranny of the male *yetzer ha-ra*.

The Talmud itself highlights the disturbing halakhic results of this reversal by showcasing the judicial resistance of two women to male tyranny in the marital bedroom. In two court appearances, outspoken wives complained that their husbands turned them over ("I set the table for him [i.e., my husband] and he turned it over!") when they had offered their bodies for sexual intercourse in the traditional sexual position, with the wife beneath her husband.[13] These husbands overturned the traditional mores that Ben D'havai's angels sought to enforce by threat of punishment on Judgment Day.

Implicit in the missionary position (the man on top) is the idea of the husband as master—*ba'al*. Ironically, then, these wives seem to prefer the subordinate position, with its traditional propriety, to being subject to the unpredictable whims of their sexually aroused husbands.

If, however, the wives are objecting to being entered from behind (i.e., turning them into a table-like position so they can be mounted from behind), then their protest may express a demand for maintaining the intimacy of face-to-face contact with their husbands, which is also the highest degree of prophetic intimacy attained only between Moses and God (Deut. 34:10). Face-to-face intercourse, the Rabbis tell us elsewhere, is characteristically a human, not an animal way, to engage in sexual relations, "For all animals have sex with his face toward her back" (*Genesis Rabbah* 20:3). If, in fact, a wife were to turn her back to her husband, she would be considered a wife of bad character, as it says: "Who is [a] bad wife? Rava says: She adorns herself setting a table for him and then turns her back to him" (TB *Yevamot* 63b). So too, the Zohar, the mystical literary masterpiece of thirteenth-century Spain, explicates the importance of face-to-face sexual union: "One who has intercourse from behind denies the [mystical] configuration (*tikkun*) of looking face-to-face . . . as it says, and *cleave with his wife* (Gen. 2:24)—*with his wife*, and not behind his wife."[14] (See chapter 5.)

In our day, we might understand the wives' demand for face-to-face lovemaking as a protest against their husbands' impersonal use and abuse of women's bodies without the interpersonal intimacy characteristic of human interaction. Regardless of the wives' motivations, however, the sugya does not focus on gender issues, but on the self-suppression or self-expression of male desire expected of the husband. While Rabbi Eliezer, Ben D'havai, and his angels attempt to restrain a husband's impulses, the majority view of the Rabbis insists on a husband's unlimited right to "consume" his wife sexually any way he desires.

Indeed, in the following verdicts issued in response to the women's complaints, the supreme halakhic authorities of the Land of Israel and Babylonia, Rabbi Judah HaNasi (Galilee, d. 217) and Rav (Sura in Babylonia, d. 247), even suppress the women's *right* to voice their own desires:

> The woman who came before Rabbi [Judah HaNasi to ask a halakhic question] said:
>
> "Rabbi, I set the table for him [my husband] and he turned it over!" Rabbi [Judah HaNasi] says: "My daughter, the Torah permitted him to you [any way he sees fit to consume you]. So as for me, what can I do?"
>
> The woman who came before Rav said: "Rabbi, I set the table for him [my husband] and he turned it over!" [Rav] said: *"What is the difference between you and a fish?!"* (TB *Nedarim* 20a–b; TB *Sanhedrin* 100b)

Rabbi Judah the Nasi shows some sympathy to a woman whose husband is trampling upon her dignity. But his half-hearted condolences—"My daughter, the Torah permitted him to you [any way he sees fit to consume you]. So as for me what can I do?"—only serve to deny his culpability for her aggrieved feelings. He blames the Torah, thus desecrating its good name, in order to escape his own responsibility as a judge and political leader to protect a vulnerable woman from indignity. In the Torah the ethical obligation to protect the widow might be generalized to the aggrieved wife.

When a woman suffering exploitation cries out, the Torah does not teach the leaders to throw up their hands and say: "So as for me, what can I do?" Rather, the social legislation of Exodus prohibits exploitation of vulnerable individuals, and God threatens with immediate retribution those who ignore a widow's or orphan's cries:

> You must not exploit widows or orphans; if you do so in any way, and they cry to Me for my help, I will surely give it. And my anger shall flame out against you, and I will kill you with enemy armies, so that your wives will be widows and your children fatherless. (Exod. 22:21–23)

Maimonides sums up the halakhic obligation to show emotional sensitivity to widows and orphans who have no husband or father to protect them:

> A person must be careful concerning orphans and widows because they are very depressed and dejected. We are cautioned concerning them, even if they are wealthy, even concerning the widow of a king and his orphans. As it says, *you shall not afflict any widow or orphan* (Exod. 22:21–23).
>
> And how shall one behave toward them? One should speak to them pleasantly and should deal with them only in a most respectful manner. One should not afflict their bodies with hard labor or their hearts with harsh words, and one should be considerate of their possessions more than of one's own.[15]

Yet Rabbi Judah HaNasi dares to say the Torah is the problem! And, what a strange accusation he makes against the Torah! After all, the Torah guarantees a wife's rights to onah (Exod. 21:9)—*her* rights, not *his*. The Mishnah, which he himself edited, construes marriage as a contract based on mutual consent, not unilateral ownership of a master over the body of his wife. Elsewhere in the Talmud and medieval codes of law, rabbis go beyond what the Torah says, exercising their rabbinic authority to legislate new decrees, suspend existing laws, punish rebellious behavior by flogging, and condemn in public improprieties not explicitly prohibited by the Torah.[16] The rabbinic interpreter and judge reign supreme over the sacred text whatever its literal meaning and limitations.

THE HORNS OF THE MORAL DILEMMA OF OUR TALMUDIC *SUGYA*

So far our sugya has constructed a halakhic dispute between two polar male ethical ideals, neither of which coheres with modern values such as human dignity, the natural goodness of the human body, or egalitarian relationships based on mutual consent. On one hand, Rabbi Eliezer and Ben D'havai attempt to restrain a husband's impulses (*yetzer*) and purify his mind from erotic thoughts, especially for husbands who are scholars. The Rabbis valorize aristocratic self-restraint as a central path to masculine heroism, character education, self-sanctification, and spirituality. Elsewhere the Rabbis condemn an uncultured husband (*am ha-aretz*) who assaults his wife as a ravenous lion devouring its prey, and depict his wife as a helpless victim bound up and delivered before a cruel and rapacious predator (TB *Pesahim* 49b; TB *Sanhedrin* 90b). However, their Rabbinic rhetoric of anxiety about male desire and their ascetic practices create unintended collateral damage by obstructing marital intimacy, interpersonal communication, and erotic lovemaking with their wives.

On the other hand, an unlimited patriarchal right of men to express their libidos in any way they desire reduces the woman to a consumable commodity. Neither Rabbi Eliezer's rushed intercourse nor these flesh-eating husbands with exotic sexual tastes are sensitive to their wives' needs. These halakhic alternatives present unpalatable choices: between self-denying male asceticism and abusive male license; between the marital bed as a public space subject to minute scrutiny and punitive intervention (by angels, zealous disciples, and ascetic rabbis) and as a man's private space (his autocratic home as his castle) where Rabbinic law has no say in moderating his sexual practice or in safeguarding his wife's self-respect. The halakhic bottom line of the sugya mandates a husband's unlimited patriarchal right to "consume" his wife sexually in accord with his idiosyncratic desires. If a husband does wish to follow Rabbi Eliezer's paradigm, that is his own choice. Rabbi Eliezer and Ben D'havai's models are preserved as aspirational halakhic paths for the pious or the Torah scholar, without obligating the nonscholar to be an ascetic or behave decently, with humane self-restraint.

MEDIEVAL CODES DEFEND WIFE'S PREROGATIVES

Despite the sugya's halakhic consensus, represented by its two highest Talmudic authorities, Rabbi Judah HaNasi in the Land of Israel and Rav in Babylonia, almost all later halakhic authorities and their codes vehemently condemn marital intercourse conducted by the husband without explicit consent from his wife. Through negotiation, couples must work out their own style of lovemaking.

Furthermore, the wife may not be pressured into engaging in "kinky" sex (which might include "turning over the table" or other male "culinary" preferences), as Maimonides legislates: "[He is obligated to divorce her] if he tries to coerce her . . . to do crazy things [during intercourse] which have no value but are just foolish."[17]

He further stipulates that a husband may not unilaterally force his wife to perform other ridiculous behaviors, like "filling up ten jugs of water and then dumping them in the garbage," for then "she will appear to be a fool" (TB *Ketubot* 72a).

Bolstering the autonomy of the wife in her marital bed, medieval codes qualify Rabbi Judah HaNasi's uncontested ruling that the Torah permits the husband to have intercourse with his wife any way *he* wants by adding the crucial proviso *"only* with the wife's consent."[18] So too, Maimonides teaches that an ethical person should conduct his marital relations on the principle of "joyful mutual consent."[19] As we saw, he also prohibits treating wives like prisoners of war or slaves who are coerced sexually by their male captors or masters:

> If she says: "I have come to loathe him and I cannot willingly submit to intercourse with him," then [the court must] force him to divorce her immediately [even by applying corporal punishment until he consents] since she [a wife] is *not like a captive who must accede to intercourse with one whom she hates* [such as a captor who has kidnapped her]. Let her go out [i.e., be divorced].[20]

Maimonides' insistence on the wife's unilateral veto on unwanted intercourse with her husband has deep roots in a parallel sugya that condemns marital rape as unethical:

> Rav Assi said: "It is forbidden to force one's wife to have intercourse." . . . Rav Ika bar Hinina said: "What does the verse, *A person without knowledge is not good* (Prov. 19:2) mean? It refers to [a husband] who forces [i.e., rapes] his wife to do a mitzvah [onah]." (TB *Eruvin* 100b)

Without full—not half-hearted[21]—consent from his wife, the husband bedding his wife is regarded as an uncouth ruffian (who today would be called a "rapist") even though he has a contractual claim on his wife to have intercourse.[22]

Later law codes turn the moral condemnation of Rav Assi into binding halakhah:

> It is forbidden for a male to coerce his wife to have intercourse, even if it is not actually rape but simply because she is not fully persuaded (*m'rutza*). Therefore a husband must appease her first before having intercourse.[23]

In the same sugya, the Rabbis insist that the wife be appeased emotionally and aroused sexually before each and every act of intercourse.[24] Elsewhere in the Talmud, the verse *One who runs too fast—sins* (Prov. 19:2) is applied to a husband who repeats his act of penetration without sufficient time between sexual acts for the woman to renew her desire (TB *Eruvin* 100b).

Birth Defects and Emotionally Defective Relationships

The finale of the sugya presents a third way to undermine the ascetic bedroom code, proclaimed at its inception by Rabbi Yohanan ben D'havai in the name of his angelic informants, that minor indiscretions in sexual modesty (kissing one's wife's genitalia, or engaging in pillow talk) cause birth defects that penalize such impudent behavior. Now, by contrast, the sugya closes by proposing an alternative catalog that attributes birth defects to moral failings in spousal relationships deficient in love and full consent.

Rabbi Levi (the Land of Israel, ca. 300 CE) catalogs nine relational lacunae that engender defects in the children or manifest moral defects in the parents as a result of emotionally damaged marital relationships:

Rabbi Levi says: "These are the children (*b'nai*) born of nine defective traits [in the relationships between their parents]: children of fear, of coercion, of hatred, of a violation of a ban, of substitution, of contention, of drunkenness, of those divorced in their hearts, of confusion, of hutzpah." (TB *Nedarim* 20b).

Or, in an alternative translation: "Rabbi Levi says: 'These are the people (*b'nai*) who manifest nine defective characteristics in their spousal relationships.'"

In the first translation, the penalties for improper intentions during intercourse fall on the offspring who develop morally defective characters or crippled physical bodies, perhaps because of the unhealthy emotional atmosphere in their homes (TB *Nedarim* 20a). For example, "the children of contention," those conceived by parents who are constantly engaged in acrimonious conflict, are the unfortunate educational victims of a home lacking in marital love and *shalom bayit* (domestic tranquility).

In the alternative translation,[25] Rabbi Levi attributes the defects not to the children, but to the parents. Grounding his list on a prophecy of Ezekiel that harshly condemns rebellious Jews (*I will sort out and remove from your midst those who are rebels and transgressors against Me*—Ezek. 20:38), Levi identifies the sinful "rebels" of Ezekiel as adults who have failed psycho-socially in their spousal relationships. For example, "the people of fear" are those who force sexual intercourse on their wives by terrorizing them with threats.[26]

Rabbi Levi's midrash gains the status of binding Jewish law in the Tur, the Spanish code of Jewish law, when Rabbi Jacob ben Asher (author of the Tur, 14th century, Spain) interprets this midrash in terms of faulty marital relations marring lovemaking. Here is a sampling from his nine explanations:

There are thoughts [during marital relations] that make one forfeit one's reward, producing relationships scarred by nine factors:

Children born of Rape: A man rapes his wife against her will [even if he first attempted to appease her and she remained unresponsive]. Rather, if he needs to have sex with his wife, he must appease her before cohabiting.

Children born of Hatred: [Hatred of the spouse even while engaging in intercourse].

Children born of Substitution: The husband hankers for a forbidden union [with a forbidden woman] and then his wife comes along [and they have sex while his mind is still on the other woman]. Some explain that this applies even where both women are his wives, and he wishes to cohabit with one and the second comes along. . . .

Children born of Strife: The couple quarrel all the time [yet they still engage in sex]. Theirs is like an illicit sexual union, for it is not out of love.

Children born of Drunkenness: Where either spouse is intoxicated.

Children born of those already Mentally Divorced: Where the husband plans to divorce his wife. . . . [and yet still initiates intercourse with her]. . . .

Sexual relations marred by any of these factors harm the offspring and [the husband] is called a sinner, even if he is obligated to fulfill the mitzvah *be fruitful and multiply* (Gen. 1:28).[27]

Like Rabbi Eliezer and Ben D'havai, Rabbi Levi constructs his list of forbidden bedroom behaviors in light of the Hellenist medical science that forms the scientific consensus from the Greeks through the Talmud, until the early modern era. The physical, mental, and moral character of offspring is determined in part by the mental state of the parents at the moment of conception.

Does the Talmud's reliance on outdated Hellenist medicine render its marital ethos outmoded for us moderns?[28] Not necessarily. While we may no longer believe in the rewards and punishments attached to Talmudic marital advice about lovemaking, new studies of the brain show that a child's brain development may in fact be shaped by environmental and emotional factors before as well as after birth. Today it's also understood that a couple's problematic emotional relationship will often adversely affect their child's development.

In sum, by concluding the sugya with the moral message of Rabbi Levi's midrash, the Talmud constrains Rav's halakhic permission for a husband to treat his wife as a piece of fish. Such behavior violates the ethos of emotional intimacy and mutual consent between husband and wife, as promulgated by Rabbi Levi's list of moral defects in love relations that displaces Ben D'havai's list of sexual improprieties in conjugal intercourse.

PRAISING THE SEXUAL HUTZPAH OF WIVES

At this point, our sugya in TB *Nedarim* 20a–b (along with its parallel sugya in TB *Eruvin* 100b) makes another U-turn, this time in terms of the ideal of female modesty. While it begins by praising the character trait of shame as the central virtue in distancing people from sin, as exemplified by Imma Shalom and Rabbi Eliezer, it now concludes by praising *hutzpadik* women, like Jacob's wife Leah, for verbally demanding sex from their husbands. Leah, the less-loved wife, tells Jacob point blank: *To me you will come for I hired you for the price of my son's mandrakes* [a species of flowers] (Gen. 30:16). Leah exchanged them with her sister Rachel in order to obtain Rachel's turn for an extra night with their shared husband, Jacob. That night, Leah lies with him and produces a child she names appropriately, if callously, "The Hireling"—*Yissachar*.

As the heroine of this sugya, Leah demonstrates how bedroom ethics directly affects the quality of offspring. Thanks to her hutzpah, Leah produces descendants who are said to be superior even to those of Imma Shalom, and even to the children born in the generation of Moses! Generalizing from Leah's case of initiative taking, Rabbi Yonatan makes this uniquely assertive woman into a precedent-setting norm for emulation by all wives:

> [The Talmudic editor asks:] Is it really true [that "the children of hutzpah," of brazen sexual intercourse, will be born with birth defects]? Didn't Rabbi Shmuel bar Nahmani say in the name of Rabbi Yonatan: "Any woman who demands [sexual intercourse] of her husband for the sake of a mitzvah is rewarded with sons that are of such excellence that even in the generation of Moshe there were none like them!" (TB *Nedarim* 20b; also TB *Eruvin* 100b)

Moshe instructs Israel to seek judges who are *wise and discerning*, but he only finds men who are *wise* (Deut. 1:13 and 15)—but not discerning. By contrast, the children of Yissachar, son of Leah (descendants born from the night with Jacob that was obtained due to Leah's bold initiative) *are* described as *discerning* as well as wise (1 Chron. 12:33).

What a U-turn! Initially, the sugya had idealized men blessed with such shame that they would not stare at women or kiss their wives' private parts. Thus Rabbi Eliezer hid the couple's bodies from each other's sight as much as possible even during intercourse. In fact, as we saw in chapter 1, Talmudic law has come to take the opposite stand about hiding one's body from erotic contact with one's spouse—so much so that it awards a divorce with full ketubah compensation to the wife if her overly modest husband refuses to remove his clothes during intercourse (TB *Ketubot* 48a). The halakhah condemns keeping one's clothes on during intercourse as an imitation of the Zoroastrian Persians who denigrate both affection and sexual pleasure.[29]

A parallel Talmudic sugya teaches that women should be even more demure than their husbands by refraining from asking their husbands for sexual satisfaction even though intercourse is the wife's marital right and the husband's marital duty (TB *Eruvin* 100b).

Some Rabbis believed that this repression grew out of the curse of Eve in the Garden of Eden. Measure for measure, Adam's wife had to be punished for speaking out too readily and telling Adam what to do in the Garden of Eden. As a result, women as a whole will naturally desire their husbands sexually, and yet be ruled by those husbands (TB *Eruvin* 100b).

In this light, one might expect the Rabbis to complete the discussion by asserting that such hutzpah would produce "children born of hutzpah," who are morally and perhaps physically defective. Nevertheless, our Talmudic discussion concludes by placing the most sexually forthright wife, Leah, on a pedestal as the model to be emulated in order to obtain the best progeny. For Rabbi Yonatan, Leah possesses appropriate audacity in insisting on a woman's marital rights, whenever she wants to exercise them.

This surprise ending in the sugya puts into question the whole string of ascetic bedroom ethics promulgated at its outset. Audaciously, the midrash casts aside the various restrictions and condemnations of free and erotic communication between husbands and wives when it comes time for a wife to demand her sexual satisfaction.

The Medieval Legal Debate

The fact that our sugya is so contradictory produces an ongoing debate among the medieval and modern codifiers of halakhah (see chapters 6, 7, and 9). As we will see, Joseph Karo, author of the Shulhan Arukh (often called simply the Code of Jewish Law), rules predominantly according to Rabbi Eliezer and Yohanan ben D'havai, as do many contemporary Hasidic groups (see chapter 7). On the other hand, earlier codes of law, such as Maimonides' Mishneh Torah, follow the halakhah of Rav and Rabbi Judah HaNasi in permitting whatever sexual style the couple desires—although their pietist advice is to voluntarily choose to follow Rabbi Eliezer. Thus for Karo, Rabbi Eliezer's position has entered the halakhic codes as an obligatory code. For Maimonides, however, Rabbi Eliezer represents an aspirational ethic recommended for those seeking a higher level of sanctity. In effect, as we will see, Maimonides' conceptual position—identifying both with the permissive view of Rav and with the aspirational program of Eliezer—is itself split like the fractured sugya. As such, the legal debate that follows is not only between Maimonides and Karo, but within Maimonides himself. Furthermore, as we will also see, Maimonides' French contemporary Ra'avad, who is less rationalistic than Maimonides, also incorporates divergent views in his systematized hierarchy of proper motivations for intercourse.

MAIMONIDES' ASPIRATIONAL ETHIC OF SEXUAL MODESTY

Maimonides recommends that scholars limit the frequency of intercourse to much less than what is permitted. Ideally, sexual engagement is to be strictly circumscribed by health and procreative constraints:

> When one has intercourse, it should only be to make one's body healthier and to produce surviving seed. So one does not have intercourse whenever one so desires but only when one knows one must express seed for medical purposes and to procreate.[30]

Maimonides also advises the pious and wise: "One should perform intercourse in shame and not with brazenness (*azut*), and then separate [from his wife] immediately."[31] Further, he notes that the visual aesthetics of love are to be minimized:

> The early pietists and the great scholars [like Rabbi Eliezer] took pride in never having looked at their own circumcised penis; others took pride in never having looked at the contours of a woman, for their minds faced away from ephemeral matters to things of truth that occupy the minds of the holy.[32]

For Maimonides the philosopher, true love is not at all about the sexual union with one's spouse; rather, eros must be sublimated into intellectual love of God. Autobiographically he wrote about himself:

Before I was formed in the womb the Torah knew me and *before I emerged from the womb, it consecrated [betrothed]* me to its study (see Jer. 1:5) and it dedicated me *to spread (the water) of its springs abroad* [i.e., to teach Torah in public]. [For Torah] she is *my beloved gazelle* and *the wife of my youth in whose love I have been infatuated from my youth* (see Prov. 5:16–19). (Letter to Rabbi Jonathan of Lunel, 1199 CE)[33]

Maimonides thus asserts that the Bible's most beautiful paeans of love for the bride of one's youth refer exclusively to the study of Torah.

All in all, Maimonides offers *two tiers of halakhic advice.* The basic obligation follows Rav in supporting joyous, mutually satisfying lovemaking. However, his aspirational counsel to those who seek sanctity is to avoid stimulating desire or to sublimate love of earthly things into passionate love for Torah:

One is not allowed to intentionally harden his penis into an erection or to stimulate himself to reflect on sexually arousing thoughts. If a sexually arousing thought (*hirhur*) enters his mind, then one should redirect his heart from these transitory things to words of Torah that are the true *loving doe* and *the mountain goat* [attributed to the love of the bride of one's youth in Proverbs 5:19].[34]

RA'AVAD'S HIERARCHY OF PROPER MOTIVATIONS FOR INTERCOURSE

Rabbi Abraham ben David of Posquières (Ra'avad, 12th century, Provence), an influential early kabbalist, opposed the introduction of Aristotelian philosophy into Jewish curricula and systematically challenged Maimonides' rationalist rulings in the code of the *Mishneh Torah*. In response to our contested sugya, Ra'avad too seeks to accommodate conflicting views of sexuality and establish priorities among them without rejecting either pole of the sugya's debate. In a style reminiscent of Catholic theologians who were the scholastics of his era and his region in France, Ra'avad undertook the task of summarizing and systematizing various medieval attitudes to onah.[35] These categories, in descending order of importance, can be applied to the motives of Rabbi Eliezer's marital practice:[36]

1. The commitment to obey God's law for its own sake, without any benefit for one's *yetzer*. This is what Ra'avad calls "the most correct motive of them all . . . to procreate in order to observe God's commandment."[37]

2. The improvement to the quality of the fetus, which men of science and Kabbalah thought derived from the quality of the intercourse.

3. The satisfaction of one's wife, when she desires him or when he is about to go on the road.

4. The channeling of one's own evil inclination into a permitted sexual act, so as to avoid performing an illicit one.[38]

While Ra'avad prefers the first motivation, namely procreation, he does *not* urge husbands to rush through the sexual act as Rabbi Eliezer does, perhaps because he disagrees with Imma Shalom's scientific recipe for producing beautiful, scholarly male offspring. Ra'avad encourages the husband to satisfy his wife's desires first, so her orgasm will precede his.[39] Ra'avad's proof text is the Talmudic adage of Rabbi Hama, son of Rabbi Hanina, who says: "God's reward for staying on one's wife's belly long enough so that she will produce her seed first [i.e., female orgasm] is male progeny" (TB *Niddah* 71a, see also 25b). Therefore, the duration of intercourse cannot be hastened, as Rabbi Eliezer's practice requires. The eugenic guidelines of Rabbi Eliezer and Rabbi Hama contradict one another, as do their concerns for the wife's sexual needs.

Yet Ra'avad, like Maimonides, is concerned lest the pursuit of sexual pleasure corrupt one's spiritual character. He then offers a path of moderation between satisfying one's wife and controlling one's evil impulse:

> One who estimates that his nature [i.e., his mental self-control] allows him—without arousing adulterous thoughts—to stay on his wife's belly so that his wife will enjoy herself and reach orgasm first—and who directs his intention to perform the mitzvah [i.e., for its own sake and not for his own pleasure], should do so, and he will be rewarded by God with male offspring. But someone who is unsure of himself in this matter and who wishes to save himself from sinful thoughts may perform a hasty intercourse and he too will be rewarded by God with beautiful sons.[40]

In other words, the ideal husband must be a consummate performer, carefully balancing between his ascetic spirituality and his altruistic devotion to execute his conjugal duties for his wife's satisfaction. Knowing how to realistically evaluate his own strengths against the power of his libido, he is capable of engaging in lengthy foreplay to arouse his wife and maximize her enjoyment, while employing scrupulous self-restraint to suppress anarchic erotic thoughts and curtail his own pleasure.

> With all we have seen about a man's responsibility to do his wife's desire and to give her joy in the mitzvah [of onah] anytime she needs it, nevertheless, we are warned that while the right hand draws us toward [desire], the left hand must help keep us at a distance, lest we be derailed to transgress the appropriate measure and drawn after it to the ephemeralities of the world and be lost![41]

In short, in differing ways both Maimonides the rationalist and Ra'avad the mystic seek to balance the tensions between the sexual legacies of Rabbi Eliezer and Rav.

Modern Applications:
Ben-Shimon, Soloveitchik, and Calderon

Our Talmudic sugya, like a good law school class, has performed its educational role with acumen—arousing a principled debate by arraying controversial polar positions and rationales one against another. It never intended to close the debate. But we, as modern readers, may yearn for resolution with a halakhic bottom line that echoes our moral concerns, and perhaps reassures us about the authority and wisdom of "the halakhah."

While, unfortunately, the jury is still out, thoughtful modern responses promote a middle path between the sugya's extremes. First, Rabbi Raphael Aaron Ben-Shimon (1848–1928, Morocco, the Land of Israel, and Egypt) rejects the abuse of wives inherent in Rabbi Judah HaNasi's Talmudic ruling and urges judges to join his crusade to reeducate abusive husbands who continue to manipulate the halakhic judicial system. (A century later this endemic problem still plagues the modern state of Israel.) Second, the Modern Orthodox halakhic philosopher Rabbi Joseph B. Soloveitchik (20th century, Belarus, Germany, and Boston) expresses concern with the abuse of sexuality within marriage and its vulgarization even if consensual. We then close with a suggestive philological remark about Rabbi Eliezer and Imma Shalom's sex life from Ruth Calderon, a secular Jewish humanist and feminist, whose concern is not halakhah, but aggadah, the narratives of the Talmud. She redeems the sugya's loveless technical description of intercourse (*m'saprim*) and its ascetic call for couples to suppress erotic conversation by means of her imaginative reinterpretation of an unusual Rabbinic term for "intercourse."

Historically, the courts in many cultures have been delinquent in outlawing and punishing abuse of spouses. Even though rabbinic jurisprudence has always prohibited and condemned spousal rape, it has often failed to enforce that ruling, and it has done too little to educate husbands about the limits on their rights to onah.

An unusual judicial crusader for the sexual rights of wives, Rabbi Raphael Aaron Ben-Shimon, chief rabbi of Cairo (1891–1921), accused his colleagues in the rabbinic establishment of allowing themselves to be pawns in the hands of abusive husbands who claimed their "rebellious wives" were refusing to fulfill their sexual duties. When systematically mistreated women abandoned their abusive husbands' beds and sought asylum with their families of origin, the rabbinic courts often failed to hear the women's counterarguments. And not only that: They often shamed the women publicly and pressured them financially to return to and pursue *shalom bayit* (domestic reconciliation) with their husbands— even when that was manifestly unattainable and the husbands had not made any behavioral changes. In his 1917 book, *Bat Na'avat HaMardut* (which means "the rebellious daughter"), Ben-Shimon surveyed his domestic strife court cases and the halakhic arguments he marshalled to oppose rabbinic courts that declared abused wives, who fled from their husbands and refused to return, to be "rebels" against their husbands. Once categorized legally as a rebel (*moredet*), a woman is pressured to reconcile herself and go home to her violent, unrepentant husband and threatened by the court with loss of her economic rights if she refuses.

In a horrific case of domestic violence reported in his book, a woman described how her husband regularly coerced her to submit to repeated acts of intercourse on the same night without her consent. Ultimately, she abandoned her house to avoid further abuse—an act her husband characterized as a breach of contract that rendered her a "rebellious wife." Ben-Shimon was asked to rule on this question: "Can this woman refuse to meet her husband's extravagant [sexual] needs without being declared a rebellious wife subject to unilateral divorce and to loss of her property [controlled by her husband] and the economic compensation guaranteed by her marriage contract?"

While, according to rabbinic practice at that time, the wife who abandons her home is automatically declared a rebellious woman, Ben-Shimon insisted that the court investigate the reasons for the wife's supposed dereliction of duty.[42] His book's subtitle, *Im B'Mered* (If She Rebels), is an acronym whose initials spell out "a wife who despises her husband because of the evil of his ways." In the court-room, at Ben-Shimon's gentle and patient urging, the woman plaintiff shared aloud her traumatic bedroom experience:

> Rabbi, am I a beast [of burden] abandoned (*hefker*) to [the will of] my husband? . . . Twelve or thirteen times in a night he performs sex with me. I am tormented, my stomach is empty, and I am kept awake all night. My stamina is at its end.[43]

"Hearing the sound of her crying and her pain, I was enraged and I trembled mightily," writes Ben-Shimon. When he interrogated her husband, the husband "couldn't understand how she could even make a complaint":

> Isn't she my wife by rights granted by my betrothal and by entering under the canopy [i.e., my marriage]?! Isn't she permitted to me by the Torah? What does it matter, if that [frequency of sexual activity] is what I want?![44]

The husband's retort echoes Rabbi Judah HaNasi's rationale for a husband's unilateral right to compel his wife to take whatever unconventional sexual position is to his liking: "My daughter, the Torah permitted him to you [any way he sees fit to consume you]. So as for me, what can I do?!" (TB *Nedarim* 20b). As a rabbinic Jew, the husband could have quoted Rabbi Judah HaNasi back to Ben-Shimon. Or, as a citizen of the British protectorate of Egypt, he could have cited the seventeenth-century British chief justice Sir Matthew Hale: "A husband cannot be guilty of a rape committed by himself upon his lawful wife, for, by their mutual matrimonial consent and contract, the wife hath given up herself in this kind unto her husband, which she cannot retract."[45]

Ben-Shimon, however, proceeded to advocate for the woman's right to human dignity. Her husband's sexual abuse should not be treated as normative onah. In his verdict, Ben-Shimon evoked the woman's suffering by playing on the triple etymological wordplay of the biblical Hebrew root: *onah*—regular marital visitation of one's wife (Exod. 21:10); *innah*—rape, coercive sex, such as degrades an unmarried young virgin (Deut. 22:29); and *innui*—to torment or persecute (Exod. 1:11–12). Thus Ben-Shimon's allusive linguistic associations to persecution make an implicit connection between this woman's suffering and the national oppression of Israel under Egyptian slave masters—persecution, bitterness, and enslavement (Exod. 1:11–14). With pathos, Ben-Shimon declares what he thinks of the husband's claim to have sex any way and as often as he likes:

> In this case [of marital intercourse, onah] there is nothing but torment (*innui*)! It is harsh and bitter enslavement! There is inadequate time between one act of sex and the next for the woman to arouse her desire for her husband. So each and every single act of his intercourse literally tortures her soul.[46]

Ben-Shimon rules that the wife can and should refuse her husband's exaggerated demands. He has a right to onah (to make love with her) but not a right to *innui* (to torture her):

I would do all I could to pressure the husband into saying "I want a divorce'" [so she could remarry]. . . . and to extract the ketubah compensation and the return of her dowry [which he owes her].

For this man, presumably, has the soul of such a beastly and low character that he will never repent from his evil ways until his strength gives out. Her refusal to have intercourse cannot be called a marital rebellion; rather, she is simply a lost soul.[47]

In essence, Ben-Shimon's responsum argues that simply expanding the *quantity* of onah generates untold pain rather than greater emotional and sexual intimacy. A numerical characterization thus has an inherent danger of missing the mark. What can be said to matter most is the *quality* of the marital relationship, one that entails harmonious interpersonal relations, sensitivity to the other's needs, and artful arousal of desire. Since neither need nor passion is easily quantified, spouses are to intuit, discuss, and synchronize their needs with those of their partners.

Ben-Shimon lamented the fate of such "a wife who can do nothing for herself but dig a grave and enter it while still alive and wait to die."[48] So he urged women abused by their husbands not to remain passive victims acquiescing to mistreatment. They were to be encouraged to liberate themselves, first by disclosing their experience to their relatives, and eventually by abandoning their marital homes.

Furthermore, during his tenure as chief rabbi of Egypt, Ben-Shimon led a campaign to convince rabbinic courts to reform the law of the rebellious wife and to no longer treat a victimized woman as though she were an arrogant rebel against her husband's authority. Recasting the legal definition of "rebellious wife," his book called upon judges to see themselves as advocates for this class of abused wives and to redeem the good name of the Torah, which he said is desecrated when judges fail to pursue justice and mercy:

God forbid that such a cruel law [and such a crooked statute that throws salt into the wounded hearts of the daughters of Israel suffering bitterly from the fate of marriage to a man of such harsh and evil behavior] shall have a place among the laws of our Torah that are pure and compassionate.[49]

Later in the twentieth century, after Ben-Shimon's death, many very prominent rabbis in Jerusalem followed in his footsteps in calling for reforms in rabbinic divorce law. Chief Ashkenazi Rabbi Isaac Halevi Herzog (1936–1959),[50] Chief Sephardi Rabbi Ovadiah Yosef (1973–1983),[51] Rabbi Eliezer Waldenberg, and Rabbi Yosef Kapah , all of whom served on Israel's state rabbinical courts (ca. 1950s–1970s), spoke out repeatedly in favor of jurisprudential policies that provide vigorous defense of mistreated wives unable to get their husbands to issue a divorce.

For example, Waldenberg argues that courts that do not compel husbands to divorce the wives they have abandoned for years in effect end up encouraging desperate women to commit adultery:

In this situation [where a wife is suffering from an abusive husband who refused to issue a divorce] a woman will not acquiesce to remain in such a miserable condition her whole life. She is likely, having no alternative, to go out to evil culture [i.e., promiscuity and adultery], God forbid, or lose control and commit suicide. In the best case this woman will remain in her devastated state, suffering many troubles. Haven't the Rabbis always tried to make every effort to enact legislation to protect the daughters of Israel?![52]

Even more forcefully, Kapah (like Ben-Shimon) urges a partial return to the aggressive policy of Maimonides, demanding courts to coerce recalcitrant husbands to release wives unwilling to remain married to men they do not love because their husbands abuse them:

How much justice, righteousness, wisdom and discernment there is in Maimonides' judgment on the [so-called] rebellious wife.... This woman has a soul, a human soul, so how can anyone imagine that she should be coerced into intercourse with someone she hates! ... Therefore, it is a mitzvah to coerce the stubborn husband with every form of coercion to separate this couple and the sooner the better.[53]

Meanwhile, for the last forty years, Israeli and North American organizations of Orthodox feminists, later coalescing as ICAR, the International Coalition for Agunah Rights, have fought ardently to "eradicate *get* recalcitrance [i.e., the husband's refusal to issue a divorce document called a *get*] and extortion in the divorce process within the framework of Jewish Law."[54] In Israel ICAR has trained a generation of knowledgeable female Orthodox advocates who represent these abused women in court. Facing often intransigent state rabbinical courts that have failed to protect *agunot* (i.e., women metaphorically and legally "chained" to their husbands by the men's refusal to grant a divorce), ICAR lobbies Israeli government committees that determine which new rabbinical judges will be appointed in order to encourage them to choose candidates known for protecting abused women's rights.

Tragically, the policies of Ben-Shimon, the passionate appeals of the above-noted Israeli chief rabbis and judges, and the political advocacy of ICAR have not yet succeeded in significantly changing the verdicts of the majority of the (mostly ultra-Orthodox) judges in Israel's divorce courts (whose jurisdiction applies to Israeli Jews only, of whatever religious persuasion). While there have been piecemeal victories, abused women are still regularly denied the right to initiate unilaterally a divorce. Often these wives have proven in court that their husbands treat them with systematic malice and beatings; that they live, without granting a divorce to their wives, with other women; and that they refuse to provide economic maintenance for their wives and children. Yet the majority of rabbinic courts in twenty-first-century Israel refrain from militantly pressuring recalcitrant husbands to issue divorces and invoke very sparingly the Knesset-approved sanctions: fines, revocation of driver's licenses and passports, freezing of bank accounts, and even imprisonment.

Ben-Shimon ends his book with a pledge and a challenge to his fellow judges to act according to their better angels in advocating on behalf of oppressed wives:

> We shall not continue along this road in torturing the souls of the daughters of Israel for no reason and we shall not fear or tremble for our holy Torah, *its paths are paths of pleasantness and all its ways are peace* (Prov. 3:17). . . . We still trust in the judges of Israel who are merciful.[55]

SOLOVEITCHIK'S PHILOSOPHY OF REDEEMING SEXUALITY

Like Maimonides, Rav Joseph B. Soloveitchik (1903–1993), one of the great modern Orthodox philosophers of halakhah, sought to find a golden mean for marital intimacy that rejects both the asceticism of Rabbi Eliezer and the anarchic sexual license of Rabbi Judah HaNasi. Unlike Maimonides, in his writings he insists that Jewish marriage belongs unapologetically to the hedonistic world of nature, and (with some exaggeration) that ascetic spiritual practice has no standing between husband and wife in Judaism:

> A covenantal marriage is a hedonic, pleasure-oriented community. Judaism did not overlook or underestimate the physical aspects of marriage. . . . The two partners owe each other not only fidelity, but also full gratification of their sexual needs. . . . The marriage must not be converted into an exclusively spiritual fellowship. Marriage with-

out carnal enjoyment and erotic love is contrary to human nature and is to be dissolved.[56]

Yet Rav Soloveitchik is equally aware that sexual liberation may result in sexual objectification and degradation for one or both spouses:

> If the sexual impulse is not redeemed and is left in its crudity, the participants in the drama are guilty of an act of mutual exploitation and vulgarization. The corruptions are interlaced and compounded with enslaving a human being, with denying him the most elementary right of personal existence. The person is depersonalized, desensitized and de-emotionalized. The climax of the hedonic sexual union is *ipso facto* an act of objectification of the personal, intimate and unique.[57]

The natural erotic impulse must not be celebrated without adapting it to an ethos of mutual human dignity. In other words, for Soloveitchik, culture need not deny nature, but it must cultivate and channel sexual impulse (see chapter 12). In order to humanize and moralize marital relationships and to achieve a covenantal relationship Soloveitchik champions the redemption of the human libido by means of halakhic restrictions on sexual desires.

CALDERON'S VISION OF LOVEMAKING AS DIALOGUE

Another modern application of our sugya emerges from Ruth Calderon, a secular Israeli feminist Talmud scholar (as well as a former centrist Knesset member, 2013–15). Notably, she is one of a number of secular Israelis seeking to make this sugya their own. Her crusade is to reclaim for secular Jews their rightful heritage of rabbinic literature over and against the ultra-Orthodox, who claim exclusive proprietary ownership over rabbinic literature understood, through their lens, as the only "authentic Judaism." Therefore, Calderon has created educational venues for young adults, secular and religious, to study Talmud and secular Israeli literature (e.g., Elul, an egalitarian *beit midrash* for religious and nonreligious men and women in Jerusalem; and the Alma Jewish Humanities College in Tel Aviv). For her (and her Israeli Jewish humanist colleagues), studying Torah means embarking on a highly personal and avowedly pluralist exploration of Talmudic stories, especially those concerned with women and intimate relationships, such as the ones in our sugya.

While questioning patriarchal domination of women in the rabbinic literature and criticizing Rabbi Eliezer and Imma Shalom's ascetic and antiseptic intercourse, Calderon nevertheless highlights the surprising term for having intercourse used by the sugya to describe Rabbi Eliezer and Imma Shalom's sexual intimacy: *m'saprim* (plural), literally, "telling a story together." As we saw, the Talmud reinterprets this verb as a mandate to engage in pillow talk designed to sexually arouse or to placate one's wife. By contrast, Calderon interprets *m'saprim* (narrating) as a euphemism for sexual relations and simultaneously as a metaphor for weaving together an interpersonal dialogue:

Lovemaking is a narrative; sexuality is a dialogue (literally, *intercourse*)[58] in which two people tell—one to the other and one with the other—a story. I think this is the most beautiful name for sex I have ever heard.[59]

Talmudic Techniques of Arousal   4

RAV HISDA'S SEX EDUCATION TUTORIAL
FOR HIS DAUGHTERS

Let your fountain be blessed, and find happiness in the wife of your youth.
She is love's doe, a graceful gazelle.
Her breasts will quench your thirst at all times;
you will always dote on her love.
—Proverbs 5:18–19

The true definition of perfect love between a man and a woman is the
exchange of positions when the lover becomes the beloved by virtue
of desire, so that the beloved becomes the lover. Then the beloved
and the lover are equal.

—JUDAH ABRABANEL (d. 1521, Italian philosopher), *Dialogues on Love*

Introduction

The classic Sanskrit sex manual, the Hindu *Kama Sutra* (ca. 400
BCE–200 CE), transmits explicit practical guidance on the art of
erotic intercourse (*kama*, one of the four goals of Hindu life, refers
to aesthetic or erotic pleasure, and *sutra*, literally, a "thread" or "line,"
refers to bundles or collection of aphorisms bound together in the
form of a manual). By contrast, the Rabbinic tradition never seeks
to maximize aesthetic pleasure as an end in itself. So while it is no
surprise that the Rabbis did not write manuals for stoking and satisfying sexual desire, it is odd and unique that the Talmud preserves
one script of a private tutorial on techniques of sexual arousal by the
famous Babylonian rabbi Rav Hisda.

As we've seen, other Talmudic Rabbis and their wives offer guidance (sometimes conflicting) on maximizing fertility, producing male offspring, maintaining modesty, suppressing erotic fantasies, and participating in pillow talk. By contrast, Rav Hisda (a student of Rav from Sura, died ca. 320 CE) imparts—and to his daughters at that!—sexually explicit guidance on how to arouse their husbands' desires.

As we will see, while Rav Hisda's suggestions are not explicated in terms of spiritual and ethical ideals, or formulated as halakhic directives rooted in Biblical or Rabbinic sources, their preservation in the Talmud and attribution to a famous scholar nonetheless elevate this ancient erotic education into a Rabbinic practice worthy of emulation. Indeed, Rav Hisda's pedagogic endeavors win a place not only in Rabbinic literature but also in contemporary Orthodox manuals for newlyweds.

Perhaps Jewish tradition should see Rav Hisda as a parent fulfilling his educational obligation to his maturing daughters by preparing them for marriage, just as a father is expected to teach his son a profession and lifesaving skills such as swimming:

> Our Rabbis taught: "The father is bound in respect to his son to circumcise him; . . . teach him Torah; take a wife for him; and teach him a craft. And some say: even to teach him to swim." (TB *Kiddushin* 29a) (*Tosefta Kiddushin* 1:11)

Understood broadly, finding a spouse for one's offspring may encompass not only arranging a good match and providing a dowry, but teaching young adults how to live harmoniously as married couples—including maintaining sexual attraction.

Hisda's Erotic Pedagogy

Rav Hisda initiates his presumably unmarried, but about to be espoused, daughters into the dynamics of foreplay and delayed intercourse with their husbands:

Rav Hisda taught his daughters. He hid a precious stone [or a pearl] in one hand and a *kura* [a measure of grain; burned dough; or a clod of earth] in the other.[1] He let them see the precious stone [in one hand], but he did not let them see the *kura* [hidden in the other hand] until he had caused them pain [by frustrating their passionate curiosity to see what was hidden]. And then he did show it. (TB *Shabbat* 140b)

Rashi explains the metaphor and the exact advice Rav Hisda imparts:

When your husband is stroking you [i.e., your body]—in order to arouse his desire for intercourse—and he is holding your breasts in his hand and the other hand [moves] toward that place [i.e., the vagina], then you should give him the breasts to multiply his desire, but the place of intercourse you should not make available to him too quickly, in order that his desire and his affection should so increase that he is pained [by denied desire]. Then turn and reveal it to him. (TB *Shabbat* 140b)

On one hand, Rav Hisda urges his daughters to share the bounty of their breasts with their husbands, as the book of Proverbs promises a young lover: *Her breasts will quench your thirst at all times; you will always dote on her love* (Prov. 5:19). On the other hand, he advises them to behave as coquettes who tease their husbands. The daughters are taught to be manipulative, alternately forward and reticent, provoking desire and denying its fulfillment to the point of pain, until finally each husband's arousal is complete and his wife is ready to satisfy him with unrestrained sexual intercourse.

What is forbidden and unavailable often provokes longing; as the Rabbis say, "the evil impulse craves only what is forbidden to it" (TJ *Yoma* 6:4). Thus, when Rav Hisda's daughters "play hard to get" by showing and yet hiding, by giving and yet holding back their husbands' access to full sexual consummation, they are intensifying their husbands' yearning and desire for them.

In stressing foreplay, Rav Hisda's technique highlights the playful agency of the woman concealing and then sharing her own body at will in order to incite her husband's desire and thereby reinforce and prolong attraction in their marriage. Rav Hisda assumes that at each stage in lovemaking, the woman holds the exclusive power to say "no" or "yes" over access to her body.

At the same time, in seeming contrast to the woman's sexual audacity which he models above, Rav Hisda also cautions his daughters to behave with modesty in monitoring their bodily functions in front of their husbands:

Rav Hisda taught his daughters: "Be modest even before your husbands. Do not eat bread before your husbands. Do not eat greens at night [for it causes bad breath]. Do not eat dates at night or drink beer at night [for they both cause diarrhea]. Do not defecate in the same place that your husbands do [for that will disgust them]." (TB *Shabbat* 140b)

At first glance, encouraging his daughters to offer their breasts to their husbands for foreplay in order to whet their sexual appetites might not seem to comport with maintaining modesty before one's husband regarding other bodily functions such as eating and defecating. Yet the common theme is Rav Hisda's awareness that feelings of desire for and disgust with one's spouse's anatomy are delicate and volatile matters. On the one hand, a hide-and-go-seek play of modesty and exposure can stoke desire. On the other hand, indiscriminate disclosure of one's bodily processes can turn the husband's attraction to the mystique of the female body into visceral repulsion. Rav Hisda's advice echoes one instruction in the *Kama Sutra*: "The woman should dress up luxuriously with many jewels and flowers. She must scent herself well; bad smell from sweat or residue between her teeth can be despicable to amorous desire."[2]

Further, Rav Hisda promulgates a norm of modesty—and not only for his daughters, but for all of Israel—that prohibits marital intercourse during daylight, when sexual partners cannot control the degree and quality of exposure of their bodies to the other's gaze:

Rav Hisda said: "It is prohibited for one to have sexual relations during the day time, as it states, *You shall love your neighbor as yourself* (Lev. 19:18)."

But [the Talmudic editor asks:] What is the point [of Rav Hisda's prooftext]?

Abbaye replied: "He [the husband] might observe something repulsive in her and she would thereby become loathsome to him" [and then divorce her].

Rava said: "But if it was a dark house [during the daytime], it is permitted; and a [Torah] scholar may darken the space by extending his cloak and having sexual relations [with his wife] underneath it." (TB *Niddah* 17a)

How is love of your neighbor connected to averting one's eyes from a spouse's blemishes? Love of your fellow, for the Rabbis, includes protecting their privacy and avoiding behavior that may cause embarrassment, as Rabbi Shimon ben Elazar says: "Make an effort to avoid seeing your fellow in the time of his disgrace" (*Mishnah Avot* 4:18). For the Rabbis, to look at one's spouse's blemishes and to let her/him see how disgusted you are by those defects may cause acute emotional stress, especially when the two of you are about to make love. The damage to the relationship caused by shame or disgust, the Rabbis fear, may even lead to divorce.

In his Israeli guidebook for Orthodox newlyweds, Rav Shlomo Aviner explains Rav Hisda's logic in contemporary psychological terms, as a product of some brides' lack of self-esteem:

There are brides who are very ashamed, owing to their feeling of modesty. Further, many think they are not beautiful and hence they are afraid that in the eyes of their husbands they are not beautiful. That is why the Rabbis commanded that the light be extinguished [during marital intercourse] for the sake of the mitzvah of *you shall love your fellow as yourself* (Lev. 19:18) [in order to avoid emotionally shaming sensitive brides with low self-esteem].

Another reason for extinguishing the light is because sight arouses and excites a male to the extreme, unlike women whose arousal comes from gentle contact with her body. In the dark the groom may be less aroused and then [he will not be rushed to orgasm before his wife has had time to become aroused by his gentle contact. When less excited sexually] he can relate to the bride with aristocratic restraint.[3]

Hiding a woman's body addresses her emotional vulnerability to shame. Her fear lest she not be beautiful in the eyes of her husband is a leitmotif throughout Rabbinic sources about maintaining marriages, because, as Rav Hisda is aware, men can be fickle. They can get bored with what is routine and readily available, like their wives' bodies, and they can be turned off by blemishes and bad smells. In short, the vagaries of desirability may threaten the commitments of love. Therefore, he suggests ways to increase the likelihood that the husband will not take sexual relations with his wife for granted. The husband, he implies, will really desire her, and appreciate his orgasmic release all the more as the consummation of their erotic play.

Among these techniques there are notable parallels between Rav Hisda's counsel and the erotic advice of the Roman poet Ovid (43 BCE–17/18 CE), renowned as one of the great lovers of the Roman world. Michael Satlow, a scholar of rabbinics specializing in marriage in the Talmudic period, explains:

Ovid suggests to women that they choose their sexual positions based on which part of their body they want their man to see. That is, a woman who thinks that she has a blemish will choose a sexual position that will conceal it. Ovid follows this with advice not to let light in, for it will expose "too much" of the body, again risking discovery of blemishes.[4]

In his commentary on family purity, Rabbi Mordechai Eliyahu (Sephardi chief rabbi of Israel, 1983–93) offers a different perspective on Rav Hisda's prohibition of intercourse in daylight. He explains that it is "not that the husband might discover a physical defect or something ugly in her body, but that the very fact of the woman revealing her [whole] body [in daylight] may lead to the husband's denigration (*zilzul*) of her body." Erotic attraction is spoiled when there is no mystery, when all is exposed and available.[5]

While for Ovid blemishes should be obscured lest they repulse the husband, the wife's more attractive features ought to be enhanced with cosmetics to stoke male desire. Yet there is a halakhic problem with using cosmetics to enhance sexual allure during the menstrual period (niddah) when a husband may not even touch his wife, let alone have intercourse. So "early elders" before the Mishnah forbade wives to adorn themselves during niddah, lest they provoke their husbands into initiating illicit sexual relations.

In contrast, Rabbi Akiba promulgated lenient halakhic rulings to make it easier for wives to maintain their sexual allure even when they are forbidden to engage in sex.[6] In opposition to the "early elders," he says that a wife may put on eyeshadow or rouge and adorn herself with colorful clothing even during her period of menstrual impurity. Otherwise, Akiba is concerned lest her lack of beauty "will lead to [marital] contention, and the husband may want to divorce her."[7] Marital security cannot be considered assured, in part because of how persnickety men can be about their lovers' appearance. The Mishnah, too, recognizes the importance of physical attraction, especially in building a new marital relationship, even when marital intimacy is temporarily prohibited, as on Yom Kippur. Thus, the Mishnah permits a new bride to wash her face, even on that holiest of fast days:

On the Day of Atonement it is forbidden to ... wash, but the king and the bride may wash their faces. (*Mishnah Yoma* 8:1)

Why may a bride wash her face? Lest she become unattractive to her husband. (TB *Yoma* 78b)

Maintaining sexual attractiveness for her husband is important for a wife, yet many Talmudic Rabbis, as we saw above (chapter 3), strongly recommend that a wife behave modestly, even in the bedroom (TB *Eruvin* 100b). Others, however, think that while there is a time to be modest, there is also a time to refrain from modesty. On the analogy of Ecclesiastes' adage, *there is a time to embrace, and a time for distance from an embrace* (Eccles. 3:5), Rav Nahman stresses the difference between the appropriate reticence of a betrothed woman in the presence of her intended husband *before* the wedding and her intentional immodesty *after* they marry and live under the same roof:

> The bride in her father's house [before entering the marital canopy] must maintain strict modesty in her husband's presence [while she is only betrothed], but when she [is married], she does *not* show modesty before her husband. (TB *Yoma* 54a)

The Rabbinic key to maintaining prolonged sexual tension and attraction within marriage is, as Rav Hisda counsels, an intentional dynamic between forbidden and permitted acts. So, too, Rabbi Meir, the student of Rabbi Akiba, explains the purpose of the laws of family purity:

> Rabbi Meir said: "Why did the Torah prohibit intercourse for seven days with a woman who has menstruated?" Because one [i.e., the husband] who is used to her will [eventually] become disgusted by her. So the Torah said: "Let her be declared impure for seven days, so that she will be beloved to her husband [when they have inter-

course after this interval] just as when she first entered the canopy of marriage." (TB *Niddah* 31b)

Alternately prohibiting and permitting intercourse in synchronization with the menstrual cycle is, for Rabbi Meir, God's trick for enhancing eros between husband and wife by alternating between withholding and opening up access to sexual union. In that sense Rav Hisda is imitating God in teaching his daughters to withhold and then expose their vagina so as to increase their husbands' desire while they are temporarily denied. Unimpeded access that is not intermittent, however, creates boredom.

So too Rav Joseph B. Soloveitchik explains that the laws of purity are designed to save marriage from banality. Secularity (*hol*), as opposed to the sanctity of objects and times, means availability for any use, at any time, at will. By contrast, what is holy is regulated, and access to it is limited for the particular purposes for which it is dedicated. The sanctity-secularity dichotomy generates an "off-and-on-again" cycle. Regarding sexual contact, this alternation generates expectation, excitement, and then pleasure.[8] Thus halakhah enhances volatile desire and permits only intermittent gratification in order to stabilize marriages.[9] Rabbi Meir's insight is captured in the Hasidic aphorism: "Constant pleasure is not pleasure."[10]

From a gender-equality perspective, Rav Hisda's advice assumes an asymmetrical social and legal reality in which the husband and only the husband may unilaterally initiate divorce. Psychologically it presupposes that men, not women, are fickle and easily bored sexually, and hence quick to divorce their wives for unsightly blemishes. Therefore, women need to be taught to avoid exposure of their less attractive sides, and men to make love only in the dark. Here, a feminist critique might legitimately object that Rav Hisda teaches his daughters to make themselves into sexual objects to pander to male desire. For their part, the Rabbis might respond that they seek to guide women realistically to manage and succeed in their marriages within a difficult social-sexual reality dominated by male flaws and prerogatives.

Even after one's daughter is married off, her marital security is not assured. Perhaps that is why the Rabbis debate whether having a daughter is a blessing or not. Rabbi Meir says that it is a blessing not to have a daughter, while Rabbi Yehuda says it is a blessing to have a daughter. Reacting to this debate, Rav Hisda chimes in assertively and very personally: "For me, daughters are preferable to sons!" (TB *Baba Batra* 141a). His investment in educating his daughters in imaginative techniques of arousal shows how seriously he takes his blessing and his responsibility for their happiness in married life.

Modern Applications for Orthodox Couples: Aviner and Shuchatowitz's Marital Guidelines and Sigala's Sensual Portraiture

In Orthodox and ultra-Orthodox communities today, 1,700 years after Rav Hisda's time, sexual modesty in public, for men, and even more so for women, has become the salient mark of their sectarian identity. Nonetheless, for some rabbis, within the marital bedroom, modesty must be abandoned to ensure erotic arousal during onah. Many innovative rabbinic authorities summon up Rav Hisda's advice as a halakhic model, granting legitimacy to the burgeoning network of counselors preparing ultra-Orthodox and Orthodox brides and grooms for marital intimacy.

AVINER'S POPULAR GUIDE FOR ORTHODOX ISRAELI BRIDES AND BRIDEGROOMS

As a student of Rav Zvi Yehuda Kook (1891–1982, son of the former chief rabbi Rav Abraham Isaac Kook), Rabbi Shlomo Aviner (born

1943, France and Israel) holds an influential position in a sector of the Israeli religious world, colloquially called "Hardal," halfway between ultra-Orthodox (Haredi) and Zionist modern Orthodox (Dati Leumi). He promotes strict personal codes of sanctity through modesty for men and women. Yet, he also published in 1984 one of the earliest and most lenient popular halakhic guidebooks for prospective Orthodox brides and bridegrooms entitled *Etzem MeiAtzamai* (Bone of my bones). Its title echoes Adam's warm welcome to the newly fashioned woman (later called Eve) even before becoming one flesh with her (Gen. 2:23). In the booklet Aviner includes some revealing remarks by an anonymous Orthodox marriage counselor who cites Rav Hisda as her paradigmatic sex educator. Initially she forthrightly describes the psychological obstacles faced by inexperienced religious brides-to-be:

> There are inner restraints about talking about these topics, and it is hard to unburden oneself from the shame. . . . Many brides are very anxious about the physical ties [with their prospective husbands] because they do not know what will happen. Therefore, the female counselors are obligated to explain to them exactly what will happen.[11]

What are the sources of anxiety reported by this premarital counselor of Orthodox brides? First, brides are reticent to engage in robust sexual activity due to their lack of knowledge about the physiology of intercourse and the dynamics of both male and female desire. Further, they are emotionally blocked by their deep religious belief that piety requires both wives and husbands to transcend their sexual impulses and dampen their passionate hunger for intimacy. The counselors identify this reticence as a recipe for marital crisis:

Sometimes the girl [the bride] is very delicate, pious and modest. . . .
Many women cannot understand that a student of Torah [like
their yeshiva-educated husband] can be such "a man possessed by
desire" [and therefore they recoil from what they feel is the groom's
sexual aggressiveness]. . . . And then the man [the groom himself]
feels bad and [treats her so gingerly that] he himself does not reach
(sexual) satisfaction.

[Embarrassed at his own powerful erotic drive, the husband] feels
that he is evil and uncouth and then he gets angry, nervous, and
tense. Finally he pours out his wrath on his wife without really knowing what he is doing.[12]

To relieve the guilt felt by pious brides, the counselor invokes the
paradigm of Rav Hisda, whom she regards as the first of her breed
of premarriage counselors. Here is her advice to a bride uncomfortable with the husband's strong libidinal drives and worried about
maintaining her own modesty:

[The bride] should not be upset; and she should not give [her
groom] a sense that he is not normal. After all, the Talmud reports
what Rav Hisda told his daughters [how to arouse their husbands'
passions]. . . . *A woman should be very liberated both for herself and for
her husband.* . . . A woman must seek to enjoy herself. . . . She must
cast aside all psychological restraints. She should not be passive, and
she must know that women taking the initiative in sexual intercourse
or women taking pleasure in orgasm belong to Judaism.[13]

The marital counselor seeks to dispel the guilt feelings at the root
of the bride-to-be's almost pathological fear of exposing her body
and touching the opposite sex, let alone being swept up in sexual
passion. Invoking Rav Hisda's precedent proves to be therapeutic
for her brides.

Like Aviner, the Haredi rabbi Moshe Aharon Shuchatowitz (late 20th and early 21st centuries, United States and Israel) is also a zealous promoter of religious "sex ed," publishing halakhic guidelines about onah for married yeshiva students and organizing premarital counseling. He too cites with approval Rav Hisda's bold precedent as a sex educator, while acknowledging that this exotic Talmudic text strikes the average pious reader as "alien to the spirit of Judaism." In his popular book *Binyan HaBayit*: *Guidance for Yeshiva Students on the Sanctity of the Jewish Home* (2003), Shuchatowitz quotes his revered master, the Steipler rav, Rabbi Yaakov Kanievsky, who identifies three practical principles to be derived from this tale of Rav Hisda:

> "Let them see the precious stone"—The woman must be active in this situation. As opposed to the Christians who hold that a woman's modesty entails her passivity, the Torah requires her to show off her precious stone.
>
> "Let them see the precious stone"—The woman must arouse her husband's sexual desire and she must respond with her active support to the man who is also seeking to arouse his own desire by engaging in foreplay with the woman's genitals.
>
> "The *kura* [alternatively translated as clod, grain, or dough], however, he did not let them see"—The woman must use her guile, her wisdom, to tantalize her husband until his desire is so aroused that it hurts.[14]

Kanievsky and some other ultra-Orthodox Litvak rabbis (who trace their brand of Talmud study to the anti-Hasidic yeshivot originating in early nineteenth-century Lithuania) generally oppose ascetic trends toward extreme *tzinus* (decorous modesty) *inside* the marital bedroom, and thus largely reject Rabbi Eliezer ben Hyrcanus's ascetic tradition. Yet none of them denigrate the importance of inordinate sexual modesty *outside* the bedroom, and especially of women's *tzinus*.[15] Rather, they distinguish sharply between situations in which sexual propriety is appropriate and those in which it is not only inappropriate but harmful. Following Rav Hisda, they argue that exposing one's body playfully in the service of the mitzvah of onah ought not to be a source of shame, but rather of joyful service of God.

Further, Shuchatowitz cites his teacher, Rav Shneur Kotler (d. 1982, Israel), who balances between advocating extreme sexual modesty in public and unapologetic erotic openness in the bedroom. Kotler affirms the traditional notion that a woman's place is in the privacy of the home, in accordance with the verse, *all the glory of the king's daughter is within* (Ps. 45:14). She must be kept under wraps like a well-protected treasure. Yet inside the palace, he insists that the affectionate relationship of husband and wife ought to be expressed demonstratively, just as the monarch revels in his jewels when securely ensconced in his treasure house.[16] Kotler explains:

> If the wife behaves with modesty and hides herself during the time of affection [onah], that is a sign that she thinks [mistakenly] that she [i.e., her body] is not to be honored. That is the modesty of the toilet [which is inappropriate behavior for the bedroom].[17]

Kotler, like Aviner's bridal counselor, questions the misplaced modesty of pious women who err in practicing stringent *tzinus* in their sexual relations with their husbands. While excessive reticence in bed with one's husband is permitted in pursuit of higher spirituality, Kotler says, that is only if it does not reduce the degree of sexual affection needed for mutually satisfying lovemaking. He sternly cautions those ascetic pietists who seek to emulate Rabbi Eliezer's extreme modesty inside the bedroom, noting that many who have tried that path of piety have failed, both in their marriage relationship and in managing their passions.[18]

Meanwhile, a new fashion, sensual portraiture, is becoming popular among some Orthodox women as a means of developing their sacred sensuality, cultivating their own hidden erotic beauty, and enhancing their sexual bonds with their husbands. Journalist Debra Kamin tells the story of an anonymous Orthodox wife (residing with four children in an Orthodox settlement in the West Bank in Israel/Palestine) who hired an Orthodox female photographer to create an erotic album for her husband.[19] While normally this married woman dresses modestly and covers her hair, in this instance, Kamin explains, she was encouraged to dress provocatively:

> Today [in her photo shoot], however, she looks different. Dressed in a lacy black negligee, her hair styled in loose waves and her eyes done up with smoky powder, she lounges on a bed in an apartment in suburban Jerusalem and gazes coyly at a photographer's camera. "Come closer," the photographer Rebecca Sigala says to her. "Imagine the lens is your husband, and give him a smile."

Kamin describes the context:

> [This Orthodox wife] has purchased today's boudoir session as an eighth wedding anniversary gift for her husband. The photos will be presented to him in an album and remain private between the two of them. The shoot begins with hair and makeup . . . a number of lacy nightdresses, and even one of her husband's unbuttoned dress shirts. But while she thinks he will be delighted by the photos, she says she wouldn't want anyone in her community to know about the experience. "It's simply too private. Intimacy is something you share just with your husband."

The Orthodox boudoir photographer Rebecca Sigala explains the religious orientation behind her unusual professional calling:

As observant Jews, we believe our sexuality is private and sacred. And since that part of ourselves is so holy, when we express ourselves within that realm, we can connect on a higher level—not just with ourselves, but with our husbands and with God.

The Israeli wife who is the subject of this album explains what this photo shoot means to her personally:

It's something I want to be able to tap into. It's about the experience I am having today, and being able to know that I'm sexy. I can lay here on the bed and feel beautiful, feel *shalem* [whole, or complete].

Similarly, an Orthodox boudoir photographer from Brooklyn reports to Kamin about the needs of her New York clientele:

For *frum* women, it can be extremely difficult to perceive themselves as beautiful. They're always having babies, or their friends are having babies and they can't, and they feel their bodies are somehow damaged. But everyone is beautiful in their own way, and by the end of the shoot, they can see themselves differently.

The halakhic basis for these women's desires to feel more attractive and, in so doing, to make themselves more attractive to their husbands is well-grounded in a broad understanding of Rav Hisda's tutorial as well as Rabbi Akiba's policies about maintaining a wife's beauty. Photographic portraiture as a tool for pious women to learn about their own sexuality and its effect on their husbands recalls somewhat Rav Hisda's use of visual aids 1,700 years ago in order to teach the pious daughters of Israel how to make themselves more erotic in their encounters with their husbands.

Conclusion

In reexamining the message of Rav Hisda and its modern applications, we have seen many attempts to encourage women to enhance, embrace, and employ (sometimes manipulatively) their own sexuality in marriage. Rav Hisda's mandate for women's forthright sexual expression may be understood as liberal or enlightened, especially when contrasted with the ascetic views of the school of Rabbi Eliezer (see chapter 3). Sometimes halakhic sexual advice is intended to help women enjoy their own onah and find the satisfaction they are owed, but much more often it is offered in order to help them win their fickle husbands' love and loyalty. The Rabbis may be more permissive in their sex education because of their assumption that men's affection and attraction can be so easily alienated by a blemish, an unwashed face, or bad breath. Therefore these so-called progressive views may also be subjected to a feminist critique of patriarchy. In substance Rav Hisda and Rabbi Akiba seek to persuade women to reshape their gender identities, physical appearance, and sexual practices around the fulfillment of male desires.

Yet the Rabbis are no less concerned for the woman's sexual satisfaction, and they demand that husbands also invest in arousing their wives' desire, as in the case of Rav jesting with his wife (see chapter 2). Later in this book we encounter the ultra-Orthodox school of twentieth-century Litvak (Lithuanian) halakhic authorities, who insistently urge husbands to satisfy their wives' erotic and emotional needs (see chapters 9–10). Aware of the danger of marital disharmony and rising divorce rates in their own communities, the Orthodox authors of many contemporary halakhic guidebooks for marriage realize that both Orthodox women and men cannot become good marital partners without more knowledge of their erotic physiology and without understanding the religious mandate to become better lovers. While we do not know precisely what was Rav Hisda's rationale for teaching his daughters about stoking erotic attraction in marriage, today's Orthodox marital educators have no doubt that teaching the art of lovemaking is indispensable for maintaining *shalom bayit*, peace and mutual love in the family.

PART THREE

Medieval Mysticism and Law

SACRED LOVE AND LEGAL LIMITS

A Mirror of the Divine Union   5

KABBALISTS' SACRED EROS OF MARRIAGE

Master of the Universe! . . . Let it be your will, our King and the
King of our forefathers, that our intercourse will be pleasing to You,
each time and hour and moment . . . so that the Holy One, blessed
be He, and his Shekhinah will be unified by us.

—Kabbalist prayer before intercourse

Introduction

An anonymous kabbalist wrote, characteristically: "If you understand the secret of a bride and groom, you will understand everything."[1] In contrast to the Talmudic conceptions of marital sexuality,
Jewish mystical tradition envisions earthly marriage as a mirror of
the heavenly divine union. On one hand, the divine union is a model
for the earthly marriage, which receives a heavenly overflow (*shefa*)
of blessing from above. On the other hand, the earthly human act
of sexual union (*zivug*) produces an active force coming from below
(*hitorerut di'ltata, theurgy*) to arouse and empower the union of the
male and female dimensions of God above. Human lovemaking primarily serves divine needs (*tzorekh gavoha*) rather than human aims
(e.g., procreation, channeling the male sex drive, fulfilling one's spousal duty, expressing emotional intimacy). *Onah* facilitates cosmic
processes to repair the world (*tikkun olam*) and perfects the human
being as the complete unification of male and female dimensions,
thus fully embodying the dual-gendered image of God.

Our necessarily brief treatment of the vast, varied field of eros and
Kabbalah will focus on its indirect and yet profound contributions
to spiritual and halakhic treatments of marital relations. Relying

primarily on the interpretations of Moshe Idel (b. 1947, Israel), Jerusalem's scholarly doyen of Jewish mysticism, we will examine the conceptual revolution, especially in Zoharic Kabbalah, that imagines God as a union of male and female forces. Unlike classic Greek notions of the passivity of the female, these medieval mystics imagine and appreciate divine feminine power.

Yet, we must be wary about identifying medieval Kabbalah with proto-feminism. While kabbalists initiated new theological theories of the Shekhinah (the divine feminine), their new sensibility did not produce a significant egalitarian transformation in medieval family life. Only in a few medieval manuals about bedroom etiquette do kabbalists direct spouses to make love with greater mutuality.

Nevertheless, today the Kabbalist imagination of divine eros has come to deeply enrich our contemporary understanding of human erotic relationships. Only recently, over the last fifty years, have modern understandings of mystical female agency begun to directly inspire egalitarian Jewish ethics of love and sacred marriage.

Midrash on the Cherubs' Erotic Embrace

Idel traces the kabbalist notion of *isomorphism*, the mirrorlike similarity in form and function of the sexual union in human and divine realms, to its roots in the Rabbinic world of Talmudic literature (3rd–6th centuries). Long before the Zohar (13th century), itself a mystical reading of the Torah, the Rabbis employed bold and explicit heterosexual imagery to illustrate the mythic activity within the Holy of Holies:

> Rav Katina says: When [the people of] Israel goes up to make a holiday pilgrimage [to the Temple in Jerusalem], the curtain is rolled back and they are shown the cherubs intertwined with one another and they are told: "Look at how you are cherished before God just like the affection (*hibbah*) of a male and a female."[2] (TB *Yoma* 54a–b)

The Talmud's depiction of the erotic embrace of the cherubs, which were placed above the ark in the Holy of Holies, evolves from the Biblical cherubim (Exod. 25:18–20; 1 Kings 6:23–28), who are described as gold statuettes with wings and faces without any gender identification. Because God speaks to Moses *from between the two cherubim* (Exod. 25:22), the cherubs are the most intimate point of access between earth and heaven. In this midrash, the auditory revelation of the divine voice to Moses, the prophet par excellence, takes on a three-dimensional visual form embodied in the pair of cherubs, portrayed in the likeness of a mature man and woman, sexual beings embracing in an act of love in the Temple.

One might expect a sexually intimate portrayal of the Divine Presence in the Temple to be consigned to esoteric wisdom. Just as the entry to the Holy of Holies is restricted to one human being, the High Priest, who enters it on only one day a year, the Day of Atonement, shouldn't the erotic dimension of divine activity in the inner sanctum of the Temple be kept secret—or perhaps known only to the esoteric circle of Rabbinic mystics like Rabbi Akiba who entered the paradise of secret wisdom?

Yet, according to Rav Katina's midrash, the embracing cherubs play a central role in a public Temple ritual. On the mass pilgrimage holidays, such as Sukkot, the Rabbis imagine, retrospectively, that the priesthood of the Second Temple teaches *all* Israel the secrets of God's inner chambers. The curtains are intentionally pulled back, literally and metaphorically, and then these secret traditions become a curriculum for popular education. In that public revelation, what is usually regarded as shameful about intercourse, especially when exposed to voyeurs, becomes a public display to teach sacred erotic symbolism that conveys ethical truths.

How did the Rabbis understand the public revelation to Israel of the hithertofore secret love life of the cherubs? Three rationales may be suggested.

First, the loving cherubs teach the people who come to God's house that God has affection for Israel. The images concretize the Rabbinic understanding of the erotic love poetry in the Song of Songs as a description of the love between the collective entity Israel and God. King Solomon's bed (Song of Songs 3:7) is interpreted in another midrash as God's bed, as the Temple itself.[3]

Second, by embracing, the cherubs broadcast an ethical message to the diverse Jews who gather on the pilgrimage holiday: to be worthy of God's love, the people of Israel must love one another. Brotherly love among the people of Israel, not sexual love between spouses, is the moral analogue to the embracing cherubs.

The first two rationales for the cherubic embrace focus on the nonsexual affection of God for Israel and the ethical value of loving one's neighbor: brotherly love of the community. Yet the gendered difference of male and female cherubim embracing also echoes the mitzvah of onah between husband and wife, so Idel suggests a third, explicitly erotic, rationale. Given that the midrash about the embrace is told *after* the destruction of the Temple, during the painful exile of the people Israel from their God and Temple, it may have been intended to reconstitute the intimacy of Temple worship in the home: "The religious role of the cherubim . . . has been transferred to human pairs . . . when [onah is] performed in purity."[4] The symbolic embrace of the cherubs can be reenacted in the embraces of individual couples, thus drawing down the Shekhinah's presence into their mini-temples: their private bedrooms. Simultaneously, the Shekhinah may now reside in multiple private dwellings, and the Divine can reveal itself to us again as we embrace, just as God once spoke to Moses from between the embracing cherubs.

The originator of this mystical ritual and sexual myth is, Idel suggests, most probably the great Rabbinic authority on the love between God and Israel, Rabbi Akiba. For Akiba, the Song of Songs is the Holy of Holies of the Bible:

All the ages are not worth the day on which the Song of Songs was given to Israel; for all the *Ketuvim* [the Writings, the third part of the Tanakh which includes Song of Songs] are holy, but the Song of Songs is the Holy of Holies. (*Mishnah Yadaim* 3:5)

If each couple proves worthy, morally and emotionally, then, says Rabbi Akiba, they will be worthy to house the divine immanence, and the Shekhinah can then find rest between them: "Rabbi Akiba said: 'Man (*ish*) and woman (*isha*)—if they merit it, Shekhinah (*ya*) is between them. If they do not merit it, fire (*esh*) is between them'" (TB *Sotah* 17a).

Generally, the Talmud does not ascribe sanctity or mystical union to what it perceives as mundane lovemaking, such as that found in the anecdotes about the bedroom practices of Rabbi Eliezer, Rav, and Rav Hisda (chapters 2, 3, and 4). Although marital intimacy is *not* treated as a sacrament or even as a metaphor for the Divine Presence, Idel believes these Talmudic midrashim about the cherubim open up a conceptual space within which marital lovemaking can be experienced as a religious act of worship endowed with the mystic power to draw the Shekhinah into one's marital bed. When medieval Kabbalah develops its dual-gendered Divinity and makes the unification of the masculine and feminine dimensions the aim of its rituals, then acts of spousal love, especially on Shabbat, gain even greater mystical potency, as they mirror and reinforce heavenly eros.

Ra'avad's Kabbalist Manual for Sexual Union

While no religious ideology is attributed to the mitzvah of onah in the Talmud, medieval halakhic works compiled by early kabbalists such as Ra'avad (Rabbi Abraham ben David of Posquières, Provence, 1125–98) combine mystical theology with Rabbinic halakhah and Greek eugenics to generate the first detailed, systematic rabbinic instructions for marital intercourse. The intersection between theosophic Kabbalah of the ten *sefirot* (dimensions) of the Divine and halakhah (12th–16th centuries) produces a uniquely Jewish brand of *Kama Sutra*, replete with practical guidance regarding conversing, kissing and hugging, preferred sexual positions, and mental intentions (Zohar III 81b). All of these actions and thoughts are deemed essential for achieving the full union of body and soul, and thus inducing the heavenly union of male and female.

Even before the Zohar was circulated (Spain, 1280 CE), the first halakhic and ethical guide for achieving sanctity in the practice of marital lovemaking was composed by the Talmudist Ra'avad (12th century, Provence). He called his manual *Sha'ar HaKedushah* (The gate to sanctity) and published it as a subsection of his book *Ba'alei HaNefesh* (Masters of the appetitive soul, i.e., the lower desires of the psyche). By interpreting, mystically and halakhically, the way God created the human being (Gen. 1–2), Ra'avad prescribes how each husband and wife should relate to one another. Initially, he observes, Adam is an organic combination of two matching faces, male and female, *du-partzufin*. Unity comes first; the male and female faces have *not* been formed as independent beings with autonomy and will. Only later does God separate them into two—a necessary stage before their reunification as a couple—so that they will recognize their common origin and collaborate. Their sexual union is not designed to return them to a utopian state of simple oneness but to advance them to a state of harmonious peace and affection between gender-differentiated yet related individuals.

To see how Ra'avad's kabbalist theology shapes his ambivalent ethos of marriage, we must delve briefly into his abstract thought system. The divine realm mirrors dramatic, dynamic dimensions in the relationship between masculine and feminine aspects of the cosmos. God must of necessity be a combination of male and female poles, since the original Adam, who was created in the image of God, is bisexual or dual-gendered, with two faces (*du-partzufin*). Those gender poles reflect the inner polarity between binary traits necessary for every system—justice and love, form and flow, strictness and compassion. Note that for the kabbalists, the feminine (in some, but not all, of its dimensions) epitomizes the execution of justice, form, and strictness, and hence activity, while in Romantic stereotypes (19th century), the woman is associated with mercy, matter, and fluidity, and hence passivity.[5]

Since the male-and-female pair derives from complementary poles of justice and mercy, they naturally and ideally seek to form a balance and a union. Yet harmony can be structured either as hierarchy or as mutual complementarity. In the first model, man and woman are one hierarchal body—he is the head and she, one of the limbs—and, as such, "since she is one of his limbs created to serve him,"[6] the man rules over her hierarchally. Yet, in the second model, man and woman are created equal and binary, so that they will tend naturally toward harmony rather than separation. Invoking the first model, Ra'avad writes about the necessary subordination of woman to man:

Adam and Eve were created *du-partzufin* [with two faces, one male and one female] so the woman would listen to her husband. . . .

For otherwise were they created as separate animals, the female would not accept the rule of the male and serve him, but rather each of them would grab food one from the other and kick one another and each go their own way with no special connection to one another since they would have each been created in one's self and for one's self.[7]

Nevertheless, Ra'avad also describes the unique emotional unity and reciprocity of human couples. While animals can procreate without building life-long heterosexual relationships of mutual love,

God wanted human beings to enjoy orderly and caring unions, so Adam and Eve were created to complete one another:

So intimacy, brotherhood and peace would prevail between them and tranquility would be in their palaces. [Had the divine attributes of justice and mercy] ... which emerged as complete opposites, pure judgment [female] and pure compassion [male], and they would have functioned independently with no connection and no mutual aid. . . . The attribute of judgment could not rise to that of mercy, nor that of mercy to judgment. . . .

But now that they have been created *du-partzufin* (double-faced) all their actions are united and equally balanced and there is no separation between them. . . . Each one approaches and becomes one with his fellow and longs and desires to be united in one dwelling [i.e., one sacred tabernacle].[8]

As a kabbalist, Ra'avad does not long to return to an original homogeneous unity or to progress forward to a total synthesis that dissolves all differences into a simple unity. Idel explains:

Being two distinct and opposite powers, the two attributes could not cooperate, had they not been originally united. However, their union entails not complete reunion, a return to their pristine situation, but a form of cooperation which does not obliterate their independent existence.[9]

This mystical theosophy imparts three lessons about male-female relations:

1. Difference is positive and primordial. The man was never conceived as the full embodiment of God's image; nor was he ever meant to be totally self-sufficient or autonomous from the woman. The woman is not an afterthought, but an essential aspect of the divine plan.[10]

2. Once separated, the nature of the re-union should not eradicate difference. Rather, the ideal is collaborative.

3. Gender relations within human marriage *must* nevertheless be hierarchal, to avoid strife between the independent wills of man and woman. Yet the outcome of hierarchy ought to be voluntary collaboration—friendship and desire, union and peace, not violent coercion and not hostile subordination of the woman to the man against her will.[11]

Ra'avad's hierarchical picture of gender relations alternates with his prescriptions regarding equality and voluntary collaboration between genders, the latter more in line with the second notion of harmony between complementary equals. While the male has greater authority, the couple's reciprocity is to extend beyond utilitarian cooperation to express ideals of mutual loyalty, love, and lifelong companionship:

> When Adam saw woman and realized that she emerged from him, he said, *Therefore a man will leave father and mother and attach himself to his wife and become one flesh* [Gen. 2:24], which means, "This one is worthy of being with me forever, and I with her, *and become one flesh*." For that reason a man should love his wife as he loves himself, and honor her and have mercy on her and guard her as if he is guarding one of his limbs [see TB *Yevamot* 62b]. So too she is obligated to serve, honor, and love him as she loves herself, for she was taken from him.[12]

On the basis of the primordial union of male and female before the separation, there is a natural affinity between male and female, so that they may collaborate out of love rather than mere obedience. Maintaining love through consensual intercourse is a halakhic requirement for Ra'avad: "Rape is prohibited even of one's own wife [if she refuses to consent freely]. Should the husband want to have sex, nevertheless, then he must appease her, and [only if and when she consents] may he engage in intercourse." Further, if they feel enmity for one another or they are in the midst of an unresolved fight and they, nevertheless, acquiesce to have sex, that is forbidden. Marital intercourse while the couple are emotionally alienated is equivalent to "an act of prostitution because it is not motivated by love."[13]

Aristotelian Jewish Philosophers versus Kabbalist Platonists

The role of the human body in the search for spirituality arouses a sharp debate among Jewish thinkers in the early Middle Ages and reflects the thousand-year dispute between the founders of Greek philosophy, the teacher Plato and his student Aristotle (4th century BCE). Most medieval Jewish philosophers, foremost among them Maimonides, viewed Aristotelian philosophy as the definitive canon of knowledge, including the sciences of the earth (physics and biology) and of the heavens (metaphysics and the Divine), whereas Platonic and Neoplatonic traditions, especially associated with Plato's *Symposium* on eros, more intensely influenced a minority of Jewish philosophers, such as Shlomo Ibn Gabirol and Judah Halevy, but the majority of medieval Jewish *mystical* thinkers. Thus, the Maimonidean school of Aristotelian philosophy and the theosophic kabbalist schools of Ra'avad, Gikatelia, and Zoharic literature took up diametrically opposed attitudes toward human sexuality and spirituality.

Aristotelian philosophy, with its strongly hierarchical differentiation and subordination between rational and physical, soul and body, reason and emotion, man and woman, active and passive, spirit and matter, is vehemently opposed to the ideas that God has both male and female dimensions and that the gendered human body (including phallus, womb, and vagina) has the same structure as the mystical divine body's ten dimensions, the ten *sefirot*. While Maimonides acknowledges the instrumental value of sexual reproduction for the preservation of the material world, he attributes no spiritual significance to the erotic union of male and female. While mandating a healthy body and commending the medicinal need for moderate sexual activity, Maimonides holds that the true calling of religion and philosophy, especially for the elites, is to enhance intellectual-cum-spiritual thinking (which characterizes the unique essence of humanity) and to minimize mundane activities that service our bodily, or animal, needs. Maimonides cites with approval Aristotle's maxim "the sense of touch is a source of shame for human beings."[14] For Maimonides, the highest form of love, passionate desire, is the genderless, nonsexual, intellectual eros to know God's mind, for God has "no body and no image of body."[15]

By contrast, Platonic love as described in Plato's *Symposium*, is an ascent on a ladder to the heavenly realm of truth and beauty that begins with the yearning for beauty manifest in erotic attraction to earthly embodiments of beauty. Only later does eros ascend the ladder of being from the concrete to the abstract and eventually arrive at the divine object of love.[16] And even after ascending beyond the early rungs of the ladder, the Platonic tradition does not necessarily denigrate those early stages. Rather than channeling, instrumentalizing, and constricting human sexuality, as the Aristotelians do, the kabbalist Platonists elevate it and transmute its eros on the way to higher realms.

For Maimonides the Aristotelian Jewish philosopher, the path to intellectual perfection and ascent to the world of pure forms begins by casting off the materiality of body represented metaphorically as a female prostitute and uniting one's mind with that which is rational and immaterial.[17] By contrast, the journey of a kabbalist mystic begins with an ardent erotic yearning for a beautiful flesh-

and-blood woman. A popular medieval kabbalist, Rav Isaac of Acco (13th–14th centuries, Spain) makes this point with great sarcasm: "One who has not felt carnal passion (*heshek*) for a woman is like a mule or even less than that, for worship of God begins when one can discern the Divine within the material world of senses."[18] On the basis of the profound experiences of human love and desire for sexual union, which mirror the dynamics of the divine realm, the theosophic school of Kabbalah directs its adepts to perform rituals and meditations (*kavanot*) that facilitate the ever-renewed union of male and female dimensions of the Divinity and thus unite earthly and heavenly worlds.

The Holy Letter: Sanctification of Sexuality

The school of mysticism embodied in *The Holy Letter* (*Igeret HaKodesh*) polemicizes against Maimonides by highlighting the correlation between transcendent and mundane processes. *The Holy Letter* (attributed traditionally to Nahmanides but probably composed ca. 1290–1310 in Gerona by Joseph Gikatelia) champions the sanctification of sexual life without denying its corporality or its driving desire:[19]

> Know that connection (*hibur*) [i.e., sexual intercourse] is holy and clean when done properly at the right time and with the correct intention. No one should think it is detestable or ugly.... Maimonides is wrong in praising Aristotle for calling the sense of touch our source of shame. God forbid, the Greek is not correct....
>
> Rather, all those who possess the Torah believe that God made everything according to Divine Wisdom and nothing was created to be condemned or ugly.... *If our sexual organs are detestable, how could the Holy One create something that is lacking or condemnable, God forbid!* ... The great secret of the cherubs is that they were intertwined one with the other in the likeness of a male and female.[20]

Coupling in order to create a child is a sacred act of imitating God the Creator:

> When the union of man to woman is worthy, then it is the secret of the construction of the world, for humanity is the partner with the Holy One in the Creation process. . . . When the union is conducted in sanctity and purity, then the Shekhinah is between them.[21]

Now, in order to produce the highest quality offspring in accord with the Greek wisdom of eugenics, *The Holy Letter* urges both the husband and the wife to achieve purity and unity of thought at the moment of intercourse:

> Therefore a husband must not rape his wife like a lion shamelessly devouring his prey, nor have intercourse when she is sleeping, but draw her heart with graceful words and entice her to reach commonality so her thoughts and his are in agreement.[22]

To instruct everyday couples in the communicative arts of wooing, *The Holy Letter* appeals to the authority and the imagery of the erotic dialogues in Song of Songs. It also analyzes the poetic song of praise Adam utters when he is first united with his wife. In the section entitled "The Fifth Way: The Quality of the Act," *The Holy Letter* teaches:

> *Set me as a seal upon your heart* (Song of Songs 8:6). I begin and tell you that it is well known that a pious and modest person will speak softly, gently, and calmly. He will never talk arrogantly. . . . Therefore, when engaging in the sex act, you must begin by speaking to her in a manner that will draw her heart to you, calm her spirits, and make her happy. Thus your minds will be bound to one another as one, and your intention will unite with hers. Speak to her so that your words will provoke desire, love, will, and passion, as well as words leading to reverence for God, piety, and modesty. . . . When the union is

performed without sufficient desire, love, and free will, the Divine Presence will not dwell there.[23]

The Holy Letter explains that mutuality of intention and desire can only be fully attained at the end of a long, step-by-step process of verbal courting and erotic foreplay:[24]

You ought to engage her first in matters that please her heart and mind and cheer her in order to bring together your thought with her thought and your intention with hers. And you should say such things, some of which will urge her to passion and intercourse, to affection, desire, and lovemaking, and some of which will urge fear of heaven, piety, and modesty.

You should attract her with charming words and seductions and other proper and righteous things. . . . And do not possess her while she is asleep, because then the two intentions are not one and her wish does not agree with yours. . . .

Do not hasten to arouse your passion until the woman's mind is ready. Engage her in words of love so that she will begin to give forth seed first [in her orgasm] and thus her seed will be like matter and your seed like form, as it is said, *when a woman gives forth seed, [then she] bears a male child* (Lev. 12:2).[25]

The apex of lovemaking is reached when the husband and wife have purified their thoughts and are ready to unite sexually. Then, in arousing her passion, he brings her to orgasm first, and then he follows with ejaculation, and thus, in accord with Greek science, he generates male offspring. Then "the two will become one in service of the mitzvah, and their thoughts will be one and the Shekhinah will be present between them."[26] Purity of thought goes with purity of body.

Recalling the Talmudic tale of Rav, who speaks playfully with his wife and satisfies both his own and her sexual desires (see chapter 3), we can see how *The Holy Letter* halakhically reaffirms and spiritualizes Rav's earthly paradigm. Similarly, the German pietist Rabbi Elazar Hasid of Worms (13th century) rejects Maimonides' denigration of sexuality and instead prescribes exuberant lovemaking with one's wife after she is purified in the water of the *mikveh*:

> After her immersion he should cause her joy, hug and kiss her, and sanctify himself in his intercourse by refraining from dirty talk and *by not regarding her as something detestable*. Rather he should take playful delight in caressing her and engaging in all sorts of hugging in order to satisfy his desire and her desire. Thus he will not think about any other woman, but only about her, for she is the woman of his bosom and he should show her expressions of affection and love.[27]

Hugging couples imitate the cherubs embracing in the Holy of Holies. Both the author of *The Holy Letter* and Rabbi Elazar of Worms have both mystical and mundane, humane reasons for urging husbands to demonstratively express their physical and emotional love for their spouses. Joseph Gikatelia (Spain, 1248–1305), from the circle of Zoharic authors, teaches that marriage with the appropriate earthly partner is a reunification of souls—souls who had once been united in the two-faced male-female Adam before God severed them and created the separation between male and female.[28]

Zohar: Reconceiving Erotic Pleasure

"There is no book in the literature of the Jewish people as erotic as the book of the Zohar," the contemporary Jerusalem-based scholar Yehuda Liebes rhapsodizes. "It is the book of *eros* that has not even one page lacking in *eros*. . . . Its humor, laughter, joy and creativity express a positive attitude to reality."[29]

Indeed, the Zohar (a quasi-novelistic interpretation of the Torah composed by a circle of mystics led by Moses de Leon, 13th century,

Spain) and its school of literature celebrate love. Eros in the Zohar is characterized by full-bodied physical contact, playful dialogue, mutual arousal of desire, and luxuriant pleasure in which the female and male each take initiative alternately. All male-female interactions, whether human or divine, are suffused with sensual aesthetic spirituality, erotic sanctity, and emotional joy.[30]

SHABBAT AS A TRIGGER FOR A REVOLUTIONARY UNDERSTANDING OF MARITAL LOVEMAKING

Melila Hellner-Eshed, Liebes's student and a professor of Kabbalah at the Hebrew University, traces the Zohar's terminology of sacred sensual pleasure—in particular, the use of the word *oneg* (enjoyment)—to its biblical and Rabbinic origins in the celebration of the sanctity of Shabbat. Isaiah the prophet promises that one who honors Shabbat by *calling it a delight* [oneg] will be rewarded: *Then you will delight* [tit'anag] *in God* (Isa. 58:14).[31] The Talmudic Rabbis concretize Isaiah's *Oneg Shabbat* by commanding that Shabbat be honored by engaging in physical enjoyments—eating, drinking, sleeping, and marital lovemaking—which celebrate the physicality and the goodness of God's Creation.[32]

Before the Talmud, the Torah never associated the observance of the sacred day of Shabbat with eating or sexual relations or any form of pleasure; it was simply a rest day. In fact, the term "Shabbat" is associated with Yom Kippur (also called *Shabbat Shabbaton*—Lev. 16:31, 23:32), a day of self-denial by withdrawal from physical pleasures like eating, drinking, and intercourse. So too, the sanctity of the Temple is preserved by prohibiting entrance to those polluted by sexual activity until they have been purified.[33] Jewish sects devoted to the Torah but not to Rabbinic oral tradition, such as the Samaritans, Karaites, and Ethiopian Beta Yisrael, prohibit sexual relations on Shabbat and, according to the apocryphal book of Jubilees 50:8, intercourse on Shabbat is a capital crime.[34]

In contrast, the Rabbinic Shabbat welcomes and mandates marital sexual intimacy as a way to honor the sacred day. Thus "Sabbath sex" becomes a social marker identifying Jews in the Roman Empire. The Greek poet Meleager of Gadara (1st century BCE) satirizes the Jews for their enthusiastic lovemaking on Shabbat (even though they will not light other fires in their homes on Shabbat): "If your lover is some Sabbath-keeper, no great wonder! Love burns hot even on cold Sabbaths."[35] Once the Talmudic Rabbis connected the dots between sacred time, physical pleasures, and marital lovemaking, the medieval Zohar elevated all lovemaking, especially on Shabbat, to a sacred act that unites both the mundane human and mystic divine couple simultaneously. Heterosexual human coupling (*zivug*) not only mimics the divine union of male and female dimensions (the sefirot of *Tiferet/Yesod* and Shekhinah) but empowers their attraction and reunification, and thereby makes them fertile so that they emanate blessings (*shefa*) on all the worlds.

MYSTICAL MARRIAGE ARTS ON SHABBAT

On Shabbat evening, mystics seek to bring the heavenly couple, the mystic sefirot, masculine *Tiferet* and feminine Shekhinah (*Malkhut*), together by imitating the cosmic union sympathetically on the human plane. In his manual of kabbalistic ritual practice, *Seder HaYom* (Order of the day), Moshe ibn Makhir (16th–17th century, Safed) recommends that husband and wife prepare for their sexual and mystical union on Shabbat by visiting the *mikveh* together just before Shabbat begins:

> The early pietists used to go down to the river in order to immerse themselves, and afterward go to greet the [Sabbath] Bride and receive an additional soul in purity and holiness. Likewise, we have found that the early pietists practiced ritual immersion with their wives [in preparation for the Sabbath] so as to bind their hearts to the same place.[36]

In sixteenth-century Safed, an anonymous marital guide inspired by the Zohar insists that the mystic enlist his wife's active collaboration in achieving proper intentionality in the sexual union: "It is incumbent to tell her to direct her mind to holiness in order to draw down a holy soul."[37] Abraham Azulai (17th century, Hebron) urges the kabbalist's wife to engage in her own mystical intentions (*kavanot*) in a complex erotic mystical ritual modeled on the purification of the High Priest Aaron (Exod. 29:20):

> [For] whoever merits [to gain] a proper woman, each and every act of intercourse emerges by her arousal. When she holds the right lobe of her husband, and the right thumb and the right toe of his leg, in order to arouse his passion, she has to intend that by holding those signs the three demons which stir his passion not for the sake of heaven will be removed from him.[38]

For Azulai, only when husband *and* wife coordinate their mental efforts, each directing their intentions to a different aspect of the Divine, can their sexual union have the desired theurgic effect (i.e., arousing the Divine by means of ritual intentions and symbolic actions that energize the supernal realm). One must be united sexually with one's earthly wife in order to be united with the supernal woman, Shekhinah, and this union produces the downpour (*shefa*) of blessings on the lower realms:

> Their desire, both his and hers, was to unite the Shekhinah. He directed [his thought] to *Tiferet* and she, *Malkhut*. His union was [intended] to unite the Shekhinah; she [the woman] directs her thought just like he does, because she was just like the Shekhinah and was uniting with her husband, the *Tiferet*.[39]

For Azulai, as earlier for Moshe Cordovero (16th century, Safed), the woman herself must have studied enough Kabbalah to properly concentrate her intentionality. For Cordovero, says Idel, "the two members of the couple not only cooperated but also interacted in a rather equal manner, transforming the spouse from an object into a partner."[40] Both are needed in order to achieve "the theurgical effect of both man and woman" on heavenly unification.[41]

These mystics of Safed are also devotees of the Zoharic artistry of cosmetics (which are also called *tikkun*, perhaps because they repair the Shekhinah's beauty). In preparation for the heavenly union, the Zohar teaches that the divine bride (Shekhinah) must be beautified by performing metaphoric rituals called *tikkuna*. Singing, banqueting, and spiritual intentions prepare the bride by symbolically adoring her, adorning her, fixing her hair, and arranging her jewelry to enhance her beauty.

Through an arcane linguistic evolution, the kabbalist term *tikkun* has given birth to the modern Jewish ideal of tikkun olam, a process by which human beings repair a broken world by acts of social justice.[42] Note, however, that *tikkun* in Zoharic Aramaic refers most often to the adornment of a woman. As Liebes explains, it is a synonym of the Greek term *kosmein*, meaning "beautifying" physically or "praising" verbally (which has also given us the English word "cosmetics"). When in the Idra (a subsection of the Zohar) the literary hero Rabbi Shimon invites Rabbi Elazar to expound words of Torah, his midrashic speech is called *takin tikkuna*, adorning the Shekhinah with beautiful words of Torah.[43] From that same Greek root, English derives the term "cosmos," which in Greek refers to the well-ordered, well-proportioned, balanced, lawful, perfected, and, hence, beautiful worlds of the natural and the metaphysical. By engaging in tikkun olam we restore the cosmos to its original beauty as a harmonious whole in which opposites are reconciled and united fruitfully.

REIMAGINING PLEASURE

The mystic Moses Cordovero (16th century, Safed) explains the Zohar's attitude to oneg: "Sexual delight is the highest form of pleasure in this world, as well as for the supernal powers."[44] But such divine pleasure and, by extension, human sexual pleasure should not be understood using a model of eating food in order to extract its power. In that consumption paradigm of pleasure and intercourse, a strictly I-it rather than I-Thou relationship, the male consumer actively incorporates the energy of the object of desire. As with food consumption, in hedonist sex, metaphorically, the man's mouth "eats up the other"—the woman as the object of desire that is absolutely subordinated to the man's will. Yet the mystics are clear that taking pleasure in God as the object of desire cannot be compared to consumption, subordination, or absorption. Instead, they developed alternative conceptions of sexual union—divine and human—that are not one-sided and exploitive and that do not end abruptly the experience of pleasure when desire is satisfied.[45]

To circumvent this consumption paradigm, the Zohar offers two alternative models of pleasure: (1) cyclical release followed by renewal of desire or (2) *devekut*, mutual attachment without obliterating difference. In the first model of pleasure, there is release at the climax of lovemaking, but the satisfaction of desire is not in its extinction but rather in a moment of respite before its renewal. Achieving perfect union is not meant to be a once-and-for-all redemption from sexuality, because then there would be no more pleasure in the relationship of lover and beloved. Pleasurable eros is a renewable resource, celebrated again and again in marital love and in its mystical analogues. Idel explains:

> Delight . . . was conceived of as a renewed experience, not an achievement that might be attained once and forever. Recurrent in Hasidic literature is the theory expressed by the dictum "*a permanent delight is no delight.*" This theory of ephemeral delight assumes . . . that no one supreme acquisition of an emotion or state should be regarded as the highest attainment.[46]

The second Zoharic model of pleasure without consumption, subordination, and absolute absorption is the two-sided relationship of devekut, that is, mutual attachment, between the two who form a union but do not obliterate one another in their unification. The physical expression of body-to-body intimacy as attachment is not the mouth that consumes, but the mouth that kisses, articulating a mingling of spirits. Idel explains:

> The kiss, the embrace, and sexual intercourse are in fact the different faces of the experience of *devekut*. In the Zohar, the kiss typically describes the desirable experience of the cleaving of spirit to spirit. This "spiritual" cleaving is sometimes understood as more exalted than the *devekut* termed *gufa-be-gufa* (body to body, i.e., intercourse). The kiss brings about the unification of the lovers' mouths and the commingling of their spirits.[47]

While intercourse achieves pleasure for the couple by allowing each partner to reach an orgiastic climax, after which desire and pleasure are consumed and extinguished, kissing and hugging offer ongoing delight in the reciprocity of mutual attachment. In that sense, hugging and kissing are not mere *fore*play before the main act of the man's penetration of the woman, but their own pleasurable, erotic, egalitarian play without end.

The kiss of devekut is cleaving without one-sided dependence. The contemporary Kabbalah scholar Joel Hecker argues that the kabbalist kiss highlights an egalitarian process of mutual give-and-take both between masculine and feminine aspects of the Divine and, by human analogy, between heterosexual lovers. While human-divine and male-female relationships are generally marked by hierarchal power, the Zohar's understanding of the kiss, in theory at least, transcends that asymmetry:

> What are kisses? It is the cleaving of spirit to spirit, and that is why a kiss is of the mouth, because the mouth is the point of egress and

the source of spirit. A kiss on the mouth is a kiss of love and the cleaving of spirit to spirit in which one never separates from the other. . . . One who does not kiss with affection is not in a state of cleaving (*devekut*). (Zohar II, 124b)[48]

The Zohar describes kisses that are mouth-to-mouth, just as the Talmudic tradition prefers the face-to-face posture of intercourse associated with intimacy and equality, which is akin to the Torah's description of Moses knowing God *face-to-face* (Deut. 34:10). Similarly, the cherubs in the Temple turn to face one another and embrace. In kissing, two become one by reliving God's first kiss of life to humanity, as Hecker explains:

> The full mystical potency of the human kiss rests upon the notion that human kisses have their origin in the primordial kisses that God first bestowed upon humanity, in which God breathed life into the inanimate lump of clay (Gen. 2:7). . . . Through kissing, the two have become one, overcoming the divisions into self and other that are the stuff of commonplace experience. . . . In the Zohar's representation of kissing, breath is exchanged by the partners such that A [male] gives of his spirit to B [female], and reciprocally B gives of [her]spirit to A.[49]

Hecker points out that the kiss is one way in which

> the Zoharic kabbalists subvert the linearity of gender and power relations. Though their medieval mindset immerses them in patriarchal hierarchies—masculine subordinating feminine, master subordinating disciple—nonetheless, they find avenues of reciprocity and equality in the meeting of one human and another across the bridge of lips.[50]

Similarly, Isaiah Tishby, the premier student of the pioneering scholar of Kabbalah Gershom Scholem (Germany and Israel, 1897–

1982), explains how the Zohar sometimes upends the usual husband-wife hierarchy in intercourse by commending the husband who follows his wife's wishes in lovemaking:

> In marital life *per se*, particularly regarding the actual time of intercourse, the Zohar gives preference to the woman and requires greater consideration of her wishes and rights.... The man must approach the place the woman has prepared for them to lay together, and even if his bed is comfortable and nicer than that, he must forgo it. Even if he has a bed of gold . . . and she has prepared her bed with stones, on the ground, with a covering of straw, he must abandon his own [bed] and lie down there so as to please her.[51]

LOVING, ZOHAR STYLE

Erotic love, in the Zohar, is associated with multiple qualities: loyalty, playfulness, creativity, laughter, joy, and even the evil impulse. According to Liebes, Zoharic love is a celebration of devekut (attachment), a term originating in the Garden of Eden, where *a man clings* [davak] *to his wife and becomes one flesh* (Gen. 2:24), but also describing Israel's devotion to God (Deut. 4:4). While the Torah describes love, human and divine, as steadfast loyalty, the Zohar is inspired by the Song of Songs to characterize love as a playful hiding and seeking, as a libidinal desire as well as a gentle affection, as a boisterous and mischievous laugh as well as a serious commitment to live together forever. The Zohar's sensibility is "humor, laughter, joy and creativity that positively affirm reality," Liebes says, and the erotic, "sexual harmony is the essence of the Zohar's power of creativity."[52]

The Zohar's spirit of playful and creative eros echoes the Talmudic description of Rav's lovemaking as "laughing and joking with his wife," but with a difference: for the Zohar, Rav's pillow talk and foreplay take on theological and cosmic significance. So, too, the Zohar gives erotic overtones to a Rabbinic midrash about God's "frolicking" (*sha-a-shua*) with the Leviathan (Ps. 104:26; TB *Avodah Zara* 3b) and describes the Creation of the world as a result of divine play (Zohar III, 58a, 60a).[53] Furthermore, the Zohar celebrates the image of King David dancing and playing before the ark (2 Sam. 6:14) as the prototype of the mystical ideal of serving as God's court jester.[54]

Liebes also highlights the libidinal aspect of the Zohar's love, its "evil impulse." Without this *yetzer*, love lacks passion, and without desire, it cannot be productive.[55] According to classical Rabbinic interpretations, the evil impulse (*yetzer ha-ra*) is not intrinsically malevolent but potentially dangerous because it has no internal limits or self-regulation. Moreover, that impulse, often identified as a sexual drive, is necessary for all creative initiatives and even fertility itself. When the Rabbis, according to the legend, once imprisoned the yetzer ha-ra with intent to destroy it once and for all so it would no longer tempt people to sin, they were compelled to release it, for without it no one would marry, build a house, or give birth. In fact, one rabbi identified God's superlative evaluation of the Creation— *Behold it is very good!* (Gen. 1:31)—with the creation of yetzer ha-ra (TB *Yoma* 69b; *Genesis Rabbah* 9:7).

In this positive evaluation of the evil impulse in the Zohar's depiction of love, Liebes finds a strong resemblance to what the Greeks call the goddess Eros and what Epicurus (341–270 BC) identifies with "a strong appetite for sexual pleasures accompanied by furor and agony."[56] The Zohar's love is alien to what Greek-speaking Christians call *agape*: love as grace, pity, and compassion; love that lacks sexual desire and neediness, because it is solely altruistic spiritual love.[57] Saint Paul praises Christian agape, which is purged of the dynamism of impatient, jealous, vengeful, sexual, passionate love:

Agape (love) is patient; love is kind; love is not envious or boastful or arrogant or rude. It does not insist on its own way; it is not irritable or resentful; it does not rejoice in wrongdoing, but rejoices in the truth. It bears all things, believes all things, hopes all things, endures all things. (1 Cor. 13:4–7)

The Zohar's sexual love is potent both humanly and theologically. The desire that brings man and woman together also realizes the true self-fulfillment of man and woman as one complete dual-gendered human being in the image of God. As the Torah says, *On the day God created the human in the image of God, male and female God created them, blessed them and called their name Human* (Adam) (Gen. 5:1–2). The Zohar explicates:

> Any image that does not embrace male and female is not the high and true image. . . . Blessings are found only in a place where male and female are found. . . . A human being is only called "Adam" (i.e., the human) when male and female come together. (Zohar I, 55b)

Physicality, not ascetic piety, then, is the proper pathway of the mystic. Cordovero, the great systematizer of the Zohar, regards "the bed of the intercourse, where the common intentions of the couple are performed, as a place of divine presence."[58] Out of the sexual and spiritual togetherness of human males and females emerge children in the image of God. In his commentary on the Siddur, *Tefillah L'Moshe*, Cordovero explains:

> Some [mistaken mystics] wished to increase the sanctity [of sexual coupling] by having intercourse through [a hole in] the sheet.[59] But beware of their pietism, lest, God forbid, it causes separation between male and female and then the children of such a coupling will be defective. Rather they should *become one flesh*, as it says. So there should be nothing at all separating them in their intimacy.[60]

How in practice do man and woman become one? According to the Zohar, by words of love and desire that pave the way to sexual union—a gradual process incumbent upon the husband to win his wife's consent:

> One who wishes to join with his wife, must first convince her and sweeten her up with words, otherwise he should not sleep with her. For the goal is that their desire should become one—without compulsion. (Zohar I, 49a)

Besides consent, sexual union also entails mutual arousal, and here the Zohar prescribes "sweet talking," seductive wooing. Interpreting Adam's first speech to the newly created woman—*And Adam said: "This time is it, bone of my bone, flesh of my flesh, so this shall be called 'woman' for she was taken from man"* (Gen. 2:23)—the Zohar elucidates:

> Come and look what it says: *Adam said: "This time!"* (Gen. 2:23)— These words of pleasantness, like a fragrance, draw her in affection and draw her to fulfill his desire and to arouse her to love him. Look how these words are filled with perfume, how many words of love such as *bone of my bone, flesh of my flesh*—show they are one and there is no separation between them at all.
>
> Now he begins to praise her: *This shall be named "Woman"*—"She is incomparable! She is the most precious one of the household. In her presence all other women are as monkeys compared to humans, but she is complete perfection. This one and no other!" . . . All sorts of words of love [that Adam speaks to Eve] . . . draw her in love, so she will cleave to him [as it says, *therefore a man will leave his father and mother and cleave to his wife and become one flesh*—Gen. 2:23– 24]. (Zohar I, 49b)

Zoharic wooing is also active and transformative—improving, coaxing, adorning, and fixing (tikkun) the Shekhinah, in contrast to Aristotelian contemplative love of beauty, which passively adores the self-contained, immutable perfection of the beloved. The Shekhinah, the object of Zoharic love, is vulnerable and changeable, unlike the Greek ideal of beauty, which is absolute, inert, and unchanging.

Let us quote at some length the Zohar's uniquely dramatic tale of courting the reticent Shekhinah, a tale embroidered with love verses from the Song of Songs, which the Rabbis viewed as a poem about God's love for Israel:

> *I am black, but beautiful, daughters of Jerusalem* [says the Shekhinah]. . . . *Do not look at me because I am blackened* (Song of Songs 1:5–6). When she is feeling great love for her beloved, because of the straining need for love which she is unable to bear, she reduces herself to such a small size that all that remains of her is the smallness of one letter, namely *yod*. Thereupon she immediately hides herself from all her hosts and regiments, saying, "*I am black*," for in this letter there is none of the whiteness which exists in the other letters. . . . Therefore she says, "*Do not look upon me*," do not gaze upon me at all, since I am merely a miniscule point.
>
> What do the powerful males in her entourage do? They roar like powerful lions. . . . As a result of their voices and their roars, her lover emerges from his palace with several gifts . . . and comes to her and finds her [in a state of diminution]—black, tiny, without form or beauty at all.
>
> He approaches her, hugs and kisses her until she awakens, a little bit at a time, with fragrances, perfumes, and joy that she loves. She is built up, transformed in her adornments, in her form, in her beauty. . . . This her powerful heroes have done [for her], as it says, *powerful heroes do his word* (Ps. 103:20) They repair (*tikkun*) her and return her to her original form. (Zohar III, 191a)

Shekhinah needs to be aroused by the lovers from below, so as to grow strong enough to willingly appear in her glory in public. Perhaps influenced by the chansons (love songs) of French troubadours of Provence and earlier Arabic poetry popular in Spain, the Zohar prescribes a double task to the masculine hero—to defend his lady (whether the heavenly Shekhinah or the earthly bride) and to awaken her love from a distance. Earthly males, like heavenly male heroes, are to serve in the divine queen's entourage. They must stimulate the reluctant Shekhinah to make an appearance and thereby overcome her reticence, low self-esteem, and modesty.[61] By drawing the Shekhinah out of her bashful state of self-abasement, the heroic male guardians literally transmute the shrunken, darkened beloved into a radiant beauty. Their powerful expressions of desire are transformative; they engage in beauty making, not just the adulation of beauty. They create worth, as well as recognizing, praising, and coveting it. While male mystics are being taught to woo the Shekhinah, one might imagine that their erotic skills could also be applied to making love to their wives, thereby mirroring the union of the divine couple. We have, however, no explicit instructions in the Zohar about human coupling, though we have seen how the Zohar interprets the rhetoric of Adam and Eve's primordial human courtship in the Garden of Eden.

ZOHARIC PRESCRIPTIONS FOR FEMALE WOOING

The Zohar also celebrates the woman's active role in exciting desire and consummating sexual union.[62] In the Zohar's imagery, the Torah, which is identified with the Shekhinah, takes on the persona of a seductive woman who excites her student, her male mystic lover, to actively pursue her. Initially, she leads him on, while withholding the exegetical secrets of Torah, and then finally she reveals herself completely without her garments:

The Torah may be compared to a beautiful and stately maiden, who is secluded in an isolated chamber of a palace, and has a lover of whose existence she alone knows. For love of her he passes by her gate unceasingly and turns his eyes in all directions to discover her. . . . She thrusts open a small door in her secret chamber, for a moment reveals her face to her lover, and then quickly withdraws it. . . .

In this manner, the Torah, for a moment, discloses herself in love to her lovers, so as to rouse them to renewed love. . . . When, finally, he is on near terms with her, she stands disclosed face to face with him, and converses with him concerning all of her secret mysteries, and all the secret ways which have been hidden in her heart from immemorial time. Then such a man becomes a true adept in the Torah, a "master of the house," for to him she has uncovered all her mysteries, neither keeping back nor hiding any single one. . . . Hence should men pursue Torah with all their might, so as to come to be its lovers.[63]

The male scholar is tantalized until he penetrates to the deepest layers of the Torah's meaning—until the Torah lays itself absolutely "bare." While the human male ultimately becomes "master of the Torah," which becomes *his* mystic spouse, the process leading up to such mastery is dominated by the initiatives of the divine Torah/Shekhinah as a powerful female figure. She is imagined as a royal princess conducting a clandestine affair with her lover outside the palace.

The Zoharic depiction starkly contrasts with certain aspects of the ideal love expressed by their contemporaries, the French troubadours: a game of refined courtship in which knights knowingly seek in vain the attentions of a demure aristocratic princess, all the while knowing she is unattainable. "For these [Zoharic] mystics," Hellner-Eshed explains, the princess who represents the mystical Torah "is revealed as an active subject. Torah is thirsty to love and to be loved; she is a maiden who knows the art of seduction."[64] The woman, both supernal (Knesset Yisrael) and earthly, is expected to take sexual initiative in seducing her male counterpart. Female arousal of the male is praised, just as it is by Rav Hisda in teaching his daughters to arouse and yet delay the gratification of their husbands' desires.[65]

Brazenly, the Zohar paints its picture of the aggressive and seductive feminized Torah by drawing on the pejorative imagery in Proverbs and transmuting it into a positive metaphor. Proverbs cautions naïve young men to be wary of the foreign prostitute who beckons: *Whosoever is a simpleton, let him turn aside here* (Prov. 9:4). Representing sin and sexual corruption, she proclaims that *stolen waters are always sweeter* (Prov. 9:17). But, as Hellner-Eshed's analysis demonstrates, the Zohar identifies this woman positively with the Torah itself, and recasts her shameless wiles as praiseworthy, when she "discloses herself in love to her lovers, so as to rouse them to renewed love."[66] She awakens slumbering Jewish mystics to embrace her mystical knowledge with the passion of a beguiled lover. Zoharic desire, as opposed to the cool masculine self-control praised in the book of Proverbs, is a highly valued emotion in the mystical experience.

DEBATING ZOHARIC MUTUALITY IN PASSION

Today's neo-Kabbalist thinkers appeal to these medieval mystical texts about the divine feminine to advocate for female agency and greater mutuality in human sexuality. Scholars, however, remain sharply divided over whether this new exegesis has authentic roots in medieval mysticism.

According to Isaiah Tishby, the Zohar portrays a mutually erotic passion between God's male and female aspects: "The lover knows that his beloved is as much in love with him, as he is in love with her." The reciprocal love between male and female flows from one to the other and then flows back again.[67]

Further, Hellner-Eshed holds that the Zohar is surprising "in its ability to capture the erotic posture of females." Its feminine images evoke an "expecting space that wishes to be filled" rather than "privation, penetration and erasure of existence so as to be integrated in the male."[68] She concludes: "It is the kabbalists who innovated, beyond the Talmudic rabbis, a new conception of explicit mutuality in the erotic relations [with the Torah]."[69]

So, too, in Idel's opinion,

> The women, under the impact of their husbands' specific agenda as dictated by the Kabbalah, did not conceive themselves as eclipsed, but actually as fulfilling an important, actually indispensable role for the well-being of the husband, namely having a son, and for the Divinity, by multiplying the divine images in the world.[70]

While Tishby, Hellner-Eshed, and Idel find proto-feminist and egalitarian motifs in some central kabbalist views of male-female relations within God,[71] Elliot Wolfson and his students categorically reject the contemporary feminists' quest for precedents drawn from medieval Kabbalah upon which to construct their egalitarian Judaism. For Wolfson, the classical Kabbalah of Zoharic literature makes the hierarchal "male-female polarity a central tenet that informs the theological imagination on the level of ritual and belief, symbol and myth," but that relationship is essentially androcentric and male chauvinist. "Not only are the masculine characteristics regarded as positive and the feminine as negative, but the latter is itself ultimately absorbed by the former."[72] The Shekhinah lacks significant autonomy, is utterly subordinate, and so no true mutuality can characterize the mystical male-female union. Nevertheless, regarding the subordinated kabbalist woman, Wolfson maintains: "This is not to deny the fact that sexual ethics in kabbalist literature reflect a genuine concern for the dignity and well-being of the woman. . . .

Man is not to treat the woman as a mere sex object, but rather as a partner [though a passive, secondary one] in the task of realizing the sacred union above and maintaining the divine image by prolonging the chain of being [below]."[73] In any case, both Idel and Wolfson concur that mystical descriptions of female agency had very little impact on the day-to-day gender relations of medieval kabbalists and their wives.[74] They both acknowledge that, within Zoharic and Lurianic literature, many texts promote the subservience of women and militate against a positive approach to male and female sexuality. Those more ascetic strands profoundly influenced the halakhic stance of Rabbi Joseph Karo, author of the Shulhan Arukh, and continue to influence his many followers to this day (see chapter 6).

RECONCEIVING EROS

In summary, according to Idel, Liebes, Hellner-Eshed, Hecker, Abrams, and their school of interpretation, by its construction of a religious ideology, a cosmic system, and a mystical practice of lovemaking, the Zohar imbues the physical eros between spouses with intellectual, emotional, ethical, mystical, and even cosmic dimensions. Quality marital intimacy renders a redemptive service for God and for the cosmos, while realizing true self-fulfillment for man and woman, who become complete as human beings only when they are "male and female together."

While religious approaches to eros are often labelled simplistically as either pro- or anti-body, pro-pleasure or anti-sex, libertine or ascetic, secular or sacred, mundane or spiritual, physical or mental, the Zohar's conception of eros transcends binary thinking. Love is reconceptualized so that sexuality is not opposed to spirituality. The divine-human and supernal-earthly polarities are transformed into a mirroring structure in which earthly pleasures complement sacred experiences.

Marital Intimacy: Zohar versus Lurianic Kabbalah

The varied schools of medieval Kabbalah present strongly divergent views of marital intimacy. On the one hand, much Zoharic literature affirms the halakhic duty of onah for mystical reasons. The highly influential *Sefer ha-Qanah* (15th century, Spain) says:

> Whoever adheres to his wife is not allowed to diminish his adherence (*devekut*). The sages said that whoever diminishes intercourse with his wife diminishes the [supernal] image and causes an exile on high and an exile for himself.[75]

On the other hand, Lurianic Kabbalah highlights a stricter attitude to sexuality.[76] For Ha-Ari, Rabbi Isaac Luria (16th century, Safed), on the earthly plane female sexual organs are associated chiefly with the danger of demonic infestation.[77] Like Luria, Joseph Karo, author of the Shulhan Arukh, commends Rabbi Eliezer's practice of minimizing physical contact with one's spouse and suppressing male pleasure during onah.

How is one to square Karo's and Luria's practices of highly constrained marital intercourse with the exuberant descriptions of lovemaking on high in the Zohar and the mystic midrashim about cherubim and Adam's pillow talk? The split between much Zoharic literature and Lurianic Kabbalah is the tension between sexualizing and desexualizing schools of thought. While in Zoharic literature, the sexualizing school of thought extols exuberant lovemaking, divine and human, in Lurianic practice, the primary aim of marital intercourse is to assure that both husband and wife are purified and sanctified. Both spouses must conquer and direct their appetites according to the practices of Rabbi Eliezer and Imma Shalom, while combining them with precise *kavanot* prescribed by Lurianic Kabbalah. In performing these sacred sexual acts, one's body, desires, and mental intentions may produce momentously positive influences on the supernal forces.

If one errs in this difficult discipline, however, one may cause great damage above and below and incur unforgiveable sin.[78] For example, if a man wastes semen outside the wife's vagina due to masturbation or semen ejaculated without penetration (see chapter 6), then, the kabbalists believed, the wasted seed would produce harmful demons, which are defective and dangerous spiritual offspring.[79] Other violations of proper marital relations include intercourse during the day and/or under artificial light at night (see chapter 4). A mystic must also observe, punctiliously, the pious Talmudic practice of aligning one's head to the east and one's right hand to the south during intercourse.[80]

Generally, Luria and his disciples are so focused on the supernal aspects of the sexual union, they pay almost no attention to the interpersonal dimension of husband-wife relations, or indeed to the woman at all. Lawrence Fine, a contemporary researcher of Lurianic Kabbalah, explains:

> The huge corpus of Lurianic texts pays virtually no attention to women as subjects or agents in their own right.... It does not appear as if the crucial role that women [as metaphors] played in the kabbalist scheme of things translated into significant regard for women as individuals with a point of view of their own.... Our [Lurianic] sources certainly do not betray any hint that a [human] woman ought to assume the kind of active role suggested by the [Zoharic] passages cited above.[81]

While the Zoharic and Lurianic schools bring divergent (respectively, sexualizing versus desexualizing) approaches to human sexuality, Daniel Abrams suggests that an ambivalent attraction-avoidance attitude to feminine sexuality is at the core of both schools of Kabbalah. Both the Zoharic and Lurianic kabbalists elevate the centrality of the feminine and her agency in such a way that any encounter with an earthly woman, her mundane embodiment, produces anxiety as well as longing. Hence they alternate between demonic and divine images of the Shekhinah:

> Kabbalistic male subjectivity seeks union and completion which only the feminine can provide and so looks with envy at what he lacks and what she offers and possesses. . . . The feminine is so envied for what she can provide that the kabbalist fears the feminine. . . .
>
> This positive valence is flipped around so that the tension within the kabbalist concerning the necessary and intermittent separation from the feminine transforms this desire and envy into a demonization of the feminine. This might explain how the feminine is revered and loved, in union, and cast so negatively, in separation. If so, then we might reassess our understanding of Kabbalistic texts as obsessed not with the masculinity of their authors, but with the feminine other, which becomes the focus of their spiritual and presumably emotional lives.[82]

Marital Intimacy: Talmud versus Zohar

The Talmud and the Zohar also present differing approaches to the roles of God and Torah study in the realm of marital relations. For example, they differ on the identity of the mythic matchmaker: Is it primarily God who brings men and women together or mystics and their wives who bring the male and female dimensions of God together?

When it comes to God's role, in Talmudic midrashim God is a matchmaker, concerned with enhancing *shalom bayit* (domestic tranquility, a peaceful family atmosphere) and overcoming human loneliness and alienation, whereas in Zoharic Kabbalah, it is human beings who actively facilitate the union of the divine bride and the divine groom.[83] In the tale of the Talmudic rabbi Yossi ben Halafta, it is God who devotes great efforts to match each human being with the proper partner:

A [Roman] matron asked Rabbi Yossi ben Halafta: "In how many days did the Holy One create his world?"

"In six days," he answered, "as it says, *In six days God created the heavens and the earth* (Exod. 20:11)."

[She asked:] "Then what has God been doing from that hour until now?"

"God sits and makes matches," he answered, "assigning a certain man to the daughter of another man, and the wife of one man to another man; and the money of one man to another."

"And that is [the sum of] his craft!?" she retorted. "Even I too can do that just the same. Look how many male and female slaves I have. In an hour, I can easily match them up!"

He responded, "Even if [matchmaking] is easy in your eyes, before the Holy One it is as difficult as the splitting of the Red Sea." Rabbi Yossi ben Halafta went away.

What did she do? She took a thousand male slaves and a thousand female slaves, made them stand in rows, and she proclaimed: "That one [I assign] to this one; and this one will marry that one." She matched them all in one night.

The next day, they came to her—this one with his brains smashed in; that one with his eye displaced; and the next one with his leg broken. She said to them, "What happened to you?" This one said, "I do not want that one"; and another said, "And I do not want this one."

Immediately she sent for Rabbi Yossi ben Halafta. She admitted to him, "There is no god like your God is! Your Torah is true, beautiful and praiseworthy. You spoke well [i.e., you were right!]."

He said: "Didn't I tell you that if it is easy to make matches in your eyes, that in God's eyes it is as hard as splitting the Red Sea!" (*Genesis Rabbah* 68:4)

Poorly arranged marriages end in strife and divorce. Matchmaking is a challenging task worthy of God, because God wishes to make peace within each couple. That is the ethical vocation of marriage to which artful lovemaking contributes.

In Zoharic Kabbalah, however, it is the mystic who expends enormous energies to hold God's marriage together. That supernal relationship of male and female *sefirot* is torn apart by jealousy, contention, and alienation (the forces of exile and judgment). In making love to their wives with the proper intentions, these kabbalists reinvigorate the romantic eros that restores the great heavenly marriage of the male and female aspects of the Divine.[84] This mirroring of heaven and earth in intercourse, says Idel, "constitutes a metaphysical eroticization of human sex."[85]

Another contrast between the worlds of the Talmud and the Zohar is apparent in their divergent pathways to male spiritual elevation. In Talmudic law and in many Rabbinic tales (TB *Ketubot* 62a–63b), the study of Torah is that path, and it is pursued with one's male *hevruta* in the *beit midrash*, not with one's wife at home. In fact, full engagement with Torah often requires that scholarly husbands curtail their marital duties for long periods in order to devote themselves to intellectual-cum-spiritual pursuits.

In contrast, the Zohar deems the mystical study of Torah and kabbalist practice of marital relations as somewhat equivalent paths to unite the gender poles of the cosmos. For Gikatelia, the love for one's *hevruta*, for one's wife, and for the Shekhinah are parallel.[86] Therefore, Abrams observes, he urges the kabbalist to study Torah and Kabbalah *with* his wife in order to enhance their total bodily and spiritual union.[87] While the male mystic's primary calling is to tend to the needs of the supernal union of male and female dimensions of the Divine, that otherworldly orientation may also have beneficial effects on the this-worldly union with his wife.[88]

A further contrast in emphasis between Talmudic and Zoharic traditions is what each considers to be the chief purpose of marital intercourse. Whereas, according to the Talmud, coupling is intended foremost for procreation and fulfillment of the marital duty of onah for one's wife, within Kabbalah, the role of *zivug* (coupling) takes on special mystical significance. Zwi Werblowsky, an academic scholar of Lurianic mysticism, describes that uniqueness:

> Kabbalism seems to have been the first ascetic system to develop a mystical metaphysic of the sexual act. Marriage is not only an honourable estate instituted of God for procreation (*be fruitful and multiply* [Gen. 1:28]) or a remedy for otherwise inevitable sins in act or in thought (Paul preaches: *Better to marry than to burn* [1 Cor. 9:7]), [and] not even a matter of companionship and mutual society, help, and comfort; [rather] it is a state of perfection without which man is incomplete.
>
> Translated into kabbalistic language this would read: Marriage is a state of perfection in which human reality duplicates and thereby promotes the divine perfection which is the union of God-and-his-Shekhinah. This latter unity, disrupted by the fall and human sinfulness, is one that has to be realized. Therefore, the sexual act in holy matrimony has an almost sacramental quality, for it is a symbol that mystically promotes the analogous divine union. A man without a wife is mystically a cripple.[89]

Yet regarding the school of Karo and Ha-Ari in particular, Werblowsky distinguishes sharply between human lovemaking and mystical lovemaking:

> Transformed, in theory, into a sacramental act, the "holy union" of husband and wife was in practice an ascetic exercise which admitted of no genuine relationship between the partners because the [Lurianic] kabbalist had to identify himself with the mystical intention of the act and not with its actuality.[90]

For Idel, nevertheless, the theosophic school of the Zohar (usually associated with Zoharic literature, the ten sefirot, and the mystical task of uniting the male and female dimensions of the Divinity) does enhance flesh-and-blood marital relationships:

The theosophical-theurgical [Zoharic] Kabbalah is concerned with idealizing present actions, licit sex included, by pointing to the correspondences between the inner processes taking place in the divine world and those taking place in the human world. This is a mirror game, in which sometimes the divine reflects the human, while at other times humans are affected by the divine.[91]

These kabbalists contribute new dimensions to the Rabbinic marital obligation—enchantment, sacralization, and mysterious empowerment. As the husband and wife enter their beds on Shabbat evening at midnight, they begin a great and fateful adventure of heroic empowerment. Idel describes this Faustian gift:

> Marriage and sexual union are imagined to have a tremendous impact on the upper worlds. This mysterious perception is one of the most important contributions of theosophical Kabbalah to the Jewish *modus vivendi*: marriage and sex are transformed into mysterious experiences reflecting a supernal *hieros gamos* [sacred marriage] whose success is crucial to the continued existence of both the divine and the lower worlds.[92]

New Age Applications: Kabbalah Centre, Zalman Schachter-Shalomi, and Dennis on Spiritualized Sexuality

For the most part, eros-enhancing mystical teachings, especially those in Zoharic literature that celebrate marital relations as a positive manifestation of the divine union, would *no longer* play a central role in rabbinic and hasidic thinking after Ha-Ari. With the birth of modern Judaism in Western Europe and North America (19th century until mid-20th century), the new religious movements—Reform, Conservative, and Modern Orthodox—and secular Jews denigrated all forms of Eastern European mysticism. In particular, modern Jewish rationalists who favored Maimonidean philosophy eschewed the Zohar's celebration of the divine marriage between male and female aspects of God and the role of human intercourse in bringing these sefirot together. In their modern eyes nothing in Judaism should sound so much like primitive polytheism and superstitious magic.

The early twentieth century, however, saw a revival of interest in Eastern spirituality, drawn both from the Buddhist Far East, such as Hermann Hesse's *Siddhartha* (1922), and from Eastern European Hasidism, such as Martin Buber's *Tales of Hasidim* (1946), *Tales of Rabbi Nachman* (1906), and *Tales of the Baal Shem Tov* (1908). These books about the individual's search for authenticity, self-knowledge, and non-Western spirituality became even more popular with the rise of the American counterculture in the 1970s.

By the late twentieth century, many in the West had lost confidence that scientific and economic progress would bring ethical progress and individual happiness, and instead sought wisdom and salvation in various religions within a newly postsecular society.[93] While the revival of religiosity has sometimes taken traditional forms, such as secularists committing themselves to authoritative Orthodox observance and distinctly traditional religious communities (Jewish *ba'alei teshuvah*; born-again or newly converted Christians, especially Pentecostalists; and renewed Muslim piety), New Age spirituality, however, has often expressed itself in free-form, highly individualistic neo-traditional practices and in eclectic beliefs drawn from the literature of global spiritual wisdom.

Since the 1990s, Jews and non-Jews, scholars and untutored individuals, have flocked to neo-Hasidic and neo-kabbalist thought and practice as paths to spiritual healing. Often, Kabbalah has been released from its original boundaries—halakhah and even Judaism. In this postmodern social and intellectual milieu, the Zohar's exuberant celebration of divine eros has frequently been harnessed as a philosophy and a therapeutic practice to enhance human love-making and the pursuit of happiness.[94] Boaz Huss, a scholar of contemporary religion and neo-kabbalism, describes the common denominators of New Age spirituality:

> One of the major characteristics of the New Age movement is the expectation or experience of a profound transformation, which is perceived as the dawning of a New Age, identified frequently as the "Age of Aquarius." . . . The anticipation of a spiritual cosmic transformation, the use of meditative and healing techniques to achieve such a transformation, psychological renderings of religious notions and the sanctification of the self . . . recur in many contemporary kabbalistic and hasidic formations.[95]

Unlike most traditional Jewish mysticism, postmodern neo-kabbalism highlights the ecstatic experience, the pleasure principle, the access of non-elites to mystical experience, and its redemptive outcome in this world in the here and now.[96] To understand the postmodern applications of Kabbalah to sexuality, one must appreciate how the erotic union of male and female is supposed to transform human consciousness and thereby not only redeem these alienated individuals but contribute to a cosmic revolution. In the following examples, we examine how today's Jewish mystic masters invoke the Zohar to reinforce human sexuality understood as a spiritual practice beneficial both for personal psychological and cosmic healing as well as for sanctifying the world.

The first example, the Kabbalah Centre, originates in the philosophy of altruism of Rav Yehuda Leib Ashlag (1885–1954, Poland, Israel), a traditional yet innovative kabbalist. After Ashlag's death, the Orthodox rabbi Philip Berg, his wife Karen (author of *God Wears Lipstick: Kabbalah for Women*, 2005), and their sons Michael and Yehuda (the latter the author of *Kabbalah on Sex*, 2011) universalized Rav Ashlag's interpretation of Kabbalah to include Jews and non-Jews equally. Since 1970, the Berg family has directed the Kabbalah Centre in Los Angeles, and from the 1990s on, it has flourished financially and institutionally, spreading Ashlag's teachings to dozens of Western countries worldwide and attracting such celebrity devotees as Demi Moore and Madonna (who visited Rav Ashlag's grave on one of her frequent visits to Israel).[97]

The second example is Reb Zalman Schachter-Shalomi (1924–2014), founder of the Jewish Renewal Movement, who (along with Arthur Green and Arthur Waskow) has plumbed the Kabbalah as a resource for promoting new standards of sacred sexuality in the postmodern world (see chapter 13).

The third example is a proposal for developing a uniquely Reform movement form of spirituality as advocated by Rabbi Geoffrey Dennis. Historically the Reform movement has always been a classically modern (but not postmodern) and rationalist (but not mystical) movement. Against the current, in 2014 Dennis called upon Liberal Judaism to incorporate an approach to sexuality inspired by neo-kabbalism.

ASHLAG'S KABBALAH OF GIVING AND RECEIVING AND THE KABBALAH CENTRE'S ALTRUISTIC SEXUALITY

Rav Yehuda Ashlag served as the spiritual inspiration for both the Kabbalah Centre and the Bnei Baruch movement (Michael Laitman) by translating mystical doctrine into personalistic psychology.[98] Reinterpreting the Zohar and Ha-Ari (whom he regarded as his direct spiritual father, whose soul had impregnated him),[99] Ashlag understood God's overflow of divine energy into the world as an expression of divine *hesed* (lovingkindness). The soul's task, he taught, is to receive that overflow and to give altruistically to others in imitation of divine generosity.[100]

The thought of creation itself dictates the presence of an excessive will to receive the immense pleasure that the Creator thought to bestow upon the soul. For the great delight to give and the great desire to receive must go hand in hand.[101]

Ashlag's altruism was motivated by the awareness that each of us is the recipient of divine generosity. As such, out of gratitude for and in imitation of divine giving, we too have a natural "will to bestow" that can trump our egocentric "will to receive." After all, whatever each of us possesses is not truly our own private possession but actually a gift that God has granted us so we can pass it on. Therefore, "the mitzvah of loving your fellow [means] we have to put the needs of our friends before our own."[102]

Yet Ashlag's mysticism is not ascetic: even in giving, kabbalist altruism does not require self-denial. We see this in how we are to "pay God back."[103] First, before passing it on to others, we must enjoy the gift that God has given so God gets the pleasure of seeing our joy in receiving, just as parents find satisfaction in watching their children delight in their birthday presents. The "will to take" and to appreciate divine beneficence by taking pleasure is as important as the "will to give" that imitates God's original act of giving.

While in Ashlag's ideal society people must place love of one's neighbor above love of oneself, no altruistic person will have to suffer deprivation because one's neighbors will in turn make it their first priority to take care of the giver's needs. For Ashlag, the Torah bound neighbors together in mutual caring as a result of the covenant at Sinai:

Each Jew obligated himself (*arevut*) at Mount Sinai to love his fellow, that is to worry about and to work for every other member of the people no less than for himself [and in fact to give priority to the needs of others over his own].[104]

Therefore [six-hundred thousand people, the number who stood at Sinai accepting the Torah] will abandon their work for the satisfaction of their own needs and worry about nothing but guarding their friends so they shall never lack a thing. Moreover, they will observe the mitzvah of *love your neighbor as yourself* (Lev. 19:18) with a mighty love in their hearts and in their souls.[105]

Of course, Ashlag knows that his ideal society of loving your neighbor *before* yourself does not function that way today, nor has it ever worked that way since the Creation, because people prefer to take and not to give. He attributes that imbalance to what Ha-Ari described as the mythic breaking of the vessels. Jody Myers, a scholar of contemporary religion, explains that Luria, as understood by Ashlag, believes there was:

A catastrophic fracturing of the one [original] soul [of Adam] into many souls, male and female, and the creation of the "lower" physical universe of our own experience. The lower world is a mirror of the upper world; [and] because of the catastrophe, both are flawed and in need of repair; and events in the lower world stimulate a reaction in the upper world. . . .

When the Desire to Receive is unrestrained, it is exceedingly selfish and aggressive, and it is called the Desire to Receive for the Self Alone. . . . Thus human society is often cruel and unjust, and history is a series of violent conflicts and imperialism [is rampant].[106]

While Ashlag teaches about the effects of the primordial spiritual and moral catastrophe in the past through which the sin of self-love (of taking without giving forward) became dominant, he also believes that today is the beginning of the messianic age in which we human beings can now mend that broken world. That is why the time has come to propagate the esoteric Kabbalah to the entire world.

At the center of Ashlag's mysticism is an interpersonal ethics founded on tikkun olam: one repairs the world through love of all human beings. This mystical philosophy must be taught to all human beings:

> To complete the task of *tikkun olam* we must welcome all human beings into the secret of the worship of God. . . . Therefore it is incumbent upon the Israelite nation to prepare itself using Torah and mitzvot and prepare also all the residents of the world until they are developed enough to take upon themselves the highest service—*love of one's fellow*, which is the ladder to achieve the goal of the Creation, namely, attachment to God.[107]

To fulfill this mystical and ethical redemption of the cosmos, Ashlag propounded a noncoercive communism. Already in 1905 as a young Polish kabbalist, he demonstrated alongside atheist communists on the streets of Warsaw. After making aliyah to Israel as an enthusiastic Socialist Zionist, he urged Prime Minister Ben-Gurion to create a truly communist state so that society would embody "from each according to their abilities and to each according to their needs."[108]

Inspired by Ashlag's messianism, his disciples, the Bergs and Michael Laitman, founded centers dedicated to teaching the art of receiving and giving love to everyone, including women and non-Jews.[109] Unlike Ashlag, though, his American spiritual heirs have separated Judaism from Kabbalah and view Jewish rituals as purely voluntary activities. Myers explains:

> Kabbalah Centre teachers suggest behaviors that conform to Jewish religious law and modern orthodox Judaism. . . . However, they assiduously avoid explicit identification with Judaism. Their recommendations and explanations are based on scientific reasoning, pragmatic individualism, and kabbalistic concepts shorn of their particularistic ethnic associations.[110]

As Myers emphasizes, the content of the practical advice the Bergs offer for sexual pleasure generally coincides with traditional halakhic restrictions on sexual behavior:

> Yehuda Berg's examples of selfish sex include a male achieving orgasm before the female partner, prioritizing one's own pleasure before one's partner's [including masturbation]; thinking of someone else while making love with one's partner; flirting with someone other than one's partner; [and] having extramarital affairs.[111]

Yet Yehuda Berg's new rationale for these traditional restrictions on inappropriate sexual practices (see chapter 3) is universalist. He believes that by refraining from such self-centered behavior, one contributes to Ashlag's project of kabbalist repair of human selfishness, with the pragmatic results of greater interpersonal love and cosmic regeneration of a healing spirituality.

Berg justifies the practice of sensual lovemaking according to kabbalist doctrines because it constitutes a hedonist path to deeper sexual satisfaction during lifelong marriages:

> For far too long, religion has equated sex with shame, guilt, and embarrassment. . . . Kabbalists held a different view. To the kabbalist, pleasing one's body was just as holy an action as pleasing one's soul. After all, it was the Creator who created both body and soul. Perhaps this is one reason why the religious establishment loathed and feared the kabbalists. . . .
>
> Kabbalah promises us a fulfilling and wild sex life, which might be more than you dare to imagine. Because let's be honest: In most relationships, great sex lasts a year . . . [Then] sex becomes routine. Sex becomes boring. For some, sex becomes no different than a household chore. . . . According to Kabbalah [however], *God intended sex to be a never-ending, passionate experience, overflowing with profound pleasure and breathless excitement.*[112]

Paradoxically, according to Berg's Kabbalah, one receives more pleasure when one is willing to restrain oneself and dedicate oneself altruistically to giving love and pleasure to one's partner first. The man in particular must give satisfaction first, and receive the woman's gift of pleasuring him only after she has received love. The halakhic recommendation that Berg is explicating here instructs the husband to let his wife achieve orgasm before he does in order to be rewarded with male offspring (TB *Niddah* 25b). Berg writes:

> A man should ensure that his wife experiences lots of pleasure during sex, and that she achieves orgasm first. According to Kabbalah, a man also has an obligation to satisfy his wife and give her sex on a regular basis. It is his responsibility, and not the other way around. If a man refuses to have sex with his wife when she requests it, it is actually grounds for divorce. Thus a woman's pleasure and her orgasm are critically important in Kabbalah.[113]

For this reason, men must learn the art of foreplay and the kabbalist notion of kissing. Here Berg urges not self-restraint but passionate kissing:

> Lovemaking without kissing and some serious foreplay is considered to be masturbation [understood as a selfish practice flawed by an excessive desire to take]. And [foreplay] cannot be simple little kisses. The kissing must be hot, passionate, and wild. Let's just say the French got it right when it comes to kissing Kabbalah style.[114]

Myers explains that for Berg, the original sin of the Garden (which humans repeat in every generation) is "to partake of the higher intensity of divine light" before having restrained "the self-centered Desire to Receive."[115] By helping one's wife to reach orgasm first, the husband can teach her the value of "Receiving for the Sake of Sharing":

When a woman reaches orgasm first, her desire, her state-of-receiving, is at its absolute peak. Now a man can impart his semen through his own orgasm, generating and sharing the maximum pleasure with his partner and with the world.

If a man climaxes first, before a woman is fully aroused, she receives limited pleasure, if any at all. Her limited pleasure, in turn, reduces the amount of Light that is revealed in our world. *If she gets nothing, the world gets nothing.*[116]

Thus, like Ashlag, Berg aims through personal redemption to transform society (*tikkun*) and the cosmos:

Believe it or not, lovemaking that embodies true sharing between a couple banishes darkness, pain and suffering from the landscape of human existence. . . . Likewise, selfish sex or abusive sex contributes only to more darkness in the world. . . .

Sex, according to Kabbalah, is the most powerful way to experience the Light of the Creator. It is also one of the most powerful ways to transform the world. . . . Kabbalah reveals how our most intensely erotic moments reverberate throughout the Cosmos.[117]

At times, however, Berg marginalizes his redemptive, altruistic message and endeavors to motivate his kabbalist consumers by appealing to self-centered, hedonistic, and materialist interests. For example, in *The Kabbalah Book of Sex*, Berg writes:

It's not about moral values. . . . Rather, it's about: What's in it for me? . . . Enlightened self-interest is our only motivation. Kabbalah is not about giving something up for some abstract spiritual ideal. Kabbalah is about learning how to have it all. When we resist the desire for immediate but short-term gratification, it's for one reason and one reason only—to attain greater pleasure over the long term![118]

In 2014 Yehuda Berg was convicted of sexually assaulting one of his students while serving as co-director of the Kabbalah Centre.

Beyond his personal moral malfeasance, Berg represents a cautionary tale characteristic of many charismatic neo-kabbalist masters who invoke mysticism to enhance sexual experiences and then exploit their female followers.

SCHACHTER-SHALOMI'S NEW AGE SPIRITUALITY AND SEX EDUCATION

Reb Zalman, as Rabbi Zalman Schachter-Shalomi is known, served as a Chabad missionary to Jewish students on American college campuses in the 1950s (along with "the singing rabbi," Reb Shlomo Carlebach). After leaving Chabad and Orthodox Judaism (1962), he founded the Boston Havurah (1968). A decade later (1978) he created Bnai Or (later renamed Pnei Or to eliminate the masculine bias in the term *b'nai*, which means, literally, "sons"). Eventually it grew into ALEPH: The Jewish Renewal Movement and a seminary for neo-Hasidic Judaism that incorporated "vernacular Kabbalah" (integrating Jewish and Far Eastern meditational techniques).

While Reb Zalman never developed a theoretical or halakhic framework for applying kabbalist sources to postmodern sexuality, he issued influential proclamations about the importance of a new ethos of lovemaking. In his aptly named book, *First Steps to a New Jewish Spirit: Reb Zalman's Guide to Recapturing the Intimacy & Ecstasy in Your Relationship with God*, he channeled and adapted the teachings of the founder of Hasidism: "The Baal Shem taught: It was revealed to me from above that the reason for the delay in the coming of the Messiah is that people do not enter the mystery of the kiss before the great loving."[119]

In this freely adapted quotation from the Baal Shem Tov, Reb Zalman conveys three messages. First, as *The Holy Letter* teaches, halakhah requires that intercourse ("great loving") must be preceded by foreplay ("kissing"). Emotional intimacy, not only sexual release or procreation, is essential to sex. Second, marital lovemaking is a mystical practice that facilitates cosmic processes of union. Third, sexual union contributes to tikkun olam, which hastens the messianic fulfillment. Thus Reb Zalman linked the perfection of erotic lovemaking (which in his movement was not necessarily restricted to marital relations) to the neo-kabbalist desire to welcome in the Age of Aquarius.

In a seminal speech at the 1994 conference of the Association of Transpersonal Psychology, Reb Zalman formulated his approach to "sacred sex":

> Sacred sex is the experience of ecstasy, *the real sexual revolution.* Sacred sexuality is about love—not merely the positive feeling between intimates, but an overwhelming reverence for all embodied life on whatever level of existence. . . . *Sacred sexuality is about the re-enchantment of our lives.* It is about embracing the imponderable mystery of existence.[120]

Reb Zalman trumpets the sacredness of sexuality for at least two reasons. On the one hand, he protests against the commercialization that disenchants physical intimacy by turning it into a self-centered consumerism of erotic sensations. On the other hand, he wishes to heal the shame associated with all sexual encounters since the expulsion from the Garden of Eden—a shame that he believes the restrictive schools of halakhah and mysticism later reinforced (see chapter 6). In a 2007 interview, he recalled the ultra-Orthodox education that first soured him toward his own urges:

> When I was a student in the yeshiva, I remember thinking of sexuality as that lousy trick that God played on us. How could God do such a terrible thing as to implant in us an urge that is so difficult to resist? I would even get "bad thoughts" from looking at the ads for Maidenform bras that were in the subway.[121]

From the Baal Shem Tov, Reb Zalman recovered a mystical technique for overcoming erotic fantasies. Known as "elevating bad thoughts," the practice distinguishes between their external form, which is evil, and their inner essence, which is good and sacred. Reb Zalman explains:

> The Baal Shem Tov once said: "When you get these bad thoughts, what's bad about them is the garments that they're in. If you take off the bad garments, you see the holy sparks behind them. And these are the ones that glitter in God's crown."[122]

Concerned with healing practices, Reb Zalman went on to experiment with a new approach, even to bar mitzvah training:

> I ask my Bar Mitzvah boys, "Do you masturbate?" And first they are a little sheepish about it and then they say, "Yes," and I say, "You know what? It is a good thing to do on the Sabbath! Take your time, put on some music, and explore your body and what feels good for you, and most important, let God in."[123]

In speaking to young teens, Reb Zalman wanted to heal their shame at having developed sexual urges and to correct the misapprehension he had learned as a young man that Judaism is necessarily ascetic. Rather, he teaches, Judaism celebrates natural desires, and even sanctifies them, especially on Shabbat, when physical pleasures and hence marital intercourse are mandated. Disregarding the absolute prohibition on masturbation in the Zohar and Karo's Shulhan Arukh (see chapter 6), he not only permits but commends teenage masturbation as a healthy preparation for Jewish manhood (bar mitzvah). Thus he hopes to enable these boys to affirm their bodies and become, as adults, the great mystical lovers of which the Baal Shem Tov spoke. If they "let God in," Reb Zalman believed, these bar mitzvah boys will discover an embodied spirituality that will enhance their initiation into Judaism.

In communicating so frankly about sexuality, Reb Zalman reaches back to the Talmudic tale of Kahana under the marital bed of Rav as an educational precedent (see chapter 2). He overrules Rav's reticence to share intimate details of his marital life and, instead, affirms the spiritual audacity of Kahana the peeping Tom:

> I fail my children when I cannot take them into our bedroom and show them how it's done . . . to make it sacred sex. Every generation learns so much from generations past about everything else, but our sexuality we have to pick up in the gutter?
>
> Elder[s] can lead younger people into seeing the relationship between sex and God, teaching how the union between man and woman, between the masculine principle and the feminine principle, can lead to a state of mystical rapture and oneness with the universe. . . . With this attitude, the wise elder can encourage people *to make love sacramentally, transforming a physical act into prayer and celebration.*[124]

Reb Zalman's kabbalist notion of sex education cannot be reduced to a liberal curriculum designed to free children from Freudian guilt. Rather, in his eyes, the celebration of sexual desire is an integral part of spiritual redemption:

> The ecological spirituality called for today is founded in a deep recognition of the unity of life—a unity that is celebrated in the act of love. Through erotic passion we overcome our habitual egoistic insularity and reach into the core of other beings.[125]

Reb Zalman transforms the call for sexual freedom into a call for sexual sanctification and mystical cosmic union through ecstasy:

> Spiritual seekers have struggled in vain to realize truth, God, or higher knowledge by escaping from what they termed the prison of the body. . . . We can learn from their mistake. . . . Sex is the gateway

to *unio mystica* [mystical union], in which there is no sense of being divorced from anything and all opposites are transcended.[126]

In one phrase, Reb Zalman's mystical Torah teaches: "Sacred sexuality is about the re-enchantment of our lives."[127]

DENNIS'S SPIRITUALIZED SEXUALITY FOR REFORM JEWS

Most modern denominations of Judaism were born in nineteenth-century Protestant Germany, a time in which Jews struggled for Emancipation and social acceptance within what they hoped would become a secular liberal democratic society. Their rabbis sought to reform and conform their religious thought and practice to Enlightenment and Maimonidean rationalism. Jews of that era rejected Eastern European mysticism as a heretical, superstitious deviation reaching its nadir in pagan-sounding kabbalist notions of the divine sexual union between the male and female aspects of God. Rabbi Geoffrey Dennis observes that the contemporary Reform movement evolved from these anti-mystical roots:

> "Erotic theology" is not a term we use much in the Reform Movement. . . . We Reformers are very much the children of medieval rationalist philosophers like . . . Maimonides who argue that God has neither body nor passion—[and] is in fact devoid of any quality that can be construed as "human."[128]

Yet today, Dennis urges Reform Jews to reclaim medieval mysticism—and, in particular, to re-envision human sexuality as

> an especially exalted, sanctified, and potentially enlightening aspect of the human experience. . . . More than that, sex potentially takes on divine qualities—through it we are deeply integrated into the

causality of the universe and how we use our sexuality has cosmic consequences, effecting the larger creation, and even divinity itself.[129]

By accessing kabbalist notions of God and eros, Dennis believes that Reform Judaism can find traditional resources for welcoming those who identify as LGBTQ:

> All these features of our erotic theology offer us starting points within our tradition from which we can begin to construct a simultaneously inclusive, healthy, and moral model of sexuality for our times. . . . Notions of God's androgyny, for example, or that God is simultaneous a Deity of laws and *Ein Sof*, divinity without boundaries, allow us to imagine how the image of God still applies to those whose sexual boundaries differ from our own . . . thus breaking the boundaries of what we think of as Judaism's conventional gender and sexual essentialism.[130]

Inspired by the most avant-garde research of academic scholars of medieval Kabbalah, Dennis highlights the fluidity of gender in Zoharic literature. Since human beings are created in the image of God, and God created humans "male and female," therefore God must be androgynous, and so too are men and women, each possessing feminine and masculine dimensions. Further, in its infinity and its fluidity the kabbalist Divinity encompasses, but also transcends, all particular categories. Such nonbinary understandings of gender are compatible with queer theory and, as Dennis insists, they constitute a Jewish affirmation of alternative sexualities.

In this same spirit Dennis proposes a new Zohar-informed pathway for Reform theology and practice:

> Erotic theology invites us, as liberal Jews, to think about sex as central, rather than peripheral, to the concerns of Torah—a positive corollary to a life-affirming religion. It is at the intersection between

tradition and modernity, between the poles of the reconditely mystical and the utterly utilitarian, that contemporary Reform Jews should look to locate how our faith and our sexuality can once again be harmoniously joined.[131]

Conclusion

As a direct result of the infusion of the worldview of the theosophic Kabbalah of the sefirot, with its focus on enhancing the erotic union of Tiferet and Shekhinah, two revolutionary changes occurred in medieval Judaism. First, the halakhah of marital onah began to mirror the sexual union of the divine marriage between the masculine and feminine dimensions of God. Passion, joy, consent, reciprocity, and prioritizing female orgasm, each of which had already appeared in the Talmud in various isolated sources, were now integrated into a detailed bedroom protocol with multiple rationales. In consequence, the legal obligation to one's wife (onah) was elevated to the highest service of God, contributing to the redemption of the mundane and divine worlds. Thus sanctity and sexuality are positively united.

Second, the image of the divine feminine was expanded and elevated by mystics, even though this conceptual and theological innovation may not have directly upgraded human marital relations in the medieval era. Nevertheless, in the late twentieth century, Zoharic literature has become a central resource for Jewish attempts to construct a new sexual ethos more in line with the American sexual revolution and the rising tide of mysticism.

Freestyle Eroticism?

PERMISSIVE VERSUS ASCETIC
MEDIEVAL CODES OF LAW

Rav said that a man is permitted [to engage in intercourse with his wife] in any way he desires . . . as long as his wife consents. . . . And if a man has found a good wife who is of the same mind with him in these matters, then . . . he fulfills the verse: [*Go and eat your bread with joy and drink your wine with a happy heart, for*] *God has already approved your deeds* (Eccles. 9:7).

—RABBI JUDAH HASID (Germany, d. 1217), *Sefer Hasidim* #509

Introduction

How freely a marital couple may shape their personal style of erotic interaction is subject to profound debate in medieval codes of Jewish law. These disagreements derive from Talmudic differences of opinion between Rabbi Eliezer and Rabbi Yohanan ben D'havai, who advocate for the restrictive position, and the majority of Rabbis, including Rav and Rabbi Judah HaNasi (3rd century), who reject the angelic code of Ben D'havai and rule in favor of the permissive stance.

Almost all early medieval Ashkenazi and Sephardi jurists legislate according to the permissive school. They affirm a tolerant approach to sexual pleasure and approve sexual foreplay and nonreproductive anal intercourse. Nor do they prohibit gazing at and kissing a woman's genitals. In effect they demote Ben D'havai and Rabbi Eliezer's Talmudic stringencies to personal pieties with no binding force. As for Maimonides (12th century), he too is liberal in his legislation, but in his moral, medical, and philosophic advice he urges scholars and pietists to minimize sexual activity far more than the halakhah demands in order to achieve greater piety, health, and rationality. In fact, he and most permissive early modern jurists recommend that select individuals, like scholars, seek a higher level of personal sanctity by adopting the ascetic practices of marital intercourse exemplified by Eliezer and Ben D'havai.

In 1565 in Safed, however, there was a great turning point in the halakhic consensus marked by the publication of Rabbi Joseph Karo's code of Jewish law, the Shulhan Arukh. Turning the tables on the long-dominant permissive tradition, Karo legislated an acutely restrictive code of marital relations reflecting his adherence to a stringent school of Kabbalah that dreads wasted male seed, in particular, and uncontrolled male libido, in general.

By their very nature, these scholastic debates are technical, but this chapter summarizes just the salient arguments and their implications for marital intimacy. A key fulcrum in the dispute is the attitude toward "wasted semen," which is spilled without entering the woman's vagina, because it violates a severe Rabbinic prohibition, as Rabbi Yohanan bar Nafha stated: "Whosoever emits semen in vain deserves death, for it is said, *Onan destroyed* [wasted his seed] *on the ground . . . And what he did was evil in the eyes of God, and God killed him* (Gen. 38:9–10)" (TB *Niddah* 13a).[1] However, the Rabbis debated whether to treat as "wasted," and hence as prohibited, the spilling of semen emitted during foreplay and intercourse that is deposited not in the vagina but instead "between the limbs." Should ejaculating such errant seed be "permitted" as a by-product of the mitzvah of arousing one's wife in foreplay and the Talmudic permission to engage in freestyle eroticism in marital onah?

The medieval intellectual and halakhic debate about appropriate sexual activity in marriage would come to fuel in surprising ways a new round of disputes between ultra-Orthodox Hasidim and Litvaks in the mid-twentieth century (see chapters 7–11).

Permissive School: Maimonides and Isaac the Tosafist

The libertarian consensus in the early medieval era originates in the explicit Talmudic decision to overrule Rabbi Yohanan ben D'havai's harsh code of bedroom decorum. The permissive jurists enthrone Rav and Rabbi Judah HaNasi's ruling that "whatever a man wants to do with his wife [in terms of sexual positions], he does" (TB *Nedarim* 20b) (see chapter 3). Rabbi Isaac Alfasi (Spain, 1013–1103), compiler of the first authoritative legal compendium of Talmudic law, skips Ben D'havai's statements altogether, while quoting Rav and Judah HaNasi as authoritative. While Alfasi cites Rabbi Eliezer's stringencies, he designates them optional forms of pietistic sanctification that have no binding force.[2]

MAIMONIDES, PHILOSOPHIC CONSERVATIVE AND LIBERAL HALAKHIST

As the next great codifier of Jewish law, Maimonides (1135–1204) reaffirms Alfasi's position:

> A husband is permitted to have sexual intercourse with his wife whether anally or between [her] limbs, or any way he wishes.
>
> And that was the answer of one of the rabbis [Rav or Rabbi Judah HaNasi] to a wife who asked him about that subject. He told her the Torah permitted him to do so.
>
> A few rabbis [Ben D'havai] wanted to decree a prohibition that it is despicable and forbidden for a husband to do those kinds of activities with his wife such as the common folk do in order to fulfill their excessive sexual appetites—namely, a reversed sexual position and kissing certain places on the body. . . . Those few rabbis disputed the ruling that the Torah permits such behavior. But the [majority of] Rabbis said one may do anything with one's wife that one desires. The Talmud ruled according to those who permitted these behaviors.[3]

At the same time, being a pietist like Alfasi, Maimonides honors the stringencies of Ben D'havai as commendable forms of *voluntary restraint* on vulgar desires that often arise during onah. But Maimonides does not compel anyone to show such noble restraint:

> Yet even though all these are permitted, the pious should modestly distance themselves from all these disgusting animal behaviors. The Rabbis condemn as wicked those who engage in these practices for their own pleasure. The final purpose of sexual relations [in Nature] is propagating the species, not solely generating erotic pleasure. . . . Therefore the pious should direct their intention to this natural end alone. The Rabbis praise that intent, they love it and they call that intention "sanctifying oneself in the act of intercourse."[4]

Further, Maimonides endorses Rabbi Eliezer's pious paradigm for purposes of health as well as personal sanctity:

> Even though a man's wife is permitted to him at all times, it befits a Torah scholar to conduct himself with holiness, and not to visit her constantly as a rooster [does with a hen]. Rather, visit her once weekly each Shabbat night, if he has the strength to do so. And when he initiates intercourse, he should [like Rabbi Eliezer] not have sex at the beginning of night, when he is satisfied and his stomach is full, nor at the end of the night, when he is hungry, but in the middle of the night, when his food has been digested.
>
> And he should not behave with excessive light-headedness, and he should not foul his mouth with vulgar talk, even in private. The prophetic tradition says, *God reminds humans of what they say* (Amos 4:13, see 2 Kings 6:12), and the Rabbis [like Ben D'havai] explain: "Even for frivolous light-headed conversation between husband and wife, one will be held accountable [on Judgement Day]."[5]

Thus, as a philosopher and doctor, Maimonides cautions males against excessive sexual activity, because the expulsion of semen drains vitality:

Semen is the power of the body, of his vitality and eyesight, and the more one expends semen, the more the body decays, one's power dissipates, and one's life force is lost.... When anyone is profligate in intercourse, old age springs on him prematurely: his strength decreases; his eyes grow dim; bad body odors waft from his mouth and armpits; his hair, eyebrows, and eyelashes shed; his beard and body hair become abundant; his teeth fall out; and his aches and pains increase.

The wisest of the doctors [Hippocrates?] says: One in a thousand die of illnesses, but a thousand from excessive intercourse.... So beware if you wish to live a good life.... Therefore, only have intercourse in order to make the body healthier and in order to propagate the seed. Do not have intercourse every time you desire it, but only when one knows one must eject semen for medical purposes, or to reproduce.[6]

Unlike ascetics such as Ben D'havai who wish to imitate disembodied angels, Maimonides endorses moderate sexual pleasure and playful pillow talk in onah:

They [husband and wife] should be [sexually united only] when both agree and both are in a happy state of mind. He should talk with her and be playful with her somewhat in order to relax her mind. Then he should have intercourse with [appropriate] shame, and not brazenly, and then withdraw immediately. Whoever behaves in this manner has sanctified himself, purified himself, and refined his character, and he will have sons who are handsome, modest, and worthy to become wise and pious. However, anyone who practices the benighted behavior of the rest of the people [the vulgar am ha-aretz] will have children like them.[7]

For Maimonides, "the way of nature" is a manifestation of divine wisdom and balance. God has planted in nature a mechanism generating pleasure as a legitimate tool to encourage procreation, and yet nature also teaches us moderation and the golden mean. Therefore Maimonides limits the unrestrained joyous lovemaking attributed to Rav in the Talmud by adding two qualifications: "somewhat, a little" and "with shame." Elsewhere he also discourages too-frequent sex ("not to visit her constantly as a rooster does"), even though such frequency is legally permitted. "In this manner," says Maimonides, the husband "sanctifie[s] himself."[8]

What is more, Maimonides sees no necessary contradiction between the natural joy of sex and the sanctity of Shabbat, for it is a mitzvah to honor the sacred day by multiplying physical enjoyment. Hence, even for intellectually oriented scholars of Torah, onah is the ideal way to observe the mitzvah of *oneg Shabbat* (the pleasures of Shabbat):

> Intercourse is part of *oneg Shabbat*; therefore, healthy Torah scholars ought to perform intercourse each Shabbat night. . . . And *anyone* who observes Shabbat . . . honors and enjoys it . . . earns a great reward in this world besides the reward stored up for the world-to-come.[9]

The historian of Jewish law Haym Soloveitchik observes that Maimonides is the first halakhist to elevate marital relations on Shabbat to the level of a mitzvah not just for scholars but for all Jews. Philosophers who might otherwise distance themselves from the shameful animality of sex should know, says Maimonides, that Shabbat should include lovemaking as oneg Shabbat:

> Maimonides literally ends [his Laws of] Shabbat by stating—to the philosophically enlightened—that not only is Shabbat not a day of ascetic practices, a mini-Day of Atonement as the Karaites believed, but its very opposite—a day chosen by God . . . on which man should not only indulge his physical nature (food and drink), but even find release for his animal instincts.[10]

For purely medical advice on fortifying male vigor in intercourse, see, at the end of this chapter, "Maimonides' Prescriptions for Medieval Viagra: Enhancing the Power of Coitus," which includes sexual-vitality-enhancing medicinal practices: massage, diet, psychological factors, and a secret rubbing ointment for maintaining an erection after ejaculation.

RABBENU ISAAC THE TOSAFIST, COMBINING SEXUAL INTIMACY AND SANCTITY

A contemporary of Maimonides from the Ashkenazi world of French Talmudists called Tosafists (composers of glosses), Rabbenu Isaac (RI), the great-grandson of Rashi (d. 1184), also acknowledges the legitimacy of the husband's desire for sexual pleasure, and therefore explicitly permits him to spill his seed in nonprocreative sexual encounters such as anal intercourse or intercourse between the limbs. In performing the mitzvah of onah (which, by law, may be practiced in almost any sexual position), spilling semen outside the vagina is *not* equivalent to the biblical sin of wasting the sperm to avoid procreation, for which Judah's sons Er and Onan were punished by death (Gen. 38:9–10). RI explains:

> [Nonvaginal intercourse such as anal ejaculation] is not categorized [as a forbidden act such] as the act of Er and Onan [who wasted their seed intentionally to avoid impregnating Tamar] unless [the husband] intends to destroy seed and practices [nonprocreative ejaculation] constantly. But if it occurs randomly and he desires to come into his wife anally, it is permitted. As it says, "Anything a man desires to do with his wife [sexually], he may do" according to his taste (TB *Nedarim* 20b).[11]

For RI, the Tosafist of Dampierre, and the latter's followers among the Talmudic commentators of France and Germany (12th–13th centuries), the right to sexual pleasure trumps the fear of wasting seed. The Italian Tosafist Isaiah of Trani (RID, 13th century) concurs with RI and explains that the sin of wasting seed refers *only* to a sinful husband whose

> intent is to avoid making his wife pregnant lest it damage her beauty.... But if his intent is to avoid causing her danger [from the health risks of pregnancy or birth] or if he wishes to satisfy his own libidinal *yetzer* (urge), then it is permissible.[12]

An anonymous Tosafist adds an acerbic defense of RI's view against ascetics who disdain these permitted sexual behaviors in their search for greater sanctity: "Anything a husband desires to do with his wife [sexually], he may do, and *there is no lack of holiness in it*."[13] In other words, the holier-than-thou pietists who pursue voluntary stringencies may not denigrate the common path of permissive halakhah as lacking in sanctity.

Ascetic School: Karo on Sanctity against Desire

Rabbi Joseph Karo (Toledo, Spain; Salonica and Safed, Ottoman Empire, 1488–1575) turns the tables on these earlier permissive rulings when he composes his classic code of Jewish law, the Shulhan Arukh. He is motivated by his disdain for and obsessive fear of male sexual desire (*yetzer ha-ra*), his mystical aspiration for spiritual purity and holiness, and his kabbalistic fear of spilling semen.

AN EXCEPTION WITHIN KARO'S LEGAL METHODOLOGY

Notably, when calculating the code's official position in almost every other field of legislation, Karo follows a unique method of determining the halakhah that defers to a consensus of traditional authorities: synthesizing the results of the top three authoritative Sephardi and

Ashkenazi law codes that preceded him.[14] He resolves disagreements among them simply by recording the majority view (two against one). Furthermore, he tabulates the preceding unanimous or majority opinions on each issue, and combines those with practical summaries of what to do, in order to produce a user-friendly digest for immediate application. Therefore the Shulhan Arukh (whose name means "the table is set") does not usually represent Karo's own halakhic philosophy. What is more, Karo generally avoids recapitulations of halakhic debates, prooftexts, or rationales to justify his conclusions, since he has already analyzed them in his earlier monumental commentaries (first, his *Bet Yosef*, 1542, on Jacob ben Asher's *Arba'a Turim* [the code known as the Tur], and later his *Kesef Mishneh*, 1575, on Maimonides' *Mishneh Torah*).

Exceptionally, Karo does *not* apply this methodology of tabulating numerically the views of previous codes when legislating about marital sexual duties. Rather, Karo revisits the Talmudic *sugya*, retrieving Ben D'havai's four angelic stringencies and singling out Rabbi Eliezer's commitment to extirpating all pleasure from his act of intercourse with his wife as the *only* halakhically sanctioned model. Therefore, Karo rules that sexual joy should not be on any husband's agenda.

In disregarding most earlier authorities, Karo's ruling on 29 is revolutionary. Selectively, he skips over Rav's jocular conversations with his wife in bed, even though they are cited by Maimonides as the dominant halakhic precedent. He deletes permissive rulings of Alfasi, Maimonides, and Jacob ben Asher. To bolster his ascetic position, Karo appeals to Ra'avad's *Ba'alei HaNefesh* as his legal authority, for Ra'avad reaffirms Rabbi Eliezer's and Ben D'havai's stringencies.[15] Nonetheless, as we will see, the motivation for this turnabout is not halakhic precedent, but Karo's own mystical religious ideology.

Karo revolutionizes the laws of onah by highlighting prohibitions more than rights and duties. He reinterprets Rabbi Eliezer's mishnaic list specifying the onah responsibilities for husbands of diverse occupations so that instead of setting the *minimum* frequency of sexual intercourse to which the wife is entitled, it determines the *maximum* permitted (or, perhaps, recommended) to the husband.[16] He states: "One should *not* make it a habit to be with his wife more than the frequency of onah set by the Torah."[17]

Introducing this legislation with a stern, pietist warning, Karo sets a tone of sanctity coupled with anxiety:

> A person should accustom himself to extra holiness, purity of thought, and proper character in order to save himself from stumbling into illicit sex. . . . Therefore, he should avoid levity, drunkenness, and erotic words.[18]

Employing pejorative language, Karo fervently warns husbands not to overindulge in intercourse beyond the required mitzvah of marital onah. He is concerned lest the mitzvah of onah become, paradoxically, the equivalent of a sinful act of fornication desecrated by improper thoughts or acts. He concurs with the ancient midrash that warns that lightheadedness (*kalut rosh*) and frivolity are "the gateway to adultery."[19] Citing Maimonides, he reiterates the pietist call to minimize frequency of onah, but this time he appears to be legislating a binding norm:

> He should not engage in too much intercourse, being with his wife constantly, for this is very defective behavior, the behavior of a crass ignoramus. Rather, one who minimizes intercourse is praiseworthy as long as he does not nullify the mitzvah of onah—unless he obtains his wife's consent [to forgo onah].[20]

Note that Karo does not deny that the halakhah obligates husbands to satisfy their wives' physiological needs. Yet, by using the language "unless he obtains his wife's consent," he hints to the spiritually oriented husband to ask his wife for an exemption.

A pious husband is thus expected to take on the Herculean burden of maintaining dual consciousness during lovemaking: avoiding any sexual pleasure for himself, even while providing for his wife's needs and indeed her legal rights for erotic satisfaction. On the one hand, Karo adopts Ra'avad's ruling that every husband is obligated to respond to his wife's sexual needs *whenever* she manifests them, even beyond the official schedule of onah: "When he realizes that she is soliciting him and seeking to please him and presents herself before him so that he will pay attention to her, he must visit her."[21]

On the other hand, Karo teaches the husband to regard intercourse as no more emotionally exciting than the usually distasteful duty to pay off a debt to one's creditor, in this case, to his wife:

> Even when he does have sex during onah, he should not intend to derive pleasure for himself, but only to act like a person paying off a debt for he is obligated to render her onah and to perform the Creator's mitzvah of procreation and to have children who study Torah and perform mitzvot.[22]

To avoid sexual arousal, Karo instructs husbands to emulate Rabbi Eliezer's choreography of onah in its most severe form:

> One should perform [one's conjugal duty] with awe and fear, as it says of Rabbi Eliezer: "He would uncover only a hand's breadth and cover a hand's breadth and perform intercourse like one coerced by a demon." That means he behaved *with awe and fear as if a demon compelled him.*
>
> Some commentators say ... he would uncover [*his* genitals] only a hand's breadth so that he would avoid rubbing his penis during

intercourse, so as to minimize his pleasure. Thus he resembled someone [having sex without desire] against his will. . . .

Other commentators say he would uncover a hand's breadth of *his wife's* [vagina], meaning he would uncover it only for the sake of intercourse [i.e., penetration] and then immediately cover it so as not to lengthen the time of intercourse. Thus he resembled someone terrified by a demon that recoils from that act so much that he shortens the intercourse.

And others interpret that he would uncover only a hand's breadth of *her* breechcloth [i.e., apron], since even during intercourse, he would require her to wear it . . . and then immediately he would cover [her again] so as to minimize his pleasure.

All these interpretations are valid and someone who is conscientious about himself should be wary of all of them.[23]

Note that Karo disregards the Talmudic prohibition against husbands demanding that their wives have intercourse while both husband and wife remain almost fully clothed, as the Persians idolaters do (TB *Ketubot* 48a). It should also be pointed out that throughout Karo's many rulings regarding a husband's duty to reduce physical, visual, and verbal contact with his wife, he never acknowledges that such an abbreviated encounter may in fact impede the wife's pleasure, thus violating her right to high-quality onah.

Karo also reinstates all the overruled restrictions of Ben D'havai as if Karo's Talmudic and halakhic forebears had not already rejected them:

[1.] It is forbidden to look at that place [i.e., female genitals, the vagina], for one who looks there has no shame and transgresses [the prophet's admonition] to *walk modestly with your God* (Mic. 6:8). . . . Even more, he incites the evil urge in himself.

[2.] And kissing the female genitals is even worse, . . . for he also transgresses the biblical commandment, *Do not make yourselves disgusting* (Lev. 20:25).

[3]. Intercourse with him-on-the-bottom and her-on-the-top is the path of arrogance, and intercourse side-by-side is the path of perversity.[24]

Karo presents each stringency without any indication that it is a voluntary form of piety. In a great many passages his strict view appears as if it were the only halakhic option, or the only religiously approved behavior. Any violation evokes from Karo damning condemnations: evil, disgusting, obstinate, arrogant, and shameless—and pejorative name-calling: an ignoramus.

As the contemporary rabbi and scholar Yaakov Shapiro astutely observes in his survey, *Halachic Positions* (2015), Karo does not actually state that these behaviors are legally prohibited but rather that "they are unspeakable and unworthy for anyone whether pious or normal and they will be punished very severely by God. His vehement condemnation covers over the lack of halakhic proof he musters despite all his erudition."[25]

UNDERSTANDING KARO'S MYSTICAL RATIONALE

Living and writing in Safed, Karo directly participated in the mystical schools active there, and their kabbalist beliefs shaped his worldview on sexuality. In particular, Karo resonates with the Zohar's negative pronouncements about masturbation, anal sex, and other crimes of wasting seed. For the Zohar, the sin of wasting seed is so horrendous that it is impossible to do penance; therefore, those sinners who waste seed are consigned to the depths of hell.[26]

More generally, Karo concurs with rigorous kabbalist traditions prevalent in Safed that semen not safely deposited into a wife's vagina is a dangerous substance. Karo's younger kabbalist colleague, Rabbi Isaac Luria (Ha-Ari, 1534–72), the founder of a new school of mysticism in Safed, is reported as saying: "All the troubles in the world, all of them, are due to this sin [of wasted semen]."[27] Eventually, these beliefs crystalize in Lurianic Kabbalah, as preserved and disseminated by Luria's primary student, Rabbi Haim Vital (1542–1620). It was believed that, empowered with misdirected procreative vitality, misplaced semen would not only pollute one's thought and one's body but produce satanic offspring who rebel against God and endanger their sinful biological fathers.[28] Therefore, spilling one's seed is worse than spilling blood in murder.[29]

Shapiro exactingly summarizes Vital's position:

> The concept of wasting seed in vain is to be expanded to include even the drips of pre-ejaculate that accumulate at the head of the penis during foreplay [outside the wife's vagina], as well as any drips of seed that may emerge after climax has subsided [after the husband has pulled out his penis from his wife]—even in the context of regular vaginal intercourse.[30]

Luria's school ritualized guilt-driven responses to misplaced ejaculate by prescribing up to eighty-four fast days as penitence for wasting seed in vain.[31]

FROM DREAD OF WASTED SEMEN TO KARO'S RESTRICTIVE LEGISLATION ON *ONAH*

Reinforced by the Zeitgeist of these popular kabbalist beliefs, Karo's anxiety over masturbation and wasted seed spills over into his legal code: "It is prohibited to spill seed needlessly and this sin is more severe than all Torah transgressions."[32] Out of his intense fear of wasted semen, Karo argues vehemently against Rabbenu Isaac (12th century) for permitting anal intercourse and nonprocreative spilling of semen during onah when the husband is in the heat of passion:[33]

> It is a difficult thing to permit [the husband] to stumble [into the sin] of emitting seed for naught, even if just occasionally. And one who cares for his soul will distance himself from this and similar matters.[34]

Since conventional halakhic decision making holds that a later authority (Karo) cannot reject the unanimous consensus of earlier authorities (RI and Maimonides), Karo needs to furnish an alternative source of ancient authority enabling him to disregard them. In his book *Bedek HaBayit* (1605), Karo proceeds to overrule RI's authority by claiming to possess a higher mystical knowledge of heavenly punishments not available to his predecessor, who lived before the publication of the Zohar (13th century, Spain). The Zohar's prohibition originates, according to mystical tradition, in the secret composition of Rabbi Shimon Bar Yohai (2nd century in the Land of Israel):

> And if Rabbenu Isaac [RI] had seen that the punishment proclaimed by the Zohar for wasting one's seed in vain is greater than that of any other violation in the Torah, he himself would not have written what he did.[35]

Besides the kabbalist traditions on wasted seed that he inherited, Karo's restrictive stances were further reinforced by mystical revelations he had heard himself. In his mystical diary *Maggid Meisharim* (The mystical preacher of righteousness), Karo recorded the nocturnal visits of the *maggid* (an angelic being, his heavenly mentor, appearing to him as the personified Mishnah). Regarding wasting seed, the mystical voice cautioned:

> Never soil too much the sign of the covenant of circumcision [i.e., the penis], even when it is permitted to you, unless it is absolutely necessary. Never touch it with your hand and never touch any part of your body below the navel. Of this take the greatest care, for you have no idea of the harm it causes.[36]

Further, this mystical visitor spurred him to acts of asceticism and cautioned him about the yetzer (the evil inclination), personified as an erotic woman. In regard to performing onah without pleasure, the *maggid* invokes the language of Rabbi Eliezer:

Take care not to enjoy your eating and drinking and your marital relations. It should be *as if demons were compelling you* to eat that food or perform that act so that if it were at all possible for you to exist without food and drink or to fulfill the duty of procreation without having intercourse, you would prefer it. . . .

You are bound to have recourse to the pleasures of the evil inclination in order to keep body and soul together, but do not bring her into your house, for if you do, she will become the dominant partner. Rather, cast her out of your house and when you need her, *you may go to her and have intercourse with her, and she will be your wife* [Deut. 21:13, the law permitting intercourse and marriage with a beautiful captive].

This means: Do not stay with her but behave like a man who cohabits with a woman in stealth. As soon as he has completed the act, he departs from her. So, too, you should not take pleasure in the evil inclination, except when it becomes absolutely necessary for the body to survive.

[The *maggid* is alluding to the Talmudic counsel: "If a man sees that his evil impulse is conquering him, he should go to a place where he is unknown, put on black clothes, wrap himself in a black cloak, and do what his heart desires, but let him not publicly profane the name of heaven" (TB *Kiddushin* 40a)].

But since *stolen waters are sweet* (Prov. 9:17), it follows that by having only occasional recourse to the evil inclination, its blandishments become even sweeter. Therefore, the verse says, *and she will be your wife* (Deut. 21:13), which means, in connection with this matter, the [sexual] relationship should be [similar to] that of a man [long accustomed to be] with his wife *where familiarity has blunted the edge of pleasure.*[37]

In short, Karo succeeded in establishing a newly dominant restrictive school embracing halakhic prohibitions against freestyle eroticism in the marital bed and suppressing the Talmudic right to do whatever one wishes to satisfy sexual desires, which his predecessors had recognized. To override entrenched legal traditions, Karo invoked the authority of his mystical knowledge and the urgency of desire-denying sexual practices that might facilitate the imminent coming of the Messianic Age expected by many mystics in Safed at that time.

Karo's legal stringency in practice is reported by his student Rabbi Elazar Azikri (1533–1600): "A woman complained that her husband had anal intercourse with her." The rabbinic court in Safed, which included Karo, "placed him under a ban, cursed him, and threatened to have him burned, and in the end expelled him from the Land of Israel."[38]

Permissive School: Reply to Karo

In response to the publication of Karo's Shulhan Arukh, which more heavily favors Sephardi jurisprudence, Rav Moshe Isserles (the ReMa, Cracow, d. 1572) composed the gloss *HaMapa* ("The Table Cloth," to cover Karo's "The Set Table"). In all European publications of Karo's Shulhan Arukh, Isserles's glosses appear interspersed within the main body of Karo's text wherever Isserles felt Karo had failed to mention prevailing Ashkenazi customs.[39] A great reverence abides for this composite code of the Shulhan Arukh with Isserles's gloss precisely because it summarizes the most updated Sephardi and Ashkenazi rulings of the period.

In the halakhic rulings on onah, Isserles dissents explicitly from some of Karo's rulings and vigorously reaffirms the permissive judgments of Maimonides and RI that Karo had intentionally deleted. Hence Isserles rules:

He may do with his wife whatever he wishes. He may have intercourse whenever he wishes, he may kiss any part of her body that he desires, and he may have vaginal or anal intercourse, or intercourse between [her] limbs, so long as he does not spill his seed for no purpose [Tur].

Some authorities [RI] are lenient and say that he may have anal intercourse, even if he spills some seed, as long as it is incidental and not habitual.[40]

In defending Isserles against Karo, Rabbi Shmuel Feibish (Poland, d. 1694) dismisses the notion that wasted seed is the most terrible sin, avowing that "the Zohar's awesome declaration that 'the sin of spilling seed is the worst of all sins' is not necessarily correct."[41] He recalls the ruling of Judah Hasid (Germany, 12th century) that, when faced with a greater sin, one may resort to intentional masturbation:

> For one afraid that [due to his overwhelming sexual drive] he will stumble into the sin of adultery or of intercourse [with his own wife] when she is menstruating (*niddah*), then it is better that he waste his seed [in masturbation], though afterward he ought to undergo penance.[42]

Furthermore, Rabbi Elijah Shapira (Prague, d. 1712) states decisively that, according to RI, there is no concept of wasting seed in marital relations at all, since ejaculation is part of a mitzvah, the purposeful activity of onah.[43]

Nevertheless, as Zvi Zohar, the Israeli professor of the history of Sephardi halakhah, observes, the permissive school of Isserles, which legislates greater license in marital intercourse, does not dissent on many of Karo's other stringencies.[44] Generally, all the prominent members of the permissive school support voluntary pietism and commend a husband seeking greater sanctity by restricting his sexual pursuits and minimizing his pleasure, just as long as his wife consents, as Karo himself also stipulates.[45] Thus Isserles concludes his lenient ruling with this advice for the pious who wish to achieve a higher level of personal sanctity: "Even though all of this is permissible, anyone who wishes to sanctify himself [by abstaining] from the permitted is called holy."[46]

Dissemination of Karo's Ideology

In the sixteenth century, the kabbalist halakhists of Safed—Rabbi Elijah de Vidas (author of *Reishit Hokhma*, d. 1592), Rabbi Elazar Azikri (author of *Sefer Haredim* and the well-known Shabbat hymn, "Yedid Nefesh"), and Rabbi Yeshaya Horowitz (author of *Shnei Lukhot HaBrit*, d. 1626)—spread Karo's ascetic kabbalistic guidelines via the recently invented Hebrew printing presses along with popular mystical rituals that appealed to all Jews (Sephardi and Ashkenazi, whether adepts of Kabbalah or novices). In an era of intense mystic messianic expectation (16th–17th centuries), many nonscholarly Jews became enthusiastic pietists seeking more stringent forms of penitence before the Final Judgment.

Naturally, Karo's halakhic-cum-mystical views came to influence the practices of Kabbalist and Hasidic heirs of the Lurianic mystical tradition (19th century, see chapter 7). More surprisingly, Karo's restrictive kabbalist-inflected legislation on onah also came to dominate the nonmystical halakhic codes in early modern Ashkenazi Europe (19th to early 20th centuries), even though they generally follow the Ashkenazi rulings of Rabbi Moshe Isserles. Examples include *Hokhmat Adam* and *Hayyei Adam* by Rabbi Avraham Danzig (d. 1820); *Kitzur Shulhan Arukh* by Rabbi Shlomo Ganzfried (d. 1886); and *Mishna Berura* by the Hafetz Haim, Rabbi Yisrael Meir Kagan (d. 1933).[47] Thus, Karo's bedroom revolution became triumphant as the mainstream prescription in halakhic compendiums written for the general nonkabbalist public.

Conclusion: Medieval Legacies and Modern Predicaments

In the mystical realm, as we have seen (chapter 5), Ra'avad's *Ba'alei HaNefesh* (12th century), *The Holy Letter* (13th century), and much of the Zohar (13th century) portray the union of man and woman, both on the heavenly and earthly levels, as a sacred act that helps heal the cosmos. The more the minds and desires of husband and wife are aligned, the greater the joy and the more excellent their offspring. Yet elsewhere in the Zohar and among many Safed kabbalists, like Karo, Luria, and Vital (16th century), there is great anxiety about libidinal thoughts that go astray in pursuit of sexual pleasure and about the dangerous forces released when semen is ejaculated for nonprocreative purposes.

In the legal codes we find three positions:

1. The nonmystics Maimonides and RI permit the husband and wife much latitude in performing intercourse in pleasurable ways. Yet for the pious elites they urge not only healthy self-restraint but ascetic piety that minimizes frequency, erotic variety, and mental arousal in performing onah as a marital duty. Indeed Maimonides as an Aristotelian rationalist denigrates the sense of touch.

2. The mystics Ra'avad and the author of *The Holy Letter* affirm the holiness of the human body and sexual desire and elevate sexual union to a sacred act in which heart and mind of husband and wife must come together.

3. It is chiefly Karo who rules that the ascetic path of Rabbi Eliezer is the *only* legitimate halakhic option, while systematically deleting from his code of law more flexible views.

In the modern era, for the majority of non-Haredi Jews who are citizens of liberal democratic Western countries, the ethos of passionate romantic and liberal democratic movements, sexual sat-

isfaction and individual autonomy in the privacy of one's own bedroom have become primary values. More generally, asceticism and an
obsessive concern to avoid personal sin and aspire to spiritual purity,
which prevailed in the zeitgeist of the medieval Christian and Jewish
era, have rapidly waned since the beginning of the twentieth century.
The sexual revolution of the 1960s has made freestyle eroticism
increasingly acceptable and commendable. Thus the gap between
medieval Jewish law and piety, on the one hand, and modern, and
especially postmodern, secular beliefs and practices, on the other
hand, has alienated many contemporary Jews from halakhic sexual
ethics. Indeed, this is also increasingly true for Jews who identify as
Orthodox as well as a minority of ultra-Orthodox!

This contemporary predicament has evoked many-sided
responses, both within the Haredi world and that of modern Jewish denominations, from Modern Orthodox to Jewish Renewal.
Haredim have attempted to close themselves off to modern romantic and erotic influences as much as they can, yet on the question
of marital intimacy, there has been a halakhic cleavage on how to
apply the medieval legacies to guide the behavior of Haredi couples. On the one hand, some of the Hasidim, most famously the
recent Gerer rebbes, have promoted vigorously the stringencies of
Karo and expanded them markedly so as to minimize emotional
and sexual intimacy between husband and wife (see chapter 7). On
the other hand, many Litvak Haredi rabbis have not only affirmed
the halakhic latitude of Maimonides, RI, and Isserles but have also
downplayed the optional ascetic piety of onah commended by Maimonides and Isserles. Indeed, these Litvaks educate their students
to elevate their own sanctity by enhancing marital joy in intercourse
and interpersonal communication as prescribed originally in the
medieval kabbalist work *The Holy Letter* (see chapters 9–11).

As we see below (chapters 12–16), liberal Jewish denominations
have altogether rejected spiritual asceticism as a value and reaffirmed

classic permissive halakhic stances (pre-Karo) and cultivated more positive pre-sixteenth-century kabbalist approaches to love and companionship that regard marital sexual union as one of the highest forms of sanctity. Yet, they too struggle to oppose unrestrained utilitarian and secular approaches to freestyle eroticism, especially regarding premarital and extramarital sex. In short, the halakhic and spiritual questions are not simple dichotomies—whether to be permissive or to be restrictive. Jewish law must balance between self-restraint, on one hand, and sacred sexual union, on the other.

Addendum:
Maimonides' Prescriptions for Medieval Viagra

Inquiry from a client: An anonymous wealthy Arab dignitary, concerned "to increase his desire [i.e., his sexual vigour] for the sake of his large number of slave girls [with whom he has intercourse],"[48] asks Maimonides, the court physician to the grand vizier of Egypt, and later to Sultan Saladin, for his medical opinion. Maimonides responds by letter in Arabic:

General guidelines: Maintain health by a life of moderation, especially in sexual intercourse. Enhance sexual vigor by increasing the body's warmth and moistness and decreasing its coolness and dryness.

Massage: "One should massage one's feet every night [and wash them with warm water] until they become red.... One should do so continuously, in summer and winter, because whenever the feet become cold or dry, the erection subsides or decreases."[49]

Diet: Food is more beneficial than medicines, because the sperm is a residue of food. Its effectiveness is enhanced when consumed after a warm bath and a glass of wine. Avoid: spinach, cucumbers, watermelon, lettuce, and vinegar. Highly recommended: carrots and spices (cumin, caraway and mustard, etc.); hot milk sprinkled with ground cloves; omelet prepared with rooster testicles; yolk of soft-boiled eggs sprinkled with the powder of pulverized ox penis.

Psychological factors: "Sadness, worry, anxiety, continuous silence, toil, exertion, and sleeplessness" are detrimental to maintaining sexual vigor, while joy, happiness, fun, and laughter increase sexual desire. "Most [detrimental to sexual desire] is intercourse with an abhorrent woman, for a man has to compel himself to do so.... Nature gets accustomed [by association, to feel a reflex of repugnance in each sexual encounter] ... and then it turns into a habit that every time that his soul desires [sex], he [responds with] languor."[50]

Ointment rub for maintaining an erection after ejaculation: "Many men suffer from issues of maintaining an erection and that interferes with producing seed, so let me mention a wonderful secret that no one else has mentioned: Take oils such as ... radish oil and mustard oil, then mix them and add some live ants, and afterwards leave it in the sun for two or three hours, and then apply it. Rub the cream on the penis two or three hours before intercourse and afterwards rinse in water.... There is nothing like it for this ailment.... May God lengthen your days in pleasures.... for the sake of God's goodness and grace."[51]

PART FOUR

Contemporary Haredim

HASIDIM VERSUS LITVAKS ON MARITAL INTIMACY

Ascetic Bedrooms   7

HASIDIC SECTS SET STRINGENT BOUNDARIES
ON MARITAL INTIMACY

The famous "hole in the sheet" mode of intercourse (TJ *Yevamot* 1:1) is probably practiced by no more than a small minority [of contemporary Hasidic Haredim], but similarly restrictive methods are not uncommon.

   —BENJAMIN BROWN, "Kedushah: The Sexual Abstinence of Married Men in Gur, Slonim, and Toledot Aharon"

Introduction

The twentieth century brought questions of love and sexuality to the center of private and public consciousness. A spousal conversation about loving feelings was portrayed as a modern romantic revolution in the 1964 Broadway musical *Fiddler on the Roof*: When Tevye, the traditional father figure from a fast disintegrating Eastern European shtetl, asks his wife of many decades, "Goldie, do you love me?," she (eventually) responds, "I suppose I do," and he echoes, "And I suppose I love you too." At the same time, passionate sexuality also became the sine qua non for the pursuit of happiness. These paradigm shifts eventually displaced the conservative ethos of marriage in both Protestant Victorian England and Jewish Eastern Europe.

Today's ultra-Orthodox—who now call themselves Haredim, meaning those who "tremble" in their devotion to God's word—are very much part of this modern universe of discourse, even as they struggle against it. Living in the midst of metropolises (New York, Antwerp, London, Tel Aviv), where they are subject to modern media (street advertisements and cell phones with internet),

Haredim distance themselves from changing notions of gender and the universal pursuit of pleasure. Their leaders recognize that they must address the temptations and competing values posed by individual freedom, consumer gratification of desires, romanticism, and feminism, because, however much they wish it were otherwise, the cultural consciousness of their followers are willy-nilly influenced by these Western trends. Sociologically, Haredim are radical neo-traditionalists who define their identity not by simple continuity with the past but by sectarian ideological hostility to contemporary secular trends—among them romantic love and sexual license. They comb premodern Jewish traditions to find precedents by which to justify their pristine ideals of stringent modesty between the genders and sanctity in marriage.

Until the Holocaust, almost all Haredi rabbis delegitimated romantic love and passionate sexuality even *within* marriage. Surprisingly, since the 1950s, the Haredi camp of Ashkenazim of Eastern European origin now living in the Land of Israel has become divided into polar approaches to sanctity, love, and sexual intimacy for married couples. For the most part, the contemporary Hasidic leadership (whose dynasties of rebbes originated mainly in Poland and Hungary) not only suppresses sexual desire and fulfillment in marital relations, but their most ascetic sects also minimize verbal and emotional communication between spouses. By contrast, key leaders of the contemporary Litvak yeshiva world (deriving chiefly from great nineteenth-century schools for advanced Talmud study originally founded in Lithuania and Belarus, the historic home of the Litvaks) increasingly educate their yeshiva-trained followers to embrace spousal sharing and mutual sexual satisfaction, per ancient rabbinic and kabbalist ideals of marital sanctity (see chapters 2 and 5). We explore Litvak understandings of marital intimacy in the next four chapters.

As we see in this chapter, there are also divergent Hasidic approaches to ascetic notions of sanctity in general and to marital relations in particular. Primarily we delve into the most radical and systematic attempt to transform the married life of a large community, the Hasidim of Gur, into a model of ascetic sanctity: the Ordinances of Kedushah (1948) issued by the fifth Gerer rebbe, Yisroel Alter (known by the title of his most famous book, the *Beys Yisroel*).

Since the Ordinances have been kept secret from people outside Gur, and the Hasidic bedroom is the Holy of Holies of privacy, one can only construct a picture of this secretive world from various piecemeal sources of knowledge. As we will see, Professor Benjamin Brown has investigated the religious ideology of the rebbe of Gur as well as two smaller hasidic sects in Jerusalem, Slonim, and Toldes Aharon, all of which share analogous (though not identical) ascetic marital practices. To discern the experience of rank-and-file female members of Gur, the sociologist-anthropologist Nava Vasserman has conducted an anthropological study of women and marriage in Gur via extensive interviews. To sample the mindset and experience of at least one male Hasidic bridegroom, we shall explore the memoir of Shulem Deen, a disenchanted hasid of the American Hasidic sect of Skver.

The Besht versus the Maggid on "Worship through Physicality"

Hasidism was a spontaneous revolutionary religious movement that emerged in the Ukraine and spread to Poland, Lithuania, and later to the backwater provinces of the Austrian and Hungarian Empires. Beginning in 1740, Rabbi Yisrael ben Eliezer, the Baal Shem Tov (abbreviated as the Besht; Ukraine, 1698–1760), emerged publicly as a charismatic teacher endowed with spiritual power (seeing from afar, fighting off demons, prognosticating the future); an ecstatic mystic (achieving *devekut*, or attachment, to God, and ascending to heaven); and a prestigious master healer (a *baal shem*, a master of the Divine Name employed in Jewish folk medicine).[1] Having developed a new form of ecstatic prayer and a theology to justify its practice, he began teaching his colleagues and disciples a new mystical path. He and his scholarly disciples were already called *hasidim*, a traditional term meaning ascetic pietists who perform the service of God beyond the minimum norms set by the halakhah and who concentrate on a general state of inner *kavanah* (mental intentionality) as much as on performance of specific mitzvot.[2] After the Besht's death in 1760, his learned disciple-cum-colleague Rabbi Dov Ber Freidman the Maggid of Mezeritch (Ukraine, 1704–72) and his circle began to establish themselves in various geographical areas. Each dynasty constructed by an independent Hasidic master had its own spiritual flavor.

Previously, Jews interested in Talmudic study had gone exclusively to the local rabbi, and those wishing to enter the rabbinate or study Kabbalah had attended a small study house in the town of a great scholar. Generally, beyond following Jewish traditions, the rank-and-file had not been deeply, spiritually engaged in Judaism, whose intellectual treasures and spiritual practices were pursued only by small elites. Now, however, the Hasidic rebbes established courts that on holidays attracted hundreds and then thousands of uneducated pilgrims. These everyday Jews did not come to study Talmud and Kabbalah or to pose halakhic questions, but rather to see the charismatic rebbe, eat with him, dance with him, sing with him, pray with him, and hear his mystical interpretations of the Torah and his homiletic stories. In personal consultations with the rebbe, supplicants asked for advice and blessings—for miraculous cures, wedding matches, and profitable business enterprises. These devotees became known as *hasidim* of a particular rebbe, though they were not themselves ascetic contemplative scholars in the original sense of *hasid*.

Usually, the rebbe was not appointed or financially supported by the local town council, and in the early generations he did not head a yeshiva. While the rebbe was sometimes a scholar of Talmud and Kabbalah, his authority derived from his connection to the heavenly powers. Some rebbes claimed that their own souls were reincarnations of the souls of the author of the Zohar, Shimon Bar Yochai, and Ha-Ari, Isaac Luria, the fountainhead of Lurianic Kabbalah.[3] Endowed with these powers, the rebbe had the ability to draw down beneficial influences (*shefa*) for the material welfare of individuals and the community.[4] For example, as the self-appointed defender of the Jewish people, the Besht reports that he ascended to heaven and met the Messiah in an attempt to enlist his aid in reversing an evil governmental decree that would have further oppressed the Jewish community. At other times of crisis he "risked his life" to ascend to heaven to stop a blood libel and the burning of the Talmud (1747–1750s).[5] In the generation after the Besht, when Hasidic courts were stabilized and hereditary dynasties established, the rebbe's authority was transmitted through his *yihus* (lineage) to his sons or to the husbands of his daughters, and the rebbe's monetary support came from his grateful Hasidim enjoying his spiritual beneficence.

INNOVATIVE TEACHINGS OF THE BAAL SHEM TOV

The Besht's initial model for leadership followed in the footsteps of traditional religious leaders of the sixteenth and seventeenth centuries: reclusive Polish Jewish pietists (already called *hasidim*) engaged in speculative Lurianic Kabbalah (16th century, Safed); itinerant preachers (*maggidim*) of repentance; and a professional class of folk healers (*ba'alei shem*, invokers of God's secret names for charms, amulets, elixirs, and exorcisms) engaged in practical Kabbalah.[6]

The old style Lurianic hasid studied the secret meanings of the Torah and practiced nonstop contemplative meditation to attach his thoughts to God (*devekut*). Thus Rav Joseph Karo, author of the Shulhan Arukh, who was often visited by a personal heavenly advisor, a *maggid*, was instructed repeatedly that "his thought adhere to God 'continually without any sort of interruption at all."[7] The historian Immanuel Etkes observes:

> The majority of the Sages of Safed shared the point of view that the path to *dvekut* involves a constant struggle against the corporeal appetites and instincts. Such a struggle is consistent with the picture of the Demonic Powers as entities that seek to ensnare man and lure him to sin. The *maggid* warns Karo as follows: "Therefore strengthen yourself against the Evil Instinct and Samael [Satan] and the [Primordial] Snake [from the Garden of Eden] who hunt after you, *for its desire is* [to rule] *you, but you must rule over it* (Gen. 4:7)."
>
> An important weapon in the battle against instinct is self-mortification and fasting, for by weakening the body the soul is strengthened. Another important means in this struggle is withdrawal from the society of man into seclusion. In general, the attainment of *dvekut* depends upon repentance and purification, on spiritual preparations that liberate one from the chains of the corporeal. Accordingly, the struggle against the corporeal through abstinence and self-mortification is a central issue in the world of these Kabbalists, one that left its stamp on their entire religious experience.[8]

This penitential spiritual discipline negated physical and especially sexual pleasures, and its devotees were preoccupied with an obsessive fear of the damage caused in heaven and in the mystic's soul by uncontrolled sexual emissions of sperm whose rectification required eighty-four fasts (see chapter 6).[9]

For example, when the popular Lurianic kabbalist book *Hemdat Yamim* (1732) was published, it evoked extreme ascetic behaviors, as reported in a memoir of the period hostile to such behavior:

Students of Talmud were transformed into practical kabbalists fasting and mortifying themselves. In place of Torah scholars, there appeared "masters of the name (*ba'alei shem*)," who blinded the eyes of the many with their enthusiasm.... The number of penitents multiplied, and they would afflict their bodies in strange ways: pounding their chests with rocks; falling to the ground during the reading of the Torah in the synagogues.[10]

But the Besht, himself a *ba'al shem*, largely broke with this moralistic kabbalist tradition. He rejected penitential fasting because, he said, it engenders black depression (*mara shehora*), which constitutes an insuperable obstacle to repentance and to joyful service of God. Unlike many Lurianic kabbalists, he did not view the body and its impulses as tools of satanic demons (*Sitra Ahra, shedim*) and the soul as exiled from God and imprisoned by the body. God's presence, he said, was immanent in everything ("No place is absent of the Divine Presence").[11]

The Besht's innovative aphorisms affirm the joy of sensual existence as a path to Hasidic worship. The historian David Biale cites characteristic adages of the Besht in his grand overview *Eros and the Jews* (1992): "It is better to serve the Lord in joy without self-mortification." "Every *mitzvah* or act of holiness starts with thoughts of physical pleasure."[12] "The soul cannot rejoice in the spiritual until the material has rejoiced in the corporeal."[13]

Regarding the evil impulses assaulting the mind and the body, Biale explains that "rather than merely suppressing such desires, the Baal Shem Tov taught, one should elevate or transform them, for they are in fact useful or even necessary tools for achieving spiritual transcendence."[14] The Besht's doctrine of elevating or redeeming the corporeal is known as *avodah b'gashmiut*, which means worshipping God through the physical world, including eating heartily, drinking intoxicants, smoking tobacco, and ecstatic group dancing.

In that spirit the Besht wrote a letter to the traditional town rabbi Jacob Josef Katz of Polonnoy (1705–83), who was suffering from spiritual depression, and discouraged this guilt-ridden scholar from further penitential fasting:

> This is the way of melancholy and sadness [because] the Divine Presence [Shekhinah] does not inspire out of sorrow, but only out of the joy of performing the commandments (*simha shel mitzvah*) [TB *Brakhot* 31a]. As it says, *Do not deny your flesh* [Isa. 58:7], God forbid, more than is obligatory or necessary.[15]

In his book *Me'or 'Eynayim* (The light of the eyes), the Besht's disciple Menahem Nahum Twersky of Chernobyl (1729/30–1797) explains the notion of worshipping God through mundane activities fulfilling our bodily "human needs":

> There is nothing in this world that does not have a holy spark within it, proceeding from the word of the blessed Holy One, making it alive. That divine spark is the taste within the thing, that which is sweet to the palate. *Taste and see that Y-H-W-H [God] is good* (Ps. 34:9). This means that when you taste or see something good, it is Y-H-W-H, the holy spark garbed within that thing. . . .
>
> Corporeal matters like eating, drinking, and the rest of human needs—if you do them just for the sake of fulfilling your desires—have no life. But if you eat to sate your soul, and raise up the eating, drinking, and other needs to God by your good intentions, then you fulfill [the verse] *Know Him in all your ways* (Prov. 3:6). "All your deeds are then for the sake of heaven" (*Mishnah Avot* 2:12).[16]

In the same era of the Besht, other preachers spoke out against the dominant asceticism of the pietists, who called themselves "hasidim." Thus Rabbi Abraham Abosh of Zamocz (late 18th century, Poland) wrote in a spirit similar to the Besht:

Sometimes the evil instinct devises a sinister method whereby a man will [be tempted to] inherit two Gehenna [hells]—one in this world and one in the world-to-come. For [the evil instinct convinces this man that] it is good and proper for him to punish himself through all kinds of tortures—with fasting beyond his strength and various types of mortifications. And it dupes him into believing that in this way he will become an acceptable and proper servant of the Lord. The truth, however, is that this is not the chosen path. . . . Instead, a man should always follow the middle path of moderation.[17]

By contrast to this preacher, who lived before the rise of Hasidism, the Besht aims not just to follow Maimonidean moderation but to transform earthly enjoyment into enthusiastic service of God, for the Divine is immanent in everything in this world, including the body and its drives. One might extrapolate from the Besht's affirmation of joyful service of God ("knowing God in all ways" through eating, drinking, and ecstatic prayer) that the Besht would affirm the joy of marital intimacy as a form of divine worship. Unfortunately, though, modern research has identified nothing explicit about his attitude to marital intercourse in the few authentic letters and more numerous oral traditions transmitted in his name. Biale, however, has identified one exceptional report of an early affiliate of the Hasidic circles named Barukh of Kosov (d. 1795), who confesses that he was transformed from an ascetic to a celebrant of sexual union. Perhaps this atypical confession may reflect the influence of teachings originating with the Baal Shem Tov's affirmation of worship through physical pleasure:

I was once listening to a humble man bemoan the fact that sexual union naturally entails physical pleasure. He preferred that there be no physical pleasure at all, so that he could engage in sexual union solely to fulfill the command of his Creator. . . . In accord with his words, I composed a simple explanation of the saying of the rabbis,

"Everyone should sanctify himself during sexual union [in what is permitted, as it says in TB *Yevamot* 20a]." I concluded that the meaning of this sanctification is that one should sanctify his thought [by] excluding... one's own physical pleasure; one should bemoan the fact that feeling such pleasure is inherent to this act....

Sometime later, however, God favored me with a gift of grace granting me understanding of the true meaning of sanctification during sexual intercourse: the sanctification derives precisely from feeling physical pleasure. Thus its secret is wondrous, deep and awesome.[18]

THE ASCETIC TEACHINGS OF THE MAGGID

Contrary to Barukh of Kosov's revelation, the Baal Shem Tov's most influential student and colleague, Rabbi Dov Ber, the Maggid of Mezeritch (1704–72), the first systematic exponent of the mystical philosophy of his master and the main architect of the movement, chose to reinforce the older ascetic traditions about marital relations, bolstered with new Hasidic theological justifications. His son Abraham was so ascetic that his nickname was the Angel (ha-Malakh).[19] According to the Maggid, even "during the act of intercourse, a man must become nothing," by which he meant that one should nullify one's materiality (*bitul ha-yesh*) and unite with the transcendent divine realm of nothingness (*ayin*).[20] Given the Besht's apparent silence about the sacred value of marital love and the Maggid's organizational prowess in convening the circle that would nurture the earliest Hasidic rebbes, it is no surprise that the new Hasidism reinforced rather than transformed the traditional Lurianic ascetic attitudes to sexual intimacy.

While Hasidic rebbes certainly did not practice lifelong celibacy (as did their religious neighbors, Christian monks and priests), they urged that the mitzvah of marital intimacy be performed in a spirit of emotional and erotic abstinence reminiscent of the Talmudic

Rabbi Eliezer and in accord with the kabbalist Joseph Karo's halakhic instructions in the Shulhan Arukh. Reducing marital sex to a passionless intercourse, the Maggid compared the performance of *onah* with one's wife to wrapping one's arm in the leather straps of tefillin (phylacteries) for morning prayer. Both rituals entail dedicating one's limbs to serve God, but neither should arouse physically pleasurable feelings:

> One should love one's wife only in the way one loves one's tefillin, namely as [an instrument for fulfilling] commandments of God, but one should not think about her. She is [merely a means to serve God] just as in the analogy of someone traveling to the market who needs a horse. But does he love the horse?! . . . So too in this world a man needs a wife in order to worship the Creator in order to earn his place in the world-to-come. But should he leave aside his work and think about her? Nothing is a greater foolishness.[21]

Shneur Zalman of Liadi (Belarus, 1745–1812), a disciple of the Baal Shem Tov and the Maggid and the founder of Chabad Lubavitch Hasidism, explained the mystical Hasidic reasons for "waging war against [the pleasures of] his body and the animal soul within it . . . in order to crush them, and to beat them into dust" in his still popular book *Tanya* (1796):[22]

> "A completely righteous man" [*tzaddik*] . . . has completely removed the filthy garments of evil, [and he is] utterly repulsed by the pleasures of this world and by men taking pleasure in gratifying their appetites instead of serving God—for these are drawn from, and flow from, the [evil] shells and the [evil] Other Side.[23]

There is a mystic, cosmic battle between the forces of the Divine and the demonic forces of the Other Side (*Sitra Ahra*), those evil "garments" and broken "shells" (*klipot*) that animate the body against one's will and entrap the soul with the pleasures of the flesh. Ascetic behavior is the human contribution to the battle. Biale describes the logic of Hasidic marital asceticism propagated under the Maggid's direction:

> Even permitted sexual acts must be divorced from desire; or, put differently, the fantasies and emotions connected with sexual arousal must be transformed into a spiritual love of God. By doing so, the act itself becomes like the performance of any other commandment.[24]

INFLUENCE OF THE MAGGID

Indeed, many of the great Hasidic masters practiced sexual asceticism within their own marriages. Even Menahem Nahum Twersky of Chernobyl, the loyal disciple of the Baal Shem Tov as well as the Maggid, explains how early Hasidim strategized to "break this desire [for women] by a virtual circumcision of the heart." They would leave their wives at home for years with the aim of

> repair[ing] their character traits, especially their fallen love [distracted from love of God to love of the world], so as to elevate it by engaging in Torah study. . . . Then they could come home [to their wives whom they had abandoned] to reproduce offspring [and thereby] to perform their Creator's commandment [to procreate] solely motivated by love of God's great name without any external [i.e., carnal] love.[25]

For example, Rabbi Nahman of Bratzlav (d. 1810), the great-grandson of the Baal Shem Tov, reported that he experienced pain rather than pleasure in the act of intercourse:

> Copulation is difficult for the true *zaddik* [i.e., spiritual virtuoso or Hasidic rebbe]. Not only doesn't he have any desire for it at all, but actually from that act he has real suffering like the suffering of

an infant during circumcision. The very same suffering, to an even greater degree, is felt by the *zaddik* during intercourse.[26]

Some of the great nineteenth-century rebbes, such as Rabbi Israel Friedman (Ukraine, 1796–1850), a great-grandson of the Maggid, who is nicknamed the Holy One of Ruzhyn, and Rabbi Mendel Morgensztern of Kotzk (Poland, 1787–1859), not only dismissed feelings of sexual pleasure during the performance of their marital duties, but, after producing children to fulfill the mitzvah of procreation, abstained from further intercourse with their wives for the remainder of their lives. Biale notes that the Kotzker rebbe held that the prohibition of adultery applied to one's spiritual marriage to God as one's Beloved; therefore, intercourse with one's legal wife was to be considered as if it were a betrayal of his marriage to God like an act of adultery committed against Shekhinah.[27]

In short, for Hasidic rebbes, other than the Baal Shem Tov and perhaps Menahem Nahum Twersky of Chernobyl, marital asceticism came to be a necessary path to spiritual intentionality in the worship of the Divine. Love of God, to the exclusion of love of one's wife, became a primary form of spirituality.[28] So it was that most Hasidic theologians came to reverse the Zohar's positive attitude to human intercourse as a mirroring and a stimulus for Divine marital union. For them, attachment (*devekut*) to God excludes a loving relationship to one's wife, for she is not mirroring but competing for the pious hasid's exclusive devotion to God.[29]

Even the Baal Shem Tov's liberating idea of serving God through our bodily existence is reinterpreted ascetically by later Hasidic writers in terms of the original self-mortifying ideal of the mystic hasid from the era before the Besht. Benjamin Brown notes:

> In many of the hasidic texts that relate to the restrictive sexual norm of *kedushah*, these [ascetic] methods [of intercourse] are presented in terms of the old hasidic ideal of "worship in corporeality" (*avodah*

begashmiyut), namely, the investment of physical acts with holiness by surrounding them with numerous restrictions.[30]

Thus we can sum up the great debate within Hasidism as between the Besht, whose this-worldly orientation to the Divine Presence shaped the earliest stage of Hasidism, and the Maggid, whose more ascetic and otherworldly spirituality came to dominate the thinking and practice of almost all subsequent Hasidic rebbes. The religious philosopher Martin Buber (Austria, Germany, and Israel, 1878–1965) would popularize the Besht's "worship in corporeality" as an existentialist mysticism whose "earthiness" is "life-embracing and world-affirming."[31] From the Besht and Menahem Nahum Twersky of Chernobyl, one can derive an embodied spirituality appropriate for validating marital love, even if they never made that explicit. By contrast, as we will see, the Maggid is the spiritual forefather of Gur's Ordinances of Kedushah.

Historic Origins: Sanctity through Stringency

Hasidism is a kind of piety whose followers voluntarily adopt more restrictive practices than the legal norm (*lifnim mishurat ha-din*) in order to perfect their souls and attach themselves to the Divine (*devekut*). As such, curbing one's sexual desires in marriage, even though the act of intercourse is commanded by the standard halakhic norms (see chapter 1), becomes the greatest challenge of the Biblical mitzvah *You shall be holy because I, Adonai your God, am holy* (Lev. 19:2). The fifth Rebbe of Gur, the author of the Ordinances of Kedushah, identifies sanctity achieved through restraint of sexual passions as "the fundamental principle of Judaism."[32]

In its Biblical context in Leviticus 18–20, *you shall be holy* is addressed to the whole community of Israel, all of whom are instructed to achieve *kedushah* by repudiating promiscuity and defilements of purity, behaviors that are attributed to the Canaanites and Egyptians. While priests were expected to maintain an even higher degree of sexual restraint, all Israelites were commanded to avoid adultery, intercourse during a woman's period, and incest. Later, the rabbinic exegetical tradition individualized, democratized, and spiritualized this quest for sanctity by exhorting each person to go beyond the behavioral taboos listed in Leviticus and to refrain from otherwise permitted sexual activities. Thus the Talmudic scholar Rava (d. 352) expounded the verse *you shall be holy* (Lev. 19:2) as: "Sanctify yourself by [forbidding] what is permitted to you."[33] Rashi (d. 1105) explained the verse as follows: "Separate yourself from forbidden sexual relations and from sin, for every time you find a way to extend a restriction on forbidden relations, you find sanctity."

What is sinful about simply observing what the Torah prescribes without going beyond its laws and prohibiting to oneself otherwise permitted behaviors? Nahmanides (Spain, d. 1270) explains that the ultimate goal of the Torah is to purify one's moral character, but merely observing the Torah's legal prohibitions punctiliously will not rescue individuals from the voracious desires that corrupt human character:

> The Torah warned about avoiding forbidden foods and sexual relations, but it permitted intercourse of a husband with his wife and consumption of meat and wine. Thus [an observant Jew] could still be possessed by desires overflowing in smutty sex (*zimah*) with his wife . . . and still get drunk on wine and be a glutton for meat [consumed as a commandment for celebrating Shabbat]. . . . One could be a vile person with the permission of the Torah [*naval b'rshut haTorah*] [i.e., without violating any explicit behavioral prohibition in the Torah.]
>
> Therefore, after the list of [formal] prohibitions [on illicit sexual relations], the Torah commanded in general, "separate yourselves

from whatever is permitted." Minimize intercourse. . . . Have sex only in accord with what is necessary to perform the mitzvah.[34]

As Nahmanides the kabbalist and Talmudist understood it, to fulfill the purpose of the Torah and to become a sacred person in character, mind, and heart, one must adopt a demanding but voluntary training regime to tame and transform one's desires. That is the reason a pious Jew seeking to enhance his personal sanctity willingly assumes greater prohibitions that circumscribe his satisfaction of natural libidinal needs. By going beyond the letter of the law, he earns the honorific title "hasid": one whose piety goes beyond the norm.

Generally the Hasidic rebbe sets higher standards of piety for himself and urges only his elite disciples to follow in his footsteps if they can. In some particularly ascetic sects, however, the rebbe decides to require *all* his Hasidim, not just the elite, to adopt higher standards of control on normal daily behaviors that may arouse erotic thoughts (*hirhurim*). Such rebbes also institute mechanisms for social control in all contacts between genders, even among pious family members, as in the case of some of the rebbes of Gur, Slonim, and Toldes Aharon.

Gur's Ordinances Police the Bedroom

Benjamin Brown, in his groundbreaking monograph, "Kedushah: The Sexual Abstinence of Married Men in Gur, Slonim, and Toledot Aharon," describes how after World War II the ideal of marital asceticism became a universal norm for followers of some influential Hasidic rebbes:

Kedushah (holiness) developed as a pietistic ideal for the virtuous few, encouraging married men to limit to the minimum the frequency and modes of sexual intercourse with their wives. . . . [Yet] today, the hasidic groups of Gur, Slonim, and Toledot Aharon radicalize this ideal by imposing it on the community as a whole.[35]

Gur's version is the most restrictive, and its mechanism of enforcement is the most systematic.

According to Brown, the historical context of Gur's revolutionary legislation must be explained as a reaction to the Holocaust. In prewar Poland the Gerer Hasidim were centered near Warsaw in the village of Góra Kalwaria (whose name means Mount Calvary, the location where Jesus was crucified in Jerusalem), so the Hasidim preferred to call the village Gur, or Ger (mountain). There, Rabbi Yitzhak Meir Alter, a disciple of the Kotzker rebbe, established his dynasty (1859–66). Thousands of pilgrims used to arrive from Warsaw on a private railroad line owned by the rebbe.[36] At the community's peak, the Hasidim of Gur were estimated at more than 100,000, the largest and most influential Hasidic group in Poland.[37]

The most famous Gerer rebbe was Yehudah Aryeh Leib Alter (serving 1870–1905), who authored the *Sefat Emet* commentary on the Torah. After the Holocaust decimated Gur's base, Alter's grandson Yisroel Alter (whose wife and children were killed by the Nazis) became the fifth Gerer rebbe (serving 1948–77). His harsh and fearsome style of leadership included slapping the faces of his hasidim, demanding absolute obedience, and extolling Judaism as "slavery to God" (*avdut laShem*).[38] The rebbe also established his own Haredi newspaper, *HaModiah* (1950). Partially because of his energetic leadership, membership in Gur would eventually recover. As of 2016, it has grown to an estimated 12,000 families,[39] most of whom live in Israel, making Gur the largest Hasidic dynasty in Israel. Thanks to its loyal electorate, Gur's political representatives in the Ashkenazi Haredi party, Agudat Yisrael, take the lead in Haredi politics through their party's participation in the Israeli government coalition, and they have served in the Israeli cabinet.[40]

In 1948—the same year of the newly established secular State of Israel—when Yisroel Alter was chosen as the fifth Gerer rebbe, he issued "The Ordinances of Holiness for [the People of] Israel." Notably, these instructions promote personal and communal kedushah as the fundamental telos of the hasid by focusing chiefly on one area of stringency: sexual relations within marriage.

Brown notes that there is no indication that such a code of marital intimacy was fostered by Gur until after the Holocaust, "and certainly not as a norm for the entire community."[41] Rather, Alter wanted to initiate an unmistakable change in the life of his whole community, and he would succeed.

STIPULATIONS IN THE ORDINANCES OF SANCTITY

The first new restrictions applied to *onah*, the frequency of obligatory intercourse in marital relations. While the Mishnah stipulated the *minimum* frequency of marital duties, based on the availability of a husband as determined by the particular demands of his livelihood (see chapter 1), the Gerer rebbe defined the *maximum* frequency, without regard to occupational distinctions, as once a month.

Since the Ordinances of Kedushah (holiness) were never officially published, and have only been communicated orally to members of Gur (more on this later), they cannot be quoted verbatim here. From his interviews with Hasidim, Brown summarizes the Ordinances' most restrictive practices:

> The couple shall have sexual intercourse maximally once a month on *leil tevilah* [the night after the wife's immersion in the *mikveh*

at the end of her halakhically prescribed menstrual period during which sexual relations and physical contact are prohibited]. Later the Ordinances were revised to permit one additional occasion for sexual relations on the Sabbath eve immediately after the night of immersion.[42] ...

The couple shall refrain from sexual intercourse from as early as the seventh month of pregnancy. After the wife has given birth, the couple shall refrain from sexual intercourse for a further period of six months.[43]

A second set of Gur proscriptions aims to minimize physical intimacy and arousal *during* intercourse:

During intercourse, the couple shall aim to minimize physical contact. The husband shall wear some of his clothes, including his *tzitzit* [considered a *segulah*—a supernatural remedy—against the sexual drive], and will not hug or kiss his wife or engage in any behaviour that is not required for the performance of the act of intercourse itself.[44]

Further, in Gur the husband is to suppress his own arousal during sexual contact by avoiding thinking about sex. Brown again: "The husband shall direct his thoughts as far away as possible from the sexual act."[45]

In addition, social intercourse between spouses is to be minimized at all times, as Brown reports:

He never walks alongside his wife in public, but [in front of her] he must always keep a distance of at least four cubits (about two meters) between them. A husband and wife should not be seen in public together; they should not sit on the same bench on a bus or the same seat in a taxi.

The husband should not address his wife by her first name. The husband should not take an afternoon nap at home when the children are not there.[46]

Since, uniquely, this code of marital behavior has never been promulgated as a formal halakhic ruling, it has not been expounded with a rationale supported by rabbinic arguments and Talmudic or kabbalist prooftexts. Rather, upon the sole authority of the rebbe himself, these Ordinances may be taught solely in face-to-face encounters by specially approved pre-marriage instructors in private conversations with young grooms (although in later years, courses for brides were added in gender-differentiated classrooms). Thus the rebbe has guaranteed personalized training and supervision, while maintaining discretion and modesty on such a delicate topic. Continuing to inculcate modesty after the wedding, the Gur community monitors adherence to the Ordinances by assigning a marriage counselor (a spiritual *mashgiah*, or supervisor) to each couple for the length of their marriage.

HISTORICAL AND SOCIOLOGICAL MOTIVATIONS FOR INSTITUTING THE ORDINANCES

Why exactly did the new Gerer rebbe of 1948 issue these new Ordinances? Here, Brown must speculate. First, he notes that in Hebrew these Ordinances are called *takkanot* (*takunes* in the Ashkenazi pronunciation), meaning new halakhic enactments by rabbinic authorities to curb unwanted trends in society. The term *takkanot* connotes "reforms," "corrections," or "repairs" in a broken society, as in the rabbinic and kabbalist term *tikkun olam*, mending or fixing a shattered world. The fifth Gerer rebbe, explains Brown, felt a social necessity to reinforce kedushah in response to the "present generation's decline into sexual permissiveness."[47]

More broadly, one may surmise that the fifth rebbe of Gur wanted to confront simultaneously a broad series of challenges: the physical decimation of his community; the dispersal of his traumatized flock and the destruction of its institutions; his followers' religious doubts in the aftermath of the apparent absence of Divine Providence to save God's most pious believers; and their questions about the significance of the apparent triumph of Jewish secular nationalism, American democracy, and hedonist modernity. The rebbe further realized that the anti-halakhic Zionist state, whose government had political and legal authority over the Gur community in Israel, regarded ultra-Orthodox Judaism as a relic with no future—and expected that Gerer children would surely enthusiastically join the ranks of the victorious modern Jewish state.

The new Gerer rebbe refused to debate the secularists theologically or to accommodate the social trends around him by making life religiously easier for his shell-shocked, depleted flock. Instead of meeting the social, theological, and political questions directly, he reinforced the militant spirit of his embattled Hasidim by ratcheting up the stringency of their marital practices. Secular Jews who cast off the yoke of mitzvot have been called *freier* (in Yiddish) or *hofshiim* (in modern Hebrew) since the late nineteenth century in Eastern Europe and thereafter in the Land of Israel.[48] Often Haredim attributed to *hofshiim* the depraved pursuit of unrestrained gratification of their desires, while the ultra-Orthodox defined themselves by rejecting the modern cult of personal freedom as nothing more than an anarchic pretext for sexual license. Therefore, Alter made higher demands for self-sacrifice (*m'sirus nefesh*) on the "love life" of his young Hasidim who might otherwise have been attracted to the self-indulgent secular freedoms of the new Jewish state. In fact, Brown reports, the rebbe "attracted youth [even] from other Hasidic groups, Lithuanian yeshivot, and even religious Zionists who were seeking a spiritual challenge, thus bolstering Ger's numbers." At this nadir in the self-confidence of Hasidism, the rebbe invigorated the youth of Gur with esprit de corps by branding them with "a badge of pride" as a militant spiritual movement toward sanctity. These youth became religious pioneers (*halutzim*), competing successfully with the call to join socialist kibbutzim promoted by the secular villain Prime Minister Ben-Gurion.[49]

Beyond these sociological hypotheses, internal religious reasons may have also guided the Gerer rebbe's decision to institute the Ordinances of Kedushah as a strategic defence of sanctity against subversive forces of temptation. Brown offers an incisive diagnosis of the Hasidic ideology of kedushah shared by Gur with its allies, the Hasidic rebbes of Slonim and Toldes Aharon.

First, in his homilies on the biblical command, *you shall be holy* (Lev. 19:2), Alter declares that the highest goal of Judaism cannot be found in the mere observance of laws, but instead in the development of a spiritual personality that aspires to personal sanctity.[50] Following the medieval mystic and moralist Nahmanides, he cautions that perfect observance of the laws of the Torah will not in any way guarantee a truly religious character. One must behave more strictly, going beyond the legal norm (*lifnim mishurat ha-din*), in order to fulfill the obligations of the heart (*hovot ha-levavot*).

Why, however, one may ask, does a *spiritual* aspiration like piety aimed at one's inner world take such draconian forms of *behavioral* control supervised minutely by the rebbe's representatives? The answer lies in the rebbe's evaluation of human nature as beset by a powerful evil impulse from within as well as by pervasive societal temptations from without. Therefore, piety is not only a function of true belief and faith in God but of strenuous training of character. This discipline consists of inculcating good habits, on the one hand, and of marshaling social pressure to enforce restrictive norms that distance sensuous attractions, on the other hand.[51]

A third rationale for the Ordinances' stringency may seem counterintuitive to Western liberals. While modern thinkers expect the norms of a community to progress with and to adjust to historical and societal conditions by accommodating human needs and natural inclinations, Gur rejects accommodation and ratchets up the level of ascetic self-sacrifice demanded for the whole community. That is the truly revolutionary goal of the rebbe of Gur—to transform a whole community, and not just its most motivated elite, into a sacred island of spiritual heroism within a highly Westernized and sexualized urban society.

How, then, does one elevate the average hasid, who is far from being a master of his passions and who lives surrounded by the "loose" standards of modern society and more lenient practices of other Haredi groups? Not by making concessions, says the rebbe of Gur.

According to the rebbe, those on a lower level of sanctity need greater restrictions. The more one suffers from sexual desires, the more permitted activities should be proscribed.[52] While the rebbe has extirpated his desires completely and so he need not be so stringent in avoiding casual interactions with women, the average hasid still beset by his yetzer must be even more wary.

Further, in an era of greater promiscuity in society generally, religious leaders should not lower standards of modesty but augment them, because, as Rav Nahum Rotstein, a prominent Gur educator in Jerusalem and head of a yeshiva, remarked in his memoir: "The generations are weakening and hence [today we] need more restrictive legislation . . . in controlling our own impulses."[53] In light of the crisis, he justifies the Ordinances as emergency regulations issued by the Gerer rebbe, whom he compares to the captain of an endangered boat:

Strong winds are blowing, and the turbulent waters sweep away everything that is good; abysses have opened up, and the boundaries that fend off promiscuity have been breached. Only the very few are holding fast, but their heads are spinning around, and all eyes turn to the captain [the Rebbe of Gur], who is guiding his ship to a safe haven.[54]

Paradoxically, the voluntary assumption of more stringent guidelines, the rebbe believes, will reinforce the spiritual power of ascetic Hasidism. One aspires to greater sanctity by turning one's face resolutely away from the mundane and toward attachment to God and Torah study.[55] Were that aim to be compromised, then Hasidism would lose all its appeal. Spiritual radicals are disgusted by concessions and invigorated by steep challenges.

A fourth rationale explains why the Ordinances focus, in particular, on making marital relations more restrictive, which is itself another counterintuitive dimension of Gur's zealous approach. Understandably, in an era of Western promiscuity and quasi-pornographic advertising in the public domain (such as posters and internet ads), it makes sense that Haredim need heightened segregation of the sexes from the earliest age, ever-stricter modesty of dress for women, and prohibitions on access to cell phones or computers with internet access. Inadvertent sexual arousal, they worry, might lead to greater promiscuity, masturbation, or even visitation of prostitutes by Hasidim.

Why, however, does the rebbe of Gur promulgate *new* restrictions on married couples whose sexual intercourse is not only halakhically permitted but religiously mandated? After all, in the Talmud early marriage is commended on the assumption that it enables greater control of erotic thoughts and thus, facilitates the defeat of the evil impulse by providing a licit sexual outlet.[56]

Gur's concern is that in the bedroom, husbands may assume that the permission to engage in the sex act for procreation liberates them to indulge in polluting erotic thoughts and behavior. After all, in public, Hasidim fear public censure, but in the unmonitored privacy of the bedroom there is no supervision.

Slonimer Rebbe's Pep Talk

In explicating the motivations for the Gerer Ordinances of Kedushah, Brown quotes the analogous thinking of Shalom Noah Berezovsky, the Slonimer rebbe (1981–2000). The Slonim dynasty began in the town of Slonim in Belarus, and already by 1873 Slonim Hasidim had begun to arrive in Tiberias, later moving to Jerusalem. Berezovsky writes with awe and nostalgia about the heroic European Hasidim who lived before the Holocaust in order to explain that the hasid is tempted more by halakhically *commanded* acts of intercourse within marriage than by adultery or promiscuity which are *forbidden* acts. The following excerpts are from Berezovsky's popular tract on ethical self-perfection, *Netivot Shalom*, as well as from two official letters he issued for the grooms of the Slonim yeshiva—one for the wedding night, "The Wedding Day Letter" (1956), and one for three months later, "The Three-Months Letter" (1957):[57]

> The early hasidim ... struggled more to resist a commandment that pleasures the body than [they struggled to resist] a transgression that gives the body no pleasure at all. ...
>
> Some of them would weep copiously every *leil tevilah* [the night of immersion when one's wife becomes pure and ready to resume *onah*]. They would repent for performing the required [and permitted sexual act] just as one repents a grave sin, lest their bodies experience physical pleasure. They feared the *kelipah* [evil force] of permission, more than the *kelipah* of prohibition![58]

Therefore, in his letters to grooms Berezovsky gives his Hasidic "soldiers" a pep talk about demonstrating heroism in the marital bed.

The bed is their frontline in the battle against the evil impulse, which argues cunningly that sexual passions are permitted in marriage:

> When confronting the enemy face-to-face, rational argumentation is of no help. . . . One should know how to act as a faithful soldier who is willing to die for the sake of victory, not sparing either his own life or that of his wife and family members. Self-sacrifice, blood, tears, and sweat are required . . . for a life of happiness and joy is a life of abstinence and purity.[59]

Just as a soldier must go beyond the call of duty to become a hero, so the hasid needs to go beyond what the halakhah permits and prohibits in sacrificing more for his higher calling. Since the field of marriage encompasses both permitted and obligatory sexual relations, in this arena a hasid has the broadest field to achieve heroic piety by conquering temptation. While in most societies sexual prowess is characteristic of masculinity, for the rebbe of Slonim, conquest of one's evil impulse is *the* test of manliness. Therefore, Berezovsky cautions grooms to treat marriage as *the* arena of a fateful battle for their souls:

> Now that you are a married man, I see that . . . you stand alone, engaged in a raging battle that is even fiercer than the previous one. For in that [first battle, i.e., before marriage], it [i.e., sexual intercourse] was prohibited, while in this [second battle, i.e., within marriage] it is permitted.
>
> Many have already been slain, and many others will be slain [in this battle]. Only the elect few whom God has preserved and planted in every generation can emerge from it [unharmed] and gloriously victorious. . . . I pray that you, my beloved, will be among them. . . . *Be strong and act like a man* (1 Kings 2:2)—a man, and not a woman.[60]

When the husband engages in sexual intercourse to fulfill the mitzvah of onah and shows "compassion" for his wife, who unlike the more spiritual hasid, craves sexual satisfaction, Berezovsky instructs him to act like Rabbi Eliezer, "as one compelled by a demon" (TB *Nedarim* 20b). He is also to avoid thinking about his wife for the rest of the day. To win the epic battle, the hasid must be prepared for self-sacrifice (*m'sirus nefesh*):

> [When facing] all manner of physical and mental temptations, resist all this with [the dedication of] self-sacrifice, for the Torah endures only in him who sacrifices himself for it, becoming cruel to himself and to members of his household. Only then ... would his mouth and heart open up with Torah and prayer.[61] ...
>
> The crucial life-or-death battle against the evil impulse, chiefly confronting ... desire, is fought between the divine soul from above, and the animal soul. Will the divine soul prevail, so one can live holy and pure, like an angel of God, or God forbid, the animal soul will prevail, and one will live like an animal?[62]

Put more positively, Berezovsky charges the Hasidic couple at the moment before they enter their home to behave as if they were priests maintaining the sanctity of their private mini-temple (*mikdash m'at*), their holy matrimony:

> Husband and wife! The Divine Presence (*Shekhinah*) dwells among them; their home is like a minor Temple; ... their table is like an altar; their bed is like the Holy of Holies; and he [the husband] is like the High Priest who enters its innermost part [the Holy of Holies] to offer sacrifices.[63]

Further, the hasid's circumcised penis is associated with the sanctity of the bris (the covenant of circumcision) and with the divine phallus, the kabbalist *sefirah* of *Yesod*. For Hasidism, heirs to Lurianic Kabbalah, great mystical significance, whether redemptive or catastrophic, is at stake in how each male conducts his intercourse. Every earthly act and thought in the bedroom has direct impact, positive or negative, on the unification of the masculine and feminine dimensions of God (see chapter 5). Brown explains that for Berezovsky, sexual license is

> the main cause of the exile, and therefore the practice of *kedushah* in respect of the sexual sphere of life, is the key to the redemption. This holds true for "the redemption of the collective" just as it does for "the redemption of the individual."[64]

So too, the rebbe of Gur believes that Jews living after the Holocaust have entered a messianic generation whose chief task is to refrain from desecrating the divine attribute of the Holy Phallus (*Yesod*) by severely restricting male sexual arousal, even if the majority of the community cannot fully live up to that heightened standard.[65]

As the term *haredi* implies, the hasid "trembles warily" lest he violate God's norm, so he takes further precautions, adding more preemptive prohibitions. As Reb Arele's son-in-law Avrom Yitshok Kohn, the rebbe of Toldes Aharon in Jerusalem, teaches:

> The difference between the *hasid* and the ordinary person is that the *hasid* says: "That which is forbidden is certainly forbidden, while that which is permitted—I nevertheless do not have to do it." The ordinary person, on the other hand, says the opposite: "That which is permitted is certainly permitted, while that which is forbidden—I can nevertheless seek permission to do it." Even that which is permitted requires a great deal of careful attention and prudence in determining how to behave rather than being eager to satisfy one's lust. And this is what the Sages meant by "Sanctify yourself by that which is permitted to you" (TB *Yevamot* 20a).[66]

Reb Arele (Aharon) Roth (Satmar, Hungary, and Jerusalem, 1894–1946) founded the hasidic community of Toldes Aharon in the Meah Sh'arim neighborhood of Jerusalem as an extremely insular, militantly anti-Zionist movement, which, unlike Gur and Slonim, refuses to vote in Israeli elections or accept governmental subsidies. In its approach to marital asceticism, however, Toldes Aharon shares a common religious ideology with Gur and Slonim that extols the "true hasid" for voluntarily renouncing what is halakhically permitted between husband and wife in order to live at a higher dimension of sanctity.

Arranged Marriages and the Women of Gur

Gur's marital relationships are rigorously constrained by observance of the Ordinances of Kedushah, and much of that burden falls on women. The sociologist-anthropologist Nava Vasserman has illuminated the lived experience of these women. From oral interviews, Vasserman uncovers the ideals and realities of their insular ultra-Orthodox world that are vastly different from contemporary Western notions of marriage: human happiness, mutuality, individualism, autonomy, and gender equality.

PARENTS ARRANGE MARRIAGES

The young women of Gur (along with young men) have little or no say in the most important decision in their lives: the choice of a marital partner. Historically, young brides have seldom had free choice of their spouse in any traditional society until the late nineteenth century, with the rise of Romanticism and the women's suffrage movement in the West. In theory, Rabbinic law (see chapter 1) disqualifies any betrothal lacking mutual consent of husband and wife. According to the Maimonidean concept of marriage, man and woman ought to enter into a legal contract between consenting adults by their own free will only after meeting and negotiating the conditions of their marriage. Parents have no official say in betrothal, and either spouse has a right to exit the marriage in case of incompatibility.[67] Further, each act of lovemaking requires the husband's renewed appeasement and wooing to win his wife's consent.

While this ideal of free choice, based primarily on the search for love and companionship, was never the social reality in Jewish families historically, in the last 120 years it has become a universal consensus. But not so in the legal framework, spiritual ideal, or sociological experience of the Gur community. Gur parents alone select a mate for their adolescent children (ages 17–19), though they will not go forward with the arrangements until the rebbe approves the match. After the match has been approved, "courting" begins and ends with the couple themselves meeting only once face-to-face, for under an hour, in a semi-private audience, just a few weeks before the official family engagement ceremony. Trusting their parents' wisdom, neither the bride nor groom would protest their parents' arrangement, which all believe is determined in heaven (*bashert*). Thereafter, the couple will not meet again until the wedding, six to twelve months later.[68] Whereas the bride will usually be given a photo of her bridegroom to dutifully cherish during this period, the bridegroom will not examine or keep a photo of the bride.[69]

GUIDANCE FOR THE WEDDING NIGHT

As the couple approaches their first night together, they have reason to be anxious. This is the first occasion in their lives in which they will converse with a member of the opposite sex outside their family, see any part of the body of the other sex, or show their own body, other than faces or hands. Note that they have not seen romantic movies or scientific diagrams of the human body; nor have they been allowed to explore the contours of their own bodies. Neither the husband-to-be nor the wife-to-be has been taught anything about the practicalities or the laws of intercourse, including the physiology of their own bodies, until the very day of the wedding—and even then, the sex act is described euphemistically and mechanically. The object of this last brief but detailed instruction is to train the man and the woman to fulfill their sexual roles without awkward interchanges.[70] In fact, in the marital bedroom no conversation of any kind is ever allowed (even though halakhah permits spouses to discuss their act of sexual union, as we saw in chapter 3).

The guidelines for intercourse require: wearing garments all the time, at least on the upper body, and fully darkening the bedroom.[71] The only approved position for intercourse is the husband on top face-to-face with his wife. The process of penetration must be quick and purposeful, devoted to a single goal—ejaculation inside the vagina. The husband is to meticulously avoid wasting semen (e.g., drops spilled outside his wife's body). Some Gur marriage counselors urge the man to rest on his elbows and fists as he holds himself above the woman to minimize physical contact even during penetration. No hugging, kissing, foreplay, or afterplay is allowed.

In a sense, this impersonal mitzvah is "egalitarian." There is to be no pleasure for either spouse—and no flexibility on the part of either husband or wife in shaping the routine of intercourse. Even though the wife is supposed to defer to her husband's wishes, the man is not supposed to express any wish for pleasure or to satisfy his sexual desires. The bridal counselors of Gur teach the brides to sanctify their bodies by sacrificing their natural desires in performing the mitzvah. Vasserman elucidates:

> The counselor reassures the bride that just as your husband uncovers his arm before putting on tefillin, so you uncover yourself for this mitzvah and your body will be sanctified to a higher purpose. She advises: "Give yourself to this mitzvah and then your children born of this night will willingly give themselves to a life of mitzvot."

M'sirus nefesh, willingness to martyr oneself, is the Hasidic ideal. The counselor promises the bride that, with God's help, she can "break nature"[72] and its impulses and "sanctify [herself] in [abstaining from sexual pleasure as much as possible even in performing] what is legally permitted."[73]

None of the love-enhancing rabbinic or kabbalist meanings of intercourse (chapters 2 and 5) are invoked in guiding these young Hasidic couples in their strictly choreographed marital relations. The sacred is defined only negatively, by abstinence and distance, and not positively, by elevating the physical union to a spiritual plane.[74]

GUIDANCE IN INTERPERSONAL COMMUNICATIONS

Gur's ethos of marriage sees no value in nurturing an intimate loving relationship, so it makes emotional communication almost impossible. It prohibits verbalization of sexual desires or dissatisfactions. All familial decisions are supposed to be made by the husband without consultation, because marriage is not supposed to be a mutual partnership in which couples discuss and negotiate their conflicting interests and perspectives. Husbands are discouraged from holding any conversation with their wives beyond managing practical issues. For those, husbands are to convey information and issue instructions dispassionately, without explication or persuasion, and wives are tasked with deferring to their husbands on all decisions without discussion. *Shalom bayit* (maintaining peace in the home) is to be achieved through the wife's submissive obedience to her husband's command. Intellectual talk about Torah is minimized, though a husband is expected to teach his wife proper halakhic conduct and to supervise her spiritual discipline. His sharing of his daily Talmudic studies with her and her recounting of her day's events to him are discouraged.[75]

For the duration of their married lives, husbands are expected to maintain physical and emotional distance, and to minimize erotic and interpersonal intimacy, lest the spirituality of their homes be disturbed. The less time a husband spends at home with his wife, the better. Husbands and wives are to avoid handing any object directly between them, even when the woman is not forbidden to him as during her menses (*niddah*). As such, one spouse places an object to be transferred on the table, and then the other spouse picks it up. In the street a wife will always walk several paces behind her husband. When walking to the same address, for a family meal or celebration, the couple will also synchronize their gait so that they will not meet or even stand simultaneously at the same stop light.[76] On the bus or airplane, they will not sit near each other; nor will a couple enter an elevator together.[77]

Since Gur places no value on identifying and fulfilling one's individual and social needs, expression of feelings and actualization of one's unique self are counterindicated. With proper willpower and obedience, a hasid and his wife learn how to repress impulses and to regard demands to fulfill one's individual needs as the product of egotistical impulses that must be repaired.

THE IDEAL MARITAL RELATIONSHIP

While contemporary Western ideals of marriage encourage couples to let difficulties surface verbally and to invest emotional work in their relationships so that they can mature and grow as individuals and as a couple, the Hasidic ideal of Gur is to accept one's partner as he or she is, for God has assigned this match by personal providence (*hashgaha pratit*) even before birth (TB *Mo'ed Katan* 18b). In the Gur wedding invitation, the bride is not described as "my heart's choice," as in modern Israeli invitations, but as the "daughter of my fate [*gili/mazali*]."

Thus, when confronted with difficulties and disappointments in marriages, couples are to bear them with patience, regarding them as spiritual trials sent by God. Since the heavenly matchmaker has arranged everything for the couple's ultimate good, one must resign oneself to marital difficulties. Divorce is seldom justified.[78] The default position is to make the marriage work, because being divorced is a terrible burden on the extended family. If there is a divorced older sister in the family, the other children will have a hard time finding a good match.

When couples disagree, women are to defer unconditionally to their husbands, just as husbands defer to the rebbe. A pious wife nullifies her will before her husband's, just as a hasid nullifies his will before the divine will.[79] Hasidic women are taught to live up to the rabbinic adage, "Who is a kosher wife? One who does the will of her husband" both in religious and economic matters.[80] Thus she fulfills God's pronouncement on Eve that *your desire will be to your husband and he will rule over you* (Gen. 3:16)—whether the text is understood as a curse for Eve's sin or as a behavior appropriate to a woman's nature for her own good (TB *Eruvin* 100b).

The daughters of Gur are taught that the spiritual blessings (*shefa*) that come to them are mediated exclusively through their husbands, just as the blessings for all Israel come through the medium of the rebbe. Therefore, a woman of Gur is not herself called a *hasida*. As Brown explains, "In Gur, only men are full-fledged hasidim, and the hasidic religious endeavor (*avodah*, worship) is their duty alone."[81] (Note, by contrast, that the rebbe of Slonim does regard women as spiritual agents. He appeals to the couple to sanctify their marital bed together: "*Husband and wife!* The Divine Presence dwells among *them*; *their* home is like a minor Temple . . . *their* bed is like the Holy of Holies."[82])

According to the gender theories of Gur, a woman's role is merely to receive passively, while a man's is to give actively (*mashpia*).[83] And

yet, the Gerer hasid is also a passive recipient and not an autonomous agent, for he is not supposed to be self-determining but obe-
dient to the rebbe in all aspects of life. Theologically, the mystical
aspiration of the hasid is to nullify his existence and his will (*bitul
ha-yesh*) before God so that the Divine can manifest itself within
his empty space (*halal panui*).[84]

THE EXTRAORDINARY ENTREPRENEURIAL
INDEPENDENCE OF THE WOMEN OF GUR

Paradoxically, while the young women have no say in choosing their
mates at the expense their autonomy, and the Ordinances demand
the husbands practice ascetic sexuality at the expense of women's
sexual satisfaction, Gerer women, more than wives in other Hasidic
sects, are known for their independence of mind, economic acumen,
and entrepreneurial success in employment outside the home, where
they are often in close proximity to secular men. Brown notes that
the wives of Gur are considered

> among Hasidic women to be somewhat freer: they dress more beau-
> tifully and are more likely to work in modern professions, such as
> fashion and computers. The very strictness of the regulations within
> the family seems to have created a space for female self-expression
> in the outside world.[85]

The unusual openness of women of Gur to participation in Israeli
economic life should dispel our expectation that the stringency of
the Ordinances would herald a general policy of withdrawal from
society. Rather, the Gerer rebbe elected to focus the severity of his
approach to sanctity only in the realm of curtailing marital intimacy.
Opposing most other forms of religious stringency, the Gerer rebbe
explained that one must be apprehensive about setting too high a
bar of strictness (*humra*), lest people who fail to live up to the most

ascetic rules end up despairing altogether of the Hasidic ideal of living a sacred life.[86] For example, the Gerer rebbe also opposed overly restrictive demands for kashrut supervision, and permitted enjoyment of the pleasures of fine wine and cigars.[87] So too the Gerer rebbe encouraged moderate policies toward collaboration with the secular Zionist state and its economy, and therefore women have been encouraged to take financial and educational initiatives *outside* their strictly patriarchal homes and bedrooms.[88]

A Disenchanted Disciple of Skver Hasidism

Shulem Deen (b. 1974), a lapsed hasid, offers yet another insider view in his first-person memoir exposing the education for marriage he received in New Square, New York. Situated in Rockland County, forty miles north of Manhattan, New Square is the American home of the Skverer Hasidic dynasty founded originally in the city of Skvira, Ukraine, in the mid-nineteenth century. In 1948, after surviving the Holocaust and immigrating to the United States, the Skverer rebbe, Yaakov Yosef Twersky (1899–1968), wary of American materialism and sexual decadence, relocated to this rural community away from the hustle and bustle of New York City. Today, his Hasidim include about three thousand families.[89] Skver has a reputation as an ascetic sect, but as we shall see, it is somewhat less stringent than Gur in its bedroom practices.

Deen, whose parents had been 1960s hippies before becoming very pious Hasidic Jews, grew up in the radically anti-Zionist community of Satmar Hasidim in Brooklyn. Later Deen moved to New Square and married there in 1993, but was expelled for his heretical views ten years later.[90] In *All Who Go Do Not Return: A Memoir* (2015), Deen offers insight into how his various instructors prepared him to become a worthy Hasidic groom. Initially, in a class of soon-to-be-married male age-mates, he was taught about the spiritual ideal of marriage. One instructor warned the prospective grooms about the horrendous punishments in hell should they violate marital purity and scorned "the sheer idiocy of those who could not resist temptations of the flesh [and] who veered from holiness and purity."[91]

Another instructor urged the prospective grooms to honor their wives according to the Talmudic maxim, "One should love one's wife as [one loves] one's body, and respect or honor her more than one's own body" (TB *Yevamot* 62b). Yet the same instructor immediately belittled this maxim by reinterpreting "*respect* her" to mean "*suspect* her":

> But how do we understand this passage? [the instructor continued] ... What it *really* means, esteemed young men, is that we must be vigilant! Respect what *she*, a *woman*, can do to a man if he does not remain careful. Let down your guard, and she will lead you into *sheol tachtis*—the abyss of sinful temptation![92]

When Deen began to doubt his emotional compatibility with his assigned bride ("I just don't think she and I have anything in common"), his favorite instructor tried to set him straight on what a man is to expect from a woman:

> You were hoping for a friend? ... A wife is to be *a helpmate* (Gen. 2:18). Your friends will still be your fellow students. ... A wife is not a friend. A wife is not something to think about excessively. To take a wife is a biblical commandment, and so we do God's will by taking one. A wife is there to assist with one's service to God, nothing more.[93]

This instructor constructed an absolute dichotomy between a study partner who is meant to be a friend and a wife who serves instrumental roles for her husband that enable him to devote his life to study.

Only on the day of his wedding was Deen instructed in private about the nitty-gritty of intercourse—technically and halakhically. His personal marriage counselor walked him cursorily through the protocols of what would be his first bedroom encounter with his bride, which was scheduled immediately after the wedding ceremony. To prepare his new wife for their first intercourse (as well as their first kiss and hug), Deen was told to conduct a perfunctory chat with her. When he asked his counselor, "Chat about what?" The counselor told him:

> It is recommended that one tell tales of the righteous. Only a few minutes are necessary. Until she gets comfortable. . . . Then you get on top, *and tell her you love her*. . . . You must kiss her twice. Once before the act and once during.[94]

When instructed to tell his bride "I love you," Deen was confused because he had been told "a wife is not a friend," not someone to think about, and then he realized: "The notion of loving my wife had never occurred to me. Marriage was a duty, no more. To pretend otherwise seemed ridiculous."[95]

When questioned, the marriage counselor shrugged and repeated: "It is the law. . . . The law says you must tell her you love her."[96] Since neither Deen nor his bride had ever been taught to value or express their emotions, professing his love perfunctorily and kissing his bride on command on the wedding night appeared to be superficial rituals.

At this point in his wedding day consultation, Deen was told to make his first intercourse curt, since intercourse with a virgin engenders a blood flow that spreads impurity on contact: "One who marries a virgin, takes possession of her [i.e., penetrative sex], and then separates from her immediately."[97] Finally, the Talmudic model of Rabbi Eliezer was invoked: "Most important of all, the mitzvah must be done the way it was done by the great sage Rabbi Eliezer: with awe and with fear, as if forced by a demon."[98]

Aware of the groom's anxieties and the intentional lack of specificity of the instructions, the marriage counselor tried to reassure Deen: "Mazel tov. If there are any problems, call me!"[99] Not surprisingly, Deen's actual wedding night was fraught with apprehension about committing inadvertent sins of impurity, about his own sexual impotence and inadequacy, and about the awkwardness of communicating intimately with a woman for the first time in his life (and hers). At the apex of that fateful night in the conjugal bedroom, technical difficulties, inadequate prior guidance, and naivete about the functioning of his and her body compelled Deen to telephone his counselor in the midst of their ungainly process of intercourse. With the help of more explicit oral instructions, Deen eventually consummated the marriage.[100]

While the rabbinic blessings recited at Deen's wedding spoke of husband and wife as "loving friends," Deen's teachers had taught him to reject such romantic expectations. In retrospect, Deen's fundamental critique of Skver's inadequate sex education concerned both the lack of preparation for interpersonal communication and the suppression of emotional and erotic desires. Much later, Deen came to view both as essential for a healthy and happy relationship.

Conclusion: Takeaways for a Modern Marriage

As we've seen, the Skver and Gur ethos of marriage is not meant to nurture intimate loving relationships through emotional communication, to express and meet husbands' and wives' sexual needs, or to promote lives of partnership between two equal persons. These Hasidic sects reject male-female friendship; a woman's dignity, spirituality, and equality; and both a man's and a woman's autonomy, sexual passions, and romantic love.

Yet, even if we profoundly dissent from these ideals, the Gur and Skver teachings can contribute to our thinking about marriage and Judaism in three ways.

First, the Ordinances of Kedushah are comprehensive, concrete, and down-to-earth in stipulating disciplined practices for married life. While rejecting their misogynist content, one might offer alternative replies to the important questions they address: How should couples conduct intimate conversations? What physical gestures should accompany lovemaking? What are the hierarchal power relations implicit in daily routines in married life that the Gur wish to reinforce and that egalitarians wish to reform? Just as marriage counselors and their how-to books offer hands-on guidance to couples from a psychological perspective, so too can Judaism address these interpersonal questions as profoundly religious and ethical questions. Like Gur, non-Hasidic Jews can also provide their followers or congregants with ongoing marriage advice while recognizing its sacred role, as some modern pastoral rabbis do (as, for example, my father, Rabbi Dr. Moshe Sachs).

Second, these Hasidic rebbes may be correct in identifying marital relations as the front line in a battle for defending sacred family values from the deleterious influences of a self-indulgent society. Many problematic aspects of human relations in postmodern, consumer-oriented society are manifest in stressful couple relationships. For example, contemporary society frequently prioritizes immediate gratification of desires above concern for its effect on others. Individuals, even after taking their marriage vows, often give preference to "me" over "us" and indulge their passions (even if adulterous) rather than demonstrate loyalty to their spouses and to the values of holy matrimony. When society stridently defends individual freedoms and sexual rights to satisfaction, then compromising with one's spouse may appear to be a betrayal of one's own autonomy and needs. While the Gur's draconian remedy to modernity's self-indulgence is, in the judgment of many, worse than the problems they address, their perspicacious diagnosis of the societal crisis in values should provoke modern Jewish leaders to find more suitable remedies.

Third, Judaism is the product of a creative battlefield of ideas and practices, and it does not have one eternal essence. Jewish culture and halakhah develop dialectically by debate and, when necessary, revolution and divergence. As Gur Hasidism shows us, as recently as 1948 a new ethos of Jewish marriage could be invented and propagated, so that today Gur's families appear to be flourishing in what is now one of the largest Hasidic communities in the world. By the same token, non-Hasidic Jews can react creatively and innovatively to a Jewish trend they abhor because it is ascetic and misogynist, and then develop alternative approaches and disseminate them systematically to their communities. In the 1950s, Litvak Haredim began to reverse the Gur's pietist trend and educate their own yeshiva students to celebrate loving and passionate marriages as the preferred path to sanctity and shalom bayit. Initiated by the doyen of Litvak scholars, the Hazon Ish (Rav Avraham Isaiah Karelitz, Lithuania, Israel, 1878–1953), the Litvak resistance to Gur engendered an alternative Haredi ideology of marriage rooted in Rav's Talmudic bedroom and in Zoharic eros, as well as in contemporary psychological insights about the emotions and desires of men and women. As we see in detail in chapters 9, 10 and 11, by revisiting the earlier halakhic and kabbalist sources censored out of Hasidic marital counseling, these Litvaks have constructed a new ethos of Jewish marriage based on spiritual and ethical ideals of *hesed*, love, sexual passion, peace, and also unification of apparent opposites like sexuality and sanctity.

Thus in the past twenty-five years a burgeoning new literature of Litvak marital guidance has emerged, with manuals for yeshiva students and their brides that aim to enhance couples' emotional and physical health and to fuel a religiously creative rethinking of the marital relationship. These Haredi marital guidebooks for grooms and brides counsel joyful marital intimacy (a modest Haredi *Kama Sutra*) and spousal communication designed to bridge the gender gap in marriage in the spirit of a Haredi *Men Are from Mars, Women Are from Venus* (see chapter 10).

Those of us who wish to live our lives in the light of traditional wisdom ought to have faith in ourselves and in Judaism that we too can reinterpret, innovate, and propagate new Jewish ways of couple intimacy. In our era of newly egalitarian gender relations and exploration of varied forms of sexuality, there is much for us to contribute critically to enrich and redirect a living Judaism.

"Break Their Evil Nature"   8

LITVAK YESHIVOT AND SALANTER'S MUSSAR
SUPPRESS DESIRE AND FAMILIAL AFFECTION

Rava says: "[Those who would possess Torah must learn from] the raven's relation to its young to make themselves cruel to their children and their household members."

—TB *Eruvin* 22a

He who has greatness is cruel. . . . Overcoming pity [is] a noble virtue. . . . When one hears a loud cry for help and pity . . . trying to lure him away from himself, . . . stay in control. Keep the height of your task free from the many lower and short-sighted impulses that are at work in supposedly selfless actions. This is the test . . . his real proof of strength.

—FRIEDRICH NIETZSCHE, *Gay Science* and *Ecce Homo*

Introduction

Immediately after the State of Israel was established, Haredi leaders nursing their terrible communal losses in the Holocaust entered an intense period of debate and innovation in Jewish marital ethics. As we saw (chapter 7), the chief Hasidic protagonist of innovation was the new Gerer rebbe. In 1948, spurning in effect the Besht's Hasidic ideas of corporeal service of God, he radicalized and universalized the Maggid's ascetic views of marriage by promulgating marital practices of self-denial. For every hasid of Gur, the spiritual battle to conquer the *yetzer* (libido) would now have to take center stage in his bedroom.

In reaction to Gur's Ordinances of Kedushah, in the 1950s three Litvak Talmudic scholars—the Hazon Ish (Avraham Isaiah Karelitz), the Steipler rav (Yaakov Kanievsky), and the Mussarnik Rav Isaac Sher—wrote adamant pastoral letters to their students instructing them that the halakhah demands that they reject marital asceticism, fulfill their conjugal duties, and enhance *shalom bayit* by embracing love and sexual satisfaction in their marriages. From that time forth, the divergent schools of Hasidim and Litvaks generated opposing guidelines for newlyweds and young couples struggling with the nitty-gritty of their love lives. This chapter is devoted to providing the historical and ideological background of the Lithuanian yeshiva world against which the Litvak paradigm shift of the 1950s was launched, just as the previous chapter surveyed the Hasidic background of Gur's Ordinances.

The seminal institutional and ideological divisions between Litvaks and Hasidim had emerged as early as 1772, with the Gaon of Vilna's ban on Hasidism. His students established what grew into a vast system of modern yeshivot, first in Lithuania and Belarus and, in the twentieth-century, around the world. These yeshivot, in turn, would produce the community of anti-Hasidic ultra-Orthodox Jews who now call themselves Litvaks, even if they no longer live in the regions around Lithuania. In the most prestigious of these Litvak yeshivot, the ethical teachings of the Mussar movement founded by Israel Salanter during the 1850s came to play a powerful role in shaping the spiritual and ethical world of their students (though its influence declined after World War II).

Despite all the polemical disagreements between Hasidim and Litvaks, before the 1950s neither side would advocate enhancing love and passion in the mitzvah of onah as a path to sanctity. Indeed, the very opposite is the case. To understand the internal about-face within the Litvak tradition after World War II, we must take the reader back to the nineteenth-century world of the Litvak yeshivot that rejected Hasidism and yet developed its own quasi-monastic attitude to family life and its own rationale for obstructing sexual and emotional intimacy with one's wife. Many forms of Hasidism, as we saw, promote marital asceticism as a response to sexual desire present even in marriage, for this evil impulse is a primary threat to the sanctity of the husband and the purity of his mind (though not of the wife), and those qualities are essential for the spiritual worship of God. For nineteenth-century Litvaks, however, the chief aim was to train an elite of Talmud scholars imbued with full-time devotion to learning, from which the obligations to and affections for one's family were a dangerous distraction, leading to the cardinal sin of wasting time that could be devoted to study of Torah (*bitul Torah*).

Furthermore, the yeshiva's educational ethos, often associated with Salanter's schools of Mussar, sought to repair the character traits of its students, cultivating extreme rationality, self-criticism, and willpower by "breaking" natural inclinations toward sex, pleasure, complacency, laziness, self-seeking pride, and even toward affection and compassion for family. Unlike Hasidim, Litvaks cultivated asceticism in marriage less to achieve sanctity or spirituality, but more to maintain unswerving dedication to intellectual excellence (*Talmud Torah*) and ethical self-perfection (*tikkun ha-midot*).

Beginning after World War II, the Litvaks changed significantly their attitudes to marital intimacy, and in the conclusion to this chapter we sample some of the new teachings of contemporary twenty-first-century Mussar teachers and their revised attitudes to marital relations.

Litvak Beginnings and the First Modern Yeshiva

Rabbi Elijah Kremer, the Gaon of Vilna in Lithuania (1720–97), the flagship teacher of the *Mitnagdim* (the Opponents), first excommunicated followers of Hasidism in successive bans in 1772, 1781, and

1797. Declaring total war against Hasidim as members of a deviant sect, the Mitnagdim also burnt Hasidic writings and periodically sought to have their leaders imprisoned. According to a hundred-year-old copy of the original broadside or street poster (*pashkvil*), the rabbinate of Vilna declared the excommunication of the newly founded Hasidic synagogues in Lithuania:

> A SEVERE BAN (*Herem*) by the Great Rabbis of Vilna with the Approval of THE GAON OF VILNA THE HASID (the Pious One) THE GRA (Rabbi Elijah) OF VILNA
>
> Our brothers the House of Israel, do you know of these innovators (*hadashim*) . . . who have banded together into a suspicious sect called HASIDIM . . . who formed separatist groups . . . and engage in many ugly customs. . . .
>
> Therefore, the leaders of our people must don the cloak of zealous-ness, zealousness for God, to destroy, TO ANNIHILATE AND TO DECLARE UPON THEM BANS AND CURSES. We have with God's help already uprooted . . . them from our place [Vilna], so too may they be uprooted from all places, so they shall not be remembered or taken into account or considered ever again. . . . One must search for them like *hometz* [bread on Passover], disintegrate them. and toss them to the winds. . . . Their dispersion will be good for the world.[1]

THE LITVAK CRITIQUE OF HASIDISM

The Opponents' critique of Hasidism singled out, among other things, worshipping God by indulging their physical desires (*avodah begashmiyut*), ecstatic prayer, magical use of Kabbalah by purported wonder-working rebbes, and, worst of all, *bitul Torah*, waste of precious time on ecstatic worship and spiritual intentionality instead of Talmud study, thereby demoting the all-consuming mitzvah of Torah study.[2]

In his anti-Hasidic polemics, the *mitnaged* Rabbi David of Makow (d. 1814) propagandized against Hasidim in these words:

All of his [i.e., the Besht's] words are directed toward a single conclusion, namely, his claim that the only true good for man is to sit upon the fleshpots . . . and to spend days of vanity just eating, drinking, and celebrating. . . . They say: "What is the divine service of the heart? It is none other than eating and praying." Thus has the holy Torah become neglected.[3]

The historian of Polish Jewry Gershon Hundert summarizes the Litvaks' attacks on Hasidim for lack of decorum:

The visage that a dignified Jewish scholar presented to the world [ought to be] dour and serious, as was appropriate in the "long and bitter exile" of the Jewish people. The Mitnaggedim [condemned] the Hasidim, [because] "all their days are like holidays," and "they waste the time of study all day in matters of silliness and laughter, . . . song . . . smoking tobacco." . . . Further: "They say, 'God forbid that one should regret a sin one has committed, lest it lead to sadness.'"[4]

Therefore, the Gaon of Vilna, who was known as a "hasid" in the older sense of a kabbalist ascetic and student of esoteric Torah, declared it "an abomination" that the Hasidim called themselves by the same honorific title.[5] While the Gaon himself did not hold an official position in the Vilna community and did not participate in an institution of higher learning (yeshiva), his unparalleled breadth and depth of knowledge of Talmud and halakhah gave him his authority.[6] And thus he initiated the great schism within Eastern European Ashkenazi Haredim, which continues to define the ideological significance of being a Litvak.[7]

In 1802 the Gaon's most influential disciple, Rabbi Haim Itzkovitz of Volozhin (1749–1821), founded the first great "modern" yeshiva, Etz Haim (The Tree of Life), in the village of Volozhin in Belarus (the region next to Lithuania and at that time within the czarist Russian Empire, along with Poland). Etz Haim had a fixed curriculum, a diverse faculty, a developed pedagogic methodology, dormitories, and yearlong studies for full-time students who came from all over Eastern Europe. For the first time, too, a yeshiva's financing was not dependent on the local community, but on a fundraising organization supported by individual donors from the whole region.[8]

Its goals were both intellectual and spiritual: to enhance analytic Talmud study (pursued night and day) for its own sake and not as a seminary to prepare rabbis, and to instill *yirah*, "fear of God," in its students. Each student was taught to become a ben Torah, a virtuous and humble exemplar of the aristocracy of Torah study.[9] In his book *Nefesh HaHaim*, Haim of Volozhin taught his students to see themselves as imitating God by creating "novel insights into the meaning of Torah (*hiddushim*)." In that sense the yeshiva's emphasis on rational analysis and individual creativity in interpretation reflected some contemporary Western values.[10]

Yet this yeshiva was also antimodern, its ideology repudiated the Jewish Enlightenment (Haskalah) and its leaders resisted the dictates of the czar's modernizing ministry of education to include the teaching of Russian and secular subjects. It zealously rejected the government's attempts to restructure the yeshiva as a professional school to prepare teachers and modern rabbis in which Talmud study would be limited to four hours per day, taught in the afternoons and evenings only. Eventually the local government officially closed the Volozhin yeshiva's doors in 1892 for noncompliance with Russification.[11]

Illustrious heads of Etz Haim after Haim of Volozhin included rabbis Naftali Tzvi Yehudah Berlin (the Netziv) and Haym Soloveitchik (grandfather of Joseph B. Soloveitchik of Yeshiva University), and its students included Haim Nahman Bialik, the poet laureate of the Zionist movement, and Abraham Isaac Kook, the first chief Ashkenazi rabbi of Israel (see chapter 12). In the aftermath of the world wars, the communist revolution, and the Holocaust, these Lithuanian-style yeshivot were transplanted to America and Israel.

THE ASCETIC PARADIGM OF THE VILNA GAON

In the late 1700s, the Gaon of Vilna, Elijah the Hasid, preached and practiced suppression of passions and minimization of this-worldly distractions in order to facilitate concentrated study. For him that meant not only disdaining mundane pleasures such as sexual satisfaction and social relations but also minimizing family affection and familial responsibilities. His own sons attested to their admiration for his stringency in their memoirs, as quoted by the historian Immanuel Etkes:

> How devoted he was in his soul to avoid the company of his household and his sons and daughters. He sought only to dwell in the pure fear of God . . . so that he never asked his sons and daughters about their livelihoods or their situations. In his life he never wrote them a letter to ask [about] their health.[12]

Etkes describes how the Gaon's family reacted to this principled abandonment:

> The sons of the Gaon of Vilna go on to praise their father for not hesitating to leave home to study Torah in isolation, although his then only son, the infant Shlomo Zalman, was lying ill. . . . That event, in his son's opinion, demonstrates the spiritual superiority of

those who "leave the paths of this world in order to labor in [the field of] Torah and mitzvot. . . . They isolate themselves in the ways of God and His Torah, until, in the sweetness they find in it, *they sever the cords of nature and throw off the bonds of love for their children.*"[13]

The Gaon of Vilna demanded no less of others: scholars were to crush their natural attachments, quash their feelings of love and compassion, and even repudiate their legal and moral responsibility for the physical well-being of their dependents. As he preached:

True heroes are men of noble heart with the fullest trust in God, constantly doing mitzvot and meditating on the Torah day and night even though their home be without bread and clothing and their families cry out: "Bring us something to support and sustain us with some livelihood!" But he pays no attention at all to them nor heeds their voice . . . for he has denied all love except that of the Lord and His Torah.[14]

To corroborate the authority of his message, the Gaon quoted the Talmudic advice of Ravah (4th century, Babylonia):

Ravah says: "Those who would possess Torah must learn from the raven's relation to its young to make themselves cruel to their children and their household members" [see Job 38:41].
  That is like Rav Ada bar Matana who was going to the house of study when his wife said: "What shall I do [to feed] your children?" He replied: "Are all the stalks in the lake used up? [i.e., if there is no bread, let them eat reeds from the lake.]" (TB *Eruvin* 22a)

The Gaon's single-minded devotion to Torah study at the expense of family became the recommended practice of the Volozhin yeshiva, and its founder, Haim of Volozhin, instructed even his married students: "Study in a distant place [far from your families] to avoid the interference and impediments of one's household." Many of these students went away to study for one to five years, while their wives worked in small businesses to support their families. For example, Rav Abraham Isaac Kook's brother-in-law reported: "My sister, the rabbi's wife, supported herself with great labor, in great poverty, and under pressure to feed her children, and yet she was always happy with her lot, and, on [Kook's] return he was stuffed full with Torah."[15]

On one level, the Vilna Gaon's asceticism can be viewed as merely pragmatic, a means of minimizing disruptions to full-time study as the highest service of God. On a deeper level, though, he aimed to perfect his character by uprooting all natural feeling and by separating body from soul. He was a rigorous ethical dualist who believed life in this world is a perpetual struggle between spirituality and human desires for corporeality, as the Vilna Gaon preached:

> The things of this world, such as eating, in which food turns into feces and excrement, or the sexual act, are intrinsically loathsome. It is only what may result from them that might be for good, such as if the only purpose of the eating is to be able to turn again to Torah study.[16]

For these Litvaks, bodily functions are disgusting and degrading, as the Vilna Gaon's student Reb Haim of Volozhin explained, they are "a great disgrace to the dignity of a human being. Now surely his soul, the spiritual part [of man], must scorn all of this with utter contempt."[17] Therefore, the Vilna Gaon's primary goal was to "break" human nature and thus completely conquer natural instincts (*yetzer*). He lionized the heroic man who suppressed animal drives and triumphed over bad habits:

> Hold on to *mussar* [pietist character training] . . . for a person lives in order *to break the [negative] traits that he has not yet broken.* Hence one must continually strengthen oneself; otherwise what is life for?[18]

His son Abraham testified that his father, "like a heavenly angel, nullified his saintly body, lest his corporeality obstruct his [spiritual] path."[19] Brute willpower, however, is not enough to break one's bad habits, so the Gaon teaches that

> to wage war against the Evil Impulse one must exercise cunning. . . . For a man who wishes to break his appetites cannot jump immediately to seize the opposite extreme and the contrary to what he is accustomed, but must gradually separate himself until he reaches the opposite extreme; and then he should break his appetite.[20]

The Gaon warns that breaking one's nature requires constant vigilance so as to see through the trappings of the yetzer's false rhetoric. In particular, the evil impulse misleads scholars by appealing to their natural compassion for their starving children, to their pangs of conscience for abandoning their lonely wives, and to their desire to have a respectable and profitable livelihood, as the Gaon explains in his *Commentary on Proverbs*.[21] Strikingly, like Nietzsche (see the epigraph at the beginning of this chapter), the Gaon of Vilna wages a battle against natural compassion and the so-called ethical claims of mercy for the weak in order to achieve greatness, which for the Vilna Gaon means the ascetic and aristocratic greatness of the *ben Torah* scholar.[22] Under no circumstances should a yeshiva scholar settle for the mediocrity of the Jewish householder who studies Torah only in the evenings but devotes his days to his business and maintaining his well-to-do and socially well-respected family.

The Legacy of Premodern Ascetic Piety

Before continuing chronologically to track the nineteenth-century Mussar movement of Salanter that shaped Litvak education on marital intimacy, it is essential to go backward in time for a brief flashback to understand what the ethos of *mussar* and hasidic piety meant *before* the emergence of the official nineteenth-century movements and ideologies of Hasidism and Mussar. Like the Hasidim, the Mitnagdim had inherited various ascetic traditions from medieval rationalist philosophers (9th–12th centuries), Spanish Jewish Sufi pietists (11th–13th centuries), German Hasidim (13th century), and Lurianic kabbalists (16th–17th centuries).[23] This composite tradition of old style Hasidim and *mussar* taught that the pietist (hasid) is to follow a long path, stage by stage, in order to become a lover of God possessed of personal sanctity and even prophecy. At the initial stage, the pietist must uproot character faults. He must turn his orientation *away* from worldly pleasures of the body and of social standing and *toward* intellectual virtues and uninterrupted philosophic meditation on the Divine. His pursuit of ever-higher levels of otherworldly sanctity shapes his relationship to women and to sexual matters.

In his famous book, *Duties of the Heart* (as opposed to mere duties of behavior, mitzvot) the Andalusian Sufi philosopher Rabbi Bahya ibn Pakuda (Muslim Spain, 1050–1120) commends cultivation of asceticism from bodily pleasures and abstinence from the world.[24] Similarly, the moralist Rabbenu Jonah Gerondi (Christian Spain, ca. 1200–63), who composed the first full-length book about repentance, urged pietists to "break physical desire" by contemplating death and the world to come:

> Since one is destined to leave the earth and his bodily desires and, in the end, to despise and abjure them, he ought to abandon them in his lifetime and make use of the earth only in the service of the exalted God.[25]

For many old-style Jewish moralists and mystics like Bahya and Jonah Gerondi, the soul's imprisonment in a body makes it subject to powerful animal impulses that are "the major obstacle to the soul's evolution," remarks the historian Patrick Koch. Koch goes on to explain that "medieval musar-writings frequently interpret withdrawal from mundane affairs as a pre-condition for self-perfection."[26]

The path of the hasid, identified as *teshuvah* (repentance), entails both a *retrospective* atonement for past sins and a *prospective* self-cleansing on the way to purity and spirituality. For example, Rabbi Elazar of Hasidei Ashkenaz (Germany, ca. 1176–1238) conceptualizes the restorative quality of penitential practice as a measure-for-measure "castigation of the flesh that nullifies transgressions by measuring the pleasures of the sin against the sincerity of the punishments."[27] For an adulterer, he prescribes the following penance:

> A person who has engaged in [adulterous] sexual relations with a married woman, for which [the Bible] imposes the death penalty, should suffer sorrow as great as death. He should sit in ice or snow for an hour each day, once or twice. In hot weather he should [cover himself in honey and] sit beside flies or ants.[28]

Quoting from the famous Spanish Jewish moralists, the anonymous anthology entitled *Orhot Tzaddikim* (15th century, Germany) sums up the ascetic tradition of the hasid's path to self-perfection:

> The one who exerts himself, as much as he can, will ascend to the levels of *hasidut* (piety). . . . That is, he will remove love of this world from his heart and replace it with love of the Blessed Creator and devote himself to the sanctification of the Name.[29]

Lurianic kabbalists and pious moralists (16th–18th centuries) systematically evaluate the severity of particular sins in terms of the damage a Jew's transgressions inflicted on the mystical realm of the Divinity. Like Elazar of Hasidei Ashkenaz, they too detail the bodily mortification necessary for restoring the upper realms that have been disturbed. One of the most important books popularizing the Lurianic kabbalist pietism of Safed, Elijah de Vidas's *Reshit*

Hokhma: Gate of Repentance (16th century, Safed), thus explains the importance of fasting for purifying the mind:

> There is no other way to crush one's limbs and [unclean] spirit but by means of the ascetic practice of fasting, that is [the reduction of] his fat and blood. . . . One should mortify oneself by not eating in order to subdue oneself and to clarify the light from darkness. This applies in particular to *talmidei hakhamim* (scholars).[30]
>
> Just as one needs to keep away from the physical aspect of the transgression, one must abstain from the thoughts [of the evil impulse]. . . . By this you learn that man is not called holy until he has sanctified himself in deed and thought [through self-denial].[31]

For the Talmud's Rabbi Eliezer, the greatest battle against the evil impulse is not in avoiding sinful acts (like adultery) or even conquering one's bodily drives, but in purifying one's thoughts, so that one is not thinking of another woman during onah with one's wife (see chapter 3). Beyond Rabbi Eliezer, the medieval and early modern pietists use physical self-torture to purify their minds so as not to think about their own wives at all or their own sexual pleasure, but only of doing a mitzvah for God precisely as commanded. They argue that by detaching oneself from the world (*ha-olam*, as they call it), one can attach oneself to the Divine and ascend to the world of pure spirituality. It is that *mussar* tradition that shaped the religious world of the Gaon of Vilna, who was therefore called Elijah the Hasid. But he added to that older pietist ideal the dimension of total devotion to Talmud study characteristic of the *Mitnagdim*.

Salanter's Mussar Movement: Yeshiva Education Curbs Natural Inclinations

The Gaon of Vilna set a personal example for breaking one's nature, but the man who most deeply shaped the educational ethos of the

Litvak yeshiva was Israel Salanter, who employed reason to construct a system for inculcating ascetic practices and mind-control exercises, without aiming at higher spirituality. After studying in modern yeshivot and being inspired by the Vilna Gaon, the educator Rabbi Israel Lipkin (1809–83, also known as Rabbi Israel Salanter, or simply the Salanter, by virtue of his roots in the Lithuanian village of Salant) established a method and a movement for religious character development entitled Mussar, his innovative educational approach to old-style pietist *mussar*. The new Mussar movement absorbs and transforms the earlier *mussar* tradition, just as the newly organized Hasidic movement absorbs and transforms the medieval hasid, which belonged to the same *mussar* tradition.

Traditional *mussar* writings had included such esteemed works as Rabbi Moshe Haim Luzzatto's *Mesillat Yesharim* (The path of the righteous, Italy, 1738), which is structured around this Talmudic saying of Pinhas ben Yair:

> Rabbi Pinhas ben Yair said: "Torah leads to wariness; wariness leads to alacrity; alacrity leads to cleanliness [from sin]; cleanliness leads to abstention (*prishut*) [from worldly affairs]; abstention leads to purity; purity leads to piety (*hasidut*); piety leads to humility; humility leads to fear of sin; fear of sin leads to holiness; holiness leads to prophecy; prophecy leads to the resurrection of the dead." (TB *Avodah Zara* 20b)

Luzzato fleshed out a full step-by-step program of spiritual development, beginning with wariness and culminating in holiness, which strongly guided the Gaon of Vilna's pietist path.

Salanter, who became the head of his own yeshiva in Vilna and later Kovno (1840s), arranged for the reprinting of *Mesillat Yesharim* (and, subsequently, the work has become a standard meditational text for yeshiva students even today).

Influenced by the Vilna Gaon's rationalistic method of exercising cunning to master evil impulses, Salanter developed a systematic educational program. He taught yeshiva students that what makes them "truly human" is the struggle to dominate instinct (yetzer) with intellect.[32] To fathom the instinctual resistance to moral education, Mussar offered a new introspective diagnosis of the competing forces within the human mind: the unconscious impulses ("dark forces") and the conscious desires ("clear forces").[33]

Using sophisticated techniques of behavior modification, some drawn indirectly from Benjamin Franklin's *Autobiography*, Salanter directed his students to conquer their libidinal nature using diverse exercises.[34] For example, he inculcated pietist aphorisms—such as "jealousy, lust, and the pursuit of honor remove a person from the world" (*Mishnah Avot* 4:28)—by demanding that students shout them loudly and fervently, and repeat them daily as their mantra. Employing exercises in visual imagination, his young male students were instilled with visceral fear of punishment in hell in order to counteract their irrational appetites, "break their evil nature," and tame their lusts.[35] In Salanter's view, critical self-observation (*heshbon ha-nefesh*) and disciplined behavioral training would radically improve his students' character. At the apex of Mussar training, an individual could achieve the state of *tikkun ha-midot* (reconstructed character traits), in which he no longer feels evil impulses at all. Death of desire was the highest aim, though it was not easily maintained. Mussar advocated constant struggle for self-mastery.

Unlike all earlier *mussar* literature, Salanter ignores medieval Jewish philosophy and Kabbalah. Further, unlike many mystics, he does not condemn irrational impulses as a manifestation of metaphysical forces of the Other Side (*Sitra Ahra*), or demonic impurity. Nor does he urge yeshiva students to love God passionately and attach themselves to the Shekhinah through ecstatic experience (*devekut*), as Hasidism does. Rational self-analysis and realistic this-worldly discipline, not inspirational spirituality, were his stock-in-trade.[36]

Notably, while traditional pietists urged that one turn a blind eye to mundane concerns with money and social relations, Salanter prioritized meticulous performance of ethical behaviors, so as to avoid even minor instances of hurtful behavior in business transactions and daily conversations (such as gossip and false praise).[37] Famously, Salanter urged Orthodox Jews to be as punctilious in observing the mitzvot between human beings as those governing the relationship between human beings and God.[38] In his expansive anthology of stories told in the Mussar movement, Dov Katz recounts Salanter's visit to a matzah factory in order to issue his seal of approval that the matzah was kosher for Passover according to the most exacting standards (including of course completing the preparation of the flour and its baking in less than eighteen minutes). In such factories, in an era when small-scale capitalism flourished in Eastern Europe, the poorly paid seasonal workers, often poverty-stricken women and children, were regularly treated harshly and exploited economically in an effort to ramp up their production and raise the factory's profitablilty:

> Once, Rabbi Salanter visited a new matzah bakery in order to check its work practices and level of *kashrut* [standards of kosher preparation of food]. He reviewed all the manufacturing procedures extensively and observed the intense labor and toil of the employees. At the end of Rabbi Salanter's visit, the bakery owner proudly asked him, "What does the rabbi say?" He answered, "The Gentiles accuse us, God forbid, of using the blood of Christian children in matzah. While this is not the case, from what I have seen here, there is indeed a violation of the prohibition on blood in food. The blood of the workers is mixed with the matzah! I will not certify this bakery as kosher!"[39]

Pointedly, Salanter criticized this factory's punctilious observance of the ritual requirements of the holiday of Passover, on which Jews remember the harsh labor they were compelled to perform in Egypt under cruel taskmasters. Ritually punctilious behavior is no excuse for morally insensitive treatment of one's fellow, whom one is commanded to love. Inspired by Salanter's moral passion, the twentieth-century philosopher of ethics Emmanuel Levinas, himself of Litvak origins, used to quote a teaching attributed to Salanter: "The material needs of my neighbor are my spiritual needs."[40]

Salanter's Legacy:
The Kelm, Navaredok, and Slabodka Schools

After Salanter's death (1883), the legacy of Mussar shaped the Litvak Haredi world through his enthusiastic disciples, who carried forth his educational regimen in yeshivot in Eastern Europe, and later in America, England, and Israel.

Divergent schools of the Mussar movement are usually divided into three traditions developed in the three great Mussar yeshivot in the towns of Kelm, Navaredok, and Slabodka in Lithuania and Belarus. By delving into the differences and similarities of each school regarding family affection and suppression of desire, we can better understand the innovations of the contemporary North American Mussar movement that seeks to adapt Salanter's mindfulness practices for non-Orthodox Jews who not in the yeshiva world (see the end of this chapter), and the radical transformation of Mussar's attitude to marital passion by Rav Isaac Sher for ultra-Orthodox yeshiva students in Israel (see next chapter).

THE KELM SCHOOL OF SIMHAH ZISSEL ZIV

In Kelm, Simhah Zissel Ziv (1824–98) taught an approach to character education based on a realistic pessimism about human nature. He called for "a war against nature, against the brutishness with which the human being is born, and a great war to conquer a power as strong and mighty as nature and bring it under the governance of reason."[41]

Yet, like Salanter, Ziv also exhibited confidence in the beneficial effects of an orderly method to overcome human weakness. His eclectic approach to character education encompassed exercises in guided imagery eliciting fear (including some fire-and-brimstone preaching about what awaits sinners in hell).[42] But, as religious and Jewish studies professor Geoffrey Claussen argues, Ziv also motivated ethical behavior by appealing to a "vision of moral perfection" characterized by "loving one's fellow as oneself—with responsive, compassionate love motivated by a powerful sense of empathy" based on the sayings of Hillel and Rabbi Akiba.[43] Like Rabbi S. R. Hirsch, the founder of Modern Orthodoxy in Germany, Ziv promoted a code of "moral decency [*derekh eretz*] in accordance with the spirit of the age" as the fulfillment of the Torah.[44] "The prime foundation in a person's life is that he instill in his heart true love of human beings, whatever religion they may be."[45]

Like Salanter, Ziv was moved by moral passion to demand that his students interrupt study to act on their ethical responsibilities. Claussen cites the following teaching:

> In one letter to his son . . . Simhah Zissel [Ziv] . . . asks his son to imagine the ideal experience of studying with the Vilna Gaon: "if a person were immersed in study with the Vilna Gaon of blessed memory, and people [in need of hospitality] were walking on their way—would it occur to him to interrupt his study with his study partner, the Gaon, and plead with the wayfarers that they agree to come in and eat and drink?"

> But, Simhah Zissel concludes, one should interrupt even an ideal study session like this one, [in order to] follow the example of Abraham [who according to Rashi abandoned his conversation with God in order to run and persuade three travelers to be his guests (Gen.18:1–5)].[46]

Nevertheless, Claussen observes, Ziv never applied his affirmations of love and moral sensitivity to relations with one's wife:

> Simhah Zissel [Ziv]'s writings, despite their focus on loving care for one's fellow, show relatively little interest in questions regarding care for one's family—especially female members of one's family. . . . He did not have much to say about the obligations of spouses to one another. Like many other traditionalist rabbis, he did not give much attention to the standard Jewish legal requirements mandating that husbands attend to their wives' needs.[47]

In fact, Ziv, like the Gaon of Vilna, taught explicitly that "the Torah is not fulfilled except when one makes oneself cruel toward one's children, like a raven (TB *Eruvin* 22a)."[48] It is said that Ziv's wife, Sarah Leah, complied with her role as his enabler. Even when she had little to feed her children, "she did not complain about her situation, and even concealed her distress from her husband so that she would not trouble him and disturb him."[49]

In contrast to this Litvak ideal of fanatic singlemindedness in Torah study and practiced cruelty and indifference to one's family's suffering, it is oft told, in praise of the first Lubavitcher rebbe, Rabbi Shneur Zalman of Liady (Belarus, 1745–1812), that while he and his adult grandson were studying, a baby suddenly began to cry. The grandson was so engrossed in his learning that he did not pay any attention to the crying baby, but Shneur Zalman heard the baby and interrupted his studies to soothe the child. On his way back from tending to the baby, he rebuked his studious grandson: "When a person studies Torah and does not hear a cry for help, something is deficient in his learning."[50] As the philosophers Daniel Rynhold and Michael Harris analyze this famous tale: "A typical *mithnaged* [Litvak opponent of Hasidism] would firmly take the side of the grandson rather than the grandfather!"[51] In fact, unlike the Lubavitcher rebbe in this tale, many other Hasidic rebbes described above (see chapter 7) showed equal disdain for the cries of their own needy families.

The second school of Mussar originated in the town of Navaredok in one of the largest yeshivot in Belarus. Its educational leader, Yosef Yozel Hurwitz (1848–1919), regarded humans as creatures enslaved by insatiable desires and passions (yetzer ha-ra) whose faculty of reason is too weak to tame.[52] Hence, he taught that individuals had to fight a total war with no compromises and no concessions to break their own natural character traits (*sheviras ha-midos*): false piety, self-righteousness, and especially false pride. To Hurwitz, "the worst thing that can happen to a person is to stay the same." For him, Talmud study was of secondary importance to moral self-criticism.[53]

The researcher David Fishman describes daily life in Navaredok:

> Their study of musar included nighttime sessions of primal scream- ing, and uncontrolled outbursts of tears, whines, and fist-pounding. And they seemed to actively pursue schemes by which to make them- selves the objects of mockery and disgust. Students would [ask the pharmacist for nails as if he ran a hardware store, or] enter a crowded grocery, push to the front, and begin reciting the afternoon Ami- dah [prayer] at the top of their lungs; or wear filthy clothes on the Sabbath, which they had intentionally splattered with mud on Fri- day afternoon; or present words of Torah to their peers which were blatantly false, contradictory, or inane.[54]

When the townspeople would upbraid students for their uncouth behavior or mock them for their stupidity, the students would ben- efit by having their pride in their intellect crushed and their piety shattered. They would learn that one should never be a conformist and never compromise one's principles to be accepted socially.

In Navaredok, as Fishman observes, radical nonconfomist disregard for what are thought to be good manners, common sense, and sensitivity to public opinion also depreciated one's responsibility to one's family:

> Students who minimized contact with their parents (e.g., who did not go home for the holidays) were praised as models of devotion to Musar. Hurwitz himself set a startling example, by leaving his wife and children behind in Slabodka [visiting them only twice a year] and sending them no financial support while he led the yeshiva [because he refused to accept a salary].[55]

As the Yiddish novelist Chaim Grade (1910–82), a former student in Navaredok, wrote: "A Musarnik must marry only to fulfill the mitzvah of 'Be fruitful and multiply'—and then he must be on his way [leaving his wife and children behind in order] to spread the Torah of Navaredok" from town to town.[56]

THE SLABODKA SCHOOL OF NOSSON TZVI FINKEL

The third school of Mussar, Slabodka, led by the master of Slabodka, Nosson Tzvi Finkel (1849–1927), was the most moderate. Finkel, a student of Simhah Zissel Ziv, founder of the Kelm school, was an inveterate optimist about humanity. Departing from classical Mussar teachings, he celebrated "the greatness of the human being" as manifest in "the power of free choice."[57] And, he affirmed the value of physical pleasures because the human body as well as the human soul and intellect reflect the wisdom of God's creation.[58] Finkel preached:

> All human beings in all the generations, after all the declines and all the deteriorations, still possess the hidden divine power of the first

Adam, for that is the true form of humanity created in the image of God.... So, every human being has the potential to rise to the level of the first human being and to enjoy all the pleasure and goodness that Adam did.[59]

Differentiating between the Slabodka and Navaredok schools of Mussar, the Jewish philosopher Rabbi Louis Jacobs put it succinctly: "In Slabodka they taught: man is so great, how can he sin? In Navaredok they taught: man is so small, how dare he sin?"[60] Brown reports an encounter between Finkel and Hurwitz in which Hurwitz concluded: "When Finkel speaks of humanity he is talking about Adam *before* he sinned in the Garden, but when I mention humanity I am referring to Adam *after* he sinned." In short, according to Hurwitz, the master of Slabodka had forgotten to leave the Garden, and so he was not acquainted with real, wild, and morally despicable human beings in need of Mussar's harsh discipline.[61]

To Finkel, "all Creation is holy and that is manifest in its physical joys as well."[62] God created the Garden of Eden as a pleasure park for humanity to satisfy all its senses, including "every tree lovely to contemplate and good to eat" (Gen. 2:9).[63] In fact, Finkel says, the angels used to pour wine and serve barbecued meat to Adam and Eve. The woman too was originally a perfect spiritual creature made of a pure material as luminescent as the stars.[64] Therefore, the path of repentance leads us back to the ideal human existence—God's sacred creation—through increased pleasure, just as we are commanded to celebrate the sanctity of Shabbat and Rosh Hashanah with physical pleasures, "for the lack of enjoyment is sin."[65]

While Salanter and most Mussar teachers educated their students to fear God and punishment in hell so as to constrain their powerful desires for pleasure with visceral images of pain, Finkel taught them to feel gratitude and love in response to God's acts of lovingkindness.[66] Yet, according to Brown, the disciples of Finkel at Slabodka did not follow in his footsteps. For the most part they reinforced pessimism about human nature, fear-based pedagogy, and ascetic self-denial, as did Salanter's original teachings of Mussar.[67]

Mussar's Apathy to Wife and Family

The fact that Mussar education suppressed a male's sexual desires is not surprising. After all, with the prominent exception of Slabodka's Finkel, Mussar teachers, wary of human nature, devised cunning stratagems to conquer desire and break bad habits. Yet it is shocking that Salanter and all his students, who prioritized love of one's fellow and meticulous stringency in ethical behavior beyond anything preached by earlier forms of *mussar* pietism, were resoundingly silent about—and, as such, indifferent to—the natural love of family and the moral and halakhic obligations to one's wife. While the Talmudic mitzvah to love and honor one's wife was well-known to any yeshiva student, Etkes, the great historian of Mussar, confesses that he never found any classical Mussar text treating the moral and emotional responsibilities to one's spouse.[68] "That . . . is particularly surprising in that Salanter and his disciples emphasized and deepened the demand for morality in human relations. Did that imply alienation from one's wife?"[69] "Perhaps so," Claussen concurs, observing that Simhah Zissel Ziv of Kelm "had relatively little interest in real-life women, and he probably saw women as inferior and as (potentially erotic) distractions from the male world."[70] The same is apparently true for Finkel, who with all his praise for the divine gifts of sensual pleasures and moral sensitivity, practiced self-denial to break his will and desire and ignored his wife, who had to support herself and their children, and whom he visited only on holidays.[71]

Why this apparent lacuna in Mussar? Although an argument grounded on the silence of sources is never fully reliable, it appears that the traditional schools of Mussar, with the possible exception of Slabodka, took a stringent view of marital intimacy due to their ascetic psychology that eschewed humanity's animal instincts, including sexuality.[72] While Salanter did not demonize the body or material existence as a metaphysical evil, as Lurianic kabbalists and Hasidim often did, he psychologized bodily impulses and stigmatized their tendency to degrade human character and distract from Torah study.[73] The Talmudic sage Rav's joyful lovemaking with his wife as legislated by Maimonides cannot plausibly be central to Mussar's educational approach. Salanter identifies the soul's innate desire for pleasure with the evil impulse, and he deems the sensuality of the self and the corporeal attractions of the world as the major obstacles to ethical ascent.[74] By extension, if a husband were to cultivate his desire for pleasure in performing marital duties and a romantic attachment to his wife, then he would undermine his spiritual quest and descend to the level of animality.[75]

Shifting Sands of Mussar: Wolbe's Yoke of Marriage and North America's Revival of Mussar

In the mid-twentieth century in Israel, and now in the early twenty-first century in North America, Mussar has undergone significant changes, especially in relation to its ethos of marital relations and its expansion beyond Orthodox practioners to a general public interested in mindfulness and character development. In the final section of this chapter we examine briefly Rav Shlomo Wolbe's Mussar guidance for Haredi Litvak newlyweds in Israel (1970s to 2000), and then mention briefly the non-Orthodox revival of Mussar in North America exemplified by Ira Stone's contemporary work on loving detachment as a trait useful for refining healthy relationships of sexual intimacy. Thus we hope to whet the reader's curiosity for this emergent Mussar movement, which is taking new forms and appealing to new audiences.

In the 1970s, Rav Shlomo Wolbe (1914–2005), one of the greatest Mussar teachers of the post-Holocaust period in Israel, pioneered in offering marital preparation talks for yeshiva students and their wives. While Wolbe's guidance for sexual intimacy on the wedding night was reserved for private oral conversations (whose content is undocumented), his Mussar talks about how a married couple can manage domestic emotional issues and adapt to each other's personality- and gender-based differences were recorded and distributed in manuals, separately, one for grooms and one for brides. Apparently, Wolbe's study of psychology in German universities (before becoming a Haredi Mussarnik in 1933) shaped his calling as a spiritual educator (*mashgiah*).

In responding to problematic influences from the West on the Haredi world, Wolbe humorously dispels the modern psychological myths prevalent even among yeshiva students about the foundations of a good marriage:

> Tell me, my dear groom, what do you think is the common basis on which you wish to build your home? Of course, [you will reply]: "Mutual understanding and love."
> Now allow me to be cruel . . . and excuse my sober approach that will explode your rosy images. . . . Reality is different![76]

Daily domestic disagreements, says Wolbe, show that mutual understanding among spouses is rare, and, in times of anger, disappointed love can become hate. Therefore, marital stability must rest on a different principle to which a husband ought to pledge himself: "I take it upon myself to bear *the yoke of my wife* in every situation and every time and I will never cast off that yoke from my neck."[77]

Similarly, the wife too must accept a yoke—the "yoke of household and the yoke of its financial support," since uniquely in history since World War II, Providence has merited the Litvak wife with the religious calling to provide monetarily for her husband and family and to enable him to devote full-time study to Talmud even after marriage.[78]

Wolbe's theory of the double yoke of marriage appears in his witty advice to a groom about to be married, based on a pun on the verb "to marry" (*nosei*), which also means "to carry a yoke" (*nosei ol*):

> Occasionally, young men ask me what they should be thinking about on their wedding day. This is what I suggest to them: When standing beneath the huppah (marriage canopy), they should undertake to bear the yoke of responsibility for their wives in every situation, and to never relieve themselves of this yoke. As the midrash taught: "*It is good for a man to bear a yoke in his youth* (Lam. 3:27)—this is the yoke of (caring for) a wife" (*Lamentations Rabbah* 3:24).
>
> In the Holy Language [Hebrew], we refer to someone who is getting married as a "*nosei isha*"—literally, one who is "carrying" a woman. This is an outstanding expression! For that is exactly what he must do—carry his wife, caring for her for all of the days of his life.[79]

Marital problems are unavoidable, warns Wolbe: "The two of you are human beings, not angels. . . . Isn't there enough explosive matter in every house—irritating, nerve wracking and generating despair—to explode, God forbid?"[80] And these tensions are exacerbated by the gender gap between traits, experiences, interests, and values of yeshiva-educated men and their wives:

> When she puts on a dress, she expects a compliment; a scarf, that he should like it. *But he does not see it at all and he does not care* at all whether it is blue or green, whether appropriate for her or not; then she is disappointed. She makes lunch for him and makes an effort to make it to his taste, but he just swallows the food and barely recalls what he ate. . . . Again she is disappointed. . . . From these little domes-

tic things grow alienation and separation and everyone lives in his own world, may God protect us!

The yeshiva student may expect his wife to be his *hevruta* study partner even if she doesn't know Talmud. . . . But the content of a woman's life is the home. No man can understand how those minor things can offer satisfaction. But that is the point: *Understand the absolute difference between a husband and his wife!* . . . Over time a couple discovers in each other things that are completely foreign, senseless . . . and irritating! One cannot change them, so one must learn to accept them and tolerate them—and that is *the yoke of the wife!*[81]

Wolbe urges husbands to conduct frequent conversations with their wives about their daily activities in order to "constantly pay attention," show sensitivity, and honor their wives (see chapter 9). Further, spouses must show appreciation for their differing vocations, namely Talmud study for men and housework for women.[82] Nevertheless, Wolbe does not have any illusions that the key to shalom bayit (domestic accord) is mutual understanding, romantic expressions of love, exchanges of compliments, or joint study of Torah. Rather, most important to marital peace are honest, realistic, and rational problem-solving conversations:

> Frequent conversation, especially in the first year of marriage, the year of adaptation and unification, is beneficial. [Wife and husband] should both accustom themselves to discuss together every problem and together to find a plan and a solution.[83]

Wolbe, however, sternly cautions the husband and especially the wife: "Never under any circumstances . . . discuss intimate issues between [you] with anyone else"—especially not with one's mother.[84]

When there are tensions, neither should get angry, shout, or bully. If the wife feels anger because the husband is apathetic to her efforts to please him or manage the household, she is to "talk to him . . . and bring him to admit that he behaved improperly."[85] In response, the husband should not argue back or fall silent but "examine himself critically to see if she is right. If so, he should request forgiveness sincerely and promise to be more careful in the future."[86]

Wolbe also offers guidance on spousal relations in light of changes in the status of women due to the contemporary division of labor. He assumes that the man is the master of the household and "the woman's nature is to want to be subordinate to her husband."[87] But, a husband must accommodate himself to a new social reality in which a woman is more independent, more educated, more self-confident, more spiritual, and often the main breadwinner.[88] Therefore, a husband ought not to expect a modern woman to obey him without her being persuaded rationally.[89] The independence of women, he warns, may also threaten the mental health of yeshiva students, since "young men in the Haredi world often feel inferior" to accomplished women like their wives who work outside the home. So men must make every effort to maintain their status as heads of the house, and trust that their wives will respect them—as long as they apply themselves seriously to their studies.[90]

In the light of the wife's intuitive knowledge of human relations, Wolbe tasks her to be the initiative-taking "architect" of a couple's married life, as its says, *The wisdom of women builds her house* (Prov. 14:1). He counsels wives: "A sign of maturity is to accept your partner as he is with his virtues and deficiencies and to behave with patience and sober perspicacity and, over time, to help him overcome his weaknesses. That is how you build a house!"[91]

NORTH AMERICA'S REVIVAL OF MUSSAR: CLAUSSEN ON GENDER JUSTICE, STONE ON LOVING DETACHMENT

In American ultra-Orthodox yeshivot, Mussar education about marital intimacy has apparently evolved (though it is difficult to corroborate new trends without documentary evidence). A former student of a contemporary Slabodka Mussar yeshiva in the United States (1990s) informed me that he sensed that "the content and tone of communications" about marital intimacy "has radically changed over the past century in the yeshiva world":

> [Before my wedding] my rebbeim [rabbis] talked to me one-on-one openly and directly about marital relations, stressing its importance, its beauty and holiness and how important it is for intimacy and shalom bayit. My teachers stressed setting the mood to evoke sexual desire and sharing physical pleasure (i.e., foreplay) and intimacy other than intercourse. When I asked my Rosh Yeshiva about a certain line written in the Shulhan Arukh which spoke about marital relations just as a means to have children, he told me to ignore it.[92]

Ignoring the stringent rulings on marital intimacy from Karo's Shulkhan Arukh is part of a general shift in the Litvak world, as we will see (chapters 9–11).

Outside the Haredi Mussar yeshiva, in the twenty-first century a new school of Mussar is being adapted and promoted as a spiritual practice primarily for non-Orthodox North American Jews. The eclectic leaders of the new Mussar movement include rabbis Avi Fertig (Orthodox), Ira Stone and Geoffrey Claussen (Conservative), as well as the anthropologist Alan Morinis. The Musar Institute founded by Morinis (1999) explains its approach in ways that echo New Age spirituality as well as Freudian psychoanalysis:

> Musar is a path of contemplative practices and exercises that have evolved over the past thousand years to help an individual soul to pinpoint and then to break through the barriers that surround and obstruct the flow of inner light in our lives. . . .
>
> The roots of all of our thoughts and actions can be traced to the depths of the soul, beyond the reach of the light of consciousness,

and so the methods Musar provides include meditations, guided contemplations, exercises and chants that are all intended to penetrate down to the darkness of the subconscious, to bring about change right at the root of our nature.[93]

Recently Stone and Claussen have begun to develop Mussar-inspired approaches to "issues of intimacy, sexuality and marital fidelity."[94] Reflecting on a significant difference in method between Salanter's classic Mussar and its contemporary non-Orthodox practitioners, Claussen writes about his intention to develop a program for gender justice employing Mussar's penchant for self-criticism:

> While the leaders of the Musar movement encouraged moral scrutiny of the self, they discouraged moral scrutiny of the traditions that they viewed as authoritative and divine. Today's non-Orthodox revival of the Musar movement can do better, encouraging us to also challenge unjust traditions. Given the historical injustices regarding sex and gender, attention to justice (*tzedek*) is an especially important component of contemporary Musar practice—inspiring us to ensure justice in our own sexual lives, and also to think critically about the unjust patriarchal traditions that so often dominate our world.[95]

In his book entitled *Cultivating the Soul*, Stone, the founder of the Center for Contemporary Mussar (2017), addresses a defect in intimate relationships through the prism of Mussar training. Characteristically, he begins with a careful observation of moral vice: "In all of our intimate relationships, it is easy to fall prey to projecting our own needs upon the other instead of seeing them as separate, complete individuals."[96]

To address such egocentricism, Stone chooses surprisingly to revive the traditional pietist *middah* (character trait) called *prishut*, which usually means turning away from this-worldly concerns, in general, and abstinence from sexual contact with one's wife, in particular. Abstracting from its classical ascetic usage, Stone redefines *prishut*: "The practice of *prishut* requires approaching those closest to us with loving detachment—a mindful separation from considering the other in light of our own needs and desires."[97]

Stone's interpretation is inspired by the Enlightenment rabbi Menachem Mendel Lefin (Levin) of Satanov (Ukraine, 1749–1826), whose 1809 book, *Heshbon HaNefesh* (Making an introspective moral accounting of one's character), employs methods for self-improvement borrowed from Benjamin Franklin's *Autobiography* (1793) that later influenced Israel Salanter, as mentioned above. Lefin defines *prishut* (separation/abstinence) in terms of a mindfulness technique to control sexually polluted thoughts, so that one may engage in marital intimacy without being overwhelmed by selfish libidinal passions: "Strengthen yourself so that you can stop lewd thoughts. Draw close to your spouse only when your mind is free, occupied only with thoughts of fulfilling your conjugal duties or procreating."[98]

As we shall see, the Litvak Revolution repudiated precisely that passionless instrumental approach to one's wife and sought instead to enhance passionate mutual desire, joy, and unity between man and woman. Yet Stone wants to develop the virtue of critical, rational distance, which he extracts from Lefin's ideal of ascetic detachment from the world. Stone considers critical detachment a necessary trait for marital intimacy, which he names "loving detachment." In considering sexually charged relations, Stone avers, we as moral persons ought to "tak[e] responsibility for our thoughts . . . understand[ing] that others are impacted by our thoughts, even when they are unexpressed."[99] To separate our self-centered erotic desires from our respect and concern for our partner, we need to cultivate loving detachment: "When we attain radical disinterestedness [i.e., selflessness rather than self-seeking] in any relationship, we . . . are fulfilled by service to the other. . . . The soul of such a person now holds both self and other."[100]

Following his classical *mussar* forebears, Stone views *prishut*, or "radical disinterestedness," as a path to holiness that connects to *kiddushin* (marital sanctification). As long as sex is not characterized by an overwhelming, passionate rush to orgasm, but by mindful self-control that respects the body, emotions, and integrity of one's partner, it is a sacred relationship: "Treating each human being through the lens of holiness involves respecting clear boundaries in our relationships."[101]

Conclusion: Paradigm Shift from Mussar's Apathy to Litvak Intimacy

Both Hasidim and Mitnagdim, advocates of Eastern European movements of religious revival (late 18th century and 19th century), emerged from a common pool of eight hundred years of *mussar* (pietist ethical training) beginning in Sufi Muslim Spain (11th century).[102] The original impetus of old-style *mussar* and Lurianic practice influenced its intellectual heirs to strive for deeply ascetic male sanctity that turned their hearts, minds, and bodies away from the mundane world and away from sexuality, and hence away from their wives and families. In the nineteenth century, Litvak mussar was transformed by Israel Salanter and his diverse, enthusiastic disciples who inspired the students of many Litvak yeshivot to embrace a new-style, modernized Mussar tradition for religious/spiritual character education. The Vilna Gaon and modern Mussar taught an intentionally cruel apathy to family in order to systematically uproot the natural feeling of affection between husband and wife and father and child, "to break one's nature."

In the last seventy years, however, there has been a paradigm shift in the Litvak world of yeshivot as couple love and shalom bayit became more central pillars of Litvak Haredi efforts to strengthen the family. After World War II, the greatest Haredi champions of an educational campaign for teaching yeshiva students about the mitzvah and the art of passionate loving relations with their wives have been, as we mentioned, Rav Isaac Sher and Rav Yaakov Kanievsky, two heads of Mussar yeshivot, and above all the Hazon Ish, who repudiated Mussar education altogether. How did that radical transformation in their attitudes emerge from the Mussar movement?

We may speculate that Sher, a disciple of Slabodka's Finkel, who was also his father-in-law, extended Finkel's unusually positive attitude to physical pleasures (though Finkel's writings never mention marital joy and sexual union). Further, Sher came to draw deeply on kabbalist sources such as *The Holy Letter* and the Zohar that celebrate sexual union as a mystical experience enhancing sanctity (see chapter 5). This is all the more notable since Salanter and most of his disciples famously avoided employing mystical texts in Mussar.

For his part, Rav Yaakov Kanievsky, a disciple of Yosef Hurwitz of Navaredok, testifies retrospectively that "I never got involved [with Mussar] on a regular basis."[103] The strongest influence on Kanievsky's deviation from Mussar was his older brother-in-law, the Hazon Ish, who criticized Navaredok Mussar in particular for overemphasizing in its sermons the attribute of fear (*yirah*) and especially for promulgating bizarre behaviors aimed to break one's pride.[104] Such practices detracted from the unceasing study of Talmud modeled by the Gaon of Vilna. To the Hazon Ish, the yoke of constant Torah study and the meticulous observance of halakhah (*dikduk ha-mitzvot*) taught fear and submission to God and control of desires much better than Mussar's obsession with breaking one's nature.[105]

What is more, the Hazon Ish rejected Mussar's radical condemnation of self-love, honor, and pleasure. To him, these tendencies are necessary components in the human organism, and to negate their place in the psyche is to undermine human existence. Rather, with greater wisdom one will discover, without the need to incite fear of punishment as Mussar does, that true honor is humility and true spiritual happiness transcends instinctual drives. The Hazon Ish was relatively optimistic about the ability to use reason to dissipate anger and desire without having to break one's nature.[106]

Chaim Grade offers additional insight into the Hazon Ish's critique of Mussar. In his novel *The Yeshiva*, Grade portrays with great historical accuracy and empathy the Hazon Ish, his own teacher in real life. In the novel the Hazon Ish's literary stand-in reprimands Tzemah Atlas, who is the literary character representing the Navaredok Mussarnik, by mounting a blistering attack on the failure of Mussar education to guide its yeshiva students' spiritual life when they mature and engage in life outside the yeshiva:

> The light of the Torah, which illuminates one's youthful years in the yeshiva, must also illuminate for him afterward in the store between the barrels of salted fish and the non-Jewish villagers. . . . The little candle standing before his Talmud folio at night will give him light for many years thereafter, when his [Mussarnik] friends who thundered through the world have long since died down and flickered out.[107]

As we will see (chapter 9), as a result of their deep critique of the marital asceticism of classical Mussar and of Gur's Hasidism, these three Litvak scholars launched in the 1950s a revolution in theory and practice: a radical reassessment of marital intimacy as a mitzvah, a worthy natural desire, and a pious path to higher levels of sanctity. Their "revolution," however, was never proclaimed as such. They never objected explicitly to the ethos of the Vilna Gaon, which preaches breaking of one's nature and extols apathy toward one's family. They never adopted modernity's cult of romantic love nor did they elevate the pursuit of marital intimacy above total devotion of men's minds to Talmud Torah. Still, as we shall see, one can read between the lines of their pastoral letters and their students' how-to books about marital love a profoundly different religious anthropology than that of the ascetic movements of Hasidism and Mussar.

Devotion and Desire 9

LITVAK REVOLUTION EQUATES
MARITAL INTIMACY WITH TRUE PIETY

Desire itself is sanctified from its impurity when it brings them together to become one flesh. It is as important an act as prayers and sacrifices, and the fire of desire between man and woman is similar to the fire on the altar over which the Shekhinah dwells.

—RAV ISAAC SHER, *Kedushat Yisra'el*, 12

Introduction

In the mid-twentieth century, three major Litvak leaders of the Ashkenazi Haredi world in Israel—all important heirs of the original Mitnagdim, who revered the Vilna Gaon and two of whom learned Mussar in their yeshivot before World War II—became surprisingly dedicated proponents of loving communication and sexually satisfying marital relations. In the 1950s and 1960s, the Hazon Ish, Rav Avraham Isaiah Karelitz (1878–1953); his brother-in-law and closest disciple, the Steipler rav, Yaacov Kanievsky (1899–1985); and Rav Isaac Sher (1881–1952) all issued pastoral letters promoting the sanctity of marital intimacy to counteract Gur Hasidism's militant spiritual ideology of marital asceticism, its restrictive Ordinances of Kedushah (1948), and its heroically self-denying piety, which had begun winning adherents even among Litvak students.[1]

These Litvak religious leaders began an unprecedented educational campaign to enhance the sanctity of conjugal intimacy, which can be understood as a response, generally speaking, to the drastic communal crisis shared by both Litvak and Hasidic Haredim after the Holocaust. The Nazis had destroyed traditional Eastern

European Ashkenazi Judaism's core institutions, murdered its spiritual leaders, and decimated its observant populations. Whether emigrating to Israel or the United States, ultra-Orthodox Jewry committed itself to revive what was now called Haredi Judaism in the image of their martyred forebears. Adherents zealously rejected modernity as a threat not only because of its atheism and secularity but because of its sexual promiscuity. Pejoratively, Haredim called non-Orthodox Jews *hofshiim*, "those who are liberated," assuming that the chief attraction of freedom was instinctual license. To defend their flock from illicit thoughts and actions, Haredim constructed self-imposed enclaves that enforced increasingly strict segregation of the sexes in schools, synagogues, transportation, and even at home. To commemorate the memory of their teachers and families martyred in the Holocaust, Ashkenazi Haredim of all sorts prioritized the rebuilding of institutions of Talmud study and ultra-Orthodox (*frum*) families with high reproductive rates in order to replenish the community's membership and retain their religious loyalty. Amazingly, the 1950s saw a revolution in the structure of the ultra-Orthodox community: The students in yeshiva became more knowledgeable and stringent than their Eastern European–born parents, and their wives worked outside the homes and supported husbands who remained for many years or even a lifetime in the yeshiva. The cloistered community in each yeshiva denigrated the practical concern with making a living. The rabbinic leadership of the yeshivas, and no longer the wealthiest Jews of the community, took over the political leadership of the Haredim.[2]

While strictly upholding these sacred policies of gender segregation, these three pioneering Litvak scholars publicly promoted, for the first time, the crucial role of emotional and sexual intimacy within matrimony as a bulwark of the Haredi family and as a path to kedushah. For their part, as Haredi religious leaders who are vehement critics of modern society, Karelitz, Kanievsky, and Sher would not, of course, have regarded their holy letters circulated among their students as proclamations of "sexual liberation." Their byword was not liberation but obligation. Their ultimate aim was not sexual satisfaction but the sanctity of spousal love. Nor would they have seen themselves as radicals or innovators, so they referenced classical texts of the Talmudic and medieval period to support their teachings.

Of these leaders the Hazon Ish was resolutely radical both in his critique of Israeli political leaders like Prime Minister Ben-Gurion and those rabbis who sought accommodation with Israeli secular society. He was also outspoken in his dissent from the Litvak Mussar traditions and the Brisker method of Talmud study at Volozhin as well as from ascetic Hasidic religious practice, as described above (see chapters 7 and 8). For example, the Hazon Ish promoted religious extremism as an ideal and rebuffed those Orthodox rabbis who sought to accommodate halakhah to modern values. Moreover, when in 1943 the Israeli chief rabbinate enacted a legal reform (*takkanah*) to Talmudic law that recognized daughters as equal heirs with sons to their father's estates, the Hazon Ish insisted that this legislation was invalid. He accused such rabbis of advancing gender equality by issuing permissive rulings due to "weakness [of faith]" and accused them of "capitulating to the heretics and taking pleasure in the heretics' approval that these rabbis are not fanatic."[3]

Further, the Hazon Ish criticized the style of Talmudic study in the Litvak yeshiva associated with innovation (*hiddush*) that encouraged intellectual creativity and abstract conceptualization, which was introduced by J. B. Soloveitchik's grandfather Reb Haim Brisker (Lithuania, 1853–1918). The Hazon Ish declared: "*Hiddush* is alien to my nature."[4] According to the intellectual historian Lawrence Kaplan, the Hazon Ish's rationale for the rejection of the Brisker method of *hiddush* was the fear that even the Litvaks have "perhaps unwittingly absorbed many of modernity's values, in particular the value of self-affirmation: self-expression, autonomy, and personal creativity."[5] While making room in the halakhah for the mitzvah of making one's wife happy, the Hazon Ish still viewed halakhic practice in general as a method for suppressing "natural character traits and inborn tendencies."[6] Nevertheless, the Hazon Ish was most innovative, especially for his place and time, in extrapolating on the Biblical mitzvah of making one's wife happy, so that the husband is commanded to engage in affectionate interpersonal communication with his wife.

This chapter explores the religious ideologies of the Hazon Ish, Kanievsky, and Sher in the context of the ever-evolving intellectual history of Jewish marital ethics. In turn, it examines their three pastoral letters, each one composed for their married yeshiva students. The order of their treatment in this chapter, however, is not strictly chronological. The Hazon Ish and Sher probably issued their letters in the same years (1950–52) at the end of their lives, though the letters lack known publication dates. We begin with the Hazon Ish because he is the most famous and influential of these leaders. His pastoral letter is the shortest, but scholars have written most about his personal biography, which illuminates his views on marital intimacy. Next, Kanievsky's somewhat longer and later holy letter (sometime in the 1960s) is examined, because, as the much younger brother-in-law and disciple of the Hazon Ish, he was most directly influenced by the Hazon Ish's positions. Last, but most innovative on marital intimacy, is Sher, who was not an influential leader of the broader Haredi community but a venerated Mussar educator. Unlike the Hazon Ish and Kanievsky, as a full-time spiritual educator (*mashgiah mussar*) he devoted significant time and effort to preparing young Haredi Litvak grooms for marriage. Understandably his pastoral letter on holy matrimony is much longer, more systematic in its conceptual framework, and surprisingly suffused with kabbalist rhetoric about the sanctity of love.

Hazon Ish's *Holy Letter*:
Championing Marital Conversation

Notably, the life experiences of Avraham Isaiah Karelitz, the Hazon Ish, would not appear to be conducive to his becoming a public champion promoting marital intimacy among yeshiva students. Uniquely, he never studied or taught in yeshiva, and his own marriage was reported to be extremely unhappy.

BIOGRAPHY OF THE HAZON ISH

Born in Kosov in Belarus (1878), Karelitz chose to study at home and never took an official job as a rabbi, even after he made aliyah in 1933. Nevertheless, from 1942 he became a Haredi *posek*, issuing important legal responsa, and from 1948 to 1953, a political leader who led the Haredi community's successful campaign against Prime Minister David Ben-Gurion's proposed legislation to draft ultra-Orthodox women. Ultimately, he also won an exemption for draft-age men from the Israeli army for as long as they studied full-time in the yeshiva.[7]

In 1906, when the Hazon Ish was twenty-seven, he was engaged, sight unseen, to the daughter of a businessman, but under false pretenses. Her father never provided the dowry as promised, and she turned out to be twenty years older than her husband-to-be. Nonetheless, and despite their incompatibility—she was uneducated, extroverted, and reportedly loudmouthed, while he was described as learned, gentle, reclusive, and silent—the Hazon Ish chose to protect her dignity and continue with the marriage. They were apparently not happy together and did not have children, but, as agreed, she ran the store so he could study at home.[8] When, as an elderly woman, her physical and mental state deteriorated, the Hazon Ish protected her honor. She burned the food, and he had

to pick out the unburned morsels, "yet he never embarrassed her."[9]
When she angrily and publicly insulted her husband in the company
of guests at the table, he never interrupted her; instead, he whispered
to his guests: "She is bitter, one must talk to her and cheer her up."[10]

THE HAZON ISH'S HOLY LETTER

In spite of his own difficult marriage, the Hazon Ish ruled that it
is the husband's obligation to attend to the emotional needs of
his wife. His unpublished Holy Letter (ca. 1950–52), bearing the
same title as that of the medieval *Holy Letter* (13th century), called
upon yeshiva students to cultivate his ideal of a ben Torah, the
noble Torah scholar whose exemplary character should be manifest in gentleness (*adinut*) and gentility (*Edelkeit*), especially in
one's relationship with one's spouse.[11] Without saying so, in effect
he repudiated the Vilna Gaon's mandate to ignore one's wife and
cultivate the virtue of cruel indifference to her needs. Rather, the
Hazon Ish understood that making the wife happy, as the Torah
itself prescribes, refers to emotional closeness as well as sexual satisfaction. Refuting the rebbes of Gur and Slonim, he affirmed the
contemporary validity of the Biblical mitzvah to devote the whole
first year of marriage to making one's wife happy:

> [During the first year of marriage] the mitzvah that *he shall be exempt
> from any obligation to be away from home* [such as military service],
> *and shall make his wife whom he has taken* [in marriage] *happy* (Deut.
> 24:5) is an obligation [not just a permitted exemption].
>
> How is he to make her happy? Her nature is to find pleasure in
> the way she finds favor in his eyes and to him her eyes are directed
> [expectantly]. Therefore he must make an effort to show her love and
> closeness in a plethora of conversation and words of appeasement.[12]

His letter was revolutionary in two ways. First, he revived an obscure and irrelevant Biblical law about exemption from military service in a national war and made it a mitzvah for each Haredi husband (though already exempt from the Israeli army) to devote his time to making his wife happy. Providing sexual satisfaction for her biological needs (*onah*) was no longer a mere legal clause in the marital agreement (see chapter 1). Now it was God's commandment. Second, the Hazon Ish offered a wholly original interpretation of making her happy (Deut. 24:5)—"to show her love and intimacy (*kiruv*) by *frequent conversation*"—and redefined talking to one's wife as a mitzvah.

BEHIND THE HAZON ISH'S ISSUANCE OF *THE HOLY LETTER*: HYPOTHESES

Why, asks the historian Benjamin Brown, is the Hazon Ish one of the first scholars to explicate and promote a detailed protocol for performing the mitzvah of making one's wife happy in the first year of marriage? Brown hypothesizes that his Holy Letter reflects his understanding of the natural gender relations threatened at that time both by the ascetic Ordinances of Kedushah of the Gerer rebbe (1948), by the egalitarian legislation (1951) of Ben-Gurion in general, and Ben-Gurion's proposal to draft all women, in particular (1948, 1951–53). In 1948, the Hazon Ish protested that drafting women "violently tears young women away from their mothers' bosoms and coerces them against their conscience." Thus the women would be "robbed of their pure and sacred character of pleasantness."[13] Brown identifies in the Hazon Ish's worldview what the West considers the romanticization of women's nature consistent with the Victorian "ideal woman" as naturally softer and gentler than men as well as more naturally ethical, aesthetic, and religious. Since women are seen as more vulnerable and passive, they are presumably less fit for leadership roles, and, therefore, according to Brown, the Hazon Ish wants to protect them from the aggressiveness of the world that characterizes men.[14]

At the same time, he wishes to replace the masculine ideal of conquest in war and in sex with a value uniquely his own—the *ben Torah*, the student of Torah, who possesses *Edelkeit* and *adinut*: gentility and gentleness, refinement and aristocratic self-restraint. Hence the Hazon Ish criticizes Haredi husbands who are insensitive to their wives' gentle nature and emotional vulnerability. He idealizes what today would be called the feminization of men, explaining that this will also make them better scholars: "One cannot enter the palace of wisdom without a sensitive eye, a sensitive heart, and a happy soul."[15]

To educate men to gentility, the Hazon Ish teaches that husbands should pay attention to "little things" in order to fill their wives' need to be loved. The yeshiva husband should "tell [his wife], whenever he leaves [the house], where he is going, and, upon his return [tell her] what he has done, and other little things and words of reinforcement—to make her heart happy."[16] A ben Torah must display noblesse oblige and *hesed* (lovingkindness), for he is obligated to please his wife, who is passive, housebound, and emotionally dependent on being loved and on finding favor in her husband's eyes.[17] Moreover, "the husband must strive to become one with his wife"—in heart, soul and body.[18]

Kanievsky's *The Holy Letter*: Marital Passion and Compassion

The Steipler rav, Yaacov Kanievsky, followed in the footsteps of his older brother-in-law, the Hazon Ish, by issuing his own Holy Letter in the 1960s.

In his letter, Kanievsky cautions against four sins prevalent in yeshiva marriages: false piety, failure to perform the mitzvah of onah properly, robbing one's wife of her contractual right to sexual pleasure, and causing her emotional anguish. Ironically, the impetus driving all these sins is the pious quest for greater sanctity through practicing more stringent self-denial than what is halakhically obligated. Of course Kanievsky agrees with the aspiration to higher kedushah and with the pietist's zealous aim to go beyond the halakhic minimum in the worship of God. He further concurs with all Haredim that one must struggle to maintain holiness by distancing oneself from sexual temptation in action and thought. Yet, like the Hazon Ish, he insists the pious pursuit of sanctity in marriage does *not* justify violating one's Biblical obligations to one's wife:

> It is true that to abstain from worldly pleasures is a great merit . . . but this does not apply unless a person fulfills his obligations as prescribed by the Torah . . . May God save us! . . .
>
> It is a criminal act of exploitation to deprive a woman of her right to sexual satisfaction, even if the husband intends by that deprivation to achieve a higher level of spirituality and asceticism. For he may not rob her [of her marital rights by minimizing the sexual contact to the barest act of physical intercourse], and [as Maimonides taught] he may not treat her as if she were a captive slave [who is raped at the will of her captor]. Such a man is comparable to a thief and a robber, as he steals from his wife that which he is obliged to give her.[19]

Furthermore, in the name of justice and compassion to his wife, the husband must engage in foreplay *before* intercourse and maintain his physical closeness *after* his own sexual climax is complete:

> The law of the Torah forbids intercourse between a husband and a wife in which the woman's desires are not gratified. He must arouse

her with hugs and kisses until she desires sexual union. Otherwise it is as if she is prey placed before a lion that tramples and devours [see TB *Pesahim* 49b].

Someone who grabs her and immediately has intercourse without developing emotional intimacy and then [after his climax] separates himself from her immediately may think of himself as angelic [in transcending his physicality]. . . . But actually while he is still satisfying his full desire and his urges are placated with complete pleasure, *his wife has not had any pleasure and she is hurting and ashamed*. . . . The truth is that inside him is buried pride. He thinks that he is on a high level, when he is only causing harm and being harmed. . . . No one can rise to higher levels [of sanctity] by means of impure and injurious sins.[20]

What is more, by engaging in perfunctory intercourse, the husband inflicts a psychological injury akin to shedding her blood:

This is *spilling the wife's blood*, for the main hope of a woman in her world is to have a loving husband. But when she sees that he is not like that, then [her pain] is almost life-threatening (*pikuah nefesh*). For she experiences overwhelming pain and anguish at being isolated [from him], as if she were a widow while her husband is still alive.[21]

To understand Kanievsky's strident accusation that causing emotional pain and embarrassment to one's wife or to one's husband (as we shall see) is akin metaphorically and comparable ethically to shedding blood, we must have recourse to the Talmudic sugya to which he obliquely refers: "Anyone who shames the face of one's fellow in public (*halbanat panim*) [literally, causes his fellow's face to blanche, to lose its red color and turn white] is like one who has shed blood" (TB *Baba Metzia* 58b). In contrast, in the English-speaking world, a similar phenomenon is called "making someone blush," which refers to one's face reddening in shame.

While the Talmud's primary exemplar of the crime of shaming someone is a public act causing a person to lose face in society, the Talmud applies the same moral condemnation to embarrassing one's wife, even in private. In discussing the ease with which one can hurt one's wife's feelings and cause her to cry, Rav says, as we saw above (see chapter 2): "A man must always be wary of causing pain to his wife, for her tears are ever-present and her sensitivity to emotional abuse is near at hand." The sugya concludes by citing Rabbi Helbo's advice about how to treat one's wife with sensitivity: "A person must always be careful to respect the honor of his wife, for the home is blessed only for the sake of the woman" (TB *Baba Metzia* 58b–59a). In his letter, Kanievsky innovatively applies the laws prohibiting shaming behavior to the wife's emotional vulnerability when her husband is obtuse to her needs for love and satisfaction. To avoid causing her embarrassment is equivalent to saving her life (*pikuah nefesh*), and to save a life trumps almost all other mitzvot in its relative importance.

What is more, Kanievsky defends the woman's right to a quality emotional relationship as much as he protects her legal claim to physiological satisfaction. For him, onah, often translated today as "marital intimacy," is not a euphemism for sex but an obligation to renew regularly a full-bodied emotional relationship of loving companionship.

While Kanievsky lashes out against self-centered yeshiva husbands, he also empathizes with their anxiety about achieving personal kedushah and reassures them that manifesting loving solicitude for their wives is compatible with attaining a higher sanctity for themselves:

When he physically embraces her for the sake of heaven out of *compassion*, so that she will not be in such pain and feel so miserable, then that behavior will not damage his own fear of heaven nor cast him into desire. Rather, it will elevate him in sanctity, and thereby he will perform the biblical mitzvah, *"follow in God's paths"* (Deut. 13:5), meaning "just as God is merciful, so you shall be merciful" (TB *Sotah* 14a). To be Godlike is not to transcend one's physicality and become angelic, but to imitate God's attributes, especially Divine compassion.[22]

Further, Kanievsky explains to pious husbands—as did the anonymous medieval kabbalist who authored the original *Holy Letter* (13th century, Spain)—that sexual intimacy does not pollute sanctity: "When one makes an effort to make her joyful during *zivug* (sexual union), both before and after [intercourse], this is *not* something disgusting, God forbid, but a mitzvah!"[23]

At the same time, Kanievsky does not wish to depict the marriage relationship as resting on the one-sided legal and ethical responsibility of the husband to perform the sex act for his wife's sake. Men too have legitimate, God-given, sexual and psychological needs. Just as the husband must concern himself with his wife's pleasure, so the wife must respond positively to her husband's desires. Kanievsky warns wives that when they refrain from intercourse, they too cause "very great pain to their husbands, which is almost like bloodshed, and the husbands will become very bitter."[24]

KANIEVSKY'S GRATEFUL LOVE VERSUS ROMANTIC LOVE

In attempting to shape his students' love lives, Kanievsky polemicizes against two alternative marital ideals, both of which he rejects. On the one hand, he is reacting against Hasidic ideologies of kedushah, whose practices of marital asceticism appeal to his students' aspirations for personal sanctity and self-sacrifice. On the other hand, he is also fearful of the opposite extreme—modernity's secular cult of promiscuity that tempts his yeshiva students to indulge in romantic passion. While the Bible and Talmud often speak frankly about the role of romantic love fueled at least in part by sexual desire (e.g., Jacob's love for Rachel), Kanievsky rejects romantic affection (*libido*) because, he believes, it is polluted with voluptuous craving. In Haredi courtship and mate selection the mystique of love and sexual attraction should play no role, though within marriage, the husband and wife are obligated to arouse and satisfy each other's erotic desires.

There is a fine but important distinction to be made here. For moderns, Kanievsky's positive orientation to sexual desire and emotional sensitivity to one's spouse is automatically identified with romantic love. Yet the rhetoric of the whole Haredi world repudiates that term as a pejorative epithet for the superficiality and licentiousness of modern ideals of love and as a failed basis for mate selection that leads, as they think, to high divorce rates in the West. Rabbi Hayyim Hirschensohn (early 20th century, New Jersey) says our Biblical father Jacob's love for Rachel was "not like love in the American tradition that comes before marriage and dies with [the onset of] marriage."[25] In the twenty-first century Rabbi Gamliel Rabinowitz, the head of the Sha'ar HaShamayim Yeshiva in Jerusalem, teaches that "love comes after marriage." (Any love before marriage, he says, "arises from sin. Generally there should be no room for 'feelings' before marriage."[26])

For Kanievsky, Haredim do not reject romance because they are ascetic about sexual desire or because sex should only be directed to procreation without emotional or erotic love. Rather, Haredim promote a mature love of "giving," not an immature romantic love of "taking" pleasure. The mature love of a married couple expresses itself in devoted gestures of caring, including providing satisfying intercourse, though it is "not motivated by desire at all, but by a good character trait (gratitude) that obligates us."[27] In that spirit, Kanievsky explicates the Talmudic maxim, "One should love his wife as [he loves] his body, and honor her more than his body" (TB *Yevamot* 62b):

It is clear that the Rabbis do not mean that you should love your wife motivated by the natural love of women, but rather . . . by the love of friendship (*ahavat haverim*), as it says, *for she is your friend, your covenantal wife* (Mal. 2:14). [Like same sex friends] the couple share common interests [and provide mutual benefits]. Each aids and is aided by the other. This is a love flowing from gratitude for goodness received (*hakarat ha-tov*).

One should imagine in his mind that if he had not found such a woman, he would have remained isolated and miserable (*galmud*). How much pain he would have had from his suffering! By having a wife, he has a settled life.[28]

The spontaneous cycle of giving and receiving goodness, expressed in concrete acts of meeting the spouse's needs, creates marital bonds of grateful love more stable than romantic love, sexual passion, or contractual duties.

INSPIRATION FROM DESSLER'S LOVE AS GIVING (*HESED*)

Apparently Kanievsky's dynamic of marital love was inspired by the popular Mussar teacher Rav Eliyahu Dessler (Kelm Yeshiva, Lithuania; Gateshead Yeshiva, UK; Ponevich Yeshiva, Israel, 1892–1953). The theology and ethics of Dessler, a great-grandson of Israel Salanter, originate in the imperative to imitate God, who is a gracious, unconditional giver (*mashpia*) to humanity:

When God created the human being, God made the human *a giver* and *a taker*. The power of giving is the supreme power among the traits of the Creator, who has mercy, who does good, and gives without receiving anything in exchange. [By contrast] the power of taking is the human desire to pull to oneself everything that comes within one's domain. This power is what people refer to as "self-love," and it is the source of all evil.[29]

In appreciation of God's divine blessings, one is expected to pass them forward to other human beings, not hoard them and exchange them solely for an adequate quid pro quo. Dessler teaches:

Joy is incomplete when one is alone, so one desires society. . . . That is why we want children—they fulfill the need to love them and to share goodness with them. Thus love and giving come together. . . . But what comes first? The love comes *from* the giving.[30]

Unfortunately, over time, marital relations often break down when the pattern of giving is disrupted. Dessler states: "Instead of giving [freely], as when they [husband and wife] first formed a connection between them, now they become takers and each one demands from the other to fulfill his/her obligations to which they committed themselves."[31] To avert this breakdown in the relationship, Kanievsky counsels, husbands should continue practicing grateful giving for what they have received, ever aware that without their wives' willingness to marry them, they would suffer as lonely bachelors.

Kanievsky thus applies Dessler's religious ideology of hesed, arising from the duty of gratitude, to the dynamic interchange of mutual emotional and physical support between spouses. Rather than denigrating bodily needs, human feelings, and the material world (as do spiritual ascetics), the divine character trait hesed reaffirms the dignity of biological and emotional human needs, and seeks to fulfill them.

For Kanievsky, these private acts of marital love contribute to *a world built on hesed* (lovingkindness) (Ps. 89:3), and Dessler's spiritual worldview has the religious power to compete with the self-denying kedushah of Gur. In contrast to so-called pious ascetics who seek to transcend their animal nature by minimizing pleasure, Kanievsky holds that one need not sacrifice one's own needs and pleasures to overcome selfishness. Giving or receiving, generosity or self-sacrifice are not zero-sum games of either-or. As Dessler taught Kanievsky, the ideal love should be viewed not as selfless, self-sacrificing altruism but as expansive sharing that encompasses both husband and wife in a broad, inclusive self:

> Whatever one gives to others is not lost to the giver, but it is an extension of self, for one feels one possesses a portion in that friend. That is the *devekut*—the glue of attraction between people that is called love. . . . For there is no gap between you and the other, for you are one.[32]

Giving to and receiving from another complements and completes a husband and wife, and the two become as one. As long as the two are in love, each one wants to give and cause pleasure to the other.[33] (See Ashlag's notion of being a giver, not an egocentric taker, in chapter 5).

Sher's Letter, *The Holiness of Israel*: Reviving Haredi Desire

The third Litvak ideologue of marital intimacy, Rav Isaac Sher (Israel, d. 1952), the head of a Slabodka Mussar yeshiva, issued *Kedushat Yisra'el* (The sanctity of the People of Israel), which is the most extensive, poetic, and mystical of the pastoral letters for married yeshiva students.

RAV SHER CONDEMNS PSEUDOPIETISTS

In *Kedushat Yisra'el* (ca. 1950–52), Sher explains:

> The world thinks that the mitzvah [of becoming holy] is only for the spiritual elite of each generation who can reach perfection, but this is a mistake! The Torah commands all Israel to be holy, and

the Rabbis identified that commandment with sexual union. . . .
Sanctity [in intercourse] is a matter of thought, and according to
each person's level of thought one can sanctify the act, so everyone
getting married is obligated to educate their minds regarding the
sanctity of thought. . . .

A husband may think of his wife as a heavenly angel [thus sanctifying his sex act] . . . or merely treat her as just another woman, as an
"other," as if she were a concubine who does not possess the image of
God [with whom conjugal relations descend to the level of animal
instincts lacking sanctity].[34]

While followers of Rabbi Eliezer perform the mitzvah of onah
as quickly as possible, because they understand sanctity as a call
for angelic purity that quashes natural desire, Sher urges yeshiva-
trained husbands to treat their wives as angels in the image of God
and therefore to honor them in a sexual union that imitates Rav in
joyful, passionate lovemaking (see chapters 2 and 3). Citing Rashi
and Nahmanides on the quality of onah required by the Torah (see
chapter 1), Sher derides the dutiful intercourse of those imitating
Rabbi Eliezer:

One who performs the mitzvah of onah merely to do his duty and be
done with it has not fulfilled the mitzvah as required by the Torah.
For the truth is that one who has intercourse without much desire
has violated [the prohibition] *he may not diminish her* [onah] (Exod.
21:10). . . . He has denied her a "time of lovemaking" (*et dodim*) . . .
and the pleasure of the physical intimacy of the husband's flesh that
his wife longs for . . . beyond the act [of copulation] itself.[35]

Like Kanievsky, Sher satirizes the would-be ascetics who mistreat
their wives in a misguided attempt to be "holier than thou":

I have heard that some who are God-fearing [Haredim] make themselves out to be pious men (*mit-hasdim*) [i.e., pseudo-Hasidim],

and make great preparations to fulfill this mitzvah for the sake of Heaven [alone] without any desire at all. The husband studies Torah and prays until midnight [on Shabbat night]. Then after midnight he comes home, wakes up his wife from her slumber, and prattles to her to placate her [so she will consent] to fulfill this mitzvah. As a result she permits him to do with her as he wishes for she knows from her mother how righteous people behave....

It is well-known that . . . she has no craving when she is deep in sleep and she is angry that her husband is disturbing her. He is doing with her whatever he wants, not what she wants. . . . Rashi explains that "he doesn't desire her very much and he has intercourse with her only to fulfill the obligatory mitzvah of onah or he persuades her to consent to intercourse when his heart is actually disgusted by her (TB *Niddah* 17a)."[36]

These so-called pious husbands are clueless about the damage they cause their wives and their offspring, Sher says:

So he performs his mitzvah as if he was compelled by a demon, and then immediately withdraws from her and flees from this impurity. He takes pride in his heart that he managed to fulfill this commandment without [an admixture of] the evil impulse and without the impurity of desire.

He later wonders why the sons he has produced in this way are wicked or stupid! The reason is that he has stumbled due to the false belief that the desire accompanying this mitzvah is very deplorable. . . . If he does not arouse his own desire with all his force to fulfill his wife's full craving, then his sons will become rebels and sinners [according to Rabbi Levi's nine causes of birth defects in TB *Nedarim* 20b; see chapter 3].[37]

In minimizing their sexual contact with their wives, these husbands are grossly insensitive to their wives' erotic needs. Sher lambasts a yeshiva student who withdraws from intercourse with his wife before she reaches her orgasm:

I told him he has *a moral duty and a legal obligation* to give her pleasure with all his might. How can he cause her such pain by withdrawing from her when she is aroused with the fire of desire to be attached to him with all her power? . . . Not only has he violated his duty of onah, he has tortured her. . . . *He should give himself over to her authority and tell her that she can do anything she wants with him.*[38]

What is more, these pseudopietists congratulate themselves on the decline of their own sexual vigor as they age, while, Sher observes, they fail to understand how denying their wives pleasure exacerbates marital discord:

> With the passage of years, when the passion of husbands has abated and love is gone, they begin to boast of their sanctity in [engaging in onah] as if "compelled by a demon." This is a total error which gives rise to numerous stumbling blocks: the wife loathes her so-called "righteous" husband and quarrels with him—about other problems, of course, since she is embarrassed to tell him what really distresses her and what she is really lacking.
>
> The result is the absence of harmony (*shalom bayit*) in the home, and the children are neglected, deprived of a good education due to the arguments. May God have mercy upon them![39]

REHABILITATING SEXUAL DESIRE AMONG HAREDIM

Lamenting that "the trait of love is not developed adequately among us [the Haredim],"[40] Sher promotes an educational campaign to redeem marriage by enhancing natural libido:

> Parents and teachers, who truly and painfully worry about the happiness of their seed, ought to teach their children and students . . . the mitzvah of igniting [the flame of love] and preparing nature [i.e., bodily desire] for the act of sanctity [onah] which is the essence of happiness in life—namely, to delight in the Lord and to sanctify

oneself in God's sanctity. . . . *For the core of sanctity is their union, which can only come about through powerful love between them, so that they become one in body and soul.*[41]

To maintain the powerful desire, which is the necessary "glue" for marital attachment (devekut) for the length of one's marriage, the couple must "behave toward one another all their lives" like the lovers in the Biblical Song of Songs who rededicate themselves to one another with the words, *I am to my beloved and my beloved is to me* (Song of Songs 6:3).[42]

> He must be like a groom and she like a bride all the days of their life. . . . and learn from Rav that in the mitzvah [of onah] a husband is to behave with levity with his wife, which is what she herself wants. It is as if he were a newlywed groom who had never had sex before, and so too she wants to be like a newlywed bride.[43]

Taking Rav as his model, Sher praises his playfulness and then turns Kahana's insulting reference to Rav's behavior—"It seems as if the mouth of [Rav] had never before tasted that dish!" (TB *Hagiga* 5b)—into a positive recommendation to husbands and wives to relive their honeymoon on every night of onah in their lives, hence he must behave "as if he were a newlywed groom who had never had sex before."

So too Sher offers practical advice to a couple about to renew marital intercourse after the menstruating wife and her husband have been forbidden to touch one another for approximately two weeks. On the night after she has purified herself by immersion in the mikveh:

> He should make this evening into a festive day (*yom tov*) and treat her with endearment as if this is the night of her marriage. . . . A couple would be wise to keep a notebook (*pinkas*) from their wedding celebration and to record all the words of love and compliments

they spoke to one another as loving companions from each day and night of the seven days of their marital festivities.

Then they should reread them on the [monthly] night of the immersion. They should also make an effort to add their own sweet and beautiful words, as it says, *Sweetness drops from your lips, my bride; honey and milk under your tongue* (Song of Songs 4:9, 11). Then [following the instructions of the German pietist Rabbi Elazar Hasid] on the night of immersion: "Make her happy, hug her, kiss her, sanctify yourself in marital intercourse . . . and delight in all sorts of expressions of affection, love, and desire."[44]

Before intercourse itself, Sher recommends recitation of a kabbalist prayer associated with *The Holy Letter* (13th century) for sexual vigor prior to sexual union:

May it be your will that the spirit of heroism emanate upon me to give my limbs and my body the courage and strength to perform the mitzvah of my onah each time. . . . So that my desire shall be accessible without fail or weakness from now and forever.[45]

In addition, Sher mentions a Talmudic recipe for organic Viagra: consuming garlic before Shabbat to multiply semen and strengthen one's sexual prowess.[46]

Ultimately, Sher says, the most important means of strengthening marital intimacy is loving communication. Repudiating Gur's Ordinances of Kedushah, he insists that one "must learn that it is a mitzvah to speak to one's wife with fabulous words of appeasement [and love]."[47] Sher teaches couples to speak to one another without shame, with words of love: "For love is natural, and it is a mitzvah to enhance and develop it properly."[48] He elucidates:

When the couple comes together, the husband ought to speak to his wife in order to convey not only "awe, piety, and chastity," but also tenderness, affection, and erotic love (*agavim*). . . . The husband must speak to his wife explicitly about her [physical] beauty such as her breasts, which are her glory. . . .

And she must respond to his words by praising his beauty manifest in all his limbs and his movements and by speaking—*with all her heart and all her soul* [adapted from Deut. 6:5]—of her love for him and of her yearning to become one with him. She takes pride before him that she is intelligent . . . and she thinks constantly about living a life of the mind (*sekhel*) in sanctity.[49]

While exchanging compliments about each other's beauty will stoke erotic desire, Sher is just as concerned that words of endearment and even physical affection characterize marital intimacy without intercourse. With unusual permissiveness, Sher rules: "Even when a man is forbidden to touch his wife during her menstrual period, he should visit or attend to her [not sexually but] with words that make her happy and give her pleasure."[50] Further,

When a woman longs affectionately for her husband who is about to go on a trip even when she is close to the onset of her period [when sexual relations are forbidden], the Rabbis permitted [the husband] to give her hugs and kisses. . . . Love is natural and it is a mitzvah to strengthen it . . . and never to ignore her when she craves it.[51]

To reinforce these sacred practices of endearment and arousal, Sher counsels "the husband together with his wife to study this letter many times to understand everything properly."[52]

CREATIVITY, UNIFICATION, AND LOVE

In *Kedushat Yisra'el* Sher identifies three dimensions of mutuality in the ideal of sexual union in marriage: (1) creativity, (2) unification, and (3) love.

1. Creativity expresses itself in the procreative duty

to create a human being upon whom God's Shekhinah dwells. It is the man's calling to arouse himself and his wife to this great act of creation by speaking to her as God spoke [in the Creation]: *Let us make the human being in our image, in our likeness* (Gen. 1:26).[53]

Learning the proper mindset of sexual union can, if successful, produce a child who will become a new Moses, but performing marital intercourse without sacred love "may, God forbid, bring into the world an evil person who is like a demon of destruction."[54] Therefore, both man and woman must approach this act with a sense of fateful responsibility.

2. Unification is the task of making man and woman physically and spiritually one, just as Adam and Eve became one flesh in the Garden of Eden. Citing the well-known Safed kabbalist Elijah de Vidas in *Reishit Hokhma* (1575), Sher explains the mystical significance of the halakhah that husband and wife must have intercourse in the nude so their bodies can attach to one another (devekut) in an unmediated fashion. In kissing there is also unmediated contact and mutuality. In the give-and-take of igniting one another's desire through direct contact, the divine *sefirot* of masculinity and femininity are conjoined without any separation:

[Unification flows] only from the force of desire that is called fire. . . . Therefore, he must ignite [in turn] the fire of desire in his wife and from her the husband will be ignited by that fire. That is the reason that kissing, which must precede sexual union, is the highest level of sanctity. . . . These holy thoughts one must root in one's heart and that of his wife, *for she too must know the sanctity of unification.*[55]

Surprisingly, Sher preaches a technique of mutual arousal that echoes the lyrics of the once controversial *Doors* song "Come on, baby, light my fire! Try to set the night on fire!" Inspired by kabbalist texts, Sher aims to integrate the call to ignite a fire of erotic passion between husband and wife into a spiritual search for kedushah.

3. Mutual love, says Sher, takes the form of altruistic caring for the needs and wants of one another; hence

> each one of the couple must forfeit their own will and make an effort to fulfill the desire of the other in order to be beloved to the other.... Through the love between husband and wife, one performs the mitzvah of *love your fellow as yourself* (Lev. 19:18).[56]

THE GARDEN OF EDEN AS A MODEL OF PURE AND SANCTIFIED SEX

Unlike many of his pessimistic predecessors in Mussar, Sher teaches yeshiva students to have confidence in their ability to combine sexuality and sanctity:

> After receiving the Torah at Mount Sinai, the holy people of Israel have the rational faculty to rule over their passion so that it becomes a means to attachment (devekut) and unification (yihud) [with one's spouse], and not an end in itself.[57]

Jews, he believes, can perform onah with the same purity as Adam and Eve in their pristine lovemaking *before* eating from the Tree of Knowledge.[58] Sher reports:

> The Rabbis say that God planted in the heart of Adam and Eve feelings of love and beauty. Then the Holy One [like the best man, *shushbin*, who arranges the wedding] braided her hair and brought her to Adam. He and she were happy with her beauty. . . . Even today at every wedding the Holy One is the true *shushbin*, making the couple happy.[59]

Sher avows that the feelings God planted in all of Israel are a "fire of desire comparable to the sacred fire on the altar, as long as the desire emerges from an [altruistic] love that wishes to cause satisfaction to the beloved."[60]

Conclusion

These twentieth-century Litvak Haredi scholars have had immense practical impact on the Litvak yeshiva world, if one is to judge from the popularity and variety of books and pamphlets about marital intimacy published and taught in the Haredi world. Today their influence continues to grow, thanks to the educational tracts of their disciples, who have propagated a halakhic art of loving, maintaining peace in the home (shalom bayit), and engaging in passionate marital relations (see chapters 10–11). Religiously, the most revolutionary contribution, especially by Sher, has been the reorientation of the understanding of kedushah within marriage away from *prishut* (ascetic withdrawal) and toward *zivug* (coupling), emotional love and intimacy, sacred passion, and spiritual union.

The Hazon Ish, the Steipler rav, and Rav Isaac Sher have thereby added a new chapter to the centuries-long battle against Hasidim. In so doing, they have also overturned the effects on marital intimacy of the pre-Hasidic pietism of a thousand years of ascetic *mussar* that inspired and dominated many of their Eastern European teachers.

Higher Purposes of Marriage 10

EDUCATION FOR LOVE, PEACE, AND SANCTITY

The Rabbis listed the nine major dimensions of failed intention in marriage, and all of them can be reduced to one dysfunction— separating the act of intercourse from the covenant of love between man and woman.

—RABBI RAFAEL MENAHEM SHLANGER, *Mishkan Yisrael*, 2:38

Introduction

In our day, the educational mission of the Hazon Ish and the Steipler rav, which is to promote a religious practice of marital love and communication among yeshiva-trained men, is being carried out by their students, rabbis Rafael Menahem Shlanger and Moshe Aharon Shuchatowitz. The intention of this chapter is to examine the detailed halakhic and pastoral works they composed in order to flesh out the revolutionary program implicit in the concise letters issued by their teachers. Employing Talmudic stories and personal anecdotes, Shlanger's *Mishkan Yisrael* (The Tabernacle of Israel, 1991) and Shuchatowitz's *Binyan HaBayit* (Building the home, 2003) offer commonsense marital advice justified by halakhic authority and legal argumentation. They reiterate their teachers' call for greater ethical sensitivity to the needs and rights of wives, and caution yeshiva students to refrain from spiritual asceticism in the conjugal bedroom. Their greatest intellectual and spiritual innovation, however, is formulating an inspirational religious ideology to motivate their practical program of marital intimacy. They, like

Sher fifty years earlier, promote a broad vision of married life whose higher purposes are love, peace, and sanctity in the world.

Shlanger and Shuchatowitz's educational strategy has two tiers: (1) the domestic microcosm of the home and (2) the macrocosm of society and beyond, of the divine cosmos.

First, by enhancing sexual and emotional bonds, they hope to countermand religious and social ills manifest in heightened domestic discord, abuse, and divorce in the Haredi community. According to Shuchatowitz, when asked to explain the "evil decree" that was causing such a high religious dropout rate among ultra-Orthodox children immediately after World War II, the Hazon Ish replied: "This is not a Heavenly decree, but a direct result of what it says in the Talmud *Nedarim* 20b," that lack of *shalom bayit* produces rebellious and sinful children.[1] Therefore, Rav Yosef Shalom Elyashiv (renowned Litvak *posek*, Jerusalem, 1910–2012) instructed Shuchatowitz to teach that Talmudic text to parents so they would know the depth of their responsibility for the "spiritual nature of their offspring" and how it "depends on the quality of the parents' relationship . . . for good or for bad."[2]

Like their teachers, Shlanger and Shuchatowitz insist that performing the mitzvah of marital intercourse ought not to be artificially separated from the qualitative emotional bonds characterizing the whole relationship. Thus a couple must sanctify itself positively both by performing marital duties with passionate love, as did the Talmudic sage Rav (see chapter 2), and by practicing the art of emotional communication on a daily basis, as prescribed by the Hazon Ish (see chapters 9 and 11).

Second, in seeking to repair the macrocosm of society, Shlanger and Shuchatowitz, who are inspired by a kabbalist worldview, teach that the couple's emotional health (shalom bayit) and degree of sexual desire contribute directly to the divine aims of cosmic peace and the indwelling of the Shekhinah that sanctifies the world.

Shuchatowitz: The Grave Sin of Rushed Sexual Performance

Shuchatowitz represents the rich heritage of oral teachings of the most illustrious Litvak scholars of the last fifty years. His personal teacher in New York, Rav Moshe Feinstein, encouraged him to make aliyah, and in Israel he studied with Rav Yaacov Kanievsky and Rav Eliezer Shach. When Rav Shlomo Zalman Auerbach commissioned him to teach about marital intimacy to yeshiva students, Shuchatowitz consulted closely with Rav Schneor Kotler (son of Rav Aharon Kotler, founder of the Litvak Yeshiva in Lakewood, New Jersey, 1918–82) and Rav Yosef Shalom Elyashiv.

Like Kanievsky and Sher, Shuchatowitz has found that many young yeshiva husbands firmly believe that they and their wives must restrain their sexual passions even in performing the mitzvah of *onah*. When he reports to them how much his exalted teachers valued robust erotic desire for onah, they are often shocked, because they had previously thought that perfunctory intercourse with their wives was acceptable, even halakhically commendable. They had believed their own piety would reach its peak if they succeeded in minimizing their own sexual arousal by rushing to ejaculation, as Rabbi Eliezer did, and then immediately withdrawing from physical contact. Since scholars are obligated to perform onah only once a week, preferably on Shabbat, and, according to Rabbi Eliezer, in the middle of the night, the students would delay their weekly marital intercourse until Friday at midnight. Often they were dead tired after a long week of study culminating in the traditional all-night study vigil Thursday night, but they were committed to performing onah at midnight and congratulated themselves on their exemplary selfless concern for their wives' sexual needs. Heroically overcoming their own physical exhaustion, they would fulfill their duty pro forma without any sexual arousal.[3]

In a vehement response to this state of affairs, Shuchatowitz instructs these yeshiva husbands to regard their rushed, sleep-deprived sexual performances as nothing better than grave spiritual and halakhic sins that may cause their offspring harm. He cites Rashi, who exposes the scandal of such so-called pious students: "As a result of sleeplessness the husband has no desire for his wife and therefore performs the mitzvah of onah perfunctorily or he tries to satisfy her when he actually [lacks any sexual attraction for her] and so he is disgusted by her."[4] Apparently, Rashi thinks that the physical act of intercourse is revolting when one is not aroused. Further, Rashi explains: "Even if she does manage to enjoy herself in onah [with her exhausted, disinterested husband], this act of intercourse cannot be regarded [as the fulfillment of the ideal marital union described in the Torah] as *the woman cleaving to the man [and becoming one flesh]* (Gen. 2:24)."[5] With sarcasm, Shuchatowitz paraphrases his students' amazement at hearing his rebuke: "Wonder of wonders! How could we have been so mistaken to think" that we were performing onah with such piety! In fact, we were doing not a mitzvah at all but "a heinous crime!"[6] To corroborate his message, Shuchatowitz cites his teacher Rav Elyashiv, who rules that such intercourse is "not a mitzvah, but a transgression."

What remedies may be proposed for sleepless husbands and listless onah? If necessary, yeshiva students should move their scheduled onah to a convenient weekday night when they are rested. Alternatively, Shuchatowitz recommends "going to sleep early" on Friday night immediately after dinner and then "getting up toward the middle of the night to perform the mitzvah" when both husband and wife are refreshed and capable of making love passionately.[7]

Shuchatowitz describes a dramatic run-in with a zealous teacher in the yeshiva who instructed his married students to strictly follow what Karo legislates in the Shulhan Arukh:

Engage in intercourse with fear and awe just as it says of Rabbi Eliezer ben Hyrcanus, who would only uncover [his or her] body one hand's breadth at a time and then cover it up again and who would behave as if he were being forced to perform intercourse against his will like one coerced by a demon.[8]

Incensed by this teacher's ascetic directives to his naive, newly married disciples, Shuchatowitz dragged the hapless, awestruck teacher before the head of the yeshiva, Rav Kanievsky himself. The Steipler rav interrogated the teacher as follows:

"When you do this act [of marital intercourse with your own wife] in fear and awe, *whom* do you fear?" The teacher answered: "I fear God, for intercourse involves the indwelling of the Shekhinah, so I do it with fear and awe."

Rav Steipler responded incredulously: "You are concerned with the indwelling of the Shekhinah?! In your house there is no Divine Presence (Shekhinah)! For we have learned that 'the Shekhinah does not dwell where there is no joy.'"[9]

The Rav continued: "If there is any 'fear and awe' in this act in your house, it is solely your wife's fear and awe before you. You are nothing but a lion that assaults and devours. Perhaps your children are even children of the nine defects in relationships with one's spouse."[10]

On halakhic, ethical, and pietist grounds, Kanievsky, as represented by Shuchatowitz, rebukes the pseudo-pious Talmud teacher for attempting to emulate Karo's pietist marital asceticism and accuses him of the sin of violating his wife's contractual needs and rights. Further, Kanievsky protests against the teacher's lack of the ethical sensitivity for one's wife expected of a Torah scholar. Instead, he ascribes to him the behavior characteristic of an uncouth ignoramus (*am ha-aretz*) who lords over his frightened wife like a ferocious lion consuming its prey. While the husband aspires to greater piety, in fact, by suppressing the joy of the mitzvah of onah, he expels the Divine Presence from his home.

The Scholar's *Onah*: Shuchatowitz versus Aviner

At first glance, Kanievsky and Shuchatowitz's halakhic stance on onah might be summarized as follows: "The great halakhic authorities decided that *in our era* one should *not* learn from the behavior of Rabbi Eliezer."[11] For example, Rav Elyashiv told Shlanger that if a husband were to imitate Rabbi Eliezer and engage in onah "as if compelled by a demon, then that woman would be regarded as one who was sexually coerced" (a victim of rape).[12] Still, the qualifier "in our era" suggests that in other eras the more pious strictures would be appropriate, whereas, unfortunately in our era people have weaker constitutions, or the temptation of sexual arousal is more acute, so that halakhic authorities have had to lower their standards. Therefore, their "leniency" in accommodating human weakness is *not* a principled repudiation of the ideal of Rabbi Eliezer's asceticism in favor of Rav's joyous onah.

Rephrasing the question, many authorities distinguish the requirements of onah not only by the era but by the class of scholars being addressed. In pursuing a higher register of sanctity, only the most spiritually elite students of Torah are expected to demand of themselves to emulate Rabbi Eliezer and obey Karo, whereas most yeshiva students and their wives in our era (which Haredim believe sorely lacks the great scholars and pietists of the previous generations of Eastern Europe) should be discouraged from "biting off more sanctity than they can chew." That is the view of Rav Shlomo Aviner, among many others, while Shuchatowitz holds that the ideal is Rav's model, even for the greatest Torah scholars of whatever class or era.

This disagreement between two contemporary scholars and popular yeshiva educators in Israel is noteworthy, because in other ways they share so much. Rav Shlomo Aviner of Jerusalem's Ateret Kohanim Yeshiva, who belongs to the Haredi-cum-Religious Zionist camp in Israel (Hardal), has pioneered in teaching and distributing psychologically sensitive guidance for marital intimacy (see his 1984 booklet *Etzem MeiAtzamai* discussed in chapter 4). Like Shuchatowitz, Aviner commends Rav's bedroom practices as the halakhic standard for average yeshiva students. Yet he is decidedly at odds with Shuchatowitz in that he expects a higher standard of erotic restraint and self-denial for those elite students and their wives truly capable of following in the footsteps of Rabbi Eliezer and Imma Shalom.

Aviner adopts a two-tiered approach that urges pious self-denial for the spiritual elite with their wives' consent and yet insists that the others—the average yeshiva couples—fulfill their duties to both the man's and the woman's sexual needs.[13] On the lower tier, Aviner acknowledges the necessity and primacy of sexual satisfaction for normal people "who struggle with their inclinations." He warns them *not* to try to practice ascetic onah with their spouses, as it destroys shalom bayit. His slogan about marriage is: "First life and afterward [ascetic] sanctity."[14]

> The couple must learn to live together in love, fraternity, affection, and friendship, including sexual union. . . . Living in love and fraternity is also a mitzvah, the mitzvah of love your neighbor. . . . On that basis—and *only* on that basis—may they construct [atop their marital house] higher stories of sanctity and purity.[15]

Yet, on the higher tier, for select couples ready for greater ascetic sanctity, Aviner encourages them that "the greater the man, the greater he should strive to be stringent."[16] While for run-of-the-mill yeshiva students intercourse during the week and even during daylight when they are fully awake is permitted, Aviner commends his elite to aspire on Friday night to achieve an ecstatic kabbalist intercourse "perform[ed] exactly at midnight," which will reveal "awesome secrets."[17]

While both Aviner and Shuchatowitz are permissive in bedroom ethics and insistent that loving companionship including sexual pleasure is a great mitzvah, their fundamental worldviews diverge. Aviner compromises, making allowances for the low capability of most yeshiva husbands only as a post facto concession (*di'avad*) for those who are "struggling with their libido and unable to extract themselves from its complications." He holds:

> One should not pressure a person [to engage in sacred ascetic practices] beyond his ability. Nevertheless, the purpose of service of God is to exert oneself as much as possible to sanctify oneself in accord with the sanctity of Israel. . . . One should not easily allow himself to lose sanctity but rather seek to increase it.[18]

Unlike Shuchatowitz, Aviner espouses the higher spiritual asceticism prescribed for the pious by Rabbi Eliezer, Yohanan ben D'havai, Maimonides, and especially Joseph Karo:

> My book, *Etzem MeiAtzamai*, is not designed to promote an ideology of hedonism based on the Torah, G-d forbid, but a guide for those in need of a permissive ruling. . . . The Rabbis "investigated human nature to its depth out of compassion for those who are broken (*m'kulkalim*)" so they provided some paths for leniencies according to the Torah. . . .
>
> While there is no prohibition of pleasure, the Torah has no ideal of desiring pleasure. . . . God does not hate the body. . . . Rather, the supreme ideal is to increase aristocratic restraint and sanctity.[19]

For Shuchatowitz, by contrast, there is no significant gap regarding onah between the intellectual and spiritual elite and the rank and file. His rabbinic masters, he assures us, the great Talmudic authorities

Rav Hisda and Rav and their heirs, all the way down to the Steipler rav, fully appreciated the positive role of their own desires and their spouses' needs in achieving sanctity. In response to the question, "Did the great scholars of Israel engage in loving their wives?" Shuchatowitz responds that "it is inconceivable that any great scholar did not love his wife!" Each one built up a domicile with "three stories of love: a loving bond, peaceful relations, and sexual acts motivated by love!"[20]

Marital Sexuality as the Synthesis of Nature and Spirituality

Shuchatowitz and Shlanger concur with the Haredi axiom that the pursuit of sanctity entails restrictions in the realm of sexual relations, as Rashi makes explicit in his Biblical commentary on the mitzvah *you shall be holy* (Lev. 19:2): "Separate yourselves from illicit sexual partners (*arayot*) and from transgression, for every place that you find a [proscriptive] fence, you find sanctity (kedushah)." Yet both agree with Maimonides that rabbinic Judaism already has enough mandatory prohibitions, so people should not take on more ascetic practices voluntarily. Both concur with Maimonides, who challenges self-denying pietists by quoting what the Jerusalem Talmud asks rhetorically: "Isn't it enough for you what the Torah prohibits, yet you wish to forbid more things on yourself?!" (TJ *Nedarim* 9). To prohibit more unnecessarily is to repudiate the goodness implicit in God's creation of nature. Therefore Shlanger objects to the ideology of ascetic kedushah that dichotomizes material and spiritual, desire and action, body and mind, wives and husbands. Instead, he champions the integration of both aspects of sanctity—"separation and union."[21]

For Shlanger, natural desires and halakhic civilization are *not* diametrically opposed, as much of traditional pietism and Salanter's Mussar movement assumes. Rather, Shlanger views marriage as a synthesis of nature and spirituality:

Marital sexuality is founded on Nature's sexual bond, and so the Rabbis appropriately call it by the term *derekh eretz*, "the way of the earth" (TB *Eruvin* 100b). Then the Torah elevated it . . . until it was called *devar mitzvah*, a matter of God's commandment. . . . Thus the Torah sanctified the union of male and female . . . raising it from a permitted act to a mitzvah that generates wholeness and sanctity.[22]

To maintain the healthy intersection of sanctity and natural drives, Shlanger and Shuchatowitz teach the avoidance of two misguided extremes: licentious nature and ascetic holiness. On the one hand, selfish, animalistic impulses may pollute the natural bonds within marriage that God wants us to nurture. Natural urges must be refined by sacred norms for marriage to fulfill its God-assigned goals. On the other hand, the anxiety that the evil impulse may corrupt marital relations is not a reason to go to the other extreme, but rather to maintain suitable caution. As Ra'avad wrote in *Ba'alei HaNefesh*, "one must not deny oneself the joy and the pleasure of this mitzvah [of intercourse with one's spouse], but simply be vigilant regarding the impulse and be careful not to try to satisfy one's full desire."[23] Shlanger explains that the overly pious husband performs the duty of onah like "one who swallows matzah whole (*akhila gasa*) and yet has not fully performed the mitzvah of 'eating' matzah, which must be consumed 'with desire so as to show that the mitzvot are beloved.'"[24] So too, Shuchatowitz quotes the medieval kabbalist *The Holy Letter*: "If the [marital] union is not consummated with much passion, love, and desire, the Divine Presence will not dwell in it."[25]

Shlanger cautions against disdain for the pleasure of intercourse itself and the denigration of the God-given sense of touch generally. While every Jew ought to strive for sanctity and turn away from vulgarity and impurity, "sexual intercourse in its [natural] reality is not deplorable and shameful. . . . Rather, the human faculties created by the Holy One are 'good.'"[26] What is more, the higher an individual's spiritual level, the more he or she can transmute bodily functions into sacred service of God.[27] Shlanger quotes Rabbi Moshe Haim Luzzato (18th century, Italy), who in his renowned work *Mesillat Yesharim* taught: "The person who sanctifies himself with the sanctity of his Creator transforms even his material acts into matters of sanctity."[28]

Covenantal Marriage

For Shlanger, marriage ought to be a sacred union imbued with mutuality, what the prophet Malachi calls *brit*, a covenant of marriage (Mal. 2:14).[29] This mutuality reaches its peak in the act of lovemaking, which, as Maimonides teaches, is achieved "by means of conversation and [erotic] play," by harmonizing "both their wills," and by embodying their intent in a sexual union manifesting "their shared joy."[30]

Consensual sex, however, is not an adequate criterion for a sacred covenant of love. Shlanger, like Kanievsky, worries that, in repudiating the pole of asceticism, a person may swing to the pole of hedonism. When an individual focuses on physicality, and control of sexual desire in marital relations, then the "covenant of love" is often reduced to a fig leaf for *z'nut*, "prostitution." Prostitution, by Shlanger's definition, is the employment of the other to satisfy one's own drives without emotional care for the other. The halakhah, therefore, provides guidelines to make sure desire itself does not undermine love.

When Maimonides writes that "one must perform intercourse with shame and not aggressively," one might plausibly argue that Maimonides thinks one should be ashamed of one's bodily functions and instinctual desires, for Maimonides also comments that "the sense of touch is the most shameful aspect of the human being."[31]

Shlanger, however, says that Maimonides' sense of shame allows husbands to have human respect for their partners, even while satisfying their own sexual needs in intercourse:

> A sense of shame guides the paths to marital union since one with a sense of shame will not violate the other's human dignity. . . . He is obligated to follow the path of union and unification with the woman for her sake and for the sake of her fullness. He does not deviate from the normal customs of the world.
>
> By contrast, an attitude of aggressiveness means doing what you will for yourself without consideration for the order of nature or for the honor and good of the other. That is what the Rabbis meant when they said: "An ignoramus assaults and then takes sexual possession (i.e., rapes) without shame" (TB *Pesahim* 49b). He lacks shame and so he takes everything for his own pleasure without appeasing his partner.[32]

Self-absorbed sexual activity disregards the dignity of the partner, who is treated as an object of consumption. One must distinguish the negative, all-consuming narcissistic desire (*ta'avah*) from the positive human desire to do lovingkindness (*hesed*) for one's partner (Prov. 18:1; 19:22). As Shlanger says, lovemaking ought to be a relationship of two subjects, in which each one "fulfills the obligation to enact a covenant of marriage through mutual will and joy as 'one soul and one body.'"[33]

Loveless Sex Desecrates Sacred Matrimony

For both Shlanger and Shuchatowitz, when marital love brings a couple together in accord with God's mitzvah, it creates a dual source of sanctity.[34] Thus, at a wedding, the betrothal (symbolized by the ring ceremony) is called *kiddushin* (sanctification) because it serves a *dual function*—separating groom and bride from forbidden relations (like incest and adultery) and uniting the couple by dedicating one particular woman to one particular man. Yet this formal legal act of dedication is inadequate to embody its name, for a truly sacred sexual union must manifest emotional union as well.

The halakhic source that treats emotionally defective marital intercourse as sinful and harmful is the Talmudic *sugya* about the nine kinds of damaged children (also see chapter 3):

> Rabbi Levi says: "These are the children born of nine defective characteristics [in the relationships between their parents]: children of fear, of coercion, of hatred, of a violation of a ban, of substitution, of contention, of drunkenness, of those divorced in their hearts, of confusion, and of audacity (*hutzpah*)." (TB *Nedarim* 20b)

Traditionally, the category of "children of coercion" refers not solely to a husband who rapes his wife but also to one who urges her to have sex when she is half-awake so that she only consents half-heartedly to his advances.[35] "Children of hatred" emerge from acrimonious marital relations. Shlanger and Shuchatowitz interpret these emotional dysfunctions broadly in terms of moral and psychological lacuna. As we saw in the opening epigraph, Shlanger explains:

> The Rabbis listed the nine major dimensions of failed intention in marriage and all of them can be reduced to one dysfunction— separating the act of intercourse from the covenant of love between man and woman. Then the act does not flow from love, and its purpose—to unite a husband with his wife and to complete a wife with her husband—remains unfulfilled. . . . It is simply a physical act similar to prostitution.[36]

By quoting classical sources, Shuchatowitz and Shlanger argue plausibly that their synthesis of love and marital sex is not a modern innovation but exactly what the Talmudic Rabbis and the medieval kabbalist mystics had in mind. For example, Rabbi Jacob ben Asher (14th century, Spain) quotes the Ra'avad, who maintains: "The act of intercourse [that generates the nine defective children] is like prostitution because it does not emerge from love." The Zohar too insists: "The proper intent in copulating is to unite his and her will." Rabbi Elijah de Vidas (16th century, Hebron) explains that "there shall be no blaming and arguing between them but only love, fraternity, peace and friendship, especially on Shabbat." Repairing their union is achieved, says the Zohar, by appeasement in which one "entreats her and perfumes her with words (both before and after intercourse)."[37]

Both Shuchatowitz and Shlanger assert that "there is a halakhic obligation to reinforce love at home as much as possible."[38] To do so, they insist that husbands and wives must make an authentic peace in their relationship and not just bury the conflicts for social reasons. Otherwise these tensions will fester and undermine the couple's emotional unity.

While shalom bayit is an important value, it may be a harmful error to persuade members of a couple whose emotional relationship has become deeply contentious to stay together at all costs. Shuchatowitz cautions that "a couple may remain together to avert social shame and the unpleasantness of divorce, but even if each one ignores the other and they refrain from quarreling, they do not love one another."[39] Their loveless alienated relationship is likely to produce acrimony and resentment and thus damage the children born of the parents' suppressed hatred.

The Higher Purposes of Onah:
Love and Unity, Humanity and Sanctity

Innovatively, Shlanger and Shuchatowitz expand the halakhic ratio-nale of onah beyond a private contractual obligation between a husband and wife regarding the frequency of sex. Rather, the Torah elevated onah from the status of a "permitted sexual activity," which a couple may forgo at will, to a positive commandment that "generates perfection/wholeness and sanctity in marriage and a sacred task that advances God's greater goal of tikkun olam."[40] That is why, says Shlanger, the Talmud permits the selling of a community's Torah scroll to finance needy individuals wishing either to study Torah or to marry.[41] Marriage and Talmud Torah are positive values commanded by God that serve not just private interests but divine ends. Therefore, a couple ought not to forgo lovemaking, even if it is legal for them to agree mutually to suspend their legal obligation to engage regularly in sexual relations.

For Shlanger and Shuchatowitz, a loving marriage contributes to three global ethical and mystical objectives: (1) love, (2) peace and unity, (3) humanity and sanctity.

1. Love: Shlanger quotes the Lurianic mystic Rav Haim Vital (16th century, Safed): "When the husband loves his wife as one loves one's own body, he performs the mitzvah of *love your neighbor as yourself* (Lev. 19:18), which includes all the mitzvot in the Torah."[42] As the Zohar teaches: "One who unites male and female . . . spreads hesed (compassion), as it says, 'the world will be founded on hesed' (TB *Brakhot* 11b)."[43]

2. Peace and Unity: "Question: Why should you get married?" asks Shuchatowitz in a hypothetical discussion with a yeshiva student. If the student thinks the purpose of marriage is procreation or being kind to your wife by satisfying her physical needs, then Shuchatowitz replies: "That is a mistake! . . . The main reason for marrying is: 'Peace.'"[44] But there is more, so Shuchatowitz asks again: "Why should you get married?" and then answers himself: "To become a Mensch." A human being is only a half until he becomes "bonded fully to his covenantal woman," as Rabbi Elazar teaches: "Anyone without a wife is not [fully] human" (TB *Yevamot* 63a).

To Shuchatowitz, forging a loving unity between husband and wife (shalom bayit) is the key to perfecting our humanity, but it is also the quintessence of Torah's telos (purpose) of making peace in all realms. The motive force of peacemaking is erotic energy, as Shuchatowitz shows by citing an ancient midrash: "It is [sexual] desire that puts peace between a man and a woman" (*Leviticus Rabbah* 18:1).[45] While this adage may be understood in the matter-of-fact manner that spouses who have quarreled may be motivated to make peace because of their desire for sexual relief, Shuchatowitz proposes that peace is generated by erotic desire in the higher mystical sense of a union between opposites at all levels—physical, emotional, spiritual, and metaphysical. The more passion, the higher the level of unity and peace within the world:

> The need for increasing the desire between man and woman is explained by the principle of unity. A little unity is not enough, rather one needs to reach the height of unity at all the levels that are possible. Accordingly, the degree of desire determines the degree of unity between the bodies until they reach the peak when they really become one [flesh]. *To arouse that desire is a great form of worship of God* as we saw with Rav. . . .
>
> But if the husband does not desire his wife so much, then [during intercourse] he is engaged not with unification but with separation (*olam d'pruda*), and therefore [his intercourse] is a sin![46]

Here lies the answer that Rav should have given to his invasive student Kahana who rebuked his master for becoming too ravenous, too enthusiastic in lovemaking. Rav should have explained that passionate lovemaking is the secret to making peace in the world.

Arousing desire between husband and wife, then, is essential for peacemaking between the couple, and in turn, peacemaking within one household is connected to peacemaking in all of Israel. Shlanger quotes the moral lesson of Rabban Shimon ben Gamliel, who says: "All who bring peace within their household are regarded as if they had brought a peace to all Israel that will reign over each and every one."[47]

Further, according to Maimonides, domestic and national peace together contribute to world peace. Therefore Shuchatowitz opens his book on marital harmony, *Binyan HaBayit*, with a chapter entitled "Great Is Peace" and a quote from Maimonides extolling domestic tranquility, shalom bayit, as the gateway to the overall purpose of the whole Torah:[48] "Great is *shalom* (peace)! For the whole Torah was given to make peace in the world as it says in the Bible, *Its ways are ways of pleasantness and all its paths are peace* (Prov. 3:17)."[49]

Moreover, Shuchatowitz explains that unification ("the essence of the mitzvah of onah is unification") and shalom bayit are the first steps to achieve what Rabbi Judah Loewe (16th century, Prague) envisions as God's grand mystical purpose for the cosmos—shalom and unity.[50]

3. Humanity and Sanctity: While sanctity also means to withdraw and separate from the mundane by prohibiting or minimizing carnal activities, Shlanger and Shuchatowitz relate marital intimacy chiefly to the sanctity of union—between male and female, sexual and spiritual, earthly and heavenly. For Shlanger, "sanctity is not only about separation, but chiefly, about relationship and union.... Evil derives from the root of division and rupture."[51] Positive sanctity flows from the Divine to the worldly by infusing the Divine Presence into the material world. The result can be described as embodying the image of God in human existence or the indwelling of the Shekhinah in the cosmos. The image of God materializes in the world in two ways: creation and procreation (Gen. 1:26–27; 5:1–3), on one hand, and sexual union that synthesizes male and female as complementary aspects of the divine image, on the other.

Shuchatowitz highlights the latter by quoting again from Rabbi Judah Loew (traditionally associated with the legendary Golem of

Prague): "Man and woman are each part of the human being and only together are they the complete human being, and to the degree that one is complete, to that degree the Shekhinah is with him."[52] Loew identifies the sexual union that makes man and woman into one flesh and the process of embodying in the world the full image of God, which is itself male and female (see chapter 5).[53]

Marital union then enables the descent of the Shekhinah into the world, as Shlanger affirms in the name of the Zohar: "Any place the mitzvah of sexual union is found, so too the Shekhinah (the Divine Presence) is found in that same place."[54] Thus the unification of man and woman has a dynamic effect on the world by drawing down the Divine Presence.[55]

When human beings come together in their full humanity, they create a space for sanctity to dwell in the midst of the world in the same way the Sacred Temple in Jerusalem is a residence for the Divine Presence. In that spirit, Shlanger calls his book for newlyweds *Mishkan Yisrael* (which means, literally, the Tabernacle of Israel, the "Dwelling Place of the Divine in the midst of Israel"), because the ultimate model for human marriage is the Holy of Holies in the Temple (which is also called the "room of beds," 2 Kings 11:2).[56] As Shuchatowitz explains, a couple's physical intimacy reenacts the relationship of the two cherubs in the Holy of Holies who, Rashi notes, are shown "embracing like a man hugging his wife between his arms" (TB *Yoma* 54a).[57] Thus, the mitzvah of building a human bayit (home) is continuous with the mitzvah for building the Divine bayit (Temple). Like the cherubs, people must behave as God desires by multiplying peace and love in the world. By guiding couples to enhance their interpersonal unity, Shlanger's book fulfills its intent "to enhance the presence of the Shekhinah in the people of Israel" and "in the bayit (the home) through the performance of the mitzvah of onah."[58]

Conclusion

Both Shlanger and Shuchatowitz, as well as Sher (see chapter 9), contextualize the laconic halakhic statements of the Hazon Ish's and the Steipler Rav's holy letters about marital harmony within a broad and uplifting spiritual calling. Repairing the whole world and fulfilling God's redemptive purposes begin at home with mundane conversations with one's spouse and a night of satisfying sexual desire.

Shuchatowitz teaches that "love of one's wife is the most natural and basic love. . . . and yet through it we are given the tools to reach supreme levels."[59] Thus the ascent to divine worship at the top of the spiritual ladder is initiated on the earthly plane by sexual desire. Shuchatowitz learns from the mystic Rabbi Isaac of Acco (13th–14th centuries), whom we quoted above: "One who has not felt carnal passion (*heshek*) for a woman is like a donkey, or even less than that, for worship of God begins when one can discern the divine within the material world of the senses."[60] That is also the visionary path of the mystic messianist, the first chief Ashkenazi rabbi of Israel, Rav Abraham Isaac Kook:

> Tranquility in the family (shalom bayit) and its joy, trust, love, peace, and satisfaction flow from the trust of a man in his covenantal wife. That leads to love of one's offspring and then to endless good influences on all fields of life for the general whole and for private individuals.[61]

Couple Communication as a Mitzvah 11

The Rebbe once acknowledged: I never would have known what love of a fellow Jew meant had I not learned it from a (non-Jewish) farmer. The farmer asked his friend: "Do you love me?" The friend replied: "Yes, I love you very much." "Then do you know what I need?" "But how am I supposed to know that?" "If you don't know what I need, then how can you help me, and if you don't help me, how can you say you love me?!"

—REBBE MOSHE LEIB SASSOVER

Conversations are negotiations for closeness.

—DEBORAH TANNEN, *You Just Don't Understand*

Introduction

Living within stringently gender-segregated enclaves, Haredi men and particularly women are systematically discouraged from verbalizing their sexual desires and anxieties, even as married couples, although most reside in the midst of an open secular society suffused with explicit expressions of sexual and psychological themes. It is not surprising that Jerusalem therapists counseling ultra-Orthodox women have told me that talking about emotional and especially sexual issues is very difficult for their clients. As we have seen in chapter 9, the holy letters composed by the Hazon Ish, Kanievsky, and Sher aim to overcome those psychological and social barriers to marital intimacy and mandate frank and supportive conversations.

Given these daily challenges in the Haredi family and armed with the prestigious rabbinic mandates (*haskamas*) from these esteemed Litvak scholars, their enthusiastic disciples have in the last thirty years composed hands-on marital guidebooks, chiefly for halakhically learned husbands, and disseminated them in dozens of publications now available in bookstores carrying sacred books (*seforim*). These Litvak educators include rabbis Rafael Menahem Shlanger and Moshe Aharon Shuchatowitz, and they and others like them have also organized now-ubiquitous courses aimed at young yeshiva grooms and their brides, trained bridal counselors, launched blogs, and participated in online discussions about marital issues (even though the official Haredi leadership prohibits surfing the internet). Such initiatives are helping many younger members of the Haredi and Hardal (Haredi–Religious Zionist) communities to talk—at least in gender-segregated contexts—about what was once regarded as unseemly to mention, lest it arouse illicit thoughts (*hirhurim*).

For contemporary American readers it is likely that Haredi marital advice will not sound particularly new or audacious. The content may come across as homespun armchair psychology reflecting standard gender stereotypes and rehashing the well-worn advice found in secular self-help books and discussed on popular talk shows. Yet its form—halakhah; its authors—Haredi rabbis; its prooftexts—Talmud and law codes; and its spiritual worldview—lovemaking that enhances sanctity and repairs the divine cosmos—are revolutionary in the Haredi world.

The Litvak scholars and educators' greatest halakhic innovation is simply this: Married couples are *commanded* to have intergender conversations about emotional issues and intimate topics of *onah*. Following the Hazon Ish, they *prescribe* precisely what Gur's Ordinances of Kedushah *proscribe*.

Flashback to Talmudic Pillow Talk

When the Litvaks speak to contemporary yeshiva students about interpersonal communication, they do so authoritatively by engaging with classical Talmudic sources. Recall the Talmudic laws of pillow talk (chapters 2 and 3), such as the infamous adage in *Mishnah Avot*, often translated as *The Ethics of the Fathers*, regarding quashing conversations with one's wife: "'Do not converse (*siha*) too much with the woman.' This refers even to one's wife" (*Mishnah Avot* 1:5). Rabbi Eliezer and Ben D'havai set the standard for minimizing spousal communication during onah itself, and Joseph Karo canonized it in the Shulhan Arukh. Finally, Gur Hasidism institutionalized the prohibition on conversation between spouses, applying it to almost all aspects of married life.

By contrast, "the great halakhic authorities" among the Litvaks, as Shlanger observes, have decided unequivocally that "*in our era* one should *not* learn from the behavior of Rabbi Eliezer."[1] Rather, as Shuchatowitz proclaims, Rav sets the halakhic standard for Litvaks on what the Torah teaches about bedroom practice—"chatting, jesting (playing, laughing, or engaging in foreplay)"—and Haredim today must say, "This is Torah and I must learn it!" (TB *Brakhot* 62a). Pillow talk is the gateway to joy (*simha*) and aroused sexual desire (TB *Pesahim* 72b), which are essential to the proper fulfillment of the mitzvah of marital intercourse.[2]

In Hebrew, *sakh vsakhak* (chatting and jesting) alliterate, such that the literary form matches the content—a playful exchange. The back-and-forth of reciprocity and rhyme in their intimate conversation shapes their lovemaking. Rashi paraphrases: "He [Rav] chatted and jested with his wife, conducting a *trivial, empty (b'teila)* conversation of persuasion leading to intercourse." Ironically, this is the same Rav whom Maimonides praises for never engaging in a "trivial, empty (*b'teila*) conversation in his whole life."[3] Perhaps, then, Rav did not consider his romantic exchange with his wife trivial. Even though it lacks scholarly content, verbal intimacy with a wife has the status of Torah that must be learned, and many rabbis legislated that without words of wooing, no man has the right to have sex with his wife.[4]

Permitted Spousal Communication: Removing Acrimony and Arousing Desire

In harmonizing between the loquacious Rav and the laconic Rabbi Eliezer, medieval halakhic codes and their modern commentators split hairs in distinguishing between prohibited, permitted, and mandatory spousal conversations (TB *Hagiga* 5b). An extended verbal exchange with one's wife is justified in Jewish law whenever it remedies characteristic squabbles and misunderstandings that obstruct marital intimacy. Such conversations serve the purposes of: (1) removing acrimony and securing the wife's consent to intercourse, (2) arousing the husband's and the wife's desire, and (3) positively enhancing their overall emotional relationship.

1. CONVERSATIONS TO ALLAY ACRIMONY AND SECURE CONSENT TO INTERCOURSE

As we have seen, the Talmud and the codes obligate a husband to placate (*ritzui, piyus*) his wife before performing onah, because otherwise coercing her into involuntary, half-hearted, or begrudging intercourse would constitute a violation of the rabbinic injunction against nonconsensual sexual contact.[5] Therefore, communication must first resolve everyday tensions and clear up a troubled emotional atmosphere that blocks sexual intimacy.

That said, the Talmud still wishes to enforce the negative warning that minimizes talk between husband and wife. The first exception to that rule permits spousal conversations solely to pacify quarrels (shalom bayit), so if one's wife is *not* upset and *not* in need of appeasement and sweet talk, then verbal communication between the couple is superfluous and hence forbidden (see chapter 2). Yet other halakhic authorities, as we shall see, adopt broader rationales for verbal conversation in marriage.

2. CONVERSATIONS TO AROUSE HIS AND HER SEXUAL URGES

Inspired by the Talmudic precedent of erotic verbal play between Rav and his wife, Rabbi Jacob Emden (18th century, Germany) prescribes intimate conversations to evoke a wife's desire for him:

> First one helps make one's wife's mind achieve tranquility, and then one arouses her joy and nourishes her with words that cause her heart joy in order that she will experience desire for him. . . . Then they make love to one another.[6]

While Emden focuses solely on the *woman's* arousal, Shuchatowitz observes that Rav is described as "gratifying *his* needs," and so he concludes:

> When Rav strengthens his desire and arouses himself, like one who has never before performed intercourse, he is engaged in a great labor of *avodah* (worship) in enhancing desire. And that intensification of desire was not only for her sake but for *his* desire, his need.[7]

3. CONVERSATIONS TO ENHANCE EMOTIONAL UNDERSTANDING BETWEEN GENDERS

The Hazon Ish discovers—or, perhaps, invents—a new commandment: to initiate extensive in-depth conversations with one's wife in order to make her happy by cultivating purely emotional intimacy. Unlike the two previous rationales associated with smoothing the path to intercourse, the Hazon Ish adds the responsibility for the new husband to learn to make his partner happy by cultivating broad and deep emotional intimacy in their whole relationship. Speaking with one's wife here is not about overcoming a localized problem (like making peace after a fight, courting her consent, or arousing erotic desire), but simply enhancing emotional closeness and love in general.

As we saw above, the Hazon Ish's revolutionary ruling derives from an oft-neglected Biblical mitzvah exempting a new husband from military service in order to make his bride happy, presumably sexually (Deut. 24:5). His interpretation, however, is grounded on an expansive explanation of the commandment by Rabbi Isaac ben Joseph of Corbeil (French author of *Sefer Mitzvot Katan*, 1277): "We learn that during the first year of marriage one is obligated to make one's wife happy . . . *in every way* that he can give her happiness" (*Sefer Mitzvot Katan: Mitzvot Lo Ta'aseh* #311).[8] The Hazon Ish explains that loving communication in addition to and perhaps more than erotic activity is crucial for a wife's happiness: "He [the husband] must make an effort to show her love and closeness in frequent/abundant conversation and appeasement."[9]

Since a Biblical mitzvah always overrides a rabbinic prohibition, the Hazon Ish's Holy Letter explicitly exempts the couple during the first year (or as long as it takes) from the rabbinic prohibition against talking with one's wife too much unless she is upset and in need of placation to consent to intercourse. Similarly, in speaking with one's wife in the first year, the husband is protected from the damage caused by unnecessary talk with a woman—namely, "injury to himself, nullification of his Torah study and eventually inheriting hell" (*Mishnah Avot* 1:5). The Hazon Ish explains:

The rabbinic prohibition, "Do not be expansive in talking . . . even with one's wife" does *not* apply when appeasing one's wife before intercourse or during the first year of marriage when one must strive to be united [with one's spouse] which is the purpose of her creation: *to become one flesh* (Gen. 2:24). Only then the Rabbis say the Shekhinah will dwell [between them].[10]

By conducting intimate conversations, the newlyweds gradually remove the pious sense of shame that makes them reticent to be intimate and become truly united. While shame and respectful honor in the presence of another, including one's spouse, are generally positive traits, the Hazon Ish cautions that these traits may also block intimate communication between spouses. Perceptively, he observes:

> *Sometimes, treating one's spouse with respect and with the awe of politeness displays lack of intimacy (closeness).* One must relate with a greater intimacy than can be accommodated in a relationship of respectful honor. Levity and light-headedness (*kalut rosh*) are more loveable than seriousness and awesome honor. One must make every effort to behave in a more intimate way and draw her closer with one's right hand rather than pushing her away with one's left. . . . One should address [her] in the familiar singular (you), not the formal plural [characteristic of polite speech in Yiddish].[11]

An affectionate conversation need not necessarily involve erotic utterances; simple sharing of daily events and feelings is enough. As previously noted, the Hazon Ish urges the husband "to tell [his wife] whenever he leaves [the house] where he is going, and, upon his return [to tell her] what he has done, and other little things and words of reinforcement—to make her heart happy."[12] Sharing small talk, rather than existential dialogue, erotic jesting, or words of conciliation after a fight, is the secret glue of a loving relationship.

The Hazon Ish's concern that a husband be attentive to the emotional needs of his wife derives from an expansive understanding of the Talmudic mitzvah of onah. The husband's obligation is to be responsive to a woman's variable sexual-emotional desires, even if unspoken. The Rabbis assume that women need not only a biological release for their drives or the pleasure of orgasm but the emotional comfort of knowing their husbands care for their wives whether they are anxious or amorous. For example, a husband has a special obligation to make love to his wife even beyond her regularly scheduled onah, especially immediately before or after he takes a trip:

> Rabbi Joshua ben Levi said: "A husband is obligated to have intercourse with his wife when he is about to go on a journey ... *because a woman longs for her husband* when he is going on a journey." (TB *Yevamot* 62b)

Knowing her husband is going away is likely, they assume, to make his wife nervous, owing to her uncertainty about when he will be back or what might happen to him on his journey. Even when the traveling husband will not have to miss one of his scheduled periods of obligatory onah, he must still make love to his wife before he leaves (at least "when the trip is long or dangerous"). The same subjective rationale applies to a husband's obligation to perform his marital duties on the night immediately after purification in the *mikveh*, since at that time the wife is presumed to "desire him more."[13] At the moment immediately before separating (before a trip) or directly after the termination of suspended intimacy (due to *niddah*), the longing for sexual and emotional union with one's spouse is presumably greatest. As the English motto has it: "Absence makes the heart grow fonder."

Traditional rabbis like the Hazon Ish have concluded that many husbands, even scholars meticulous in doing their conjugal duty, are mistaken in thinking that their wives simply want sexual satisfaction when actually they want to be assured that they have a loving relationship. Therefore the rabbis advise husbands to devote an extended period to demonstrating caring behavior for their wives in the period leading up to the time allotted for onah.

The Tur, the medieval Spanish code of Rabbenu Jacob ben Asher (14th century), warns that "Torah scholars must be *careful* to fulfill the mitzvah of marital duties."[14] Commenting on "being careful," Rabbi Joel Sirkis (17th century, Poland) wonders why Rabbenu Jacob directs his warning specifically to scholars who are usually more punctilious in observing the law: "But why [does Rabbenu Jacob] bother to say ['be careful' to Torah scholars]? Of course, Torah scholars are obligated to fulfill their marital duties once a week, from Shabbat night to Shabbat night."[15]

Sirkis replies to his own question:

It seems to me that "to be careful" means to be cautious about observing the mitzvah, even before the night arrives. One should show added love and affection to one's spouse. It goes without saying that one should avoid fights, God forbid, from the afternoon even before the onset of Shabbat. . . . [But also] be careful to pursue love and brotherhood between him and her all of the time leading up to Shabbat, so that there will be no reason [such as a marital quarrel] to cancel intercourse on Shabbat itself.[16]

Aviner's Advice:
Making a Study of One's New Spouse

Shlomo Aviner, a leading Jerusalem rabbi of Religious Zionism (and a student of the Religious Zionist mystic Rav Tzvi Yehuda Kook), is among those who praise the Hazon Ish's innovative affirmation of intimate marital communication as a mitzvah incumbent upon the husband to make his bride happy. To explain why this mitzvah falls asymmetrically on the groom more than the bride, Aviner makes an astute sociological and psychological observation about contemporary marriage patterns among yeshiva students. His yeshiva students, who marry young (by their early twenties), often study for many years in a *kollel*, a special full-time program at the yeshiva for married students. Hence they continue their daily contact with their male study friends (especially their Talmud *hevruta*, meaning companion or friend with whom one shares all one's most intimate secrets). By contrast, their wives usually move out of their parents' homes into apartments with their husbands far from their birth homes and relatives where they are almost immediately busied by raising their children. Aviner informs these new husbands:

> This obligation [to make your wife happy] falls in particular on the bridegroom, since his new wife's form of life has changed much more than his. Generally she has been cut off from many more of the things that made her happy when she was single.[17]

While the mitzvah to make your wife happy is asymmetrical in gender terms, with the husband active and the wife passive, Aviner rephrases his advice to couples in egalitarian, bilateral terms. He recommends that to make each other happy, a Hardal Religious Zionist yeshiva couple, who have probably not known each other intensively or for a long period before marrying, must first "study" one another. As Aviner observes: "There are people married fifty years who still don't understand one another ... because they never studied one another."[18] Therefore, a new couple must make a study of one another:

> In the first year of marriage one must dedicate special attention to this issue because the bride and groom do not know one another very well and they haven't assayed their mutual expectations. . . . .

But it is not so simple to know what truly causes the other joy. Beware of those who say what they think one "must" do to make the other happy and, if the other is not pleased, then s/he must be completely stupid. . . . *No one can decide for the other what will make the other happy. Rather, one must listen humbly to what the other says*, and conclude from that what is expected. . . . Each person has an inner world of joy and sadness, of ambitions and desires that is the world of the "I." No one else is permitted to belong to that inner world. [Getting to know what brings joy to one's spouse] cannot be done at a distance in a theoretical way. It comes only from frequent and living encounters. . . . At all times the couple must inscribe in the depths of their souls the aspiration to make the other happy—*with one's whole heart and soul* (Deut. 6:5).[19]

For Aviner, spousal communication opens the way to total, loving devotion, which he compares implicitly to the total love for God prescribed in the *Shema* (Deut. 6:4–5).

That said, emotional love and understanding are not enough if the couple's unhappiness stems from unsatisfied sexual needs. Solving sexual issues, says Aviner, requires knowledge about human sexuality as well as frank interpersonal communication about one's erotic preferences:

To learn about sexual problems and to prepare for marriage, Rav Moshe Feinstein [the great Haredi halakhic authority, d. 1986] approves the reading of medical literature "to make sure his wife will have pleasure and to increase *shalom bayit* (domestic tranquility)."[20]

In pursuit of knowledge about sexuality Kahana hid under Rav's bed, and so too newlyweds must seek out essential knowledge about one another in sexually explicit, problem-solving conversations. Although Aviner is known in Israel for promoting stringent modesty in women's dress, even from age twelve, he believes that once a couple is married, modesty should not prevent them from openly discussing sexual issues.[21] In his popular guide to Orthodox Israeli bridegrooms, *Etzem MeiAtzamai*, Aviner urges troubled couples to be frank:

> If there is some incompatibility, then the couple should converse together out of love and affection to reach a solution. While some think it is prohibited to speak with one's wife about these matters because it is immodest, that is a mistaken view. . . . It is all part of the mitzvah to enhance love and peace.[22]

Aviner summarizes the marital counseling offered by Rav Abraham David Wahrman (d. 1840, Ukraine):

> A husband interested in a particular form of intercourse, who is fearful that this might not be comfortable for his wife, ought not to rely on her silence as a sign of consent. Rather "he should discuss this with her in explicit terms once and for all."
>
> Just as the daughter of a scholar [like Rav Hisda's daughters] should not be ashamed to show "some reticence and distance and delay somewhat" [in satisfying her husband's desire], so she should not be ashamed to tell her husband if the sexual position [he has chosen] is uncomfortable [for her].[23]

For Aviner, the virtue of modesty is misplaced in marriage if it prevents frank communication between partners to increase their sexual compatibility.

Shuchatowitz's Advice: Acknowledging Gender Differences in Marriage

Most contemporary Orthodox thinkers believe there is an essential gap between the genders, rooted in the divine plan of Creation. For example, Rav Naftali Tzvi Berlin ("Netziv," head of Volozhin Yeshiva in Lithuania, 1816–93) explains that God created "two creatures, male and female . . . to teach us that the male as a species is not at all similar in its traits to the female species."[24] For that very reason, Shuchatowitz insists that spousal communication between man and woman is the crucial first step to bridging this natural dichotomy and laying the foundations for shalom bayit within a new couple's relationship.

THE HAREDI *MEN ARE FROM MARS, WOMEN ARE FROM VENUS*

Notably, Shuchatowitz's gender analysis echoes some of the observations and strategies of the psychologists John Gray in *Men Are from Mars, Women Are from Venus* (1992) and Deborah Tannen in *That's Not What I Meant! How Conversational Style Makes or Breaks Relationships* (1992). In his book *An Intimate History of Humanity* (1995), the intellectual historian of manners Theodore Zeldin summarizes Tannen's approach:

> [Tannen] concludes that they [opposite genders] cannot understand each other; that they mean quite different things when they speak; that women want comfort from those they converse with, while men seek solutions to problems. . . .
>
> Sexes "play different games"; their dissatisfactions are not due to personal defects but to "gender differences." The two sexes are brought up in "different cultures" and have to realise that . . . they speak different languages. She . . . cites the sad statistic that American married couples, on average, spend only half an hour a week "talking to each other."[25]

Like Tannen, Shuchatowitz laments that most couples do not understand one another because men and women are speaking different languages. Only by deliberately studying one another's perspectives can a couple achieve shalom bayit, and thereby embody the fullness of humanity created in the dual-gendered image of God:

> However, what happens in reality? Instead of a man learning the female perspective on the Creation, he insists stubbornly that he remain in his narrow male perspective even after marriage, and he misses the main purpose of marriage.[26]

Even worse, observes Shuchatowitz, each side usually tries to induct the other into their own gendered perspective, "even though one can never succeed in turning a man into a woman or a woman into a man." At the worst, he says, the husband will turn his wife into a bad wife, a resentful wife, "a bitch" (klafta), or the wife will turn the husband into a worn-out rag.[27]

Spousal conversations during the first years of marriage are intended to enable each spouse to benefit from "a year-long private tutor" in better understanding the other. Yet, Shuchatowitz comments, almost humorously, that the Torah thought optimistically that mutual acquaintance could be accomplished in one year, because the husband was exempt from military service for one year in order to devote himself to making his new bride happy (Deut. 24:5). Yet, in our troubled days, getting to know "the other side of the coin" might take two or five or ten years, or even their whole lives:

> During their whole lives lived in mutuality, each must learn about the other half. The result will be a whole human being (TB Yevamot 63a)—a person who has both a male and female perspective on the whole of Creation.[28]

Often young couples come to Shuchatowitz after just a few weeks of matrimony to complain that their match was a mistake, because they do not agree; they are too different. He tells them frankly:

You are right about all those differences! Men and women are really different, but love is the attraction of opposites, and when those differences are united in peace, they complement one another and bring about completeness without dissolving the differences.[29]

Then he counsels each spouse not to try to change the other, but to appreciate the gift that God has given them and "to honor one another, each in his or her own way—a woman as a woman and a man as a man . . . and thus to build a stable and complete household."[30]

KEY DIFFERENCES BETWEEN MEN AND WOMEN

For Shuchatowitz, the key differences between men and women manifest themselves in three ways: (1) their divergent responses to physical connection and desire, (2) their varied perspectives on emotional connection, (3) the amount of time necessary after an acrimonious exchange to make up and return to harmony.

First, Shuchatowitz elucidates the asymmetry of male and female patterns of arousal:

[Unlike male desire] a woman's passion for her husband is not a natural impulse, but the result of a husband's diligent work to arouse that desire each time. . . . Then she will willingly enter into a fully voluntary covenant with her husband.[31]

Here Shuchatowitz is conveying characteristic Orthodox assumptions about women's sexual desire. Similarly, in his book *Marital Intimacy* (1996), the Yeshiva University–trained rabbi Avraham Peretz Friedman speaks of women's slower ascent to orgasm and longer descent thereafter, and from that purported fact, he deduces a particular halakhic and moral obligation for men:

The Torah legislated a formal Torah obligation on a husband to slowly, gently, and lovingly escort his wife up the mountain [i.e., to her climax] and to continue the act of emotional intimacy long after intercourse is ended, until the emotional descent is complete.[32]

Further, according to a widely held stereotype, Shuchatowitz assumes that a woman cannot separate sex from love, while a man can:

> A woman's erotic nature functions by a dynamic that is the opposite of the man's, for he can start with the sexual alone and be satisfied with that alone. A woman, though, must first be aroused with an emotional connection and only later physically.... For her, the mitzvah of onah begins long before the act of intercourse and finishes long after it....
> [Otherwise] the wife will feel degraded and despised. For her, the whole relationship will become a great experience of compulsion and suffering... a stinging insult to her dignity.[33]

Addressing this point earlier, the Hasidic rebbe Eliezer Hager of Vizhnitz (1891–1946) counsels husbands to demonstrate to their wives that, for them, lovemaking is not solely a matter of securing men's own physical release:

> Even *after intercourse* [the husband] should continue to chat lightly and lovingly with her in order that she not think that his whole intent in speaking this way earlier was for the sake of his own pleasure. Therefore, to counter this mistaken notion, he should continue to appease her even after intercourse.[34]

To Shuchatowitz, a third characteristic difference between the genders is the time necessary to overcome acrimony. The Talmudic adage says: "A man is easily appeased, a woman is not easily appeased" (TB *Niddah* 31b). Therefore, Shuchatowitz concludes that *a husband must apologize even if it is his wife's fault.* That is why it is the husband's duty to take the initiative in seeking reconciliation after an argument.[35]

In sum, Shuchatowitz maintains that women are more concerned with emotional love and men more concerned with a physical hunger for sex. Given these differences, Shuchatowitz emphasizes the need for active listening skills followed by attempts to satisfy the differing needs of each spouse. Each spouse must be particularly attentive to his or her partner because what the recipient *most wants* may be something the giver *least* appreciates and needs for him or herself.

Haredi Educators Combine Sanctity and Intimacy

Like Hasidic rebbes, the rabbinic leaders of Litvak Haredim and Hardal (Haredi-Zionist Orthodox) are militant in defending their besieged camps against Western assimilation and desecration of Israel's *kedushah*. Therefore, they are fanatic in maintaining standards of modesty (*tzinus*), especially in the public sphere. Yet, many Haredi Litvaks and Hardal rabbis are *simultaneously* making concerted efforts to educate their disciples that kedushah in matrimony is fully compatible with mutuality and joyful sexuality in the privacy of the bedroom and with sensitivity and respectful emotional intimacy in spousal relationships overall. For them there is no contradiction between stringent gender segregation in society generally and sexual and emotional intimacy in marriage. Litvak Haredi educators like Shuchatowitz and Shlanger (contra Aviner) insist that the path of Rav is the *higher* halakhic telos (goal), whereas the path of ascetic marital relations of "the exceptional ones" is often motivated by an arrogant false piety that violates the halakhah. Pleasurable sex with one's spouse is not a sign of laxity, self-indulgence, or weakness of will, but of strict performance of the letter and spirit of the law of onah. The broad understanding of the conjugal duties encompasses the mitzvah of making one's wife happy and that, in turn, entails in-depth, frank, and loving conversation between husband and wife.

In evaluating the new Litvak ethos of marital lovemaking, however, one must be careful *not* to confuse Litvaks and their Haredi-cum-Religious-Zionist fellow travelers with liberal Modern Orthodox Jews or moderate Israeli Religious Zionists. While outsiders might characterize Litvak marital guidelines and rhetoric as more "permissive," "lenient," "liberal," and "realistic," many Litvaks and their fellow travelers would never employ such adjectives to describe their own positions. In their minds, they have not lowered their religious standards to accommodate the instinctual life (yetzer) indulged without shame by advocates of the American sexual revolution, or offered a more liberal approach that expands the couple's individual freedom. They do not wish to be seen as more progressive or up-to-date than their Hasidic opponents. Rather, most Litvak teachers, especially the Hazon Ish, heartily commend those who seek out ever-more stringent (mahmir) ways of sanctifying their lives and excoriate the promiscuity of Western sexuality.

In the case of marital life, however, these Litvaks hold that the path to greater kedushah lays in a sacred sexuality, in mutually satisfying onah, and in emotional communication that advances greater peace and hesed, at home and in the world. Unification and integration, rather than extreme suppression of desire and increased separation, are the watchwords of holy matrimony. Therefore, these Litvaks firmly oppose multiplying new restrictions in the sexual realm of marriage, as Gur Hasidism does. The obligatory laws of the Torah and Talmud have already defined a golden mean between permitted and prohibited sexual practice. God does not wish to add more prohibitions, lest these undermine the positive nature of sexuality as God created it.[36]

Here these Litvaks concur with Maimonides' legal policy against issuing prohibitions indiscriminately and assuming blindly that the more severe ruling is always preferable:

When one who is indubitably a fool attempts to prohibit more and more things, such as prohibiting food and drink beyond what the Torah prohibits, or prohibiting intercourse beyond what the Torah prohibits. . . . then he is doing bad things without knowing it. He will arrive at the other extreme and leave behind the [golden] mean completely. . . . As Rabbi Isaac said: "Isn't it enough for you what the Torah prohibited? Yet you take on yourself voluntarily to prohibit more things?!" (TJ *Nedarim* 9:4).[37]

Thus, many Israeli and North American Haredi guidebooks for newlyweds discourage stringencies and affirm that natural desires and sacred life are mutually reinforcing.

For example, Yirmiyohu and Tehilla Abramov, ultra-Orthodox educators who founded the organization Jewish Marriage Education (in 1993), aim to resolve the classic halakhic tension between marital duties and sanctity (kedushah) by bringing God into the bedroom. In *Mishpahteinu—Koheinu* (*Our Families Are Our Strength*, 1997) they bid couples to enhance their lovemaking as a means to rise to spiritual heights:

> Marital relations do not block sanctity, but they bring sanctity. The Torah teaches that one can achieve spiritual heights in marriage by virtue of satisfying marital relations. At the moment of the physical coupling the Shekhinah is present between the couple. In the house, which is analogous to a small temple, the bedroom is the Holy of Holies.[38]

In general, these new-style Litvak marital educators, who counsel couples not to confuse modesty with feeling shame about one's physiological urges, have circled back to the original rationale of the anonymous mystical medieval manual, *The Holy Letter* (see chapter 5):

> Just as the hands when they write a Torah scroll are honorable and praiseworthy and yet when they steal or do indecent acts, they are indecent, so too were the organs of intercourse of Adam and

his wife before they sinned. So too each limb is honored when it does good and condemned when it does evil. Thus the organs of intercourse in the First Adam were originally good. . . . For ugliness comes from human activities . . . and are not original attributes of the [organs] themselves.[39]

It is the intent, not the activity as such, which generates sanctity in marital lovemaking, albeit within halakhically permitted boundaries. Marital lovemaking—joyous, humorous, communicative, mutual, and consensual—is the halakhic golden mean for Litvaks.

Litvak Revolution or Haredi Crisis Management?

Viewed historically from outside the Haredi world, we have clearly discerned a deep Litvak reform in Jewish thought and law about marital intimacy. Yet, as we noted, these Litvak scholars might present their campaign as *a reform of Haredi behavior* that is sinful, but never as *a reform of the Torah*, whose law is perfect and eternal. Therefore, they employ varied rhetorical strategies to persuade their constituencies of the validity and continuity of their new emphasis on marital communication and sexual intimacy. Generally, these rhetorical justifications fall into two categories.

APPROACH 1: POSING NEWLY FORMULATED TEACHINGS AS AUTHENTICALLY REPRESENTING THE ORIGINAL POSITION OF THE TORAH AND TALMUD

The first strategy downplays "changes" by claiming that their position is identical with the original position of the Torah and the Talmud, which later pseudo-pietists misunderstood. Thus, the Hazon Ish and the Steipler rav issue more "lenient" rulings about marital intimacy, yet claim to be ruling more "strictly" about the halakhah of onah than ascetic schools like Gur Hasidim. So too, their heirs, Shuchatowitz and Shlanger, detail the recommended marital practices and cite rabbinic sources validating this revolution—without calling it a reform, without even speaking directly about Gur's ascetic marital policies which appear to have triggered their campaign, and without confronting head-on the Western sexual revolution.

APPROACH 2: ADJUSTING EROTIC NORMS TO CHANGING SOCIAL REALITIES

A second strategy speaks of addressing changing social realities and erotic norms. For example, as we saw above, the American Litvak halakhic authority Rav Moshe Feinstein (Belarus, United States, d. 1986) responded to the greater desire for sex in the modern world, which influences Haredim as well, by issuing a small adjustment to the halakhah of onah—doubling the frequency of onah for scholars from once a week on Shabbat to twice a week (see chapter 1).[40]

In the same spirit of accommodation, the Sephardi Haredi rabbi Hanan Aflalo of Yeshivat Ateret Hakhamim of Holon, Israel, discourages heroic asceticism in marriage and argues that this kind of halakhah is, by its original design, subject to change:

> To maintain abstinence from the wife on weekdays and to fight the evil impulse and wait for intercourse on Shabbat is like vinegar to the teeth and like smoke in the eyes even for many scholars of Torah.... Who can say: "I am a hero to go against the trend"?... The power of thoughts and sexual musing is too strong. Even those who try to delay [their desires] and to keep to once a week in accord with the Shulhan Arukh damage their ability to be diligent in Torah study....
> *Any good advice that appears in [sacred] texts can change.* It is not like an absolute law. So, for any student of Torah who wishes to have intercourse on an additional day [besides Shabbat], there is no obstacle and no prohibition, especially if the wife is desirous on other days.[41]

More alarmed and shrill in their diagnosis of social reality—and more radical in the action to be taken in response—are Haredi marriage educators, who decry society's imminent social crisis exacerbated by the contemporary sexual revolution. In such crises they urge halakhic authorities to take more authority and exercise greater halakhic flexibility or greater stringency, depending on their diagnosis. As educators, they believe that they have a mission to spread their redemptive truth.

For example, contemporary Litvak educators, like the American rabbi Yaakov Shapiro and the anonymous Israeli author of the online book *Devar Seter* (A secret message), fear that shalom bayit will be damaged and the divorce rate will continue to rise within the Haredi world due to sexually unsatisfied spouses. They worry about an abandonment of Orthodoxy by younger generations who see halakhic Judaism as too stringent, and especially as anti-sex. These educators openly promulgate a *more lenient* school of halakhic practice precisely because "the evil impulse of today is not similar to the one of yesterday, and human nature is not the same today as yesterday."[42] They speak explicitly of making accommodations by selectively preferring Rav's model of marital intimacy over Rabbi Eliezer's.

The author of *Devar Seter* further argues that when pietist norms are foisted on everyone indiscriminately, they desecrate the good name of Judaism and halakhah such that Orthodox *and* secular people both believe unnecessarily that "religion is paranoid and hateful toward sex." It is unacceptable that Orthodox couples who enjoy sex often feel "heavy pangs of guilt" as if they were violating the halakhah.

Therefore halakhic Judaism must engage in *heshbon ha-nefesh*, a moral accounting, about its own failings regarding the laws of modesty.[43] In his self-published book *Halachic Positions* (2015) and on his website, Shapiro (who became ultra-Orthodox Chabad in his youth) calls for adapting Haredi sex education to an era of heightened sexual awareness by rejecting Karo's halakhic stringencies. Shapiro maintains that times have changed:

> The Jewish spiritual leadership in every generation is expected—nay, obligated—to address the unique needs of its time. Childish naivete in matters of sex in general, and stringency in marital sex in particular, may have helped keep people of past centuries "in line" or "closer to G-d." But in present—and dare I say, future—generations, with sexual awareness at unprecedented heights, continuing to perpetuate such naivete and imposing such stringency can have the exact opposite effect.[44]

Instead, "a Jewish couple needs to know, now more than ever, that G-d understands, accepts and loves them even with their expanded sexual consciousness and curiosities."[45] Therefore, Shapiro boldly suggests that "reclaiming sexual exploration within marriage *as something holy* may just prove a key factor in preserving Judaism into the next generation—and beyond."[46] In accord with his book title, *Halachic Positions*, he encourages couples to "choose for themselves" their own position "between basic law and strictest piety, as appropriate to the unique spiritual and physical dimensions of [your marital] relationship."[47]

According to Shapiro and the author of *Devar Seter*, improving the "public relations" (i.e., the sanctification of God's name in public, *kiddush HaShem*) of an embattled Judaism in the modern age requires that rabbinic authorities refrain from advocating unnecessary prohibitions. The author of *Devar Seter* speaks of being inspired by Rav Abraham Isaac Kook, who advanced this approach in his response to his generation of Zionist socialist secularists (early 20th century), saying:

I know very clearly the characteristic of this generation that when they see that whatever we permit is based on the depth of the law, then they will know that whatever we prohibit is because of the truth of the law of the Torah. There will be many who will cleave to the Torah and obey their teachers.

However, that will not be the case if they discover that many things that should be permitted according to the law were not permitted because the rabbis did not care about the burden and the pain caused to the Jewish people [by unnecessary prohibitions] and just left things under prohibition. From this [unnecessary stringency] emerges, God forbid, desecration of God's great name. It leads many to challenge laws that are core to the Torah because they suspect the rabbis could permit them, if they only wanted. Thus the law is made crooked.[48]

Applying the same strategy to Haredim today, the author of *Devar Seter* campaigns on his blog (note: it is an unprecedented practice among Haredi scholars in Israel to use blogs to argue for halakhic views) as well as in his books to reject unnecessarily ascetic halakhic rulings. While maintaining anonymity to avoid controversy and social ostracization for his lenient views, he insists that "halakhah does not hate marital love" and that an unhealthy sexual purism in marriage relationships is *not* the way to sanctify marriage.[49]

Conclusion

Over the last seventy years, the Litvak Revolution's understanding of the mitzvah of onah has contributed to an ongoing transformation in Haredi ideology, education, and practice of marital relations. These changes have been nothing short of revolutionary, though they are not universally accepted in the Litvak yeshiva world. The historian of halakhah Haym Soloveitchik, as we noted above, speaks of the demise of a thousand-year "ascetic ideal [that] held sway over

Jewish spirituality,"[50] though Hasidic sects like Gur continue to militantly contest this new trend.

It is important to note, however, that most Litvak Haredi educators are still much more invested in reinforcing modesty and resisting the anarchic eroticism that increasingly pervades Western societies in which their youthful students, both male and female, reside than in preparing those soon-to-be-married for healthy relations with the opposite sex and for managing their own erotic urges. Overwhelmingly, the institutional weight of the Haredi world enhances the fear of yetzer and promotes modesty and gender segregation, and embraces the ideal of sanctifying instinctual life through self-denial and stringent halakhic pietism. To date, only a dedicated and innovative minority of educators are attempting to lay the foundations for emotional and sexual intimacy through how-to guidebooks, crash courses, and private counseling before the wedding. Whether this revolution-in-the-making has reached its tipping point remains to be seen.

PART FIVE

Modern North American Rabbis

CONFRONTING THE SEXUAL REVOLUTION

Redeeming Sexuality through Halakhah 12

MODERN ORTHODOX PHILOSOPHERS OF JEWISH LAW SANCTIFY PLEASURE WITHIN MARRIAGE

The ethic of marriage is hedonistic, not monastic. . . . [Nevertheless] the sacred is an outgrowth of the sacrificial action performed by the married partners when there is an act of withdrawal at the hour of carnal madness and concupiscence.

—RAV J. B. SOLOVEITCHIK, *Family Redeemed*

Introduction

In transitioning from Part Four, "Contemporary Haredim: Hasidim versus Litvaks on Marital Intimacy," to Part Five, "Modern North American Rabbis Confronting the Sexual Revolution," we have remained in the same century (post–World War II to the present) and the same type of scholarly Jewish elite, rabbis as halakhic authorities. Yet our geographical focus now moves from Israel to North America (for the most part) and our chosen rabbinic spokespeople no longer represent antimodern Haredi religious ideologies but varied progressive or liberal, modern denominations. Our halakhic investigation largely shifts from the quality of *marital* intimacy to the permissibility of *nonmarital* sexual relations. The societal issues faced also change. While Haredi Litvaks combat the challenge of pious asceticism *within* marriage preached and practiced by Hasidic sects, liberal rabbis confront secular promiscuity *outside* marriage celebrated and exemplified by the majority in North American society.

The terminology "liberal" is somewhat ambiguous because the term "liberal" (literally, "free") is used in so many ways in contemporary parlance. For this book, "liberal rabbis" (lowercase) refers to modern rabbis who are ideologically committed to modern values of freedom, democracy, and individual self-fulfillment, whose roots or analogues (such as human dignity implicit in the creation of man and woman in the image of God) can be found in classical Jewish texts or which can be adapted and integrated within Judaism. Rabbinic liberals explicitly oppose their view of Judaism to that of Haredim and some right-wing Orthodox who reject modern values and vehemently repudiate accommodations to Western culture. Thus, Modern Orthodox rabbis (the subject of this chapter) are, broadly speaking, "liberal." "Liberal Judaism" (capitalized) is used to describe the informal alliance of Conservative, Reform, Reconstructionist, and Jewish Renewal rabbis who reject Orthodox ideology and call openly for a more pluralist Judaism and halakhic reform—piecemeal or wholesale (chapters 13–16). Within each movement some rabbis are more liberal and others more conservative regarding how far and fast and in what manner to adapt Jewish attitudes about sexuality to progressive ideologies like feminism. While committed to modern values, these liberal rabbis are nonetheless critical of negative trends affecting Jewish families within contemporary society, as the Haredim are, but they are not at all nostalgic for premodern, undemocratic forms of Judaism and their patriarchal marital structures.

The majority of modern liberal rabbis also concur with Haredim that sexual licentiousness outside marriage is unholy as well as psychologically and socially unhealthy, though they would not support across-the-board sex- or gender-segregated institutions. Only a minority of contemporary liberal rabbis assert that halakhah must adapt (capitulate?) to the reality of widespread nonmarital sexual relations. Thus, North American liberal rabbis concur with contemporary Litvaks (see chapters 9–11) both in affirming the positive role of love and sexuality in holy matrimony and in condemning sexual licentiousness. Like the Haredi Litvaks, liberal rabbis of all denominations aspire to a higher ideal of sanctity in couple love, and, like the Litvaks, liberal denominations have gone beyond merely issuing legal rulings to publish popular educational guidebooks about loving intimacy.

But the halakhic opponents, constituencies, and halakhic questions faced by Litvaks in promoting marital intimacy differ sharply from those with whom North American liberal rabbis must spar. In simplistic political terms, one might say that when discussing sexuality and sanctity, liberal North American rabbis are looking over their left shoulders toward so-called progressive secular Western society, while Litvak Haredim in Israel are looking over their right shoulders toward so-called superpious ascetic Hasidic sects.

For example, Litvak Haredim must contend against the idealization of sexual self-denial by Hasidic Haredim, while modern rabbis feel no urgent need to issue halakhic rulings to justify erotic pleasure and interpersonal communication within marriage, because they have already repudiated the premodern Jewish ideal of ascetic piety. In fact, liberal rabbis maintain that erotic sexuality and spirituality are positively correlated. Their major challenge is how to modify or reinterpret Jewish sexual ethics and halakhah in light of modern sensibilities that prioritize individual freedom, sexual happiness, and gender equality.

In general, North American rabbis also share with all Haredim the worldview that sexual intimacy is a religious matter and sex should not be secularized and privatized without regard for classical Jewish values. Unlike Haredim, however, liberal rabbis believe that ideally these decisions should be made by the couples themselves, but that religious teaching and halakhah ought to have a voice in shaping these individual choices about sexual ethics and family values.

Of course, in seeking to persuade their constituencies to accept the beneficent authority of halakhah, the North American liberal rabbinate—including the Modern Orthodox—faces vastly different challenges than the Haredim. Haredi authorities can reasonably presume their audience of yeshiva graduates is deeply committed to halakhah and *kedushah*. Among college-educated North American Jews, however, halakhic observance and aspirations toward personal holiness cannot be taken for granted, especially when these impinge on bedroom behavior.

This trend holds true equally for the North American–born constituency of Modern Orthodoxy, especially since the age of marriage has been increasingly postponed from the teens in Talmudic families and in Eastern European communities up until the mid-nineteenth century to the mid-to-late twenties and even thirties today. Although reliable statistics on premarital practices of Modern Orthodox singles are not available, anecdotal evidence suggests that many singles behave in ways that deviate from their rabbis' prescriptions, even when they maintain their religious commitment to daily prayer, Shabbat, kashrut, and Torah study. A proverbial discussion topic among Orthodox singles in New York since the 1960s is the scandalous "tefillin date," in which young men in their twenties go out on a date at night with their tefillin (leather straps and tiny boxed scrolls used in weekday morning prayers) in tow in the hope that they may spend the whole night in bed with their date.[1]

As the historian of halakhah Haym Soloveitchik points out, for over a millennium,

> the ascetic ideal held sway over Jewish spirituality. While there was a sharp division in traditional Jewish thought over the stronger asceticism of mortification of the flesh, the milder one of distrust of the body was widespread, if not universal. The soul's control over the flesh was held to be, at most, tenuous, and without constant exercises in self-denial, there was little chance of man's soul triumphing over the constant carnal pull. The thousand-year struggle of the soul with the flesh has finally come to a close.[2]

What has changed most of all in the West, and therefore in modern denominations of Judaism, is the demise of the spiritual ideal of asceticism, and its concomitant disdain of the body and its libidinal impulses. Natural drives and the human body are no longer regarded as the polar opposites of spirituality and sanctity. Therefore, Jewish sexual ethics and halakhah must be rethought. What Haredim generally and North American liberal rabbis continue to share is a common philosophic and halakhic question: How should the relationship between sanctity and sexuality shape guidelines for sexual intimacy? That is the topic of this book and the following chapters.

Toward a Modern Orthodox Philosophy and Practice of Sanctified Sex

Modern Orthodox philosophers have devoted much thought to developing a positive halakhic orientation to nature in general and to the body in particular. Haym Soloveitchik's father, Rabbi Joseph B. Soloveitchik, the premier philosopher of halakhah and the preeminent Talmud teacher at Yeshiva University (YU), affirms the hedonist values of marriage in Judaism and rejects ascetic tendencies attributed falsely to the Torah, which he stigmatizes as monastic. Similarly, his colleague Rabbi Eliezer Berkovits, also a refugee from Berlin, praises passionate marital sexuality when pursued with self-control and respect for one's partner. They both highlight the quality of onah as the key to humanizing and sanctifying sexual impulses.

In conceptualizing marriage as a sacred realm of interpersonal intimacy, Modern Orthodoxy mandates both appropriate self-restraint before entering under the canopy and joyous sexual fulfillment thereafter. Contemporary couples, however, must submit to the regulations of the halakhah that redeem sexuality from its deleterious tendency to become promiscuous and vulgar. Thus Modern Orthodoxy prescribes a Maimonidean golden mean between celebrating God's creation of sexuality and resisting the demeaning promiscuity of the sexual revolution. Not asceticism, but disciplined self-restraint and periods of postponed gratification are needed to redeem the innately positive aspects of sexual desire from its narcissistic and anarchic tendencies and elevate them to sacred activities.

While the philosophic change in Modern Orthodoxy has been profound, the adjustment of halakhic practice has been more problematic. Within the marital bedroom, Modern Orthodox rabbis have generally adopted the model of Rav's erotic sexual union without any controversy. Yet regarding premarital physical expressions of affection, and especially intercourse, there has been militant resistance to halakhic flexibility, even among most of the liberal wing of Modern Orthodoxy, at least until very recently.

The first American Orthodox rabbi to publicly call for closing the gap between Modern Orthodoxy's ideology of positive sexuality and the asceticism of traditional halakhic practice was Rabbi Irving (Yitz) Greenberg. In a controversial interview published in Yeshiva University's student paper in 1966, he delivered an incisive analysis of the religious dilemmas of Americanized college-aged Orthodox Jews and then offered a bold proposal to address their issues. He was immediately rebuffed even by his liberal Orthodox colleague Rabbi Aharon Lichtenstein. Thereafter YU and its affiliate rabbinical institutions of Modern Orthodoxy totally rejected Greenberg's ideas for reform. His resulting marginalization in centrist Modern Orthodox institutions ended up impeding public discussion on modernizing the halakhah on sexual relations in the Modern Orthodox world for almost fifty years.

In retrospect, that incident signaled the steady shift rightward within American Orthodoxy from a positive commitment to integrating liberal democratic values and Eastern European halakhic Judaism to an increasingly conservative attitude toward progressive trends, especially Jewish feminism. Led by the faculty of the YU rabbinical seminary (RIETS), this more militant trend has come to dominate its rabbinic graduates (the Rabbinical Council of America) and its affiliated synagogues (like Young Israel) within what today is called Centrist Orthodoxy.

Keeping in mind these later developments, we first look at Greenberg's controversial proposal for halakhic change on sexual relations (1966), which was suppressed for half a century, and its recent revival in an innovative Orthodox website and podcast entitled *The Joy of Text*. While Greenberg and his heirs are viewed today as Orthodox outliers, the continuation of this chapter explores the innovative halakhic ideologies of more central figures in Modern Orthodox philosophy, Soloveitchik and Berkovits, whose celebratory hedonistic understandings of marital union exist alongside strict prohibitions against premarital physical intimacy.

Finally we cycle back again to Rabbi Aharon Lichtenstein, J. B. Soloveitchik's son-in-law, who rebuffed Greenberg's controversial challenge to halakhic practice on premarital sexual encounters. While more conservative in his style of Modern Orthodoxy, he too advocates his father-in-law's affirmative approach to human sexuality in Judaism. In addition, his Israeli student Rabbi Raphael Ostroff produced a groundbreaking educational book, *LaDaat Le-Ehov* (To know how to love, 2013), devoted to enhancing the marital intimacy of Modern Orthodox couples.

Greenberg's Proposal to Modernize American Orthodoxy's Sexual Ethics

In the early 1960s, Greenberg and his YU colleague, the Talmudist Aharon Lichtenstein of YU's rabbinical seminary, sought to forge a new, modern, and distinctly American Orthodoxy.[3] Greenberg and Lichtenstein feared that the faculty of New York's preeminent Orthodox and ultra-Orthodox yeshivot, which were staffed by refugee Eastern European–born scholars coming from prewar Litvak yeshivot, could not appeal to American-born college-aged students. Most of these immigrant scholars did not speak English well, and did not understand culturally or appreciate American society's practical mindset, its cult of personal choice and its pursuit of happiness. Often they actively opposed the desire of North American Jews to integrate into Western society not only professionally, but socially and culturally. As a result, many children of European refugees were leaving the Orthodox practice of their parents and grandparents.

Greenberg and Lichtenstein further believed that dynamic teachers, like their revered teacher Rav Joseph B. Soloveitchik, who are capable of integrating Western philosophy, American democracy, and halakhic Judaism, could not only keep those students in the fold but would attract thousands more. Halakhah offered a fulfilling way of life and a persuasive sophisticated worldview when understood as Soloveitchik presented it in his neo-Kantian essay, *Halakhic Man* (composed in 1944), and his existentialist essay, *The Lonely Man of Faith* (1965).

In April 1966 Greenberg gave a controversial interview to the YU student newspaper, *The Commentator*, entitled "Dr. Greenberg Discusses Orthodoxy, YU, Vietnam and Sex." In the interview, Greenberg challenges the halakhic decision makers (*poskim*) of Modern Orthodoxy to replace the pervasive asceticism of Eastern European piety born of suspicion of natural impulses with a positive appreciation of natural sexual desires. Greenberg asserts:

> Today the Poskim [halakhic decision makers] should recognize that there is nothing wrong with sex *per se*, and should promulgate a new value system and corresponding new halachot about sex. The basis of the new value system should be the concept that experiencing a

woman as *tzelem Elohim* [someone created in the image of God] is a mitzvah, just as much as praying in Shul [the synagogue]. The Poskim should teach people that the depth of one's sexual relationship should reflect the depth of his [personal] encounter. . . .

Sex has come to be considered a secular activity only because Poskim have abdicated their responsibility in examining its true meaning. Sex is a religious activity; it is the expression of relationship and caring for the other; we abuse it by ignoring it.[4]

In calling for a renewed halakhic appreciation of the human body, Greenberg protested that "the negative attitudes" to the body expressed by rabbis Eliezer ben Hyrcanus (Talmud, 1st century) and Joseph Karo (Shulhan Arukh, 16th century) "have won out in our thinking."[5]

We [Orthodoxy] have come to view sex not just with *tziniut* [modesty] but with shame. How else can we understand the almost universal shunning of this topic in public or private at YU? . . . .

[We need to learn from the positive values of contemporary civilization about] the expression of communication and love in the husband-wife relationship with a particular emphasis on *a new mutuality and significance for the woman*. Here we have failed, for we have not related the halakhah to such a concern. . . .

We should reemphasize (or rediscover) the positive strand in halakhah, the strand expressed so beautifully by Tanach's [i.e., the Bible's] use of sexual imagery as the allegory of the highest relationship of G-d and Israel, and shift the emphasis to the positive value of sex as a mode (among many) of encounter rather than exploitation.

Thus [the Talmudic maxim] *Kadesh at'zmecha b'mutar lach* ["sanctify yourself (even) in what is permitted"] would come to mean . . . [that] our permitted sexual relationship, *b'kedushah* [in holiness] . . . [ought to be] more reciprocal, more tender. Calling such a sexual relationship a religious act is quite legitimate.[6]

Greenberg proceeded to rebuke modern Orthodox authorities for failing to carry the mission of halakhah into uncharted waters in order to sanctify the secular:

> The purpose of halachah is to transform the mundane into the holy.... But today, there are some [contemporary] experiences which halachah doesn't cover adequately. ... The Poskim aren't meeting their responsibility in updating and fully applying our law codes. This inaction represents a denial of one of the basic tenets of Judaism: that our tradition may be applied to any situation.[7]

In light of modern sensibilities about mutuality in lovemaking and respect for women's equality and dignity, Greenberg argues, halakhists must reject Rabbi Eliezer's model of minimalist intercourse that assumes the wife will consent to and support her husband's passionless piety. Instead, Rav's paradigm of making love to his wife with verbal endearments (TB *Brakhot* 62a) ought to be "expanded on the grounds that a wife's expectations are higher in our society and more would be needed to please her."[8] Greenberg was intimating that educated women in a democracy rightfully demand more intellectual interaction, more sexual satisfaction, and more involvement in decision making in their relationships.

Had Greenberg not said more, he probably would not have stirred up a wasp's nest of reactions, for at this point he had only called for a change of outlook regarding greater *marital* intimacy. But Greenberg also believed that the urgent crisis for young Orthodox students required immediate halakhic reform to permit *physical expressions of affection prior to marriage*. Otherwise, the prevailing halakhah was liable to push Jewish college students out of the Orthodox fold just when America was at the cusp of the sexual revolution. Greenberg, who was not a halakhic authority, wanted adjustments made in guidelines for American Orthodox Jews who go on dates, go steady, and have long engagements before finally marrying ten to fifteen years after puberty.

Traditional halakhic practice prohibits common North American dating practices: being alone with someone of the opposite sex (*yihud*), touching in any way (*negia*), let alone kissing or hugging, and, of course, premarital intercourse. The Torah's prohibition on *negia*, physical contact, begins once a woman has had her first period, when her body is considered impure and the Torah prohibits a man from having sex with her unless she has been immersed in the mikveh. Since single women were strongly discouraged from going to the mikveh, touching before marriage was prohibited. This rendered impossible American-style dating (hand-holding, kissing, hugging, and petting as expressions of physical affection). Greenberg expressed his concern this way:

> [The Bible] doesn't look upon sex as an evil; the prohibition of *negia* is based on a technical halacha—that a girl is in a state of *niddah* [impurity during and after her period] until she performs *t'vilah* in the *mikveh* [immersion in the ritual bath]. [But] unmarried girls are not permitted go to the *mikveh*.[9]

As Greenberg later commented: "The negative phenomenon of promiscuity is real. But people have real sexual needs as well."[10]

Speculating, Greenberg suggests that the classical Rabbis had no serious halakhic objection to limited physical intimacy before marriage except for their fear of intercourse with a woman who was impure due to her menses. He implies obliquely, without stating it explicitly, that single women should purify themselves monthly so that holding hands with their dates could be approved halakhically. One might even construe his ambiguous statement as an authorization for premarital intercourse after immersion.

Acknowledging the daring nature of his proposed policy, Greenberg conceded that issuing such new directives entailed moral risks:

"No value system is free of its practical problems, and this new value system might lead to an increased tendency by some to violate halachah."[11] For example, an engaged couple who permit themselves to hug and kiss might be so sexually aroused that they engage in spontaneous, unintended intercourse.

Nonetheless, Greenberg continues:

Still, this new approach to sex, even with its problems, would be much better than our present suppression of such deep and meaningful activity. Indeed, I believe that more people would end up observing [the laws], for they would see the relevance and rationale in the new halachic categories.[12]

The interview evoked zealous rebuttals, the most important and personally painful of which came from his closest ally, Lichtenstein, who wrote a rejoinder in the next issue of the student paper.[13] On one hand, as Lichtenstein would later write, he agreed with Greenberg's generally positive attitude to sexual intimacy: "With regard to the basic phenomenon of sexual experience . . . our instincts and our attitude are clearly positive. We have no qualms."[14] Both concurred with Soloveitchik that the Jewish approach to marital sexuality affirms pleasure and rejects asceticism, but they did not agree about premarital sexual contact, or about whether halakhah could or should be more permissive.

Lichtenstein vigorously condemned the implications of Greenberg's permissive attitude to premarital physical intimacy and the "public criticism of the halakhah, matters about which you or I have no business issuing manifestos."[15] He added elsewhere: "On both halakhic and ethical grounds . . . we [as Orthodox Jews] reject non-marital sexuality as transient, vulgar, and possibly exploitative, devoid of interpersonal commitment or social and legal sanction."[16]

In a reply to Lichtenstein in the same YU newspaper (May 1966), Greenberg declared officially that he had not intended to advocate for permitting sexual relations outside of marriage.[17] Nevertheless, he later admitted in private and published interviews that he did have the reform of premarital sexual practices in mind.[18]

This acrimonious exchange would silence Modern Orthodox public discussions on intimacy before marriage for nearly half a century. In 2018, Dr. Jennie Rosenfeld, author of *The Newlywed's Guide to Physical Intimacy* (2011), lamented:

> Today, more than forty years later [after Greenberg's interview], there are no new laws [about premarital sexual intimacy for Modern Orthodox youth].... With the lack of guidance in this context, individuals are left to struggle alone with their sexual decision-making, perhaps wanting to make moral choices, but lacking any moral compass to help them in this difficult endeavor.[19]

While Greenberg continued to publish and lecture voluminously for forty years, he never returned to the subject of sexual ethics. Then in a 2014 interview with the Orthodox feminist sociologist Sylvia Barack Fishman, published in *Yitz Greenberg and Modern Orthodoxy: The Road Not Taken* (2019), he took an even more radical step: proposing a new halakhic category, "positive sinning," to guide serious couples exploring a committed relationship involving premarital sex. He cautioned, though, that "the depth of emotional attachment should dictate the extent of physical involvement."[20]

> If a single man or woman finds another appropriate individual to whom they are attracted and with whom they want to deepen the connection, they proceed. [On one hand] the term *positive sinning* is an acknowledgement that they are going beyond what is currently permitted and is in that sense a violation.
>
> On the other hand, it is positive in that it reflects a desire to meet the Torah's values and goal of sexuality ... to know another person as *tzelem elokim* [the image of God]. It is not a casual or exploitative

or abusive contact. All interaction is for connection, relationship building with an implied goal of becoming a permanent, stable commitment which enables lifetime marriage and family creation.

Laws regulating sexuality (indeed, all halakhot) are not some electrified barbed wire fence which means that to try to go beyond the current boundary is to be instantly electrocuted. Rather the couple should realize that ultimately they stand before God who will judge their behavior. . . . The mitzvah—the good—in knowing a *tzelem elokim* and confirming it in the other and deepening it in one's self in part through sexual expression outweighs the negative in breaching a norm that is not constructive, often counterproductive, in an age of extended years of singlehood.

The goal is *covenantal sexuality*—in which the pleasure and self-expression [are] nurtured by [a] relationship . . . [that] grow[s] out of appreciating the value, uniqueness and equality of the other. . . . The pleasure given or taken is not hedonic or selfish but part of a deeper embrace of life and of the other. . . . This positive halakhic approach also means that the holiness dimension in sexuality is not expressed in withdrawal and restriction only. . . . In the covenantal approach the holiness is deeply infused into the sexual expression which is permitted. Carried out in this spirit, sexuality and intercourse . . . [are] one of the highest forms of encountering Shekhinah—of recognizing God's presence and increasing it in the world.[21]

Linzer and Marcus's Podcast, *The Joy of Text*

It took until the early years of the twenty-first century for a separate trend of Modern American Orthodoxy called Open Orthodoxy to emerge, in which the need for more liberal halakhic rulings on issues of sexual intimacy, raised by Greenberg in 1966, could finally be openly discussed.

The institutional shifts necessary for this change in Liberal Modern Orthodoxy and the most liberal wing of centrists of Modern

Orthodoxy began with Blu Greenberg and Rabbi Avi Weiss and their students, a new generation of liberal Orthodox Jews. In a belated Orthodox response to the feminist revolution (1970s) in which so many Jewish women took an active role, Blu Greenberg (Yitz Greenberg's wife) founded the Jewish Orthodox Feminist Alliance (JOFA) in 1997. Since the conservative rabbinical establishment at YU continued to condemn any halakhic reform on women's issues as well as issues of sexual practice, Weiss, a fearless and hence notorious Jewish social activist (particularly in the Free Soviet Jewry Movement) called for a movement of Open Orthodoxy that same year. In 1999 Weiss established the male rabbinical school Yeshivat Chovevei Torah Rabbinical School (YCT), and in 2009 Yeshivat Maharat, the equivalent women's seminary.

To this day, right-wing and centrist Orthodox institutions refuse to recognize graduates of these seminaries and polemicize against what has become, in effect, a separatist breakoff from YU Orthodoxy. In this context, reform of halakhah relating to sexual intimacy has again become a topic of public discussion within a philosophically open Orthodoxy.

In 2005, the Orthodox Forum, a conference of centrist and liberal Orthodox academics concerned with contemporary issues (founded in 1989 by then YU president Norman Lamm), convened a conference on the cutting-edge issue of changing relationships between men and women. As part of this conference, the predicament of increasing numbers of unmarried Orthodox singles (in their late twenties and thirties) was presented by Jennie Rosenfeld and Koby Frances, based on interviews with these singles.

Later, Rosenfeld and Frances created the organization Tzelem (In the Image of God), which promotes a curriculum for teaching "healthy attitudes toward the body, sexuality, and intimacy" within liberal Orthodox day schools in America.[22] The term *tzelem* recalls what Greenberg wrote in 1966: "The basis of the new value system should be the concept that experiencing a woman as a *tzelem Elokim* is a mitzvah."[23]

In 2015, Rabbi Dov Linzer, rosh yeshiva of YCT, and Bat Sheva Marcus, president of JOFA, inaugurated *The Joy of Text*, which would soon become a popular website and podcast for halakhically informed discussions about contemporary sexuality.[24] *The Joy of Text* raises sensitive issues long taboo in the Modern Orthodox world: physical affection during dating, foreplay in marital lovemaking, sexual positions, and modified practices of couple intimacy during *niddah*.[25] For example, in one of the halakhic study texts Linzer prepared for the website, he quotes a contemporary Israeli Haredi responsum permitting and recommending that a single religious woman living together with a secular Jew visit the mikveh after her period, a position for which Greenberg had been condemned when he hinted at it in 1966.[26] What long-term effect these open halakhic discussions will have within various wings of Modern Orthodoxy remains to be seen.

Berkovits: Humanizing Sexual Relationships

Although Modern Orthodoxy did not respond positively to Greenberg's challenge to halakhic authorities to issue more flexible guidelines for premarital sexual intimacy, two of its foremost philosophers of halakhah—the German-educated European philosophers Rabbi Eliezer Berkovits (1908–1992) and Rav Joseph B. Soloveitchik (1903–1993)—did, like Greenberg, affirm sexuality within marriage as natural and sacred and called for treating women with respect as dignified egalitarian partners created in the image of God.

Berkovits, a disciple of Rabbi Yehiel Weinberg (a student of Slabodka Mussar and author of the responsa *Seridei Esh*; Poland, Germany, and Switzerland, 1884–1966), was ordained in the Modern Orthodox Hildesheimer Rabbinical Seminary in Berlin. Simultaneously, he earned a doctorate in philosophy from the University of Berlin. His theology, *Faith after the Holocaust*, was published in 1973, and his seminal essay, "A Jewish Sexual Ethics," was published three years later.

Berkovits's unique halakhic approach to sexuality developed in response to the American proponents of radical sexual liberation who ridiculed bourgeois restraints on premarital sexual relations and celebrated natural desires freed of social conventions. Dismissing traditional religious restraints as neurotic obsessions laced with guilt and shame, they repudiated the classical Greek and rabbinic ideal of mastering one's *yetzer* as unhealthy repression. To them, freedom was not a product of self-control, but of sexual release. Nonmarital sexual expression was to be praised whether or not it occurred within the confines of committed love relationships.

While Berkovits vigorously rejects this militant ethos of promiscuity, he does *not* denounce the aim of true sexual liberation. He affirms that guilt and shame should be removed from natural human sexuality, for it is God's creation, which is good in itself unless abused. He aspires to integrate the physiological and the spiritual, but, for this very reason, he draws a clear distinction between mere instinctual gratification and truly liberated lovemaking.

For the sake of human dignity and interpersonal intimacy, the impersonal drive of libido must be *personalized*. Otherwise, sexual drives will dehumanize both the person in the throes of desire and the sexual partner exploited to satisfy unbridled passions. Within a moral relationship characterized by trust, love, and commitment, ethics must limit the reign of indiscriminate satisfaction of human desire. Then, the sanctification of nature will abide.

Berkovits, the philosopher and the halakhist, chooses atypically to convey his message by analyzing a rabbinic narrative about a prostitute and yeshiva student in a glamorous exotic brothel. Berkovits claims that this story "contains all the basic principles of a Jewish sex ethics."[27]

Here is an abbreviated version of the Talmudic narrative, often entitled, "The Tzitzit and the Harlot."

PROLOGUE: Rabbi Nathan said ... "Go and learn the [principle that the performance of every mitzvah has an earthly reward and an otherworldly reward] from the commandment of tzitzit [i.e., attaching fringes or tassels with ritual knots to the four corners of one's garment]."

ACT ONE: ... Once a certain man, who was scrupulous about the commandment of tzitzit, heard that there was a harlot in one of the [distant] cities by the sea who takes 400 gold pieces for her reward [i.e., her hire]. He sent her 400 gold pieces, and she fixed a time for his appointment. . . .

When he entered, she prepared for him seven beds [or six] of silver and the highest of gold, and between each bed there was a ladder of silver, but the topmost ladder was of gold. [She ascended and sat on the topmost bed, and she was naked. He too ascended in order to sit naked opposite her.]

ACT TWO: ... And when they arrived [ready] for that event, his four tzitzit [the knotted tassels on his garment] appeared to him like four accusing witnesses[28] and slapped him on the face! He slipped down [from the seventh bed] and sat on the ground. Then she too slipped down and sat on the ground.

She said to him: "By the Roman Capitol! [*or* By the goddess of love, Agape/Isis!] I will not let you go until you tell me what blemish you saw in me!"

He said: "By the [Temple] service! I have not seen any blemish in you, rather there is no woman as beautiful as you in the whole world! But God has given us one commandment [called tzitzit]. . . . Now they (i.e., the four tzitzit on my four-cornered garment) have appeared to me as four [accusing] witnesses!"

She said to him: "By the [Temple] service![29] I will not let you go until you write down for me your name, the name of your city, [the name of your teacher], and the name of your study house (*beit midrash*) where you study the Torah!" He wrote down for her his name, his city, and his house of study where he learned Torah. [Then he returned home by himself].

ACT THREE: ... She arose and apportioned all her wealth: a third to the [Roman] government, a third to the poor, and a third she took with her in her hand. [She distributed her possessions] except for those bedsheets [which she took with her] and then she went to the house of study of Rabbi Hiyya.

She said to him: "Master, make me a convert!" He said to her: "My daughter, perhaps you have set your eye on one of the students?" She took out the written note [that the student had given her at her request and gave it to the rabbi]....

HIS HAPPY ENDING (Version A)[30]: He [Rabbi Hiyya] said to *him* [the student]: "Arise and claim your acquisition! Those beds which she prepared for you illicitly, she shall prepare for you permissibly!" Such is the reward [for observing the mitzvah of tzitzit] in this world; as for the world-to-come, I know not how much it is.

HER HAPPY ENDING (Version B)[31]: He [the Rabbi] said to *her* [the newly converted woman]: "Arise and claim your acquisition!"

[The head of the yeshiva or the narrator concludes]: "Those beds which were prepared for him illicitly, she will prepare for him permissibly! Such is her reward in this world; and as for the world-to-come, I know not how much it is."[32]

THE CRITIQUE OF FAKE SEXUAL LIBERATION

Berkovits interprets this unusual Talmudic tale, scene by scene, in order to show that the character of the yeshiva student in this ancient tale is making the same mistake that North American college students of today do in expecting to find sexual liberation in a casual hook-up without love or commitment. While Berkovits acknowledges that the "contemporary sexual rebellion [of the 1960s] that wishes to do away with the taboos of this civilization has its justification,"[33] the purported cure to societal repression (euphemistically named "free love") that promises personal liberation and guiltless intimacy, in fact, enslaves humanity in two senses.

First, unlimited desire dominates and eviscerates the autonomous self that set out on that quest:

> Man falls into the thralldom of mighty impersonal forces when he liberates himself from social taboos. The sex act is not so much an act of letting go. It is not man who acts; rather it is something that happens through man [as if compelled by a demon].[34]

Second, the liberated person enslaves others through the utilitarian commodification of persons used as a means to satisfy his desire. Thus both the user and the used, the student as a consumer and the woman who is consumed, are depersonalized, even if they act freely by mutual consent and he pays her 400 zuz. When they strip themselves of their identities and clothing and climb to the highest bed, "nudity . . . meets nudity; his sexual desire meets her greed."[35]

> It is an accommodation between a man who has been reduced to the pleasure principle, and a woman who has been reduced to cupidity. . . . *What could be more impersonal than an appointment between lust and greed?*[36]

TRUE LIBERATION IS LIBERATION
FROM ENSLAVING ECSTASY

Atop the highest bed, the moment before the student is to sink into sexual reverie with the prostitute, he is awaked by a call to repent for his actions. The slap of the tzitzit calls the student back to his authentic self as the lover of tzitzit who has a relationship with God. Berkovits suggests that the agency of the fringes is symbolic of the student's inner resistance: His conscience rebukes him at the moment of anticipated sexual ecstasy. So "he tears himself away and sits on the ground."[37]

At that moment he also releases the woman herself from her role as a prestigious product of the sex industry. Abruptly, just as the capitalist market is about to turn natural lovemaking into an artificial commodity exchange between two persons who do not see each other as persons, the student withdraws from the role he is playing and descends from the golden bed. In reaction, she steps out of her role and follows him to the floor.

After stripping themselves of their commercial roles, both the "consumer" and the "product" are enabled to encounter one another, face to face. Now, they see in each other two flawed persons ashamed of what has happened: "They sit there, still naked, but no longer in the nudity of lust and desire, but in *the nakedness of their frail humanity amidst the ruins of their human dignity*."[38] At that moment she too is liberated: "*As she meets him as a person, she finds herself as one. . . .* She comes out of it a changed human being. And so, we assume, does he."[39]

THE HUMANIZING POWER OF DIALOGUE

Having regained her autonomy, the woman begins to examine first her former client's core identity and then her own. Berkovits says their I-it relationship is now redeemed by virtue of an honest I-Thou dialogue in accord with Martin Buber's existentialist paradigm.[40] "When he first appeared at her door [as the man who sent her money], he was nameless." But after their collapse onto the floor, her questions probe his individual identity—his name, his city, his rabbi, his house of study where he learns Torah.[41] She no longer sees him as a client or as a naked male but as a particular person clothed in a biography and as a disciple who possesses a significant other—his teacher.

Her questions test his willingness to take responsibility for himself. She asks him to "write it all down for her on a piece of paper," which she can show to his teacher, thus revealing his sinful secret. Nevertheless, "he placed it into her hand" as one "entrusts something precious into safekeeping."[42] Now she releases him to go to his true home, and she begins her search for a core identity beyond her commercial role as a glamorously sexy woman.

SEXUALITY IS HUMANIZED

The story could have ended with this chaste friendship and perhaps the prostitute's repudiation not only of her profession but of sex itself, as occurs in many ancient Christian tales of the same era about penitent prostitutes who become nuns after encountering a holy monk.[43] With such an ending, the tale's message would then have been about spiritual redemption accessed by transcending the impurity of the sexual body.

No, protests Berkovits. This is a Jewish tale, and its happy ending must be a marriage in which passionate sexuality and holy matrimony are integrated. The tzitzit were not preaching abstinence; nor did they denigrate the student's yetzer (libido). Rather, they merely warned him that desirous, roving eyes must be controlled to avoid the depersonalization of pornographic sex.

The woman and the student can now look at one another with new eyes, without exploitive intent. Now they discover beauty and desire that are neither chaste nor prurient:

When he first heard about her, she was the celebrated prostitute . . . the anonymous symbol of sex to him. But now, sitting opposite each other on the ground, he recognizes her as the most beautiful woman he ever saw. *He acknowledges her in her full feminine dignity and is able to appreciate her beauty without the eyes of lust.*[44]

In place of lust, which dehumanizes, comes his respect for this particular female's dignity and at the same time a genuine, disinterested appreciation of her erotic beauty. And this woman now sees him as a human being with a conscience, self-control, and a spiritual tradition, whom she can love.

Following the student back to his teacher, Rabbi Hiyya, the reformed prostitute speaks openly about her desire for marital relations: "She does not hide the fact that she desires the man, but the whole man."[45] Approving her desire, the rabbi pronounces his blessing over her and announces the reward: "the sensual enjoyment of their union" on her erotic sheets, now adorning the marital bed that has been sanctified between them. Berkovits comments:

The humanizing of the impersonal [in marriage] does not in any way take away from enjoyment of the sexual act. It does not attempt to "spiritualize" the act. In fact, the enjoyment itself is part of the living realization of Judaism.[46]

Rabbi Hiyya does not ask this woman to divest herself of elements of her previous identity as an erotic woman: her glamorous sheets or the money she had earned as a prostitute. Rather, he instructs her to bring her sheets to her marital bed as a culmination of the process of her transformation.

The couple succeeds in converting what began as a merely financial or biological exchange into a lasting marital union constructed on the corrupt foundations of their first "date." Emerging out of this illicit liaison, they both come to realize that they sought something deeper than an ephemeral tryst. They confess and embrace their flawed biographies on their path to marital union.

More generally, from Berkovits's analysis we can deduce that the aim of marriage should not be the shedding of previous identities *in toto* but the construction of a dialogic relationship from two diverse points of view. The twoness is not lost in *becoming one flesh*; rather, marriage synthesizes the concrete particularities of bodies and experiences. Thus marriage is the product of rededication, not eradication, of expansive growth of the original self to encompass another, not dissolution of each self into what Berkovits denigrates as the alchemy of romantic infatuation or sexual reverie.

THE MAN'S OR THE WOMAN'S AGENCY?

After the conversion, Rabbi Hiyya authorizes the betrothal, an acquisition made with the 400 zuz paid for a sexual union not yet consummated. The bride is acquired as usual—or is it the groom? This Talmudic tale appears in variant manuscripts with alternative happy endings. In one version Rabbi Hiyya tells the student to arise and claim his bride with those same sheets she had intended to use as a prostitute. According to Berkovits, the student, who restrained his desire in the golden bed, has now transformed what was forbidden—when acquired through commercial exploitation (I-it)—into what is permitted and sacred in a passionate union of onah following an act of sanctification, *kiddushin*, the betrothal.

In the alternative second version of the happy ending, Rabbi Hiyya speaks, not to his student, but to the convert, saying, "Arise and claim your acquisition!" Thus he acknowledges the reformed prostitute's legal claim to acquire the student as her husband; he tells her to claim *her* purchase. Unlike the Talmudic pattern of marriage in which women play only passive roles, this redemptive narrative presents the woman as a liberated, self-determining agent: She changes her profession, goes in search of the student, chooses her religion, picks her own husband, and "takes" him (a technical term for betrothal, or marriage). In so doing, she can have a truly equal relationship with her husband. In fact, she might even be said to be master (*ba'al*) of her husband by acquiring him in marriage.

SANCTITY AND LIBERATION UNITE
IN JEWISH SEXUAL ETHICS

For Berkovits, what makes casual, nonmarital sex an anathema is not guilt about violating religious rules or fear of heavenly punishments, but desecration of the potential for a sacred I-Thou relationship of love. To achieve a human relationship worthy of sexual union, the couple must be willing to make the supreme commitment, the act of betrothal called, appropriately, kiddushin (sanctification):

> The highest form of the personalization of the relationship between man and woman finds its expression in their complete dedication to each other. It includes unquestioning trust in one another, the full acceptance of one's partner in his or her comprehensive humanity.
> *A love that does not have the courage to commit itself "forever" is lacking in trust, in acceptance, in faith.* [Only after commitment can one achieve] the climax in man's striving for sexual liberation.[47]

In approving the kiddushin, Rabbi Hiyya (whose name means "To Life!") blesses the couple's union and the woman's newly redeemed bedsheets for use in the sacred bed of matrimony. By analogy, Berkovits gives his blessing to sexual liberation as long as it truly liberates individuals from the sexual obsessions that dehumanize them and their partners. Only by controlling the objectifying sexual drive within halakhic limits does one have the potential to love another person ethically, genuinely, and humanely. Then "their life together makes room . . . for a God not of asceticism or of life-denying spirituality, but of life-affirming and life-desiring sanctification."[48]

Soloveitchik: Redeeming Natural Sexuality

Soloveitchik studied and deeply absorbed Western philosophy—integrating Kant and Kierkegaard into his religious philosophy of halakhah. Without denying his Litvak Haredi roots, he fully embraced the ideal synthesis between "Yeshiva" and "University" that combines Torah and secular human wisdom. At YU he became the leading Modern Orthodox Talmudist, although he generally refrained from issuing halakhic directives. His most sustained analysis of marital sexuality is found in *Family Redeemed* (published posthumously in 2000).

COMMONALITIES WITH BERKOVITS, SHER, AND SHLANGER

Like Berkovits, who was inspired by Buber's I-Thou relationship, Soloveitchik condemns sexual activity that involves "the depersonalization of the Thou." Therefore, variety in sexual partners is "the most depersonalizing and vulgarizing factor." Marriage is sacred and simultaneously humanizing because it demands "exclusiveness in sexual life," and thus "the conquest of the powerful instinct of sexual promiscuity hallows the sex union."[49]

Moreover, Soloveitchik's understanding of the intersection of halakhah and human sexuality also shows remarkable continuities with the antimodernist and anti-Zionist Litvak Haredi educators Sher and Shlanger (see chapters 9–11), despite Soloveitchik's modern existentialist and Zionist nationalist views. All three share the common traditions of the Lithuanian yeshivot. (For example, Soloveitchik's family roots derive from the Brisker Talmudists of Volozhin: His paternal grandfather was Chaim Soloveitchik; his great-great-grandfather was Naftali Tzvi Yehuda Berlin, the Netziv; and his great-great-great-great grandfather was Haim of Volozhin).

Soloveitchik and Shlanger share the same characterization of the modern predicament, namely, Orthodox Jews must avoid two dangerous polar extremes: the Western sexual revolution that celebrates unrestrained hedonism and self-serving personal freedom, and halakhic asceticism within marriage that devalues God's creation—the human body—and deforms legally mandated love relations between spouses.

Like Shlanger and Shuchatowitz, Soloveitchik and Berkovits repudiate the pessimistic path of those ascetic Haredim who suffer from an irrational anxiety about the evil impulse and whose fear nourishes paranoid distrust of human rationality and strength of will. Soloveitchik and Berkovits condemn an ascetic ethos in marriage not only as unhealthy and unnatural but as heretical because it rejects the goodness of Creation and of the human being into which God, with wise providence, planted sexual desire. Both affirm this-worldly life regulated by halakhah, as Soloveitchik writes: "Holiness means the holiness of earthly, here-and-now life. . . . Performance of commandments is confined to this world, to physical, concrete reality, to clamorous, tumultuous life, pulsating with exuberance and strength."[50] Similar to the Besht's notion of *avodah begashmiyut* (corporeal worship of God with all the bodily functions), Soloveitchik states that "man worships his Creator with his body, his eating and his sexual activity."[51]

Both Soloveitchik and Shlanger see the revelation of Torah as God's gift of *tikkun*, repairing nature's deficiencies. The halakhah provides a process of remediation and perfection for the still imperfect human formed by the Creator. Everything God made has a positive potential, but it must be refined and actualized by civilizing processes, as exemplified in the following Rabbinic story:

> Rabbi Hoshaya was asked: "If circumcision is so precious, why was it not given to Adam?" . . .

He replied: "Whatever was created in the first six days requires further *tikkun* (preparation, refinement): [raw] mustard needs sweetening; legumes need sweetening; wheat needs grinding; and *the human being too needs tikkun.*" (*Genesis Rabbah* 11:6)

Just as mustard seeds become beneficial for human consumption only after they have been refined with the aid of agricultural knowledge, so too human sexuality must be reformed by halakhic wisdom in order to elicit its positive potential and eliminate its deleterious side effects. Halakhic restrictions on sexual practice civilize instinct, and a discipline of self-control dignifies humanity even in the fulfillment of its bodily desires. Rules are necessary, even though God's Creation is good, because in nature, instinctual drives are not rationally self-guided; they must be trained. Soloveitchik explains:

We detest unruly, chaotic, boundless and unsatiated desire . . . which desires only to enjoy, no matter what or how. . . . Sexual activity can be a sinful affair of the most crass and devastating consequence. Thus *the Halakha was compelled not only to redeem but to remedy the sexual impulse.*[52]

THE DYNAMICS OF HOLINESS

Soloveitchik teaches that while, on one side, one must be wary of untamed desire, on the other, one must not be terrified by the power of *yetzer ha-ra*. After all, God declared the Creation, an orderly natural world, *very good* (Gen. 1:31). Soloveitchik teaches: "Judaism was opposed to any maiming of the natural life for the sake of some transcendental goal, since holiness arises out of the naturalness of man."[53]

While pessimistic monks, medieval pietists, and many Haredim focus on the difficulties of resisting the wiles of the evil impulse, Soloveitchik as a Maimonidean exudes confidence in the human ability to master impulses when reinforced by halakhah's wise guidelines and character training. Soloveitchik writes: "Judaism's philosophy of carnal existence is an *optimistic* one," and he "foresees its undreamed-of progress and improvement" as long as a human being "redeems himself, body and soul, by employing the knowledge and technique available to him."[54]

Employing Kierkegaard's dichotomy, Soloveitchik distinguishes between the aesthete and the ethicist. An aesthetic civilization of cultured hedonism is at odds with the sacred ethical civilization developed by the halakhah. For example, an aesthete partaking in multiple erotic encounters cultivates "an instinctual reaction of an excited heart to the shocking sudden encounter with beauty."[55] The aesthete relates to each sexual partner in the mode of transient I-it commercialism rather than of an ongoing I-Thou relationship. For the erotic consumer seeking endless varieties of sexual experience, *life without commitment is serial prostitution.*

By contrast, marriage introduces an ethical and sacred dimension to human existence in which sex can be regulated and restrained by mutual love and care and sanctified by an exclusive covenant with one partner. Soloveitchik writes:

> Marriage, charged with the task of redeeming the erotic experience, tries to free the latter from the *whimsicality of the eros* and from the *capriciousness of the aesthete.* The task of marriage is to teach man to find love in identity and continuity . . . in reply to a metaphysical ethical summons.[56]

> The purpose of the halakhic imperative is not to label man's sensual body as impure and thus reject it, but to purify it and draw it closer to God.[57]

In marriage, the body becomes "the wellspring of *kedushah.*"[58] Furthermore, "the sanctity of the soul, of the spiritual personality, can be realized only via the sanctification of the body."[59]

A human being does not become sanctified by a metaphysical union with the invisible nor by mystical unification with the infinite, nor by an ecstasy that embraces the whole world, but by bodily life, by animal activities, and by the concretizing of halakhic values in this world.[60]

Yet, Soloveitchik cautions that bodily instincts seek immediate gratification and know no inherent boundaries, so "the dynamics of holiness" entail some acts of self-denial. It is necessary to sacrifice immediate gratification "by refusing to yield to the powerful push of the flesh and by resisting the rush of primitive lust."[61] In marriage, its sanctity commences with the sacrifice of the freedom of desire.[62]

> The prohibition against adultery is the basis of married life according to Halakha. If one would stipulate in the marriage agreement that adultery would be permitted, the stipulation would be null and void. *To marry means to give up freedom of choice with respect to one's sexual gratification.*[63]

Nevertheless, halakhic self-discipline ought not to be confused with repressive self-denial. It must serve the original natural impulse whose satisfaction leads to "a holy life."[64]

> *A covenantal marriage is a hedonic, pleasure-oriented community.* Judaism did not overlook or underestimate the physical aspects of marriage. On the contrary, once sacrificial withdrawal from the sinful erotic paradise of change and variety is completed, the natural element in marriage comes to the fore. The two partners owe each other not only fidelity, but also full edification of their sexual needs.[65]

What is more, Soloveitchik explains, halakhah declares invalid a "marriage without carnal enjoyment and erotic love," for it is "contrary to human nature."[66]

Soloveitchik concurs with Maimonides' condemnation of the misguided Jewish ascetics, whose "practices resemble Christian monastic practice":

> Fools . . . mortify their bodies with all sorts of tortures and thought to acquire virtues and to come closer to God *as if the Blessed One hates the body and wants to destroy it*. . . . *The Torah is perfect, reviving the soul* (Ps. 19:7). . . . [and its aim] is to perfect the natural human being by following the [golden] mean.[67]

In the same spirit, Soloveitchik declares (with unjustified exaggeration):[68]

> Self-torture, mortification of the flesh, revulsion towards the world, the condemnation of natural drives or the deadening of the senses and the repression of the exercise of the natural faculties of man— nothing of that sort was ever preached by Judaism.[69]

In fact, the followers of Rabbi Eliezer do apparently value marital asceticism and sexual self-denial as the path to sanctity, while treating women, even their own wives, as a dangerous temptation. By contrast, Soloveitchik would probably concur with Martin Buber, who wrote:

> Creatures are placed in my way so that I, their fellow creature, by means of them and with them find the way to God. . . . God wants us to come to Him by means of the [women] he created [as potential spouses] and not by renunciation of them.[70]

Lamm's *The Jewish Way in Love and Marriage*

While Soloveitchik's own reflections on redeeming sexuality through halakhic marriage were not published until after his death, his student and colleague at YU, Professor Maurice Lamm (d. 2016), captured his message and made it accessible to a contemporary generation in his Jewish best seller, *The Jewish Way in Love and Marriage* (1980). Like Soloveitchik, Lamm argued not by quoting laws, but by appealing to Jewish insights about the paradoxical dimensions of human experience:

> Sex is the most powerful, all-pervasive force in human experience. It may be intensely personal, meaningful, and creative at one moment, and depersonalized, meaningless, and careless the next. Much of its glory is that it can bring us as close as we may get in life to experiencing the mystery of our mortality, and because of this it is sanctified.
>
> Yet it can also be a blind, nearly irresistible force seeking wanton release on the biological level, and in this way its sanctity is perverted. Paradoxically, sex—the most chaotic, powerful, and untutored drive—can only be fully experienced when it includes an element of discipline and precision.[71]

Lamm insists that the sex act be mutually consensual, but that freedom from coercion in and of itself is not enough to make the libido meaningful or sacred: "Mutual consent . . . is simply mutual exploitation. It has met the test of liberty . . . but it has failed the test of meaning, sensitivity, decency, and responsibility to the future."[72]

Therefore, like Soloveitchik, Lamm condemns premarital intercourse as "sexual adventurism."[73] The halakhic constraint on desire in the context of marital commitment is the path to sanctity: "Love seeks eternity, sanctity, rootedness in a transcendent power. . . . Love will not be fulfilled until it reaches that ultimate moment, the total commitment of marriage."[74]

Simultaneously, while acknowledging the dangers of sexual yetzer, Lamm, like Soloveitchik, celebrates God's mandate for sexual desire: "There is nothing shady about the sexual appetite legitimately expressed. . . . It is ordained by God Himself as the means for the perpetuation of the human race and for the ultimate expression, of human love."[75]

Lichtenstein's "Of Marriage" and Ostroff's *To Know How to Love*

Even though Rabbi Aharon Lichtenstein (1933–2015, United States and Israel), as mentioned above, critiqued Greenberg's audacious halakhic proposals for reform in rabbinic sexual ethics, he was by no means a right-wing Orthodox thinker and halakhic *posek*. He objected to Greenberg's public challenge to *poskim* to liberalize premarital practices, and yet, like Greenberg, wholeheartedly concurred with his father-in-law Soloveitchik's affirmative worldview that halakhah mandates the religious value of natural desires (hedonism and sexuality) as long as they are redeemed and sanctified by halakhic structures. In his seminal article, "Of Marriage Relationships and Relations" (2007), Lichtenstein wrote:

> Impelled by our spiritual instincts, and animated by the faith instilled in us by our Torah mentors, we opt for *consecration rather than abstinence*. . . . We are challenged to sanctify—by integrating sexuality within total sacral existence, characterized by . . . divinely ordained denial and realization, and by infusing the relationship itself with human and spiritual content. This is by no means the easier course. May we have the wisdom and the commitment to render it the better.[76]

LICHTENSTEIN'S CELEBRATION OF ROMANTIC LOVE

Unlike Haredi rabbis such as Yaakov Kanievsky, Lichtenstein celebrates romantic love within marriage, though he too rejects the "lusty passion" of extramarital affairs lionized by Romanticism's English writers like William Blake and D. H. Lawrence (whom

Lichtenstein studied when earning his doctorate in English literature at Harvard):[77]

> *We assert the value of romantic love, its physical manifestation included,*
> *without flinching from the prospect of concomitant sensual pleasure;*
> *and we do so without harboring guilt or reservations.*[78] We insist, of
> course, upon its sanctification . . . within the context of [the] suffu-
> sive *kedushah* of carnal experience.[79]

While convinced that halakhic Judaism celebrates passionate,
romantic, and yet controlled and sanctified marital sexuality,
Lichtenstein is surprised (and perhaps disappointed?) that rabbinic
codes offer no significant legal directives about how to build marital
relationships:

> A corpus of halakhot spell[s] out the respective rights and duties
> [between spouses]. . . . However, as regards *many of the issues which*
> *confront and concern many contemporary couples, we find relatively*
> *little imperative direction.*[80] They have been relegated to the realms
> of *devar ha-reshut* [matters of permission], an area of . . . personal
> preference . . . subject to the discussion, predilection, and decision
> of individual couples.[81]

For Lichtenstein, this lacuna has the positive result that the halakhah leaves "room for flexibility and mutual choice" and therefore
couples are free to adjust their bedroom practices according to their
own preferences and those of their particular communities.[82]

Along with other liberally inclined students of Soloveitchik (like
Rav Shlomo Riskin), Lichtenstein made aliyah to Israel (1972), and
he and Riskin each created many liberal Orthodox Religious Zionist
yeshivot, rabbinical schools, and women's yeshivot (Yeshivat Har
Etzion; Midreshet Lindenbaum; Ohr Torah Stone Institutions). In
his community in Efrat, Riskin appointed Jennie Rosenfeld, author

of *The Newlywed's Guide to Physical Intimacy*, as the first official Orthodox female spiritual advisor (equivalent in many ways to a rabbi) in Israel (2015). Emerging from these prestigious Israeli rabbinic institutions inspired by Soloveitchik's philosophy of halakhah, some students have begun to address educationally the halakhah of marital intimacy. For example, a student of Lichtenstein at Yeshivat Har Etzion, the halakhic ethicist Rav Yuval Cherlow (Rosh Yeshiva [the head] of Amit Orot Shaul in Tel Aviv, and co-founder of Tzohar, an organization of liberal-minded Religious Zionist Orthodox rabbis who conduct user-friendly weddings) has since 2001 answered more than 30,000 internet questions, many about sexual issues, and his responsa were later published in book form.

OSTROFF'S GUIDEBOOK TO MARITAL LOVEMAKING

Lichtenstein's student Raphael Ostroff, a centrist Religious Zionist rabbi, believes that sustained sexual intimacy and excitement are imperatives for maintaining emotionally healthy marital relationships that may last for forty to fifty years, given contemporary life expectancy. In his groundbreaking book *LaDaat LeEhov*, Ostroff attempts to repair the lacuna in marital halakhah, translate Soloveitchik and Lichtenstein's philosophical worldview into a practical manual for Orthodox couples, and teach the art of romantic, guilt-free marital lovemaking.[83] This most sexually explicit and practical halakhic guide for Modern Orthodox married couples in Israel integrates lenient legal directives, the spiritual objectives of marital union, and the mechanics and art of sexual intercourse (illustrated with anatomical charts portraying male and female genitalia). The book also includes a dictionary of anatomical terms along with their rabbinic euphemisms; a list of common sexual dysfunctions and their remedies; and descriptions of the physiological dynamics of male and female orgasm.[84] Ostroff speaks explicitly about varying sexual experiences and tastes in order to help couples fulfill the qualitative requirements of the mitzvah of onah.

"IT IS TORAH AND I MUST LEARN IT!"

Compared to Ostroff's book, Litvak Haredi manuals are intentionally reticent in describing and prescribing erotic behavior. In fact, when yeshiva students ask Shuchatowitz to prescribe specific techniques for marital sex, he purposefully refuses:

> I never answer them. This is no time to imitate or put on a show like an entertainer. This requires sincerity that emerges from one's soul. Only the man himself knows how to appease his wife truly using the brains and the talents God gave him. Every imitation—even though it may appear more professional—has no value compared to what emerges from the man himself. This is appropriately named in the halakhah—"private matters between him and her."[85]

Ostroff, however, sides with Rav Kahana's desire to know firsthand and in detail about the Torah's practice of marital relations—"It is Torah and I must learn it!" He imparts specific—and comprehensive—physiological, sexual, psychological, and halakhic knowledge about these previously unmentionable "private matters." Also, to counter the silence and shame about sex which are characteristic of Orthodox institutions, Ostroff founded an NGO, Merkaz Yahel, the Center for Jewish Intimacy, to train professionals to counsel married Orthodox couples.[86] Key obstacles to such explicit conversations are the prejudices and naivete of yeshiva students, who, like the youthful Kahana, are shocked by the thought that their rabbinic masters "enjoy desire, pleasure, and joy in their marital relations."[87]

Ostroff identifies three factors that lead Orthodox Jews to "think of great scholars as if they had no evil instinct, no sexual desire, in fact, no desire at all."[88] First, "the Christian influence on our thought process [introduces] the [misleading] assumption that the more sacred one is, the more one must separate from one's wife, while the more one expresses desire, the more impure one is."[89] Therefore, Ostroff concurs with Soloveitchik that we must repudiate anything resembling the ascetic marital practices of Christianity.[90] Second, as Rav Kook argues, ultra-Orthodox Judaism during the Exile from the Land of Israel (after 70 CE) "disconnects between the life of the body and the life of the spirit,"[91] and develops a guilt-ridden, overly spiritualized religious consciousness. By contrast, Kook affirms: "Every natural quality of the body and of the soul must be healthy and vital."[92] In particular, "the sexual drive is rooted in holiness that is incredibly strong. . . . Its secular aspect, and certainly its unclean aspect, will be totally nullified before its holy aspect."[93]

Third, Ostroff castigates "the conservative [religious] educational system that gives no [social or educational] place to express and to deliberate about these topics [i.e., marital intimacy] within a sacred framework."[94]

Ostroff rules authoritatively that "the husband and the wife may always discuss matters of sexual intercourse during sexual relations."[95] Furthermore, he asserts: "There is no contradiction between openness between couples in the inner sanctum of their bedroom and their modesty toward the outside world."[96]

The best Talmudic precedent for Ostroff's frank sex education is Rav Hisda: "Rav Hisda explains [the secret of male desire] to his daughters with stupendous openness, to the point of offering explicit sexual counseling."[97] Ostroff elucidates Rav Hisda's motivation:

Rav Hisda explains to his daughters that if they are too revealing to their husbands, exposing all their secrets [at once], then the husbands will feel that they have conquered it all, and then they will lose interest. Rather a wife must know *how to guard the dimensions of mystery and modesty* with her husband in order to succeed in drawing his eyes towards her and strengthening his desire for her.[98]

The wife must be a full partner in the dynamic of revealing and concealing, drawing forward and pushing back, in order to achieve the goal of magnifying desire and empowering the husband's pleasure.[99]

ENCOURAGEMENT OF ONGOING SEXUAL EXPERIMENTATION

For Ostroff, Rav Hisda's anxiety that male desire is fickle and that his sons-in-law may lose interest in their wives is magnified in our era of monogamy, extended longevity of lifelong marriage, and lax attitudes to extramarital affairs. Taste is idiosyncratic, and desire often necessitates variation. So Ostroff encourages ongoing experimentation and consultation with sex therapists to expand erotic variety in marital lovemaking.

As a Talmudic precedent, Ostroff cites Rabbi Yohanan bar Nafha's culinary metaphor to explain why a wife should collaborate with her husband's preference of anal intercourse and why any sexual position is permitted, just as one may prepare one's meat or fish in any way that is tasty for one's palate (TB *Nedarim* 20b). From this prooftext, Ostroff concludes:

It is permitted [with the wife's consent] for the husband to do different things with his wife; to have variety; to have pleasure.[100]

Just as one is free to enjoy food according to one's own taste, and it is inconceivable to predetermine how someone prepares his food, so too in the realm of sex[ual consumption], one is free to manage one's

tastes and preferences as one sees fit. One should not dictate to him/
her how to realize his/her desire.[101]

While conservative halakhic authorities rely on Karo's Shulhan Arukh to prohibit or restrict many of these options, Ostroff
unapologetically sets aside Karo and sides with Moshe Isserles, who
ruled:[102]

One may [with her permission] do anything one wants with his
wife [in the act of intercourse]: one may have sexual relations at any
time; kiss any and every limb; enter vaginally or anally or between
[her] limbs.[103]

UNPRECEDENTED APPROACHES

To operationalize this halakhic ruling, Ostroff lists in great detail
variations on marital intercourse—by diverse forms of foreplay,
by sexual act, by position, by degree of undress, by location in the
house, by time of day, and by use of erotic apparatuses—a level of
specification unlike any other halakhic guidebook to date.

Additionally, Ostroff's book models a co-ed educational approach
that is almost unprecedented (with the exception of Isaac Sher's
Kedushat Yisrael):

This book is meant for a [married couple] to read together. Study of
this book aims to bridge gaps between men and women in marital
relations. The book is to be read slowly and deliberately, so that its
content may be digested, that a couple may experiment with its
suggestions, with the objective of generating a full understanding
between spouses.[104]

Moreover, unlike most Orthodox rabbis, Ostroff adopts four
unusual educational policies. First, wisdom from non-Jewish
sources, especially sex therapists, is fully incorporated and acknowledged as essential for Jewish normative practice. Second, he admits

unapologetically that "some of the guidance of our rabbinic masters (Hazal) is not appropriate for today's society."[105] Third, he refrains from halakhic authoritarianism. When asked a halakhic question about marital relations, he tells the questioner: "I teach all the laws and you decide what you can observe now and what, not."[106] Fourth, in the footsteps of Lichtenstein, Ostroff shifts the locus of halakhic decision making in the bedroom from the *authority of the rabbi*, who issues only generalized rulings, to the *discretion of the couple*, who know their own unique situation and can decide their particular norms by mutual consent:

> In the context [of marital intercourse], the *question* is not what is permitted and what is forbidden, but what is appropriate and worthy, what is commendable and acceptable. The *answer* varies from couple to couple and even from one cultural world to another.
>
> The basic rule is that within the realm of the [halakhically] permitted, whatever is agreeable to the couple is accepted as long as it does not cause one of the spouses to feel uncomfortable. It is natural that some feel comfortable with certain sexual practices, while others find those disgusting.[107]

Orthodox Women's Internet Responsa

In a spirit similar to Linzer, JOFA, and Ostroff, the pluralist forum of Israeli Orthodox rabbis, called Beit Hillel, launched the website Meshivat Nefesh (Refreshing and responding to the soul) in 2017 to field women's questions about religiosity and halakhah, including issues of sexual intimacy before and after marriage. Meshivat Nefesh provides, for the first time, access to popular responsa written by expert women respondents who are themselves teachers of Talmud and halakhah in women's yeshivot.

Among the many exchanges, the following question by a young woman who had recently become Orthodox exemplifies the concerns about the ascetic image of Judaism expressed by Greenberg in 1966. A young woman asked candidly:

> I understand what is forbidden in Jewish marital relations, but I do not understand what is permitted. . . . I understand that Judaism very much sanctifies couple relations, but it sounds to me very cold or too gentle. . . . [Apparently physical intimacy is] mainly for the sake of the mitzvah.
>
> I want to ask: Do religious couples also flirt and laugh? Does the husband pick her up and does she laugh out loud? Does he tickle her and does she hug him? . . . Do they merely love each other, or are there desire, boldness and craziness? . . . It sounds like their love is so gentle and calculated. . . . I am not a gentle woman; I am a little crazy; and I love that.

Via the website, Rabbanit Uriah Mevorah, a halakhic counselor at Rabbi Shlomo Riskin's Lindenbaum Women's Yeshiva in Jerusalem and a doctoral student in gender studies at Bar-Ilan University, reassures the questioner:

> Your question is wonderful and it reflects a very healthy instinct regarding intimacy and sexuality. . . . The truth is there is no reason, halakhic or religious, to make the atmosphere heavy between couples. . . . The Torah itself chose the word "laugh" (*tzhok*) to describe sexual contact between Isaac and Rebecca. . . . More halakhic authorities mandate boldness than disqualify it . . . Many of the religious people I know are filled with humor, joy of life, and a love of mischief, so I assume their intimate relations are no different.[108]

A second letter reveals the widespread dilemma of unmarried Modern Orthodox Zionist women struggling with the demand for abstinence before marriage during their extended dating period as well as the psychological importance of this women's website as a place to unburden their hearts and engage in frank discussion:

Question: I am almost 28 years old and I have never had a couple experience which is something I very much want. While I am not observant of the laws against *negia* [physical contact with the opposite sex], I have never slept with anyone. [But] I am not sure I can hold out until I am married.

On some of my dates more and more men who define themselves as religious tell me that they have already slept with other women and that it is important for them to have sex especially before marriage, so as to become acquainted with that dimension of being a couple.... Is it permitted halakhically to sleep with someone or have some sexual contact before marriage? If I do so, will I no longer be considered a religious woman?

Thank you, this website is very very important.

Via the website, Rabbanit Hannah Godinger (Rosh Yeshivat Drisha, the women's yeshiva of Rosh Zurim, Israel) reassures the questioner:

With pain I read your candid words . . . You are right about the difficult challenge posed by reality in the modern world (marriage at an older age, love as the critical criterion for marriage, women's more developed awareness of their sexuality, etc.). . . . Don't feel alone and guilty in your thoughts and desires. . . .

The phenomenon of these men who say they have slept with many women and wish to sleep with you is cheap and they show no respect for the intimacy between a man and a woman who love one another. . . . Sometimes we think that if we release something in our physical behavior, then a door will be opened in our couple relationship. But the truth is that usually that thought is an illusion. . . .

Halakhic loopholes and leniencies for intercourse before marriage are problematic and they are not compatible with the spirit and logic of the halakhah. But I do not wish to conclude my response with a simple halakhic prohibition. You must keep in mind that the purity and beauty of the physical encounter within a context of covenantal marital commitment is a counterbalance to the powerful [animal] *yetzer* and desire that makes all of us happy but also challenges us. . . .

Each person should define his image of the moral world by which he wishes to behave. But the fact that we do not always live up to that standard is not the whole story. . . . People fall and then rise again. . . . But the fact that we stumble does not define us as "not religious."

I pray that the Holy One, *the healer of broken hearts* (Ps. 147:3), will give you the strength to confront these challenges in the present and will find you a marital partner with whom to build a faithful and happy home.[109]

Characteristically, most liberal Orthodox halakhists are not willing to countenance halakhic reforms that allow for nonmarital sex, even for women in difficult emotional situations. They are, however, deeply empathetic with the contemporary dilemmas of women seeking counsel and support. No guilt is imputed to the questioner, nor does the rabbanit rebuke her for violating the laws of negia.

Conclusion

Even though Greenberg's lonely cry for change back in 1966 has not yet borne fruit in Orthodox halakhic reform, it has heralded seminal works by centrist and liberal Orthodox halakhic thinkers who reject asceticism and affirm the goodness of God-given human sexuality when sanctified within halakhic marriage: Berkovits's "A Jewish Sexual Ethics" (1976), Lamm's *The Jewish Way in Love and*

Marriage (1980), Soloveitchik's posthumously published *Family Redeemed* (2000), and Lichtenstein's "Of Marriage Relationships and Relations" (2007). More practical advice for Modern Orthodox married couples is offered in English by Rosenfeld's *The Newlywed's Guide to Physical Intimacy* (2011) and in Hebrew by Ostroff's *LaDaat LeEhov* (2013). No authoritative halakhic work has emerged to guide expressions of nonmarital physical affection, but many forums for counseling and open discussion have proliferated, such as the podcast *The Joy of Text* (in English) and the websites Meshivat Nefesh and Yuval Cherlow's popular internet responsa (in Hebrew).

Looking beyond the Modern Orthodox world, at least four religious themes raised by Greenberg have been prescient for the sexual ethics developed by his American colleagues, rabbis of non-Orthodox Liberal Judaism who have confronted the sexual revolution in nonmarital relations, as we see in the following chapters.

First, interpersonal ethics is the essential axiom for all sexual relations. Promiscuous sexual relations, even consensual ones, should be prohibited because those involved do not treat their partners as creatures in the image of God (*tzelem*).[110] The tzelem is the uniqueness of the individual, and true love seeks to know the other in his or her uniqueness and full vitality.

Second, reciprocity—not merely the satisfaction of wives' biological needs and legal rights—is the hallmark of couple love.

Third, the Song of Songs is a positive model of human sexuality, not merely an allegory for God-Israel relations, and it ought to have normative force in Jewish sexual ethics.

Fourth, the role of the sacred in human sexuality is to mandate "marital love as a value in holiness." As a relationship partakes of greater life-enhancing intimacy, it becomes more sacred. Sanctity in love is most accessible in a marital relationship because total commitment to mutual care reinforces trust.

Struggling with Sexual Liberation

LIBERAL JUDAISM'S RABBIS TACKLE OMINOUS AND LIBERATING DIMENSIONS OF THE SEXUAL REVOLUTION

> Premarital sex transforms the sexual act from . . . an expression of
> the highest level of intimacy and love into a run-of-the-mill sensual
> experience, casual or irregular, available at any time and with any
> partner. . . . Far from strengthening the institution of marriage, a
> premarital relationship undermines it at its most basic. If marriage
> is to survive . . . it must be the only theater for experiencing the most
> intimate interplay of love and sex.
>
> —RABBI ROBERT GORDIS, *Love and Sex*

Introduction

Most of the non-Orthodox rabbis of North American Liberal Judaism came of age in the 1960s in the midst of countercultural movements among their fellow students. While these movements deeply
inspired them, their excesses—especially with regard to sexuality—
frightened them. They too longed for sexual liberation from guilt,
yet many recoiled from the sexual anarchy that undermined the
building of relationships. In the bestselling *The Second Jewish Catalog* (1976), Rabbi Herschel Matt (Conservative) introduces the
chapter on Jewish sexuality with characteristic ambivalence: "The
sexual revolution . . . has increased our knowledge, awareness and
frankness, [and] decreased many of our fears. . . . And yet in spite of
all the good in the sexual revolution . . . there is much that is bad."[1]

As congregational rabbis they struggled between their commitment to Jewish tradition and their constituencies' general indifference to Judaism as a set of binding norms, especially in the bedroom.

It was a great spiritual and professional challenge to formulate a policy regarding the permissibility of engaging in sexual intercourse outside marriage and to identify a value-based approach to counsel others empathetically about these personal decisions. The law committees of the Conservative and Reform associations of rabbis ruled out sexual liaisons outside marriage, while most nondenominational rabbis approved them under certain conditions. All these Liberal rabbis, however, agreed on the need to set stringent moral and spiritual criteria for sexual intimacy in order to sanctify loving relationships and to engage in Jewish education about sexual ethics.

This chapter focuses on how these Liberal rabbis understood the problems posed by sexual liberation. Then I discuss those rabbis who called for a new code of sexual ethics not rooted primarily in traditional halakhah, including Eugene Borowitz (Reform), Eric Yoffie (Reform), Arthur Green (Havurah, ordained Conservative), Michael Strassfeld (Havurah, ordained Reconstructionist), and Arthur Waskow (Fabrangen, ordained Jewish Renewal). In chapters 14 and 15 I address proposals for internal halakhic reform to update Jewish sexual ethics suggested by leading spokespeople of Liberal Judaism in this realm: Elliot Dorff, Danya Ruttenberg, and Jeremy Kalmanofsky (Conservative); Mark Washofsky and Eric Yoffie (Reform); and David Teutsch (Reconstructionist). Chapter 16, the final chapter, is devoted to a radical critique of the patriarchal structure of halakhic marriage advanced by feminist theologians Judith Plaskow and Rachel Adler (Reform).

Problems Raised by Sexual Liberation

For centuries, the traditional family has been structured as an intersection and alliance between sex, childbirth, love, and marriage. In 1960s America, however, generational assaults on bourgeois values such as sexual propriety and marital respectability and the availability of the contraceptive pill—began to pry apart the triumvirate of sex, procreation, and marriage. Lord Rabbi Jonathan Sacks (Orthodox) describes the new sociological and value predicament born of the sexual revolution:

> Sex has become, for the first time since the conversion to Christianity of the Roman Emperor Constantine, an almost value-free zone. Whatever happens between two consenting adults in private is, most people now believe, entirely a matter for them. The law may not intervene; neither may social sanction. It is simply not other people's business. . . .
>
> What marriage brought together has now split apart. There has been a divorce between sex and love, love and marriage, marriage and reproduction, reproduction and education and nurture. Sex is for pleasure. Love is a feeling, not a commitment. Marriage is now deeply unfashionable.[2]

"Truthfully, what the nation experienced in the '60s was not a sexual revolution, but a sexual revolt," explains Deborah Roffman, the high school sex educator and author of *Sex and Sensibility: The Thinking Parent's Guide to Talking Sense About Sex* (2000). In her aptly titled essay, "Making Meaning and Finding Morality in a Sexualized World," she notes the unfortunate result of the rush to experiment with sexual liberation:

> We tossed out the old ideas but failed to replace them with anything specific enough to make an ethic out of. Is it surprising, then, that sex is now so frequently depicted as an amoral enterprise—simply another form of entertainment or recreation, deserving no moral reflection of any kind?[3]

In North American Jewish communities in particular, a high percentage of politically liberal, college-educated, middle- and upper-middle-class young people abandoned wholesale Judaism's traditional family values and sexual mores. The threat to the family was particularly worrying to Liberal Judaism's denominations, Reform and especially Conservative, which had flourished and built countless new synagogues in the 1950s and 1960s because they accommodated the bourgeois norms of suburban married life (with unliberated, stay-at-home wives).

Noting in 1995 that "in our generation, issues of sexual ethics have taken on an aura of enormous anxiety," Rabbi Arthur Waskow, Jewish social justice activist, founder of the Fabrangen Havurah (1971, Washington DC), and co-founder of the Jewish Renewal Movement (1993), agrees with Roffman: "Definitions of what is permissible, what is honorable, what is hurtful, what is criminal have all been changing with great speed."[4] While the characteristic historic American response to such value anarchy has been "make up your own mind; individual choice rather than a communal ethic," Waskow argues that an individualistic response without a communal framework is inadequate.[5] Due to their failure to innovate as a community regarding the sexual revolution, he criticizes "the various religious traditions [as] not ... very useful sources for a healing, sacred sexual mode of behavior."[6]

Similarly, the prominent feminist Jewish theologian Judith Plaskow observed in 2000 that Jews who want "meaningful guidance from tradition" feel "abandoned by institutions that ought to serve as sources of sustenance."[7] In 2005, Rabbi Eric Yoffie, then president of the Union for Reform Judaism (URJ), told his movement:

> In popular culture ... a social ethic known as "hooking up" ... severs sex from any pretense of a relationship. It means getting physical without getting emotional. It means never having a healthy relationship. ... More often than not, hookups leave [our children] depressed, confused, and guilty. But very few of them see the synagogue as a place to go for support, or their Judaism as a source of comfort and direction. And they wonder why. ...

The problem . . . may be that we are not very good at saying "no" in Reform Judaism. We are the most creative and forward-looking movement in Jewish life, but in the realm of personal behavior, we are reluctant to ever use the word "forbidden." . . . The concept of autonomy leaves us unable to set limits and make sound judgments.[8]

Formulating Liberal Rabbinic Responses

For non-Orthodox Liberal rabbis, the sexual license exercised among their younger (and often older) congregants has been particularly distressing, because they also have been caught on the horns of a dilemma between passionately held yet conflicting values. They have always been politically and religiously supportive of expanding the *right* to individual choice through socially progressive legislation for gender equality, but they have counseled their followers to *choose* wisely and ethically and not to avail themselves fully of the legally permitted sexual freedoms, especially intercourse outside of marriage. They have pursued their religious and political calling in vociferous opposition to conservative-minded North American clergy (Evangelical Christians, traditional Catholics, and right-wing Orthodox Jews) who view the sexualization and liberalization of modern society as an existential, spiritual, and ethical threat to religion. Liberal rabbis have applauded the Supreme Court's expansion of civil liberties concerning abortion, birth control, and gay and lesbian rights, even as they have insisted that religious teaching should have a voice in shaping individual choices about sexual ethics and family values; sex is not to be secularized and privatized without regard for communal values. They have welcomed a revival of natural sexuality freed of Victorian guilt and shame, even as they have deplored the secularization of sexual intimacy and its decoupling from spirituality. Even though both Conservative and Reform ideologies generally embrace historical change and progress and readily adjust Jewish communal norms, these modern rabbis lament the rapid deterioration of religious family values in the name of narcissistic sexual liberation.

In aspiring to the sanctity of eros, they have sought to persuade their constituencies to voluntarily accept the beneficent authority of halakhah, the wisdom of tradition, and the strictures of conscience regarding sexual intimacy—including limiting intercourse to committed loving relationships—without instilling guilt about erotic pleasure. They have also struggled to balance their own halakhically rooted calls to action with the nonhalakhic stance of their denominational rank and file. Since the 1970s, Liberal congregants have often become eager consumers of religiously creative life-cycle events and supporters of Jewish reforms for gender equality and inclusivity for LGBTQ Jews. Yet, almost none of these congregants would ask—or necessarily want to hear—what their Liberal rabbis had to say about how to conduct their own intimate sex lives. Nevertheless, Liberal Judaism's rabbis have felt a moral, religious, and social calling to speak to these generational questions about sexual intimacy and sanctity, whether as halakhic authorities, theologians, cultural and social critics, or pastoral ethicists. It is to the religious ideologies and halakhic views of the Liberal rabbinic elites, not their constituents or the Jewish cultural history of their era, that we devote these next few chapters.

Borowitz: Covenantal Sexual Ethics

The Reform theologian, philosopher, and educator Eugene Borowitz (1924–2016) was the first American rabbi to systematically confront issues of sexual ethics, even before the unsettling effects of the sexual revolution became acute in the late 1960s. His 1956 guidebook, *Choosing a Sex Ethic*, written for Jewish college students, protests with prophetic pathos against the corruption of the

Western culture of love and takes a "stand against our society's sick sexuality" that "everything should be tried, and sex is no different from travel or restaurants."[9]

> Too often our civilization is amoral about sex and not infrequently teaches shamelessness and the *abolition of all guilt*. It considers immediate pleasure the highest goal and has little sense of personal integrity through a lifetime and almost no concern for the individual as the channel for historic human destiny. By glorifying genitality and exploiting our repressions, contemporary society has largely stripped sexuality of its mysterious power to expose us to *transcendence*.[10]

Borowitz, however, does not call for a return to traditional halakhic attitudes toward sexuality. In his view, traditional halakhah has created unnecessary and unhealthy guilt, and set unrealistic standards of self-restraint and delayed gratification. Therefore, both American culture and rabbinic Judaism need to be reformed in light of the Biblical heritage of "covenantal ethics."

> The Jewish [i.e., biblical] teaching on sexuality continues to express with compelling power the mandates of existence under the Covenant. . . . It invests our sexual lives with sanctity, raising our animality beyond the human to where something of the divine image may be seen in us.[11]

In making decisions about whether to engage in sexual intimacy, Borowitz says that binary halakhic ethics—permitted or prohibited—is no longer relevant.[12] Instead of a "single, synthesizing principle," he argues, "what we require is something far more pluralistic; a *ranking* rather than a comprehensive rule; a *hierarchy*."[13]

Three kinds of sexual intimacy possess varying degrees of ethical legitimacy, he says, and these may be ranked in terms of their ascending aspirations toward sacred living: (1) mutual consent for sexual pleasure; (2) mutual consent *and* love, even without matrimony; and (3) marriage as the ultimate sacred relationship.

First, the bare minimum of sexual morality requires *mutual consent for sexual pleasure.* For Borowitz, this arrangement is "an obvious ethical advance over permitting any form of coercion or exploitation."[14] Since sex is fundamentally "good," sexual relations are moral when they accord with the Kantian criteria of free will and dignity for each partner so that autonomous humans are treated as ends, not means.

Second, a higher ethical level involves *love* as well as mutual consent, so that "lovemaking" is not only moral but *personal.* Borowitz employs Martin Buber's I-Thou/I-it distinction to characterize a humanistic ethic of love in which the lovers treat each other as fully human persons, not as sex objects to be exploited as an "it" appropriated selfishly by an egocentric "I." Thereby, Borowitz constructs a second tier of sexual ethics that aspires to a fully human relationship and not a merely instrumental one often characterized by exploitation, even if both individuals consent to provide each other pleasure mutually:

> My Jewish concern for the moral dignity of persons . . . means to be a whole person . . . a real person. . . . It is wrong to settle for anything less. . . . If they are not concerned with each other as persons but only as sex partners, they are treating each other as "its" and thus, despite their free consent to the intercourse, are being unethical to each other as full human beings.
>
> How much truer the act would be if their sexual activity arose from what they meant to one another; if sex were not the reason for their intercourse but rather the natural outgrowth of all that they shared with one another. There is a radical difference between loving someone because he is sexy and having sex with someone because of your love.[15]

Like Berkovits and Soloveitchik (see chapter 12), Borowitz espouses and adapts Buber's ideal of the I-Thou relationship from Buber's book *Ich und Du* (Germany, 1923, where *du* is German for the familiar second person). There, Buber distinguishes between an erotic relationship (I-it), in which one is absorbed in a monologue of egotism, and a love relationship (I-Thou), in which two persons encounter one another in a dialogue between Thou and Thou. In the merely erotic relation, the "I" is preoccupied with his or her romantic feelings of being in love and the satisfaction of libidinal desires by using the "it."

As Buber says: "In every [erotic] situation one is not [fully] present to the other; . . . one merely enjoys oneself in the other." By contrast,

> True marriage always arises by the revelation by two individuals of the Thou to one another. . . . I and Thou take their stand . . . in the solid give-and-take of talk. . . . Here are gazing and being gazed upon, knowing and being known, loving and being loved in which the couple are fully present to one another and living in a mutual relation with one another.[16]

Third, the highest ethical level is marriage as a *sacred* relationship. To Borowitz, sanctity is achievable when personal love is sealed by a vow for *long-term commitment and mutual responsibility*, which, he believes, is possible solely in marriage:

> To affirm and uplift a person for a time is no small thing in our world, but *to love him for life* and be loved in return is to make both persons, finally, fully what they might be. Great daring is required to bind one's future to another. . . . Though I esteem love greatly, I believe men can reach an even more significant level of personal existence. . . . A person must live his life not only in the present. . . .

Man is more than moments of meaning. He is that integrity of self which carries on from birth to death. . . .

My Jewish faith asserts [that] . . . a whole person must include not just what one is and can enjoy but equally the enduring relationships and continuing commitments through which alone one can mature.[17]

Love by itself is wholly absorbed in the present, but it gives rise to an anxiety about future abandonment. In response to the predicament—immortalized in Carole King's song, "Will You Still Love Me Tomorrow?"—Borowitz would respond: "The most ethical form of human relationship I know is love-for-life." The best structure for love-for-life is monogamous marriage, and so a marital commitment is "the best criterion for the validity of sexual intercourse."[18] Note that Borowitz transcends Buber's I-Thou relationship by adding halakhic commitment and institutionalized marriage. For Buber, all institutions and all laws degenerate necessarily into alienated I-it relations, fixed forms lacking sincerity and personal spirituality, so true love, true community, and true sanctity must remain spontaneous and wholly present without foreclosing the future. By contrast, Borowitz extols long-term commitments.

In sum, Borowitz applies three different ethical standards to sexual behavior: (1) a binary Kantian ethics of free will (in which coercion is by definition immoral because it dehumanizes one's partner); (2) a Buberian ethics of humanistic love (in which an I-Thou relationship precludes I-it sexual relations); and (3) an aspirational ethic of Biblical covenantal sanctity (founded on a long-term committed marriage in which human partners treat one another responsibly as fully created in the image of God).

Borowitz's book is called *Choosing a Sex Ethic*, not a "Jewish" sex ethic, and his arguments do not presuppose halakhic commitment. As a professing liberal Jew, he is dedicated to the Western ideal of personal autonomy in decision making, and so he denies the heteronomous authority of Jewish law to legally obligate individual Jews. Nevertheless, Borowitz is also deeply committed to Jewish covenantal values that transcend the liberal Kantian ethics of autonomy. He is suspicious of the new American norms of sexual behavior that focus solely on "me," and he confesses: "I have less trust in contemporary wisdom and more in Judaism's independent validity."[19] Therefore he affirms Biblical "covenantal personalism" and employs that religious axiom to countermand secularized promiscuous sex that dehumanizes relationships.[20]

Green: New Halakhah and New Kabbalah

When Borowitz composed *Choosing a Sex Ethic* (1956), most suburban American Jews, as the children of immigrants who had "arrived" socially and economically, were uninterested in halakhah, in religious engagement with Judaism, or with any social critique of contemporary American culture. By the late 1960s, when college youth were developing a counterculture, they opposed as illegitimate their assimilated parents' values. Publicly they protested racial discrimination (civil rights), capitalist materialism (social justice activism), military imperialism (Vietnam War protests), and bourgeois morality (that condemned their youthful sexual revolution).

When the American "seeker generation" began to explore alternative non-Western sources for wisdom, community, and spirituality, an elite cadre of young Jewish intellectuals began to experiment with their own creative return to tradition through text study, neomystical practice, and informal nonsynagogue communities. They founded communes such as the Havurah (in Boston and New York) and the Fabrangen (Washington DC), whose illustrious "graduates" would emerge in the 1970s as leading faculty members of the Jewish studies movement expanding the academic study of Judaism.

Rabbi Arthur Green (Conservative) co-founded the Boston Havurat Shalom (1968). Later he would become a professor of mysticism at Brandeis University, head of the Reconstructionist Rabbinical College, founding head of the Boston Hebrew College Rabbinical School, and simultaneously a popular neo-Hasidic theologian.

In Boston's Havurat Shalom, three of its members, Michael and Sharon Strassfeld and Richard Siegel, edited three consecutive volumes of *The Jewish Catalog* (1971, 1976, and 1980) for their contemporaries, who purchased more than 500,000 copies. Since this renaissance of Jewish consciousness was flowering in the midst of the era of sexual liberation, the editors decided that Jewish sexual ethics had to be addressed for their mass American Jewish student audience, and chose Rabbi Arthur Green to compose the main entry in *The Second Jewish Catalog* (1976).

In his seminal article, "A Contemporary Approach to Jewish Sexuality," Green sought to generate a new kind of Jewish sexual ethics inspired by his study of Kabbalah at Brandeis University rather than by his Talmudic training at the Jewish Theological Seminary. He baldly declared that traditional Judaism's sexual ethics holds *no* attraction for his do-it-yourself seeker generation (1970s):

> The Catalog [is] twofold: . . . a guide to traditional Jewish living, drawn with some leeway from the traditional sources, and . . . a reflection of the neo-traditional Jewish life-style that is evolving among certain young-in-spirit American Jews, in *havurot*—alternative communities. . . .
>
> While these circles have tended toward traditionalism . . . we are postmodern rather than premodern Jews, and *our life-style is hardly to be considered halakhic* . . . in the full sense. . . . It is in the areas of sexual relations and the place of women that this discrepancy between fully halakhic traditionalism and the neotraditionalism of these "new Jews" is most clearly seen.

The halakhah has generally viewed all forms of nonmarital intercourse as *beilat zenut*—harlotry. Among the many young unmarried
[however] there is hardly a thought of condemnation concerning
premarital sexuality, including intercourse (even without deep love
commitment!), provided it is carried out within the general bounds
of interpersonal decency. . . . These Jews . . . have, rather guiltlessly,
had any number of sexual partners.[21]

In fact, Green's proposed "New Halakha," a three-page essay in a
popular New Age format, resembles no classical Jewish legal text,
for it derives its authority wholly from the couple's consent, without
any attempt to reinterpret classical halakhic precedents or principles.
For Green, "Jews who find the old standards inoperable for them
find themselves bereft of moral guidance in this area and . . . are in
need of a new and realistic approach."[22]

Since traditional laws and ideas are irrelevant to his generation,
and the contemporary cult of naturalism and sexual liberation sets
no standards, Green turns for inspiration to another source of wisdom: New Age mysticism rooted in classical Kabbalah:

The greatest and potentially most divine mystery accessible to most
humans is the *mystery of sexuality*. . . . Kabbalists see the very origins of the universe as a never-ceasing process of arousal, coupling,
gestation, and birth within the life of a God who is both male and
female, and proclaim this complex inner flow of divinity, described
in the most graphic of sexual terms, to be the highest of mysteries.
All this imagery provides for the Jew an ideal of sexuality.[23]

Green's values recapitulate many themes Borowitz raised twenty
years earlier (though he had never read Borowitz).[24] Like Borowitz,
Green criticizes the reduction of sexual behavior to the satisfaction of biological needs. While Borowitz finds inspiration in the
dialogic philosophy of Martin Buber, Green utilizes the language

of Kabbalah—which itself had been intentionally suppressed by modern rabbinic schools from Reform to Orthodox, and ignored by the universities—precisely as Far Eastern mysticism first begins to penetrate American culture.

His mandate is to re-enchant sexuality within a context of individual freedom in the service of a Jewish countercultural revolution against America's culture of sexual consumption:

> We Jews should stand opposed to the current moves toward the "demystification" of sexuality which seek to define coupling as a purely biological function. We are made most fully human by the fact that this act, shared by us with the animal kingdom, can be raised in our consciousness to the rung of . . . the sublime mystery of union. Sexuality at its fullest is brimming with religious *kawanah* [spiritual intentionality].[25]

While Green's ideal of sexual love aspires to be robustly sublime and sacred, his ethics are minimalist, constructed on the Kantian axiom of autonomy. Only mutual consent is needed to validate sexual intimacy. Contra Borowitz and most Conservative rabbis (see chapters 14–15), Green accepts premarital sex, even if its aim is simply to supply sensual pleasure without love. He argues from a position of realism:

> It is clear that *we cannot advocate celibacy for all who are not in love.* Given the world in which we live, they would simply ignore such pious pronouncements, rightly noting that it is usually the *self-righteousness of the happily married* that stands behind them. . . .
>
> What do we say to the adult who has not found a person to share the depths of love? . . . What do we say to the widowed or divorced person, used to loving sexual fulfillment, who is now driven to distress partially by sexual loneliness?[26]

Green goes so far as to validate all consensual sexual relations, even "open relationships," which are not monogamous. Yet, he cautions that, while engaging in sexual relations to assuage one's physiological needs, one may coarsely disregard the feelings of the other partner who might be expecting lasting love and exclusive loyalty. Green asks liberated individuals to be morally sensitive to the consequences of self-centered promiscuity:

> Intimacy perforce involves . . . interpersonal responsibility. The whole area of sexuality . . . is one of tremendous personal vulnerability. . . . Any ethic that says that I am responsible only for myself, but not for the other, is abhorrent to Judaism. . . .
>
> However open we may be with regard to alternative sexual life-styles . . . a marriage that one partner unilaterally decides is "open" [while deceiving the other] is in fact not open at all, and makes a mockery of the traditional values of fidelity, honesty, and responsibility.[27]

Like Borowitz, Green too invokes a sliding scale of standards to accommodate the variety of human situations rather than the traditional binary logic typical of halakhah that categorizes all behaviors as either permitted or forbidden:

> Living in a world where we cannot advocate either ideal sex or no sex as the alternatives, what we must begin to evolve is *a sliding scale of sexual values*. . . . At the top of this scale would stand the fully knowing and loving relationship, while rape—fully unconsenting and anonymous sexuality—would stand at the bottom. Somewhere near the middle of the scale, neither glorified nor condemned, would be the relationship of two consenting persons, treating one another with decency, fulfilling the biological aspects of one another's love-needs, while making no pretense at deeper intimacy.[28]

Green's rejection of ascetic spirituality and his realism concerning human sexual needs leave no room for the obsessive fear of sin stressed by traditional pietism (see chapter 8): "Only at or near the bottom of the scale (rape) would we speak of sin; in other relationships we would do better to note the *inadequacies* of our situation than to bemoan our *sins*."[29]

In sum, what Green calls a "new halakhah" is, by his own admission, radically different in form as well as content from the traditional role of Jewish law which specifies authoritative and explicit standards for permitted and prohibited behavior:

> This kind of new halakhah ... is in its very liberalism more difficult and in some ways less immediately gratifying than the old. It does not remove our insecurities by telling us what we may and may not do. Rather, it leads us to self-examination and encourages growth.
>
> By maintaining the ideal of true and full sublime sexuality, we may be able to continually infuse ourselves with higher strivings, while not self-righteously condemning anyone who, through the circumstances of his/her life, stands at a different point in our flexible scale of intimate values.[30]

Out of his neo-mystical recovery Kabbalah, Green promotes individualized guidelines to sacred sexuality rather than a code of law to regulate sexual behavior. His hope is that *aggadah* (nonhalakhic Jewish literature), especially mystical texts, will eventually generate an appropriate new halakhah, which cannot yet be envisioned.[31]

Strassfeld: Sexual Togetherness as *Tikkun Olam*

Like Borowitz and Green, Rabbi Michael Strassfeld (Reconstructionist, co-editor of *The Jewish Catalog*) is not naive about the dangers of sexual liberation, but he largely welcomes its personal and spiritual benefits as part of the kabbalistic forces of regeneration within a deeply fractured world: "Ultimately we need to acknowledge sexuality as a powerful force that also provides the opportunity for two people to touch the deepest parts of each other's being."[32]

In his 2002 neo-mystical guidebook, *A Book of Life: Embracing Judaism as a Spiritual Practice* (inspired by the neo-Hasidic theologian A. J. Heschel), Strassfeld explains his two-fold approach to sexual relations:

> [There are] two complementary ways to look upon sex before marriage: The first . . . sex as a source of pleasure is not denied us by the Torah. We are to enjoy this world and see it as God's gift to us. . . . [But] there is "*junk sex*," just as there is "junk food"—that which seems fine, but actually is not good for us.
>
> The second way of viewing sex is as a means to *kedushah*. . . . It is a holy connection between two people that brings a sense of wholeness and unity, even if only for a brief period. . . . [Sex can be] an *act of togetherness*. . . . That is no small thing in a world of brokenness . . . where we experience existential aloneness. . . .
>
> The possibility that the masks that we wear and the walls that we have erected should be removed to allow for the joining of two people in warm embrace is an opportunity that should not be restricted only to those who are married.[33]

Strassfeld's neo-kabbalist approach, inspired by the Lurianic idea of "broken vessels," regards the world we live in as "life in exile, a world of separation" (*alma d'pruda*). On the interpersonal level, this alienation manifests itself in "the masks we wear and the walls we have erected." The redemptive process for human, cosmic, and divine worlds takes place, as Luria teaches, in every small act of *tikkun olam*, through the unification (*yihud*) of the male and female aspects that have become alienated.

While Borowitz's remedy to the sexual revolution is to promote a three-tiered scale of individual ethical decision making, Green calls programmatically for a new halakhah inspired by a new Kabbalah for a generation who could find no relevance in traditional sexual ethics (though he never produced such a new halakhic guidebook). Strassfeld begins with a broader diagnosis of what is ailing his generation. Their liberation of libido is shallow, and their free love is often a futile attempt to escape a deeper malaise—human alienation. The Lurianic myth of a fractured world offers a metaphor for the profound problem of our age. As his remedy, Strassfeld composes a daily spiritual practicum to achieve personal redemption. Within that attempt at self-examination (*heshbon ha-nefesh*) and self-improvement (*teshuvah*), erotic love plays an important role in bridging the existential loneliness that separates and isolates one from the other and thus contributes piecemeal to a process of interpersonal tikkun olam.

Waskow: A Life-Cycle Approach to Sex Ethics

Like Borowitz, Arthur Waskow (social justice activist and Jewish Renewal rabbi) is a *communitarian liberal*, strongly committed to maximizing the good of society and not just individual autonomy. In his view, individuals ought to learn to evaluate their sexual practices and then behave with an eye to the effects of their behavior on the public good.

As such, Waskow does not view sexual choices as merely private decisions. Rather, sexual ethics ought to contribute to the good of the individual, the couple, the society, and even the cosmos.

While Borowitz's flexible policy evaluates the permissibility of sexual intimacy in terms of individual consent, quality of love, and length of commitment, Waskow proposes a situational ethics in which, at different *stages in the adult life cycle*, there are different moral choices to be made about sexual intimacy.

Since sexual ethics reflects a social policy, Waskow commences his analysis by identifying urgent contemporary problems of the Jewish collective. In North American Jewish society individuals face growing periods of life without a partner, beginning with the gap between the age of sexual desire (sixteen and declining) and the average age of marriage (close to thirty and climbing), leading to a prolonged period without a spouse before marriage. Then, increasing life expectancy and rising divorce rates generate long periods without a spouse after divorce or widowhood. To Waskow, this complex social reality markedly contrasts with the marital practices upon which rabbinic norms and laws were promulgated: child marriages performed before the dawn of sexual awareness; short life spans; frequent death of young wives in childbirth, and consequently frequent remarriage. Given these new social realities, Waskow described in 1995 three basic strategies from which he thought the North American Jewish community must choose.

POLICY ONE: PRACTICING CELIBACY FOR LONG PERIODS

Waskow argues that the official responsa committees of Conservative and Reform rabbis wish to sustain traditional halakhic and bourgeois norms that prohibit sexual intimacy outside of marriage. They uphold a public policy of "just say no," even though they know it is untenable. For long periods of many American Jews' lives, they are not yet married, no longer married, or never married. Most Jews today reject abstinence, and many become alienated from a Judaism that in effect preaches celibacy. Sardonically, Waskow sums up: "Who wants to be part of an institution that looks with hostility or contempt on the source of much of one's most intense pleasure, joy, and fulfillment?!"[34]

Furthermore, Waskow wants the official community to approve sexual relations, not just realistically tolerate them:

> It is important consciously to erase the sense of shame and guilt or of estrangement from religious communities and traditions that has often shadowed nonmarital sexual relationships, shame and guilt so strong that the last thing many people wanted was to bring God into the bedroom. . . . Only sexual expressions rooted in coercion, dishonesty, violence, hatred of self or other, are ipso facto sinful.[35]

POLICY TWO: NO COMMUNAL POLICY

Unable to reach consensus on permitting premarital sex, by default the community relegates decisions about sexual ethics to the private domain. Effectively, it "accepts the fact that many unmarried people are sexually active—without creating standards of ethical behavior for unmarried sexual relationships or creating ceremonial or legal definitions of them."[36]

But Waskow rejects policy two, insisting that even today, people want ethical guidelines, public rituals for their most important relationships, and communal approval.

POLICY THREE: CREATE NEW JEWISHLY AFFIRMED FORMS OF SEXUAL RELATIONSHIP OTHER THAN MARRIAGE

To meet individuals' needs for communal values, Waskow promotes the third policy option: greater flexibility with sexual liaisons—in accordance with today's "New Life Cycle": adolescence, young adulthood, married adult, and aging adult. Each stage in life ought to be characterized by appropriately different values and ethical guidelines:

[Stage 1.] a time of dating and first sexual experiences enabling fluid relationships without commitments;

[Stage 2.] a time of living together (*pilegesh/zug*), with commitment but without permanence and without children, and hence without matrimony;

[Stage 3.] a time of marriage (*chuppah*) with long-term commitments celebrated by elaborate communal rituals of affirmation.[37]

For example, while older teenagers should be allowed graduated sexual experiences without commitment, they must be educated to maintain moral standards, such as honesty with their partner (about sexually transmitted diseases, about lack of commitment to going steady, etc.). They must obligate themselves not to have sex without full, mutual consent. Regarding committed couples—before, instead of, or after marriage—Waskow suggests that the Jewish community encourage them to institutionalize their *zug* (couple) relationship by sanctifying their living together with a communal ritual (distinctly different from marriage) and by formalizing their commitment to care for one another with a contract that protects each other's rights (like the prenuptial agreements often composed by widows or widowers remarrying late in life). Waskow suggests that for the couple that has decided to live together, "the ceremony for acknowledging the *zug* might include the ceremony of dedicating a home, *chanukat ha'bayit*, in which a *mezuzah* is affixed."[38]

While Borowitz as well as rabbis Mark Washofsky and Elliot Dorff (see chapters 14–15) restrict the honorific term "sacred" and communal recognition to marriages and discourage intercourse without *kiddushin*, Waskow commends communally approved sexual relations at each of the three stages of the new life cycle. Their hierarchy reflects ascending levels of sanctity worthy of broader social recognition for each type of couple in the community. The higher the stage, the deeper its spirituality and intimacy, and hence the more elaborate its communal ritual celebration. He states, "Judaism can affirm that at different times of life, it is possible for individuals reasonably to pursue different basic sexual relationships."[39] Moreover, "it is possible to create holiness at every level."[40] Thus Waskow works out a detailed halakhic system delineating multiple models and stages in the spirit of Borowitz's suggestion that "what we require is something far more pluralistic; a *ranking* rather than a comprehensive rule."[41]

What makes Waskow's new halakhic sexual ethics unique among the rabbis (with the exception of the Reconstructionists) is its ultimate source of authority—the community. His Jewish ethics are not based "on the past alone," on Jewish laws and precedents (for in his view they are already outmoded); nor on "a small elite of rabbis alone" (as if they were "up there" with God); nor on the autonomy of each individual. Rather, "as the modern world has taught us, a whole community should be democratically involved in shaping communal values and laws."[42] Given that realities are constantly in flux and today's crisis in sexual norms is causing great individual and social distress (a broken world), it is up to the community to select policies to fix the misfit between tradition and contemporary human needs. For Waskow, the Jewish social justice activist, such a progressive policy of reform is an example of tikkun olam.

Conclusion

Liberal Judaism's rabbis seek to combat the wanton dimensions of the sexual revolution with a two-pronged approach. On one hand, they welcome the elimination of moral guilt and shame from interpersonal sexuality as long as respect and mutual consent prevail. Religiously, they celebrate the natural joys of sex as an expression of God's goodness in creating human sexuality. In the spirit of neo-

Kabbalah, they elevate sexual union to a redemptive spiritual plane, as did *The Holy Letter* in medieval Spain.

Yet, on the other hand, all of these rabbis display spiritual discomfort with the "new normal" in which nonmarital intercourse ("hooking up") is simply a means to satisfy the individual's instinctual needs. (In 2018, 69 percent of Americans reported that a sexual relationship without marriage is morally acceptable.)[43] In response, all of these rabbis condemn an indiscriminate hookup culture and espouse an aspirational ethic of kedushah tied to the quality of the interpersonal relationship.

Where they disagree is on the communal policy to be adopted. Many Conservative and some Reform rabbis wish to reserve the highest act of sexual intimacy for the highest level of mutual commitment—marriage—and to prohibit all nonmarital sexual intercourse. Others, like Green and Waskow, see the possibility of degrees of sanctity in various loving sexual relations, even without marriage.

Sliding-Scale Sex Ethics   14

LIBERAL HALAKHAH BALANCES MARITAL SANCTITY AND THE REALITIES OF NONMARITAL SEX

We [rabbis] are trained to give a halakhic ruling by looking into the Shulhan Arukh [the Code of Jewish Law]. . . . Nobody taught us how to issue a ruling when it's not a question of what is forbidden or permitted but instead is a matter of identifying the lesser prohibition. How do we establish *a hierarchy of transgression* which helps us decide how to help our questioners navigate a Judaism that's more complex than the one most halakhic decision-makers imagined, or cared to address?

—RABBI YSOSCHER KATZ, Yeshivat Chovevei Torah Rabbinical School

Introduction

Does God Belong in the Bedroom? asks Rabbi Michael Gold (Conservative) in his popular book, so titled—especially if "God" is represented by rabbinic authorities perusing and prohibiting acts of sexual intimacy between couples. Most members of the Reform and Conservative movements—the overwhelming majority of affiliated North American Jews—would answer with an unequivocal, resounding "no."

Generally speaking, Liberal Jews neither follow the halakhah on a daily basis, nor study rabbinic sources. Nevertheless, non-Orthodox rabbis as spiritual and communal leaders regularly appeal to Jewish tradition and law to guide their congregants in making moral and spiritual decisions in their private and public lives. At a minimum, they ask their congregants to give Liberal Judaism's halakhah what

Rabbi Mordecai Kaplan, founder of Reconstructionism, called "the right to a vote, but not the right of a veto," when they are making autonomous decisions on their own bedroom behavior.[1] In each of the movements, the rabbinic associations set halakhic standards for how their own rabbis ought to behave in conducting weddings. But their biggest challenge was to determine what they ought to teach when confronted with sexual behavior that falls short of their halakhic ideals.

For example, in the quotation opening this chapter, Rabbi Ysoscher Katz (originally a Satmar hasid, today a Modern Orthodox rabbi) suggests that rabbinic counselors should sometimes offer multitiered complex options rather than render unambiguous legal decisions about what is prohibited and what is permitted.[2] When one's constituency believes and behaves in ways that are at odds with the ethical tradition of their religious leaders, as in the case of nonmarital sexual activity, the loyalists of tradition who wish to be relevant educators must find a middle way and advise their community on how to balance the desire for erotic intimacy with higher spiritual aspirations for sanctity. A two-tiered approach must set limits to the sexual revolution and its excesses, and yet accommodate the explosive libido that has been liberated by the radical autonomy of each couple.

The halakhic project of non-Orthodox rabbis determining sexual ethics based on Jewish law may appear irrelevant to a wide swath of Liberal Judaism's constituency and, therefore, make the halakhic rulings of Liberal rabbis appear superfluous. Nonetheless, this chapter demonstrates how Liberal halakhic thinking enriches educational discourse and ethical deliberation about sanctity and intimacy. It explores how different rabbinic leaders under the wide umbrella of Liberal Judaism interpret and seek to promulgate halakhah about sexual intimacy for a constituency that practices and believes what mainstream college-educated North Americans do.

Sexual Ethics through Jewish Values Clarification

Without legal force or communal consensus, today's Liberal halakhah functions best as an educational guideline to sexual ethics. Stipulating clear behavioral directives in nuanced situations is always difficult, and intimate relationships are subject in practice only to one's own personal supervision and the scrutiny of one's conscience.[3] Therefore, Eugene Borowitz, Arthur Green, and Arthur Waskow emphasize the need for a sliding scale that varies in its content according to the type, quality, and life stage of the relationship (see chapter 13); each couple can then customize these moral maxims for their situation. Liberal Judaism's rabbis often promote Jewish values to supplement or sidestep issuing legal rulings.[4] As Rabbi David Teutsch (Reconstructionist) maintains: "Contemporary thinking about sexual ethics does not begin with norms. . . . [but] with values and ideals."[5]

Contemporary values education about sexual ethics first appears in the margins alongside Arthur Green's essay on Jewish sexuality in *The Second Jewish Catalog* (1976). The *Catalog's* editors list values (such as love, knowing, honesty, degradation, and consent) as normative criteria by which to determine a Jewish approach to sexuality, though they lack halakhic specificity.[6] Since then, Liberal rabbis have composed many such values lists in their teaching manuals. The Reform Movement's Central Conference of American Rabbis (CCAR) Ad Hoc Committee on Human Sexuality singles out ten Jewish values through which "*sh'leimut* (wholeness) [can] be realized: *B'tzelem Elohim* (in the image of God), *Emet* (truth), *B'riut* (health), *Mishpat* (justice), *Mishpachah* (family), *Tz'niut* (modesty), *B'rit* (covenantal relationship), *Simchah* (joy), *Ahavah* (love), *K'dushah* (holiness)."[7] The committee is creating an analogue to the Ten Commandments, particularly for regulating intimate relationships in order to enhance the rationality and mutuality of decision making between partners. Informed, reasoned, and negotiated values clarification, rather than authoritarian commandments of do and do not, becomes the most important process for the practice of both marital and nonmarital Jewish sexual ethics.

Note that the contemporary values approach is not wholly alien to the traditional halakhic approach to marital relations. For example, the *Sheva Brakhot* (nuptial blessings) specify the aspirational values of "love and brotherhood, peace and companionship," and the Talmud includes a list of prohibited emotions ("fear, coercion, hatred, contention, drunkenness") during conjugal lovemaking (see TB *Nedarim* 20b in chapter 3). Over time, these same value recommendations have often become halakhic norms enforceable by law (see chapter 10).

The Reform and Conservative movements have each produced values clarification curricula designed for adolescents and young adults. In 2007, Reform educators published "Sacred Choices: Adolescent Relationships and Sexual Ethics" in response to the public policy sermon on adolescent relationships and sexual ethics delivered in 2005 by URJ president Rabbi Eric Yoffie (quoted in chapter 13). Posing the central question, "What does it mean to view my life—my body, soul, and sexuality—as well as those of others, as gifts from God?,"[8] the curriculum adapts Borowitz's typology of sexual relationships from his book *Choosing a Sex Ethic* (see chapter 13) to help students clarify their amorphous relationships:

> The Five Levels of Sexual Relationships: [(1) Conquest without consent; (2) Healthy Orgasm; (3) Mutual Consent without exclusivity; (4) Love with exclusivity; and (5) Marriage with public commitment] represent a continuum of holiness, the lowest level being the least holy [or a desecration of the sacred] and the highest level being the most holy.[9]

In 2010, Rabbi Elliot Dorff and Rabbi Danya Ruttenberg (Conservative) published the textbook *Sex and Intimacy: Jewish Choices, Jewish Voices* to engage singles and couples in halakhic ethical thinking by deliberating about concrete cases illuminated by Jewish values. For example, Rabbi Uzi Weingarten's essay in the volume uses Maimonides to guide students to discuss the moral limits of persuading a partner to consent to sexual intimacy under false pretenses:

> One person may not deliberately act with the intention of giving an erroneous impression—what we would call "leading a person on"—even if nothing is said (Maimonides).[10] . . . Thus, one who acts in a way that, by commonly accepted standards, implies romantic commitment has an obligation to clarify the truth to the other. One cannot simply claim, "I never said we were going steady." Actions speak louder than words, especially in matters of the heart. . . . The subject of romantic and sexual relationships is so tricky precisely because there are no hard and fast rules, and there are huge gray areas that could lead to heartbreak for one or both people.[11]

These Liberal curricula of sex education avoid giving commandments or issuing a code of law, but rather present cases and suggest values and guidelines for deliberation by their learners. In rabbinic law committees, however, the rabbis of Liberal movements have issued halakhic rulings based on classical precedents.

Conservative and Reform Responsa

Besides educational endeavors to teach sexual ethics through values clarification, in the last quarter of the twentieth century a small cadre of Conservative and Reform rabbis began to formulate halakhic codes of practice for sexual intimacy rooted in legal precedents. Conservative rabbis (such as Dorff and Jeremy Kalmanofsky) and

Reform rabbis (such as Mark Washofsky) have led their rabbinical movements in issuing halakhic rulings and setting policy on marital ethics for their colleagues, though some rabbis in their movements may not concur. While conceptually these responsa often reiterate positions, values, and social analyses already pioneered in Borowitz's philosophic treatise *Choosing a Sex Ethic*, they now take the form of authoritative halakhic discourse produced by official organs of the movements and justified with Talmudic precedents and medieval codes of law.

In formulating halakhah for Liberal Judaism, the rabbis authoring these responsa dissent sharply from conservative Catholics, Protestant Evangelicals, and many Orthodox rabbis who condemn *all* nonmarital sexual relations as unconditionally prohibited, morally wrong, and spiritually corrupting. In 1998, for example, Catholic canon law was expanded to designate anyone who questions the absolute prohibition on sex before marriage as deserving of excommunication.[12] By contrast, while the responsa committees of Conservative and Reform Judaism forbid premarital sex, Liberal Judaism carefully avoids the traditional rabbinic rhetoric that labels all sexual impropriety as prostitution (*zenut*) and speaks derisively of unmarried couples "living together in sin." Instead, Conservative and Reform rabbinic leaders reaffirm the traditional halakhic hierarchy that condemns less severely casual sexual promiscuity (generally regarded as a rabbinic prohibition but only a misdemeanor) from capital crimes like adultery or incest (a Biblical prohibition).[13]

Consider, for example, the official position formulated by Elliot Dorff—a Jewish philosopher at the Ziegler School of Rabbinic Studies (Conservative), and ethicist and chair of the Rabbinical Assembly (RA)'s Committee on Jewish Law and Standards—in his paper, "*This Is My Beloved, This Is My Friend*: A Rabbinic Letter on Intimate Relations" (published by The RA Commission on Human Sexuality in 1996). Pointedly, Dorff refuses to condone nonmarital relationships of any kind and urges his constituency to postpone intercourse until marriage, yet he understands and values the moral qualities that ought to govern the morality of long-term nonmarital sexual relationships, even while urging his constituency to postpone intercourse until marriage.[14] Rabbi Sheldon Marder (Reform) elucidates the pastoral style of Dorff's letter:

> For North American liberal rabbis, "pastoral" means being a good, active listener. [Dorff] is distinguishing himself as *a listening heart* [the trait of King Solomon the wise judge (1 Kings 3:9)] who listens to the people he is addressing, tries to understand their feelings, and sympathizes with them. The letter clearly sets standards, but it also moves the discussion from being only halakhic into the realm of spiritual care.[15]

Like Borowitz, Dorff evaluates the desirability of various sexual behaviors in terms of their place within an evolving, full-bodied, loving relationship. While intercourse among teenagers cannot be regarded as this kind of responsible love relationship, sexual relations between members of a loving adult couple committed to living together is much closer to the highest ideal of marital commitment. Still, even for those who live together, Dorff advocates strongly for proceeding to holy matrimony as the exclusive context for intercourse. To him, *only* marriage, with its full commitment of spouses to one another, creates a *sacred* relationship—by which he also means a fully Buberian I-Thou human relationship.[16] Thus Dorff reaffirms what Rabbi David Feldman (Conservative) declares passionately in *The Second Jewish Catalog*:

> Marriage . . . prevents the ultimate human relationship from being trivialized; it does the same for sex itself. The holy and essentially human character of the sexual relationship obtains when the sexual is part of an umbrella of relationships—physical, emotional, social.

Being the most intimate, the sexual is reserved for the most total of relationships.

While the idea of living together without marriage may be attractive to lovers who are impatient with commitment or exclusivity, with social status, or with long-run considerations, those who share society's goals and religion's ideals will see the ceremony and certificate [of marriage] as their allies.[17]

In his anthology, *Reform Responsa for the Twenty-first Century*, Rabbi Mark Washofsky—professor of Jewish law at the Reform seminary Hebrew Union College-Jewish Institute of Religion and chair of the CCAR Responsa Committee—contributes two relevant responsa. When asked, "Should long-term relationships between mature adults be discouraged?," his Reform responsum expounds a highly conservative axiom: "Rabbinic Judaism has consistently opposed non-marital sexual relationships, no matter what type of affinity existed between the man and the woman," because they undermine the classic Jewish difference between holy and profane.[18]

This Jewish view differs dramatically from that of a society prepared to recognize an element of *k'dushah* in long-term nonmarital relationships, [which is a] commitment which may be eroded upon the slightest whim, . . . and [within which eventually] marriage becomes readily disposable.[19]

While Washofsky is fully aware both of the minority halakhic views that permit a legal arrangement for living together (*pilegesh*) and of the growing consensus since the 1990s among Reform Jews that living together is normal and even desirable as a prelude to marriage, his committee denies rabbinic recognition to nonmarital sexual relationships.[20] He also reaffirms the countercultural vocation of Reform Judaism and protests against the historic tendency of Liberal Jewish denominations to uncritically accommodate social reality.[21]

Subsequently, Washofsky's Reform responsa committee addresses this corresponding problem brought by a Reform congregational rabbi:

> A retired heterosexual couple has approached me to perform a commitment ceremony for them in lieu of a wedding ... to affirm their mutual love and commitment ... [and to] validate [their relationship] in the eyes of our faith and also in the eyes of their family.[22]

In response, the committee rules that the Reform rabbi should not conduct a Jewish "commitment ceremony" to authorize their living arrangement:

> Our faith offers no other ritual means than marriage for "validating"—i.e., sanctifying—a heterosexual relationship. ... The rabbi should not arrange a commitment ceremony for them. ... Judaism has always been at pains to make sharp, clear-cut distinctions between what is *kadosh* [holy] and what is not.[23]

Still, the Reform responsa committee, like Borowitz and Dorff, never impugns the *ethical* standing of stable amorous relationships not sanctified by matrimony:

> While we would neither sanction nor sanctify such relationships, we are cognizant that they will continue to exist, as they have throughout Jewish history. ... Indeed, we do not deny that such relationships could possess ethical standing, insofar as they are not marked by manipulation, deceit, or foreseeable harm. The absence of *kedushah* [sanctity] should never imply a vacuum of *musar* [morality]: the two individuals involved in this relationship ... are subject to a moral obligation to accord one another the fullest measure of respect, honesty, and consideration.[24]

Opposing the CCAR Responsa Committee's binary approach, in 1996 another forum of Reform rabbis, the CCAR Ad Hoc Committee on Human Sexuality, publicly characterized sexual intimacy as "covenantal" within committed nonmarital love relationships: "A sexual relationship is covenantal when it is stable and enduring and includes mutual esteem, trust, and faithfulness . . . grounded in fidelity and the intention of permanence."[25] The Ad Hoc Committee also counseled that "each Jew should seek to conduct his/her sexual life in a manner that elicits the intrinsic holiness within the person and in every relationship."[26] Sanctity is not found only in marital relations.

Similarly, in Yoffie's 2005 URJ biennial address to professional and lay leaders of Reform congregations, he explicitly rejected preaching to teenagers that "sex before marriage is forbidden" and implicitly approved nonmarital sex when practiced by unmarried adults within sacred—that is, holy and ethically respectful—relationships:

> Judaism tells [students] that they are created in the image of God, and each and every one of them is unique, of infinite worth, and entitled to respect. It tells them that the guiding principle of sexuality in the Jewish tradition is *K'doshim tih'yu*—"You shall be holy" (Lev. 19:2) which means that sexuality is linked to blessing, commandment, and God. It tells them that in our tradition, both partners in a sexual relationship must be sensitive to the sexual needs of the other. . . .
>
> Reform Judaism must make what is forbidden as clear as what kind of sexual relationship is sacred: High school students should not be having sexual relations. Our teens are not adults. They are beset by . . . pressure from friends, a desire for approval, and an uncertain sense of self. . . . [and] not yet ready for the loving, mutual relationships that make sex an experience of holiness. . . .
>
> The Reform Movement has dedicated itself to promoting the equality of our women and all women. But this is worth nothing if Jewish girls define their worth by how they please boys. . . . In Judaism, a woman never exists to be a subordinate vessel to the man. . . .

They are created in the image of God, and each and every one of them is unique, of infinite worth, and entitled to respect. . . .

[But] we do *not* tell our kids that *sex before marriage* is forbidden. Since many of them will not marry for fifteen years after the onset of puberty, it is unreasonable to suggest that this traditional standard should be maintained for young people who are adults.[27]

Three Tiers of Liberal Sexual Ethics

In the face of de facto social deregulation of sexuality and the freedom to do whatever feels good, whatever "comes naturally," and whatever gives instinctual gratification, North American Liberal Judaism has formulated its own ethical code for a liberated generation. Liberal Judaism employs a tripartite system of halakhic categories to regulate sexual intimacy: (1) what is forbidden, immoral, and intolerable; (2) what is permitted, recommended, and sacred; (3) what is tolerable and moral, but not permitted or mandated.

The first category applies to exploitive sexual relations (date and marital rape, seduction, adultery, and prostitution). The second category, the aspirational ideal of sacred sexuality (*l'hatkhila*), limits intercourse solely to marriage. In the third category, sexual relations are neither permitted nor recommended but merely tolerated. With this gray area, rabbis seek to guide Jews who are going to engage in nonmarital sexual relations anyway to select the most ethical and least spiritually injurious option within the range of nonmarital sex. Here we find a wide swath of mutually consensual, sometimes loving, unmarried relationships (occasional sex, premarital sexual relationships, and living together) that most Liberal rabbis will not celebrate ritually, since they do not believe they merit the honorific characterization as sacred.[28]

In the Torah, adultery is indisputably a capital crime, a major violation of the Ten Commandments (Exod. 20:14; Deut. 5:17), though it applies only to wives who have extramarital affairs and not to husbands who are permitted to maintain polygamous sexual relations. In practice, Talmudic courts did not prosecute adulterers, but the Rabbis did penalize the adulteress and her paramour by legislating that after committing adultery, a married woman "is defiled and forbidden to her husband, and she is forbidden to her paramour" (TB *Sotah* 26b). Even if she repented and made up with her cuckolded husband, he had to divorce her and she could not marry the adulterer. By contrast, the husband's infidelity is not regarded as a crime of adultery against his wife or God, and so the adulterous husband need not divorce his wife and may, subsequent to divorce, marry his paramour. (Even today, in Israeli state religious divorce courts, which rule on the basis of Orthodox halakhah, male infidelity is considered only a misdemeanor).

Most Liberal rabbis demand a higher bar than traditional halakhah in condemning infidelity. First, insisting on gender equality, they apply the term "adultery" equally to a married man who has an affair, and, second, they condemn sexual betrayal equally whether a couple is married or simply living together.

Further, Liberal Judaism's halakhic demand for fully consensual intercourse has become more stringent in light of the Me Too movement (since 2017), which protests vociferously against people (especially powerful men) abusing their social privilege to take sexual advantage of persons over whom they wield authority. Non-Orthodox rabbis concur wholeheartedly with the standards promoted by Rabbi Michael Dratch (Orthodox), the chairman of the Task Force on Rabbinical Improprieties of the Rabbinical

Council of America and the founder, in 2005, of JSafe: The Jewish Institute Supporting an Abuse Free Environment:

> Jewish law rules that people should engage in sexual relations willingly; [thus] it prohibits a husband to force his wife to have intercourse.[29] And the bar for consent is set high. If a wife . . . is not *fully* agreeable to intercourse, sexual relations are prohibited. All of this means that if a husband or wife is interested in having sex, it is his or her responsibility to seduce [i.e., persuade or woo] the partner and earn consent. However, if these advances are rebuffed, they must be stopped. "No" means "no." Nonconsensual sex is rape (TB *Nedarim* 20b).[30]

In sum, the halakhic intolerance of Liberal Judaism for sexual infidelity, abuse, and exploitation is reinforced by three normative rationales: contemporary Kantian ethics of human dignity and human autonomy, Buberian dialogic philosophy of I-Thou, and feminist ethics.

TIER TWO: PERMITTED, RECOMMENDED, AND SACRED RELATIONS

Washofsky and the CCAR Responsa Committee hold that sexual intercourse should only be permitted within the bounds of a sacred relationship.[31] They reaffirm that, even today, "We consider premarital and extramarital chastity to be our ideal."[32] Therefore they refuse to conduct ceremonies for nonmarital relationships:

> We will not be party to steps that undermine Jewish marriage or that diminish ambitions for sanctity in Jewish lives. . . . Once long-term non-marital relationships are found to be fully acceptable and "partially holy" by society, people have little need for the strictures of marriage.[33]

So too, Dorff, as a member of the RA Responsa Committee (Conservative), affirms the halakhic ideal that sexual intercourse entails the highest form of companionship and trust, hence, it is only safe and sacred within the bounds of holy matrimony:

> Only after Adam had experienced the pain of aloneness, despite all his possessions, would he be ready to appreciate the need for companionship and interdependence as the essential path of personal fulfillment. Sex is one of the ways in which this companionship is expressed. . . .
>
> The tradition understood, however, that *sex not only involves physical enjoyment; it is also an intense form of communication* through which a husband and wife convey their love for each other. It is precisely because this communicative aspect is essential to human sexuality that *licentious sex is effectively a lie*, for here the couple clearly do not mean to undertake the fundamental commitment to each other conveyed by their sexual union.
>
> Even if two people verbally declare to each other that their sex act is only for physical pleasure with no intention of further commitments, what they are conveying with their bodies belies what they have said with their lips. Such a situation, in other words, is rife with the potential for miscommunication, misunderstood intentions, and deeply hurt feelings. Undoubtedly, that is one reason that the Jewish tradition wants sex to be restricted to marriage.
>
> The Jewish tradition mandates that sex be restricted to marriage for very good reasons. . . . Marriage (*kiddushin*) is holy precisely because a man and woman set each other apart from all others to live their lives together, taking responsibility for each other, caring for each other, and helping each other live through life's highs and lows. They also take responsibility for the children they bear.[34]

TIER THREE: TOLERABLE AND MORAL, BUT NOT PERMITTED OR MANDATED RELATIONS

While Dorff denies halakhic validity to nonmarital sexual relations, his pastoral letter begins by acknowledging the social consensus among younger North American Jews, which he calls aptly "The Reality of Sex Outside Marriage." He understands compassionately that this reality is often embraced as a remedy to unbearable loneliness and frustrated instinctual needs, that many Jews regard living together as a beneficial prelude to marriage, and that many such relationships are ethically and emotionally supportive. Therefore, he states,

> We must also deal realistically, supportively, and therapeutically with the many who fall short of that ideal. . . . Although Judaism clearly would have Jews restrict intercourse to marriage, singles in our society generally do not abide by that norm. . . . [But] it is not an either-or situation, in which one either abides by all of what Judaism has to say about these matters or follows none of it.
>
> On the contrary, precisely those values that lead Judaism to advocate marriage—honesty, modesty, health and safety, love, and holiness—still apply to sexual relations outside marriage; they are just harder to achieve in that context. Indeed, precisely because unmarried couples cannot rely on the support of a marital bond to foster those values, it is all the more critical that if they engage in sexual intercourse, they must consciously strive to live by them. Even though their behavior will not be ideal by Jewish standards, to the extent that they can make those values real in their lives, they will be preserving their own humanity, their Jewishness, and their own mental and physical health, as well as that of their partner.[35]

For Dorff, rabbis must reach out pastorally beyond the halakhah to help sexually liberated North Americans who, he believes, are often floundering without a moral compass for determining worthy sexual behavior. So too, in the Reform movement, Washofsky closely parallels Dorff's pastoral letter in acknowledging living together as a morally acceptable relationship, while insisting it is not desirable as a sacred spiritual practice and should not be halakhically authorized or ritually celebrated by a rabbi. Washofsky aspires to sacred Jewish relationships that are more than merely ethical:

Judaism asks far more from each one of us than ethical behavior alone. It asks us to distinguish our sexual behavior in the most exalted—*kadosh*—context possible. This unequivocally implies that marriage should be the goal for our sexuality.[36]

However, not all Reform and Conservative rabbis agree with the responsa issued by their respective movements. The CCAR Ad Hoc Committee on Human Sexuality honors sexual intimacy within committed nonmarital love relationships as "covenantal." For these rabbis, there is sanctity in living together. This gray area is not only to be condoned as tolerable and ethical, but welcomed as commendable and sacred. Similarly, in the Conservative movement there are some dissenters from Dorff's position. After reading Dorff's letter denying that nonmarital relationships can be imbued with sanctity, Arthur Green, a Conservative rabbi and author of the article on sexual ethics in *The Second Jewish Catalog*, resigned in protest from the RA.[37] In chapter 15 we explore in greater depth and breadth approaches to living together advocated both within Reform and Conservative Judaism as well as Reconstructionist and Jewish Renewal movements.

Traditional Halakhah and Contemporary Conservative Jews

In the footsteps of Dorff's nuanced halakhic response to the complex challenges of the sexual revolution (1996), Rabbi Jeremy Kalmanofsky (Congregation Ansche Chesed, New York City) published a more detailed halakhic analysis entitled "Sex, Relationship and Single Jews" in *The Observant Life: The Wisdom of Conservative Judaism for Contemporary Jews* (2012).[38] He acknowledges the yawning gap in values between the traditional rabbinic world and contemporary America regarding romantic and sexual relationships: "Single people today face different problems and possibilities than our sages ever imagined.... Few topics illustrate this disjunction more clearly than do the halakhot concerning unmarried people and their intimate lives."[39] Yet, for him to admit that Jewish law has nothing relevant to say to contemporary Jews would be to admit the bankruptcy of the Conservative movement:

> Failing to give guidance in these areas would turn the realms of love and sex, for the vast majority of Jews from their late teens into their twenties and thirties and beyond, into *halakhah-free zones*. It would be to concede that the traditions of Jewish law have nothing to say to the modern situation. That would be faithless.
>
> Those who walk the path of halakhah must hope that ancient and medieval norms still retain the capacity to sanctify us, refine us, and help us build a better society.[40]

The motto of the Conservative movement, "tradition and change,"[41] obligates its rabbinic leadership to search out halakhic precedents to accommodate, in part, the social norm of sexual activity among single Jews today. So Gold, Dorff, and Kalmanofsky resort to the long history of Jewish law adapting itself to the gaps between its legal norms and its communities' changing practices. In crisis situations both for individuals and communities, halakhic authorities have often circumvented overly stringent laws by distinguishing between two tiers of norms: the ideal ruling "according to the book" (*l'khat-hila*) and the "second best," after-the-fact legal accommodation to reality (*di'avad*) in a time of stress.

GOLD'S HALAKHIC APPROACH TO SEXUALLY ACTIVE SINGLE JEWS

While most liberal rabbis hold to the norm *l'khat-hila* that restricts sex to marriage, they also admit that nonmarital sex may be condoned under the de facto category of *di'avad*. Rabbi Michael Gold (Conservative) explains: "While taking a public stand on behalf of sex within marriage . . . a rabbi called upon to counsel an unmarried person on sexual matters must do so with sensitivity and compassion, not judgment."[42]

As an example, Gold cites the Talmudic policy of halakhic leniency for sinners who cannot or will not restrain their sexual desires:

> Rabbi Ilai said: If a man sees that his evil impulse is conquering him, he should go to a place where he is unknown, put on black clothes, wrap himself in a black cloak, and do whatever his heart desires, but let him not publicly profane the name of heaven. (TB *Kiddushin* 40a)

Rav Ilai (Land of Israel, ca. 250 CE) counsels those who cannot overcome their desires "to go and do whatever his [or her?] heart desires," but that ruling is only due to necessity (*di'avad*). The Talmud does not understand Rav Ilai's advice as permitting anyone (*l'khat-hila*) to engage in casual sex (e.g., visiting prostitutes) whenever one feels like it. While Gold might object to resorting to sex workers, he is forgiving, after the fact, of premarital sex practiced by committed couples.

KALMANOFSKY'S HALAKHIC APPROACH TO SEXUALLY ACTIVE SINGLE JEWS

Similarly, Jeremy Kalmanofsky (Conservative) seeks a middle path for halakhah to accommodate—at arm's length—responsible partners who choose to live together, even though they intentionally violate his own ruling prohibiting nonmarital intercourse:

> If marriage is the ideal venue for sex, and if promiscuity is deemed altogether forbidden, might there be some middle ground status to

assign to sexual relations that take place within a committed relationship that is not a marriage? . . . Is there a *di'avad* condition, a non-optimal but legally defensible sexuality for single people?[43]

Kalmanofsky has solid halakhic precedents for ruling more leniently, since most halakhic authorities regard the prohibition against sexual relations between singles as a minor infringement of a rabbinic, rather than a Biblical, prohibition.[44] He justifies lowering traditional rabbinic "fences" prohibiting any physical contact (*negia*) between unmarried singles, because the contemporary community simply cannot and will not abide by them.[45] As the Talmud says, "A court must not enact a decree unless most of the public can fulfill it" (TB *Baba Kama* 79b). Thus he condones, halakhically, noncoital sexual intimacy for a couple living together.[46]

While showing flexibility, Kalmanofsky still engages the law with reverence and responsibility, prohibiting as well as permitting without capitulating whenever his congregants are uncomfortable with traditional halakhic constraints. Even if the prohibition on intercourse among singles is only a rabbinic prohibition, he argues "that certainly does not mean we should take it lightly, but it means we should see this prohibition in perspective."[47] He clarifies:

> Promiscuous sex without commitment is a physical pleasure that deliberately avoids both the spirituality of ultimate intimacy and the commandment of procreation. *Z'nut* [prostitution], therefore, is a degraded version of sexual intercourse.[48] This is why traditional halakhah forbids licentious sex,[49] and why Conservative halakhah affirms the prohibition . . . [of sex with] multiple partners in the same time period or . . . of sex without emotional engagement or meaningful, enduring commitment.[50]

Generally, Kalmanofsky is unafraid to advocate strong prohibitions to his permissive congregants whenever he believes leniency will have adverse ethical outcomes. For this reason, he has no tolerance for occasional adultery or "open marriages" in which a couple agrees in advance that either spouse may engage in extramarital affairs.[51] Also, he uncompromisingly upholds Biblical family purity laws for singles and married couples (no intercourse during menses; and afterward, ritual immersion before resuming intercourse).[52]

Unmarried couples ought ideally to refrain from sexual relations. Once they do engage in intercourse, however, Kalmanofsky rules that, like married couples, they should uphold the halakhic standard of marital intimacy that permits sexual union only when their emotional relationship is not flawed by acrimony, hate, fear, or lack of full consent:

> Unmarried people should uphold these same norms in their sexual relationships. If these are ignored, sex will be *cold-hearted* when it should be tender, *crass* when it should be modest, *deceptive* when it should be sincere, *unthinking*—or, God forbid, nonconsensual—when it should be the product of mutual feelings of passion and love. *Without mutual commitment to these values, a sex partner can become only a warm body to exploit for one's own immediate comfort....* Such an orientation fundamentally degrades one's partner by turning him or her into an object.... Exclusive fidelity is first on that list of virtues and is presumed in every Judaic discussion on sex and holiness, while infidelity is universally regarded as poison.[53]

Realistic Halakhah Condones Lesser Sins to Avoid Greater Sins

Dorff's and Kalmanofsky's policies for accommodating lesser infractions of the halakhah in order to avoid more flagrant violations have a long pedigree. In many situations one must guide those under one's tutelage in how best to violate the law, how to sin, but less heinously, while minimizing legal culpability and interpersonal damage. Rabbi Robert Gordis (Conservative) offers this mundane example of an authentic parental dilemma:

> Many a modern mother, suspecting that her daughter going out on a date may engage in sexual relations, has been confronted by the dilemma of whether or not to advise her daughter on the use of a contraceptive before she leaves for the evening. In most cases, the mother has opted for discretion [and instructed her about birth control techniques to prevent unwanted pregnancy].[54]

In partially accommodating single Jews engaging in sex, Liberal rabbis follow policies modeled by Maimonides (Egypt, 12th century) and the Rashba (Rav Shlomo ibn Aderet, Spain, 13th century), who in their responsa are often lenient and flexible in condoning and containing illicit practices when those involved are not likely to abide by the letter of the law.

MAIMONIDES' PRECEDENT

Like the Conservative rabbis today, Maimonides also faced significant gaps between ideal standards of his code of law and the actual sexual behavior practiced by the members of the Jewish community in Egypt under his jurisdiction. Once, Maimonides was asked about a Jew who had purchased a "beautiful" non-Jewish slave who was living in his courtyard. Rumor suggested he was sleeping with her, though Jewish (not Muslim) law clearly forbade such intercourse. Given such rumors, the Mishnah forbids the master from liberating and converting the slave and subsequently marrying her, so as not to reward Jewish men who take sexual advantage of their pagan female slaves.[55] Yet Maimonides ruled to waive that prohibition:

While the court should coerce him to remove her [the slave woman] from his courtyard, [if he refuses, then the court should coerce him] to liberate her from slavery [which automatically converts her to Judaism] and then he can marry her properly. [This is my ruling] *even though this constitutes a kind of sin.*[56]

Audaciously, Maimonides justifies his court's decision to circumvent the law and unequivocally prescribes committing a lesser rather than a greater sin. Quoting the Talmudic adage, "It is better to sip the broth of a forbidden stew than to eat the forbidden meat within" (TB *Yoma* 82a), Maimonides argues that a rabbi should permit a minimal violation of the law to contend with a sinner's overpowering desire for the forbidden. The Jewish slave master will not or cannot rein in his desire, so Maimonides legalizes the master's sexual intimacy with the slave utilizing a shady but lawful maneuver.[57]

Further, as Rashi teaches, when a conquering soldier receives in spoils "a beautiful captive woman," the Torah permitted him to marry her, "but only begrudgingly," because

the Torah speaks [i.e., legislates] after taking into consideration the evil impulse. For were the Holy One [i.e., the Torah] not to permit [marriage to the beautiful captive under these special conditions], then the Hebrew soldier would [probably] marry her anyway, in violation of the prohibition [against marrying idol worshippers].[58]

Analogously, Maimonides not only permits the sinful master to marry his former slave paramour but instructs the court

to help him—with gentleness and softness—to marry her, and to set the date for the wedding, for this is deemed an emergency situation in which 'one must act for God by violating your Torah' (TB *Temurah* 14a), and we pray that God will repair our corruptions.[59]

Despite Maimonides' philosophic disgust with excessive sexuality, his realistic halakhic flexibility reflects his judgment that sexual relations are the most recalcitrant field of human behavior to legislative control: "No prohibition in all the Torah is as difficult to keep as that of forbidden sexual relations."[60]

RASHBA'S PRECEDENT

For his part, Rav Shlomo ibn Aderet (Spain, 1235–1310) recommends that leaders choose sagaciously when, how, and to whom to direct their admonitions:

> To eliminate the stumbling blocks of the people . . . one cannot treat all the persons by the same measure. . . . Turning a blind eye on a sinner is sometimes a mitzvah. . . . So the judge must be wary lest his fiery zealousness for God burn in him and thereby cause him to neglect the good and appropriate path. . . . The profit and the loss must be weighed; moderation, consensus and consultation are needed.[61]

In short, a politic leader, even a judge representing God's Torah, must choose his battles carefully. The recalcitrance of libido-driven transgressors, especially when reinforced by social norms contradicting traditional halakhic norms, has compelled rabbinic leaders both in ancient times and now to modulate their responses. Rabbis have long employed a strategic policy of what we now call "pastoral halakhah" by encouraging those who cannot simply refrain from transgressions to choose lesser infractions over greater ones.

Test Case 1: Adultery Revisited

In this and the next chapter, we examine three test cases in which Liberal halakhists struggle with whether to permit what traditional halakhah condemns unconditionally as adultery: (1) forgiving adulterers after repentance in order to rehabilitate the original marriage,

(2) spouses agreeing to conduct a marriage of polyamory or permitted sexual affairs, and (3) permitting the caretaker spouse of a permanently incapacitated spouse to take a lover. The diagnoses of these particular cases depend on one's general understanding of the primary reason for prohibiting adultery.

While most Liberal rabbis treat adultery as a red-letter crime, their rationales tend to be different than the reasons embedded in the Torah. They do not accept the patriarchal rationale that adultery is an act of theft of another man's property (Deut. 5:18); rather, they regard adultery as the arch-crime against the sacred I-Thou relationship of marital trust and a threat to Israel as *a kingdom of priests and a holy people* (Exod. 19:5).[62] The place of adultery in prophetic ethics, an important religious authority for Liberal Judaism, is implicit in the prophet Malachi's description of marriage as a *covenant with your friend* (Mal. 2:14). Gold sums up this judgment:

> In Judaism, adultery is the ultimate crime against a family [because it] undermines the basic trust on which the marital bond is built.... Even if adultery occurs with one's partner's consent, Judaism would find such liaisons abominations. That is why Joseph [as a slave] tells Potiphar's wife [who attempts repeatedly to seduce him] that adultery is *a sin against God* (Gen. 39:9).[63]

Liberal rabbis also factor in the consequences of extramarital affairs. Gold confesses: "As a rabbi, I have seen too many marriages crash on the shoals of an affair. It is vital that rabbis today make a statement that adultery is wrong."[64] In upholding their own strict anti-adultery code, Liberal rabbis contend with three increasingly frequent dilemmas.

In the first dilemma, a rabbi confronts partners who wish to be reconciled to one another after one or both have participated in an adulterous affair. Rabbinic law removes the jurisdiction over forgiving the sin of adultery from the hands of the victimized spouse.

The court is supposed to compel a husband to divorce his wife if she has had an affair, for it is an abomination for a woman to return to her husband after intercourse with a third party.[65] While Gold acknowledges that "Jewish law leaves no room for forgiveness," he and many other Conservative rabbis argue that repentance and family maintenance are higher considerations favoring leniency after the betrayal.[66] He states, "In my rabbinic counseling, I always try to save a marriage. . . . They can begin anew, for central to Judaism is *teshuvah*. . . . Forgiveness and rebuilding after an indiscretion are possible and desirable."[67]

A second dilemma is discussed by David Greenstein (Conservative, faculty of the Academy for Jewish Religion's rabbinical seminary), who discovered a historic trend among early modern traditional rabbis to let adulterous couples reunite despite the unforgiving Talmudic prohibition of rapprochement after adultery. In an intriguing nineteenth-century responsum about a woman who committed adultery, repented, and confessed to her rabbi, the authorities are asked: Must the rabbi break up the marriage by informing her husband and pressuring him to divorce her immediately? Greenstein summarizes the responsum of Rabbi Shlomo Kluger (ultra-Orthodox, Poland, d. 1869):

> Kluger . . . applies the value of protecting human dignity to the woman. While she has sinned and become forbidden to her husband, she should not be shamed. She must inform her husband quietly and then the husband can divorce her quietly.
>
> If, however, the woman is too embarrassed to admit her sins to her husband, the rabbi must help the woman find an appropriate way *to repent while yet staying in the marriage*. But the rabbi must *not* reveal the facts to the husband, "even though from the legal standpoint it is right to do so, because we have no power to uphold the law properly."[68]

While Greenstein concurs in part with Kluger's policy that refrains from coercing or publicly shaming those involved in adultery, he opposes Kluger's decision to keep the wife's secret from the cuckolded husband. Instead, Greenstein commends a policy of telling the truth to the spouse of the adulterer:

> Many people in our society would consider this to be a matter to be settled between the couple. Without condoning the adulterous actions, we would rather let the hurt party decide whether he or she wanted to end the marriage or whether he or she would rather try to somehow reconcile with the adulterous spouse. . . . [By informing him or her of the infidelity] we would rather allow them the freedom to choose.[69]

Rabbi Walter Jacob (Reform, co-founder of the Abraham Geiger College rabbinical school in London) struggled with a painful question arising from another dilemma related to adultery: May a rabbi, contra Jewish law, officiate at a divorced adulterer's wedding with his adulterous lover, even though his public behavior will, he believes, be interpreted as implicitly condoning adultery? In 1986 Jacob chose to rule in a Solomonic fashion that incorporates the conflicting values of condemning adultery as a betrayal of a covenantal marriage and yet facilitating *teshuvah* and remarriage:

> The sources are clear in their prohibition of adultery (Exod. 20:13) and of marriage between the adulterous party and her lover.[70] . . . Despite these strictures . . . tradition gives its grudging consent by stating that if, nevertheless, the adulterous parties marry, they are not compelled to divorce.[71]
>
> The rabbi may find herself in a difficult position as she is duty-bound to strengthen family life and defend the sanctity of marriage. If she, however, refuses to marry this couple, they may simply opt to live together, as is frequent in our time, and that will not help their

situation or the general attitude towards family life. Therefore, the rabbi should officiate at such a marriage, while at the same time discussing her own hesitations in keeping the tradition. She may insist on some special counseling [for the adulterers] before the ceremony. She should insist that it be a simple ceremony and one which places special emphasis on the seriousness and sanctity of marriage.[72]

In each of these cases, Liberal rabbis steer a tricky path, simultaneously attempting to reaffirm the prohibition on adultery while helping their congregants make the halakhic, moral, and interpersonal best of an undesirable situation.

Test Case 2: Open Marriage and Polyamory

Liberal Judaism has also begun to address questions of "open marriage" and "polyamory"—"consensual and emotionally intimate non-monogamous relationships in which both women and men can negotiate to have multiple partners."[73]

For many modern Jews, the doctrine of free choice overrides Biblical and rabbinic notions of what is sacred and what is abominable in sexual relations. If marriage or living together is a relationship defined *solely* by mutual consent of the sexual partners without regard to sanctity, then at least in principle couples may elect to forgo the demand for exclusivity.

In his recent Reconstructionist code of Jewish law, *A Guide to Jewish Practice*, vol. 1, *Everyday Living* (2011), Rabbi David Teutsch (founding director of the Center for Jewish Ethics of the Reconstructionist Rabbinical College) argues that, historically, bilateral monogamy, in which husband and wife are both prohibited from sexual relations with anyone else, never had a privileged status in Judaism. Even when Rabbenu Gershom enacted his ban on male polygamy for Ashkenazim in Christian Europe (ca. 1000 CE), its promulgators never viewed it as a step toward gender equality, enhanced marital intimacy, or higher sanctity; rather, they wanted to reinforce a second reform: prohibiting divorce without the wife's consent.[74] (Polygamy would have allowed the husband to take a second wife without having to grant a divorce to his first wife.) Therefore, Teutsch holds, *polyamory is an egalitarian extension of traditional Jewish male polygamy, so all partners of whatever gender may agree to an additional partner.* An open marriage simply allows, by mutual consent, casual sexual relations akin to the male's traditional resort to a second wife, a sex worker, or a kept woman, which the halakhah never treated as a moral or legal equivalent to adultery.

For Teutsch, mandating polyamory would also solve the problem of historic gender inequality in the history of halakhah, which prohibits adultery only when applied to married women:

> The traditional form of the Jewish wedding explicitly commits the woman—but not the man—to sexual fidelity. She is *mekudeshet,* "set aside" for him, but the reverse is not true, [though contemporary] egalitarian versions of the wedding vows and the *ketubah* imply that *both* husband and wife are committed to marital fidelity.
>
> The other *egalitarian* solution to the inequality in the traditional marriage agreement would be to require fidelity of *neither* partner.[75]

Teutsch prefers the second solution. If one dismisses the patriarchal notion of a husband's exclusive right to his wife's sexuality and the idea that a married woman with multiple sexual partners defiles Israel's sanctity, then the absence of sexual egalitarianism in Jewish tradition may be resolved.

Most other Liberal rabbis, however, object to both polyamory and polygamy because they undermine both traditional halakhah and modern Jewish values, especially the primacy of the Buberian ideal of I-Thou relationships as the basis for the sanctity of marriage. In addition, polygamy exacerbates pre-existing asymmetries of power between the original spouses, even if the woman too can have multiple husbands. Equality is hard enough to achieve with a dyad whose partners are never equally endowed, let alone a threesome or more.

Polyamory, one may argue, also disregards Biblical and Western romantic understandings that true love (*with all your heart, all your soul and all your might*—Deut. 6:5) is necessarily and appropriately possessive. Jealousy is inseparable from the emotional dynamic of love, as in the case of Leah's and Rachel's jealousy of one another (Gen. 29:30, 30:1). Even when spouses agree to an open marriage, it is a different matter when they actually face the reality of their beloved's amorous relationship with a third party. Someone is liable to be emotionally devastated, and the couple's mutual love and dignity may be deeply compromised. Teutsch acknowledges that often, even in an polyamorous marriage, a man or woman may feel betrayal, "deep pain, and a breakdown in trust," when a spouse takes another lover. Nonetheless, he maintains that, ethically and rationally, neither partner who agreed in advance to an open marriage has a right to expect exclusivity.[76]

Conclusion

In sum, the official responsa committees of the Conservative and Reform rabbinate have issued halakhic prohibitions on nonmarital (premarital, extramarital, or postmarital) sexual relationships. Yet these rabbis acknowledge that by promulgating an all-encompassing prohibition, their halakhic rulings leave the overwhelming majority of their community, who do practice nonmarital sex, without a moral compass. It is important to distinguish between committed relationships (living together), which are often caring and ethical, and casual intercourse (hooking up "for fun"), which may be depersonalized and at times exploitive.

Out of pastoral responsibility for their communities, these halakhically committed Conservative and Reform rabbis offer extralegal guidelines to those who decide to engage in prohibited nonmarital sex. They counsel them to maximize the moral quality of their nonmarital relationships, but many do *not* condone unreservedly what they consider to be unhalakhic and spiritually impaired practices. They often apply a sliding scale of situational ethics to match the amorphous condition of sexual partners, who vary from sixteen-year-olds living with their parents to thirty-year-old adults living together to forty-year-old divorcees to eighty-year-old widows. They offer a checklist of Jewish values for couples to apply to themselves, since the subjective quality of each emotional bond varies.

Many nonscholars are confused by the plethora of options suggested by Liberal Judaism's guidelines for sexual relations, and traditionalists often protest that the fuzziness of Liberal halakhah vitiates its claim to be regarded as halakhah. Yet Liberal rabbis maintain that normative ambiguity and lack of halakhic consensus can become virtues in facing the fluidity, individuality, and complexity of modern relationships. In helping couples make their own decisions, the Torah's flexibility—and hence realism—can be a blessing assuring perpetual relevance. As the Talmud reasons:

> If the Torah had been given *hatukha* [i.e., cut and dried, totally explicit and clear], then there would have been no leg to stand on [i.e., there would have been no leeway to apply it freshly to varied situations].... Instead the Torah is interpreted [amorphously] with forty-nine facets for impurity and forty-nine facets for purity. (TJ *Sanhedrin* 4:2)

In this spirit, Dorff and Ruttenberg argue that halakhic literature often maintains indeterminacy intentionally in order to address the nuances of intimate relationships such as "I-Thou relationships

[that] have no pre-set boundaries." Dorff concludes their book *Sex and Intimacy* on this point:

> In Judaism, every aspect of human life is a holy piece of Torah, worthy of thought, study, and consideration—and sex is certainly no exception. And yet ... it is no small task to figure out what that view means on the ground, how to translate our aspirations for a sacred sexuality to the messy, complex reality of our interpersonal lives.[77]

Legalizing Living Together?   15

COMPETING RABBINIC POLICIES

All paths should be presumed to carry danger. There is no path forward that is without crookedness or ambushes. Some [rabbis] say: "What do I need this trouble for? I will [refrain from making any legal innovations], watch my step and not sin, and I will have saved my soul."

But the Sages have expounded: *And to him who blazes a path I will show the salvation of God* (Ps. 50:23)—This refers to those who light lamps for the multitude.

—RABBI ABRAHAM JOSHUA HESCHEL, *Heavenly Torah: As Refracted through the Generations*

Introduction

Faced with the rapid rise of Jewish couples choosing to live together without benefit of marriage, Liberal rabbinic thinkers have been debating since the 1980s the pros and cons of an audacious and original halakhic proposal composed more than 250 years ago by a brilliant, maverick Orthodox rabbi from Germany, Jacob Emden (1697–1776). Emden demonstrates with great erudition that the halakhah never prohibited living together in sexual intimacy without marriage. His responsum not only condones but urgently commends the reinstitution of the *pilegesh* (literally, the concubine), so that a man and a woman may choose to enter a legal arrangement for a long- or short-term sexual partnership *without* need for formal marriage or subsequent divorce in case of separation. They can and should, however, make a civil agreement to protect her material maintenance, their offspring's reputation, and the exclusivity of her sexual relationship with him for its duration.

461

For Emden, his legal maneuver enables any man, married or single, even a rabbi like himself, to have a mistress, "kept woman," paramour, or lover (whichever term is in vogue), and thus provides him a safe outlet for libidinal drives (and perhaps romantic longing?) that might otherwise harm society. Surprisingly, Emden claims that the pilegesh arrangement is equally attractive to men and to women. For married Ashkenazi men, to whom polygamy has been prohibited since 1000 CE, it offers access to an additional sexual and emotional attachment; and for single women, it provides a sexual partnership with an easy escape hatch—without the legal complications of divorce and the man's consent—should this intimate relationship become undesirable or abusive for her.

Despite the derogatory connotations of the old-fashioned word pilegesh (the Biblical "concubine"), some twentieth-century rabbis believe Emden's pilegesh can be reformatted and repurposed for a fully egalitarian society to mandate and regulate the sexual relations of living together. Other contemporary rabbis, however, vociferously condemn the revival of a patriarchal institution, both because of Emden's sexist motives and because of its potentially disastrous competition with the institution of holy matrimony.

Our concern here is not to analyze the halakhic validity of pilegesh or weigh the prognosis for such a policy's impact on traditional marriage. Rather, after presenting Emden's historic proposal, this chapter compares the divergent responses of North American Liberal rabbis to his responsum, and their evaluation of the contemporary phenomenon of living together—before, instead of, after, or even alongside marriage.

Historical Background: The *Pilegesh*

To set the stage for discussing Emden's innovative responsum (scandalous in his age and ours), let's consider the Biblical origins of pilegesh and its medieval revival in Spain (11th–14th centuries). In Biblical usage, the term *pilegesh* (concubine) is not a female slave (*shifkha*, or *amah*). Sometimes, *pilegesh* refers to a *secondary wife within a polygamous marriage*, whose role is to produce heirs when the primary wife is barren. For example, Bilhah and Zilpah, former slave attendants (*shifkha*) of Rachel and Leah, became secondary wives (*pilegesh/isha*) to augment the production of children when Rachel and Leah could not give birth (Gen. 29:24,29; 30:9; 35:22). In a royal harem, however, a *pilegesh* (but not a wife, *isha*) refers to hundreds of secondary consorts in King Solomon's and King Ahashverosh's harems who fulfill the king's sexual desire. In addition, multiple wives in a harem fulfill the reproductive aim of generating heirs or the foreign policy goal of sealing alliances with foreign monarchs by marrying their daughters as wives (1 Kings 11:1,3; Esther 2:14,17).

Unlike these kinds of Biblical pilegesh, which are not analogous to the contemporary practice of living together, a third type of Biblical pilegesh is a man's primary sexual partner, who lives in his home, not as a secondary wife but as his sole consort, apparently with her father's approval. She is comparable to a common-law wife in the English or Israeli system of law. The pilegesh of the town of Giv'ah (Judg. 19:1–3) is a good example. When she is dissatisfied with her husband, she leaves him on her own initiative and goes back to her family of origin. The only way her male consort can retrieve her is "to speak to her heart" and persuade her to return voluntarily to his home. She is not a secondary wife for procreation, a mistress for sexual pleasure, a sex worker, or a slave. She is his lone spouse, the sole woman to whom he is emotionally attached, but, unlike a formal wife, she can leave him or return to him as she wishes, without divorce proceedings or coercion (Judg. 19:1–3).

While the Rabbis of the Talmudic era never mention any woman in Rabbinic society who is an actual pilegesh, in the medieval world of Jewish Spain (ruled by Muslims and later by Christians), *pilegesh* was the term for a widespread rabbinically regulated phenomenon—the "kept woman" who typically entered voluntarily into a sexually exclusive bond with a wealthy married Jewish businessman or rabbi.[1] While in Islamic lands a slave concubine was a legally recognized sexual partner for polygamous Muslim men alongside their official wives (up to four wives, but unlimited slave concubines), for Jewish men in these lands the only halakhically permitted sexual relations were with Jewish women who were not slaves and who consented voluntarily to the extramarital arrangement called pilegesh. Alongside the primary wife, the pilegesh provided a second sexual and emotional partner, whom the man was financially obligated to support, along with their common children, who were his legitimate heirs. The pilegesh was obligated to maintain exclusive monogamy (on her part) during the period of their bond (and to practice ritual immersion in the community *mikveh* after the conclusion of menstruation and prior to returning to intercourse). Unlike a formal marriage, no betrothal (*kiddushin*) or formal marriage contract (*ketubah*) was involved. As such, no sacred status attended this arrangement, and when it was no longer desirable, divorce was not necessary, simply a cessation of living together determined unilaterally by either partner.

Even before the expulsion of the Jews of Spain (1492), this custom fell into abeyance in Spain. Among Ashkenazi Jewry, the pilegesh arrangement was never adopted, just as the Catholic Church never accepted mistresses as a legal option in Christian society, even though princes and popes often had mistresses. In line with Church law, Ashkenazim insisted on strict bilateral monogamy (at least since the edict attributed to Rabbenu Gershom, ca. 1000 CE).

Emden, however, was a leading Ashkenazi rabbi living in a German principality four hundred years after the demise of the institution of the pilegesh in Spain. In the Age of Reason, in the same country and period in which the Orthodox rationalist philosopher

Moses Mendelssohn was becoming famous by demonstrating that even Jews can belong to the enlightened Protestant world of modernity, Emden's call for a *return to male polygamy* seemed anachronistic and scandalous.

Emden's Pathbreaking Halakhah: Enhancing Marital Lovemaking and Legalizing a Paramour

Jacob Emden, whose acronym is YAVETZ—YAcov (Jacob) son of (VEn) the *hakham* TZvi, an internationally acclaimed scholar—describes and commends two polar experiences of sexuality usually thought to be contradictory. On one hand, he envisions marital union in terms of mutual erotic intimacy founded on a husband's legal obligation to show sensitivity to his wife's feelings and sensual needs. Love is sacred, and its highest fulfillment is achieved when celebrating Shabbat pleasures and simultaneously facilitating the mystical union of masculine and feminine aspects of the Divine (see chapter 5).

On the other hand, Emden describes the ravenous, powerfully egocentric and hedonistic male libido. If this libido is not satisfied within marriage, he warns, it may lead to dangerous violations of the sanctity and social order of the community of Israel. Since, he argues, monogamous marriage is an inadequate outlet for masculine desire, having a mistress is socially and spiritually useful for all males and for society.

EMDEN'S JEWISH *KAMA SUTRA* FOR SHABBAT EVENING

Emden's approach to marital intimacy is found in a detailed erotic guide to the mitzvah of lovemaking with one's wife on Shabbat. No ivory tower scholar, Emden seeks to teach his bedroom ethics to his whole community by printing his manual for marital onah, entitled

Hadar HaMitot, Mitot Kesef (The bedroom and silver beds), within his classic self-published prayer book, *Siddur Beit Yaakov* (1747). Guidelines for onah appear as a subcategory within his commentary on the mitzvah of *Oneg Shabbat* (the sensual pleasures mandated on Shabbat) along with sumptuous dining and extended hours of sleeping.[2] He explains why Friday night is the most appropriate time for *onah*, its desired frequency, its proper positions and the foreplay to precede it, how soon after a meal intercourse becomes appropriate, and the necessary diet for procreation of healthy progeny. Further, he discusses how sexual relations can, with proper kabbalist intentions, become an exalting mystical experience.[3] He states: "Know that the marital union, when done properly with the right timing and intention, is sacred and pure. One should not think sexual union is despicable and ugly, God forbid!"[4]

Emden's advice is to be read by Jewish husbands weekly at the synagogue, just before going home to share Shabbat dinner with their wives. They can then make love with their wives on Shabbat night—the ideal time for onah for scholars and mystics. Strikingly, Emden highlights emotional and sensual preparations for lovemaking and mutuality in mind and heart:

> A husband should soothe/appease/arouse his wife and please her with words that gladden the heart and intensify her longing for him—in a spirit of sacred purity. The greater their mutual love during their union, the greater the intelligence of the resultant offspring. Their mutual desire generates warmth; intelligence is the product of warmth of heart and sharpness of the mind. When husband and wife are at one in their purity, they achieve perfect union of mind/intention on a religious basis, and they will bear children that reflect the purity of the ideas that they conceived.[5]

For Emden, not only the intelligence of the child is shaped by the quality of the parents' sexual union but so too the child's moral traits. If the father or mother is wicked, their offspring will likely follow suit and thus desecrate God's holy name by their bad behavior. By carefully following Emden's instructions, however, their lovemaking can bring about sanctification of God's name in the world. Therefore, a couple's sexual relationship is a crucial test of their self-control, their sensitivity to one another, and their collaboration in producing offspring capable of honoring God's name in the world.[6]

While traditional medieval texts (like *The Holy Letter* and *Ba'alei HaNefesh*) had highlighted the purity of thought at the moment of intercourse, slowly arousing one's wife to desire, and appropriate pillow talk (see chapter 5), Emden explicated in greater detail the physical gestures of affection necessary to enhance the union of body and mind. Like an Enlightenment scientist, he catalogs kissing under two classifications and teaches husbands to observe their wives' physical responses to foreplay:

> Intimacy should come at the climax of hugging and kissing. There is no intercourse without preparing it with hugging and kissing. There are *two kinds of kissing*: the one before the sexual union is designed for the husband to appease his wife and to awaken the love between them, and then there is kissing during the sexual union.[7]

Since it is the man's duty to bring his wife step-by-step to orgasm, he needs a recognizable indication of his success in her arousal: "That will be apparent to him by attending to her breathing and [the light in] her eyes. Then they make love to one another."[8]

In sum, for Emden, sexual union is not merely a release for excess male drives or an instrument for procreation of high-quality offspring; it is a supremely sacred end in itself:

> True scholars, who stand in God's confidence, know that this act (sexual union) is important and good as well as advantageous to the soul as well. There is no comparable value in all other acts of

man when this act is performed with pure intentions and innocent, wholesome thoughts; certainly it is called *holy*. There is in it no flaw, nor depreciation, nor reproach.⁹

EMDEN'S CONFESSIONAL AUTOBIOGRAPHY:
A SCHOLAR'S STRUGGLE WITH HIS *YETZER*

To understand the personal significance of Emden's pathbreaking preoccupation with sexual intimacy and gratification, we must look at his remarkably candid autobiography, *Megillat Sefer*. Here he recounts his trials and tribulations, his personal tragedies—a failed betrothal, a disappointing wedding night, and an attempted seduction thwarted—that may have shaped his halakhic work.

His three joyless marriages occurred in the shadow of his failed espousal at age sixteen to someone he describes rhapsodically as "a learned and intelligent woman, verily without equal in all the land of Germany."¹⁰ After his father revoked the betrothal he so desired, Emden was married off at age seventeen to another bride his father had chosen, and then suffered a bout with impotence: "My wedding [day] ... was not a day of my heartfelt joy. For during onah I lacked virility and I agonized over it for several days. ... I was thus deprived of happiness and joy."¹¹ His own expectations of a passionate love life with a wise woman had been dashed. Perhaps, to save others from such disappointment, Emden, adopts the amorous Talmudic model of Rav's lovemaking—the ideal his own marital life likely never achieved—in composing his halakhic prescriptions for sexual union on Shabbat. In his autobiography he broods about his periodic bouts of depression, which, he feared, derived from his own father's melancholic state at the moment of Jacob's own conception. Hence Emden was very concerned that husband and wife be joyful and truly of one heart and mind at the time of sexual union, in particular because their state of mind would influence the mental state of the child conceived at that moment.

In his autobiography Emden also discusses the other side of sexual intimacy—animal lust rather than emotional love. He recounts how he was sorely tempted to stray during a trip away from home in Prague in 1722:

> I was a man at the prime of my strength and passion. There was a very pleasant beautiful woman before me who demonstrated all manner of love and closeness many times. . . . If I had wanted to fulfill my desire for her, I was absolutely sure she would not reveal my secret. I controlled my instinct, conquered my passion and determined to kill it. . . . "Blessed be the Lord who gives strength to the weary" for I was saved from this flaming fire![12]

In his prayerbook *Siddur Beit Yaakov*, Emden acknowledges the utility of marital intercourse in safely channeling anarchic urges a man cannot always suppress by willpower alone. He quotes with approval from Ra'avad's *Ba'alei HaNefesh* (12th century):

> Someone who intends to have [intercourse with his wife] in order to fence in his evil impulse which threatens to overwhelm him has earned merit. He satisfies himself with what is permissible [i.e., intercourse with his wife] and not with what is prohibited [i.e., a prostitute, adulteress, or idolater].[13]

Ra'avad, however, exempts true scholars from the need to channel their desires into marital intercourse, because he says they have sufficient willpower to master their impulses without recourse to channeling their drives into sex.[14] Yet, while Emden once demonstrated his ability to resist temptation, he is not as confident as Ra'avad in a scholar's self-restraint. Therefore Emden extends Ra'avad's dispensation for men in need of greater frequency of onah to include scholars.

Emden also addresses a health issue caused by abstinence from sexual relations: "Maybe he will get sick if he does not engage in intercourse."[15] Like Maimonides, Emden sees regular intercourse as a necessary component to male health, because a man's *yetzer* is essential to human nature as the Creator intended it: "The yetzer is present within Adam for his own good, and it is not possible to exist without it."[16] Since each couple's healthy need for sex differs in accord with the variable strength of the husband's and the wife's individual desires, the frequency of their scheduled onah ought to be adjusted accordingly:

> The frequency of onah is set for everyone according to one's capability and one's enjoyment and in accordance with what the Rabbis thought the wishes (*da'at*) of the woman are so that she would be appeased/satisfied by fulfilling her sexual desire.
>
> If the husband needs to do more of this act [of sexual intercourse], he has permission to add [to the frequency of onah] as long as his intention is to save himself from sin. . . . [So too] if she needs this [sexual intimacy] and she makes an effort to persuade him [i.e., she lobbies him] and adorns herself before him, he is obligated to make her happy with this mitzvah, even if it does not fall at the time of his [halakhically obligated frequency of] onah.[17]

For Emden, men must reckon realistically with their evil impulse, estimating its needs and channeling its satisfaction, monitoring their health needs to facilitate necessary outlets for their libido, and diligently observing and fulfilling their wives' variable desires. What is more, with proper restraint, passionate marital lovemaking on Shabbat can achieve sanctity in accord with mystical science:

> One needs to exercise extreme care to stand against this yetzer in order to bring it into the Covenant. . . . Yet at the proper time, on Shabbat night, . . . love is awakened due to the fire of desire from

the left side; this is the side of holiness. By virtue of the holy fire, the yetzer, which is supported by that [left] side, is sanctified. It is like something added from the profane to the sacred and thereby made pure. When one behaves during the act of onah according to all we have written above *one greatly sanctifies oneself in having sex.*[18]

Each act of intercourse affords an opportunity for sanctifying oneself and one's sexual urges, not through ascetic self-denial, but through passionate and appropriately balanced mutual lovemaking. To the kabbalists, like Emden, it is vital to balance the polar tendencies between the right and the left side of the dynamic multidimensional human (and divine) persona, both of which maintain a tension between the attributes of reticence (i.e., holding back yetzer) and of arousal (i.e., stoking desire).

EMDEN'S RESPONSUM ON
REVIVING THE HALAKHIC *PILEGESH*

The law of the pilegesh (exemplified in the Bible by Jacob, Emden's namesake) enables men to simultaneously maintain a formal marriage relationship and a contractual but nonmarital relationship. According to Emden, that legal option was never abrogated. Furthermore, he insists, the law is *not* a form of slavery, economic exploitation, or prostitution, but an honorable arrangement based on mutual consent and benefit:

> *Pileg-esh*—as the term connotes—is *p'lag isha*, a half wife [without kiddushin, formal betrothal, and ketubah, marriage contract] . . . in an exclusive relationship with a man for a certain time and for certain benefits, all of which are determined between the two of them. . . . If she renders herself sexually accessible to anyone else, then she certainly becomes like a prostitute [and that is prohibited].[19]

Aiming to meet the male need for more sexual outlets and thus avoid illicit relations with married women, Jewish prostitutes, or non-Jews, Emden proffers a policy designed to bring *relief to all men but especially to Torah scholars*, like himself, who have a more capacious need for sexual satisfaction: "Even more so do Torah scholars need to know of this option, for 'those who are greater than their fellows [in Torah study], their yetzer [lustful inclination] is that much greater, too' (T B *Sukkah* 52a)."[20]

Yet Emden also commends the pilegesh arrangement for three other potential benefits. First, men and women can have a committed sexual relationship without the legal burdens of marriage. Should the relationship sour, they can disengage without the painful, costly, and lengthy procedures of a contested divorce:

> Both parties might then prefer the pilegesh relationship to a marital one. . . . Perhaps he does not wish to be bound by the weighty responsibilities of marriage; and the woman too prefers this form of relationship to marriage so that if the man mistreats her, she can simply leave the relationship instantly, without the hassles of acquiring a *get* from him in accordance with all the intricate details this involves. *By simply leaving him, she is free of him in so light a manner. . . .*
>
> The moment she ceases cohabitation with the one she was with, the prohibition [of exclusivity] is lifted by word alone [i.e., by his or her declaration that the agreement is null without the documentary procedure of a *get*], and she may marry or live with another man. By the mere act of her leaving his house and no longer having intercourse with him, she automatically resumes her status as a single woman— after waiting the three-month period [to determine whether she is pregnant from the man she left].[21]

While a divorce requires the husband's and, for Ashkenazim, the wife's consent, here the pilegesh may leave a man unilaterally, whenever "she simply wishes to leave him," without his permission and without having to prove he is at fault because "he has abused her or he has not upheld whatever they agreed between them."[22] Implicitly Emden recognizes that halakhic divorce laws are chauvinist or at least unequal and, by contrast with the status of a married woman, such an arrangement gives the pilegesh greater unilateral freedom over her own sexuality and her significant relationships.

Second, a pilegesh relationship protects the woman with an enforceable civil contract. Even without kiddushin and ketubah, she is guaranteed the man's economic support for her private lodgings by virtue of a mutually binding, mutually negotiated agreement.

Third, the children of the pilegesh are considered legitimate as long as she refrains from sexual relations with another man during their arrangement. What is more, should she commit an act of infidelity while they are living together, it would not constitute adultery, and so (unlike the children born from an affair involving a married woman) the children born of such infidelity would not be considered *mamzerim* (illegitimate offspring).

To those rabbis who would prohibit living together lest it lead to greater sexual crimes, Emden protests that their logic is backward:

On the contrary, [the reinstitution of the pilegesh] would be a mitzvah, because it removes obstacles that lead to sinfulness. . . . It would allow alternative options of sexual relations that are not in violation of Torah principles, and reduce, not increase, sexual immorality. . . . In some situations the Talmudic Rabbis declared it is better even for a colleague to trespass a secondary prohibition than to end up trespassing a major one. . . . And here we are dealing with an issue [pilegesh] about which anyway there is *no prohibition* even by the Torah.[23]

Audaciously, Emden dismisses Maimonides' claim that the pilegesh is prohibited: "Where in the Talmud is there such a decree? What court ever made such a ruling? At what time was this legal tradition ever taught?"[24] Rather, Emden argues that the pilegesh was always acceptable in the Babylonian Talmud and many rabbis such as Ra'avad and Nahmanides recognized its validity (contra Maimonides and Karo).[25]

Admittedly, one significant halakhic objection to permitting nonmarital sexual relations is the fear that an unmarried woman will not purify herself in the mikveh after her menstrual cycle and before having intercourse with the man who made this arrangement with her. Emden, however, counters that a pilegesh will not avoid the mikveh any more than a married woman might:

> If the couple [the married man and his mistress] adhere to all that has been said above, there will be no burden of guilt or sin to bear whatsoever in this regard. She should feel no more ashamed of immersing herself at the proper times than her married sisters.[26]

While his halakhic reasoning is impeccable, Emden is surely too sanguine about his society's willingness to accept single women visiting the mikveh and to welcome their offspring, rather than calling them prostitutes and their children mamzerim. Even where the halakhah is inclusive, Orthodox communities are often not.

In conclusion, Emden proved himself a remarkable halakhic leader and educator regarding human sexuality. In his prayerbook he teaches husbands how to engage their wives in mutual passionate lovemaking *within* marriage. In his singular halakhic responsum, a tour de force of original exegesis and social policy, he acts as a legal activist shaping social policies for quasi-marital relationships *outside* marriage. He accommodates male libido capaciously and unapologetically, while also radically expanding a woman's options in living with her chosen significant other. Thus he argues forcefully for a pilegesh's legal autonomy and hence for her greater equality and freedom than a married woman. Even though he knows his proposal will arouse vociferous opposition from his conservative colleagues, Emden concludes the responsum with manifest civil courage: "In my opinion, it is a great mitzvah to publicize the fact that the pilegesh arrangement is halakhically permissible."[27]

Indeed, while the publication of Emden's prayerbook, with its sensuous guide to Oneg Shabbat, aroused no hackles, his (in)famous responsum about reinstituting the practice of the concubine created a controversy. Unsurprisingly, almost no other rabbi approved his proposal for a pilegesh as a paramour alongside one's wife, and it was never implemented anywhere in that form. Yet his arguments were cited by rabbis from the turn of the twentieth century on in order to find a halakhic category for libertarian Western practices of nonmarital sexual relations. Zvi Zohar, an Israeli professor of early modern and modern Sephardi halakhic traditions, has cited several Sephardi rabbis who invoked Emden's pilegesh model to make their rulings about modern couples living together outside wedlock in, for example, modern Alexandria.[28] We do not have space to explore Sephardi responsa, since this chapter is devoted to North American Ashkenazi rabbis as a dimension of their struggle with the modern sexual revolution (chapters 12–15).

On Living Together: Contemporary Halakhic Debate

While the societal issues Emden addressed in eighteenth-century Germany are significantly different from those facing the liberal rabbinate in twentieth- and twenty-first-century North America, his responsum has been reclaimed—or rebuffed—by modern and postmodern rabbis facing difficult situations in which traditional halakhic practice appears inadequate. Leading non-Orthodox North American rabbis, such as Arthur Waskow (Renewal) and Eugene Borowitz (Reform), believe Emden's legal ingenuity can be applied beneficially to the contemporary situation of living together, while

Solomon Freehof (Reform) and Jeremy Kalmanofsky (Conservative) reject Emden's proposal out of hand as a misguided attempt to sanction living together as a legitimate alternative to sacred matrimony, and as a chauvinist travesty of women's rights.

MORAL OBJECTIONS TO THE RETURN TO POLYGAMY

To many modern rabbis, much is objectionable about Emden's proposal to revive the pilegesh. First, the reinstatement of a retrograde form of polygamy in which the man conducts simultaneous sexual liaisons sets two women against each other by institutionalizing *structural jealousy* between the wife and pilegesh, who are competing for the same man's loving attention. That jealousy will prevail regardless of whether the second woman is a full wife or a pilegesh/lover. The Biblical tales of Leah and Rachel, Sarah and Hagar, and Hannah and Peninah demonstrate how destructive such polygamous competition can be for family stability, the dignity of the co-wives, and marital love and trust.

Second, from the Buberian perspective, Emden's pilegesh is demeaned, because she becomes a sex object in an *I-it relationship*. Instead of enhancing sexual intimacy within the I-Thou emotional bonds of marriage, license is given to sexual release unburdened by the entangling, long-term commitments of marriage.

Third, contrary to Emden's claim, the pilegesh option exacerbates *gender inequality* by circumventing the progressive Ashkenazi anti-polygamy legislation of Rabbenu Gershom (which Emden attributes to the unworthy foreign influence of Christian values on Jewish law). Rabbenu Gershom's ban on taking a second wife and his simultaneous ban on the husband's unilateral right to divorce his wife compelled both husband and wife to agree to a divorce or else both would be deprived of alternative sexual outlets. Emden's responsum, however, allows a husband whose wife does not agree to divorce to take another woman as a pilegesh "on the side." Thus, he reinstates the double standard regarding men's and women's sexual options. After all, only men may have a pilegesh alongside their married spouse. Further, women who do consent to be "kept," or mistresses, are probably socially and economically disadvantaged relative to the married men who "keep" them. Thus Emden's arrangement may encourage these privileged men to think they are "entitled" to abuse their power differential over these women.

Fourth, Emden recommends the pilegesh arrangement in order to satisfy the needs, above all, of great rabbis! Thus he makes superfluous the ethical virtue of *self-restraint*, even for the spiritual elite and dismisses the sanctity of self-control and mastery of anarchic impulses. Instead of praising the rabbinic hero "who conquers his yetzer" (*Mishnah Avot* 4:1), the responsum exploits a legal loophole to facilitate the satisfaction of male yetzer, while circumventing the dampening effect of social shame.

Fifth, in the eyes of key Reform and Conservative rabbis as well as almost all Modern Orthodox rabbis, the pilegesh system bolsters *competition* with the endangered institution of marriage and its ideal of total devotion to one's married spouse (I-Thou) by removing the stigma from sexual promiscuity practiced under the guise of living together. Living together advances the secularization and instrumentalizing of short-term sexual relations of convenience instead of reinforcing the sanctity and humanity of long-term marital relationships of loving commitment.

One classic Reform halakhic authority, Rabbi Solomon Freehof (1892–1990), not only rejects living together, but labels it, pejoratively, "simply living in adultery."[29] Without going to that extreme in name calling, many North American Conservative rabbis concur that there is a slippery slope between permitting living together and condoning casual sex. Since, in principle, the pilegesh can be a very short-term arrangement, living together may not really be all that different from promiscuity. So, Conservative rabbi Jeremy Kalmanofsky asserts:

> Halakhic tradition unambiguously condemns sex outside of marriage as *z'nut*, a pejorative term meaning "harlotry" or "licentiousness." ... Traditional authorities universally agree that sex between single people—including consenting adults—is forbidden at least by rabbinic enactment, and some consider it banned by Torah law.[30]

Therefore, Kalmanofsky argues forcefully:

> Conservative Jews should reject this suggestion on moral grounds. An exploitative system like concubinage—applied however loosely or metaphorically—can provide no model for intimate relationships of dignity and mutuality. Perhaps the modern *pilegesh* arrangement would not be exploited so basely, but such arrangements seem more likely to invite abuse than to foster care and responsibility.[31]

In the face of sexual libertinism, these Liberal rabbis feel a religious calling to enhance the *kedushah* of marriage, whose "holiness and consecration, separateness and exclusivity," will, hopes Reform rabbi Mark Washofsky, contribute to its "stability and permanence."[32] While these rabbis may sound to the children of the 1960s sexual revolution like social conservatives or even anachronistic halakhic reactionaries, they are actually better understood as modernists trying to hold back the tsunami of postmodern relativism that reduces sexual relations to convenient private arrangements: "hook-ups," longer or shorter, for satisfying biological and emotional needs. Washofsky's CCAR responsum makes his philosophy of marital halakhah clear: "Judaism is not to bless 'reality' but rather to call upon us to transcend it, to uplift the potential for human dignity and human greatness. In this task, Judaism must, not infrequently, take a position that is countercultural."[33]

Inspired by kabbalist motifs and the Buberian philosophy of I-Thou dialogue, these North American rabbis define the essence of a sacred union as a covenant of loving intimacy, of mutual communication, commitment, and responsibility for each other's well-being. Only that positive spiritual and interpersonal union constitutes positive sanctity. Having set that high bar for a human relationship and identified it with the rabbinic ideal of sanctity and intimacy in marriage, these rabbis do not want to cheapen that aspiration by conducting ceremonies that "bless" and honor lesser relationships like living together.

CONTEMPORARY VIEWS ADAPTING EMDEN'S HISTORIC CALL FOR THE REVIVAL OF THE *PILEGESH* TO LIVING TOGETHER

While Emden envisioned a legalized mistress *alongside* his wife, some contemporary rabbis wish to employ his legal precedent to validate living together *before* or *instead* of marriage as an egalitarian arrangement in which sexual intimacy may express a loving, committed, exclusive union. Already in 1956 Reform rabbi Borowitz argued that the historic pilegesh was a respectable model of friendship and stability that conferred meaning on sexual life:

> [*Pilegesh*] was no temporary affair of two friends spending occasional nights or weekends together. . . . They were legally man and "demi-wife." . . . This arrangement . . . provides structure and stability as a kind of friendship rather than of love. . . . The formality and binding quality of marriage were missing, but the relationship had relative permanence and a socially sanctioned structure. . . . One can see how near to it were marriage and fidelity.[34]

Fifty years later, Rabbi Shlomo Zacharow, who later became the head of the Halakhah Committee of the Israeli Masorti (Conservative) Rabbis, reaffirmed the halakhic acceptability of the pilegesh. In his unpublished student responsum (2000), Zacharow attests that many halakhic authorities do *not* view intercourse outside marriage as prostitution. While they condemn women who make themselves available to any man, the majority do not view intercourse between a couple "going steady" or living together as prostitution. They only insist that a woman visit the mikveh after her period ends and before intercourse, whether she is married or not.

Zacharow rules:

> We regard physical contact between members of a couple as an instrument that can contribute to the sanctity of their bond, but not as an end in itself. Steady couples are not examples of "promiscuity" (*hefkerut*) but of "[girl/boy] friendships" among singles.[35]

Clearly, his ruling does not permit a married man to have a mistress on the side, and he does not wish to replace marriage (which enables a couple to raise children and fulfill the mitzvah of procreation) with living together in a pilegesh arrangement. Rather, he wants to recognize the halakhic legitimacy of a temporary but monogamous sexual relationship for "a divorced man or widower who has already fulfilled the mitzvah of procreation or a single person who still intends to fulfill that mitzvah in the future" within a marital arrangement. These nonmarital couples, however, must be "educated to keep the laws of *niddah*" (refraining from intercourse during and after menses until the woman purifies herself in a ritual bath) and thus "discover how it contributes a dimension of sanctity to their [nonmarital] relationship."[36]

While Maimonides leads a substantial camp of halakhists prohibiting any nonmarital sexuality as a Torah-based prohibition, modern rabbis have a legitimate option to follow an equally distinguished but more permissive school. In sum, Zacharow declares: "We are following in the footsteps of Nahmanides [the thirteenth-century halakhic precedent invoked by Emden] in ruling that we should not forbid something that was permitted by the Torah, especially in our contemporary social situation."[37]

Other rabbis also hold that Emden's proposal can be repurposed to resolve the systemic lacunae in the rabbinic marital system, which lacks alternative models of communally approved and regulated sexual relations for those wanting a committed but nonmarital relationship.

First, the pilegesh option can simplify convoluted halakhic divorce proceedings that cause so much pain, especially for women, and alienate so many from Judaism. To this point, the most far-reaching and high-ranking Orthodox proposal for reinstating the practice of the pilegesh was sponsored by the Orthodox Sephardi rabbi Yaacov Moshe Toledano (rabbi in Tangiers, Cairo, and Tel Aviv, and Israel's minister of Religious Affairs, 1958–60).[38] To circumvent the problem of the *agunah* (an abandoned wife lacking a divorce), Toledano proposed a court-initiated enactment (*takkanah*) empowering each couple to marry in Israel either through kiddushin (a traditional marriage requiring divorce) or the institution of the pilegesh:

> In my judgment the best legislative enactment in our era is to return and permit the pilegesh.... Many rabbinic authorities have written and permitted it, including more recently the Ya'avetz [Emden]....
>
> Of course, all this depends on the will of the couple, who will choose whether [to bond together] under kiddushin ("under the law of Moshe and Israel") or under the pilegesh arrangement. The latter method will make [procedures for] marrying and separating much easier, with less expense, whenever they wish to do so. May there be many joyful marriages in Israel! ...

Let us arrange the pilegesh through the rabbinic court to avoid promiscuous intercourse (*z'nut*) and [to formalize, without divorce proceedings, the subsequent] separation of a couple [joined under a pilegesh arrangement].[39]

In effect, the proposed pilegesh arrangement would function like a civil marriage with no-fault divorce. For those who criticize the oppressive Israeli rabbinic courts, with their monopolistic control over marriage and divorce among all Jews in Israel, opting for the pilegesh arrangement liberates Jewish Israelis from religious coercion.

The second advantage is the institutionalization of living together as a halakhic analogue to the Western category of common-law wife or the Israeli status of "publicly known couples" (*yeduim b'tzibur*).[40] So too the pilegesh arrangement may be distinguished clearly from promiscuity, since the couple living together demonstrate they will take responsibility for one another by signing a civil contract to regulate their mutual moral, legal, and financial obligations—thus defending women against exploitation.

The third benefit of the pilegesh is relief from the moral anxiety and guilt felt by pious single Jews who wish to engage in sexual union during the long periods before they marry (if they ever do) or after they have divorced or are widowed. Professor Zvi Zohar urges Religious Zionist rabbis in Israel to authorize unmarried couples in their late twenties and thirties to avail themselves of an adapted pilegesh arrangement, because they "should not be considered sinners." Kalmanofsky summarizes Zohar's proposal (though he dissents from it):

Zohar notes that in the Israeli national-religious community [modern Zionist Orthodox] people appropriately delay marriage until they attain emotional and financial maturity, but have sex nonetheless. Zohar sees concubinage [pilegesh] as a way for well-intentioned people to remain within Torah norms by committing to exclusive, ethical sexual relationships without marriage, a solution that would also allow them to observe *niddah* laws [attending a mikveh after menstruation] without embarrassment.[41]

Similarly, in the North American Jewish Renewal Movement, Rabbi Gershon Winkler (formerly ultra-Orthodox) addresses the sociological phenomenon that "a great percentage of the adult population is single due to divorce or career and academic involvement" and "most single Jewish people today do have sex," but as a result many "feel that they are doing something Jewishly wrong."[42] He dedicated his book to promote Emden's proposal:

> To think that God expects people to suspend their burning sensuality for five, sometimes ten years until they find a suitable marriage partner is to accuse the Creator of being totally oblivious to the physical and emotional needs of the Creations. After all, *the Torah was given to humans, not angels* (TB *Brakhot* 25b).
>
> Judaism has always cherished the institution of marriage. . . . Nonetheless, the pilegesh relationship is a viable alternative to marriage for those who are not ready for it or for whom it is not feasible, for whatever reasons. . . . *Pilagshut* is an alternative that imbues a nonmarital relationship with sacredness and sexual responsibility.[43]

In his defense of Emden and the possibility of sanctity without marriage, Winkler appeals to his belief in God's realism and decency. Concurring, Rabbi Arthur Waskow (Renewal) holds that the pilegesh relationship—which he calls *zug*, the "couple" relationship—provides an honorable halakhic model from which to establish a sacred grounding of nonmarital sexual relationships that adhere to patterns of honesty, health, contraception, intimacy, and holiness. When the pilegesh relationship is reformatted to realize open and egalitarian negotiations, Waskow agrees that it helps circumvent patriarchal features of traditional kiddushin and allows either the woman or the man to end the relationship without the complications of public divorce.[44]

Test Case 3: Caring for the Caretaker
Whose Spouse Is Incapacitated

While none of the Liberal or Jewish Renewal rabbis (except for David Teutsch; see chapter 14) wants to follow Emden's responsum in validating a mistress *alongside* a wife or husband, pastoral and halakhic voices give serious thought to accepting a lover or facilitating divorce and remarriage when one's spouse develops extreme physical and mental disabilities (such as Alzheimer's) that may make them unavailable for sexual relations and emotional intimacy for many years. When divorce and remarriage are not morally desirable solutions, some Liberal rabbis mandate non-marital relationships alongside marriage that they do *not* regard, morally speaking, as adulterous betrayals of love and responsibility for one's long-term spouse.

Michael Gold (Conservative) formulates the ethical dilemma rabbis must consider:

> What about the case in which one partner in a marriage is incapacitated and unable to have sex? Is the other partner permitted to take a lover for sexual fulfillment, or must he or she first seek a divorce? *Is someone who wishes to remain married out of love or loyalty to a lifelong spouse condemned to a life of celibacy?*[45]

While traditional Judaism teaches that a woman's marital fidelity must be absolute and her adultery pollutes a sacred relationship of trust, Gold believes there is room for compassion and understanding toward dedicated married spouses who ignore the law and become involved in an extramarital relationship while continuing to serve as loyal caregivers of their spouses with dementia. Refusing to pass judgment in such a pastoral situation, Gold feels rabbis should abide by Hillel's famous dictum, "Do not judge another until you stand in that person's place."[46]

More boldly, Rabbi David Teutsch (Reconstructionist) insists that rabbis show not only pastoral understanding but public leadership by developing a policy on this matter to proactively guide their constituents. Teutsch supports consensual polyamory when it is a *joint* decision of "couples [who] agree to suspend the part of their marriage vows that deal with fidelity . . . when one partner becomes uninterested in sex or has a physical disability that prevents such activity."[47] In the case of a spouse suffering from Alzheimer's, he approves a *unilateral* decision by the healthy spouse to take a lover, but only "as long as the healthy partner cares for the ailing spouse." Only then can "the healthy partner . . . develop a sexual relationship with someone else without violating marriage vows, for under these conditions this does not significantly harm the institutionalized partner."[48] Thus Teutsch develops his policies by weighing the real-life alternatives in such predicaments in terms of their utility, rather than by engaging in a classic halakhic discussion.

A traditional halakhic analysis of the case of a spouse with Alzheimer's, exemplifying both pastoral compassion and innovative halakhic flexibility, can be found in a timely, aptly titled essay, "When Alzheimer's Turns a Spouse into a Stranger: Jewish Perspectives on Loving and Letting Go." Summarizing their halakhic position on the subject, authors Rabbis Elliot Dorff (Conservative) and Laura Geller (Reform) explain their struggle with the legal, ethical, and pastoral issues regarding a seventy-year-old woman who needs and wants an alternative relationship of love and sexual intimacy while she continues loyally and bravely to tend to her husband who suffers from Alzheimer's.[49] Her friends and adult children are morally and emotionally conflicted about her desire either to divorce her ailing husband in order to remarry or to remain married to her incapacitated husband while simultaneously caring for him and conducting a loving sexual liaison with another man.

Dorff and Geller's responsum begins with a diagnosis of a Jewish values conflict: on the one hand, one must avoid shaming one's incapacitated spouse or divorcing him in his hour of need in order to remarry, yet, on the other hand, the bereft caregiver/spouse is very lonely and God long ago recognized that for human beings *it is not good to be alone* (Gen. 2:18).[50] It seems theologically and morally unjustifiable to allow legal obstacles to prevent fulfillment of the need for human fellowship for this woman anchored (literally, an *agunah*) to such an incapacitated husband.

Dorff and Geller sort through four traditional legal options: rethinking (1) polygamy, (2) pilegesh, (3) adultery, and (4) divorce. First, making an exception to the ban of Rabbenu Gershom and permitting polygamy would allow a healthy male spouse to marry a second wife, but that would not help the woman in this case, for no married woman has ever been permitted a second husband in Jewish law. Second, reinstituting the option of the pilegesh alongside the marriage is patriarchal and unegalitarian, so, they think, modern Jews would not consent to this solution. Third, circumventing the prohibition of adultery can be achieved by restricting sexual relations with the lover to nonvaginal penetration, but that is not satisfying to all couples. So Dorff and Geller prefer the fourth option: loosening the standards for divorce, which normally entail mutual agreement of both mentally fit spouses, by inserting a conditional clause for automatic divorce in case of incapacitation into the original ketubah, or by adding this proviso by mutual agreement when dementia is first diagnosed: "By reframing this kind of divorce as a *get al tanai* [an agreement to conditional divorce in case of mental incapacitation], a healthy couple could proactively make clear what their wishes would be if this situation arose."[51]

Nevertheless, there are moral and emotional complications to divorcing a spouse with Alzheimer's, such as guilt experienced by a healthy spouse moving on with life while the incapacitated spouse is in need. Therefore, Dorff and Geller add to their halakhic solution a ceremony for the couple to sign a conditional *get al tanai* preceded by a discussion among themselves and with their families and clergy:

> Conversations about the challenges [of] this next stage of life might well be difficult, but through employing Jewish values, Jewish law, and Jewish ritual . . . we can touch the Divinity that is present in all the experiences of our lives and remind ourselves how Judaism brings meaning and purpose to our lives.[52]

Conclusion

In seeking ways to keep halakhic Judaism relevant to a new generation, these modern rabbis seek both to accommodate new social realities and yet to educate and inspire Jews to strive for higher aspirations and more restraint in their sexual relationships. As we saw, some Liberal rabbis call for celebrating the commitment of loving couples that choose to live together openly, even without marriage, and thus acknowledge the sanctity of living together.

In so doing, Zacharow, Waskow, Borowitz, Zohar, and Winkler have selectively adapted Emden's model. Although his issues with sexuality are different from theirs, they seek to emulate his courageous and innovative style of rabbinic leadership, in several ways. First, Emden begins by making a thorough diagnosis of the social situation. Second, he exhibits frank and empathetic recognition of people's sexual needs, including his own. Third, he demonstrates great facility in reinterpreting the halakhic diversity within a tradition of two thousand years. Finally, and, most importantly, Emden displays courageous leadership and hutzpah in proposing new halakhic policies to help the community channel libidinal drives, even though he knows most rabbis will condemn his initiative.

Following in Emden's footsteps, these Liberal rabbis diagnose their own situations and apply their own values regarding sexual ethics. While rejecting the halakhic and moral legitimacy Emden grants to a husband's need for a mistress as an additional sexual outlet, they acknowledge that when couples are not ready for marriage, they have legitimate erotic and emotional needs that should be both permitted and regulated within an ethical framework of mutual responsibility and monogamy. Only Waskow has taken the additional initiative to ritualize the act of living together as a couple within a communal framework celebrating their bonds.

By contrast, other Liberal rabbis, inspired by the unique sanctity of marital intimacy and the Buberian philosophy of I-Thou dialogue, feel a religious calling to enhance the exclusivity of the institution of marriage. Dorff and Kalmanofsky, Freehof and Washofsky, representing their respective denominations' law committees, reject Emden and the practice of nonmarital sexual relations, lest these encourage sexual license and displace the sanctity of marriage. While in pastoral and educational contexts they may counsel flexibility and accommodate individual choice, their public responsa strictly prohibit intercourse in a relationship lacking full marital commitment. Here they take a religiously courageous countercultural stance protesting against libertarian promiscuity in North American culture. Dorff and Geller's subtle treatment of the wife of a man with Alzheimer's is a fine example of that pastoral sensitivity within conservative halakhic constraints.

Liberal rabbis—whether more halakhically conservative or flexible—share the commitment to employ the Jewish legal tradition to meet contemporary phenomena, whether by accommodation or resistance. For them, the authority of halakhah and the concern for Jewish continuity are not strictly legalistic, but guided by a commitment to propagate central Jewish values for the benefit of modern Jews.

Behind these halakhic debates within the North American rabbinate lies a larger societal issue challenging all Western societies, as pointed to by the religious and social thinker and former chief rabbi of the United Kingdom, Jonathan Sacks. In his book *Morality: Restoring the Common Good in Divided Times* (2019), he identifies the late 1960s, when the sexual revolution arose as the fulcrum of a social climate change in morality thus: "When the 'I' takes precedence over the 'We,' the result is weakened relationships, marriages, families, communities, . . . and entire societies."[53] Marriage, he argues, is the most representative institution in this ethical sea change:

> Marriage is fundamental to the moral enterprise because it is the supreme example of the transformation of two "I's" into a collective "We." It is the consecration of a commitment to care for an Other. It is the formalization of love, not as a passing passion but as a moral bond. . . . A covenant is a relationship [based on] *the logic of cooperation*. That is what differentiates marriage and the family from economics and politics, the market and the state, which are about *the logic of competition*.[54]

For Sacks, as for many of the rabbis discussed above, this covenant of marriage is sacred to Judaism and also an essential link in the stability and survival of a Western civilization based on the common good. It is for that practical reason that he decries the practice of living together:

> Marriage is often derided as a mere formality, a "piece of paper," while cohabitation has come to be portrayed as an equivalent or substitute. Sadly, it is not so. In Britain, the average length of marriages that end in divorce is between eleven and twelve years, and the average length of marriages as a whole is thirty years. The average length of cohabitation in Britain and the United States is less than five years. The formal act of commitment that constitutes marriage makes a difference to the strength and durability of the relationship.[55]

What the sexual revolution and the subjectification of all ethical behavior have done is to undermine the commitment to social morality that is essential for a vibrant liberal civil society. And that, for Sacks, is a crucial moral argument for maintaining the sanctity of the marriage covenant.

In this chapter we have seen the cleavage between two rabbinic camps. On one hand, those like Sacks, Kalmanofsky, Dorff, and Washofsky, who reject living together (even if a halakhic precedent could have been found in Emden) precisely because it is a popular option today that reinforces a sexual revolution that undermines marriage and societal stability. On the other hand, Waskow, Winkler, and Zacharow accept this inevitable social development, give it halakhic form and validity, and seek to reshape living together into a human relationship characterized by sanctity, ethical integrity, and stable loving commitment.

A Feminist Alternative to   16
Halakhic Marriage

JEWISH THEOLOGIANS RETHINK THE
MARRIAGE CONTRACT AND GENDER BIASES

How beautiful it is that the second human being was taken from
the very substance of the first, so that nature might teach that all
are equal. Among human beings this is the property of friendship
that there is neither a superior nor an inferior.

—AELRED OF RIEVAULX (English monk, d. 1167), *On Spiritual
Friendship*, I, 57.

Introduction

Now we conclude our book with a radical critique of and presentation of alternatives to halakhic marriage. Our spokespersons are two
prominent North American feminist theologians of Judaism: Professor Judith Plaskow and Rabbi Rachel Adler. These religious leaders are not only feminists but radical feminists, not interested only
in Jewish law but in Judaism's basic views of God and of the practice
of justice, power, and gender in marital law and values. Note that the
term "radical" here is not meant pejoratively, but in recognition of
these women's program to bring about a sweeping paradigmatic shift
from traditional teachings. Radicals, whose name derives from the
Latin for "root," wish to uproot existing patterns in society because
they judge them to be essentially corrupt and, in the case of halakhic
marriage, fundamentally patriarchal and abusive of women.

The modern political term "radical" is used to distinguish a political revolutionary from liberals and conservatives.[1] Generally, liberals

aim to expand liberty and equality by gradual reforms and piecemeal legislation from within existing legal traditions and institutions, while conservatives seek to maintain the status quo against liberal reforms or to roll back so-called progressive changes. By contrast, radicals challenge the basic institutions at their root in search of alternatives, and they introduce radical new ideals that transform the meaning of tradition.

Let us give examples of radical transformation of Jewish marital law from our book so far. First, the editor of the Mishnah, Rabbi Judah HaNasi, ruled in a radical way that recognizes the libertarian sexual rights of husbands. When a woman complained to him that her husband was behaving contrary to tradition and to propriety by "turning the tables" on her (anal sex or the woman on the top of the man in intercourse), Rabbi Judah HaNasi established for the first time the right of husbands to free choice in their sexual positions (TB *Nedarim* 20b, see chapter 3). In the sixteenth century, however, in opposition to the acceptance of Judah HaNasi's position, which had become the standard halakhic practice, Joseph Karo in his *Shulhan Arukh* radically restricted the right to male pleasure, foreplay, and freestyle intercourse. In 1948, the rebbe of Gur Hasidism translated Karo's halakhah into a radical social ideology and systematic practice, prohibiting, in effect, lovemaking (though not intercourse) and emotional intimacy in marital relations (see chapter 7). In the 1950s, the Litvak counterrevolution in turn established a new paradigm shift in the mitzvah of marital intimacy, broadly understood, though as we noted, the Litvaks would never call themselves liberal reformers, revolutionaries, or even innovators (*ba'alei hiddushim*). They rejected Karo's legal revolution and Mussar's asceticism and returned to Rav's joyful model of onah, enriching it with a deep concern for emotional intimacy between husband and wife (see chapters 9–11).

Finally, beginning in the 1960s, North American liberal rabbis (from Modern Orthodox to Reform) resisted the radical implications of the sexual revolution, but they did introduce many liberal, egalitarian reforms into halakhic marriage inspired by liberal feminism and the ideal of gender equality. Yet most of them took relatively conservative positions in their preaching and responsa and reinforced the traditional legal prohibitions discouraging nonmarital sexual relationships in order to buttress the beleaguered institution of holy matrimony. For them, the sanctity of marital intimacy ideally fulfills Buber's I-Thou covenantal relationship, while sexual liberation often licenses promiscuous I-it relations. Therefore, most Liberal rabbis of all modern denominations highlighted and celebrated the *kiddushin* (literally, the sanctification ceremony of halakhic betrothal) traditionally recited when the groom gives a ring to his bride, saying "You are hereby sanctified to me by the laws of Moses and the people of Israel," while adding rituals to express the bride's agency (see chapters 12–15).

By contrast, radical feminists, like Plaskow and Adler, oppose halakhic marriage in principle, especially kiddushin. Its form is, according to their analysis, irremediably patriarchal. Therefore, they reject liberal reforms as inadequate to counteract the pervasiveness and profundity of what is wrong with the classic Jewish marriage tradition.

Plaskow, a former professor of religious studies at Manhattan College, asserts that when liberal Jewish feminism focuses merely on political and legal reforms, it misses the deep cultural and theological roots of discrimination against women in Judaism. Therefore, liberated Jewish women must return to Sinai as autonomous agents to rewrite their own Torah. Working together in self-governing women-only groups, they can review and then reform traditional laws, and invest them with their present community's own living authority.[2] Plaskow wants women, through rewriting their covenant with God and reimagining a Divinity untouched by male chauvinism, to uproot the heterosexual and binary gender biases that undergird patriarchal Judaism in general and traditional marriage in particular.

Adler, a professor of modern Jewish thought at the Hebrew Union College-Jewish Institute of Religion, also seeks to transform Judaism itself in light of feminist discourse, and not merely to remedy particular gender injustices in law and ritual. She, like Plaskow, begins with a deep diagnosis of the patriarchal biases in classical Judaism, and proposes a new theology and poetry (*aggadah*). But she also wants to construct a new ethical praxis (halakhah) in critical dialogue with Jewish classical law. At its apex, her feminist theology and ethics of Judaism radically re-envision the marriage contract as a *b'rit ahuvim*, a mutual covenant of love, without kiddushin.

Radical Jewish Feminism versus Liberal Judaism: Revolution or Reform?

By no means is the debate between Liberal rabbis and radical feminists a dispute about the validity of Jewish feminism and its positive role in the evolution of Judaism toward greater egalitarianism. Women's participation in Liberal Judaism includes being counted in the minyan, receiving *aliyot* to the Torah, taking leadership on synagogue boards, and participating in life-cycle rituals, as well as being ordained rabbis and cantors. In marriage ceremonies, too, women have gained a voice through double ring ceremonies (in which the bride as well as the groom verbally sanctifies the relationship) and more egalitarian *ketubot* (in which women are treated as equal partners in the relationship and not as housewives to be supported by their husbands). Women's rights to divorce their husbands and avoid *agunah* status have also been acknowledged. Further, since the 1980s, these Liberal denominations, each in its own way and at its own pace, have extended rabbinic marriage to include the LGBTQ community by making Jewish matrimonial law more inclusive and reconceiving rabbinic understandings of sexuality.

Nevertheless, Liberal Judaism in general has not treated kiddushin itself as an oppressive and chauvinist feature in need of reform, but rather as an important index of the sanctity of rabbinic marriage, to be extended, in most denominations, to LGBTQ marriage ceremonies. For Liberal Judaism, not unlike Modern Orthodoxy and contemporary Haredim, the sanctity and exclusivity of marriage is a central idea employed to combat what they consider the corrupting influence of unregulated sexual relations in the secular, postmodern West.

The radical feminist structural critique of marriage, by contrast, insists that kiddushin (halakhic betrothal) manifests male hegemony, symbolized by the ring in the acquisition of the wife as chattel. Women have been designated as male property in order for men to control their sexuality, lest they endanger men's power and male spirituality. Since the traditional rabbinic male aims at mastery of his libido (*yetzer ha-ra*) and defense of his own sanctity (*kedushah*), women, for the Rabbis, have been categorized as a tempting source of erotic arousal that undermines male self-control and thus leads to desecration of Israel's individual and collective sanctity. Therefore, feminists warn, sacred sex is often a rationale for abuse of women, though an alternative positive understanding of sanctity can enhance egalitarian marital sexuality.

Radical Jewish Feminism versus Secular Feminism: Sacred or Private Relationships?

While Adler and Plaskow seek to liberate erotic relationships from oppressive male chauvinist halakhic institutions and to empower the couple to construct a consensual covenant, they do not want to reduce the sexual relationship to a purely secularized private transaction. They wish to free halakhic marriage from that traditional notion of sanctity associated with male control of a woman's sexuality, but not to eliminate egalitarian dimensions of holy matrimony.

Therefore, both Plaskow and Adler have decided to fight a *two-front war* critical both of Jewish patriarchal traditions and secular modernity's sexual license. They refuse to choose exclusively either pole of this false dichotomy between Judaism and sexual liberation. They repudiate the sanctified sex of halakhah that, they claim, demands the suppression of desire and the subordination of women. Nor will they acquiesce to a radical feminism that insists on unregulated free love subject only to the consent of adult partners and free from almost all social and legal constraints. Early feminists like Mary Wollstonecraft, Mary Gove Nichols, and famously Emma Goldman (1869–1940), the Jewish anarchist, all wished to abolish marriage as an institution that irreparably enslaves women and to teach about birth control so as to separate lovemaking from reproduction. Goldman celebrates erotic love and repudiates marriage:

> Marriage and love have nothing in common; they are as far apart as the poles; are, in fact, antagonistic to each other. . . . Love, the strongest and deepest element in all life, the harbinger of hope, of joy, of ecstasy; the defier of all laws; of all conventions; the freest, the most powerful molder of human destiny. How can such an all-compelling force be synonymous with that poor little State and Church-begotten weed, marriage?[3]

In confronting halakhic marriage, Plaskow seeks to liberate Jews in general from the oppressive yoke of male rabbinic authority and women in particular from a halakhah that sanctions male acquisition of a women's sexuality. Yet in facing the Western cult of personal freedom, Plaskow knows that liberation of the libido from traditional norms often releases a torrent of abuse of women, destroys healthy intimacy, and desecrates sacred relationships. Law can be tyrannical, but anarchic freedom also endangers humane relationships:

> If the Jewish tradition says sex is a powerful impulse that needs to be controlled, certain strains in modern culture say it is healthier to act out our impulses. If the tradition says men may have affairs but women may not, certain strains in modern culture give women "permission" to be promiscuous on male terms. If the tradition says sex has a place in life but it must not be allowed to take over, modern culture offers sex as a panacea for all that ails us.
>
> But when sex is understood as a particular impulse that we act out instead of control, the result is an alienated sexuality that can never rescue us from the alienation in the rest of our lives. If greater genital expression were really the solution to our social miseries . . . we would expect ours to be the happiest society around.[4]

So Plaskow warns against the utopian lure of sexual liberation for some feminists:

> It is tempting for a feminist account of sexuality to deny the disruptive power of the erotic, and to depict the fear of it in rabbinic thought as simply misplaced. But it is truer to experience to acknowledge the power of sexuality to overturn rules and threaten boundaries. . . .
>
> The unification of sexuality and spirituality is sometimes a gift . . . [when practiced with] the exercise of respect, responsibility, and honesty—commensurate with the nature and depth of the particular relationship—as basic values in any sexual relationship.[5]

Yet, having exposed the dilemma between excessive control and profligate liberation, Plaskow selects the pole of freedom that does not "repress sexual feelings":

I am not arguing here for free sex or for more sexual expression, quantitatively speaking. I am arguing for living dangerously, for choosing to take responsibility for working through the possible consequences of sexual feelings rather than repressing sexual feeling.[6]

Even while promoting a policy of living dangerously, in practice, Plaskow upholds three conservative doctrines close to the conservative bent of most Liberal rabbis. First, she says, "by no means" does feminist liberation mean "a sexual ethic of anything goes."[7] Second, she recognizes that while the traditional ideal of "heterosexual marriage" suppresses women and individuals who are not heterosexual, it is to be commended for its "celebration of long-term partnerships" because they are "the richest setting for negotiating and living out the meanings of mutuality, responsibility, and honesty amidst the distractions, problems, and pleasures of daily life."[8] Plaskow declares: "I believe that radical mutuality is most fully possible in the context of an ongoing, committed relationship in which sexual expression is one dimension of a shared life."[9] After Jewish marriage has been fundamentally restructured to remove inequality, then "the same norms [of mutual, exclusive fidelity between couples] that apply to heterosexual relationships [ought] also [to] apply to gay and lesbian relationships."[10] Precisely in appealing to the sacred, Plaskow, like Adler, departs from mainstream secular feminism:

Work that tries to bring together sexuality and the sacred is a minority strand in feminist writing, but it is a strand with considerable power not only to challenge traditional dualisms but also to generate alternatives to the energy/control paradigm of sexuality. . . .

Acceptance and avowal of a link between sex and spirit is by no means foreign to Jewish experience. In the mysteries of the marriage bed on Sabbath night; in the sanctity of the Song of Songs; [and] for mysticism, in the very nature and dynamics of the Godhead; sexual expression is an image of and path to the holy.[11]

Plaskow rejects negative connotations of sanctity: "Leviticus 18 [listing prohibited sexual relations] offers no positive vision of holy sexuality. Instead, holiness is defined as avoiding defilement."[12] By contrast, as a unitive thinker, Plaskow affirms that truly holy sexual acts unite one human being with another and with the Divine:

> The question becomes: Can we affirm our sexuality as the gift it is, making it sacred not by cordoning off pieces of it, but by increasing our awareness of the ways in which it connects us to all things? . . .
>
> We see sexuality as part of what enables us to reach out beyond ourselves, and thus as a fundamental ingredient in our spirituality. . . . The deeper vision offered by the Jewish tradition [is] that sexuality can be a medium for the experience and reunification of God. . . .
>
> The erotic aspect of human life is spiritual, because it expresses the power and desire for communication, and it demands that relationship will be based on mutuality, responsibility, and honesty.[13]

Plaskow's Approach: Women Returning to Sinai

In her seminal work of feminist Jewish theology, *Standing Again at Sinai: Judaism from a Feminist Perspective* (1991), Plaskow holds that a liberal feminism focusing merely on political issues misses the deep cultural and theological roots of discrimination against women. It is not enough to make reforms in the existing covenant originating supposedly in the Divine Revelation at Sinai. Rather, a new constitutional convention must be convened in which women return to Sinai as autonomous agents to rewrite their own Torah. Plaskow explains rabbinic Judaism's misogyny in relation to sexuality:

> Men's sexual impulses are powerful—"evil"—inclinations in need of firm control. Women's very bodily functions are devalued and made the center of a complex of taboos: their gait, their voices,

their natural beauty are all regarded as snares and temptations and subjected to elaborate precautions.[14]

Men define their own sexuality ambivalently—but they define it. And men also define the sexuality of women which they would circumscribe.[15]

For that reason, radical Jewish feminists insist that the pathology of halakhic marriage requires drastic surgery, not cosmetic reforms such as the introduction of a double ring ceremony. The feminist Jewish thinker Mara Benjamin explains the deep alienation from liberalism felt by radical Jewish feminists such as Plaskow:

> So-called egalitarian liberals have not appreciated adequately the righteous indignation and alienation of radical feminists reacting to chauvinist notions of sexuality inherent in Judaism. Jewish feminist theological work began with the feminist revolution and with the activists who aimed for nothing less than a dismantling of patriarchal social structures.[16]

Like Eugene Borowitz, Arthur Green, Arthur Waskow, and Jeremy Kalmanofsky, both Plaskow and Adler share the sociological observation that contemporary North American Jews find rabbinic attitudes and laws about sexuality outmoded and hence irrelevant to their lives. Yet, radical Jewish feminists maintain, these traditions have not become *irrelevant* simply because modern Jews have adopted liberal values and practices. Rather, paradoxically, these outdated attitudes and laws are *hyper-relevant*, because chauvinism is at the core of ongoing oppression of women that is far from passé either in Liberal Judaism or the democratic West. As Plaskow writes:

> Troublesome as inherited sexual values are for Jews of both sexes, however, they are especially troubling for women; for these values are a central pillar upholding Judaism as a patriarchal system, and

the stigma and burden of sexuality fall differently on women than on men.[17]

While Liberal Judaism and liberal Jewish feminism often cull the tradition to highlight its most progressive values and recover its marginalized voices extolling women, Plaskow chooses "to focus on a central oppressive element in my tradition rather than on some emancipatory theme."[18] She maintains that Liberal Judaism's tactics, repairing laws piecemeal, are inadequate to the tasks of restoring female dignity and liberated women's relationship to Judaism. Plaskow and Adler assert that Biblical and rabbinic matrimony is essentially about male acquisition (*kinyan*) of the woman's sexual and procreative services. Therefore, *tikkun olam* (repair of the world) within Judaism must begin with radical self-criticism and repentance, revolutionary legislation, and revisionist theology regarding marriage, God, and sexuality.

Historically, as we have shown, important Talmudic and medieval schools of rabbinic law have legislated greater gender mutuality in marital sex (see chapters 2, 4, 5). Yet, Plaskow insists whatever egalitarian rhetoric can be found in the otherwise patriarchal Talmudic tradition is disingenuous, a fig leaf, a benign despotism masquerading as a paternal concern for women's best interests (about which male rabbis claim to know best). She declares that "for the Bible and for the rabbis, good sex is sex that supports and serves a patriarchal social order."[19] Not only is the rabbinic law's telos, its original purpose, the domination of women, but the authors of its coercive authority are not by accident exclusively male. Passionately, Plaskow protests: A male-only power structure has no right to present its self-serving oppressive tradition as the *authentic* Jewish tradition of the community *when half the community has been disenfranchised.*[20] Revolutionizing the Jewish power structure of halakhah, decision making about sexual relations must be transferred from rabbis to autonomous communities, by which Plaskow means, self-governing women-only groups. Once empowered, women will wish to reform traditional laws whose validity will then derive not from the authority of past rulings by men (precedent), but from the will of women who wish to invest themselves with the present community's own living authority.[21] Now, however, what is needed is liberation *from* halakhah itself, not minor adjustments of its ceremonies.

Furthermore, Plaskow argues, essential to the patriarchy of the halakhah is its bias for the exclusivity of heterosexuality. Since heterosexuality always privileges men, it is by its nature oppressive to women's sexuality. Hence she calls for the deconstruction of traditional notions of human sexuality in order to eliminate the discriminatory language of binary genders. For example, she rejects the Biblical ideal of *becoming one flesh* in a male-female sexual union (Gen. 2:24) and the kabbalist celebration of a male-female synthesis that Modern Orthodox and Liberal rabbis have invoked to promote egalitarian notions of marriage. Instead, Plaskow advocates a "new theology of sexuality" with fluid, multivalent categories rather than binary genders.[22] Rather than amending Judaism's constitution, which was composed by men, women must return to Mount Sinai to establish their own covenantal Torah whose foundations are purged of patriarchal axioms and patchwork reforms.

Adler's Approach: Redeeming Tradition for Egalitarian Holiness

Generally, Rachel Adler, author of *Engendering Judaism: An Inclusive Theology and Ethics* (1998), concurs with Plaskow's trenchant critique of rabbinic marriage and her protest at the exclusion of women from the foundations of Jewish law, for "we did not participate in making the rules, nor were we there at the beginning of the party."[23] Both Adler and Plaskow grew up going to nonegalitarian

Reform temples. As a young adult, Adler chose Orthodoxy, and it was from within liberal Orthodoxy that she initially called for feminist reform within halakhah. Only later did she leave Orthodoxy, and eventually she became a Reform rabbi in 2012. Adler cautions against the naivete of "some feminists [who] optimistically believed that halakhic change alone would remedy gender injustice in Judaism."[24] She contends: "It is very difficult to argue in androcentric terms without being inexorably dragged to androcentric conclusions."[25]

Nevertheless, Adler holds that, in a thoroughgoing gendered reconstruction of Judaism, traditional legal and poetic texts can be redeemed and repurposed for a liberated egalitarian practice. Therefore, she directs *some* of the intellectual energy of Jewish feminism *away* from criticism of halakhic discrimination and "*back to the sources*" and the traditional tools for their reinterpretation (hermeneutics):

> For the most part, the hermeneutics of classical texts has been strangely neglected as a component of Jewish feminist theology.... Consequently, I am concerned ... with mending and healing Judaism by encountering, renewing, and reclaiming the holiness in texts.[26]

Contra some of Plaskow's declarations, Adler is confident that halakhah itself *can* be redeemed and that traditional texts, even problematic ones, can be transformed for bridge building to a better world:

> It is not necessary to discard Judaism or its texts to make a world of meaning in which women and men are equal subjects. Instead, our task is theological: to read these texts as believing Jewish women and men today without evading or denying their patriarchal past and to seek in them *redemptive meanings* to propel us toward a more just and loving future.[27]

In the spirit of Yale philosophy of law professor Robert Cover, Adler proclaims that "the ultimate goal [of halakhah] . . . is not judgment but restoration. I propose to restore these texts as sources of a trajectory toward holiness."[28] To Cover and Adler, law is not a positivist collection of legal precedents designed to reflect and maintain the existing power distribution, but an aspirational movement, a bridge from a patriarchal past to a messianic future fueled by an egalitarian prophetic vision. The two components of tradition, both halakhah and aggadah (nonlegal thought, midrash, and narrative), are not homogeneous "systems," but multivalent "texts," open to innovative reinterpretation. Adler is not an *essentialist* in diagnosing and revamping patriarchal motifs in classical Judaism, for she does not claim that Judaism has one unchanging essence defined at its origin by an authoritative source, such as the Revelation of God at Sinai. Rather she is a *constructivist* who sees Jewish culture as a work-in-progress that is constantly developing through the reconstructive efforts of all the members of its community of interpretation. Intentionally and unintentionally they are arranging the heterogeneous traditions that constitute their building materials and they are importing new resources through cross-cultural exchanges. In that sense, Adler defines her Jewish feminist task as the construction of a concrete praxis for egalitarian marital relationships in dialogue with a creative exegesis of Biblical narrative *and* rabbinic halakhah.

While at times Plaskow sounds like an essentialist in condemning halakhah in itself as irremediable, in other contexts, she too shares Cover's reformist "metaphor of the law as a bridge between our present moral universe and those *alternative universes* a people might create through concerted communal action."[29] From that perspective Plaskow acknowledges the carnivalesque multiplicity of Jewish attitudes to sex and envisions a process of transformation from within the Jewish laws of sexuality.[30] Elsewhere, she writes:

Every attitude toward sexuality from the freest to the most inhibited is found somewhere in Jewish writing. . . . It is necessary to find a path through contradiction and ambivalence, avoiding elevating one side of the ambivalence as truer or more fundamental than the other.[31]

A New and Renewed Aggadah for Covenantal Love

Some assert that to heal patriarchal halakhah, a new aggadah (a new narrative of ideas) is needed. Arthur Green found his new aggadah in a renewed mystical tradition that he called a New Kabbalah and on which he hoped to found a New Halakhah of Jewish sexuality. By contrast, Adler and Plaskow look primarily to Biblical poetic texts that manifest mutuality and erotic passion, such as the Song of Songs with its playful female sexuality. For religious authority, they appeal to the prophecy of Hosea (8th century BCE) to eschew the concept of marriage as the acquisition of the woman; and they discover in both Malachi (5th century BCE) and the rabbinic nuptial blessings (ca. 3rd–5th century CE) a model of marriage as a loving covenantal friendship.

RECLAIMING THE SONG OF SONG'S CELEBRATION OF EROS

Adler credits the pathbreaking Protestant feminist Bible scholar Phyllis Trible for the insight that the Song of Songs is a cycle of "poem[s] about lovers in a garden [that] redeems the love story that went awry in the Garden of Eden. In this setting, [Trible] contends, there is no male dominance, no female subordination, and no stereotyping of either sex."[32] Adler elucidates:

The hierarchical relations established in the Eden story are overthrown in the Song. Eden's gender polarities are inverted or dissolved. *Your desire shall be for your husband*, Genesis 3 decrees, *and he shall rule over you* (Gen. 3:16). The Shulamite exults, *I am for my beloved and his desire is for me* (Song of Songs 7:11).

For the lovers in the Song, desire and power are shared attributes. Reciprocally, they praise each other's bodies in lingering detail, from head to foot. Reciprocally, they speak imperatives. . . . Both are clothed in images of power, the man as a king; and, in a splendid subversion of gender stereotyping, the female as a triumphant army (Song 1:4,12; 6:10).[33]

Here in the Song of Songs the woman is compared not to a snake maliciously seducing her husband but to a playful lover arousing his desire for mutual play:

We see the lovers, as we never see Adam and Eve, playing together. Their play is physical, even childlike. . . . Whereas Adam and Eve conceal themselves in terror and shame from a punishing God, the lovers of the Song play at concealment, teasing each other with endless games of peekaboo and hide-and-seek.[34]

In the Garden of Eden sinful behavior proceeds in a linear causal mode from crime to guilt to punishment. Intimacy and unity give way to shame and hiding, followed by exposure and accusation, denial and blame, and finally alienation and exile under the curse of hierarchy and mortality. The woman's illicit desire for the Tree of Knowledge is iniquitous and rebellious, so her special curse is to crave sexual knowledge of her husband, and her desire enslaves her to his arbitrary rule. The Garden of Eden has a tragic misogynist ending, while the Song of Songs is joyful and egalitarian, alive with expectation without fear of betrayal or of the evil impulse.[35] Plaskow, like Adler, extolls the sexual freedom of the Song of Songs expressed without guilt or shame:

Unlike the Garden of Eden, where Eve and Adam are ashamed of their nakedness and women's subordination is the punishment for sin, the Garden of the Song of Songs is a place of sensual delight and sexual equality. Unabashed by their desire, the man and woman of these poems delight in their own embodiment and the beauty surrounding them, each seeking the other out to inaugurate their meetings, each rejoicing in the love without dominion that is also the love of God.[36]

Famously, by employing allegory, the Rabbis transmute this mundane romance into a sacred spiritual love affair between God and Israel, thus emptying it of its Biblical authority as a liberating mandate for human lovemaking. Reversing the Rabbis' interpretive footsteps, Plaskow and Adler reclaim the Song of Song's original celebration of human and humane eros as "the wellspring of both feminist theology and feminist sexual ethics."[37] And yet, while the liberated theology of eros in the Song of Songs may contribute to the rejuvenation of egalitarian Jewish attitudes to sexuality, its vision is confined to private, nonmarital lovemaking and excludes the institution of marriage. And while it may celebrate a feminist idyll, "the sacredness of mutuality," sexuality is not merely a private matter. Gender is political and theological as well as personal and secular.

Therefore Plaskow, like Adler, cautions that loving mutuality cannot be realized in the marriage bed until the Jewish feminist replaces discriminatory halakhic social structures with "justice for women in those institutions that legitimate and surround it."[38] Plaskow calls on radical feminist theologians to take up their vocation in challenging the rabbinic travesty of a

> Judaism that . . . defines sexuality in terms of patriarchal possession and control. Where women's sexuality is seen as an object to be possessed and sexuality itself is perceived as an impulse that can take possession of the self, the central issues surrounding sexuality will necessarily be issues of control.[39]

Halakhah deforms the loving friendship within marriage by structuring the relationship around power and control, so love cannot flourish without justice.[40]

Just as the classical prophets rebuked the religious and political establishment in their era, so too, the radical feminist must assume that prophetic mantle in the present. For Plaskow and Adler, the revolutionary challenge to gender oppression in marriage and commodification of women is first broached by the prophet Hosea. His theological rejection of enslavement to polytheism and the pagan god Ba'al may be translated into a contemporary mandate for egalitarian marriage, as Prime Minister David Ben-Gurion (1886–1973) argued in 1953. While the Biblical, rabbinic, and modern Hebrew word for husband is *ba'al*, which literally means "master/possessor," Ben-Gurion insisted that the term *ishi*, "my man,"—the equivalent of *ishti*, "my woman" (wife)—be used instead:

> May 5, 1953 20 Iyar, 5713
>
> Dear Secretary of the Treasury [Levi Eshkol],
>
> I signed today a tax form entitled: "Declaration of the Worker for Determining Tax Deductions." It said: "Name: *Ba'al* [husband] and *Ishti* [my wife/woman]." In my opinion, it should say: "*Ishi* (my man) and *Ishti* (my woman)." The word *Ba'al* means master but also refers to the idolatrous [Phoenician] god. That word does not fit the honor of the woman who is completely equal in her rights to the man. Let us follow the words of Hosea the prophet: *And on that day—you shall call Me, Ishi (my husband), and you will no longer call Me, my Ba'al* (Hosea 2:18).
>
> With great respect,
> David Ben-Gurion[41]

Inspiring Ben-Gurion's egalitarian reform in the Israeli tax bureaucracy is Hosea's prophecy that Israel's servitude to the Canaanite god Ba'al will be replaced with the monotheistic metaphor of a bilateral covenantal marriage between Israel and God. For Israel to restore its covenant with God, not only must the object of worship change but so too the quality of the relationship and the metaphor for the God-Israel marriage. Therefore, Hosea formulates a reconsecration ceremony characterized by mutual love, faith, and justice that redefines the ideal of matrimony:

> *I will betroth (espouse) you to me forever;*
> *I will betroth you in justice and law, in goodness and love (compassion).*
> *I will betroth you in faithfulness, and then you will know God.*
>   (Hosea 2:21–23, 25)

Adler too wants Hosea's liberating theological imagination to inspire a legal, cultural, and theological revolution that banishes traditional patriarchy from Jewish marriage by reviving the idyllic language of *ishi*, "my man," which Adam introduces in the Garden of Eden when he names woman, *isha*, his other half (Gen. 2:23):

> *Ishi* and *Ishti*, "my man" and "my woman," are equivalent and nonhierarchical terms of relationship.... The shocking change from "my *ba'al*" to "my man" ... prophesies a time when marriage will not be a relationship of master to subordinate, owner to property, or omnipotent giver to extractive dependent.... The prophesied resolution of the war between the sexes is to usher in a new covenant of universal harmony.[42]

A New Halakhah: *B'rit Ahuvim*

Adler invents a new halakhic form of marriage that is fully egalitarian and yet has deep Biblical and Rabbinic roots. Her radical feminist reenvisioning of marriage originates in the prophet Malachi's poetic description of one's spouse as *my companion and the wife of my covenant* (*haverati v'eshet b'riti*) (Mal. 2:14). The Aramaic Targum translates "companion" (*haver* or friend) as "partner" (*shutaf*). In that same spirit of contractual mutuality, several ancient ketubah documents from the Land of Israel found in the medieval Cairo Geniza (an archive for discarded Hebrew texts, ca. 10th–13th centuries) use that same language—*shutaf*—to describe marriage as a legal partnership. As the Geniza scholar Mordechai Friedman observes, the term *shutaf* describes a contractual relationship, comparable to a business collaboration between equal partners, either of whom can withdraw from the partnership at will (even though traditional halakhah does not allow the wife to unilaterally divorce her husband).[43]

While Adler repudiates marriage as *kinyan*, the "acquisition" of a woman symbolized by the husband's giving of a ring, she does not wish to leave love solely in the realm of poetry and prophecy. Nor does she reject the idea of the *contract*, whose origins stem from the commercial world. Marriage needs institutionalization, and legal metaphors capture the dimensions of obligation and commitment necessary for just and reliable relationships. Like Maimonides (see chapter 1), Adler believes contracts can be employed to protect fairness, reciprocity, and justice, including facilitating each spouse's unilateral freedoms of both entrance *and* exit from marriage: "Like all covenants, a marriage agreement [ketubah] must embody some of the characteristics of contracts, articulating standards for an ethical relation and laying out some of what the partners most need and want."[44]

From the ancient legal metaphor of partnership Adler then develops a contemporary model of marital partnership between two autonomous adults—a model she names *b'rit ahuvim*, the Covenant of Lovers:

> The *b'rit ahuvim* specifies both the standards of righteousness and the desires of the partners . . . [that] specify the obligations that will

form the fabric of the marriage. The partners must be able to make some promises to one another, even though promises are sometimes broken. And if a marriage loses its qualities as a *shutafut*, a partnership, people must be free to dissolve it.[45]

Adler discards the romantic imagery of the incorporation into one body that unites husband and wife, as expressed in the mythic Garden of Eden imagery: *they shall become one flesh* (Gen. 2:24). Instead, she insists on preserving twoness in the couple:

> We have just reached a point in history where it is possible to envision, and sometimes to realize, marriages in which two remain two; marriages that are not incorporations, but covenants.... This intention is not reflected in an *act of acquisition*. It can only be expressed by an *act of covenanting*.[46]

Unlike a purely business "contract" for exchanging services, a "covenant" is a commitment of exclusivity between people for "lasting, monogamous unions."[47] Adler explains that "we need a wedding ceremony that embodies the partners' intentions to sustain and strive with each other all their lives, to endure like the protagonists of the stormy but ultimately redemptive covenant marriage of biblical prophecy."[48] As with the covenant between God and Israel, relationships between people may be stormy, promises may be broken and occasionally marred by betrayals, and yet, even afterward, relationships can be healed. Like Hosea, Adler expresses her faith in the resilience of a loving union: "To the extent that this covenantal commitment is realized in the relationship, it can survive breaches in contractual obligations."[49]

Beyond the interpersonal connection of spouses, Adler highlights the *communal* aspect of marriage made explicit in the *Sheva Brakhot*, the seven rabbinic nuptial blessings. Just as the house of the husband and the wife is connected to the House of Israel, so the joy of the private couple is tied to the joy, but also the brokenness, of the whole community:

> The *b'rit ahuvim* is not a private arrangement, but a commitment entailing communal responsibilities. While its stipulations can be tailored to the needs of particular couples, it embodies a standard of righteousness based upon how a conscientious progressive community interprets and lives out its Jewish obligations. As a *bayit b'Yisra'el*, "a household among the people Israel," *b'rit* partners share with other Jewish households a responsibility for the continuity and well-being of the people Israel and for participating in its task of *tikkun olam*, repairing the world.[50]

CONSERVATIVE RABBIS ADOPT *B'RIT AHUVIM* AS AN OPTIONAL EGALITARIAN ALTERNATIVE TO *KIDDUSHIN*

On April 14, 2020, the Rabbinical Assembly's Committee on Law and Standards adopted Rabbi Gail Labovitz's responsum, "With Righteousness and Justice, with Goodness and with Mercy, Options for Egalitarian Marriage within Halakhah." Its innovation is the approval of Adler's *b'rit ahuvim* as a halakhically acceptable mode of effecting a valid marriage without kiddushin (understood as a unilateral male acquisition of exclusive sexual rights to a woman without the husband's reciprocal obligation).[51]

Motivating this historic change in the halakhah of the Conservative movement is the contemporary understanding that marriage is "a partnership of equals" and the aspiration to ensure that "Jewish men and women have an opportunity to commit to each other in their understanding of how to achieve those essential values in relationship."[52] The responsum is titled "With Righteousness and Justice, with Goodness and with Mercy" in order to evoke the revolutionary prophecy of Hosea 2:21–22. Thus, a radical feminist critique of kiddushin by a Reform rabbi has persuaded the official halakhic organ of the Conservative movement to legitimate an alternative mode of marriage—without condemning or invalidating the traditional kiddushin ceremony that Adler herself seeks to uproot.

RENEWED RABBINIC NUPTIAL BLESSINGS

Adler, like Borowitz, Elliot Dorff, and Joseph B. Soloveitchik, affirms the *sacred* dimension of marriage, beyond its contractual duties. She distinguishes between the two ceremonies performed consecutively at the contemporary wedding, each represented by its own cup of wine with different blessings. For Adler, what is sacred in marriage is not the prohibitions—characterizing the first blessing in the first ceremony, kiddushin, but the affective life lived together—the nuptial blessings recited in the second ceremony over the second cup, *nisuin*.

In the halakhic marriage ceremony of kiddushin, the giving and accepting of the ring and the husband's formula "you are hereby sanctified to me" establish the legal exclusivity of the wife's sexual loyalty to her ba'al (husband as proprietor), constructed by analogy to a commercial acquisition. The groom's presentation of a ring to his bride (not a double ring ceremony of mutuality) symbolizes the consummate act of acquisition (kiddushin), and it always follows immediately after the blessing stipulating the prohibition on adulterous violations of a wife's oath of fidelity. This aspect of sanctity is yoked to prohibition, propriety, and property. Even though kiddushin can be understood as the negative but necessary side of sanctification as exclusivity, both Adler and Plaskow reject the traditional kiddushin ceremony out of hand because it expresses exclusivity as a one-sided acquisition of sexual access to a woman by the property-owning husband.

For Adler, however, positive emotional bonds should be placed at the heart of sacred marital vows, as symbolized by the second ceremony in marriage (*nisuin*), when both groom and bride enter the huppah (canopy), which signifies living together in the marital house in a *sacred relationship*:

> In contrast to the prosaic legal machinery that effects *kiddushin*, the second half of the Jewish wedding ceremony is poetic and allusive. It consists of a series of celebratory blessings recited over a [second] cup of wine. . . . What the blessings celebrate is not "*taking*" but "*wedding*," a conjoining that, according to the prophets, supersedes the rule of acquisition-marriage. This, and not *kiddushin*, is the union from which redemption flows.[53]

CELEBRATING THE RABBINIC VISION OF THE HUPPAH

While Adler and Plaskow repudiate the rabbinic vision of kiddushin with its traditional language facilitating the man's sanctification of his exclusive legal relationship with the woman, they wholeheartedly celebrate the rabbinic vision of the huppah, the canopy of "loving companions in the Garden of Eden." To them, the union between groom and bride reenacts the reunion of the male and female aspects of God's image as described in Creation: *And God created the human in his image, in the image of God he created him, male and female he created them* (Gen. 1:27). And, as phrased in the Talmud:

> Blessed are You, Adonai our God, Ruler of the universe, who has formed humanity in his image patterned after his image and likeness and has established from Adam an eternal construction, the woman. Blessed are You Adonai, shaper of humanity. (TB *Ketubot* 8a)

While Adler starkly contrasts the two gardens in the Song of Songs and in Eden, she is able to endorse the metaphor of the Garden of Eden in the *Sheva Brakhot* (Seven Blessings), because here the Rabbis identify it not with the sinful tale of sexual knowledge, female temptation, and divine curse of male hegemony found in Genesis 3, but selectively, with the rhapsodic story of shame-free sexual union in Genesis 2. The Rabbis entreat God to restore that lost erotic friendship born before Adam and Eve sinned:

> Make these loving friends (*re'im ahuvim*) happy as You made your creations in the primordial Garden of Eden happy. Blessed are You, Adonai, who makes the groom and the bride happy (TB *Ketubot* 8a).

Under the canopy of an egalitarian marriage ceremony of friendship and partnership, the Garden of Eden's curse of male subjugation of woman (Gen. 3:16) disappears from sight—as does, surprisingly, the procreative blessing of male and female (Gen. 1:28). Here, the Rabbis do not bless hierarchy or reproduction, but mutual joy, each with the other, in a private happiness that spills over into what Adler calls communal redemption:

> Blessed are You, Adonai our God, Ruler of the universe, who created joy and happiness, groom and bride, merriment, song, affection and delight, love and brotherhood, peace and friendship. Adonai, our God, may there soon be heard in the cities of Judah and the outskirts of Jerusalem the voice of joy and the voice of happiness, the voice of the groom and the voice of the bride, the rapturous voices of grooms from their bridal chambers, and of young people feasting and making music.
>
> Blessed are You, Adonai, who makes the groom happy together with the bride. (TB *Ketubot* 8a)

For Adler, the poetic imagery of the Seven Blessings connects this couple's union both with the primordial Creation and with messianic expectations for the people Israel's redemption:

Wedding is the beginning and end of time shaped into a circle and wreathed around the bridegroom and the bride. Wedding is creation and redemption, the origin of all bonds and their perfect mending, the first encounter of lover-equals . . . with the lover . . . no longer calling [the husband] "my *ba'al*" (my possessor, my owner).[54]

Multiform Sexuality, Gender Fluidity, and Hybridity as Divinely Blessed

As a Jewish theologian, Plaskow builds her radical gender-egalitarian message on two religious axioms of Divine Creation. First, one's moral and sexual duties to one's spouse derive from the theological belief in the sanctity of the body created in the image of God (Gen. 9:5–6) combined with the Biblical mitzvah, *You shall be holy as I am holy* (Lev. 19:2). From that axiom we learn that "as our bodies are holy, we shall not do violence to others."[55]

Second, Plaskow interprets God's indiscriminate affirmation of the goodness of "all" of Creation to mean that a wide variety of sexual desires occurring in nature have been affirmed normatively in the verse, *And God saw all that God had made: Behold it is very good!* (Gen. 1:31). Therefore, she rejects the Torah's attribution of binary heterosexual structures to humanity and the Godhead (Gen. 1: 27), and repudiates legal and ethical norms that claim that heterosexuality is the only sacred and natural form of sexuality. Thus Plaskow finds Jewish theological roots for her affirmation that gender fluidity, hybridity, and multiform sexuality are divinely blessed:

We affirm that human sexual diversity is part of the richness and diversity of life. We envision a society in which sexual behavior, whether heterosexual, bisexual, homosexual, or celibate, is all considered healthy; and in which sexual ambiguity, including hermaphroditism, androgyny, and transgenderedness, is affirmed and neither feared nor despised.[56]

In her survey of fifty years of feminist Jewish theology, Mara Benjamin observed in 2020 that "many contemporary trans, nonbinary, and queer Jews have found the Rabbis' recognition of multiple genders promising both socially and theologically."[57] Elliot Rose Kukla, the first transgender Reform rabbi, so explained in a public dialogue with Plaskow:

In the Mishna, Rabbi Yossi says that the androgynous [a person possessing a bisexual body] is neither essentially male nor female but a "created being of its own." This phrase is a classical legal term for exceptionality; it is an acknowledgment that not all of creation can be understood within binary systems.

In my reading, it is also a theological statement . . . that God creates diversity that is far too complex for humans to understand or ever fully categorize. There are parts of each of us that are uncontainable. All of us—whether we see ourselves within or between male and female genders—are uniquely "created beings of our own." This idea allows for infinite gender identities that are all created in the image of God.[58]

Jay Michaelson (b. 1971), journalist, pundit, Jewish Renewal rabbi and professional religious LGBTQ activist, comments aptly on fluidity's revolutionary threat to the basically conservative binary orientation of Biblical and rabbinic Judaism:

The liminal . . . is terrifying. . . . Some cultures sacralize these chaotic, anarchic, and death-linked moments, but others—surely including biblical Israel—seek to circumscribe it. Biblical Judaism sanctifies not the ecstatic but the formal, not the chaotic but the ordered. . . . *God saw that it was good* [Gen. 1:18]—because now it was ordered, where before it was not. . . .

This is how it must be, for in a religion of civilization, the notion of boundary is essential. One does not organize clans, tribes, and nations without a healthy respect for hierarchy, law, and propriety—and within the Jewish tradition, the respect is deified. . . . Such binaries of pure and impure, male and female, dark and light, Israelite and foreigner, and sacred and profane are the essence of the Levitical writings. . . . The borders drawn around sexual behavior are of the same type.[59]

Thus, Plaskow, along with other radical Jewish gender activists (especially followers of the school of the feminist philosopher Judith Butler, author of *Gender Trouble*) and proponents of queer theories of sexuality and gender, advocate for fluidity, hybridity, and permeability in Judaism. That makes them intractable philosophical opponents of the practitioners of classical halakhic thought and practice, whether Modern Orthodox or Liberal, who defend the Torah's and the Rabbis' heritage of legislating binary structures of permitted and forbidden behaviors. This cavernous divergence between radical theologians of gender fluidity and binary halakhists is evident by comparing the views of Plaskow, Kukla, and Michaelson (above) with the argument of Rabbi Mark Washofsky, chair of the CCAR committee on halakhah, in his rationale for rejecting living together without the sanctity of marriage:

> These sharp distinctions [between sacred and profane] are particularly important for Judaism. Just like the clear boundaries between God and humanity, humanity and animals, life and death, and good and evil, the boundary between the holy and the ordinary seeks to help us categorize our lives with clarity and avoid unnecessary intermingling. The distinction is based upon the premise that when the holy and the ordinary become blurred, it becomes impossible to recognize and properly to appreciate the holy when we encounter it. Experiences that partake of both the holy and the ordinary cease to be either *kodesh* or *chol*.[60]

On the horizon in the twenty-first century is a radical disagreement among North American rabbis over the nature of sexuality.

Most contemporary liberal halakhic thinkers of all modern denominations root their advocacy for a more egalitarian partnership in marriage in Biblical and mystical conceptions of the basic binary of male and female that God created in God's image and of their heterosexual union into one flesh as celebrated in rabbinic marriage. Most hold that halakhic categories are essential for holding off the anarchic trends of the sexual revolution, though some accept the need for a sliding scale of guidelines. However, contemporary postmodern discourses about spirituality and sexuality condemn such binaries as misrepresentations of "nature" that are morally oppressive because they are essentially both hierarchical and chauvinist, as reflected in particular in the halakhah's preference for heterosexuality. The next generation of rabbinic debate may focus on the desirability of a postmodern paradigm shift away from binary sexuality. The question will be whether these fluid, hybrid views can and should be incorporated broadly in the stream of Jewish continuity and within the diverse halakhic traditions about marital intimacy.

Conclusion

We complete our study of contemporary halakhic attitudes to interpersonal intimacy and sanctity at a historic crisis point and crossroads. With the notable exception of the Hasidim, especially Gur and Slonim, today's leading Jewish halakhic ideologies of marital life have reached a momentous apex in the positive sacralization of mutuality in marital relations. Both Litvak ultra-Orthodoxy in Israel and the modern liberal rabbinate of North America (from Modern Orthodox to Jewish Renewal) regard intimate loving conversation and mutual joyous physical and emotional pleasure between spouses as legal norms and aspirational goals for Judaism. They often take their inspiration from kabbalist motifs about intensifying the union of male and female dimensions, so that while kabbalist sources about couple intimacy were marginal to actual marital norms in the medieval era, they have borne rich fruit in twentieth- and twenty-first-century Jewish teachings about real-life couples, including the innovative Litvak guidebooks for newlyweds.

Both Jewish feminists and liberal rabbis welcome the liberation of sexuality from ascetic guilt and support the feminist revolution in so far as it both enhances the affirmative value of loving sexuality and reforms gender biases in the halakhic structures of marriage and divorce. Progressively, liberal rabbis and their denominations have adjusted marital ceremonies to express greater egalitarianism. More radical halakhic changes have been enacted regarding who may be married officially (especially regarding gay and lesbian Jews).

Yet certain radical Jewish feminist theologians and some liberal rabbis often disagree in evaluating the core definition of halakhic marriage, perhaps because they approach the sexual revolution with different preconceptions. Radical feminists like Plaskow and Adler understand the halakhah of kiddushin as the emblematic act of acquisition of exclusive rights to a woman's sexuality.[61] To them, kiddushin must be eliminated from wedding ceremonies, both to nullify patriarchal hegemony—laws and social structures that oppress women—in marriage, and to liberate Judaism from the view that female sexuality is essentially subversive to male self-control.

For most modern rabbis, however, from Soloveitchik to Borowitz, and from Kalmanofsky to Washofsky, the potential for abuse in the anarchic atmosphere of the sexual revolution is the greater concern. For these rabbis, marital commitment—societally regulated desire that does not demean and suppress the hedonistic pleasures of marital lovemaking—is the royal road to kedushah. And so, by reaffirming the sanctity of marriage, they wish to redeem sexuality not *from* halakhah but *through* law. For them, kiddushin symbolically represents the essential sanctity of marriage, both in its negative and positive dimensions, both in prohibiting promiscuity and adultery and in sanctifying the I-Thou relationship embedded in intimate lovemaking. Of course, Plaskow and Adler are also well aware of the destructive nature of unrestrained instinctual drives, even in so-called liberated communities. Yet their greater concern is the oppressive male power that permeates halakhah.

In response to what they see as the rigidity and gender bias of Jewish law, Plaskow prefers the approach of a situational ethics that varies from couple to couple, whereas Adler advocates for an alternative marriage ceremony, sans kiddushin, but still characterized by holiness and legal commitment. In general, we can differentiate Plaskow and Adler by contrasting their intuitive responses to attempts to redeem marital halakhah. Plaskow, inspired by Buber's antinomianism, tends to be suspicious of law. As Adler once observed, "Plaskow is profoundly ambivalent about halakha."[62] Adler, however, "adopts a more affirmative attitude to the halakhic medium."[63] She advocates for a contractual framework of marriage, *b'rit ahuvim*, without kiddushin as a binding covenantal partnership. In her alternative ceremony, she promotes a synthesis of playful, aesthetic, feminine sexuality (Song of Songs) and egalitarian halakhah, symbolized by the huppah (canopy), its blessings (*Sheva Brahot*). The couple shares a pouch that represents the pooling of resources in a common partnership (*shutafut*).[64] The Conservative movement's rabbis have also authorized this halakhic alternative to kiddushin.

Whatever their disagreements, both Plaskow and Adler insist that improving the quality of loving interpersonal relationships between partners cannot be addressed as a private matter. Society in general, and Jewish law, narrative, and theology in particular must be critically scrutinized and appraised to make men and women aware of the depth of the problem. Then thought patterns (aggadah) and legal practices (halakhah) must be reconstructed. Only then can true love be attained and maintained in marriage, only after women achieve societal justice.

Conclusion

AGGADAH AND HALAKHAH OF MARRIAGE

No aspect of humanity is more sacred and worthy of being elevated than the bond of the marriage covenant. Therefore the Perfect Torah wishes to guide us not by coercion and force to build the house of Israel, but rather by an inner recognition that enters our sacred souls, so that we will perceive how great and valued the sacred covenant of matrimony is, as it says, for *Adonai witnesses between you and the wife of your youth* (Mal. 2:14).

—RAV ABRAHAM ISAAC KOOK, *Eyn Aya*, Shabbat #75

The two-thousand-year Jewish debate about marital intimacy is inspired by aggadah as much as halakhah. Guidelines for the bedroom are shaped by divergent worldviews of sexuality and sanctity as well as legal arguments and precedents. Thus rabbinic policymakers construct a protocol for private acts of lovemaking (halakhah) in light of their idealistic rationales (aggadah) for marital *onah*. (While the term *aggadah* has been reduced in modern Hebrew parlance to "Jewish folklore," it originally referred to all rabbinic literature that is not legal in form, whether folklore, imaginative interpretation of Biblical narratives, or tales about rabbis and about God.) Today Jewish thinkers also use aggadah to describe Jewish worldviews implicit in nonlegal texts or underlying the reasons for laws—*ta'amei ha-mitzvot*.[1] In the sense of a worldview, the spectrum of the aggadah of Jewish marriage is composed of diverse understandings of emotional and physical needs and spiritual aspirations in which human intimacy is intertwined with grand purposes: love and joy, peace and unity, libido and sanctity, reproduction of the

Jewish people and propagation of the human race, elevation and humanization of sexual desire, gender justice and mutual consent, communication and I-Thou dialogue, and personal and national holiness. The challenge for Judaism's visions of *shalom bayit* and marital intimacy will be their success in translating these aspirations into nuanced halakhic practice and sensitive educational guidance.

In this summary chapter to *Sanctified Sex* I will first review what we have discovered about the aggadah of rabbinic marriage, notably four tugs-of-war between different worldviews in tension:

1. **Gender justice versus gender equality.** In the Talmud, pursuing marital justice means legislating women's sexual rights and revising the marriage contract to counterbalance men's economic and legal advantages. Contemporary Jewish feminists, however, often view those same laws and even their so-called liberal reforms as patriarchal and paternalistic and therefore they pursue gender equality by radically restructuring the ceremonies and laws of marriage.

2. **Sexual playfulness versus spiritualized sanctity.** The styles of onah modeled in the Talmudic bedroom tales of Rav and Rabbi Eliezer contrast two rabbinic ideals, passionate eros stoked by joyful pillow talk as opposed to desireless sex without arousal designed to protect the male's spiritual mindset from unseemly physical drives (the *yetzer*).

3. **Negative versus positive sanctity in the institution of marriage.** In the Torah and the Talmud, marriage itself is not yet a matter of sanctity. It is not until the mystics imbue sexual union in marriage with positive holiness that the Jewish understanding of marriage comes to affirm that sexual love can be sacred.

4. **Negative versus positive sanctity in sexual relations.** While rabbinic ascetics and philosophers aspire to holiness that separates itself from the polluting physicality of sex, kabbalists and contemporary neo-kabbalists see sexual union as the highest act of spiritual union.

In the second half of this conclusion I will revisit two debates about the *halakhah of marriage*: Whose prerogatives are supposed to dominate in the marital bed—male hegemony or female rights? And, how might the halakhah of marital relations best contribute to the urgent task of counseling couples to develop marital practices like frequent communication that enhance emotional and erotic dimensions of their relationship?

Aggadah of Gender Justice versus Gender Equality

For the Torah and Mishnah, a central aim in legislating onah, defining its frequency and quality as the wife's right and the husband's duty, is to enhance gender justice, though not full gender equality. Within a patriarchal society where husbands have greater advantages, Biblical and rabbinic laws of onah contribute to greater gender justice for women in three ways:

First, recognizing that wives have sexual desires and emotional needs for personal intimacy.

Second, enfranchising wives through the marriage contract to demand fulfillment of these desires and needs as their legal rights and hence as contractual duties of their husbands.

Third, mandating that all sexual relations in marriage be consensual by stipulating that every act of intercourse must be preceded by foreplay and pillow talk in order to arouse female desire and assure mutual agreement.

When unmet, these quantitative and qualitative needs are grounds for a wife's right to divorce. But when treated as aspirational goals, the halakhic definition of the quality and quantity of onah serves another function by setting a high bar for couples striving to augment their marital relationship and erotic life.

By introducing legal standards, the Rabbis demonstrate that the woman, the more vulnerable and disadvantaged partner in marriage, must be protected and her free will respected. The negotiated contract of marriage aims to provide a wife with security in the form of structured expectations, duties, and rights as a ballast to counter what the Rabbis saw as a man's often fickle affections and arbitrary whims.

Like the Torah and Talmud, the modern rabbis of North America (Liberal Orthodox to Reform and Renewal) maintain the inviolability of contractual obligations between spouses, though they are much more inclusive and egalitarian in their demand for gender justice. Women play a more active role in the ceremony, often by giving a ring to the groom, and LGBTQ commitment ceremonies are celebrated by some liberal rabbis, though not always in the form of a halakhic marriage with *kiddushin* and a traditional *ketubah*. Liberal rabbis struggle to adapt and reform the halakhic system in differing degrees by stretching it through evolution rather rewriting it through revolution.

Liberal rabbis have also added a new chapter to the aggadah of marriage by adopting Martin Buber's ideal relationship, I-Thou, as the criterion for a sacred relationship and thereby they have condemned exploitive I-it sexual relations as dehumanizing. Sexual relations are degraded, they assert, when there is no mutual consent between equal partners, because they violate the Talmudic and Kantian principles that human dignity entails autonomy over one's body. Beyond that, the innovative claim of liberal rabbis is that even consensual sex between adults can be dehumanizing. Accompanying the most intimate physical act, intercourse, must be the deepest interpersonal relationship characterized by the totality of an I-Thou relationship and a marital commitment. While these modern rabbis disagree among themselves as to whether to endorse sex within marriage alone or also lovemaking between committed but unmarried couples living together, most withhold their religious approval from casual sex and hook-ups lacking wholehearted commitment and sanctity. As Eugene Borowitz writes: "The most ethical form of human relationship I know is love-for-life."[2] Only then are sexual *relations* worthy of the name sacred *relationship*.

After the rise of Jewish feminism, a revised understanding of the aggadah of gender justice requires total equality in marriage. For radical Jewish feminists like Judith Plaskow and Rachel Adler, gender equality begins not with specific halakhic reforms in a system invented solely by men, but with women empowering themselves to make laws on sexual relations for themselves. Since rabbinic marriage, its aggadah and its halakhah, is exclusively heterosexual, and hence, for radical Jewish feminists, necessarily patriarchal, they argue that Jewish marriage must be reinvented. Its new aggadah must be inspired by the Song of Songs, where, as Adler writes, there is "no male dominance, no female subordination, and no stereotyping of either sex."[3] Since, according to the radical feminists, traditional kiddushin (the rabbinic invention of betrothal) takes the form of male acquisition of a wife as his exclusive sexual property, as chattel, rabbinic marriage must be reconceived without kiddushin. As an alternative, Adler proposes the *b'rit ahuvim*, the Covenant of Lovers, in the form of an egalitarian legal partnership in the spirit of Hosea's prophetic demand for equality and freedom, *You shall call Me Ishi* [my husband], *and you will no longer call Me my Ba'al* [my master] (Hosea 2:18). Since the rabbinic worldview as well as its law is biased toward the binary structure of heterosexuality, Plaskow proposes that its aggadah be replaced with contemporary understandings of the fluid nature of sexuality and queer gender identity.

Aggadah of Sexual Playfulness versus Spiritualized Sanctity

The law of onah conceptualizes human beings in terms of their basic sexual needs and the Rabbis regulate their fulfillment through enforcing consensual marriage contracts. The Talmudic tales of rabbinic bedroom decorum are less about needs and duties than desires and aspirations. Some tales authorize mutual playfulness in word and deed, while others condemn desire and dialogue in order to protect the spiritual project of the scholar seeking to transcend his body and purify his mind even in the midst of the shameful sex necessary for procreation.

For Rav and his wife and for Rav Hisda and his daughters, in marriage human beings should behave as *homo ludens* (people who play), and so they ought to cultivate erotic playfulness that elevates the fulfillment of natural needs to the level of high culture. Laughter, pillow talk, and the give-and-take of seduction humanize libidinal release and enrich desire. Rather than denigrating the body and regarding sex as shameful, Rav shows that desire in marital relations is to be celebrated as an art of lovemaking ("chatting, playing, jesting and gratifying needs," TB *Hagiga* 5b). For Rav, however, sexual union is not related to sanctity, as it would be for medieval mystics. Unlike his hutzpadik student Kahana, who, from under Rav's bed, criticized his master's passions, Rav did not think marital sex either enhances or detracts from the spiritual goals of a scholar.

For Rabbi Eliezer and Imma Shalom, by contrast, performance of onah is not an art but a science of eugenics in which purity of thought—unpolluted by sexual arousal, spousal conversation, or physical intimacy—generates beautiful offspring. Hence, Rabbi Eliezer executes intercourse "as if a demon were coercing him" (TB *Nedarim* 20a). Further, for Rabbi Yohanan ben D'havai, the highest aspiration in intercourse is to live up to angelic standards; hence, the male quest for spirituality places severe limits on husbands' intimate interactions with their wives—prohibiting them from kissing their wives' genitalia and engaging in any conversation. While the Talmud defines these ascetic practices as optional, Rav Joseph Karo (16th century) understands them as obligatory halakhic norms to achieve personal sanctity by strictly policing the deleterious by-products of procreative intercourse—wasted semen, physiological pleasure, and wayward erotic thoughts. His aggadic ideal is spiritual mastery of a man's sexual impulses by "minimizing his pleasure," lest his mind and soul be conquered by his anarchic *yetzer*.[4]

The price exacted for such an uncompromising pursuit of ascetic male spirituality is paid, first, by women in terms of lost intimacy with their husbands, but also by men alienated from their own bodies. Medieval halakhists almost never mentioned the trade-off between men's ascent on the ladder to heaven and women's emotional abandonment and their marginalization from the sacred center. In the nineteenth century small Talmudic elites of the Litvak yeshiva world, especially the Gaon of Vilna and the Mussarniks, explicitly trumpeted the suppression of affection for wives and children, "making themselves cruel" (TB *Eruvin* 22a), as a worthy sacrifice for scholars committed to the life of the mind.

In the twentieth century, post-Holocaust Hasidim of Gur, Slonim, Toldes Aharon, and Skver constructed a community-wide ethos of sanctity, the Ordinances of Kedushah, which preemptively quashed intimacy of any kind for *all* hasidic spouses, not merely for self-selected Torah scholars. The aggadah of the rebbe of Slonim is "self-sacrifice, blood, tears, and sweat . . . for a life of happiness and joy is a life of abstinence and purity."[5] Hasidic piety is aspirational, going beyond the demands of the law; but its enforcement by social sanctions is more draconian than any law, and its totalitarian indoctrination of men and women excludes consideration of any alternative aggadah or halakhah of marriage. Its pious wish is to suppress all erotic thoughts.

By contrast, both Litvak Haredim and North American Jewish feminists have reaffirmed the imaginative playfulness of Rav's erotic onah by returning to its Biblical, Rabbinic, and kabbalist roots, while also highlighting more sharply its mutuality. Isaac Sher, the Litvak Haredi Mussarnik, connects the "ecstasy in this [sexual] act," mutual orgasm, to the ability of the couple "to imagine themselves in the Garden of Eden."[6] He explains:

> She is filled with love and pleasure arising from sanctity and spiritual elevation so that when she reaches the apex of the act [of intercourse] she is fully intoxicated, hovering in the world of imagination. Then she dreams pleasant dreams illustrated with beautiful images of angels filled with light and radiance flying above her and feting her with the very same pleasures as in the Garden of Eden itself.[7]
>
> So too the man can in this desire, in this act, and with this woman be filled with elevated thoughts and elevated illustrations of love and sanctity in their unification.[8]

Jewish feminist theologians find in the Song of Songs the original aggadah infusing Rav's bedroom ethos. Adler comments: "Whereas Adam and Eve conceal themselves in terror and shame from a punishing God, the lovers of the Song play at concealment, teasing each other with endless games of peekaboo and hide-and-seek."[9] Plaskow adds: "Unabashed by their desire, the man and woman of these poems delight in their own embodiment and the beauty surrounding them ... each rejoicing in the love without dominion that is also the love of God."[10]

Aggadah of Negative versus Positive Sanctity in the Institution of Marriage

In the Torah and the Talmud, marriage had not yet become a matter of positive sanctity, even though many contemporary rabbinic preachers of all denominations rhapsodize over the spiritual significance of the act of kiddushin solemnized by the husband pronouncing the formula, *Harei at mekudeshet li, b'tabba'at zu, k'dat Moshe v Yisrael* ("You are hereby sanctified to me by this ring according to the law of Moshe and Israel"). Rav Joseph B. Soloveitchik (20th century, Modern Orthodox) is not alone in writing: "Marriage is a sacred institution. The term *kiddushin* [betrothal], sanctification, attests to the quality of sanctity which is implied in the marital contract."[11]

Historically, however, that commonplace idea of rabbinic marriage as holy matrimony is anachronistic. While marriage has always involved negative sanctity, prohibiting a married woman's adultery as a defilement of Israel's holiness, asserting the positive sanctity of a marital sexual union and a loving relationship is a revolutionary kabbalist motif not found in the Talmudic era. The Talmudic historian Moshe David Herr denies that kiddushin ever meant sanctification of the marriage.[12] Rather, Biblical and rabbinic marriages were understood as secular, private arrangements (mainly financial), without consecration.[13]

Thus the rabbinic marriage ceremony is not a *sacramentum*. It differs from that of Romans, whose hearth was sacred and so too their marriage, and from that of Catholics, whose marriage is a sacrament that only a priest representing God can validate.[14] The Talmudic marriage (like the Sunni marriage ceremony) requires no clergy, no sacred space, no sacrifice, no ritual or mandatory blessing (even though these are now customary), no public affirmation (other than two witnesses to testify, if necessary, to the betrothal).[15] With or without kiddushin there is no difference in the status of the offspring: even the son born out of legal wedlock has full rights to inherit from his father. While, legally, kiddushin is obligatory, it does not require a particular sacred formula; and the medieval tradition of saying "you are hereby sanctified to me according to the law of Moshe and Israel" and the giving of a ring to the bride are not essential.[16] Furthermore, no dimension of divine grace, holy spirit, or positive sanctification is ascribed to the sexual and emotional union, and therefore divorce entails no abrogation of an inviolable sacred union, as the Catholic Church teaches ("What therefore

God has joined together, let not man put asunder"—Mark 10:6–9).
Maimonides observes pragmatically: "It may happen that husband
and wife do not agree, live without love and peace, and do not enjoy
the benefit of a home; in that case he is permitted to send her away
[i.e., divorce her]."[17]

By contrast to the Talmud, the prophet Malachi's vision of marriage as a sacred covenant of companionship reemerges among
medieval kabbalists and contemporary rabbis of all denominations, beginning with *The Holy Letter* (13th century, Spain). Rabbi
Eugene Borowitz, the doyen of American Reform theologians,
acknowledges this historic transition in the sanctity of marriage.
While for him, "the act of marital intercourse" is connected to
"the highest expression of holiness of which people are capable,"
he frankly admits that "sacred sexuality in our early [biblical and
Talmudic] Jewish books" is absent until "the mystics endowed sexual
intercourse with sanctity."[18] The kabbalists transformed the Jewish understanding of marriage by affirming a positive sanctity that
encompasses sexual love.

Aggadah of Negative versus Positive Sanctity in Sexual Relations

Sanctity may be oriented both negatively and positively toward
sexuality depending on one's pessimistic or optimistic worldview.
On the one hand, the fearful view believes that relationships are
threatened by anarchic sexual drives *within* human beings, especially
the dark male *yetzer ha-ra* (the evil impulse), and by foreign cultural
and religious influences from *without*, such as idolatrous Canaanite
incest, Roman orgies, or contemporary sexual license. Therefore,
sanctity is primarily separation of physicality and desire from the
spiritual and the intellectual. Yet, on the other hand, the hopeful
approach trusts that human desire may be elevated within a marriage

of mutual responsibility and exclusivity to advance higher purposes beyond pleasurable sexual release, and thus achieve a sanctity that synthesizes body and spirit.

In the Talmudic world, sanctity regulates marriage in two ways, both negatively. First, the sanctity of Israel prohibits certain sexual partners (incest with family members and adultery with married women) and certain times for intercourse within marriage (*niddah*). Secondly, sanctity as the aim of ascetic pietists requires them to minimize the frequency of onah and, during marital intercourse, to minimize its length and pleasure, lest husbands' desires be inflamed and their minds distracted by erotic thoughts. The negative understanding of sanctity and sexuality is dualistic, touting the intractable battle of body versus soul and idealizing the sanctity of the male spiritual "I."

Only in the Zohar and the mystical halakhic manuals of *The Holy Letter* and Ra'avad's *Ba'alei HaNefesh* does holy matrimony come to mean the positive expression of sanctity in marital lovemaking. While acknowledging and adapting the eugenics advice of Imma Shalom, the manuals infuse onah with a spiritual dimension that reinforces (rather than suppresses) mutuality: of desire (with foreplay and patient arousal of female orgasm), of thought (synchronizing man and woman's intentions), and of full consent and love. These kabbalists tout the private pleasures of marital intercourse as key vessels for enhancing cosmic goals of unity over division, peace over conflict, and love over hate in the whole earth and in heaven. When man and woman become one, they achieve full humanity by embodying the image of God, which is itself male and female, as the Zohar teaches: "Any image that does not embrace male and female is not the high and true image."[19] The positive mystical approach to sanctity and sexuality rejects the dichotomy of matter and spirit, earthly and heavenly, and instead celebrates their integration in a dynamic union of opposites. Its ideal is *the sanctity of "we"* and the loving union of body and soul, immanence and transcendence, and male and female.

These kabbalist visions have found new expression in the modern age. From the 1950s on, a leading cadre of ultra-Orthodox Litvak scholars, reacting against the rebbe of Gur's Ordinances of Sanctity and his marital asceticism, have restored the aggadah of the medieval kabbalists and renewed the basic Talmudic commitment to the marital obligation of onah. For the Hazon Ish, Hasidic piety that goes *beyond* the law by restricting marital intimacy more than necessary is pseudo-piety that violates God's law because it results in the husband failing to make his wife happy. Onah allows a couple to achieve mystical unity with the Divine when an earth-bound husband and wife learn to bridge their gender differences and understand each other through honest, caring communication. Further, Sher's aggadah of marriage, which aims to overcome division and bring unity to the cosmos, is fueled by sexual passion. Without passion, performing what is supposed to be the mitzvah of onah becomes a crime, as Rabbi Moshe Aharon Shuchatowitz writes, "if the husband does not desire his wife so much, then he is engaged not with unification but with separation, and therefore [his intercourse] is a sin!"[20]

Like the Zoharic kabbalists, modern rabbis, especially neo-kabbalists, sanctify sexual union in marriage when it achieves mutuality of heart, mind, and body. Unlike the ascetic Hasidism of Gur with its heroic ethic of *kibbush ha-yetzer*, conquest and extirpation of natural impulses (*Mishnah Avot* 4:1), the neo-Hasidic modern philosopher Rabbi Abraham Joshua Heschel teaches human beings to strive not for "self-conquest but self-dedication, not suppression of emotion but its redirection."[21] In the spirit of Heschel his teacher, Arthur Green in *The Second Jewish Catalog* calls for a New Kabbalah as the aggadah to inspire a New Halakhah of sexuality:

The greatest and potentially most divine mystery accessible to most humans is the *mystery of sexuality*. . . . Kabbalists see the very origins of the universe as a never-ceasing process of arousal, coupling, gestation, and birth within the life of a God who is both male and female, and proclaim this complex inner flow of divinity, described in the most graphic of sexual terms, to be the highest of mysteries. All this imagery provides for the Jew an ideal of sexuality.[22]

But these modern rabbis also recognize, as did their forebears, the dangers of egotistical libidinal drives that use and abuse bodies without care for or commitment to partners. To them, the individual's preoccupation with selfish pleasures without regard to a partner's dignity derives in part from the separation between sex and sanctity. Green cautions against a negative dimension in the contemporary sexual revolution: "We Jews should stand opposed to the current moves toward the 'demystification' of sexuality which seek to define coupling as a purely biological function."[23] Therefore, liberal rabbis of all denominations campaign with countercultural zeal against the negative cultural influences of unrestrained sexual liberation, exploitation, and coercion (as condemned by the Me Too movement). While repudiating asceticism, they refuse to condone unbridled hedonism. As Soloveitchik argues: "Sexual activity can be a sinful affair of the most crass and devastating consequence. Thus the Halakha was compelled not only to redeem but to remedy the sexual impulse."[24]

Halakhah of *Onah*:
Male Prerogative versus Female Right

As in the competing philosophies of aggadah about rabbinic marriage surveyed above, so too in halakhah there is an internal tug of war between various strains.

In the ethos of Gur Hasidim, a woman is taught to live up to the Rabbinic adage, "Who is a kosher (worthy) wife? One who does the will of her husband."[25] She is expected to defer to her husband's instructions in ritual practice, economic decision making, and the bedroom. Thus she fulfills God's pronouncement about Eve: *Your desire will be to your husband and he will rule over you* (Gen. 3:16).

Furthermore, Plaskow and Adler assert that this male hegemony is not an exceptional stringency of Hasidic sectarians, but the patriarchal essence of Biblical and Rabbinic matrimony as symbolized by the Mishnah's identification of the betrothal (kiddushin) with male acquisition (*kinyan*) of the woman's sexual and procreative services. At least one renowned modern Talmudist (19th century, Belarus), the Netziv, Rabbi Naftali Zvi Berlin, holds that a wife is obligated, like a female slave, to fulfill her husband's sexual demands at any time.[26] Although he doesn't at all regard wives as concubines, the doyen of twentieth-century ultra-Orthodox halakhic authorities, Rabbi Moshe Feinstein, rules, nevertheless: "The wife is obligated to serve *his* sexual needs *at any time* that he wishes, even if it is not the scheduled onah, as long as she is healthy."[27] So too, a famous Talmudic precedent maintains that a husband may choose whatever sexual position he prefers over his wife's objections. As Rabbi [Judah HaNasi] says: "My daughter, the Torah permitted him to you [anyway he sees fit to consume you]. So as for me, what can I do?" (TB *Nedarim* 20b).

Nevertheless, Maimonides and Feinstein insist that the husband's sexual prerogative is not absolute but conditional—"*only* with the wife's consent."[28] Maimonides adds that a wife may demand from the court that her husband be instructed to divorce her, if she so wishes, "if he tries to coerce her . . . to do crazy things [during intercourse] which have no value but are just foolish."[29]

A prevalent strain in rabbinic legislation holds that sexual rights guaranteed by the law *are only for wives*—perhaps because men usually get their way even without judicial intervention. Thus the mishnah that defines the frequency of conjugal duties solely stipulates the wife's contractual rights to onah (*Mishnah Ketubot* 5:6), and in the Talmud malfeasance by denying onah is grounds for divorce. While some rabbis assume implicitly that a husband also possesses equivalent rights to scheduled intercourse, Rabbi Moses ben Joseph di Trani (Greece, d. 1585) states baldly: "It is *her* right, *not* his right."[30] Therefore, a husband who desires intercourse may propose sexual intimacy, but has no legal power to compel his wife and so must woo her. The Shulhan Arukh concludes: "A husband may not possess his wife sexually unless she consents freely. If she is not desirous of intercourse, then he must court her until she is willing."[31]

Even beyond this mishnah's stipulated frequency of onah, a woman also has a right to additional sexual satisfaction, and a husband must be ever sensitive to her desires. As Rashi explains: "Even if it is beyond her scheduled onah, [he is obligated to provide intercourse] whenever the husband sees that his wife desires it" (TB *Pesahim* 72b).

THE BOTTOM LINE

According to Maimonides, the bottom line on the question of who calls the shots in the marital bed is the wife's freedom to say "no" to a husband's sexual advances, as he rules unequivocally:

> If she says: "I have come to loathe him and I cannot willingly submit to intercourse with him," then [the court must] force him to divorce her immediately since she is *not like a captive who must accede to intercourse with one whom she hates.*[32]

In sum, in Jewish law there are conflicting views on the prerogatives of husband versus wife. While in halakhic debates some rabbis reinforce male sexual hegemony in marital relations, many others legislate one-sidedly in favor of the wife's right to onah whenever she feels the urge.

In real life, married couples have different patterns for resolving conflicting sexual needs and desires. In a traditional society, disagreements over sexual practices are resolved either by the wife's unilateral deference to her husband's wishes (since in rabbinic tradition a wife is generally discouraged from verbalizing her sexual demands—TB *Eruvin* 100b) or by negotiation and mutual consent.

Halakhah of Caring Communication

The halakhic guidelines about when, what, and in what style spouses should converse has been most hotly debated since the Talmudic era. Over the last 1,800 years, two polar positions on marital communication stand out: restrictive versus affirmative. In our contemporary era, both positions have generated inventive dimensions in the halakhah of onah.

Restrictive: We've seen some of the stern Talmudic warnings, such as: "Do not converse (*siha*) too much with the woman . . . even one's own wife. . . . Anytime a person converses too much with women—it causes him damage, nullifies words of Torah, and eventually he inherits hell" (*Mishnah Avot* 1:5). Ascetic Rabbis threatened couples that their bedrooms were "bugged"—God would be quoting their pillow talk back to them, for which they would be punished in Heaven—and they counseled silence during intercourse as a pious discipline (TB *Nedarim* 20a). In the mid-twentieth century as well, the rebbe of Gur instructed his Hasidim to minimize discussion with their wives at any time, especially avoiding oral communication during onah, and to depersonalize marital relations by blocking verbal intimacy between spouses: "The husband should not address his wife by her first name."[33]

Affirmative: By contrast, in the Talmud, in medieval kabbalist manuals about onah, in modern rabbinic how-to handbooks, and in Liberal Judaism's sex-education curriculums, conversations with one's spouse have been *mandated* to enhance true emotional and erotic intimacy in loving relationships. The rationales for this affirmative practice of spousal dialogue reflect nuanced appreciation of couple communication for a variety of reasons.

1. Maintaining or restoring shalom bayit. The Hazon Ish urges the husband "to tell [his wife] whenever he leaves [the house] where he is going, and, upon his return [to tell her] what he has done, and other little things and words of reinforcement—to make her heart happy."[34] Other rabbis mandate conversations that precede intercourse as a means of remedying stress, airing and apologizing for past grievances, and thus restoring shalom bayit.

2. Enhancing eros in one's wife. According to Rabbi Yohanan, a husband must win his wife's consent to onah by wooing her as modeled by "the rooster who woos/appeases/courts [the hen] before performing intercourse" by prancing, stretching his wings, and scraping his feet (TB *Eruvin* 100b). The Zohar recommends that one court one's wife verbally with extraordinary compliments as modeled by Adam when he first wooed Eve: "Now he begins to praise her: *This shall be named 'Woman' (Gen. 2:23)*—she is incomparable! In her presence all other women are as monkeys compared to humans, but she is complete perfection. This one and no other!"[35]

3. Encouraging wives to make their desires known to their husbands. In the Talmud, Rabbi Yonatan encourages wives to be assertive in persuading their husbands to perform their timely marital duties. Citing Jacob's wife Leah, who demands sex explicitly—*To me you will come for I hired you* for the night (Gen. 30:16)—as exemplifying the value of sexual hutzpah, he promises: "Any woman who demands [sexual intercourse] of her husband for the sake of a mitz-vah is rewarded with sons of excellence!" (TB *Nedarim* 20b; also TB *Eruvin* 100b). While accepting Rabbi Yonatan's argument, the Talmud seeks to harmonize this ethos of female assertiveness with the conservative midrash that holds that women are cursed since the Garden of Eden: *Your [the woman's] desire is to your husband, but he shall rule over you* (Gen. 3:16). Therefore "she may demand sex in her heart [silently], while he makes his sexual demands in his mouth [verbally and explicitly]" (TB *Nedarim* 20b; also TB *Eruvin* 100b). The standard halakhic compromise commends the modest wife to intimate her desire for onah by indirect communication, specifically by employing nonverbal body language (TB *Eruvin* 100b; Rashi on *ritzui*). While silencing women's, not men's, verbal expressions of sexual desire, a characteristically gender-biased policy, wives are still encouraged to take initiative to obtain their sexual satisfaction and to encourage procreation by signaling to their husbands about their sexual urges. As we saw in chapter 4, the Orthodox boudoir photographer Rebecca Sigala helps *frum* (religious) wives prepare sexy albums for their husbands' eyes alone that nonverbally but effectively communicate their love and desire:

> Dressed in a lacy black negligee, her hair styled in loose waves and her eyes done up with smoky powder, she lounges on a bed in an apartment in suburban Jerusalem and gazes coyly at a photographer's camera. "Come closer," the photographer Rebecca Sigala says to her. "Imagine the lens is your husband, and give him a smile."[36]

4. Negotiating differences in sexual practices. Elliot Dorff and Danya Ruttenberg's couples study book, *Sex and Intimacy*, offers a hypothetical case study of a husband and wife who differ radically in their desires for and their comfort level in participating in certain sexual behaviors such as spanking, role playing, and using degrading language. Given these differences, they educate couples to study texts together and negotiate their divergent paths to mutual orgasm.[37]

5. Negotiating differences resulting from the gender gap. Many Haredim regard the gender gap as a permanent and divinely mandated difference. Thus the Hazon Ish mandates spousal conversations to help husbands and wives "learn" each other's divergent expectations and needs, just as yeshiva students "learn" Talmud with analytic acumen. At least for the first year they should investigate each other's world, so the husband will know how to fulfill his halakhic obligation to make his wife happy.[38] In fact, conversations aimed at reaching a comfortable modus vivendi based on mutual understanding may take two to ten years, admits Shuchatowitz.

6. Negotiating emerging differences as each spouse changes over time. Unlike Haredim who think gender differences are fixed, modernists believe that each spouse never stops changing. The poet Rainer Maria Rilke expresses this well:

> Self-transformation is precisely what life is, and human relationships, which are an extract of life, are the most changeable of all, rising and falling from minute to minute, and lovers are those in whose relationship and contact no one moment resembles another.[39]

Therefore, communicating and negotiating differences become life-long disciplines necessary for the longevity of marital life. While such conversations may build bridges, they do not often erase dissimilarities. As Rilke observes:

> Marriage [is] not about creating a quick community of spirit by tearing down and destroying all boundaries. . . . Once the realization is accepted that even between the closest human beings infinite distances continue to exist, a wonderful living side-by-side can grow up, if they succeed in loving the distance between them which makes it possible for each to see the other whole and against a wide sky![40]

Rilke's insight into the need to honor "infinite distances" between unique individuals is also characteristically rabbinic. The rabbis said: "God created each human being in the image of the first human being and yet no one is identical with any other" (*Mishnah Sanhedrin* 4:5). As Rabbi Maurice Lamm explains in *The Jewish Way in Love and Marriage*, Rilke's image of "living side-by-side" counterbalances the romantic and Biblical ideal of becoming *one flesh* (Gen. 2:25) by echoing God's intent to create woman as *a helpmate opposite him* (Gen. 2:18). Lamm states: "An opposite independent person with whom one chooses to side at will" is necessary for "true *yihud* (unifying) love [that] embraces, [but] never stifles, one's individuality."[41]

Managing the dynamic differences between two unique individuals when yoked together in marriage necessitates wise advice and disciplined marital practices. In my judgment, when rabbis over the last 1,800 years have functioned as educators and pastors, more than as lawgivers and spiritual inquisitors, and when they have promoted affirmative practices, rather than restrictive piety, they have made positive contributions to cultivating spousal love. Achieving couple communication is, according to Soloveitchik, the key to marriage as true friendship and true partnership in building community:

> The union between Adam and Eve . . . established a community of destiny, of feelings . . .—a union of two lonely hearts which beat with the same rhythm. . . . A person needs a *haver li-de'agah* [a friend to share one's anxiety] . . . in whom one can confide both in times of crisis . . . and in times of glory. . . . Of course, marriage, if it is to last, [must also be] a community of commitments . . . dedicated to a great vision and a noble idea.[42]

Halakhah's Labors of Love

Resources of marital wisdom such as Rabbinic aggadah and halakhah seem all the more vital, given that the persistence of love within marriage does not appear to be a natural phenomenon found in the vast majority of human relationships. Perhaps long-lasting love entails a great and rare miracle, as the American Jewish humorist Sam Levenson once quipped: "Love at first sight is easy to understand; it's when two people have been looking at each other for a lifetime that it becomes a miracle."[43]

Many Western romantics think that their match was, so to speak, made in heaven, and that love conquers all. In a different way, many traditional Jews since the time of the Talmud have trusted that God has chosen their mates—that "forty days before the fetus is formed a heavenly voice announces this daughter is to be married to that person" (TB *Sotah* 2a)—and thus couples are naturally and supernaturally *bashert*, destined for this partner by divine providence. Therefore, as Hava Vasserman, an anthropologist of the Gur Hasidim, observes, when Gur couples are confronted with difficulties and disappointments, they are taught to bear them with patient resignation and faith, since the heavenly matchmaker has arranged everything for the couple's ultimate good.[44]

Yet the Talmud itself observes that the romantic love of the honeymoon period seems destined to evaporate: "When our love was strong, we could lay together [on a bed] the width of a sword, but now that our love is no longer strong, even a bed sixty-feet wide is not enough for us" (TB *Sanhedrin* 7a). Therefore the Talmud warns us not to approach the vicissitudes of love and marital strife fatalistically. Just as the Rabbis say, "If the ladder is rickety, don't rely on miracles" (TB *Kiddushin* 39b), so, by analogy, marriages are usually rickety and fragile, even dangerous, and in need of constant repair (*tikkun*). The danger in a mismanaged marriage is noted by the mystic playwright and pietist Rabbi Moshe Hayyim Luzzato (Italy, 1707–46), who says, "All things between husband and wife are in themselves the Holy of Holies, but human beings can turn them into the source of all impurity."[45] Thus, the continued success of matrimony is not predetermined by Providence having found the right match but requires diligent devotion—prescience, skilled craftsmanship, and regular tending. As Rilke writes, "Those who love must act as if they had a great work to accomplish," and the Zohar teaches, "There is no labor like the [sacred] labor (*avodah*) of love."[46]

While to the Zohar, human labor devoted to the service of God is necessary to bring together the male and female dimensions of the Divine, on the earthly level, in my opinion, much of the halakhah and aggadah of onah teach us that the labors of love necessary to cultivate and maintain a flourishing love relationship are spiritual and emotional, physical and imaginative, verbal and erotic. Essential to our "homework," our homemaking labor, is the regularity of onah as lovemaking performed willingly with declarations of affection and expressions of delight and desire. Marital communication is necessary to identify and solve problems and share intimacy. Then, by healing the microcosm of rickety marriages, sexual intimacy may also contribute to the higher purposes of *tikkun olam*: enhancing peace in the cosmos and repairing humanity's brokenness.

Notes

Introduction

1. Reported to the author by Dov Zinger of Tekoa (July, 2015, at Hartman Institute). See Zohar I, 50a.
2. Adler, *Engendering Judaism*, 190. See T B *Ketubot* 8a.
3. See Maimonides, *Mishneh Torah*: Marriage 12:6.
4. Perel, *The State of Affairs*, 36; see Giddens, *The Transformation of Intimacy*.
5. Plaskow, *Standing Again at Sinai*, 179, 181.
6. Teutsch, *A Guide to Jewish Practice*, xx.
7. Maimonides, *Guide for the Perplexed* 3:31.
8. Maimonides, *Mishneh Torah*: Laws of Substitute Offerings 4:13.
9. See Greenberg, *Wrestling with God and Men: Homosexuality and the Jewish Tradition*; and Lisa Grushcow's anthology, *The Sacred Encounter: Jewish Perspectives on Sexuality*.
10. See Fonrobert, *Menstrual Purity*.
11. See Boyarin, *Carnal Israel*; and Diamond, *Holy Men and Hunger Artists*.
12. Sher, *Kedushat Yisra'el*, 18.
13. Zohar III, 81b.

1. Legislating Marital Sexuality

1. Plutarch, *Advice to Bride and Groom*, 756e, 769a–e.
2. Rashi on Gen. 2:23, based on T B *Yevamot* 62b.
3. Adapted from the translation by Fox, *The Five Books of Moses*.
4. Idel, *Kabbalah and Eros*, 20.
5. Friedman, *Commentary on the Torah*, 242. Biblical philology, however, defines *onatah* as "oil, ointment," that is, her cosmetics (see Paul, "Exodus 21:10 A Threefold Maintenance Clause," 52).
6. Nahmanides on Exod. 21:9–10.
7. Sher, *Kedushat Yisra'el*, 6.
8. Ritba, *Hidushei HaRitba* on T B *Ketubot* 48a.

9. Diamond, "Nahmanides and Rashi," 193–224.

10. Nahmanides on Gen. 2:18.

11. Nahmanides on Gen. 2:18, 24.

12. Diamond, "Nahmanides and Rashi," 209.

13. Maimonides, *Mishneh Torah*: Marriage 15:7; Yom Tov Asevilli (Ritba) on TB *Yevamot* 61b.

14. Isaac bar Sheshet Perfet, *Responsa of Ribash* #15; see Isserles on *Shulhan Arukh*: Even HaEzer 154:10.

15. Maimonides, *Mishneh Torah*: Marriage 4:1.

16. Maimonides, *Mishneh Torah*: Marriage 3:19. See TB *Kiddushin* 41a; TB *Yevamot* 57b.

17. Maimonides, *Mishneh Torah*: Marriage 3:1.

18. Maimonides, *Mishneh Torah*: Marriage 10:7.

19. Maimonides, *Mishneh Torah*: Marriage 12:6.

20. Maimonides, *Mishneh Torah*: Marriage 12:5–7.

21. Maimonides, *Mishneh Torah*: Marriage 12:6.

22. Maimonides, *Guide for the Perplexed*, 3:49.

23. Gershom, *Responsa of Meor haGolah*, #42.

24. Karo, *Shulhan Arukh*: Even HaEzer 1:10.

25. "Bigamy and Polygamy," Jewish Virtual Library, https://www.jewishvirtuallibrary.org/bigamy-and-polygamy, accessed September 20, 2020.

26. Maimonides, *Mishneh Torah*: Divorce 1:1–2.

27. Gershom, *Responsa of Meor haGolah*, #42.

28. Maimonides, *Mishneh Torah*: Marriage 14:8; see Divorce 2:20.

29. Maimonides, *Mishneh Torah*: Marriage 14:2.

30. Feinstein, *Igrot Moshe*: Even HaEzer, 3, #28.

31. Feinstein, *Igrot Moshe*: Orah Haim, 4, #75.

32. Feinstein, *Igrot Moshe*: Even HaEzer, 3, #28.

33. Mabit, *Kiryat Sefer*, Marriage Laws 14, cited in Stav and Stav, *Avo Beitekha*, 403ff. See TB *Nedarim* 15b.

34. Ra'avad, *Ba'alei HaNefesh*, 124.

35. Maimonides, *Mishneh Torah*: Marriage 15:1.

36. Cited in Medini, *Sdei Hemed*, 337.

37. De Boton, *Lekhem Mishne*, gloss on Maimonides, *Mishneh Torah*: Marriage 14:2.

38. Cited in Frankel, *Simha Temima*, 103n2.

39. Nietzsche, *Human, All Too Human*, 158.

40. Mill, *Collected Works*, 18:223–24.

41. Mill, *Collected Works*, 10:156.

42. Mill, *Collected Works*, 19:402–3.

43. Illouz, *Why Love Hurts*, 18–19, 161.

44. Sofer, *Mahane Haim Responsa 2*, Even HaEzer #41.

45. Feinstein, *Igrot Moshe*: Orah Haim, 4, #75.

46. Feinstein, *Igrot Moshe*: Even HaEzer, 3, #28.

47. Joseph di Trani, *Responsa of the Maharit*, 1:5.

48. Feinstein, *Igrot Moshe*: Even HaEzer, 3, #28.

49. Feinstein, *Igrot Moshe*: Even HaEzer, 3, #28.

50. Feinstein, *Igrot Moshe*: Even HaEzer, 3, #28.

51. Cited by Abraham Hirsch ben Jacob Eisenstadt of Byelostok, *Pitkhei Teshuvah* on *Shulhan Arukh*: Even HaEzer #76 (3).

52. Feinstein, *Igrot Moshe*: Even HaEzer, 3, #28.

53. Perel, *Mating in Captivity*, 215.

54. Perel, *Mating in Captivity*, 215.

55. Perel, *Mating in Captivity*, 215.

56. Young and Young, *Sexperiment*, 5.

57. Young and Young, *Sexperiment*, 51, 40.

58. Young and Young, *Sexperiment*, 60.

59. Young and Young, *Sexperiment*, 4.

60. Young and Young, *Sexperiment*, 35.

61. Young and Young, *Sexperiment*, 61, 62.

2. Talmudic Proprieties of Pillow Talk

1. In parallel descriptions of erotic intimacy between spouses, the term *sahak* (played) and the gloss "hugged, kissed and conversed about empty things," that is, erotic talk, are equivalent (*Avot d'Rabbi Natan*, A Chap. 2; B Chap. 3).

2. Moshe Halbertal, "Philosophical, Political and Human Perspectives on the Notion of Home," presentation delivered at Paideia, The European Institute for Jewish Studies in Sweden, "Home: A Simple Notion Contested" Conference, September, 2016, https://www.youtube.com/watch?v=P_bwIWUelT8.

3. Maimonides, *Mishneh Torah*: Neighbors 2:14.

4. Kass, *The Beginning of Wisdom*, 109.

5. Maimonides, *Mishneh Torah*: Marriage 14:5; see *Commentary on the Mishnah: Ketubot* 7:3; and T B *Ketubot* 71b–72a.

6. Epstein, *Arukh HaShulhan*: Orah Haim #3 (13).

7. Elijah, *Hidushei HaGra, Imrei Noam* (citing T B *Brakhot* 7b) cited in Schottenstein, *Talmud Brakhot* 2:62a.

8. T J *Brakhot* 2:8,5c (22b), cited by Friedman, "The Further Adventures of Rav Kahana," 255.

9. Maimonides, *Mishneh Torah*: Character Traits 4:19.

10. Kosman, *Woman's Tractate*, 131–32, 127–28.

11. Zeldin, *An Intimate History of Humanity*, 102–3.

12. Tzefira, "Coercion in Sexual Relations," 24: 222–27.

13. Karo, *Shulhan Arukh*: Even HaEzer, #25.

14. Sher, *Kedushat Yisra'el*, 20.

15. Quran 4:24; T B *Yevamot* 37b. See also Encyclopaedia of Islam under divorce and marriage.

16. See Cohen, *Zakhu Shekhina Beineihem*, 44–52.

17. Maimonides, *Mishneh Torah*: Marriage 15:17.

18. Muffs, *Love and Joy*, 121–94.

19. Maimonides, *Mishneh Torah*: Marriage 14:8. See also Joseph di Trani, *Responsa of the Maharit* 1:50.

20. Maimonides, *Guide for the Perplexed*, 2:36, 40.

21. Maimonides, *Mishneh Torah*: Character Traits 5:4.

22. Maimonides, *Mishneh Torah*: Marriage 15:18; see Forbidden Intercourse 21:13.

23. Elazar Hasid, *Sefer HaRokeah Hagadol*: Teshuvah, #14.

24. Maimonides, *Mishneh Torah*: Forbidden Intercourse 21:12; see T B *Nedarim* 20b.

25. Personal communication with the author's wife, Marcelle Zion, a marital therapist.

26. Sirkis, *Bayit Hadash Commentary* on Tur: Orah Haim #280.

27. Hirsch, *Commentary on Avot*, 1:5.

3. Modesty or License in the Marital Bed

1. Samuel, "Lidmuta shel Imma Shalom," 125.

2. Tractate *Kallah Rabbati* as translated by Yaakov Shapiro in Shapiro, *Halakhic Positions*, 47–48.

3. See Gen. 30:37–42; Gen. 31:11–12; *Genesis Rabbah* 26:7.

4. Nissim Gaon, cited in Bezalel Ashkenazi, *Shita Mekubetzet* on TB *Nedarim* 20a–b; Maimonides, *Mishneh Torah*: Prohibited Intercourse 21:10; Karo, *Shulhan Arukh*: Orah Haim #240:7, and Even HaEzer #25:3.

5. Ruth Calderon lecture, Hartman Institute, Jerusalem, July 1, 2015.

6. Heschel, *Abraham Joshua Heschel: Essential Writings*, 54–56.

7. Cited in Steinsalz Talmud, TB *Nedarim* 20b, 119–20.

8. Muffs, *Love and Joy*, 122.

9. Brezis, *Between Zealotry and Grace*, 255ff.

10. Qumran Thanksgiving Hymn 1QH 3.30ff, http://orion.mscc.huji.ac.il/cave /megila4.shtml; see also Jubilees 4:21.

11. Calderon lecture, Hartman Institute.

12. Meiri, *Beit HaBehira*, on TB *Pesahim* 49b.

13. Shapiro, *Halachic Positions*, 54, 59–60.

14. Zohar 3: 259a.

15. Maimonides, *Mishneh Torah*: Character Traits 6:10.

16. Maimonides, *Mishneh Torah*: Rebels 2:4.

17. Maimonides, *Mishneh Torah*: Marriage 14:5.

18. Maimonides, *Mishneh Torah*: Forbidden Intercourse 21:9.

19. Maimonides, *Mishneh Torah*: Character Traits 5:4.

20. Maimonides, *Mishneh Torah*: Marriage 14:8.

21. Tractate *Kallah* 1:8; Ra'avad, *Ba'alei HaNefesh*, 121; TB *Eruvin* 100b.

22. Contra Naftali Berlin's claim that one's wife is obligated, like a female slave, to fulfill her husband's sexual demands at any time. *Meishiv Davar* 4: #35, based on TB *Nedarim* 15b. But most halakhic authorities do not specify a wife's obligation to satisfy her husband. *Responsa Mabit* 1, #5; Maimonides, *Mishneh Torah*: Character Traits 5:4; Stav and Stav, *Avo Beitekha*, 403ff.

23. Epstein, *Arukh HaShulhan*: Orah Haim #240, Even HaEzer #25.

24. Sirkis, *Bayit Hadash* gloss on Orah Haim #240 #4; Avraham David Wahrman of Buczacz, *Ezer M'kudash*, Even HaEzer #25 (2).

25. See *Igeret HaKodesh* [*The Holy Letter*], attributed to Nahmanides.

26. TB *Nedarim* 20b; Epstein, *Arukh HaShulhan*: Even HaEzer #25:9.

27. Jacob ben Asher, Tur: Even ha-Ezer #25; see Karo, *Shulhan Arukh*: Orah Haim #240.

28. Henkin, *Responsa Bnai Banim* 4: 16 #4.

29. Kiel, *Sexuality*, 103–4.

30. Maimonides, *Mishneh Torah*: Character Traits 3:2.

31. Maimonides, *Mishneh Torah*: Character Traits 5:4.

32. Maimonides, *Mishneh Torah*: Forbidden Intercourse 21:24.

33. Maimonides, *Responsa of Maimonides*, 3, #57.

34. Maimonides, *Mishneh Torah*: Forbidden Intercourse 21:19.

35. Cohen, "Rationales for Marital Sex," 65ff.

36. Hoshen, "External Structure versus Binary Structure in Sexuality," 15.

37. Ra'avad, *Ba'alei HaNefesh*, 116.

38. Ra'avad, *Ba'alei HaNefesh*, 116–17.

39. Ra'avad, *Ba'alei HaNefesh*, 120.

40. Ra'avad, *Ba'alei HaNefesh*, 120.

41. Ra'avad, *Ba'alei HaNefesh*, 124.

42. Karo, *Shulhan Arukh*: Even HaEzer 77:2; Ben-Shimon, *Bat Na'avat HaMardut*, 20–22.

43. Ben-Shimon, *Bat Na'avat HaMardut*, 14.

44. Ben-Shimon, *Bat Na'avat HaMardut*, 14.

45. Hale, *History of the Pleas of the Crown*, 629.

46. Ben-Shimon, *Bat Na'avat HaMardut*, 15.

47. Ben-Shimon, *Bat Na'avat HaMardut*, 15.

48. Ben-Shimon, *Bat Na'avat HaMardut*, 9.

49. Ben-Shimon, *Bat Na'avat HaMardut*, 5, 130, 132.

50. Herzog, *Heikhal Yitzhak*, Even HaEzer #1.

51. Yosef, *Yabia Omer*, III, Even HaEzer #1.

52. Waldenberg, *Tzitz Eliezer*, IV, #21.

53. Kapah, *Commentary on Maimonides Mishneh Torah*, Marriage 14:14.

54. ICAR mission statement, The International Coalition for Agunah Rights, http://www.icar.org.il/.

55. Ben-Shimon, *Bat Na'avat HaMardut*, 132, 105.

56. Soloveitchik, *Family Redeemed*, 50.

57. Soloveitchik, *Family Redeemed*, 93.

58. The term "intercourse" derives from medieval Latin's *intercursus*, which literally means the "act of running between," like a "*cur*-rent" running back and forth.

59. Calderon, *A Talmudic Alpha Beta*, 80. See TB *Brakhot* 3a.

4. Talmudic Techniques of Arousal

1. Marcus Jastrow translates: "a grain seed"; Michael Sokoloff: "a measure of grain"; Ritba on TB *Shabbat* 140b: "burned dough (charcoal)"; Adin Steinsalz: "a clod of earth"; Shlomo Aviner: "a small fish."

2. Kamasutra 4.1.23:24, cited in Prabhu, "Significance of Sexual Pleasure," 30.

3. Aviner, *Ahoti Kallah (Leil Klulot)*, 58.

4. Satlow, *Tasting the Dish*, 303, citing Ovid, *The Art of Love* 3:769–92.

5. Mordechai Eliyahu, *Darkhei Tahara*, cited in Har-Shefi, "Kavanah v'Hitkavnut b'Yahasei Ishut," 151.

6. Admiel Kosman notes that a married woman who does not adorn herself for her husband "will be cursed" (*Tosefta Nashim, Kiddushin* 1:11); a married woman may not take a vow that she will not wear colorful clothing (*Mishnah Ketubot* 7:8); and when a married woman no longer adorns herself, it is regarded as a sign that her sexual relations with her husband have ceased (*Sifrei* Numbers, *Beha'alotekha* 99). Rabbi Hiyya says, "Women are only for beauty and childbearing" (TB *Ketubot* 59b). See Kosman and Sharbat, "Two Women Who Were Sporting with Each Other"; and Kosman, *Gender and Dialogue in the Rabbinic Prism*, 75.

7. *Sifra* (end of *Metzora*, 9:12, 79c); see also TB *Shabbat* 64b.

8. Soloveitchik, "Tzeiruf," 244–49.

9. Dreyfus, "The Covenant and the Yetzer," 137.

10. Baal Shem Tov, *Keter Shem Tov*, no. 121, 69.

11. Aviner, *Etzem MeiAtzamai*, 23–24.

12. Aviner, *Etzem MeiAtzamai*, 24.

13. Aviner, *Etzem MeiAtzamai*, 24.

14. Shuchatowitz, *Binyan HaBayit*, 75.

15. Shuchatowitz, *Binyan HaBayit*, 79–82. See *Midrash Leviticus Rabbah* 20:11; see TJ *Yoma* 5a.

16. See Psalm 45:10–16.

17. Shuchatowitz, *Binyan HaBayit*, 80.

18. Shuchatowitz, *Binyan HaBayit*, 81.

19. All the quotes in this section originate in Debra Kamin, "In the Boudoir with Orthodox Jewish Women," *The Guardian*, September 2, 2015.

5. A Mirror of the Divine Union

1. Anonymous kabbalist (New York, manuscript, JTS, ca. 1896), cited in Idel, "Eros in Moshe Cordovero" (unpublished manuscript). The prayer in the epigraph of this chapter is attributed to an anonymous kabbalist gloss cited by Idel, *Kabbalah and Eros*, 234.

2. See also Neis, *The Sense of Sight in Rabbinic Culture*, 92.

3. *Midrash Tanhuma* (Buber), Numbers 17a.

4. Idel, *Kabbalah and Eros*, 33.

5. Scholem, *Reshit ha-Kabbalah*, 79.

6. Ra'avad, *Ba'alei HaNefesh*, 14.

7. Ra'avad, quoted by an anonymous student in British Museum Manuscript #768, 14a; Oxford Manuscript #1956, 7a; and Ra'avad, *Ba'alei HaNefesh*, 14.

8. Ra'avad, quoted by anonymous disciple in British Museum Manuscript #768, 14a; Oxford Manuscript #1956, 7a.

9. Idel, "Eros in Moshe Cordovero."

10. Idel, *Kabbalah and Eros*, 86.

11. Idel, *Kabbalah and Eros*, 71.

12. Ra'avad, *Ba'alei HaNefesh*, 15.

13. Ra'avad, *Ba'alei HaNefesh*, 121.

14. Maimonides, *Guide for the Perplexed*, 2:36.

15. Maimonides, *Mishneh Torah*: Foundations of the Torah 1:8, 2:2; Repentance 10:3, 6.

16. Plato, *The Symposium* 210a-d.

17. Maimonides, *Guide for the Perplexed*, 3:8.

18. Vidas, *Reshit Hokhma*, Part 1, *Gate of Love*, chap. 4, 262.

19. Idel, *Kabbalah and Eros*, 74.

20. *Igeret HaKodesh*, chap. 2, 323, 326.

21. *Igeret HaKodesh*, chap. 2, 323, 326.

22. *Igeret HaKodesh*, chap. 6, 335–37.

23. *Igeret HaKodesh*, chap. 6, 335–37.

24. See Zohar, III, 81b.

25. *Igeret HaKodesh*, chap. 6, 335–37.

26. *Igeret HaKodesh*, chap. 6, 335–37.

27. Elazar Hasid, *Sefer HaRokeah HaGadol*, Teshuvah #14, 27.

28. Gikatelia, *Sod reuya hayta Bat Sheva l'David*, 181–86.

29. Liebes, "Zohar and Eros," 80–81.

30. Zohar II, 155a—b.

31. Hellner-Eshed, *A River Flows from Eden*, 279.

32. See TB *Shabbat* 117–18b; TB *Ketubot* 62b.

33. See Lev. 15:16–18; Temple Scroll 48:7–12, http://dss.collections.imj.org.il/temple?id=0; TB *Baba Kama* 82a; TB *Niddah* 38a–b.

34. Kosman, "The Israelite People Shall Keep the Sabbath," 153–54n50.

35. Meleager of Gadara, cited in Stern, *Greek and Latin Authors on Jews and Judaism*, 1:140.

36. Moses ibn Makhir, *Seder HaYom*, 21b, cited in Fine, *Physician of the Soul*, 203.

37. Cited in Idel, *Kabbalah and Eros*, 221.

38. Idel, *Kabbalah and Eros*, 249.

39. Abraham Azulai, *Or ha-Hamah*, 2:12c, cited in Fine, *Physician of the Soul*, 202.

40. Idel, "Eros in Moshe Cordovero," chap. 13.

41. Cordovero, *Tefillah L'Moshe*, folio 213a.

42. Fine, "Tikkun: A Lurianic Motif in Contemporary Jewish Thought," 52.

43. Liebes, "Zohar and Eros," 112–13.

44. Cordovero, *Or Yakar*, 194, cited in Idel, "Eros in Moshe Cordovero."

45. Idel, *Kabbalah and Eros*, 229.

46. Idel, *Kabbalah and Eros*, 229.

47. Idel, *Kabbalah and Eros*, 296.

48. Cited in Hecker, "Kissing Kabbalists," 190.

49. Hecker, "Kissing Kabbalists," 190.

50. Hecker, "Kissing Kabbalists," 190.

51. Tishby, *The Wisdom of the Zohar*, 2:611–12.

52. Liebes, "Zohar and Eros," 99, 78.

53. Liebes, "Zohar and Eros," 81.

54. Liebes, "Zohar and Eros," 82–83.

55. Liebes, "Zohar and Eros," 83, 101.

56. Epicurus, cited in Lindberg, *Love: A Brief History through Western Christianity*, 3.

57. See Lindberg, *Love: A Brief History through Western Christianity*, 160–61.

58. Idel, "Eros in Moshe Cordovero."

59. The tanna Rabbi Yosi (2nd century, Land of Israel) was obligated to engage in intercourse with his deceased brother's widow via a hole in a sheet. On one hand, he fulfilled his levirate obligation to marry his widowed, childless sister-in-law and provide an heir for his childless brother. Yet, on the other hand, he minimized the incestuous sexual pleasure of such intercourse by separating his body from hers with a perforated sheet, lest his desire sully the mitzvah he was performing (TJ *Yevamot* 1.1, 2a).

60. Idel, "Eros in Moshe Cordovero."

61. Tishby, *The Wisdom of the Zohar*, 2:611–12.

62. *Tikunei Zohar*, 67.

63. Zohar II, 94b, from Scholem, *The Book of Splendor*, 89–91.

64. Hellner-Eshed, "If You Awaken and Arouse Love: The Language of Arousal in the Book of the Zohar," 333–34.

65. Idel, *Kabbalah and Eros*, 210.

66. Hellner-Eshed, "If You Awaken and Arouse Love," 333.

67. Tishby, *The Wisdom of the Zohar*, 2:611–12, citing Zohar III, 143a–b.

68. Hellner-Eshed, *A River Flows from Eden*, 202–3.

69. Hellner-Eshed, "If You Awaken and Arouse Love," 333.

70. Idel, "Eros in Moshe Cordovero."

71. Idel, *Kabbalah and Eros*, 146.

72. Quoted in Tirosh-Samuelson, "Gender in Jewish Mysticism," 205.

73. Wolfson, "Woman: The Feminine as Other in Theosophic Kabbalah," 190.

74. Wolfson, "Woman: The Feminine as Other in Theosophic Kabbalah," 169.

75. *Sefer ha-Qanah* 98b, cited in Idel, *Kabbalah and Eros*, 230.

76. Idel, *Kabbalah and Eros*, 230.

77. See Vital, *Etz Hayim* and *Sha'ar ha-Mitzvot*.

78. Vital, *Ta'amei HaMitzvot, Parshat Breshit* 15b, cited in Fine, *Physician of the Soul*, 197.

79. The demons born to man from the wasted seed of masturbation are considered his illegitimate sons (*banim shovavim*, "mischievous sons"). At the death and burial of their father who wasted the seed, they claim their share of the inheritance; and may also injure the legitimate sons. Thus arose the custom of circling the dead at the cemetery to repulse the demons and also the custom (dating from the 17th century in a number of communities) of not allowing the sons to accompany their father's corpse to the cemetery for burial lest they be harmed by their illegitimate, demonic step-brothers. https://www.jewishvirtuallibrary.org/demons-and-demonology.

80. The head of the conjugal bed must face north, according to *Shulkhan Arukh*: Orah Haim #240.

81. Fine, *Physician of the Soul*, 203–5.

82. Abrams, "A Light of Her Own," 29.

83. Idel, *Kabbalah and Eros*, 237.

84. Idel, *Kabbalah and Eros*, 237.

85. Idel, *Kabbalah and Eros*, 245.

86. Gikatelia, *Sod HaReut*, 181–86. See also Horowitz, *Shnei Lukhot HaBrit, Ki Teitze*.

87. Abrams, *The Female Body of God*, 176.

88. Abrams, *The Female Body of God*, 180.

89. Werblowsky, *Yosef Karo: Lawyer and Mystic*, 134.

90. Werblowsky, *Yosef Karo: Lawyer and Mystic*, 135, 137.

91. Idel, *Kabbalah and Eros*, 93.

92. Idel, *Kabbalah and Eros*, 235.

93. Garb, *The Chosen Will Become Herds*, 101.

94. See Merissa Nathan Gerson, "Better Sex Through Kabbalah," *Tablet Magazine*, December 4, 2014, https://www.tabletmag.com/jewish-life-and-religion/187223/better-sex-through-kabbalah.

95. Huss, "The New Age of Kabbalah," 111.

96. Garb, *The Chosen Will Become Herds*, 110, 119, 120.

97. Garb, *The Chosen Will Become Herds*, 16n31.

98. Garb, *The Chosen Will Become Herds*, 29.

99. Yehuda Leib Ashlag, *Sefer Pri Hakham*, 2: 121, cited in Garb, *The Chosen Will Become Herds*, 29.

100. Myers, "Marriage and Sexual Behavior in the Teachings of the Kabbalah Centre," 261.

101. Ashlag, *Introduction to the Book of Zohar*, 2:119.

102. Ashlag, *Introduction to the Book of Zohar*, 2:119.

103. Garb, *The Chosen Will Become Herds*, 53–54.

104. Ashlag, *Matan Torah*, 2.

105. Ashlag, *Matan Torah*, 34.

106. Myers, "Marriage and Sexual Behavior," 262.

107. Ashlag, *Kuntres Arevut*, 37–38.

108. Ahituv, "Rav Ashlag and Levinas on the Duty to One's Fellow," 471.

109. Myers, "Marriage and Sexual Behavior," 264.

110. Myers, "Marriage and Sexual Behavior," 259.

111. Myers, "Marriage and Sexual Behavior," 266. See Berg, *The Kabbalah Book of Sex*, 197, 204, 219.

112. Berg, *The Kabbalah Book of Sex*, 5–6.

113. Berg, *The Kabbalah Book of Sex*, 219.

114. Berg, *The Kabbalah Book of Sex*, 220.

115. Myers, "Marriage and Sexual Behavior," 271.

116. Berg, *The Kabbalah Book of Sex*, 221.

117. Berg, *The Kabbalah Book of Sex*, 221 and 6.

118. Berg, *The Kabbalah Book of Sex*, 179.

119. Schachter-Shalomi, *First Steps to a New Jewish Spirit*, 116.

120. Zalman Schachter-Shalomi and Eve Ilsen, interviewer, "Sacred Sex: Making Love Can Be a Gateway to Unity with the Great Mysteries," interview with Rabbi Zalman Schachter-Shalomi, *Yes* magazine, October 20, 1997, https://www.yesmagazine.org/all-issues/.

121. Zalman Schachter-Shalomi, "Sexuality and Holiness," in *The Rebbe Looks Back & The Rebbe Looks Forward*, a three-part interview of Reb Zalman (June 13, 2007) by Alter Shoresh Barry Barkan, https://www.youtube.com/watch?v=7SO0VRZwHq8.

122. Schachter-Shalomi, "Sexuality and Holiness."

123. Schachter-Shalomi, "Sexuality and Holiness."

124. Schachter-Shalomi, "Sexuality and Holiness."

125. Schachter-Shalomi, "Sexuality and Holiness."

126. Zalman Schachter-Shalomi and Eve Ilsen, "Sacred Union: The One in the Many," *Yes* magazine, October 27, 1997, http://www.yesmagazine.org/issues/sustainable-sex/sacred-sex, accessed February 15, 2018.

127. Schachter-Shalomi and Eve Ilsen, "Sacred Sex."

128. Dennis, "Your Love Is Sweeter Than Wine: Erotic Theology in Jewish Tradition," 131.

129. Dennis, "Your Love Is Sweeter Than Wine," 139.

130. Dennis, "Your Love is Sweeter than Wine," 139.

131. Dennis, "Your Love is Sweeter than Wine," 141.

6. Freestyle Eroticism?

1. See TB *Yevamot* 34a–b; Rabbenu Nissim on TB *Sanhedrin* 58b.

2. See Isaac Alfasi, *Sefer HaHalakhot on* TB *Nedarim 20a–b*, cited by Shapiro, *Halachic Positions*, 65, 94.

3. Maimonides, *Commentary on the Mishna*: Sanhedrin 7:4.

4. Maimonides, *Commentary on the Mishna*: Sanhedrin 7:4; see Maimonides, *Mishneh Torah*: Forbidden Relations 21:9.

5. Maimonides, *Mishneh Torah*: Character Traits 5:4.

6. Maimonides, *Mishneh Torah*: Character Traits 4:19; 3:2.

7. Maimonides, *Mishneh Torah*: Character Traits 5:4.

8. Maimonides, *Mishneh Torah*: Character Traits 5:4–5.

9. Maimonides, *Mishneh Torah*: Shabbat 30:14–15; see TB *Ketubot* 65b.

10. Soloveitchik, "Mishneh Torah: Polemic and Art," 340.

11. Isaac the Tosafist, Tosafot on TB *Yevamot* 34b; Maimonides, *Mishneh Torah*: Forbidden Sexual Relations 21:9. Note the phrase in Maimonides about "not wasting seed" may be a late addition probably not compatible with his halakhic views. See Linzer, *Joy of Text*, https://library.yctorah.org/2018/03/the-i-didnt-know-you-could-do-that-episode-part-2-joy-of-text-31/.

12. Isaiah of Trani, Tosafot RID on TB *Yevamot* 12a, cited in Pachter, *Shimirat HaBrit*, 95. See also Rosh on TB *Yevamot*, 3:10; Netziv Berlin, *Responsa Meishiv Davar* 2:88; and Feinstein, *Igrot Moshe*: Even HaEzer 1:63.

13. Tosafot Yeshanim (of Sens, France) on TB *Nedarim* 20a–b (cited in Shapiro, *Halachic Positions*, 141).

14. These three codes are: Isaac Alfasi, *Sefer HaHalakhot* (1088); Maimonides, *Mishneh Torah* (1180); and Jacob ben Asher, *Arba'a Turim* (1340).

15. Ra'avad, *Ba'alei HaNefesh*, 119–20. See Shapiro, *Halachic Positions*, 172–73.

16. Rosenberg (Shagar), "*Mitzvat Onah*," 34.

17. Karo, *Shulhan Arukh*: Orah Haim #240:1.

18. Karo, *Shulhan Arukh*: Even HaEzer #25.

19. *Midrash Derekh Eretz*, Zuta, chap. 3.

20. Karo, *Shulhan Arukh*: Even HaEzer #25.

21. Karo, *Shulhan Arukh*: Even HaEzer #240:1.

22. Karo, *Shulhan Arukh*: Even HaEzer #25.

23. Karo, *Shulhan Arukh*: Orah Haim #240.

24. Karo, *Shulhan Arukh*: Orah Haim #240.

25. Shapiro, *Halachic Positions*, 148.

26. Zohar, *Parshat Vayeshev* and *Vayehi*, based on TB *Niddah* 13a–b. See Zohar I, 61b–62a, 219b; II, 263b.

27. Cited in Pachter, *Shmirat HaBrit*, 6n2.

28. Vital, *Etz Haim*, Heikhal 7, Gate 9, 211b; *Sha'ar HaKavanot* #7, 362–64.

29. Vital, *Sha'arei Kedushah* 2:, Gate 6, 20a.

30. Shapiro, *Halachic Positions*, 152.

31. Vital, *Shaar Ruakh Hakodesh*, Tikkun 27, cited in Shapiro, *Halachic Positions*, 152.

32. Karo, *Shulhan Arukh*: Even HaEzer 23:1.

33. Tosafot, TB *Yevamot* 34b, s.v. *Vi'Lo*.

34. Karo, *Beit Yosef*: Even HaEzer 25.

35. Karo, *Bedek HaBayit* on Tur: Even HaEzer 25:2. See Karo, *Shulhan Arukh*: Even HaEzer 23.

36. Karo, *Maggid Meisharim*, translated by Jacobs, *Jewish Mystical Testimonies*, 132.

37. Karo, *Maggid Meisharim*, translated by Jacobs, *Jewish Mystical Testimonies*, 131, 146.

38. Elazar Azikri, *Sefer Haredim*, cited in Pachter, *Shimirat HaBrit*, 175–76.

39. Based on author's email communication with Professor Zvi Zohar, August 24, 2020.

40. Isserles, gloss on *Shulhan Arukh*: Even HaEzer #25:2.

41. Feibish, *Beit Shmuel*, gloss on *Shulhan Arukh*: Even HaEzer #25:2.

42. Feibish, *Beit Shmuel*, gloss on *Shulhan Arukh*: Even HaEzer #25:2.

43. Shapira, *Eliyah Rabbah*, gloss on *Shulhan Arukh*: Orah Haim #240:2.

44. In an email communication with the author on August 24, 2020, Zohar observed that in *Shulhan Arukh*: Orah Haim 240, "where Caro really goes all-out against pleasure and against spilled seed, etc.—there are no dissenting *glossa* of ReMa [Isserles]."

45. Karo, *Shulhan Arukh*: Even HaEzer 25.

46. Isserles, gloss on *Shulhan Arukh*: Even HaEzer #25:2.

47. Shapiro, *Halachic Positions*, 161–63.

48. All of the quotations in this sidebar are from the Arabic in a translation found in Maimonides, *On Coitus*, in *The Medical Works of Moses Maimonides*, XI. The rest of the text is the author's summary, drawn from both this English translation of the Arabic letter, 26–34, 40,48, 52; and from a Hebrew translation of a variant version of the Arabic letter reprinted in Maimonides, *Kitavim Refuiim*, vol. 4.

49. Maimonides, *On Coitus*, #10 (Arabic), 52.

50. Maimonides, *On Coitus*, #3 (Arabic), 32.

51. Maimonides, *K'tavim Refuiim* 4:60, 62.

7. Ascetic Bedrooms

1. Etkes, *The Besht*, 47, 249–51.

2. Etkes, *The Besht*, 153, 194–202.

3. Etkes, *The Besht*, 50, 72.

4. Etkes, *The Besht*, 256–57.

5. Hundert, *Jews in Poland-Lithuania in the Eighteenth Century*, 168–71; Etkes, *The Besht*, 7.

6. Hundert, *Jews in Poland-Lithuania in the Eighteenth Century*, 163; Etkes, *The Besht*, 43–45.

7. Etkes, *The Besht*, 120.

8. Etkes, *The Besht*, 121.

9. Hundert, *Jews in Poland-Lithuania in the Eighteenth Century*, 135, citing Isaiah Horowitz (1555–1630, Central Europe and Israel), *Shnei Luhot HaBrit: Sha'ar Otiot* #350.

10. Brawer, *Galitsiyah viyehudeha*, 203, cited in Hundert, *Jews in Poland-Lithuania in the Eighteenth Century*, 124.

11. Hundert, *Jews in Poland-Lithuania in the Eighteenth Century*, 172–75; Baal Shem Tov, *Keter Shem Tov*, #51.

12. Baal Shem Tov, *Tzava'at HaRibash*, #56, 10; Jacob Joseph of Polonnye, *Toldot Yaakov Yosef*, 151a; Jacob Joseph of Polonnye, *Ben Porat Yosef* 66b; all cited in Biale, *Eros and the Jews*, 131.

13. Baal Shem Tov, *Sefer Shivhei HaBesht*, 105.

14. Biale, *Eros and the Jews*, 131.

15. Hundert, *Jews in Poland-Lithuania in the Eighteenth Century*, 173–74.

16. Menahem Nahum Twersky, *Me'or 'Eynaim*, *Bereshit* #5, *Mattot* #1, and *Lekh Lekha* #1, quoted in Green, "Buber, Scholem, and the Me'or 'Eynaim"; and Green, *The Light of the Eyes*.

17. Nadler, *The Faith of the Mithnagdim*, 79–80.

18. Barukh of Kosov, *Amud HaAvodah*, 29b, cited by Biale, *Eros and the Jews*, 125.

19. Nadler, *The Faith of the Mithnagdim*, 83.

20. Baal Shem Tov, *Tzava'at HaRibash*, #101.

21. Baal Shem Tov, *Tzava'at HaRibash*, #35, cited in Biale, *Eros and the Jews*, 136.

22. Shneur Zalman, *Tanya: Likkutei Amarim*, chap. 10, cited in Claussen, *Modern Musar*.

23. Shneur Zalman, *Tanya: Likkutei Amarim*, chap. 30, cited in Claussen, *Modern Musar*.

24. Biale, *Eros and the Jews*, 133.

25. Menahem Nahum Twersky of Chernobyl, *Me'or 'Eynaim*, Lekh Lekha, 24.

26. Nahman of Bratzlav, *Shivhei HaRan*, #17, cited in Biale, *Eros and the Jews*, 135.

27. Menahem Mendel of Kotzk, *Emet v'Emunah*, #635, cited in Biale, *Eros and the Jews*, 134.

28. Biale, *Eros and the Jews*, 141–44.

29. Biale, "Hateshukah L'Sagfanut BaTenuah HaHasidit," 215, 221.

30. Brown, "Kedushah," 476.

31. Green, "Buber, Scholem, and the Me'or 'Eynaim."

32. Brown, "Kedushah," 485.

33. Cited in TB *Yevamot* 20a, where brothers-in-law are urged not to enter levirate marriages with widowed, childless sisters-in-law.

34. Nahmanides on Lev. 19:2.

35. Brown, "Kedushah," 475.

36. Biale, *A New History of Hasidism*, 344, 417.

37. Farbsteyn, *Hidden in Thunder*, 82.

38. Brown and Shalem, "Gur BaAretz," 622, 625.

39. Wodziński, *Historical Atlas of Hasidism*, 192, 198.

40. Brown and Shalem, "Gur BaAretz," 641.

41. Brown, "Kedushah," 477.

42. Biale, *A New History of Hasidism*, 717.

43. Brown, "Kedushah," 478. Biale, *A New History of Hasidism*, 717, specifies only a "three-month" prohibition after birth.

44. Brown, "Kedushah," 478.

45. Brown, "Kedushah," 478.

46. Brown, "Kedushah," 478; Biale, *A New History of Hasidism*, 717.

47. Biale, *A New History of Hasidism*, 718, citing Yisrael Alter's "Letter of Guidance and Strengthening" [Hebrew], *Tsefunot* 5 (Tishrei 5750/1989): L 63.

48. Fisher, *Hilun v'Hiloniut*, 112–16.

49. Brown, "Kedushah," 479; Biale, *A New History of Hasidism*, 718.

50. Brown, "Kedushah," 485–86.

51. Brown, "Kedushah," 494.

52. Alter, *Beit Yisra'el: Leviticus*, 158.

53. Nahum Rotstein, *Avnei Zikaron*, 395, cited by Vasserman, *I Have Never Called My Wife: Marital Relations in Gur Hasidism*, 290.

54. Nahum Rotstein, Letter 1, cited in Brown, "Kedushah," 506.

55. Berezovsky, *Netivot Shalom*, 1:112.

56. See TB *Kiddushin* 29b–30a.

57. Brown, "Kedushah," 492, 490.

58. Berezovsky, "Wedding Day Letter," cited in Brown, "Kedushah," 493.

59. Berezovsky, "Three-Months Letter" §10, cited in Brown, "Kedushah" 494.

60. Berezovsky, "Three-Months Letter," §1and 10, cited in Brown, "Kedushah," 490, 494.

61. Berezovsky, "Three-Months Letter," §5-6-7, cited in Brown, "Kedushah," 493. Berezovsky's Talmudic citations include TB *Eruvin* 22a; TB *Shabbat* 83b; TB *Gittin* 57b.

62. Berezovsky, *Netivot Shalom*, 1:111.

63. Berezovsky, "Three-Months Letter," §4, cited in Brown, "Kedushah," 493.

64. Brown, "Kedushah," 488, citing Berezovsky, *Netivot Shalom*, 1:110.

65. Brown and Shalem, "Gur BaAretz," 630.

66. Kohn, *Divrei Kedushah*, chap. 5, 9, quotes the definition of the true *hasid* from Reb Aharon II of Karlin, the Beys Aaron, cited in Brown, "Kedushah," 494.

67. See Zion, *Marital Friendship and Covenantal Partnership*, 39–124.

68. Vasserman, "The 'Abstinent' Society," 276–79.

69. Vasserman, "The 'Abstinent' Society," 311.

70. Vasserman, "The 'Abstinent' Society," 301, 311.

71. Vasserman, *I Have Never Called My Wife*, 292.

72. Ra'avad, *Ba'alei HaNefesh*, 113.

73. Vasserman, "The 'Abstinent' Society," 283ff, citing TB *Yevamot* 20a.

74. Vasserman, "The 'Abstinent' Society," 340–41.

75. Vasserman, "The 'Abstinent' Society," 288–89.

76. Vasserman, "The 'Abstinent' Society," 283ff.

77. Vasserman, "The 'Abstinent' Society," 324.

78. Vasserman, "The 'Abstinent' Society," 298.

79. Vasserman, "The 'Abstinent' Society," 276–79.

80. *Midrash Tana d'bei Eliyahu* 9.

81. Brown, "Kedushah," 478.

82. Berezovsky, "Three-Month Letter," §4, cited in Brown, "Kedushah," 493.

83. Vasserman, "The 'Abstinent' Society," 283.

84. Berezovsky, "Three-Months Letter" §1, cited in Brown, "Kedushah," 489.

85. Biale, *A New History of Hasidism*, 718.

86. Brown and Shalem, "Gur BaAretz," 629.

87. Biale, *A New History of Hasidism*, 718.

88. Brown and Shalem, "Gur BaAretz," 628–30.

89. Wodziński, *Historical Atlas of Hasidism*, 199.

90. Berger, *The Pious Ones*, 2, 158, 194; Shaul Magid, "My Teacher's Son: A Memoir of Heresy Is Marked By a Father's Unnerving Piety," *Tablet*, April 15, 2015, https://www.tabletmag.com/sections/arts-letters/articles/shulem-deen-dovid-din.

91. Deen, *All Who Go Do Not Return*, 37.

92. Deen, *All Who Go Do Not Return*, 37.

93. Deen, *All Who Go Do Not Return*, 39.

94. Deen, *All Who Go Do Not Return*, 48.

95. Deen, *All Who Go Do Not Return*, 48–49.

96. Deen, *All Who Go Do Not Return*, 48–49.

97. Deen, *All Who Go Do Not Return*, 47.

98. Deen, *All Who Go Do Not Return*, 47.

99. Deen, *All Who Go Do Not Return*, 51.

100. Deen, *All Who Go Do Not Return*, 51–52.

8. "Break Their Evil Nature"

1. "'Severe Ban' Approved by the Vilna Gaon—Printed Sheet against Chassidim," Kedem Auction House, https://www.kedem-auctions.com/product/severe-ban-approved-by-the-vilna-gaon-%E2%80%93-printed-sheet-against-chassidim/, accessed February 12, 2020. Capitalization in the original.

2. Hundert, *Jews in Poland-Lithuania in the Eighteenth Century*, 197–202; Etkes, *The Gaon of Vilna*, 5, 73–74, 93, 154, 167–68.

3. Nadler, *The Faith of the Mithnagdim*, 84–85.

4. Hundert, *Jews in Poland-Lithuania in the Eighteenth Century*, 201, citing Wilensky, *Hassidim umitnaggedim*, 1:39, 54–57; 2:60, 75.

5. Hundert, *Jews in Poland-Lithuania in the Eighteenth Century*, 204; Etkes, *The Gaon of Vilna*, 2.

6. Etkes, *The Gaon of Vilna*, 2, 12.

7. Etkes, *The Gaon of Vilna*, 5, 8.

8. Etkes, *The Gaon of Vilna*, 204; Stampfer, *The Lithuanian Yeshiva*, 14–22.

9. Etkes, *The Gaon of Vilna*, 206.

10. Wurzburger, "The Centrality of Creativity in the Thought of Rabbi Joseph B. Soloveitchik," 227.

11. Stampfer, *The Lithuanian Yeshiva*, 208.

12. Etkes, "Marriage and Torah Study among Lomdim," 154, 171.

13. Etkes, "Marriage and Torah Study among Lomdim," 154, 171.

14. Elijah, the Vilna Gaon, *Commentary on Proverbs*, cited in Etkes, "Marriage and Torah Study among Lomdim," 154, 171.

15. *Elijah, the Vilna Gaon, Seder Eliyahu*, 20, 75, cited in Etkes, "Marriage and Torah Study among Lomdim," 153.

16. Elijah, the Vilna Gaon, *Sefer Mishlei im Biur ha-GRA*, 10:16, cited in Nadler, *The Faith of the Mithnagdim*, 87.

17. Haim of Volozhin, *Ruah Haim* (Vilna, 1859), 6–14, cited in Nadler, *The Faith of the Mithnagdim*, 87.

18. Elijah, the Vilna Gaon, *Commentary on Proverbs* 4:13, cited by Brown, *Lithuanian Musar Movement*, 37.

19. Abraham ben Elijah of Vilna, *S'arat Eliyahu*, 11a, cited in Nadler, *The Faith of the Mithnagdim*, 88.

20. Elijah, the Vilna Gaon, *Commentary on Proverbs* 11:22, 4:15, cited in Etkes, *Rabbi Israel Salanter and the Mussar Movement*, 22.

21. Elijah, the Vilna Gaon, *Commentary on Proverbs* 23:30.

22. Nietzsche, *The Gay Science* #266; *Ecce Homo* 1:4.

23. Biale, *Eros and the Jews*, 86–148.

24. Koch, *Human Self-Perfection*, 167.

25. Jonah Gerondi, *Gates of Repentance* 2:XVII, 103.

26. Koch, *Human Self-Perfection*, 170.

27. Koch, *Human Self-Perfection*, 133.

28. Elazar, *Sefer HaRokeah HaGadol*, 27. See also Judah Hasid, *Sefer Hasidim* #19.

29. Anonymous, *Orhot Tzaddikim*, 64 cited in Koch, *Human Self-Perfection*, 205.

30. Vidas, *Reishit Hokhma*: Gate of Repentance, chap. 4, #10, 1:755.

31. Vidas, *Reishit Hokhma*: Gate of Love, chap. 11, #64, 1:633, cited in Koch, *Human Self-Perfection*, 134.

32. Israel Salanter, *Or Yisrael*, 224, cited in Englander, "Changing Concepts of the Ultra-Orthodox Body," 796.

33. Etkes, *Rabbi Israel Salanter and the Mussar Movement*, 96.

34. Salanter, *Igeret Mussar*, cited by Brown, *Lithuanian Musar Movement*, 47. Salanter arranged for the reprinting of Menahem Mendel Lefin's *Book of Moral Accounting* (*Sefer Ḥeshbon Ha-Nefesh*), which cites Franklin's *Autobiography* (see Sinkoff, *Out of the Shtetl*, 134–161; and Etkes, *Rabbi Israel Salanter and the Mussar Movement*, 125).

35. Etkes, *Rabbi Israel Salanter and the Mussar Movement*, 99, 102, 126, 290.

36. Brown, *Lithuanian Musar Movement*, 47–49; Etkes, *Rabbi Israel Salanter and the Mussar Movement*, 93, 97.

37. See a nuanced examination of these questions in Claussen, *Modern Mussar*.

38. Etkes, *Rabbi Israel Salanter and the Mussar Movement*, 209.

39. Gisser, "Social Kashrut," 14; Katz, *Tenu'at Ha-Musar*, 1:329.

40. Levinas, *Nine Talmudic Readings*, 99.

41. Ziv, *Sefer Hokhmah U-Musar*, 1:57, cited in Claussen, *Sharing the Burden*, 44.

42. Claussen, *Sharing the Burden*, 7.

43. Claussen, *Sharing the Burden*, 8, 141, 145.

44. Claussen, *Sharing the Burden*, 30.

45. Ziv, *Sefer Hokhmah U-Musar*, 2:6–8, cited in Claussen, *Sharing the Burden*, 145.

46. Claussen, "The Promise and Limits of Rabbi Simhah Zissel Ziv's Musar," 159–60, quoting Ziv, *Hokhmah U-Musar*, 1:288.

47. Claussen, *Sharing the Burden*, 177.

48. Ziv, *Hokhmah U-Musar*, 1:47, cited in Claussen, "The Promise and Limits of Rabbi Simhah Zissel Ziv's Musar," 161.

49. Katz, *Tenu'at Ha-Musar*, 2:64, cited in Claussen, "The Promise and Limits of Rabbi Simhah Zissel Ziv's Musar," 159.

50. Amital, *Commitment and Complexity*, 53.

51. Rynhold and Harris, *Nietzsche, Soloveitchik, and Contemporary Jewish Philosophy*, 114n150.

52. Brown, *Lithuanian Musar Movement*, 100–101.

53. Quoted in Fishman, "Musar and Modernity: The Case of Navaredok," 52.

54. Fishman, "Musar and Modernity," 44.

55. Fishman, "Musar and Modernity," 54; Katz, *Tenu'at Ha-Mussar*, 5: 173.

56. Grade, *The Yeshiva*, 44.

57. Finkel, *Or HaTsafun*, 2:214, cited in Brown, "Gedulat Ha-Adam v'Ha-Ktanato," 247.

58. Brown, "Gedulat Ha-Adam v'Ha-Ktanato," 244, 252.

59. Veritger, *Ha Saba MiSlabodka*, 117, cited in Brown, "Gedulat Ha-Adam v'Ha-Ktanato," 246.

60. Louis Jacobs, "The Musar Movement," *Wikipedia*, https://en.wikipedia.org/wiki/Musar_movement, accessed February 15, 2020.

61. Brown, *Lithuanian Musar Movement*, 111.

62. Finkel, *Or HaTsafun* 2:123, cited in Brown, "Gedulat Ha-Adam v'Ha-Ktanato" 249.

63. Katz, *Tenu'at Ha-Mussar*, 3:151, 154.

64. Katz, *Tenu'at Ha-Mussar*, 3:103–4.

65. Finkel, *Or HaTsafun*, 2: 127, cited in Brown, "Gedulat Ha-Adam v'Ha-Ktanato," 249–50; Katz, *Tenu'at Ha-Mussar*, 3:155.

66. Brown, "Gedulat Ha-Adam v'Ha-Ktanato," 250.

67. Brown, "Gedulat Ha-Adam v'Ha-Ktanato," 253–71.

68. Etkes, "Marriage and Torah Study among Lomdim," 172.

69. Etkes, "Marriage and Torah Study among Lomdim," 116.

70. Claussen, *Sharing the Burden*, 178.

71. Katz, *Tenu'at Ha-Mussar*, 3:159, 164.

72. Englander, "Changing Concepts of the Ultra-Orthodox Body," 707, citing Finkel, *Or HaTzafun*, 2:218, and Salanter, *Or Yisrael: Writings of Rabbi Israel Salanter*, 119.

73. Etkes, *Rabbi Israel Salanter and the Mussar Movement*, 97–98.

74. Friedman, *Nafshi Yatza Bedabro*, 493, cited in Englander, "Changing Concepts of the Ultra-Orthodox Body," 795.

75. Englander, "Changing Concepts of the Ultra-Orthodox Body," 707, citing Finkel, *Or HaTsafun*, 2:218; and Salanter, *Or Yisrael: Writings of Rabbi Israel Salanter*, 119.

76. Wolbe, *Talks on Guidance for Grooms*, 1.

77. Wolbe, *Talks on Guidance for Grooms*, 2.

78. Wolbe, *Guidance for Brides*, 42; and in the Foreword by Shmuel Carlebach, 11–13.

79. Shlomo Wolbe, *Alei Shur*, 2:218, cited in Moshe Hauer, "Six Conversations about Marriage: A Guide," Orthodox Union, September 5, 2012, https://www.ou.org/life/relationships/marriage/six-conversations-about-marriage-guide-moshe-hauer/.

80. Wolbe, *Guidance for Brides*, 22.

81. Wolbe, *Talks on Guidance for Grooms*, 2–4.

82. Wolbe, *Talks on Guidance for Grooms*, 6.

83. Wolbe, *Guidance for Brides*, 20, 27, 30.

84. Wolbe, *Guidance for Brides*, 59–60.

85. Wolbe, *Guidance for Brides*, 28–29, 31.

86. Wolbe, *Talks on Guidance for Grooms*, 29.

87. Wolbe, *Guidance for Brides*, 35.

88. Wolbe, *Talks on Guidance for Grooms*, 20.

89. Wolbe, *Talks on Guidance for Grooms*, 34.

90. Wolbe, *Talks on Guidance for Grooms*, 5, 20–21.

91. Wolbe, *Guidance for Brides*, 55.

92. March 1, 2020, email communication (author prefers anonymity).

93. The Mussar Institute website, https://mussarinstitute.org/about-mussar/, accessed October 10, 2020.

94. Stone et al., *Cultivating the Soul*.

95. Personal communication from Claussen to the author on April 13, 2020.

96. Stone et al., *Cultivating the Soul*.

97. Stone et al., *Cultivating the Soul*.

98. Lefin, *Heshbon HaNefesh*, translated by Stone in *Cultivating the Soul*.

99. Stone et al., *Cultivating the Soul*.

100. Stone et al., *Cultivating the Soul*.

101. Stone et al., *Cultivating the Soul*.

102. Russ-Fishbane, *Judaism, Sufism, and the Pietists of Medieval Egypt*, 43–45, 89–91.

103. Brown, *The Hazon Ish*, 131n6.

104. Brown, "Kedushah," 500; Brown, *The Hazon Ish*, 86.

105. Brown, *The Hazon Ish*, 152.

106. Brown, *The Hazon Ish*, 153, 157.

107. Grade, *Tzemah Atlas* (Hebrew), 391–92, cited in Brown, *The Hazon Ish*, 140.

9. Devotion and Desire

1. Brown, *The Hazon Ish*, 825.

2. Friedman, "Haredim Confront the Modern City," 74–96.

3. Karelitz, *Kovetz Igrot*, 1:111f (letter #96), cited in Kaplan, "The Hazon Ish," 165.

4. Karelitz, *Shevi'it*, siman 7, cited in Kaplan, "The Hazon Ish," 154n27.

5. Kaplan, "The Hazon Ish," 150.

6. Karelitz, *Emunah U-Vitahon*, 4:8, 167.

7. Brown, *The Hazon Ish*, 1–2, 78–93.

8. Brown, *The Hazon Ish*, 30–32.

9. Brown, *The Hazon Ish*, 65.

10. Brown, *The Hazon Ish*, 79.

11. Brown, *The Hazon Ish*, 109, 830.

12. Karelitz, *Igeret HaKodesh* #1, cited in Brown, *The Hazon Ish*, 824–25.

13. Karelitz, *Kovetz Igrot*, 1:111, cited in Brown, *The Hazon Ish*, 828.

14. Brown, *The Hazon Ish*, 809, 830, 836.

15. Brown, *The Hazon Ish*, 109–10, quoting Karelitz in *Hazon Ish*, ed. Greineman, 1:12.

16. Karelitz, *Igeret HaKodesh* #1.

17. Brown, *The Hazon Ish*, 826.

18. Karelitz, *Igeret HaKodesh* #1, cited in Brown, *The Hazon Ish*, 824–25.

19. Kanievsky, *Igeret Hakodesh*, #1. See Maimonides, *Mishneh Torah*: Marriage 14:8.

20. Kanievsky, *Igeret Hakodesh*, #1.

21. Kanievsky, *Igeret Hakodesh*, #1.

22. Kanievsky, *Igeret Hakodesh*, #1.

23. Kanievsky, *Igeret Hakodesh*, #1.

24. Kanievsky, *Igeret Hakodesh*, #2.

25. Marc B. Shapiro, "Some Recollections of R. Jehiel Jacob Weinberg, Love Before Marriage, and More," *Seforim* (blog), https://seforimblog.com/2016/05/some-recollections-of-r-jehiel-jacob/, quoting Hirschensohn, *Apiryon* 3 (1926), 29.

26. Rabinowitz, *Tiv ha-Emunah*, 142.

27. Kanievsky, *Igeret Hakodesh*, #1.

28. Kanievsky, *Igeret Hakodesh*, #1.

29. Dessler, *Mikhtav MiEliyahu*, 1, 32.

30. Dessler, *Mikhtav MiEliyahu*, 4, 35–36.

31. Dessler, *Mikhtav MiEliyahu*, 6, 38.

32. Dessler, *Mikhtav MiEliyahu*, 4, 37.

33. Dessler, *Mikhtav MiEliyahu*, 6, 38.

34. Sher, *Kedushat Yisra'el*, 21–22.

35. Sher, *Kedushat Yisra'el*, 6.

36. Sher, *Kedushat Yisra'el*, 6–7, and the bracketed supplements, 4, 7.

37. Sher, *Kedushat Yisra'el*, 6–7, and the bracketed supplements, 4, 7.

38. Sher, *Kedushat Yisra'el*, 20–21.

39. Sher, *Kedushat Yisra'el*, 20–21.

40. Sher, *Kedushat Yisra'el*, 12.

41. Sher, *Kedushat Yisra'el*, 25.

42. Sher, *Kedushat Yisra'el*, 16.

43. Sher, *Kedushat Yisra'el*, 20.

44. Sher, *Kedushat Yisra'el*, 19, citing Elazar Hasid, *Sefer Rokeah*, Teshuvah #14.

45. Sher, *Kedushat Yisra'el*, 23, citing *Shnei Luhot HaBrit*, *The Prayer Book on Shabbat Evening*, and *The Holy Letter* (13th century).

46. Sher, *Kedushat Yisra'el*, 24.

47. Sher, *Kedushat Yisra'el*, 27.

48. Sher, *Kedushat Yisra'el*, 12.

49. Sher, *Kedushat Yisra'el*, 15.

50. Sher, *Kedushat Yisra'el*, 24.

51. Sher, *Kedushat Yisra'el*, 12.

52. Sher, *Kedushat Yisra'el*, 18.

53. Sher, *Kedushat Yisra'el*, 11.

54. Sher, *Kedushat Yisra'el*, 11.

55. Sher, *Kedushat Yisra'el*, 12.

56. Sher, *Kedushat Yisra'el*, 16, 20,12.

57. Sher, *Kedushat Yisra'el*, 26.

58. Brown, "Kedushah," 502.

59. Sher, *Kedushat Yisra'el*, 29–30.

60. Sher, *Kedushat Yisra'el*, 21.

10. Higher Purposes of Marriage

1. Shuchatowitz, *Binyan HaBayit*, 42.

2. Shuchatowitz, *Binyan HaBayit*, 42.

3. Shuchatowitz, *Binyan HaBayit*, 76.

4. Rashi on TB *Niddah* 17a.

5. Rashi on TB *Sanhedrin* 48b on *davak* (Gen. 2:24).

6. Shuchatowitz, *Binyan HaBayit*, 76.

7. Shuchatowitz, *Binyan HaBayit*, 78.

8. Karo, *Shulhan Arukh*: Orah Haim #240:8. Karo skips over the Maimonidean obligation of a husband to give his wife love and joy during intercourse, even though Karo usually quotes Maimonides.

9. See Psikta Zutra, Toldot 27 #10; TB *Shabbat* 30b; and *The Holy Letter* (chap. 6): "If the sexual union is not performed with much passion, love and desire, then the Shekhinah does not dwell in it."

10. Shuchatowitz, *Binyan HaBayit*, 70–71.

11. Shuchatowitz, *Binyan HaBayit*, 70–71; Shlanger, *Mishkan Yisrael*, 2:69.

12. Shlanger, *Mishkan Yisrael*, 2:69.

13. Knohl, *Et Dodim*, 2–3.

14. Aviner, *Etzem MeiAtzamai*, 8, 115.

15. Aviner, *Etzem MeiAtzamai*, 1.

16. Aviner, *Leil Klulot*, 38–39.

17. Aviner, *Leil Klulot*, 38–39, citing Avraham Gombiner, *Magen Avraham* gloss on *Shulhan Arukh*: Orah Haim #240 (20).

18. Aviner, Letter dated Elul 5777, reprinted in fifth edition of *Devar Seter* [A word of secrecy], 7, 2011, https://static1.squarespace.com /static/56763c8d1c1210f594d7084f/t/58bd15cf44024365b338083f /1488786898911/48-1Dk33JHjhg.pdf, accessed February 15, 2018.

19. Aviner, *Etzem MeiAtzamai*, 16.

20. Shuchatowitz, *Binyan HaBayit*, 43.

21. Shlanger, *Mishkan Yisrael*, 1:13.

22. Shlanger, *Mishkan Yisrael*, 2:20.

23. Ra'avad, *Ba'alei HaNefesh*, #4.

24. Shlanger, *Mishkan Yisrael*, 2:26–27, quotes Maimonides, *Mishneh Torah*: Hametz and Matza 6:12.

25. *Igeret HaKodesh* [*The Holy Letter*], 2:335–37.

26. Shlanger, *Mishkan Yisrael*, 1:54–55.

27. Shlanger, *Mishkan Yisrael*, 2:90.

28. Luzzato, *Mesillat Yesharim*, chap. 26, cited in Shlanger, *Mishkan Yisrael*, 2:90.

29. Shlanger, *Mishkan Yisrael*, 2:14.

30. Maimonides, *Mishneh Torah*: Marriage 15:17; Character Traits 5:4, cited in Shlanger, *Mishkan Yisrael*, 2:26–27.

31. Maimonides, *Mishneh Torah*: Character Traits 5:4; Maimonides, *Guide for the Perplexed*, 3:8.

32. Shlanger, *Mishkan Yisrael*, 2:48.

33. Shlanger, *Mishkan Yisrael*, 2:26,48, citing Zohar I, 81b.

34. Shlanger, *Mishkan Yisrael*, 1:12–14.

35. Shlanger, *Mishkan Yisrael*, 2:40.

36. Shlanger, *Mishkan Yisrael*, 2:38.

37. See Tur: Orah Haim, 240; Zohar III, 81a; Vidas, *Reishit Hokhma*, The Gate of Sanctity #16, 875; Zohar I, 49.

38. Shuchatowitz, *Binyan HaBayit*, 44.

39. Shuchatowitz, *Binyan HaBayit*, 44.

40. Shlanger, *Mishkan Yisrael*, 2:20.

41. Shlanger, *Mishkan Yisrael*, 1:24, citing TB *Megillah* 27a.

42. Vital, *Sha'ar ha-Likutim* on Ekev 8.3, cited in Shlanger, *Mishkan Yisrael*, 2:93.

43. Zohar III, *Numbers: Naso* 145.

44. Shuchatowitz, *Binyan HaBayit*, 28–29.

45. Nissim Gaon on *meisim shalom babayit* in TB *Shabbat* 152a.

46. Shuchatowitz, *Binyan HaBayit*, 109.

47. Avot d'Rabbi Natan A 28, cited in Shlanger, *Mishkan Yisrael*, 1:24.

48. Shuchatowitz, *Binyan HaBayit*, 25.

49. Maimonides, *Mishneh Torah*: Hanukkah 4:14.

50. Shuchatowitz, *Binyan HaBayit*, 106.

51. Shlanger, *Mishkan Yisrael*, 1:13.

52. Maharal, *Hidushei Aggadot*, 2:59.

53. Shuchatowitz, *Binyan HaBayit*, 30–33, 240.

54. Zohar on Genesis 176a, cited in Shlanger, *Mishkan Yisrael*, 2:6.

55. Shuchatowitz, *Binyan HaBayit*, 108.

56. Shlanger, *Mishkan Yisrael*, 2:6.

57. Shuchatowitz, *Binyan HaBayit*, 37–38.

58. Shlanger, *Mishkan Yisrael*, 2:6.

59. Shuchatowitz, *Binyan HaBayit*, 140.

60. Shuchatowitz, *Binyan HaBayit*, 140.

61. Kook, *Eyn Aya*: Shabbat, 2 #106.

11. Couple Communication as a Mitzvah

1. Shlanger, *Mishkan Yisrael*, 2:69.

2. Shuchatowitz follows his Lithuanian teachers: Rav Yosef Shalom Elyashiv, Rav Eliezer Shakh, and Rav Yaakov Kanievsky, the Steipler Rav.

3. Maimonides, *Mishneh Torah*: Character Traits 2:4; TB *Yoma* 19b.

4. Maimonides, *Mishneh Torah*: Character Traits 2:4.

5. TB *Eruvin* 100a; Maimonides, *Mishneh Torah*: Prohibited Intercourse 21:12.

6. Emden, *Siddur Beit Yaakov*, 159a.

7. Shuchatowitz, *Binyan HaBayit*, 65..

8. Frankel, *Simha Temima*, 20–21, 87–88, 90–91, 99. See Maimonides, *Sefer HaMitzvot*, Positive Mitzvah #214.

9. Brown, *The Hazon Ish*, 824–25, citing Karelitz, *Igeret HaKodesh* #1.

10. Brown, *The Hazon Ish*, 824–25, citing Karelitz, *Igeret HaKodesh* #1.

11 Brown, *The Hazon Ish*, 824–25, citing Karelitz, *Igeret HaKodesh* #1.

12. Karelitz, *Igeret Hakodesh* #1.

13. Rashi on TB *Brakhot* 24a.

14. Jacob Ben Asher, Tur: Even HaEzer 280; TB *Ketubot* 62b. See also Tur: Even HaEzer #76.

15. Sirkis, *Bayit Hadash*, gloss on Tur: Even HaEzer #280.

16. Sirkis, *Bayit Hadash*, gloss on Tur: Even HaEzer #280.

17. Aviner, *Panim el Panim*, 87–88.

18. Aviner, *V'Ahavta L'Reiakha Kamokha*, 55.

19. Aviner, *Panim el Panim*, 87–88.

20. Aviner, *Etzem MeiAtzamai*, 6, citing Feinstein, *Igrot Moshe*: Even HaEzer 1: #102.

21. "Leave Girls Alone," *Jerusalem Post*, October 15, 2019, https://www.jpost .com/israel-news/leave-girls-alone-604628.

22. Aviner, *Etzem MeiAtzamai*, 6, 13.

23. Wahrman, *Ezer M'kudash* on the *Shulhan Arukh*: Even HaEzer #25b, cited by Aviner, *Etzem MeiAtzamai*, 6, 13.

24. Berlin, *HaEmek Davar*, Gen. 1:27.

25. Zeldin, *An Intimate History of Humanity*, 40.

26. Shuchatowitz, *Binyan HaBayit*, 31–32.

27. Shuchatowitz, *Binyan HaBayit*, 31–32.

28. Shuchatowitz, *Binyan HaBayit*, 31–32.

29. Shuchatowitz, *Binyan HaBayit*, 151.

30. Shuchatowitz, *Binyan HaBayit*, 136.

31. Shuchatowitz, *Binyan HaBayit*, 151. See TB *Sanhedrin* 22b.

32. Friedman, *Marital Intimacy*, 81–85.

33. Shuchatowitz, *Binyan HaBayit*, 151.

34. Eliezer Hager, *Damesek Eliezer*, cited in Friedman, *Marital Intimacy*, 81–85.

35. Shuchatowitz, *Binyan HaBayit*, 60, 63.

36. Eibeschutz, *Sefer Ya'arot Devash*, Part 1, Derush 1.

37. Maimonides, *Shemonah Prakim*, 4:180–81.

38. Abramov and Abramov, *Mishpahteinu—Koheinu*, 24.

39. *Igeret HaKodesh*, 324.

40. Quoted in *Devar Seter*, 11.

41. Aflalo, *Responsa Asher Hanan*, Parts 6–7, #72, 414–16.

42. Hurvitz, *Sefer HaBrit*, Part 2, Essay 12, Chapter 9 on the Path of Sanctity, cited in *Devar Seter*, 8.

43. *Devar Seter*, 105–6.

44. Shapiro, *Halachic Positions*, 5–6.

45. Shapiro, *Halachic Positions*, 5–6.

46. Shapiro, *Halachic Positions*, 5–6.

47. Shapiro, *Halachic Positions*, 5–6.

48. Kook, *Responsa of Rav A. I. Kook, Orah Mishpat* #112, cited in *Devar Seter*, 136n37.

49. *Devar Seter*, 126.

50. Soloveitchik, "Rupture and Reconstruction," 81.

12. Redeeming Sexuality through Halakhah

1. Sztokman, *The Men's Section*, 66; Fishman, "Modern Orthodox Responses to the Liberalization of Sexual Mores," 234.

2. Soloveitchik, "Rupture and Reconstruction," 81.

3. Singer, "Debating Modern Orthodoxy at Yeshiva College," 113–26.

4. Irving Greenberg, "Dr. Greenberg Discusses Orthodoxy, YU, Vietnam and Sex," *The Commentator*, April 28, 1966, 7.

5. Irving Greenberg, Letter to Editor, *The Commentator*, May 12, 1966, 8–9. See Karo, *Shulhan Arukh*: Orah Haim 240: 2, 3, 5, 7, 9, 10, 12, 15, cited by Greenberg.

6. Greenberg, Letter to Editor, 8–9.

7. Greenberg, "Dr. Greenberg Discusses Orthodoxy, YU, Vietnam and Sex," 7.

8. Greenberg, "Dr. Greenberg Discusses Orthodoxy, YU, Vietnam and Sex," 7.

9. Greenberg, "Dr. Greenberg Discusses Orthodoxy, YU, Vietnam and Sex," 8–9.

10. Fishman, "Modern Orthodox Responses to the Liberalization of Sexual Mores," 228, citing her interview with Greenberg, Jerusalem, June 1, 2014.

11. Greenberg, "Dr. Greenberg Discusses Orthodoxy, YU, Vietnam and Sex," 8–9.

12. Greenberg, "Dr. Greenberg Discusses Orthodoxy, YU, Vietnam and Sex," *The Commentator*, April 28, 1966. 8–9.

13. Greenberg, "Modern Orthodoxy and the Road Not Taken," 25.

14. Lichtenstein, "Of Marriage Relationships and Relations," 24–25.

15. Aharon Lichtenstein, "Lichtenstein to Greenberg," *The Commentator*, June 2, 1966, 7–8.

16. Lichtenstein, "Of Marriage Relationships and Relations," 24–25.

17. Greenberg, Letter to Editor, 8–9.

18. Fishman, "Modern Orthodox Responses to the Liberalization of Sexual Mores," 230.

19. Rosenfeld, "From Prostitution to Marriage and Back Again," 295ff.

20. Fishman, "Modern Orthodox Responses to the Liberalization of Sexual Mores," 250.

21. Fishman, "Modern Orthodox Responses to the Liberalization of Sexual Mores," 252–53.

22. Fishman, "Modern Orthodox Responses to the Liberalization of Sexual Mores," 239.

23. Greenberg, "Dr. Greenberg Discusses Orthodoxy, YU, Viet Nam, & Sex," 6–10.

24. *The Joy of Text*, a project of The Lindenbaum Center for Halakhic Studies, is sponsored by Maze Women's Health and Yeshivat Chovevei Torah Rabbinical School.

25. Dov Linzer, "Thinking about Mikveh before Marriage," *Joy of Text* (podcast) 2:11, November 10, 2017. http://jpmedia.co/thinking-mikveh-marriage-episode/. Source sheet available at https://library.yctorah.org/2017/11/thinking-about-mikveh-before-marriage-joy-of-text-211-2/.

26. Linzer, "Thinking about Mikveh before Marriage" source sheet, citing Teshuvot of Rav Hanan Aflalo 8:60.

27. Berkovits, "A Jewish Sexual Ethics," 120.

28. "Accusing witnesses" appears only in *Sifrei* Numbers 115.

29. "By the [Temple] service!" does not appear in all manuscripts.

30. Rabinowitz, *Dikdukei Soferim*; *Sifrei* Numbers 115.

31. See variants cited in *Sifrei* Numbers 115 (Horowitz edition).

32. The unbracketed English text derives from Sifrei Numbers 115, while bracketed inserts are cited from TB *Menahot* 44a. Parentheses are editorial additions. Translation by Noam Zion.

33. Berkovits, "A Jewish Sexual Ethics," 114.

34. Berkovits, "A Jewish Sexual Ethics," 114.

35. Berkovits, "A Jewish Sexual Ethics," 117.

36. Berkovits, "A Jewish Sexual Ethics," 117.

37. Berkovits, "A Jewish Sexual Ethics," 118.

38. Berkovits, "A Jewish Sexual Ethics," 118.

39. Berkovits, "A Jewish Sexual Ethics," 118.

40. Berkovits, "A Jewish Sexual Ethics," 118.

41. Berkovits, "A Jewish Sexual Ethics," 118.

42. Berkovits, "A Jewish Sexual Ethics," 118.

43. Bar-Asher Siegal, *Early Christian Monastic Literature*, 178ff.

44. Berkovits, "A Jewish Sexual Ethics," 118.

45. Berkovits, "A Jewish Sexual Ethics," 120.

46. Berkovits, "A Jewish Sexual Ethics," 114.

47. Berkovits, "A Jewish Sexual Ethics," 123.

48. Berkovits, "A Jewish Sexual Ethics," 128.

49. Soloveitchik, *Family Redeemed*, 49.

50. Soloveitchik, *Halakhic Man*, 33–34.

51. Soloveitchik, *U-Vikkashtem Mi-Sham*, 115.

52. Soloveitchik, *Family Redeemed*, 76.

53. Soloveitchik, *Family Redeemed*, 77.

54. Soloveitchik, *Family Redeemed*, 76.

55. Soloveitchik, *Family Redeemed*, 47–48.

56. Soloveitchik, *Family Redeemed*, 47–48.

57. Soloveitchik, *U-Vikkashtem Mi-Sham*, 111.

58. Soloveitchik, *Family Redeemed*, 74.

59. Soloveitchik, *Family Redeemed*, 73.

60. Soloveitchik, *On Repentance*, 42

61. Soloveitchik, *Family Redeemed*, 75.

62. Soloveitchik, *Family Redeemed*, 63.

63. Soloveitchik, *Family Redeemed*, 49.

64. Soloveitchik, *Family Redeemed*, 63–64.

65. Soloveitchik, *Family Redeemed*, 49–50.

66. Soloveitchik, *Family Redeemed*, 49–50.

67. Maimonides, *Introduction to Avot*, chap. 4.

68. Rynhold and Harris, *Nietzsche, Soloveitchik, and Contemporary Jewish Philosophy*, 131.

69. Soloveitchik, *Family Redeemed*, 76.

70. Buber, *Between Man and Man*, 52.

71. Lamm, *The Jewish Way in Love and Marriage*, 25.

72. Lamm, *The Jewish Way in Love and Marriage*, 31.

73. Lamm, *The Jewish Way in Love and Marriage*, 134.

74. Lamm, *The Jewish Way in Love and Marriage*, 120.

75. Lamm, *The Jewish Way in Love and Marriage*, 141.

76. Lichtenstein, "Of Marriage Relationships and Relations," 30.

77. See https://www.thelehrhaus.com/commentary/the-rational-theology-of-rav-aharon-lichtenstein/.

78. Lichtenstein, "Of Marriage," 27–29.

79. Lichtenstein, "Of Marriage," 24–25

80. Lichtenstein, "Of Marriage," 4.

81. Lichtenstein, "Of Marriage," 2–3.

82. Lichtenstein, "Of Marriage," 2–3.

83. Ostroff asked this author to cite his pseudonym in this book.

84. Ostroff, *LaDaat LeEhov*, 63ff, 75ff.

85. Shuchatowitz, *Binyan HaBayit*, 65.

86. Fishman, "Modern Orthodox Responses to the Liberalization of Sexual Mores," 239.

87. Ostroff, *LaDaat LeEhov*, 44.

88. Ostroff, *LaDaat LeEhov*, 44.

89. Ostroff, *LaDaat LeEhov*, 45.

90. Soloveitchik, *U-Vikkashtem mi-Sham*, 104, cited in Lichtenstein, "Of Marriage," 26.

91. Ostroff, *LaDaat LeEhov*, 45.

92. Kook, *Shemonah Kvatzim*, 2:305; and "HaOneg v'HaSimha" and "Pahad," in *Or HaYakar v' Ikvei haEder*, 116–21.

93. Kook, *Shemonah Kvatzim*, 1:356, cited in Ben-Pazi, "Holiness Streams toward the Future: Sexuality in Rav Kook's Thought," 162.

94. Ostroff, *LaDaat LeEhov*, 45, 57, 109.

95. Ostroff, *LaDaat LeEhov*, 174.

96. Ostroff, *LaDaat LeEhov*, 45.

97. Ostroff, *LaDaat LeEhov*, 53–54.

98. Ostroff, *LaDaat LeEhov*, 52.

99. Ostroff, *LaDaat LeEhov*, 54.

100. Ostroff, *LaDaat LeEhov*, 191–92.

101. Ostroff, *LaDaat LeEhov*, 190.

102. Ostroff, *LaDaat LeEhov*, 195.

103. Isserles's gloss on *Shulhan Arukh*: Even HaEzer #25.

104. Ostroff, *LaDaat LeEhov*, 17–18.

105. Ostroff, *LaDaat LeEhov*, 24.

106. Ostroff, *LaDaat LeEhov*, 234.

107. Ostroff, *LaDaat LeEhov*, 234.

108. Responsum by Uriah Mevorah, Meshivat Nefesh Responsa, https://www.meshivat-nefesh.org.il/post-142/, accessed October 2, 2020.

109. Hannah Godinger, Meshivat Nefesh Responsa, https://www.meshivat-nefesh.org.il/post-6/, accessed October 6, 2020.

110. Author interview with Yitz Greenberg, Jerusalem, September 13, 2018.

13. Struggling with Sexual Liberation

1. Matt, "Sex and Sexuality: Introduction," 92.
2. Sacks, *The Home We Build Together*, 210.
3. Roffman, "Making Meaning and Finding Morality in a Sexualized World," 57.
4. Waskow, *Down-to-Earth Judaism*, 243.
5. Waskow, *Down-to-Earth Judaism*, 243.
6. Waskow, *Down-to-Earth Judaism*, 243.
7. Plaskow, "Decentering Sex," 23–24.
8. Eric Yoffie, Sermon at 68th Biennial Convention of the Union for Reform Judaism, November 8, 2005, Houston TX, https://ericyoffie.com/conversion/.
9. Borowitz, *Choosing a Sex Ethic*, 101–4.
10. Borowitz, "Reading the Jewish Tradition on Marital Sexuality," 369.
11. Borowitz, "Reading the Jewish Tradition on Marital Sexuality," 358–59, 363.
12. Borowitz, *Choosing a Sex Ethic*, 117.
13. Borowitz, *Choosing a Sex Ethic*, 104.
14. Borowitz, *Choosing a Sex Ethic*, 105.
15. Borowitz, *Choosing a Sex Ethic*, 105–6.
16. Buber, *I and Thou*, 45–46, 103.
17. Borowitz, *Choosing a Sex Ethic*, 109–12.
18. Borowitz, *Choosing a Sex Ethic*, 113.
19. Borowitz, "Reading the Jewish Tradition on Marital Sexuality," 358.
20. Borowitz, "Reading the Jewish Tradition on Marital Sexuality," 357–58.
21. Green, "A Contemporary Approach to Jewish Sexuality," 96–97.
22. Green, "A Contemporary Approach to Jewish Sexuality," 98.
23. Green, "A Contemporary Approach to Jewish Sexuality," 98.
24. Author interview with Arthur Green, Jerusalem, January 24, 2019.
25. Green, "A Contemporary Approach to Jewish Sexuality," 98.
26. Green, "A Contemporary Approach to Jewish Sexuality," 99.
27. Green, "A Contemporary Approach to Jewish Sexuality," 99.
28. Green, "A Contemporary Approach to Jewish Sexuality," 99.
29. Green, "A Contemporary Approach to Jewish Sexuality," 99.
30. Green, "A Contemporary Approach to Jewish Sexuality," 99.
31. Green, "A Contemporary Approach to Jewish Sexuality," 99.
32. Strassfeld, *A Book of Life*, 369.
33. Strassfeld, *A Book of Life*, 368.

34. Waskow, *Down-to-Earth Judaism*, 317–18.

35. Waskow, *Down-to-Earth Judaism*, 340.

36. Waskow, *Down-to-Earth Judaism*, 317–18.

37. Waskow, *Down-to-Earth Judaism*, 317–18.

38. Waskow, *Down-to-Earth Judaism*, 341.

39. Waskow, *Down-to-Earth Judaism*, 31.

40. Waskow, *Down-to-Earth Judaism*, 338–42.

41. Borowitz, *Choosing a Sex Ethic*, 104.

42. Waskow, *Down-to-Earth Judaism*, 310–11.

43. Brady Kenyon, "Poll: 69% of Americans Support Sex outside Marriage," CBS News, June 8, 2018, https://www.cnsnews.com/news/article/brady-kenyon/poll-69-americans-support-sex-outside-marriage.

14. Sliding-Scale Sex Ethics

1. Kaplan, "Can Judaism Survive without Supernaturalism?," 17.

2. Ysoscher Katz, email on the Torat Chayim LISTSERV, September 13, 2018.

3. *You shall fear God* applies to mitzvot "given to the heart" (Rashi on Lev. 19:14).

4. See Sakowitz, "CCAR Ad Hoc Committee on Human Sexuality," 241–46; Waskow, *Down-to-Earth Judaism*, 283–84; Dratch, "Task Force on Rabbinical Improprieties (RCA)"; Weingarten, "Doing What Is Right and Good," 16–22, 134–35; and Teutsch, *A Guide to Jewish Practice*, xx.

5. Teutsch, *A Guide to Jewish Practice*, xx.

6. Strassfeld and Strassfeld, *The Second Jewish Catalogue*, 97.

7. Sakowitz, "CCAR Ad Hoc Committee on Human Sexuality." 241–46. Selig Sakowitz co-chaired the committee (1993–2000) and published its resolution in 2001.

8. Novak Winer, "Sacred Choices," 24.

9. Novak Winer, "Sacred Choices," 28–29.

10. Maimonides, *Mishneh Torah*: Character Traits 2:6.

11. Weingarten, "Doing What Is Right and Good," 18–21.

12. *National Catholic Reporter*, July 17, 1998, cited by Carroll, *Constantine's Sword*, 320.

13. Gold, *Does God Belong in the Bedroom?*, 49.

14. Dorff, "This Is My Beloved, This Is My Friend," 30–35.

15. Email communication from Rabbi Sheldon Marder to the author, December 2018.

16. Dorff, "This Is My Beloved, This Is My Friend," 30–35.

17. Feldman, "Sex and Sexuality," 95.

18. Washofsky, *Reform Responsa*, 1:257.

19. Washofsky, *Reform Responsa*, 1:263.

20. Washofsky, *Reform Responsa*, 1:261.

21. Washofsky, *Reform Responsa*, 1:264.

22. Washofsky, *Reform Responsa*, 2:261.

23. Washofsky, *Reform Responsa*, 2:265.

24. Washofsky, *Reform Responsa*, 2:265.

25. Washofsky, *Reform Responsa*, 1:267.

26. Sakowitz, "CCAR Ad Hoc Committee on Human Sexuality," 241.

27. Yoffie, Sermon at 68th Biennial Convention.

28. Gold, *Does God Belong in the Bedroom?*, 56.

29. See TB *Eruvin* 100b; Ra'avad, *Ba'alei HaNefesh*; Maimonides, *Mishneh Torah*: Character Traits 5:4, Marriage 15:17; Karo, *Shulhan Arukh*: Even HaEzer #25:2; Magen Avraham on Tur: Orah Haim 240 (7); Zohar, I, 49b, 148b; III, 225b; *Kallah Rabbati* 1:11.

30. Dratch, "A Bit of Heaven Here on Earth," 135–36. See Teshuvot Maharit 1:5.

31. Washofsky, *Reform Responsa*, 1:257–60.

32. Washofsky, *Reform Responsa*, 1:262.

33. Washofsky, *Reform Responsa*, 1:263–64.

34. Elliot Dorff, "The Reality of Sex Outside Marriage," My Jewish Learning, https://www.myjewishlearning.com/article/the-reality-of-sex-outside-marriage/. Also reprinted in Dorff, *Matters of Life and Death*, 38, 136.

35. Dorff, *Matters of Life and Death*, 137–38.

36. Washofsky, *Reform Responsa*, 1:265.

37. Author interview with Arthur Green, Jerusalem, January 24, 2019.

38. Kalmanofsky, "Sex, Relationship and Single Jews," 632–46.

39. Kalmanofsky, "Sex, Relationship and Single Jews," 656, 632–33.

40. Kalmanofsky, "Sex, Relationship and Single Jews," 656, 632.

41. Waxman, *Tradition and Change*.

42. Gold, *Does God Belong in the Bedroom?*, 91.

43. Kalmanofsky, "Sex, Relationship and Single Jews," 643.

44. Kalmanofsky, "Sex, Relationship and Single Jews," 643. See Karo, *Shulhan Arukh*, Even HaEzer 26:1.

45. Kalmanofsky, "Sex, Relationship and Single Jews," 645.

46. Kalmanofsky, "Sex, Relationship and Single Jews," 635–36.

47. Kalmanofsky, "Sex, Relationship and Single Jews," 643.

48. Dorff, *This Is My Beloved, This Is My Friend*," 31.

49. Rashi on Lev. 19:29, Deut. 23:18; Maimonides, *Mishneh Torah*: Marriage 1:4; *Sefer Mitzvot*, Lo Ta'aseh #351, see Tur: Even HaEzer #26 contra Ra'avad; Nahmanides on Lev. 19:29; Responsa of Rashba #284.

50. Kalmanofsky, "Sex, Relationship and Single Jews," 643.

51. Kalmanofsky, "Sex, Relationship and Single Jews," 645.

52. Kalmanofsky, "Sex, Relationship and Single Jews," 645.

53. Kalmanofsky, "Sex, Relationship and Single Jews," 644.

54. Gordis, *Love and Sex*, 164.

55. *Mishna Yevamot* 2:8.

56. Maimonides, *Responsa*, #132.

57. Maimonides, *Responsa*, #132.

58. Rashi on Deut. 21:10–14; TB *Kiddushin* 22a.

59. Maimonides, *Responsa*, #132.

60. Maimonides, *Mishneh Torah*: Forbidden Sexual Relations 22:18.

61. Rashba, *Responsa of Rashba*, 5: #238.

62. See Exod. 19:6; Lev. 20:10, 18:20; Deut. 5:17, 22:13–21, 21:18, 24:1–4.

63. Gold, *Does God Belong in the Bedroom?*, 60, 69–70.

64. Gold, *Does God Belong in the Bedroom?*, 69–70.

65. See *Mishnah Sotah* 5:1 ("just as the adulteress is forbidden to her lover, so is she forbidden to her husband"); Karo, *Shulhan Arukh*: Even HaEzer #11.1, 178.17; Jer. 3:1, Deut. 24:1–4; and Maimonides, *Mishneh Torah*: Forbidden Relations 3.2.

66. Fine, "Marriage," 619. See Gordis, *Love and Sex*, 182; Dorff, "*This Is My Beloved*," 117.

67. Gold, *Does God Belong in the Bedroom?*, 53. See Adler, *Engendering Judaism*, 164.

68. Greenstein, "Equality and Sanctity," 9.

69. Greenstein, "Equality and Sanctity," 10.

70. See TB *Sotah* 27b; TB *Yevamot* 24b; Karo, *Shulhan Arukh*: Even HaEzer #11.1, 178.17.

71. Karo, *Shulhan Arukh*: Even HaEzer #11.2ff, and commentaries 159.3; *Otzar HaPosqim*: Even HaEzer 11.1,44.

72. Jacob, *Contemporary American Reform Responsa*, #192, 286.

73. Sheff, *The Polyamorists Next Door*, x.

74. Gershom, *Responsa of Meor haGolah*, #42.

75. Teutsch, *A Guide to Jewish Practice*, 220, 225.

76. Teutsch, *A Guide to Jewish Practice*, 220, 225.

77. Dorff and Ruttenberg, "Conclusion: The Ethics of Sex," *Sex and Intimacy*, 141–42.

15. Legalizing Living Together?

1. Ellinson, *Non-Halachic Marriage*, 69, citing Responsa of Rabbenu Nissim #68 and of Rabbi Yehoshua ibn Shueib, *Tzedah laDerekh* III, klal 3, perek 2.

2. Maimonides, *Mishneh Torah*: Shabbat 30:14, see TB *Ketubot* 65b.

3. Schacter, "Rav Jacob Emden: Life and Major Works," 292–93.

4. Emden, *Siddur Beit Yaakov*, 158b.

5. Emden, *Siddur Beit Yaakov*, 159a.

6. Emden, *Siddur Beit Yaakov*, 158a.

7. Emden, *Siddur Beit Yaakov*, 159b.

8. Emden, *Siddur Beit Yaakov*, 159a.

9. Emden, *Responsa of Ya'avetz, Mor u-Kets'ia Orah Haim*, #240.

10. Emden, *Megillat Sefer*, 58, cited in Schacter, "Rav Jacob Emden," 33–34.

11. Emden, *Megillat Sefer*, 144a, cited in Schacter, "Rav Jacob Emden," 37.

12. Emden, *Megillat Sefer*, 82–83, cited in Schacter, "Rav Jacob Emden," 55–56.

13. Ra'avad, *Ba'alei HaNefesh*, 117.

14. Ra'avad, *Ba'alei HaNefesh*, 117.

15. Emden, *Siddur Beit Yaakov*, 159a.

16. Emden, *Siddur Beit Yaakov*, 158b.

17. Emden, *Siddur Beit Yaakov*, 158b.

18. Emden, *Siddur Beit Yaakov*, 1560b.

19. Emden, *Responsa of Ya'avetz*, 2:, #15.

20. Emden, *Responsa of Ya'avetz*, 2, #15.

21. Emden, *Responsa of Ya'avetz*, 2, #15.

22. Emden, *Responsa of Ya'avetz*, 2, #15.

23. Emden, *Responsa of Ya'avetz*, 2, #15.

24. Emden, *Responsa of Ya'avetz*, 2, #15.

25. See TB *Yoma* 18b; Maimonides, *Guide for the Perplexed*, 3:49; Maimonides, *Mishneh Torah*: Marriage 1:4, with Ra'avad gloss; *Rashba Responsa* (attributed to Nahmanides) #280, #284; *Nahmanides Responsa* #2.

26. Emden, *Responsa of Ya'avetz*, 2, #15.

27. Emden, *Responsa of Ya'avetz*, 2, #15.

28. Rabbi Rafael Birdugo (Morocco, 18th century) and Rabbi Eliyahu Hazan (Alexandria, Egypt, ca. 1884) ruled that, regarding unmarried Jewish couples who have entered an exclusive sexual relationship, it is appropriate in many cases to apply the permitted pilegesh category. Hazan states that he now realizes that Emden was inspired by the Holy Spirit! Hazan, *Ta'lumot Lev* 3:32. Cited in Zohar, "Halakhic Positions Permitting Pre-Marital Sexual Intimacy."

29. Freehof, "Unmarried Couples and Temple Membership" (#51), 242.

30. Kalmanofsky, "Sex, Relationship and Single Jews," 637.

31. Kalmanofsky, "Sex, Relationship and Single Jews," 642. See also Schindler, "Responsum on Intimate Relations without Kiddushin and Huppah," 82.

32. Washofsky, *Reform Responsa for the Twenty-first Century*, no. 5764.4, 2:264.

33. Washofsky, *Reform Responsa for the Twenty-first Century*, no. 5756.10, 1:264.

34. Borowitz, *Choosing a Sex Ethic*, 108.

35. Zacharow, "Kesher Beino l'Veina L'lo Nissuim."

36. Zacharow, "Kesher Beino l'Veina L'lo Nissuim."

37. Zacharow, "Kesher Beino l'Veina L'lo Nissuim."

38. Feldblum, "Ba'ayat 'Agunot u-Mamzerim," 203–16.

39. Toledano, *Otzar Hahaim*, 6:209, cited in Ellinson, *Non-Halachic Marriage*, 91.

40. See Shava, "The Y'dua B'Tzibur as His Wife," 3–36, cited in Schindler, "Responsum on Intimate Relations without Kiddushin and Huppah," 84, 88.

41. Kalmanofsky, "Sex, Relationship and Single Jews," 642.

42. Winkler, *Sacred Secrets*, 96–97.

43. Winkler, *Sacred Secrets*, 96–97.

44. Waskow, *Down-to-Earth Judaism*, 307–8.

45. Gold, *Does God Belong in the Bedroom?*, 55.

46. Gold, *Does God Belong in the Bedroom?*, 55.

47. Teutsch, *A Guide to Jewish Practice*, 220–21.

48. Teutsch, *A Guide to Jewish Practice*, 220–21.

49. Dorff and Geller, "When Alzheimer's Turns a Spouse into a Stranger," 558. For pastoral advice on spouses with Alzheimer's, see Address, "With Eyes Undimmed and Vigor Unabated," 537–48.

50. *Mishnah Baba Kamma* 8:1, 6; and see TB *Baba Kamma* 85a–86b.

51. Dorff and Geller, "When Alzheimer's Turns a Spouse into a Stranger," 561.

52. Dorff and Geller, "When Alzheimer's Turns a Spouse into a Stranger," 549–64. See Richard F. Address, "Till Death Us Do Part? A Look at Marriage Rituals When a Partner Has Alzheimer's Disease," American Society on Aging, www

.asaging.org/blog/till-death-us-do-part-look-marriage-rituals-when-partner
-has-alzheimer's-disease, accessed April 2, 2019.

53. Sacks, *Morality*, 17.

54. Sacks, *Morality*, 61–62.

55. Sacks, *Morality*, 64.

16. A Feminist Alternative to Halakhic Marriage

1. "The Roots of 'Radical,'" Word History, Merriam-Webster, https://
www.merriam-webster.com/words-at-play/radical-word-history#:
~:text=The%20Origin%20of%20'Radical'&text=Radical%20was
%20first%20an%20adjective,or%20proceeding%20from%20a%20root.
%22, accessed October 20, 2020.

2. Plaskow, "Authority, Resistance, and Transformation," 69–82.

3. Goldman, *Marriage and Love*, 1, 8. Cited in Gornick, *Emma Goldman*, 79.

4. Plaskow, *Standing Again at Sinai*, 206. See also Harrison, "Misogyny and Homophobia," 150.

5. Plaskow, *Standing Again at Sinai*, 204, 207.

6. Plaskow, *Standing Again at Sinai*, 204–5.

7. Plaskow, *Standing Again at Sinai*, 207.

8. Plaskow, *Standing Again at Sinai*, 207. Contra Plaskow, see Levitt, "Love the One You Are With," 251–56.

9. Plaskow, *Standing Again at Sinai*, 207.

10. Plaskow, *Standing Again at Sinai*, 208–9.

11. Plaskow, *Standing Again at Sinai*, 193, 197.

12. Plaskow, "Sexuality and Teshuva," 297.

13. Plaskow, *Standing Again at Sinai*, 205, 207–9, 202.

14. Plaskow, *Standing Again at Sinai*, 195.

15. Plaskow, *Standing Again at Sinai*, 191.

16. Benjamin, "Tracing the Contours of a Half Century of Jewish Feminist Theology," 27.

17. Plaskow, *Standing Again at Sinai*, 191.

18. Plaskow, "Authority, Resistance, and Transformation," 73.

19. Plaskow, "Authority, Resistance, and Transformation," 198.

20. Plaskow, *Standing Again at Sinai*, 161.

21. Plaskow, "Authority, Resistance, and Transformation," 69–82.

22. Tirosh-Samuelson and Hughes, *Judith Plaskow*, 21–22.

23. Rachel Adler, "I've Had Nothing Yet, So I Can't Take More," *Moment*, September 1983.

24. Adler, *Engendering Judaism*, 44.

25. Adler, *Engendering Judaism*, xx.

26. Adler, *Engendering Judaism*, xxv.

27. Adler, *Engendering Judaism*, 114.

28. Adler, *Engendering Judaism*, 21. Also see Cover, "Nomos and Narrative."

29. Plaskow, "Sexuality and Teshuva," 297.

30. Plaskow, "Sexuality and Teshuva," 298.

31. Plaskow, *Standing Again at Sinai*, 178.

32. Adler, *Engendering Judaism*, 133–38. See Trible, *God and the Rhetoric of Sexuality*, 161.

33. Adler, *Engendering Judaism*, 136.

34. Adler, *Engendering Judaism*, 136.

35. See Waskow, "Eden for Grown-Ups," 259ff.

36. Plaskow, *Standing Again at Sinai*, 199.

37. Adler, *Engendering Judaism*, 135.

38. Plaskow, *Standing Again at Sinai*, 199.

39. Plaskow, *Standing Again at Sinai*, 197–98.

40. Plaskow, *Standing Again at Sinai*, 197–98.

41. Letter accessed at "David Ben-Gurion in Favor of Women's Equality," Israel Post, courtesy of the Tax Museum and the Ministry of Finance, Jerusalem, https://www.israelpost.co.il/unforget.nsf/lettersbycategory/a10ff8701947e6e342256c7e004d6878?opendocument, accessed June 20, 2019.

42. Adler, *Engendering Judaism*, 165–66.

43. Friedman, *Jewish Marriage in Palestine*, 1:19–30; 2:212–17; Adler, *Engendering Judaism*, 180.

44. Adler, *Engendering Judaism*, 192.

45. Adler, *Engendering Judaism*, 193–94.

46. Adler, *Engendering Judaism*, 192–93.

47. Adler, *Engendering Judaism*, 80.

48. Adler, *Engendering Judaism*, 192–93.

49. Adler, *Engendering Judaism*, 193–94.

50. Adler, *Engendering Judaism*, 193–94.

51. Labovitz, "With Righteousness and Justice," 4, 46–47.

52. Labovitz, "With Righteousness and Justice," 7, 47.

53. Adler, *Engendering Judaism*, 181.

54. Adler, *Engendering Judaism*, 190.

55. Plaskow, "Sexuality and Teshuva," 301–2.

56. Plaskow, "Sexuality and Teshuva," 301–2.

57. Benjamin, "Tracing the Contours," 21.

58. Kukla, in Plaskow and Kukla, "Remapping the Road from Sinai," 4, cited in Benjamin, "Tracing the Contours," 21.

59. Michaelson, "On the Religious Significance of Homosexuality," 214–15.

60. Washofsky, *Reform Responsa*, 1:262.

61. In this author's scholarly opinion, Plaskow and Adler are incorrect in their assumptions about the patriarchal nature of the mainstream, historical, halakhic understanding of marriage. See Zion, *Marital Friendship and Covenantal Partnership*, 39–124.

62. Adler, *Engendering Judaism*, 46.

63. Ross, *Expanding the Palace of Torah*, 143, 154.

64. Adler, *Engendering Judaism*, 193.

Conclusion

1. Zion, *Romantic Rabbis*, 35ff.

2. Borowitz, *Choosing a Sex Ethic*, 113.

3. Adler, *Engendering Judaism*, 133–38.

4. Karo, *Shulhan Arukh*, Orah Haim 240.

5. Brown, "Kedushah: The Sexual Abstinence of Married Men in Gur, Slonim, and Toledot Aharon," 494.

6. Sher, *Kedushat Yisra'el*, 22.

7. Sher, *Kedushat Yisra'el*, 18.

8. Sher, *Kedushat Yisra'el*, 22.

9. Adler, *Engendering Judaism*, 136.

10. Plaskow, *Standing Again at Sinai*, 199.

11. Soloveitchik, *Family Redeemed*, 63.

12. Herr, "Marriage in Its Socio-Economic Aspects According to the Halakhah," 37–38.

13. Gafni, "The Institution of Marriage in Rabbinic Times," 14–15.

14. Witte, *From Sacrament to Contract*.

15. Berger, "Two Models of Medieval Jewish Marriage," 59–84.

16. "There is no legal requirement that in *kiddushin* one intends to perform a mitzvah of the Torah, but simply to acquire a wife." Feinstein, *Igrot Moshe*: Even HaEzer 1: #74.

17. Maimonides, *Guide for the Perplexed*, 3:49.

18. Borowitz, "Reading the Jewish Tradition on Marital Sexuality," 360–61.

19. Zohar I, 55b.

20. Shuchatowitz, *Binyan HaBayit*, 109.

21. Heschel, *Between God and Man*, 126.

22. Green, "A Contemporary Approach to Jewish Sexuality," 96–99.

23. Green, "A Contemporary Approach to Jewish Sexuality," 96–99.

24. Soloveitchik, *Family Redeemed*, 76.

25. Tana d'bei Eliyahu 9.

26. Berlin, *Meishiv Davar* 4: #35, based on TB *Nedarim* 15b.

27. Feinstein, *Igrot Moshe*: Orah Haim, 4: #75.

28. Maimonides, *Mishneh Torah*: Forbidden Intercourse 21:9.

29. Maimonides, *Mishneh Torah*: Marriage 14:5.

30. Stav and Stav, *Avo Beitekha*, 403ff.

31. Karo, *Shulhan Arukh*: Even HaEzer 25.

32. Maimonides, *Mishneh Torah*: Marriage 14:8.

33. Brown, "Kedushah" 478; Biale, *A New History of Hasidism*, 717.

34. Karelitz, *Igeret Hakodesh* #1.

35. Zohar I, 49b.

36. Debra Kamin, "In the Boudoir with Orthodox Jewish Women," *The Guardian*, September 2, 2015.

37. Dorff and Ruttenberg, *Sex and Intimacy*, 113.

38. Karelitz, *Igeret HaKodesh* #1, cited in Brown, *The Hazon Ish*, 824–25. See Shuchatowitz, *Binyan HaBayit*, 31–32.

39. Rilke, *Letters to a Young Poet*, 36.

40. Rilke, *Letters to a Young Poet*, 33–34.

41. Lamm, *The Jewish Way in Love and Marriage*, 126.

42. Soloveitchik, *Family Redeemed*, 27–29.

43. Levenson, *Lifetime, Love, For Her*.

44. Vasserman, "The 'Abstinent' Society," 298.

45. Luzzato, *Yalkut Yedi'ot HaEmet*, 321.

46. Rilke, *Letters to a Young Poet*, 33–36; Zohar III, 267a.

Bibliography

Abrabanel, Judah. *Dialogues on Love.* Quoted in Andrew Gluck, *Judah Abrabanel's Philosophy of Love and Kabbalah.* Lewiston IL: Edwin Mellen Press, 2012.

Abramov, Yirmiyohu, and Tehilla Abramov. *Mishpahteinu—Koheinu.* Jerusalem: Hinukh L'Hayei Mishpaha, 2004. Also published in English as *Our Family, Our Strength: Creating a Jewish Home.* Jewish Marriage Education, 2007.

Abrams, Daniel, ed. *The Female Body of God in Kabbalist Literature.* Jerusalem: Magnes Press, 2004.

———. "A Light of Her Own." *Kabbalah: Journal for the Study of Jewish Mystical Texts* 15 (2006): 7–29.

Address, Richard. "With Eyes Undimmed and Vigor Unabated: Sex, Sexuality, and Older Adults." In *The Sacred Encounter,* edited by Lisa Grushcow, 537–48. New York: CCAR Press, 2014.

Adler, Rachel. *Engendering Judaism: An Inclusive Theology and Ethics.* Philadelphia: The Jewish Publication Society, 1998.

Adler, Rachel, and Robin Podolsky. "Sexuality, Autonomy, and Community in the Writings of Eugene Borowitz." *Journal of Jewish Ethics* 1, no. 1 (2015): 114–36.

Aelred of Rievaulx. *Spiritual Friendship.* Edited by Marsha Dutton. Collegeville, MN: Liturgical Press/Cisterian Publications, 2010.

Aflalo, Hanan. *Responsa Asher Hanan.* [In Hebrew]. Holon, Israel: n.p., 2004.

Ahituv, Yoska. "Rav Ashlag and Levinas on the Duty to One's Fellow." [In Hebrew]. In *B'Darkhei Shalom,* edited by Benjamin Ish-Shalom, 469–83. Jerusalem: Beit Morasha, 2007.

Alter, Yisrael. *Beit Yisra'el.* Jerusalem: Beit Yisrael Publishers, 1980.

Amital, Yehuda. *Commitment and Complexity: Jewish Wisdom in an Age of Upheaval: Selections from the Writings of Rabbi Yehuda Amital.* New York: KTAV, 2008.

Ashlag, Yehuda Leib. *Introduction to the Book of Zohar: Volume Two.* Toronto: Laitman Kabbalah Publishers, 2005.

———. *Kuntres Arevut.* Tel Aviv: n.p., 1934.

———. *Matan Torah.* Tel Aviv: n.p., 1934.

———. *Sefer Pri Hakham*. Bnai Brak: n.p., n.d.

Ashkenazi, Bezalel. *Shita Mekubetzet*. 12 vols. Jerusalem: Horev, 1987.

Aviner, Shlomo. *Ahoti Kallah (*including *Leil Klulot)*. Jerusalem: Sefriat Hava, 2002.

———. *Etzem MeiAtzamai*. Jerusalem: n.p., 1984.

———. *Panim el Panim: Pirkei Ahava bein Ish v Ishto*. Jerusalem: n.p., 1983.

———. *V'Ahavta L'Reiakha Kamokha*. Jerusalem: n.p., 2000.

Baal Shem Tov, Israel. *Keter Shem Tov*. New York: Kehot Publishing Society, 2004.

———. *Sefer Shivhei HaBesht*. Jerusalem: n.p., 1942.

———. *Tzava'at HaRibash*. New York: n.p., 1975.

Benjamin, Mara. "Tracing the Contours of a Half Century of Jewish Feminist Theology." *Journal of Feminist Studies in Religion* 36, no. 1 (Spring 2020): 11–31.

Ben-Pazi, Hanoch. "Holiness Streams toward the Future: Sexuality in Rav Kook's Thought," *Nashim* 21 (2011): 160–78.

Ben-Shimon, Refael Aharon. *Bat Na'avat HaMardut*. Jerusalem: n.p., 1917.

Berezovsky, Shalom Noah. *Netivot Shalom*. Jerusalem: Yeshivat Beit Avraham Slonim, n.d.

Berg, Yehuda. *The Kabbalah Book of Sex and Other Mysteries of the Universe*. Los Angeles: Kabbalah Centre International, 2006.

Berger, Joseph. *The Pious Ones*. New York: Harper Perennial, 2014.

Berger, Michael. "Two Models of Medieval Jewish Marriage: A Preliminary Study." *Journal of Jewish Studies* 52, no. 1 (Spring 2001): 59–84.

Berkovits, Eliezer. "A Jewish Sexual Ethics." In *Essential Essays on Judaism*, edited by David Hazony, 103–28. Jerusalem: Shalem Institute, 2002.

Berlin, Naftali Tzvi Yehuda (Netziv). *HaEmek Davar*. Jerusalem: M. Kuperman, 2005.

———. *Meishiv Davar*. Warsaw: n.p., 1894.

Biale, David. *Eros and the Jews*. New York: Basic Books/HarperCollins, 1992.

———. "Hateshukah L'Sagfanut BaTenuah HaHasidit." In *Eros, Erusin v Isurim*, edited by Yisrael Bartal, 213–24. Jerusalem: Zalman Shazar Institute, 1988.

———, ed. *A New History of Hasidism*. Princeton NJ: Princeton University Press, 2017.

Bickart, Noah Benjamin. "'Overturning the Table': The Hidden Meaning of a Talmudic Metaphor for Coitus." *Journal of the History of Sexuality* 25, no. 3 (September 2016): 489–507.

Borowitz, Eugene. *Choosing a Sex Ethic*. Bnai Brith Hillel Foundations, 1956.

———. "Reading the Jewish Tradition on Marital Sexuality" (1982). In *The Sacred Encounter*, edited by Lisa Grushcow, 355–70. New York: CCAR Press, 2014.

Boyarin, Daniel. *Carnal Israel: Reading Sex in Talmudic Culture*. Oakland: University of California Press, 1993.

Brawer, Abraham Yaakov. *Galitsiyah viyehudeha: Mehkarim betoledot Galitsiyah viyehudeha*. Jerusalem: n.p., 1956.

Brezis, David. *Between Zealotry and Grace*. [In Hebrew]. Jerusalem: Bar-Ilan University Press, 2015.

Brown, Benjamin. *The Gdoilim: Leaders Who Shaped the Israeli Haredi Jewry*. [In Hebrew]. Jerusalem: Magnes Press, 2017.

———. "Gedulat Ha-Adam v'Ha-Ktanato: Temurot B'shitat HaMussar shel Yeshivat Slabodka." In *Yeshivot and Battei Midrash*, edited by Immanuel Etkes, 243–71. Jerusalem: Zalman Shazar Center, 2006.

———. *The Hazon Ish: Halakhist, Believer, and Leader of the Haredi Revolution*. [In Hebrew]. Jerusalem: Magnes Press, 2011.

———. "Kedushah: The Sexual Abstinence of Married Men in Gur, Slonim, and Toledot Aharon." *Jewish History* 27 (2013): 475–522.

———. *Lithuanian Musar Movement: Personalities and Ideas*. [In Hebrew]. Tel Aviv: Universita Meshuderet, Israeli Defense Department, 1966.

Brown, Benjamin, and Haim Shalem. "Gur BaAretz—HaBeit Yisrael v'Shikuma shel Hasidut Gur b'Eretz Yisrael." In *The Gdoilim*, edited by Benjamin Brown, 617–43. Jerusalem: Magnes Press, 2017.

Buber, Martin. *Between Man and Man*. New York: Macmillan, 1965.

———. *I and Thou*. New York: Scribner's Sons, 1958.

Calderon, Ruth. *A Talmudic Alpha Beta*. [In Hebrew]. Tel Aviv: Yediot Ahronot, 2014.

Cancian, Francesca. *Love in America*. Cambridge: Cambridge University Press, 1987.

Carroll, James. *Constantine's Sword*. New York: Mariner Books, 2002.

Cherlow, Yuval. "Premarital Guidance Literature in the Internet Age." In *Gender Relationships In Marriage and Out*, edited by Rivkah Blau, 131–72. New York: Yeshiva University Press, 2007.

Claussen, Geoffrey. *Modern Musar: Contested Virtues in Modern Jewish Thought*. Philadelphia: The Jewish Publication Society/University of Nebraska Press (forthcoming).

———. "The Promise and Limits of Rabbi Simhah Zissel Ziv's Musar: A Response to Miller, Cooper, Pugh, and Peters." *Journal of Jewish Ethics* 3, no. 1 (2017): 154–77.

———. *Sharing the Burden: Rabbi Simhah Zissel Ziv and the Path of Musar*. Albany NY: SUNY Press, 2015.

Cohen, David. *Zakhu Shekhina Beineihem: The Nazir*. [In Hebrew]. Jerusalem: Ariel Publisher, 1906.

Cohen, Jeremy. "Rationales for Marital Sex in Ra'aBaD's Ba'alei ha-Nefesh." *Jewish History Journal* 6, nos. 1–2 (1992): 65–78.

———. "Sexuality and Intentionality in Rabbinic Thought of the 12th–13th C." [In Hebrew]. In *Marriage and Family in Halacha and Jewish Thought*, Teuda XIII, edited by Menahem Friedman, 155–72. Tel Aviv: Tel Aviv University Press, 1997.

Cohen, Martin, ed. *The Observant Life: The Wisdom of Conservative Judaism for Contemporary Jews*. New York: Rabbinical Assembly, 2012.

Cordovero, Moshe. *Tefillah L'Moshe*. Premislany, Russia: n.p., 1891.

Cover, Robert. "Nomos and Narrative." *Harvard Law Review* 97, no. 1 (November 1983): 4–68.

Deen, Shulem. *All Who Go Do Not Return: A Memoir*. Minneapolis MN: Grayfish Press, 2015.

Dennis, Geoffrey. "Your Love Is Sweeter Than Wine: Erotic Theology in Jewish Tradition." In *The Sacred Encounter*, edited by Lisa Grushcow, 131–44. New York: CCAR Press, 2014.

Dessler, Eliyahu. *Mikhtav MiEliyahu*. Vol. 1. Jerusalem: The Committee for the Publication of the Writings of Rabbi E. L. Dessler, 1991.

Diamond, Eliezer. *Holy Men and Hunger Artists: Fasting and Asceticism in Rabbinic Culture*. New York: Oxford University Press, 2003.

Diamond, James. "Nahmanides and Rashi on the One Flesh of Marital Union— Lovemaking vs. Duty." *Harvard Theological Review* 102, no. 2 (2009): 193–224.

Dorff, Elliot. *Love Your Neighbor as Yourself*. Philadelphia: The Jewish Publication Society, 2003.

———. *Matters of Life and Death: A Jewish Approach to Modern Medical Ethics*. Philadelphia: The Jewish Publication Society, 1998.

———. *"This Is My Beloved, This Is My Friend": A Rabbinic Letter on Intimate Relations*. New York: Rabbinical Assembly, 1996. Available at https://www.rabbinicalassembly.org/sites/default/files/assets/public/publications/this-is-my-beloved.pdf.

Dorff, Elliot, and Danya Ruttenberg, ed. *Sex and Intimacy: Jewish Choices, Jewish Voices*. Philadelphia: The Jewish Publication Society, 2010.

Dorff, Elliot, and Laura Geller. "When Alzheimer's Turns a Spouse into a Stranger: Jewish Perspectives on Loving and Letting Go." In *The Sacred Encounter: Jewish*

Perspectives on Sexuality, edited by Lisa Grushcow, 549–64. New York: CCAR Press, 2014.

Dratch, Mark. "A Bit of Heaven Here on Earth." In *Sex and Intimacy*, edited by Elliot Dorff and Danya Ruttenberg, 133–40. Philadelphia: The Jewish Publication Society, 2010.

Dreyfus, Yair. "The Covenant and the Yetzer." [In Hebrew]. In *And He Named Them Adam*, edited by Zohar Maor, 124–43. Efrat, Israel: Bina Leitim Institute of Yeshivat Siah Yitzhak Shagar, 2004.

Eibeschutz, Jonathan. *Sefer Ya'arot Devash*. Warsaw: Y. Galdeman, 1968.

Elazar Hasid. *Sefer HaRokeah HaGadol*. Jerusalem: B. Shneersohn, 1967.

Elijah, Vilna Gaon (GRA). *Seder Eliyahu: Commentary on the Haggadah of Pesah*. [In Hebrew]. Prague: Franz Shalal, 1815.

———. *Sefer Mishlei with the Gra's Commentary on Proverbs*. [In Hebrew]. Vilna: Tzvi Ma'atz, 1926.

Ellinson, Getsel. *Non-Halachic Marriage*. [In Hebrew]. Tel Aviv: Dvir Press, 1975.

———. *Woman and the Mitzvot*. [In Hebrew]. Jerusalem: Jewish Agency, 1986.

Emden, Jacob. *Megillat Sefer*. Warsaw: Shuldberg Brothers, 1897.

———. *Sh'elot Ya'avetz, Mor u-Kets'ia Orah Haim*. Altona, Germany: Aaron Katz Publisher, 1739–49.

———. *Siddur Beit Yaakov*. New York: Mesora Torah Publishing, 1904.

Englander, Yakir. "Changing Concepts of the Ultra-Orthodox Body: Rabbi Avigdor Miller as a Test Case." *Journal of the American Academy of Religion* 82, no. 3 (September 2014): 771–810.

Epstein, Yehiel Mihel. *Arukh HaShulhan*. Tel Aviv: Yitzu Sifrei Kodesh, n.d.

Etkes, Immanuel. *The Besht: Magician, Mystic, and Leader*. Waltham MA: Brandeis University Press, 2005.

———. *The Gaon of Vilna: The Man and his Image*. Oakland: University of California Press, 2002.

———. "Marriage and Torah Study among Lomdim in Lithuania in the Nineteenth Century." In *The Jewish Family*, edited by David Kraemer, 153–78. New York: Oxford University Press, 1989.

———. *Rabbi Israel Salanter and the Mussar Movement*. Jerusalem: Magnes, 1984; Philadelphia: The Jewish Publication Society, 1993.

Falk, Marcia. *Love Lyrics from the Bible*. Boston: Brandeis University Press, 2004.

Farbsṭeyn, Ester. *Hidden in Thunder*. New York: Feldheim Publishers, 2007.

Feinstein, Moshe. *Igrot Moshe*. 9 vols. New York: Mordechai Feinstein (self-published), 1974–2011.

Feldblum, Meyer. "Ba'ayat 'Agunot u-Mamzerim—Hatza'at Pitaron." *Dinei Yisra'el*, 19 (5757–58) [1998]: 203–16.

Feldman, David. "Sex and Sexuality." In *The Second Jewish Catalog*, edited by Sharon and Michael Strassfeld, 91–99. Philadelphia: The Jewish Publication Society, 1976.

Ferziger, Adam. "The Road Not Taken and The One Less Traveled: The Greenberg–Lichtenstein Exchange and Contemporary Orthodoxy." In *Yitz Greenberg and Modern Orthodoxy: The Road Not Taken*, edited by Adam Ferziger, 254–88. Boston: Academic Studies Press, 2019.

Fine, David. "Marriage." In *The Observant Life*, edited by Martin Cohen, 611–31. New York: Rabbinical Assembly, 2012.

Fine, Lawrence. *Physician of the Soul, Healer of the Cosmos—Isaac Luria and his Kabbalist Fellowship*. Stanford CA: Stanford University Press, 2003.

———. "Tikkun: A Lurianic Motif in Contemporary Jewish Thought." In *From Ancient Israel to Modern Judaism: Intellect in Quest of Understanding—Essays in Honor of Marvin Fox*, Vol. 4, edited by Jacob Neusner et al. (n.p.: Scholar's Press, 2012).

Finkel, Nosson Tzvi. *Or HaTsafun*. 5 vols. Jerusalem: n.p., 1978.

Fisher, Esther. "'His Yetzer Is External, Her Yetzer Is Internal': Gendered Aspects of Sexual Desire in Rabbinic Literature." [In Hebrew]. PhD diss., Bar Ilan University, 2014.

Fisher, Yohi. *Hilun v'Hiloniut*. Tel Aviv: HaKibbutz HaMeuhad, 2015.

Fishman, David. "Musar and Modernity: The Case of Navaredok." *Modern Judaism Journal* 8 (1988): 41–64.

Fishman, Sylvia Barack. "Modern Orthodox Responses to the Liberalization of Sexual Mores." In *Yitz Greenberg and Modern Orthodoxy*, edited by Adam Ferziger, 224–53. Boston: Academic Studies Press, 2019.

Fonrobert, Charlotte. *Menstrual Purity: Rabbinic and Christian Reconstructions of Biblical Gender*. Stanford CA: Stanford University Press, 2000.

Fox, Everett. *The Five Books of Moses*. New York: Schocken Books, 1995.

Fraade, Steven. "Ascetical Aspects of Ancient Judaism." In *Jewish Spirituality: From the Bible through the Middle Ages*, edited by Arthur Green, 253–88. New York: Crossroad Publishing, 1986.

Frankel, Avraham. *Simha Temima*. Jerusalem: n.p., 1976.

Freehof, Solomon. "Unmarried Couples and Temple Membership" (#51). In *Reform Responsa for Our Time*, edited by Mark Washofsky, 238–44. Cincinnati OH: Hebrew Union College Press, 1977.

Friedman, Avraham Peretz. *Marital Intimacy: A Traditional Jewish Approach*. Northvale NJ: Jason Aronson, 1995.

Friedman, Alexander Zusia. *Mayana shel Torah*. Tel Aviv: Peer Publishers, 1990.

Friedman, Menachem. "Haredim Confront the Modern City." In *Studies in Contemporary Jewry*, vol. 2, edited by P. Medding, 74–96. Bloomington: University of Indiana Press, 1986.

Friedman, Mordechai Akiva. *Jewish Marriage in Palestine: A Cairo Geniza Study*, vols. 1 and 2, *The Ketuba Traditions*. Tel Aviv: Tel Aviv University Press, 1980.

Friedman, Richard Elliot. *Commentary on the Torah*. San Francisco: HarperSanFrancisco, 2001.

Gafni, Isaiah. "The Institution of Marriage in Rabbinic Times." In *The Jewish Family*, edited by David Kraemer, 13–30. New York: Oxford University Press, 1989.

Garb, Jonathan. *The Chosen Will Become Herds*. New Haven CT: Yale University Press, 2009.

———. *A History of Kabbalah: From the Early Modern Period to the Present Day*. New York: Cambridge University Press, 2020.

Gerondi, Jonah. *The Gates of Repentance*. Jerusalem: Feldheim, 1967.

Gershom. *Responsa of Meor haGolah*. New York: Shlomo Eidelberg, 1956.

Giddens, Anthony. *The Transformation of Intimacy*. Stanford CA: Stanford University Press, 1992.

Gikatelia, Joseph. *Sod reuya hayta Bat Sheva l'David* and *Sod HaReut*. In *The Female Body of God* [in Hebrew], edited by Daniel Abrams, 181–86. Jerusalem: Magnes Press, 2004.

Gisser, Avi. "Social Kashrut." *B'Ma'agalei Tzedek Journal* (Heshvan, 5766/ 2006): 14–19. http://www.edah.org/mtzenglish.pdf.

Gold, Michael. *Does God Belong in the Bedroom?* Philadelphia: The Jewish Publication Society, 1992.

Goldman, Emma. *Marriage and Love*. New York: n.p., 1911.

Gordis, Robert. *Love and Sex: A Modern Jewish Perspective*. New York: Women's League for Conservative Judaism, Hippocene Books, 1978.

Gornick, Vivian. *Emma Goldman: Revolution as Way of Life*. New Haven CT: Yale University Press, 2011.

Grade, Chaim. *The Yeshiva*. Indianapolis IN: Bobbs-Merrill Company, 1976.

Green, Arthur. "A Contemporary Approach to Jewish Sexuality." In *The Second Jewish Catalog*, edited by Sharon and Michael Strassfeld, 91–99. Philadelphia: The Jewish Publication Society, 1976.

———. "Buber, Scholem, and the Me'or 'Eynaim: Another Perspective on a Great Controversy." Forthcoming.

———. *The Light of the Eyes: Menahem Mendel of Chernobyl*. Stanford CA: Stanford University Press, 2020.

Greenberg, Irving. "Modern Orthodoxy and the Road Not Taken: A Retrospective View." In *Yitz Greenberg and Modern Orthodoxy*, edited by Adam Ferziger, 7–54. Boston: Academic Studies Press, 2019.

Greenberg, Steven. *Wrestling with God and Men: Homosexuality and the Jewish Tradition*. Madison WI: University of Wisconsin Press, 2004.

Greenstein, David. "Equality and Sanctity: Rethinking Jewish Marriage in Theory and in Ceremony." *G'vanim* (Beth Chayim Chadashim Newsletter, Academy for Jewish Religion) 5, no. 1 (May 2009): 1–34.

Grushcow, Lisa J., ed. *The Sacred Encounter: Jewish Perspectives on Sexuality*. New York: CCAR Press, 2014.

Hale, Matthew. *The History of the Pleas of the Crown*. [In Latin]. London: Sollom Emlyn of Lincoln's-Inn Esq. Printed by E. and R. Nutt, and R. Gosling (assigns of Edward Sayer, Esq.), for F. Gyles, T. Woodward, and C. Davis, 1736.

Harrison, Beverly. "Misogyny and Homophobia." In *Making Connections: Essays in Feminist Social Ethics*, edited by Beverly Harrison and Carol Robb, 135–51. Boston: Beacon Press, 1985.

Har-Shefi, Avishar. "Kavana v'Hitkavnut b'Yahasei Ishut." In *And He Named Them Adam* [in Hebrew], edited by Zohar Maor, 144–192. Efrat, Israel: Bina Leitim Institute of Yeshivat Siah Yitzhak Shagar, 2004.

Hauptman, Judith. *Reading the Rabbis: A Woman's Voice*. Boulder CO: Westview Press, 1998.

Hecker, Joel. "Kissing Kabbalists: Hierarchy, Reciprocity, and Equality." In *Studies in Jewish Civilization. Vol. 18, Love—Ideal and Real—in the Jewish Tradition from the Hebrew Bible to Modern Times*, edited by Leonard J. Greenspoon, Ronald Simkins, and Jean Cahan, 171–208. Omaha NE: Creighton University Press.

Hellner-Eshed, Melila. "If You Awaken and Arouse Love: The Language of Arousal in the Book of the Zohar." [In Hebrew]. *Kabbalah: Journal for the Study of Jewish Mystical Texts* 5 (2000): 327–52.

———. *A River Flows from Eden: The Language of Mystical Experience in the Zohar*. Translated by Nathan Wolski. Stanford CA: Stanford University Press, 2011.

Henkin, Yehuda Herzl. *Bnai Banim Responsa*. [In Hebrew]. Jerusalem: Self-published, 1945.

Herr, Moshe. "Marriage in Its Socio-Economic Aspects According to the Halakhah" [in Hebrew]. In *Mishpehot Bet Yisrael*, 37–46. Jerusalem: Ministry of Education and Culture, 1976.

Herzog, Isaac Halevi. *Heikhal Yitzhak Responsa*: Even HaEzer. [In Hebrew]. Jerusalem: Agudah L'Hotzaat Kitvei I.H. Herzog, 1960–67.

Heschel, Abraham. *Abraham Joshua Heschel: Essential Writings*. Maryknoll NY: Orbis Books, 2013.

———. *Heavenly Torah: As Refracted through the Generations*. New York: Continuum, 2006.

Hirsch, S. R. *Commentary on Genesis*. London: Isaac Levy, 1959.

———. *Commentary on Avot*. New York: Philipp Feldheim, 1967.

Horowitz, Isaiah. *Shnei Lukhot HaBrit*. Warsaw: Y. M. Alter, 1930.

Hoshen, Dahlia. "External Structure versus Binary Structure in Sexuality: The Approach of the Rishonim and the Talmudic Sources." [In Hebrew]. *Mo'ed Annual Jewish Studies* 15 (2005): 63–84.

Hundert, Gershon. *Jews in Poland-Lithuania in the Eighteenth Century: A Genealogy of Modernity*. Oakland: University of California Press, 2004.

Hurvitz, Pinhas Eliyahu. *Sefer HaBrit*. Lemberg, Russia: n.p., 1859.

Huss, Boaz. "The New Age of Kabbalah." *Journal of Modern Jewish Studies* 6, no. 2 (2007): 107–25.

Idel, Moshe. "Eros in Moshe Cordovero." Forthcoming, title undetermined.

———. *Kabbalah and Eros*. New Haven CT: Yale University Press, 2005.

———. *The Privileged Divine Feminine in Kabbalah*. Berlin: Walter de Gruyter, 2019.

Igeret HaKodesh [*The Holy Letter*]. Vol. 2 of *Kitvei HaRamban*. [In Hebrew]. Jerusalem: Mossad HaRav Kook, 1986.

Illouz, Eva. *Consuming the Romantic Utopia*. Oakland: University of California Press, 1997.

———. *Why Love Hurts: A Sociological Explanation*. Cambridge, UK: Polity Press, 2012.

Irshai, Ronit. "Theology and Halakhah in Jewish Feminisms." In *The Cambridge Companion to Jewish Theology*, edited by Steven Kepnes, 297–315. New York: Cambridge University Press, 2020.

Isaac bar Sheshet Perfet. *Responsa of Rivash*. Jerusalem: n.p., 1975.

Jacob ben Asher, Ba'al HaTurim. *Arba'a Turim* (with glosses). Warsaw: n.p., 1861.

Jacob Joseph of Polonnye. *Toldot Yaakov Yosef*. [In Hebrew]. Korzec, Russia: n.p., 1780.

————. *Ben Porat Yosef.* Korzec, Russia: n.p., 1781.

Jacob, Walter. *Contemporary American Reform Responsa.* New York: CCAR Press, 1987.

Jacobs, Louis. *Jewish Mystical Testimonies.* New York: Schocken, 1997.

Jaffee, Martin. *Torah in the Mouth: Oral Tradition and Early Rabbinism.* New York: Oxford University Press, 2001.

Kalmanofsky, Jeremy. "Sex, Relationship and Single Jews." In *The Observant Life*, edited by Martin Cohen, 632–56. New York: Rabbinical Assembly, 2012.

Kanievsky, Yaakov. *Kovetz Igrot HaKodesh.* Bnai Brak: n.p., 1968.

Kapah, Joseph. *Commentary on Maimonides' Mishneh Torah: Book of Women, Marriage.* [In Hebrew]. Jerusalem: Machon Mishnat HaRambam, 1987.

Kaplan, Lawrence. "The Hazon Ish: Haredi Critic of Traditional Orthodoxy." In *The Uses of Tradition: Jewish Continuity in the Modern Era*, edited by Jack Wertheimer, 145–74. Cambridge MA: Harvard University Press, 1992.

Kaplan, Mordecai. "Can Judaism Survive without Supernaturalism?" *Journal of Jewish Education* 27, no. 2 (1956): 10–23.

Karelitz, Avraham Isaiah. *Emunah U-Vitahon.* Translated by Yaakov Goldstein. Jerusalem: Am HaSefer, 2008.

————. *Hazon Ish.* Edited by Shmaryahu Greineman. Jerusalem: n.p., 1997.

————. *Kovetz Igrot HaKodesh* [The Holy Letters]. Bnai Brak: n.p., 1968.

Karo, Joseph. *Bedek HaBayit*, gloss on *Arba'a Turim.* Cracow, Poland: Y. Prostitz, n.d.

————. *Beit Yosef*, gloss on *Arba'a Turim.* Warsaw: n.p., 1861.

Karo, Joseph, and Moshe Isserles. *Shulhan Arukh.* Vilna. Poland: Rosenkranc and Szryftizecer, 1928.

Kass, Leon. *The Beginning of Wisdom.* New York: Free Press, 2003.

Katz, Dov. *Tenu'at Ha-Musar.* 5 Vols. Jerusalem: Feldheim Publishers, 1996.

Kiel, Yishai. *Sexuality in the Babylonian Talmud, Christian and Sasanian Contexts in Late Antiquity.* New York: Cambridge University Press, 2016.

Knohl, Elyashiv. *Et Dodim.* Ein Zurim, Israel: Machon Shiluvim, 2002.

Koch, Patrick. *Human Self-Perfection: A Re-Assessment of Kabbalistic Musar-Literature of Sixteenth-Century Safed.* Los Angeles: Cherub Press, 2015.

Kohn, Avrom Yitshok. *Divrei Kedushah.* Jerusalem: n.p., n.d.

Kook, Abraham Isaac. *Eyn Aya.* Jerusalem: Mossad HaRav Kook, n.d.

————. "Lights for Rebirth, Orot." In *The Zionist Idea*, edited by Arthur Hertzberg, 427–31. Philadelphia: The Jewish Publication Society, 1959.

———. *Or HaYakar v'Ikvei haEder*. Jerusalem: Mossad HaRav Kook, 1966.

———. *Responsa of Rav A. I. Kook: Orah Mishpat*. Jerusalem: Mossad HaRav Kook, 1979.

———. *Shemonah Kvatzim*. Jerusalem: n.p., 1999.

Kosman, Admiel. "The Israelite People Shall Keep the Sabbath: The Homiletical Rationale for Shabbat Observances, from Second Temple Times to the Talmudic Era." In *V'Shamru*, edited by Martin Cohen, 109–84. New York: Matrix, 2019.

———. *Gender and Dialogue in the Rabbinic Prism*. Berlin: Walter de Gruyter, 2013.

———. *Woman's Tractate*. Jerusalem: Keter, 2007.

Kosman, Admiel, and Anat Sharbat. "Two Women Who Were Sporting with Each Other." *Hebrew Union College Annual* 75 (2004): 37–73.

Kraemer, David, ed. *The Jewish Family*. New York: Oxford University, 1989.

Kraemer, Joel L. *Maimonides*. New York: Doubleday, 2008.

Kuper, Levi Yitzhak. "Admor miMunkacs." In *The Gdoilim*, edited by Benjamin Brown, 259–91. Jerusalem: Magnes Press, 2017.

Labovitz, Gail. "With Righteousness and Justice, with Goodness and with Mercy, Options for Egalitarian Marriage within Halakhah." Responsum of Rabbinical Assembly by the Committee on Jewish Law and Standards on Even HaEzer 27:1. April 14, 2020. Available at https://www.rabbinicalassembly.org/.

Lamm, Maurice. *The Jewish Way in Love and Marriage*. San Francisco: Harper and Row, 1980.

Laqueur, Thomas. *Making Sex: Body and Gender from the Greeks to Freud*. Cambridge MA: Harvard University Press, 1990.

Levenson, Sam. *Lifetime, Love, For Her*. n.p., n.d.

Levi, Yair. "Mussar, Education and Counseling: Rav Shlomo Wolbe." [In Hebrew]. In *The Gdoilim*, edited by Benjamin Brown, 736–65. Jerusalem: Magnes Press, 2017.

Levinas, Emmanuel. *Nine Talmudic Readings*. Translated by Annette Aronowicz. Bloomington: Indiana University Press, 1990.

Levitt, Laura. "Love the One You Are With." In *Passionate Torah*, edited by Danya Ruttenberg, 245–58. New York: New York University Press, 2009.

Lichtenstein, Aharon. "Of Marriage Relationships and Relations." In *Gender Relationships In Marriage and Out*, edited by Rivkah Blau, 1–35. New York: Yeshiva University Press, 2007.

Liebes, Yehuda. "Zohar and Eros." [In Hebrew]. *Alpayyim* 9 (1994): 67–115.

Lindberg, Carter. *Love: A Brief History through Western Christianity*. Malden MA: Oxford Blackwell Publishers, 2010.

Linzer, Dov. *The Joy of Text*. https://library.yctorah.org.

Luther, Martin. *Luther's Works*. Minneapolis: Fortress Press and Concordia, 1957.

Luzzato, Moshe Haim. *Mesillat Yesharim*. New Jersey: n.p., 1995.

———. *Yalkut Yedi'ot HaEmet*. Vol. 1. Warsaw: Ahava, 1936.

Maharal [Judah Loew]. *Hidushei Aggadot of the Maharal*. London: Dfus HaHinukh, 1960.

Maharit [Joseph MiTrani]. *Sh'eilot v'Teshuvot ha-Maharit*. Lvov, Poland: n.p., 1861.

Maimonides. *K'tavim Refuiim*. Vol. 4. Jerusalem: Mossad HaRav Kook, 2006.

———. *Commentary on the Mishna*. [In Hebrew]. Translated by Joseph Kapah. Jerusalem: Mossad HaRav Kook, 1963–67.

———. *Guide for the Perplexed*. Translated by Shlomo Pines. Chicago: The University of Chicago Press, 1963.

———. *Introduction to Avot*. [In Hebrew]. Jerusalem: Mossad HaRav Kook, n.d.

———. *Mishneh Torah*. Jerusalem: Mossad HaRav Kook, n.d.

———. *Mishneh Torah* (with classic glosses). 14 vols. Warsaw: Mordekhai Kalonberg, 1886.

———. *On Coitus*. Vol. 11 of *The Medical Works of Moses Maimonides*, edited and translated by Gerrit Bos. Boston: Brill, 2019.

———. *Responsa of Maimonides*. [In Hebrew]. Vol. 3. Edited by Joshua Blau. Jerusalem: Mikitzei Nirdamim, 1961.

———. *Sefer HaMitzvot*. Translated by Joseph Kapah. Jerusalem: Mossad HaRav Kook, n.d.

———. *Shemonah Prakim (Commentary on Ethics of the Fathers)*. Jerusalem: Mossad HaRav Kook, 1960.

Maor, Zohar, ed. *And He Named Them Adam: Love Relationships from a New Jewish Point of View*. [In Hebrew]. Efrat, Israel: Bina Leitim Institute of Yeshivat Siah Yitzhak Shagar, 2004.

Matt, Herschel. "Sex and Sexuality: Introduction." In *The Second Jewish Catalog*, edited by Sharon and Michael Strassfeld, 91–99. Philadelphia: The Jewish Publication Society, 1976.

Medini, Haim. *Sdei Hemed*. [In Hebrew]. London: n.p., 1951.

Meiri, Menahem. *Beit HaBehirah*. Zikhron Yaacov, Israel: Torah Educational Center, 1977.

Menahem Mendel of Kotzk, *Emet v'Emunah* [in Hebrew]. Jerusalem: n.p., 1972.

Michaelson, Jay. "On the Religious Significance of Homosexuality; or, Queering God, Torah, and Israel." In *The Passionate Torah*, edited by Danya Ruttenberg, 212–28. New York: New York University Press, 2009.

Mill, John Stuart. *Collected Works of John Stuart Mill*. Edited by J. M. Robson. Toronto: University of Toronto Press, 2006. Accessed from Online Library of Liberty, https://oll.libertyfund.org/titles/mill-collected-works-of-john-stuart -mill-in-33-vols.

Moses ibn Makhir, *Seder HaYom*. Lublin: n.p., 1876.

Muffs, Yochanan. *Love and Joy: Law, Language and Religion in Ancient Israel*. New York: The Jewish Theological Seminary of America, 1992.

Myers, Jody. "Marriage and Sexual Behavior in the Teachings of the Kabbalah Centre." In *Kabbalah and Modernity*, edited by Boaz Huss, 259–82. Leiden: Brill, 2010.

Nadler, Allan. *The Faith of the Mithnagdim*. Baltimore MD: Johns Hopkins University Press, 1997.

Nahman of Bratzlav. *Shivhei HaRan*. Jerusalem: n.p., 1989.

Nahmanides. *The Chumash Torat Chaim*. Jerusalem: Mossad HaRav Kook, 1981.

———. *Responsa Attributed to Nahmanides* (actually composed by Rashba). [In Hebrew]. Tel Aviv: Sifriyati, 1988.

Neis, Rachel. *The Sense of Sight in Rabbinic Culture*. Cambridge: Cambridge University Press, 2013.

Nietzsche, Friedrich. *Ecce Homo*. Cambridge: Cambridge University Press, 2005.

———. *The Gay Science*. Cambridge: Cambridge University Press, 2001.

———. *Human, All Too Human*. Cambridge: Cambridge University Press, 1996.

Novak Winer, Laura. "Sacred Choices: Adolescent Relationships and Sexual Ethics: The Reform Movement's Response to the Need for Faith-Based Sexuality Education." *American Journal of Sexuality Education* 6 (January 2011): 20–31.

Ostroff, Raphael (pseudonym, Avraham Shmuel). *LaDaat LeEhov* [To know how to love]. [In Hebrew]. Jerusalem: n.p., 2017.

Otzar HaPoskim on Shulhan Arukh: Even HaEzer. Jerusalem: n.p., 1947

Pachter, Shilo. "*Shimirat HaBrit*: The History of the Prohibition on Wasting Seed." [In Hebrew]. PhD diss., Hebrew University, 2006.

Pardo, Ariel. "The Invisible Partner: Jewish Sex Manuals and Jacob Emden's Mitot Kesef." Master's thesis, Brandeis University, 2017.

Paul, Shalom. "Exodus 21:10 A Threefold Maintenance Clause," *Journal of Near Eastern Studies* 28, no. 1 (January 1969): 48–53.

Perel, Esther. *Mating in Captivity: Unlocking Erotic Intelligence.* San Francisco: HarperCollins, 2006.

———. *The State of Affairs: Rethinking Infidelity.* San Francisco: Harper, 2017.

Plaskow, Judith. "Authority, Resistance, and Transformation: Jewish Feminist Reflection on Good Sex." In *Judith Plaskow, Feminism, Theology, and Justice,* edited by Hava Tirosh-Samuelson, 69–82. Leiden: Brill, 2014. Also in *The Coming of Lilith: Essays on Feminism, Judaism, and Sexual Ethics, 1972–2003.* Edited by Judith Plaskow. Boston: Beacon Press, 2005.

———. "Decentering Sex: Rethinking Jewish Sexual Ethics." In *God Forbid: Religion and Sex in American Public Life,* edited by Karen Sands, 23–41. New York: Oxford University Press, 2000.

———. "Sexuality and Teshuva: Leviticus 18." In *Beginning Anew,* edited by Gail Reimer, 290–302. New York: Touchstone/Simon and Schuster, 1997.

———. *Standing Again at Sinai: Judaism from a Feminist Perspective.* San Francisco: HarperCollins, 1991.

———. "Towards a New Theology of Sexuality." In *Twice Blessed: On Being Lesbian, Gay and Jewish,* edited by Christie Balka and Andy Rose, 141–51. Boston: Beacon Press, 1989.

Plaskow, Judith, and Elliot Rose Kukla. "Remapping the Road from Sinai." *Sh'ma: A Journal of Jewish Ideas* 38/646 (December 2007): 2–5.

Plutarch. *Advice to Bride and Groom. Coniugalia Praecepta* II. Cambridge MA: Loeb Classical Library, Harvard University Press, 1928.

Prabhu, Vikas. "Significance of Sexual Pleasure in Human Sexuality: An Understanding in the Light of Emphasis on Sexual Pleasure in the Kamasutra." Master's thesis, Christ University, Bangalore, India, 2013.

Ra'avad (Rabbi Abraham ben David). *Ba'alei HaNefesh: Sha'ar HaKedushah.* Jerusalem: Mossad HaRav Kook, 1964.

Rabinowitz, Gamliel. *Tiv ha-Emunah.* Jerusalem: n.p., 2007.

Rabinowitz, R. *Dikdukei Soferim.* Multiple volumes. Munich: H. Russel, 1867–86.

Raz, Pinhas. *Ish v'Isha She-Zakhu.* Jerusalem: n.p., 2011.

Rashba (Shlomo ibn Aderet). *Responsa of the Rashba.* [In Hebrew]. Bnai Brak, Israel: n.p., 1958.

Rilke, Rainer Maria. *Letters to a Young Poet.* Translated by Jane Bannard Greene and M. D. Herter. Reprinted in *Rilke on Love and Other.* Edited by John Mood. New York: W. W. Norton, 1975.

Ritba (Yom Tov ben Avraham Asevilli). *Hidushei HaRitba.* Jerusalem: Mossad HaRav Kook, n.d.

Roffman, Deborah. "Making Meaning and Finding Morality in a Sexualized World." In *Sex and Intimacy*, edited by Elliot Dorff and Danya Ruttenberg, 53–60. Philadelphia: The Jewish Publication Society, 2010.

Rosenberg, Shimon Gershon (Shagar). "Mitzvat Onah." In *And He Named Them Adam* [in Hebrew], edited by Zohar Maor, 193–233. Efrat, Israel: Bina Leitim Institute of Yeshivat Siah Yitzhak Shagar, 2004.

Rosenfeld, Jennie. "From Prostitution to Marriage and Back Again." In *The Intellectual Legacy of Rabbi Dr. Irving (Yitz) Greenberg*, edited by Shmuel Yanklowitz, 295–342. New York: Urim Publications/KTAV, 2018.

———. "Talmudic Re-Readings: Toward a Modern Orthodox Sexual Ethic." PhD diss., Yeshiva University, 2008.

Ross, Tamar. *Expanding the Palace of Torah: Orthodoxy and Feminism*. Philadelphia: The Jewish Publication Society, 2004.

Rotstein, Nahum. *Avnei Zikaron la-Bar Mitzvah*. Jerusalem: Mifal Torat Eretz Yisrael Darkhei Simhah, 2003.

Rozen Zvi, Ishay. "Do Women Have a *Yetzer*?" In *Spiritual Authority*, edited by H. Kreisel, 21–34. Jerusalem: Ben-Gurion University Press, 2010.

Russ-Fishbane, Elisha. *Judaism, Sufism, and the Pietists of Medieval Egypt*. Oxford: Oxford University Press, 2015.

Ruttenberg, Danya, ed. *The Passionate Torah: Sex and Judaism*. New York: New York University Press, 2009.

Rynhold, Daniel, and Michael Harris. *Nietzsche, Soloveitchik, and Contemporary Jewish Philosophy*. Cambridge: Cambridge University Press, 2018.

Sacks, Jonathan. *The Home We Build Together: Re-creating Society*. New York: Continuum Press, 2009.

———. *Morality: Restoring the Common Good in Divided Times*. New York: Basic Books, 2020.

Salanter, Israel. *Or Yisrael: Writings of Rabbi Israel Salanter*. [In Hebrew]. Edited by Yitzhak Blazer. n.p.: 1890.

Sakowitz, Selig. "Central Conference of American Rabbis Ad Hoc Committee on Human Sexuality" In *The Sacred Encounter*, edited by Lisa Grushcow, 241–46. New York: CCAR Press, 2014. Originally published in *CCAR Journal* 48, no. 4 (Fall 2001): 9–13.

Salmon, Yosef. "Ish Milhama: R. Moshe Leib Diskin." In *The Gdoilim* [in Hebrew], edited by Benjamin Brown, 301–11. Jerusalem: Magnes Press, 2017.

Samuel, Miriam. "Lidmuta shel Imma Shalom." *Shma'atin Journal* 182 (2012): 125–32.

Satlow, Michael. *Tasting the Dish: Rabbinic Rhetoric of Sexuality*. Atlanta GA: Scholars Press, 1995.

Schacter, J. J. "Rav Jacob Emden: Life and Major Works." PhD diss., Harvard University, 1988.

Schachter-Shalomi, Zalman. *First Steps to a New Jewish Spirit: Reb Zalman's Guide to Recapturing the Intimacy and Ecstasy in Your Relationship with God*. Woodstock VT: Jewish Lights, 2013.

Schindler, Pesach. "Responsum on Intimate Relations without Kiddushin and Huppah." [In Hebrew]. In *Teshuvot Va'ad Hahalakhah shel Knesset HaRabbanim B'Yisrael* , vol. 4, edited by Golinkin, 81–86. Jerusalem: Masorti Movement, 1992.

Schofer, Jonathan. *The Redaction of Desire*. Leiden: Brill, 2003.

Scholem, Gershom, ed. *The Book of Splendor: Basic Readings from the Kabbalah*. New York: Schocken Books, 1972.

———. *Reshit ha-Kabbalah*. Jerusalem: Magnes, 1948.

Schremer, Adiel. *Male and Female He Created Them*. Jerusalem: Zalman Shazar Center, 2003.

Shapira, Elijah. *Eliyah Rabbah*. Jerusalem: Mekor HaSefarim, 1999.

Shapiro, Marc. "HaTamim: R. Yaacov Yisrael Kanievsky, 'HaSteipler.'" In *The Gdoilim*, edited by Benjamin Brown, 663–74. Jerusalem: Magnes Press, 2017.

Shapiro, Yaakov. *Halachic Positions: Sexuality and Jewish Law*. Vol. 1. Self-published , 2015.

Shava, Menashe. *Seugyot Nivharot B'Dinei Ishim, Mishpaha and Yerusha*. Tel Aviv: Dionon, 1984.

Sheff, Elisabeth. *The Polyamorists Next Door*. Lanham MD: Rowman and Littlefield, 2014.

Sher, Yitzhak Isaac. *Kedushat Yisra'el*. n.d., n.p. Available at http://www.bhol.co .il/forum/topic.asp?whichpage=13&topic_id=2466988&forum_id=19616.

Shlanger, Raphael Menachem. *Mishkan Yisrael*. 2 vols. Jerusalem: n.p., 1991.

Shneur Zalman of Liadi. *Tanya—Likutei Amarim*. Vilna: n.p., 1900.

Shuchatowitz, Moshe Aharon. *Binyan Habayit: Guidance for Yeshiva Students on the Sanctity of the Jewish Home*. Jerusalem: n.p., 2003.

Sifrei [Midrash]. Edited by Saul Horovitz. Leipzig, Germany: G. Fock, 1917.

Singer, David. "Debating Modern Orthodoxy at Yeshiva College: The Greenberg-Lichtenstein Exchange of 1966." *Modern Judaism* 26, no. 2 (May 2006): 113–26.

Sinkoff, Nancy. *Out of the Shtetl: Making Jews Modern in the Polish Borderlands*. Providence RI: Brown Judaic Studies, 2020.

Sofer, Chaim. *Mahane Haim Responsa*. [In Hebrew]. Jerusalem: n.p., 1975.

Soloveitchik, Haym. "Mishneh Torah: Polemic and Art." In *Maimonides after 800 Years: Essays on Maimonides and His Influence*, edited by Jay Harris, 312–43. Cambridge MA: Harvard University Press, 2007.

———. "Rupture and Reconstruction: The Transformation of Contemporary Orthodoxy." *Tradition* 28 (Summer 1994): 64–130.

Soloveitchik, Joseph B. *Family Redeemed: Essays on Family Relationships*. Edited by David Shatz and Joel B. Wolowelsky. New York: Toras HoRav Foundation/ KTAV, 2000.

———. *Halakhic Man*. Philadelphia: Jewish Publication Society, 1983.

———. "The Lonely Man of Faith." *Tradition* 7 no. 2 (Summer 1965): 5–67.

———. *On Repentance*. [In Hebrew]. Edited by Pinchas Peli. Jerusalem: World Zionist Organization, 1974.

———. "Tzeiruf." In Soloveitchik, *Divrei Hagut v'ha-Arakhah*. Jerusalem: World Zionist Organization, 1981.

———. *U-Vikkashtem mi-Sham*. In Soloveitchik, *Ish ha-Halakhah-Galui v'Nistar*. Jerusalem: World Zionist Organization, 1979.

Stampfer, Shaul. *The Lithuanian Yeshiva* [in Hebrew]. Jerusalem: Zalman Shazar Center, 2005.

Stav, David, and Avraham Stav. *Avo Beitekha: Marriage and Family Law* [in Hebrew]. Jerusalem: Maggid, 2017.

Steinsalz, Adin. *Talmud Bavli*. Jerusalem: The Israel Institute for Talmudic Publications, 1991.

Stern, Menahem. *Greek and Latin Authors on Jews and Judaism*. Jerusalem: Israel Academy of Sciences and Humanities, 1976.

Stone, Ira, et al. *Cultivating the Soul*. Philadelphia: Center for Contemporary Mussar. Forthcoming.

Strassfeld, Michael. *A Book of Life: Embracing Judaism as a Spiritual Practice*. New York: Schocken, 2002.

Strassfeld, Sharon, and Michael Strassfeld, eds. *The Second Jewish Catalog*. Philadelphia: The Jewish Publication Society, 1976.

Sztokman, Elana Maryles. *The Men's Section: Orthodox Jewish Men in an Egalitarian World*. Waltham MA: Brandeis University Press, 2011.

Tannen, Deborah. *You Just Don't Understand: Women and Men in Conversation*. New York: William Morrow, 2001.

Teutsch, David. *A Guide to Jewish Practice*. Vol. 1, *Everyday Living*. Wyncote PA: Reconstructionist Rabbinical College Press, 2011.

Tikunei Zohar. Constantinople: n.p., 1719.

Tirosh-Samuelson, Hava. "Gender in Jewish Mysticism." In *Jewish Mysticism and Kabbalah: New Insights and Scholarship*, edited by Frederick Greenspahn, 191–230. New York: New York University Press, 2011.

Tirosh-Samuelson, Hava, and Aaron Hughes, eds. *Judith Plaskow: Feminism, Theology, and Justice*. Leiden: Brill, 2014.

Tishby, Isaiah, ed. *The Wisdom of the Zohar [Mishnat HaZohar]: An Anthology of Texts*. 3 vols. Translated by David Goldstein. The Littman Library of Jewish Civilization. New York: Oxford University Press, 1989.

Treggiari, Susan. *Roman Marriage*. New York: Clarendon Press/Oxford University Press, 1993.

Trible, Phyllis. *God and the Rhetoric of Sexuality*. Philadelphia: Fortress Press, 1978.

Tzefira, Yigal. "Coercion in Sexual Relations." [In Hebrew]. *Tehumim* 24 (2004): 222–27.

Vasserman, Nava. "The 'Abstinent' Society—*Hevrat HaKedusha*: The Process of Building a Home among Ger Hasidim in Israel." [In Hebrew]. PhD diss., Bar-Ilan University, 2010/11.

———. *I Have Never Called My Wife: Marital Relations in Gur Hasidism*. [In Hebrew]. Jerusalem: Ben-Gurion University Press, 2015.

Veritger, D. N., ed. *HaSaba MiSlabodka: Toldotav, Shitotav, Ma'amrav*. [In Hebrew]. New York: n.p., 1986.

Vidas, Elijah. *Reishit Hokhma*. Vol. 1. Jerusalem: Vagshal Publishing, 1997.

Vital, Haim. *Etz Haim*. In *Kol Kitvei HaARI*. Jerusalem: n.p., 1988.

———. *Sha'arei Kedushah*. Istanbul: n.p., 1793.

———. *Sha'ar ha-Kavanot*. In *Kol Kitvei HaARI*. Jerusalem: n.p., 1988.

———. *Sha'ar ha-Mitzvot*. In *Kol Kitvei HaARI*. Jerusalem: n.p., 1988.

———. *Sha'ar ha-Likutim/Pesukim*. In *Kol Kitvei HaARI*. Jerusalem: n.p., 1988.

———. *Ta'amei HaMitzvot*. In *Kol Kitvei HaARI*. Jerusalem: n.p., 1988.

Wahrman, Avraham David. *Ezer M'kudash on the Laws of Divorce*. [In Hebrew]. Bilgoraj, Poland: M. Horowitz, 1932.

Waldenberg, Eliezer. *Tzitz Eliezer*. [In Hebrew]. Jerusalem: n.p., 1984.

Washofsky, Mark, ed. *Reform Responsa for the Twenty-first Century*. Vols. 1 and 2. New York: CCAR Press, 2017.

Waskow, Arthur. *Down-to-Earth Judaism: Food, Money, Sex and the Rest of Life*. New York: William Morrow, 1995.

———. "Eden for Grown-Ups: Toward a New Ethic of Earth, of Sex, and of Creation." In *Passionate Torah*, edited by Danya Ruttenberg, 259–66. New York: New York University Press, 2009.

Waxman, Mordecai, ed. *Tradition and Change: The Development of Conservative Judaism*. New York: Burning Bush Press, 1958.

Weingarten, Uzi. "Doing What Is Right and Good." In *Sex and Intimacy*, edited by Elliot Dorff and Danya Ruttenberg, 16–22. Philadelphia: The Jewish Publication Society, 2010.

Werblowsky, R. J. Zwi. *Yosef Karo: Lawyer and Mystic*. London: Oxford University Press, 1962.

Wilensky, Mordekhai. *Hassidim umitnaggedim: Letoledot hapulmus Beineihem*. Vols. 1 and 2. Jerusalem: n.p., 1990.

Winkler, Gershon. *Sacred Secrets: The Sanctity of Sex in Jewish Law and Lore*. Northvale NJ: Jason Aronson, 1998.

Witte, John. *From Sacrament to Contract*. Louisville KY: Westminster John Knox Press, 1997.

Wodziński, Marcin. *Historical Atlas of Hasidism*. Princeton NJ: Princeton University, 2018.

Wolbe, Shlomo. *Alei Shur*. Jerusalem: Bais HaMussar, 1974.

———. *Guidance for Brides*. [In Hebrew]. Bnai Brak: Seminar Or HaHaim, 1976.

———. *Talks on Guidance for Grooms*. [In Hebrew]. Jerusalem: Beit HaMussar of H. Lehmann, 1990.

Wolfson, Elliot. *Language, Eros, Being: Kabbalistic Hermeneutics and Poetic Imagination*. New York: Fordham University Press, 2005.

———. "Woman: The Feminine as Other in Theosophic Kabbalah: Some Philosophical Observations on the Divine Androgyne." In *The Other in Jewish Thought and Identity, Constructions of Jewish Culture and Identity*, edited by Laurence Silberstein, 166–204. New York: New York University Press, 1994.

Wurzburger, Walter. "The Centrality of Creativity in the Thought of Rabbi Joseph B. Soloveitchik." *Tradition* 30, no. 4 (1996): 219–28.

Yosef, Ovadiah. *Yabia Omer Responsa*. [In Hebrew]. 10 vols. Jerusalem: Midrash Bnai Zion, 1954–2009.

Young, Ed, and Lisa Young. *Sexperiment: Seven Days to Lasting Intimacy with Your Spouse*. Nashville TN: FaithWords/Hachette Book Group, 2012.

Zacharow, Shlomo. "Kesher Beino l'Veina L'lo Nissuim." Rabbinic diss., Schechter Rabbinical Seminary in Jerusalem, 2000.

Zeldin, Theodore. *An Intimate History of Humanity*. London: Penguin/Random House/Vintage, 1995.

Zion, Noam. *Marital Friendship and Covenantal Partnership*. Cleveland OH: Zion Holiday Publications, 2018.

———. *Rabbinic Family Disrupted by Love of Torah*. Cleveland OH: Zion Holiday Publications, 2018.

———. *Romantic Rabbis: How to Study Talmudic Tales of Love and Lust*. Cleveland OH: Zion Holiday Publications, 2018.

Ziv, Simhah Zissel. *Sefer Hokhmah U-Musar*. 2 vols. New York: n.p. 1957.

Zohar, Zvi. "Halakhic Positions Permitting Pre-Marital Sexual Intimacy." [In Hebrew]. *Akdamot* 17 (2006): 11–31.

Index

desire (*cont.*) 331, 344, 347–48, 353, 505–7; to give, to receive (Ashlag), 170–74, 300–302; redeemed, 105, 376–84, 385–91; revived, 302–14; and shared desire, xxxviii, 11, 59, 107, 144; shalom bayit, 328; spontaneous or scheduled, 23, 32, 36–37, 51; suppressed, 72–74, 93, 186–87, 190–99, 218–20, 235, 261–65, 380; and Viagra, 204–5

Dessler, Eliyahu, 300–302

devekut, 146–49, 159, 211–22, 265, 302, 309–10

De Vidas, Elijah, 201, 309, 326

Dorff, Elliot, 425, 433–36, 442–45, 448, 458–59

Dratch, Michael, 440–401

Elazar Hasid of Worms, 56, 59–60, 63, 141

Eliezer ben Hyrcanus, 65–78, 105, 193–94, 235, 246–47, 263, 303, 315–20, 335–36, 369, 391. *See also* Imma Shalom

Elijah, Vilna Gaon, 47–48, 252–55, 257–60, 263–64, 268–69, 283–84, 529

Elijah de Vidas. *See* De Vidas, Elijah

Emden, Jacob, 337, 487–90; biography of, 461, 464, 468–71; prayerbook of, , 465–68. See also *pilegesh* (concubine)

ethics, sexual: Ashlag on, 171; Berkovits on, 377, 379–85; Borowitz on (covenantal), 410–15; Buber on, 413–4; Dessler on, 300–302;

feminist, 494, 507; liberal, 439–43; Maimonidean golden mean, xxxv, 92, 103, 186–88; Modern Orthodoxy, 367–72, 404; mystic, 157–58; prophetic, 452, 504, 527; situational, 458, 521; and Talmudic shame, 71; Waskow (life-cycle), 422–26; and values clarification, xxx, 431–32

Etkes, Immanuel, 214, 257–58, 273

Feinstein, Moshe, 22–23, 30, 31–35, 315, 343, 353–54, 536

feminism, xxiv, 28–29, 83–84, 102–3, 157–58, 362, 366, 491–505, 529–30; and patriarchy, 280, 326, 452, 456, 462, 483, 486, 491–96, 500–507, 520–21, 525–27, 536

Finkel, Nosson Tzvi, 271–73, 283. *See also* Mussar, Eastern European schools of

Freehof, Solomon, 476–77, 488

Geller, Laura, 485–87

gender: differences, 31–35, 242–43, 275–79, 344–49, 541; fluidity, 180, 516–19; hierarchy/equality/justice, 131–36, 148, 280, 456, 508–9, 525–27; in Song of Songs, 505–7. *See also* LGBTQ persons

Gur (Ger), 203, 236–44, 247–49, 251, 287, 301, 335, 357, 492, 536, 538, 543; arranged marriages in, 162, 237–38; entrepreneurial women in, 243–44; marriage relations in, 240–43; Ordinances of, 211, 222, 224–33, 243, 248, 292–93, 307, 334, 529,

Ostroff, Raphael, 367, 395–400

patriarchy. *See* feminism
Perel, Esther, xxv, 36–37
pilegesh (concubine), 461–65, 471–83, 486
Plaskow, Judith, 408–9, 491, 493–508, 513–14, 516–18, 520–21, 527, 530, 536
pleasure: con, 65, 71–72, 95, 186–88, 193–94, 197–98, 215–21, 233, 240, 292, 320, 407, 411–12, 442; pro, 30–31, 53–55, 103, 115, 118, 141–43, 145–47, 169, 172–74, 272–74, 295–96, 303–5, 389, 394, 398, 421, 530;
privacy. *See* modesty and exposure
polygamy, polyamory. *See* marriage

Ra'avad (Abraham ben David), xxxiii, 24, 94–96, 131–36, 191, 202, 322, 469, 474
Rabbi (Judah HaNasi), 14, 66, 70, 81, 83, 84, 91, 99, 183, 185, 492, 536
Rashba (Shlomo ibn Aderet), 449, 451
Rav: bedroom, 43–44, 51–52, 81, 91, 183, 328, 335, 528; worldview, 44–46, 53–56, 60–62
Reconstructionist movement (RRC), xxx, 362, 431, 455–57
Reform movement (CCAR, URJ, HUC-JIR), xxix, xxx, 168, 179–81, 362, 406–15, 423, 427, 429, 431, 439, 443, 454–55, 443, 454–58, 475–79, 492–93, 517–18, 532
Rilke, Rainer Maria, xxi, 541–42, 544
Roffman, Deborah, 407–8

Rosenfeld, Jennie, 373, 375, 393
Ruttenberg, Danya, 433, 458, 540

Sacks, Jonathan, 407, 489–90
Salanter, Israel, 252, 260, 263–67, 272–74, 281, 283. *See also* Mussar, Eastern European schools of
Schachter-Shalomi, Reb Zalman, 168, 175–79
sex/sexuality, xxv, 4; education 43–44, 108–9, 129, 177–78, 244–47, 395–400, 431–33, 539; premarital 364, 366–67, 371–73, 377, 392, 405, 417–18, 424, 434, 441; procreation and infertility, 14–16. *See also* desire; ethics, sexual; LGBTQ persons; liberation, sexual; Maimonides, lovemaking; marriage, conjugal intercourse (*onah*); *pilegesh* (concubine)
Shabbat: mystical, 143–45, 165; *onah*, 186, 188, 304, 307, 315, 353, 465–68, 470–71; *oneg*, 142–43, 177, 186, 188, 223, 272; shalom bayit, 56, 62, 326, 341
Shapiro, Yaakov, 195–96, 354–55
Shekhinah: arousal, 153–55, 309; between man and woman, xxi, 127–28, 130–31, 139–40, 143–45, 181, 221, 235, 287, 339, 351; feminist analysis, 157–58, 161, 163–64; joy, 216, 317; sanctifying the world, 314, 329–30, 374
Sher, Isaac, xxxviii, 11, 52, 252, 275, 283, 287, 290, 302–11, 386, 529–30
Shlanger, Rafael, 313–14, 318, 321–31, 334–35, 386–87